Marriage and the Family

Marriage and the Family

Marcia Lasswell *California State Polytechnic University, Pomona*

Thomas E. Lasswell *University of Southern California*

D. C. HEATH AND COMPANY *Lexington, Massachusetts Toronto*

International Standard Book Number: 0-669-04373-7

Library of Congress Catalog Card Number: 81-82992

Dedication

Without our "tree of life," this book could not have been written.

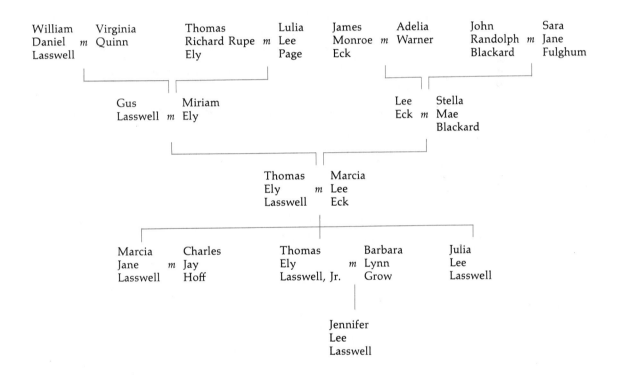

Preface

Of all human experiences, marriage and being a member of a family are nearly universal. These institutions occur in some form in every society, and virtually every individual in a given society experiences some form of them. Certainly no one has ever grown up in a childless family!

Each of us has spent over thirty years involved in marriage and family life through our personal family lives and through teaching, counseling, research, reading, and writing. We have come to view both marriage and family life as constantly changing mosaics, and we are optimistic about the changes that we see in the United States.

Although we feel positively about the state of marriage and the family, we are not unaware of the problems and the challenges facing American marriages and families. However, our focus has consistently been on helping people to work out difficulties rather than on lamenting change or gloomily pronouncing the failure of these two institutions to meet everyone's ideals. The viability of marriage and of family living cannot be seriously questioned. Even though the meanings and functions of these institutions will change, change is certainly nothing new nor is it cause for alarm, for it is one of the most critical indications of life.

One of us is a psychologist; the other, a sociologist. Both of us are marriage and family therapists. Our belief is that people looking forward to marriage and parenthood, as well as those in satisfying relationships and surely those in pain over their personal marriage or family crises, are entitled to the most valid and reliable information available. To this end, we hope this book will be of benefit.

Orientation

There are a number of strong theoretical positions taken by leaders in the field of marriage and the family. We have used the major theories as impartially as possible to explain the various points of view drawn from research and clinical material. We question whether any one existing theory can cover all aspects of topics as complex as marriage and the family; instead, we feel that many theories have special insights to offer. Although the chapters in this book are in a life-cycle sequence, we do not wish to imply that we are partial to developmental theory. We have leaned on systems theory, social interaction theory, developmental theory, and cognitive theory, and we have tried not to omit any of the major theoretical explanations that seemed to facilitate understanding of the subject matter at hand.

We are concerned with the application of research findings and clinical data to couple and family organization, everyday life, and decision making. We have stressed the diversity of ways in which single persons, couples, and families live in the United States. We hope that the text will help students to understand their choices and to make decisions that lead to increased satisfaction and happiness in their lives.

Study Aids

Key terms have been defined in glossaries at the end of each chapter. In addition, each chapter has internal section summaries to aid reader comprehension. Concepts are illustrated with familiar examples from everyday life. Numerical data from research and from government population reports are presented in a variety of tables and diagrams. There are three appendixes, which may be used as supplementary reading or as additional chapters.

For those who are interested, a study guide is available. Prepared by Ruth Talley, it provides self-test questions, review items, key terms, and chapter objectives for each chapter. For instructors there is an instructor's guide, which offers a large bank of test questions.

Acknowledgments

We gratefully acknowledge the valuable contributions of our talented colleagues in the field of marriage and the family who tirelessly carry out research that makes a book such as this possible. The early reviews of the manuscript helped us immeasurably to sharpen our efforts. We wish to thank Kathleen Campbell, Department of Home Economics, Bowling Green State University; Brent C. Miller, Department of Family and Human Development, Utah State University; Elizabeth Thomson, Department of Sociology, University of Wisconsin; Kenrick S. Thompson, Department of Sociology, Northern Michigan University; Nancy Voigt Wedemeyer, Department of Home Economics, University of Texas; and Anthony P. Jurich, Department of Family and Child Development, Kansas State University. Understanding of the genetic aspects of human sexuality was enhanced by discussions with Charles Oxnard, University of Southern California, and Charles Hoff, University of South Alabama, although neither should be held responsible for our presentation in the text.

George Abbott, our editor, along with Sylvia Mallory and Esther Agonis of D. C. Heath and Company, was of invaluable assistance. Our special thanks also go to our assistant Patricia Tice, who was always willing to help and to smile when the deadlines came, and to Sydney Alter, for her aid and encouragement.

Marcia Lasswell
Thomas E. Lasswell

Brief Contents

Detailed Contents

Marriage
and the Family

At Piggott, Ark., Monday evening, J. A. Northington and Mrs. S. R. Benson were quietly married. Mrs. Benson is a refined and highly respected lady of Gibson. Mr. Northington is one of Campbell's most prominent merchants. The marriage occurred much earlier than first intended, on account of Mr. Northington's housekeeper unexpectedly leaving.

—Dunklin Democrat,
 Kennett, Missouri,
 May 16, 1901.

1 · Marriage and the Family in the United States

This is a book about some of the experiences of nearly all Americans—experiences that usually involve deep emotions and that most people consider some of the most important in their lives. The reality of these life experiences lies in the beliefs, feelings, and behaviors of those who experience them, as well as in the social and legal meanings given to marriage and the family.

Love, *sexual intercourse, commitment, cohabitation, marriage, childbearing, parenting, family, dissolution*, and *child custody* are terms for experiences about which most people have strong feelings. Even people who have not had a particular experience often have strong beliefs about how people who do have this experience should behave and feel. This chapter presents an overview of the topics of love, sex, marriage, and the family, including the issues central to our personal and social judgments about them.

4

*1/Marriage and the
Family in the
United States*

The United States census defines a *family* as "a group of two persons or more related by birth, marriage, or adoption and residing together."[1] Much of the material in this book is based on information gathered by researchers using that definition. Although such a definition permits the collection of general statistics, it tells us nothing about some of the most important features of our own family relationships—how we ought to feel about one another (and how we do feel), how we ought as a family to interact with the rest of society (and how we do interact). In other words, for most of us there is much more to the concept of "family" than legal marriage, birth or adoption, and common residence. This book is concerned with personal and **social** feelings and behaviors related to family living, the ways that family rules and roles emerge, common problems families have, and ways of dealing with those problems.

One popular definition of marriage is that it is an institutionalized process whereby given men and women ceremonially begin, and generally maintain, a mutual relationship suitable for the purpose of founding and sustaining a family.[2] Some questions may be raised about the applicability of this definition to modern American society. For many people, marriage seems to be as concerned with the public legitimation of sexual relationships and cohabitation as with the founding and sustenance of a family. A marriage may exist for a number of years both before and after children are a part of it; many people now marry with the intention of remaining childless. However, even if one or both members of a couple are sterile, they may still be subject to both personal and social pressures to represent themselves as married if they intend to live together for a long time. In fact, in all the fifty states marriages continue to be valid whether children are born or not; moreover, if children are born, a marriage continues to be valid until it is dissolved by death or divorce, often many years after the children have left the home.

There are two legal forms of marriage in the United States: ceremonial and nonceremonial. A **ceremonial marriage** is one in which the principals state before witnesses that they intend to take one another as marriage partners. Although all states require some form of license in order to register a marriage in the public records, the qualifications for obtaining it differ from state to state (see Chapter 6). Some states require the presence of an authorized officiant; many permit the couple themselves to conduct their ceremony.

In those states providing for **nonceremonial ("common-law") marriages**, the legal status of a marriage can be based on **cohabitation** (living together) and/or **consummation** (engaging in sexual intercourse) over a specified period of time. In such states, having children and establishing other kinds of marital relationships are not required for a marriage to be recognized as legal and valid. In at least one state (Iowa), the courts have ruled that marriage can be established by a couple who are competent to marry (legally of age, not married to someone else, and so forth), simply by their telling witnesses that they are married or by their representing themselves publicly as husband and wife. According to the Constitution of the United States, these marriages must be

5

Changing Patterns
of Love and Marriage
in the United States

recognized as legal and valid in all states whenever they are contracted in any state where they are legal. Regardless of where the partners live, common-law marriages can be dissolved only in the same ways that ceremonial marriages are dissolved in the couple's state of residence.

In general, the customs of a society seldom conflict directly with its laws. In other words, laws shape behavior and behavior shapes laws, even in such fundamental areas of our lives as marriage and the family. On the other hand, there have always been minorities in the United States that have codes of beliefs or behaviors that differ from the laws to a greater or lesser extent. For example, the Roman Catholic Church may define a marriage as not valid until or unless it has been ceremonially sanctioned according to the Church's own prescriptive codes, regardless of the legal status of the couple. Other examples could be drawn from communes, group marriages, and the customs of various religious and **cultural** groups whose norms for contracting marriage differ to a greater or lesser extent from those of the state in which they occur.

It is difficult—perhaps impossible—to view social phenomena such as marriage and the family without a cultural bias. Nevertheless, suppose that we were the first arrivals from the earth on some distant planet inhabited by apparently intelligent beings whose language, however, is completely incomprehensible to us. Because of our own cultural biases, one of our early wishes might be to distinguish persons who are married from those who are not. If we are unable to speak their language, what observable behavior might give us clues? What can one observe about a person that indicates that he or she is married? If we are looking for an analogy with the rest of the animal kingdom, we might begin with terms like *mating* or *pairing*.

"Pairing," in particular, suggests a cultural bias—the assumption of **monogamy**. This concept implies sexual exclusiveness, which is not necessarily a requirement for marriage. In fact, an early study by anthropologist George Murdock found that in a world sample of 554 societies, monogamy was the preferred style in only 135.[3] We might be closer to deciding who was married, therefore, by emphasizing the enduring nature of the relationships we observed rather than by looking for monogamous relationships.

Clearly, marriages everywhere must endure or be intended to last through *some* appreciable time span in order to qualify as "real" marriages. This time span must represent a defined period in the human life cycle. Marriage is, therefore, a developmental, enduring (though dynamic) social relationship between two or more people in a social system.

What *kind* of social relationship is marriage? How can an objective observer distinguish marriage from other forms of patterned human social interactions? Four criteria, primarily social in nature (although not entirely lacking in cultural components), may help to characterize marriage:

1. The persons involved expect and usually achieve some form of sexual access to one another for an indefinitely long period, either as a basis for

6

*1/Marriage and the
Family in the
United States*

or as a symbol of their social relationship. If there are exceptions to this generalization, they are considered matters of individual peculiarity rather than of social prescription.

2. The persons involved have an economic relationship, including some understanding about the allocation of their energies and incomes, and an agreement about the communality or exclusiveness of their material goods, services, items for consumption, and real or personal property.

3. The persons involved relate to one another in patterns that are predominantly *symbiotic*; that is, they are mutually supportive and interdependent, with each apparently contributing in some specific (and perhaps also general) ways to the welfare of the other(s).

4. Although they are dynamic and subject to change, the responsibilities and patterned functions of the relationship tend to be stable over an enduring period—a one-day relationship probably would not count unless the persons involved intended it to last longer and its termination was due to an external event such as the death of one of the partners.

In addition to these primarily social criteria for a marriage relationship, seven features are usually found in conceptualizations of marriage in the United States that have somewhat stronger cultural overtones.

1. The relationship is **heterosexual**. That is, if the foregoing criteria are applied to persons relating to one another who are of the same sex, most people (and all existing state laws) deny that the systems constitute a legally recognized marriage.

2. The relationship is monogamous. Although many societies do not concur, this is the only legal pattern in the United States. Only one pair of partners can participate in a marriage at a time; additional relationships are considered to be extramarital, **bigamous** (with one person having two partners), or **polygamous** (with one person having many partners), by definition. Consequently, group marriages are not legally recognized, nor do most people consider such relationships to be marriages.

3. The relationship is usually thought to be directed toward the establishment of a family, especially through procreation or the adoption (either formal or informal) of children. This assumption may be changing in our society, but it is still the case more often than not.

4. There is a division of tasks in the relationship, with specified (and usually cultural) roles allocated to participants in an organized way.

5. The participants in the relationship "love" each other; or, at least, love was a factor in their selection of each other as mates.

6. The persons involved in a marriage have a common residence. They conceptualize a common dwelling place as "home."

7. Persons with certain kinship (or sometimes other) relationships cannot be partners in a marriage, even though they meet all of the other social

7

*Changing Patterns
of Love and Marriage
in the United States*

criteria. Marriages that are defined as **incestuous** are prohibited by law in every state.

These seven criteria make the conditions for marriage more specific and hence tend to reduce the number of persons conceptualized as being socially "married" at any given time.

This book is concerned with the legal and moral rights and obligations of marriage and the family and with the statistics related to marriage and its termination. It is also concerned with the feelings and behaviors of people who are involved in marriage and family relationships, and of men and women who pass laws or establish policies that affect marital organization or dissolution.

Changing Patterns of Love and Marriage in the United States

Many cultural changes have occurred with respect to love and marriage in the United States within the past hundred years. Unfortunately, they have not been as well documented as one might wish, largely because the capabilities of social science to measure long-term cultural changes have been, for the most part, recently developed. Even the record keeping of such important human milestones as marriage and divorce has been carefully done only since the turn of this century. Much of the information that was not recorded by government agencies or scholarly studies, therefore, has been gained from deduction, from reported memories of older persons, or from descriptions in the literature of the time. These sources are often inaccurate because of the impact of time on perception and also because of the biases of the reporters and writers of history, typically white, upper-class, well-educated men. Some experts on family life trace the beginnings of the systematic study of the family to Charles Darwin's 1859 work, *The Origin of Species*.[4] In response to Darwin's biological evolutionary ideas, early studies were large-scale, cross-cultural attempts to find universal laws about marriage and the family.

Later in the United States, social problems and their effects on marriage and the family became the focus of research and writings in the newly developing fields of sociology and of marriage and the family. The studies became more and more sophisticated in research techniques and analyses as facts about American family life were collected. Changes were noted by comparing past with present, and trends were forecast for the future.

Some of the most striking examples of changes noted by the twentieth-century sociologists were in popular views of love, marriage, and the family, and in the notions of what *model* has been favored for each. To describe these

8

*1/Marriage and the
Family in the
United States*

changes in popular notions accurately, it was—and still is—necessary to take into consideration the many social class and ethnic differences that have always existed in the United States. These differences have been present since the founding of the country; yet many people assume that post–Civil War Americans were culturally homogeneous and that the great variations in marriage and the family are of fairly recent origin.

One has only to review the evidence to see just how unjustified the assumption is that there are or ever have been universal models of love, marriage, and family organization in the United States. One could hardly expect the Irish-Catholic immigrant blue-collar worker who came to Boston as late as the turn of the twentieth century to have the same model for his or her marriage and family as the Mississippi-born descendant of a black slave. We *know* more about differences today because of television and the ease of travel from place to place, but the differences have always been there.

It is possible that recent advances in the literacy of the population and in mass communication may be tending to make U.S. society *more* culturally homogeneous. Today, the southern black may be as likely to have a college education or to wear clothes made in New York or to read *The Joy of Sex* as is the Irish factory worker in New England. Popular stereotypes still persist, however.

When we think of the Irish-Catholic blue-collar immigrant mentioned before, our stereotypical impression is likely to be that he looked forward to marriage when he became economically self-sufficient; that he expected to be married in a religious ceremony; that he expected never to dissolve his marriage in divorce; that he hoped for a large number of children; that he expected his wife and perhaps later his older daughters to take care of all the housekeeping, making and mending of clothing, child care, and similar activities even if they were employed outside the home; that he probably expected his wife to be a virgin at marriage whether or not he himself was sexually experienced; that he quite possibly expected never to see his wife totally nude, even during lovemaking; that he expected his wife and children to obey his commands without question; that he expected to resort to force or corporal punishment if it was necessary to control the behavior of family members. With what contemporary model shall we compare this? One possible comparison would be with Irish blue-collar workers migrating to the United States in 1982. Alternatively, we could try to measure changes in the U.S.-born descendants of the Irish worker just described. In any case, it is certain that many differences would be found between early families and any contemporary ones with whom they were compared, since patterns are always evolving.

The mosaic of **microcultures** in the United States contains many tiles; the picture is complicated by racial, ethnic, religious, educational, and geographical differences that make it difficult for one to shape any general statements about the culture of the society as a whole, particularly with respect to ideals such as love and models for family organization.

Family sociologists have built a strong case for the fact that there has been a widespread shift in the popular conceptualization of the family in the United States. It has been proposed that the family model is generally moving from an *institutional* to a *companionship* one.[5] Although many kinds of changes are described, the emphasis has been on the main shift from the all-encompassing family to one composed of a group of relatively liberated people whose chief ties are affectional. The all-encompassing family was one that prepared its young members for life in society and maintained its social unity through a high degree of economic and functional interdependence of family members. The companionship family, which depends on other institutions for much of this preparation, concentrates instead on nurturance and affection.

Other major areas that seem to be in a state of change are ideal patterns related to mate selection, sexual freedom, gender roles in society, romanticism, the degree of mutual interdependence of marriage partners, mixed marriages, and the definitions of masculinity and femininity. Although the differences from the patterns of the past are striking, they are more impressive for the number of people that are affected than for the novelty of the ideas themselves. Because they are documented in literature and films and are openly discussed in classrooms and on television, the changes are highly visible. Thus, even small differences take on significant proportions.

Social Changes Related to Love and Marriage

There have been social as well as cultural changes in patterns of love and marriage; these have resulted from a variety of social events. Data on vital statistics, legislative changes, economics, and population movements are examples of information collected about social change that have had profound implications for family life; much of this information has been carefully recorded.

Among the important social changes noted in the past century are those in the rural-urban distribution of the population. In its early days the United States was primarily an agricultural nation. Just after World War II, in 1946, almost one-third of the population still lived on farms. By 1979, however, only about one family in twenty-eight lived on a farm. Less than half the families in the United States lived in urban areas in 1910; today, over 90 percent of families live in such areas.[6]

Although this dramatic move away from the farm was not the result of changing ideas about love, marriage, and the family, it certainly had a profound effect on all of these. Many customs that were functional for a satisfactory life on the farm are inappropriate or unsatisfactory for city living. For instance, patterns of mate selection have changed, in part because of the greater mobility of young people.[7] The physical locations in which courtship, marriage, childbirth, terminal illness, and death occur are drastically different.

Partial employment of both the young and the aged had a very different meaning on the farm fifty years ago from that in contemporary metropolitan centers. Members of the generation moving away from the farm had ingrained

11

*Changing Patterns
of Love and Marriage
in the United States*

in them as children sentiments appropriate to farm life at the time, such as reliance on the family unit to meet most vital needs. Urban children of today, on the other hand, are often exposed to situations in which reliance on the family may be either inappropriate or inefficient.

Even today, children in rural areas typically do not need to deal with busy thoroughfares in the same way that city children do. Children on farms can usually roam some distance from home quite safely, with the assurance that almost anyone encountered can help them find home if they get lost. In contrast, in today's urban environment, children's leaving the immediate area of familiar adult supervision can pose the threat not only of getting lost but also, perhaps, of physical danger.

It was not unusual for isolated farm children half a century ago to know from an early age the partners that they would eventually marry. Contemporary urbanites, however, often first meet their potential mates as adults living alone or apart from their families; sometimes the parents do not even meet before the partners have married. Clearly this is not the result of any conscious effort of the persons involved to make changes in their patterns of love, marriage, and family living. It is instead the result of complex economic and political factors and their effects on human needs and values.

Life Expectancy

The number of years that a person born in a given year can expect to live has changed dramatically since the turn of the century. In 1900, the average person in the United States was expected to live to about age forty-seven. A boy born today in this country can expect to live to be about sixty-nine on the average; a girl born today has an expectation of living nearly eighty years.[8] Even though this change is primarily due to a large drop in infant mortality, the increasing numbers of persons who live beyond their child-rearing years, of men who live until retirement, and of widows all have important implications for love, marriage, and family living, as will be discussed in a later chapter.

In 1890, half the women who ever married were dead before they were fifty-three, and many still had children living at home when they died.[9] Some were already widows, of course, since men also died early. Today, half the women who have ever married live to be well over seventy-five. They live to see their own children grown and to have grandchildren and perhaps great-grandchildren. Most women outlive their husbands by ten years or more. Such factors, coupled with the migration from farms (where even the very old are usually still partially employed) to urban areas (where the old may have almost no economic contribution to make to the family), have had a profound impact on the customary ways of life of all family members, old and young alike.

Today, since both men and women usually live for many years after their children leave home, the "empty nest" poses problems for many middle-aged married couples, who have to reorganize their lives after their children's departure. The postparental period often gives a couple a new lease on life. They

may have more time, more money to spend on themselves, and more opportunity to get to know each other as a couple again. The decrease in child-rearing responsibilities gives them the opportunity for new activities, more leisure time, a job shift, or a host of other pursuits. A new look at postparental adjustments and traditional customs for relating to older family members has been the focus of a great deal of research in the past few decades.[10]

Characteristics of People Who Marry

Throughout the twentieth century there have been about 10 marriages per year per 1,000 population. Unusual circumstances have occasionally caused departures from this rate, such as the extremely low rate during the Depression of the 1930s (9 per 1,000) and the extremely high rate (12 per 1,000) that peaked in 1946, immediately after World War II. The actual number of marriages has been increasing since 1977. In 1980, the largest annual number of marriages ever was recorded in the United States; 1979 was the second-highest year and 1946 the third highest. This increase was noted in every region of the United States.[11] For the country as a whole, there have never been more than two marriages a year for every hundred people or fewer than one marriage for every two hundred people. The usual rate is about one marriage per year for every hundred people.[12] Although the rate has not shown any major long-term trends in the twentieth century, this situation in itself may be remarkable, since

13

*Changing Patterns
of Love and Marriage
in the United States*

we have observed that age distributions have changed considerably during the twentieth century. There have been marked increases both in the fraction of the population past childbearing age and in the number of females who survive from birth to childbearing age. The long-term stability of the marriage rate leads us to suspect, therefore, that there must be changes in the characteristics of the persons who marry. This is borne out by the data, as we shall see.

The median age at first marriage for men in 1890 was slightly over 26 years. This means that approximately half of all men who married were under 26 years of age, and half were over 26. Over the years that followed, the median age of first marriage for men steadily declined, reaching a low of 22.5 years in 1956, a decline of more than 3.5 years from the 1890 figure. Beginning about 1960, a small upward trend began, resulting by 1980 in a median age at first marriage for men of over 24 years.[13]

It is interesting to associate this information with the remarkable changes in the median number of years of education. Since in 1890 most males went to work rather than to high school, a large fraction of males around the turn of the century had been more or less self-sufficient (that is, had finished school and were presumably working on the farm or in other kinds of employment) for twelve or more years before they married. In contrast, today's figures show that half the males who marry will have been self-sufficient for six years or less. This circumstance is due partly to the later age at which males leave school and partly to their lower median age at marriage. This drastic reduction in the period of independent bachelorhood has many implications for patterns of courtship and marriage, as we will discuss in a later chapter.

Much less change has been observed in the median age of first marriage for women than for men. In 1890, median age at first marriage for women was 22 years. A slow decline followed, to a low of 20.1 years in 1956, which was followed in turn by a slow rise to 20.8 years in 1968 and 20.9 in 1972. Currently, the median age at first marriage is about 22.0 for women. Thus, the age at marriage for females is just about the same now as it was a hundred years ago.[14] Following our previous logic, we can note that young women a century ago spent seven or eight single years at home or employed after they had finished school, whereas today many young women spend only about three years.

The general implication of the above findings for both men and women is that today there is a more immediate transition from the family of one's parents and siblings to the family created with a marriage partner, and thus a much shorter period of self-sufficiency, than there was at the beginning of the twentieth century. This change is of great importance for the establishment of personal identities on the part of young people. For example, the likelihood that a young person will marry before establishing a mature adult identity is believed to be a main factor in the high failure rate of youthful marriages. The

14

*1/Marriage and the
Family in the
United States*

recent increase in age at first marriage for both men and women may mark the beginning of a trend toward a longer transition period from dependency on parents until marriage; however, it is still uncertain what this increase means.[15]

Changing Birth Rates

On average, the first child born to a marriage arrives slightly later than his or her counterpart of a decade ago. At present, about half the firstborn children arrive within seventeen months after marriage. There has been no significant change in the average spacing between the first and second children of women who have only two children. There has, however, been a significant increase in the length of time between the most recent birth to a mother of four or more children and the birth of the preceding child.[16]

The birth rate in the United States has declined since 1800, although during the twentieth century birth rates have fluctuated from one birth per year for every sixty people—the all-time low, reached at the peak of the Depression in 1933—to one birth per year for every forty people, a figure reached during the postwar baby boom in 1947. After 1957, when the baby boom ended, the crude birth rate decreased steadily until 1976. Although it has been increasing gradually for the past few years, it appears destined to stay relatively low for the foreseeable future.[17] Collectively, these data suggest that there is considerably more family planning than there was even a decade ago, especially since much of the recent increase in the birth rate has been accounted for by first births to women over thirty years old. It is not insignificant that the birth control pill was mass marketed in 1966, providing its users with a more effective means of planning their families.

It is important to note that since the population has shifted from rural to urban, parents increasingly find their children no longer to be economic assets. In the past it was more costly to raise a large family in the city than it was on the farm. Many believe that economic factors play a most important role in the reduction of the birth rate.

Changing Divorce Patterns

In 1890, there was 1 divorce for every 2,000 people in the population.[18] The rate of divorces has increased more or less steadily until the present, when there are about 5 divorces per year for every 1,000 people.[19] This is higher than the previous peak of 4.3, which occurred immediately after World War II. Divorce is about ten times as common as it was in 1890, but the number of years that the average person remains in his or her first marriage has increased dramatically. Unfortunately, information on abandonment, desertion, and separation without divorce is neither consistent nor reliable; however, it is estimated that these forms of family disruption occur as often as legal divorce and may have occurred even more often in the nineteenth century. Marital disruption overall, however, most often occurs because of the death of one of the

15

*Changing Patterns
of Love and Marriage
in the United States*

partners, even though for younger couples divorce is more likely to end their marriages.

Divorces account for about two-thirds of the recorded disruption of marriages among nonwhites in the United States today, while they account for only about one-third of the disruption of marriages among whites. The proportion of women between the ages of thirty and forty-five who report disrupted marriages is approximately three times as high for the nonwhite population as it is for the white population.[20] This is thought to represent an economic factor more than a racial or ethnic one. As noted earlier, the greatest likelihood of family disruption exists among couples in which the man has not finished high school and has a low income. Interpretations of these data are complicated—undoubtedly, some of the change is due to the increased potential length of the marriage period. Some, however, is probably due to changes in ideals, which were discussed earlier.

Summary

■ There are many definitions of marriage and the family—legal, religious, formal, informal—but the most frequently used definitions emphasize the enduring nature of the relationship and the fact that persons living together in marriage and the family form a dynamic social system.

■ Four social criteria help to define marriage:

a. The persons involved have some agreement about sexual access to each other and to others.
b. They are economically involved both as an earning and as a consuming unit.
c. They are mutually supportive of each other's welfare.
d. The relationship is stable over a period of time; or, at least, the couple intends it to be.

■ In addition to these four general criteria, marriages in the United States are heterosexual, monogamous, and usually directed toward the establishment of a family; they involve task division; they must not involve certain kinship relationships (defined as incest). Further, the partners maintain a common residence and begin with a basis of love.

■ Although there has never been only one model for marriage or only one suitable family pattern, currently the models are more varied than ever. Marriage and the family have been affected by changes that have occurred in this century, such as the population shift from farms to urban areas. Children have become more an economic liability than an asset, and the birth rate has fluctuated with the economy; more women are in the labor force; mate selection has become more a personal choice based on love than a family matter. Finally, the divorce rate has risen.

16

1/Marriage and the
Family in the
United States

The State of Health of
Marriage and the Family

The family is a prominent feature of every society. Very little happens in people's lives that is not affected by the family and that does not, in turn, affect the family. In an ongoing process, not only is the family molded by society into whatever forms are functional, but also families contribute significantly to the success of the society to which they belong. Families not only prepare future citizens but also nurture and sustain adults engaged in the day-to-day business of the society.

Perhaps more than any other feature of the family, its endurance as an institution stands out. This endurance both provides individual family members throughout their lives with a feeling of continuity and roots and gives them a sense of leaving a heritage that future generations can use as a similar path to establishing their identities. Each family lives in historical time, not only making its own fate but also being influenced daily in important ways by world events—wars, economic ups and downs, and other less dramatic public occurrences.[21]

Family sociologists look to historical facts to explain the present and to predict future trends. The use of family history—formerly a largely neglected area—to understand how families change across generations has increased markedly since World War II.[22]

The early family literature gave great weight to an idealized version of past family life. More recently, however, research using family history has set the perspective straight. Those who compared the present with an idealized past—which was viewed as more wholesome and more satisfying for families—drew the conclusion that current family life had "glaring deficiencies."[23]

The literature has been filled with predictions that the family is disintegrating so rapidly that it will soon cease to function as an institution.[24] The high divorce rate has been cited as evidence of the "death of the family," along with what has been interpreted as a serious erosion of family support systems within kinship networks. The variety of forms the family has taken in the past few decades—single-parent families, step families, dual-paycheck families, communal families, cohabiting families—has been seen as evidence of the breakdown of the American family system. The fact that the same varieties are present (and may always have been present) in other societies has been ignored by the alarmists or has been cited by them as evidence of the inferiority of those societies.[25]

There are currently a great many types of families in the world that seem to function at least somewhat satisfactorily. Moreover, this apparently has always been true. The standards against which so many critics of current family life measure the family's deterioration, then, seem to be derived from unrealistic ideals rather than from careful observations of historical social reality.[26]

There is little question that the traditional American family system has undergone significant modifications. Paradoxically, the flexibility of the family, one of its most striking features, has been seen by some as proof of the family's demise. Such critics view social change and the adaptability of social institutions to change as signs of disintegration rather than of strength.[27]

What has been occurring is not the death of the family but rather a powerful struggle by family units to adapt to societal conditions and to the needs of individual family members. The adaptability of the family keeps it alive and is the reason that, no matter what the odds, the family has endured over time and across cultures. Many family-life specialists—and we are among them— believe that the family is thriving. We do not deny that there are serious problems, but we have confidence in the resiliency of contemporary families. Experts are not alone in this belief. In a recent survey of 4,000 persons representative of a much larger population, the immediate family was given first priority in the lives of over 75 percent of the respondents.[28] This and other pieces of research leave little question that Americans believe in and support the family and, moreover, depend on family life to fulfill a variety of important needs that our society does not meet in any other way.[29]

The American belief in the family, demonstrated by the widespread concern for its welfare, as well as other characteristics of the family—including its problems—is the subject of this book. We will discuss how the family unit still fulfills basic survival needs for the young but has changed from a total institution to a support system that meets needs of companionship, love, and intimacy. In a comprehensive statement of family life in the United States today, the director of the National Institute of Mental Health has said:

> *The family gives each newborn its primary nurturing environment, and as time passes, is each child's primary socializing agent, shaping its capacity for personal relations, interpreting and mediating the vast and complex outside world. Beyond these recognized functions we largely take for granted, the family exerts other powerful influences. It can provide us with a continuity of identity throughout our lives—a present network of relatedness, roots into the past, and branches to the future. It is a platform for each member's stages of growth and the intimate arena for learning to recognize and adjust to these stages in others. It has an internal dynamic quality, its functions changing over time according to its members' needs and enduring long after its members have dispersed. Externally, the family affects other people and institutions, both as the family unit collectively engages with the world and as its members sally forth, imprinted by their family ways. And the idea of family itself has been extended, providing a unifying function for new combinations of people who choose to call themselves a family.*[30]

18

*1/Marriage and the
Family in the
United States*

The nature of the unifying functions around which individuals come together as families has shifted perceptibly in the twentieth century. As noted previously, early definitions of the family often emphasized its utilitarian functions—the economic aspects of the family unit. Even during the first thirty years of this century, and throughout the Depression of the 1930s, the definition of the family was often colored by its practical functions.[31]

Although millions of Americans still live in poverty, and inflation may again be forcing families to focus on economic issues, since the 1940s the major emphasis has been increasingly on the emotional aspects of family life. In her thoughtful discussion of this change, family sociologist Lois Pratt has commented that families still have difficulty in giving their members all the necessary emotional nourishment but that multifamily forms have developed in an effort to accomplish this task.[32] Although the heavy emotional demands made on each family unit have the potential to create serious problems, most families are motivated by the necessity to do for their members what no other institution can. The forms families take must vary to meet the unique demands of different times and situations, and of the individual members' need to learn to care for themselves and for each other and to have healthy contacts outside the family boundaries. Therefore, not only may one family differ from another, but each family also changes its form over time.

To determine what makes families strong, cohesive, functional support systems for their members, a study was made of 130 such families.[33] Six qualities stood out clearly:

1. Most important was the members' *appreciation for one another.* Students of **social psychology** will recognize at once the important findings of research on affiliation and liking: we like people most who like us; we want to be with those who make us feel good about ourselves and who support rather than criticize us.[34] Family members who openly appreciate each other enjoy being together.

2. Because family members enjoyed each other, they *arranged their personal schedules* so that they had time together as a family. Each of the strong families regularly spent time together as a family, although what they did together was by no means routine. They also spent time together spontaneously. Most family members lead busy lives, and each person must make a positive effort to find family time.

3. Strong families are characterized by positive *communication patterns,* as will be discussed in Chapter 7. Positive communication involves openness, genuineness, active listening, respect, interest, and the airing of differences. The important thing is not the quantity of communication—provided there is adequate coverage of concerns and interests—but rather that family members share meaning and agree on the quality of the communication.

4. The well-functioning families provided evidence of strong family feeling and *high family commitment*. Since the family is a small group, small-group research can be used to explain the cohesiveness of strong families. Cohesiveness derives from the belief of members that some of their important needs (being liked and appreciated, for example) are met by belonging and that the group they belong to is a "winning team." The presence of these factors induces members to invest time and energy in the family.[35]

5. In the strong families there was a sense of a power and a purpose greater than themselves—a *spiritual orientation*. This is not to say that they were necessarily religious or churchgoing people. However, they defined themselves as having values that are generally associated with religion.

6. Finally, these families were able to face their problems and to *deal positively with crises*. They were striking in their adaptive abilities and in the nourishment and care they provided for family members during times of trouble.

The same dire predictions that have been made about the demise of the family have been leveled at the institution of marriage as well. The futurist F. M. Esfandiary has said, "Marriage . . . must go. . . . No variation will work."[36] Family sociologists and certain authors commenting on the American scene have suggested that marriage is an institution in decay.[37,38] There have been many suggestions for improving contemporary marriages, ranging from so-called **trial marriages** to legislation designed to make getting married more difficult.

Certainly there are many unhappy marriages, and an increasing number of marriages end in divorce. In response to a recent poll, 1.7 percent of never-divorced men and 2.8 percent of never-divorced women reported that they were "not too happy." However, 71.3 percent of the men and 70 percent of the women in the sample described themselves as "very happy." The figures for those who had been divorced and remarried indicated slightly less happiness in their current marriages; even so, less than 7 percent reported being "not too happy."[39]

Although many marriages end in divorce, in 1979 85 percent of married men and 88 percent of married women between ages fifty-five and fifty-nine were still married to their first spouses.[40] Although the increase in life expectancy is largely responsible for these figures, it is also a positive sign that more and more silver and golden wedding anniversaries are being celebrated each year. Evidently not all marriages are in trouble, if, as these statistics indicate, the average marriage is lasting longer—even though divorce is an option—and an overwhelming number of couples report that they are happy in their marriages. Since over 90 percent of all Americans marry at least once and most divorced persons remarry, it seems obvious that Americans overwhelmingly prefer being married to any other life-style.[41]

20

*1/Marriage and the
Family in the
United States*

Marriage and Family Research and Theory

Partly because of concerns about the effects of social change on marriage and the family and partly because the problems noted earlier prompt a general concern, most research in the areas of marriage and the family has been problem oriented. It has been estimated that for every 100 studies investigating families only 1 has been of a positive nature whereas 99 have been concerned with problems.[42] Marriage and family research has contributed to a better understanding of the family as an enduring unit, although more research on successful marriages and families is needed to complete the picture.

The hundreds of studies have yielded a steady supply of facts. Until relatively recently, in fact, marriage and family research was long on facts but short on **theory**. At first researchers borrowed theories from other disciplines to help interpret the facts derived from marriage and family research. Recently, however, the field of marriage and the family has generated theories of its own in addition to using existing theories to good advantage in explaining contemporary family life and expected trends.[43] During the past decade, marriage and family theories have become more sophisticated and have expanded to include dozens of "minor" theories in an attempt to interpret findings on subjects that are only peripherally related.[44] Throughout this book there will be references to contemporary theories on various phenomena of family life. Although there is no general agreement about which theories offer the best possibilities for explaining family behavior, we have chosen a few to use here in explaining aspects of marriage and family life.

Theories are best viewed as statements that attempt to explain concisely findings from various pieces of research that somehow are related—systems of ideas that link concepts together in order to explain certain related facts. They attempt to demonstrate cause and effect and to suggest further areas of research that may sharpen the initial theory. Frequently two or more theories appear to be in conflict with each other. More often than not, however, the apparent conflict results from the fact that the theories are approaching a given topic from very different directions. Rather than disagreeing, then, often the theories simply are addressing separate parts of the problem.

With topics as large and diverse as marriage and the family, many theories are probably needed: it is unlikely that any one theory could ever be comprehensive enough to take all factors into consideration. However, the search continues for an "all-purpose general family framework" to unify and consolidate knowledge about marriage and the family.[45] We are less certain than some of our colleagues that the pursuit of a unified, all-encompassing theory is the most appropriate goal at present, and we are even doubtful that it is now possible to find one theory that is simultaneously broad enough to cover all aspects of marriage and the family and specific enough to be useful.[46]

Throughout this book we will refer to theories that have been used to explain how people interact in their family relationships. We have selected the major theories as well as a few others that reveal our particular biases. In a recent review of marriage and family theories, it was suggested that there are three kinds of theoretical approaches that currently are judged to have a major impact on our understanding of issues of marriage and the family.[47]

Symbolic Interaction Theory

Many family theorists believe that this may be the most influential theory, on the basis of the number of research projects employing this approach.[48] A distinguishing feature of the interactionist approach is the belief that we acquire a complex assortment of symbols in our minds (words, meanings, gestures, objects) and use these symbols to understand our environment and the people in it, including ourselves. We learn how to act, react, and adjust by the use of these symbols—most of which are a part of the environment into which we are born. We are "socialized" to accept and understand the vast array of symbols we will have to use.

Symbolic interaction theory has been widely used to explain mate selection as an evolving process dependent on a person's learning to evaluate potential partners through symbols. It is through symbols that information is gathered and categorized. Choices are then determined by the meanings each person gives to his or her own behavior and to that of others.

Exchange Theory

This point of view has grown in popularity in the past decade. It has been suggested that exchange theory has the potential to be the "grand, all-encompassing" framework that has so far been elusive.[49] At the risk of oversimplifying a complex theoretical orientation, we can say that exchange theory basically emphasizes the concepts of rewards and costs in any interaction. The sociologist Peter Blau describes exchanges as "voluntary actions of individuals that are motivated by the returns [that the exchanges] are expected to bring and typically do in fact bring from others."[50] People seek rewarding exchanges and attempt to keep the costs lower than the rewards.

Most studies on family decision making have used exchange theory as a basis for explaining how and why decisions are made.[51] Each person has certain resources (money, talent, wisdom, affection) that may be used as rewards for the desirable behaviors of the other. Such rewards may become sources of power in couples' decision making, for example. Exchange theory has also been widely used as a basis for helping couples in conflict. Much successful marital therapy concentrates on maximizing the rewarding aspects of the relationship for each partner while minimizing the drawbacks.[52] Exchange theory has

22

1/*Marriage and the
Family in the
United States*

helped scholars understand a variety of marital and family issues in which a clear focus on rewards and costs is evident. Critics of exchange theory point out, however, that not all issues lend themselves to such a clear analysis: many interrelationships appear to be based on highly complicated factors that are often beyond the conscious awareness of the individuals involved.[53]

General Systems Theory

This theory emphasizes the nature of the family as a system with boundaries that delineate it from elements outside itself. Both the system and the boundaries change constantly as children are born or leave home and as husbands, wives, and children go outside the family to work or to school and bring others into the family through marriage and friendships. Systems theory has been used, for example, to describe the impact on a marriage of the addition of a new member through the birth of the first child.[54] The presence of a new baby transforms a couple into a family, increases the possibilities for interaction, and modifies the relationships in ways that may be dramatic.

A family system has standards, rules, goals, and methods of communicating that serve as means of control of the family's members. When one member of a system varies his or her responses to the standards, the other members will change in reaction, often putting pressure on the straying member to conform again. Although the direction of change of the system as a result of a change in one or more of its members is not always predictable, it seems certain that there will be some response.[55]

The systems approach has gained in popularity immensely in recent years, although critics of systems theory point to the many questions it leaves unanswered and to the lack of documentation of many of the cause-and-effect statements that have been made.[56] These criticisms have not dampened enthusiasm for systems theory, however. Those who support this approach—and we are among them—have suggested that general systems theory will continue to develop and grow in importance.[57]

Other Theories

In addition to the three major theories described so far, there are three others that have been used frequently and that offer valuable insights into the functioning of marriage and the family. We mention these here so that they will be familiar to the reader when they are cited in later chapters.

These six are by no means all the theoretical points of view that have made important contributions to the understanding of marital and family life; rather, they represent our own biases. Psychoanalytic theory, for example, has certainly had a strong influence on systems theory, among others. Similarly, social learning theory and the behavioral theories are clearly influential in exchange theory. The following three theoretical approaches have been used less frequently than the three major ones described earlier; nevertheless, they offer many explanations about marriage and the family.

Developmental Theory.   The life-cycle changes of individuals who marry and have families have been investigated as important factors in marital and family interrelationships and satisfactions.[58] Not only are the individual changes seen as important, but it has been proposed that, beyond the importance of the individual changes, changes in the marital life cycle (birth of first child, school entrance of children, departure from home of last child, retirement, and so forth) affect interpersonal issues between family members.[59] Almost all text-books on marriage and the family, including this one, proceed from the topic of courtship to those of love, mate selection, marriage, child rearing, and finally the "empty nest" and aging. Developmental theory explains each stage of the life cycle as the product of an orderly sequence of preceding events. Such an approach is useful in describing how the life cycle is tied to changes in relationships—both as cause and as effect.

Conflict Theory.   This approach has gained in popularity in the past decade as family researchers have attempted to explain marriage and the family in terms of the competing needs of the members who make up the system.[60] This theory proposes that the very nature of marriage and the family, which brings together individuals with unique backgrounds and separate needs and desires, provides a setting for conflict in the form of competition, tension, and power struggles. Resolution of the conflict allows for growth and for relationships that are satisfying in new ways. In particular, male-female roles lend themselves to exploration from the perspective of conflict theory. It is argued, for example, that gender-role inequality is based on the differences between the sexes that lead to conflict between men and women.[61]

Cognitive Theory.   A central feature of this theoretical approach is that a person's thinking affects not only behavior but also emotions. In many ways cognitive theory resembles symbolic interactionism because the meaning one gives to another's action is believed to determine one's response to that action, more than the objective situation or even the other person's intended meaning.[62] **Phenomenology** is a term used to describe this process, whereby one's unique perception of reality becomes the basis for one's actions. This approach has been particularly helpful in providing a perspective for marriage and family therapy.[63] Behavior therapy, which is often used with troubled marriages and families, is closely linked to cognitive theory; both emphasize the translation of behavior and emotions into cognitive terms and the mapping of explicit ways to rethink and hence to change old behaviors.

Summary

- The health of the family as an institution, and family life-styles today, are powerful factors in determining the nature not only of individual family heritages that will be handed down, but also of future society and culture.

- The current alarm about the "poor health" of the American family, as

24

*1/Marriage and the
Family in the
United States*

measured by high divorce rates, may be inappropriate. Widespread concern about the survival of the family indicates a healthy social interest, however.

■ Although divorce rates have increased over the past century, so has the average number of years that first marriages last. Other severely disruptive family problems, such as infant mortality, abject poverty, and deadly communicable diseases, have declined. Thus we believe there is less misery in families now than in the past.

■ Over the past fifty years, the unifying functions of the American family have shifted from primarily protective, religious, educational, survival, and economic activities to primarily affectional and companionship activities.

■ Both the researcher's and the lay person's concepts of the family include some ideas about what a family does, how it developed its current form, and how it works. These understandings are formally called *theories.* Currently, the most prominent theories or groups of theories favored by scholars are (1) interactionist theory, (2) exchange theory, and (3) general systems theory.

■ Theories that help explain family structure and function but are less inclusive than the foregoing are (1) developmental theory, (2) conflict theory, and (3) cognitive theory.

Challenges to the Family of the 1980s

Family-life specialists have recently begun to emphasize the need for planning for the future of the family. In recent years *family policy* and *family action* have become topics of interest. Both are concerned with the problems faced by families resulting from the impact of regulations and changes produced by government, other social institutions, and other aspects of the society at large. A major emphasis of the White House Conference on Families in 1980 was the investigation of how families are faring and what families need. Important issues raised included the problems of poverty, the availability of health care, and support for the many types of families that exist in our society. The conference encouraged the strengthening of all forms of the family rather than criticism of family forms other than the two-parent nuclear family. The National Council on Family Relations developed proposals for the conference that reflected the concerns of specialists for the future of the American family. Topics covered included: two-earner families, the needs of the elderly, families and health-care legislation, day-care policies, the impact of divorce, family violence, family-life education, and the needs of special families.[64]

In a recent survey, family-life specialists named the following as among the major challenges facing professionals in their attempts to aid families in the 1980s.

1. to help people to have commitments to family and spouses that are strong enough to see them through crises, and to maintain a belief in lasting commitments to each other
2. to educate young adults who have not had models of a good marriage or a functional family so that they might avoid repeating the problems of their parents
3. to help those without a family support system to develop a **surrogate** family support system to meet their needs, and to help people reach out to others to overcome isolation and loneliness
4. to help the family deal with economic stress, family violence, and incest
5. to develop more programs for specific groups such as single parents, stepparents, and remarried couples
6. to aid those who feel they must divorce—for example, by promoting new patterns in separation agreements and in support and custody arrangements
7. to create a "family of the future" that will permit the greatest possible amount of individuality, autonomy, and self-fulfillment to all family members[65]

26

*1/Marriage and the
Family in the
United States*

The last concern may be the greatest challenge of all—to help in creating families that will permit individuality, autonomy, and self-fulfillment while still preserving the family as a unit. In the diverse population of the United States, many families—particularly minority families and single-parent families—do not conform to mainstream, middle-class family models (which have dominated views of marriage and the family for generations).

Pluralism seems to be a key to the future of marriage and the family. A shift toward pluralism may be the single most significant change we will see in marriage and family systems in this decade.[66] Most of us are only beginning to deal well with changes in marital, sexual, and family models; many still insist on conventional, traditional patterns. It is, of course, difficult to predict the future. The value of past and current data in looking ahead is undermined by the likelihood of occurrence of unforeseeable events that may interrupt the steady path of any trend. Wars and economic conditions, for example, may drastically alter a trend that has previously provided easy projections from one generation to the next. With the understanding that long-range forecasts are imprecise and often inaccurate, many family specialists still believe that trends are our most accurate predictors of the future. On the basis of trends, it is forecast that during the 1980s there will be a continued loosening of conventional expectations for male-female roles;[67] increasing variety in sexual and marital experiences;[68] continuation of the low birth rate;[69] continuation of parent-child involvement and mutual bonding;[70] and a leveling off of divorce rates.[71]

We think it safe to predict that marriage and the family will survive in good shape and that social scientists will continue to be fascinated by the many forms of the family and by the problems and the successes of its members. Advances in research are expected in the next decade that will contribute significantly to the understanding of marriage and the family and to the quality and stability of American family life, no matter what form it may take.

Glossary

Bigamy The state of being married to two persons at the same time. Bigamy is forbidden by law in all fifty states of the United States.

Ceremonial marriage A formal declaration in the presence of witnesses of the intention to be spouses. Most states require that ceremonial marriages be registered or licensed to be legally valid.

Cohabitation A life-style in which two unrelated people live at the same residence. Because *cohabitation* frequently implies a sexual relationship between the persons living together, the word is not usually used in reference to the members of a family.

Consummation The fulfillment of a marriage through the act of sexual intercourse.

Cultural   Referring to ways of believing and behaving that are generally accepted as right or proper in a social collectivity. Judgments of "right" or "proper" may apply to social behaviors, to ways of thinking and feeling, to symbols, or to technologies.

Heterosexual   Pertaining to different sexes.

Incest   Sexual activities between those of such close kinship that laws and customs forbid them to marry or to engage in coitus.

Microculture   The ways of living of a societal sub-group (such as an ethnic group or a particular family group).

Monogamy   A form of marriage in which there is one spouse at a time for each person.

Nonceremonial ("common-law") marriage   In legal terms, an unregistered or unlicensed marriage; often a marriage that becomes legally recognized after a couple cohabits for a specified period.

Phenomenology   A point of view that behavior is responsive to an individual's perceptions rather than to objective reality.

Pluralism   The belief that reality consists of many kinds of distinct elements with many explanations for those elements.

Polygamy   The sanctioned marriage of a person or persons to more than one other person at a time.

Social   Referring to the interactions of two or more persons or to the relationships between or among them.

Social psychology   The study of human behavior as it is affected by social environments—especially by group interaction.

Surrogate   A person or object that substitutes for another. Foster parents, for example, may be surrogates for biological parents when the latter are unavailable or unfit.

Symbolic interactionism   The theory that human behavior is a product of thinking and communication that takes place through a system of organized symbols meaningful to those who interact.

Theory   A summarizing statement used to explain complex phenomena linked together in such a way as to produce a specific effect or effects.

Trial marriage   A tentative or conditional relationship (usually cohabitation) intended to determine whether or not a formal marriage is desirable.

It is true, of course, that the increased activity of women in economic life tends to reduce the differences between male and female roles, but the cause of the alteration in these roles lies also in the decline of the ancient values and the unshackling and unmasking of a masculine hunger for emotional gratifications.

—Jules Henry,
Culture against Man

2 · Male-Female Similarities and Differences

We are born male or female, but we learn to be masculine or feminine. This chapter will explore the biological differences and similarities between males and females and will consider how we learn sex roles and what it means to be a man or a woman in our society. We are beginning to learn that the differences between the sexes are fewer than we once thought and often less important in limiting the behavior of either males or females. To what extent do the differences that exist have a biological basis, and to what extent do they arise from social expectations?

By the age of three, most children know clearly what sex they are. Children get direct impressions about gender from parents and other significant people in their environment, and they are quick to imitate attitudes. By age three, they also know many of the "proper" masculine and feminine ways to behave. They can tell us, for example, that mommies cook and clean (even if they also have jobs outside the home) and that daddies are big and strong and "go to work" (even if they also do all the home maintenance and yard work).

Although we make fewer distinctions today between the behaviors considered appropriate for one sex or the other, it is slow and arduous to swim against the tide of so many years of tradition. In most societies throughout history, women have tended the home (with sojourns into the fields for food gathering); men have built houses, gone hunting to bring home meat for the table, and defended the family against attack.

Some historians claim that a division of labor between the sexes is "natural" because of the physical differences between men and women. They point out that men are better suited to physical labor and combat because they are, in general, bigger and stronger than women. Women, who have the unique biological capability to bear and nurse children, have been given the task of caring for the children they bear. Since the responsibilities assigned to women are better accomplished in a safe and stable environment, it has been functional for them to combine home care with child care. The factors of size and strength in men and of pregnancy and lactation in women thus have been basic to the division of labor. As a result, these historians point out, every society throughout history has organized men's and women's work around these differences.

Boys and girls are brought up surrounded by the traditions and customs of their parents. Their early training and the examples of adult behavior they observe reflect these customs. In the past, children typically grew up expecting women to do the work compatible with child care—homemaking and food production—and men to perform tasks that took them outside the home for prolonged periods, even if they were significantly involved with their children when they were at home.

Modifications in the ways young children are socialized are most likely to occur as a result of changes in the roles of adults. Life-styles in the United States have changed in response to economic changes and have in turn led to adaptive changes in family life. Very gradually, there have come to be fewer distinctions between the behaviors considered appropriate for each sex. A simple example of such a change is found in the relative ease with which men can now feed infants.

The development of mechanical refrigeration for safer storage of milk, of pasteurization, of vulcanization (for the manufacture of acceptable artificial nipples) combined with advances in the sciences of hygiene and nutrition make it possible to feed infants satisfactorily without depending on a lactating mother or wet nurse. There was undoubtedly a lag of a few years during which both men and women thought it was "odd" or "peculiar" for a man to *want* to feed an infant or for a woman to want a man to do so. Now, however, most members of both sexes are quite comfortable with the idea of a man feeding a baby, even though this represents a reversal of a long-standing pattern.

Similarly, there is now a greater acceptance of women working outside their homes and of men performing a greater share of home and child care than in the past. These changes signal shifts in popular attitudes about masculinity and femininity. Thus although some hospitals still issue blue name bracelets to boy babies and pink to girls, and although members of each sex begin to be treated differently almost immediately, the capabilities of the two sexes are now increasingly seen as similar as a result of cultural, economic, and social changes and technological developments.

It is interesting that the acceptance of changes in the roles of men and women seems to be increasing among people at all social and economic levels. Usually basic role changes begin among more highly educated persons and trickle down very slowly to those with less education. Probably because of the economic nature of work roles, however, attitudes seem to be changing in all groups.[1]

Changes in sex-role behavior in the United States have been gradual. Even though today the average woman is likely to be involved with reproduction for only a minimal period of time (and about one woman in eight has no children), ideologically many Americans still cling to the notion that a woman's role is basically that of mother and a man's primarily that of provider. Recent opinion polls have made this very clear: 75 percent of respondents supported the idea that "it's up to the man to be the main provider in the family," and 82 percent believed that "a woman with small children should go to work only if the money is really needed."[2] These sentiments seem to have changed as much as they have primarily because the money really is needed by married women with small children and the growing number of single mothers. As more and more mothers enter the labor force for this reason, public opinion reflects more tolerance of those who, besides needing to work, choose to work outside the home.

Although all known societies distinguish between men's and women's roles, there is great variation from one society to another (and within a given society over time) about what is considered masculine or feminine behavior. It is interesting to note that beyond the obvious biological differences (men do not get pregnant), there is no universal agreement about what is correct or good behavior. There is not even a consensus on what is functional, since now as in the past both men and women have a wide variety of approved activities, many of which overlap their sex roles. What may be accepted behavior for men and women in one society may be frowned on in another. Likewise, what is shocking behavior in a society at one historical period may be acceptable within the same society at another time.

People in most societies have used the obvious sex differences as a rationale for polarizing the concepts of masculinity and femininity. Consequently, these concepts have tended to diverge from each other as much as possible. **Sexologist** John Money comments on the application of this polarity to the ways males and females are legally identified:

> As registered on your birth certificate and other documents, your sex denotes, on the basis of the anatomy between your legs, your civil status as either male or female. You are given no other option. . . . On to it has been grafted the cultural practice, universally taken for granted in our culture, of maximizing the differences, behavioral included, between the sexes, rather than maximizing the similarities.[3]

The extent to which the observed differences between men and women arise from genetic factors as opposed to social learning is a complicated and still controversial question. For the sake of clarity, it may be easier to discuss the issues involved by distinguishing four aspects of male-female similarities and differences: (1) *sex* (the biological state of being male or female); (2) *gender* (a term that describes one's self-concept and social presentation as male or female) and gender role; (3) *sex preference* (sometimes called sexual orientation); and (4) the concepts of *masculinity* and *femininity*. The designation of these four categories allows us to see where they overlap and how easy it is to confuse one with another or to assume that if one is present in a particular form, then the other three must invariably follow suit.

Sex

One's sex is determined by the coincidence of many qualities. To determine sex, "one must assay the following conditions: **chromosomes**, external **genitalia**, internal genitalia (e.g., **uterus**, prostate), **gonads**, hormonal states, and secondary sex characteristics. (It seems likely that in the future another criterion will be added: brain systems.)"[4] Not until 1976 did scientific discoveries unravel the puzzle of how germ cells cause a human embryo to differentiate the male sex organs from those of the female.[5] Earlier, it was known that at about six weeks after fertilization the undifferentiated gonadal tissue in the male embryo begins to form **testes**, whereas in the female the tissue stays undifferentiated for another six weeks or so. The 1976 discovery was of a substance (H-Y antigen) produced by the Y chromosome that programs embryonic cells to differentiate. Without this programming, which causes the testes to form, both XX and XY embryos would eventually differentiate female sex organs.

In about the third month of pregnancy, however, the fetal testes secrete two substances. One suppresses the development of ducts that would otherwise grow to become the uterus and the **fallopian tubes**. (It is rare, but not unheard of, for a child to be born with testes as well as a uterus and fallopian tubes.)

The second substance secreted by the fetal testes is **androgen**, which stimulates growth of the ducts that eventually develop into male genitalia. Should this androgen secretion fail, the XY (male) fetus could have testes but no penis.

In the female fetus, **ovaries** become differentiated approximately three months after fertilization and begin to produce **estrogens** that encourage growth and the eventual development of a uterus and fallopian tubes.

If either the testes or the ovaries fail to produce appropriate hormones, there is a potential for abnormalities of the genital or reproductive organs. A condition involving ambiguous external genitalia is called **hermaphroditism**. The baby with such a problem is born looking "sexually unfinished," in John Money's description.[6] The external genitalia of a hermaphrodite may show some characteristics of both sexes. If such babies are mistakenly not assigned to the sex indicated by their chromosomal composition, they may be brought up by their parents with a gender identity that is genetically inappropriate.

Nearly everyone is assigned to a sex immediately upon birth. This assignment is universally made on the basis of the appearance of the external genital organs. A baby's sex is announced at once; no one would think of waiting for a microscopic examination of the baby's chromosomes before saying "It's a girl!" or "It's a boy!" From that moment on, the child's social experiences and self-concept will be profoundly affected by the announced sex.

At **puberty** the hormonal system mobilizes to develop secondary sex characteristics such as body hair, voice changes, and breast development. At this point, erroneous sex assignment becomes apparent. Early corrective surgery may be performed to construct the appropriate genitalia for whichever sex was assigned at birth, and in some instances hormone treatment can be used to suppress later changes. If such surgery has not been done soon after birth, it can be performed when an error in sex assignment becomes obvious. When a child has had a **gender identity** that does not match his or her chromosomal sex, it is usually simpler for a specialist to change the appearance of the genitalia surgically than for the young person to undo years of believing that he or she was of the opposite sex.

Some societies view a person with genital abnormalities as belonging to a "third gender" and allow such persons to perform roles of either males or females—or both—and to dress in any way they wish. Such individuals can marry other persons assigned to either sex and may receive a special recognition in the society.[7]

Gender

Gender is a term that has psychological or cultural rather than biological connotations. If the proper terms for sex are "male" and "female," the corresponding terms for gender are "masculine" and "feminine"; these latter may be quite independent of (biological) sex. Gender is the amount of masculinity or femininity found in a person, and, obviously, while there are mixtures of both in virtually all humans, the normal male has a preponderance of masculinity and the normal female a preponderance of femininity.[8]

American children and adults alike assess persons' genders in everyday interaction by their behaviors and appearances. The ways in which they dress, talk, posture their bodies, groom themselves, and relate to others are all evidence of people's genders.

Gender role is the overt behavior one displays in society, the role which he plays, especially with other people, to establish his position with them insofar as his gender and their evaluation of his gender is concerned. While gender, gender identity, and gender role are almost synonymous in the usual person, in certain abnormal cases they are at variance. One problem that arises to complicate our work is that gender behavior, which is for the greatest part learned from birth on, plays an essential part in sexual behavior, which is markedly biological, and at times it is very difficult to separate aspects of gender and sex from a particular piece of behavior.[9]

The hormones from the fetal testes and ovaries have important effects on gender. They play a major role in programming **neural** pathways in the brain that will eventually direct the behavior of the individual through his or her lifetime. These hormones do not necessarily *preordain* behavior but do appear to *predispose* certain behavioral patterns. Research is currently proliferating rapidly in an attempt to determine just what brain differences result from the variation in hormones and whether or not these biological differences are programmed in such a way that they will resist alteration through later learning. There are intriguing questions about the existence of biological differences that create a "male" or a "female" brain and make certain types of behavior more likely in one sex or the other.[10]

Aggression

A widely studied question is that of the total effect of androgens on the brain and on behavior. **Testosterone** is an androgen that stimulates the development of secondary sex characteristics in males (making the average male larger, more muscular, and stronger than the average female). This hormone has been linked to aggression in a variety of animals.

Every rancher or farmer knows that a castrated bull becomes a more docile animal because its testicles have been removed. Cat owners believe that their male cats have fewer fights when they are castrated. The decrease in aggression is attributed to the absence of the testosterone formerly supplied by the animal's testicles. Consequently, this hormone has been called the "aggression hormone."

It has been hypothesized that the Y chromosome programs the gonads in such a way that testosterone is produced, with the obvious effect that testes grow and the probable effect that distinctively male brain characteristics develop simultaneously. The association of these brain characteristics with aggressive behavior is still hypothetical, but the evidence for it is increasing. According to this theory, male animals not only are programmed to produce testosterone in amounts large enough to make them behave more aggressively than females, but also, because males are genetically larger and stronger on the average, they are more capable of effective aggression.*

Although the evidence that *human* males may be more aggressive because of brain differences is still controversial, there is a long-standing folk belief that boys are generally more aggressive than girls. Boys invariably are reported to be more physically active and to play more boisterously. Studies of children in many countries have noted that this male-female difference shows up before the age of three and lasts into young adulthood. Even data on older adults show that men are more likely to be involved in crimes of violence and in accidents than are women.[11]

Other research that gives important evidence of the relationship of testosterone to aggression has shown that female animals that have been injected with testosterone have become more aggressive and boisterous. Males normally produce five times as much testosterone as do females, but it is not uncommon for a female to produce enough to display physical characteristics or behaviors that are stereotypically male.

Of course, no experiments are conducted in which large doses of testosterone are given to human females to see if they will become more aggressive. A few clinical cases of girls who were "androgynized" during fetal development have been studied, however. **Androgynization** sometimes occurs when a pregnant woman has a tumor on one of her ovaries or on her adrenal cortex (the outer layer of the adrenal gland, which secretes a small amount of androgen). Babies born to such women sometimes appear to be hermaphrodites at birth.

Some apparent hermaphrodites have undergone corrective surgery so that they could live as females. To date, artificial female genitalia have been constructed more satisfactorily than have artificial male genitalia. Many apparent hermaphrodites assigned as females have been unusually "tomboyish," many have been excellent athletes, and many have conformed to a more masculine image than other girls with whom they have been compared.[12]

The findings on androgynization raise interesting speculations about what seem to be gender differences that affect behavior in later life. Some observers have been so impressed with these data that they have hypothesized that male dominance over females is the natural order of things. Others have suggested

---

*Male animals castrated early in life typically grow to be significantly larger and heavier than their uncastrated counterparts, suggesting that the effects of testosterone on growth are linked to the developmental stage of the affected animal.

that women can never be aggressive enough to make it in a man's economic world. However, although the power of hormones is indeed impressive, the power of humans to build strengths and to overcome obstacles resulting from inherited traits is even more impressive. Human behavior in all its complexities (especially gender-role behavior) clearly involves many more factors than hereditary variables alone can account for.

Children learn a gender identity at an early age, and few question the gender to which they were assigned at birth. Even a very young child can become visibly upset by being referred to as a member of the opposite sex. Besides knowing their own genders, children also learn early to assign others in their environment to their correct genders. At first they may use superficial clues like clothing or hairstyle, but they eventually become more sophisticated in such identification.

One's self-image as male or as female develops as a result of comparing one's own body and behavior with those of others; interacting with others who also distinguish maleness from femaleness; and learning from teachers, books, the mass media, and other sources. In this way a cognitive bridge is formed from sex assignment that is biologically determined to gender identification that is learned.

Transsexual Persons

Transsexual persons represent exceptions to the rule of acceptance of one's assigned sex and the development of gender identity. Such persons feel that they have the body of one sex but the mind (or the "soul") of the other—"women trapped in the bodies of men" or vice versa. They often seek hormonal and surgical treatment to align the two conflicting definitions of themselves. In the past twenty-five years, thousands of such transformations have taken place, although they continue to be medically, psychologically, and legally controversial.

Males who wish to become females can take estrogen to stimulate breast growth and to feminize their bodies in other ways. Surgery can be performed to enlarge breasts, to remove the testes and penis, and to create an artificial vagina. It is not yet possible to construct a penis that will erect naturally or testes that produce sperm; for females who wish to become males, however, these organs can be simulated for the sake of appearance, and the breasts can be removed. When clothed appropriately, a person of either sex can then attempt to pass for a member of the other sex. Sometimes size of feet and hands or height seems unusual, but seldom beyond the limits of normal variation within each sex.

The term **transvestism** has been used to describe the occurrence of cross-dressing (primarily that of males who dress as females). Not even a small percentage of those who enjoy dressing as members of the opposite sex can be construed as transsexual, although most transsexual persons have cross-dressed prior to surgery and many report feeling quite comfortable in the

Renee Richards

clothing of the opposite sex. For women in the United States, dressing in male clothing is so common and so acceptable that it is seldom even thought of as transvestism. In fact, it is often fashionable for women to emulate masculine dress, although in many localities "masquerading" as women is a crime for which men can be prosecuted.

Summary

■ Each person is born genetically male or female. This is called one's *biological sex* and may be ultimately defined by the presence of XX or XY chromosome combinations in the person's body cells.

■ H-Y antigen is produced by Y chromosomes in the fetal germ cells; this process causes testes to form in an embryo. The fetal testes then secrete a chemical that suppresses the development of a uterus and fallopian tubes. The fetal testes also produce androgen, which stimulates the development of male genitalia. The fetal ovaries produce hormones that inhibit the development of male genitalia and stimulate the growth of female genitalia.

■ Sex assignment is made at birth on the basis of the appearance of the external genitalia. Hermaphroditism is caused by failure of the fetal testes or the fetal ovaries to differentiate male and female sex organs completely. Babies in whom differentiation is lacking or partial may have genitalia with some characteristics of both sexes and may occasionally be assigned at birth to the sex that is the opposite of their chromosomal sex.

- Hormones from the fetal testes and ovaries play a major role in brain development; their effects appear to predispose males and females to certain differences in behavior and attitudes. One of these is thought to be a difference in aggressiveness.

- Gender identification is the self-image that a biological male or a biological female develops normally as a result of sex assignment.

- Transsexual persons do not develop a gender identification that matches their original sex assignments. Some undergo surgery to alter their genitalia so that they more closely resemble members of the opposite sex.

Sex Preferences

Just as one's sex and one's gender identity are not always perfectly matched, sometimes one's gender role and *sex preference* may not correlate, either. Sex preference refers to the individual's preference for partners in sexual activities. In this society it has generally been considered normal and natural for people to prefer **heterosexual** partners for sexual interaction—that is, for men to be attracted to women and for women to be attracted to men. Yet historical and cross-cultural accounts tell us that preference for sexual activity with partners of one's own sex (**homosexuality**) is well known in all societies.

Ancient Greek society recognized that members of the same sex might be sexually attracted to each other, although the approved pattern was that of **bisexuality**: being attracted to members of one's own sex exclusively was not accepted as natural.[13] The assumption of bisexuality allowed for sexual intimacy with both one's own and the opposite sex. It was from writings of the female Greek poet Sappho, who lived with other women on the island of Lesbos and left accounts of their sexual intimacies, that the term **lesbian** is derived.

Even though bisexual and homosexual activity may be as old as humanity and may have been widely accepted throughout history, in recent times this behavior has not been accepted in the United States. Until very recently in this country, a man or woman whose sexual preference was not exclusively for the opposite sex was thought to have a personality disorder. Not until 1975 did the American Psychiatric Association take such behavior out of the category of mental disorder. As a result, many men and women who may have engaged in (or may have thought about engaging in) a sexual act with a person of the same sex were made to feel that they were abnormal. As far back as 1948, Kinsey found that one in every three males in his study had engaged in one or more homosexual experiences in adolescence and that approximately one in twenty had had such an encounter as an adult. In a comparable study of women in

1953, up to 6 percent reported a homosexual experience.[14] These numbers represent a high proportion of men and women who may have been left with guilt and anxiety.

Most current research indicates that although there are some men and women who deny ever having thoughts of or actual sexual experiences with partners of their own sex—in other words, who are 100 percent heterosexual—such persons are clearly not in the majority. On the other hand, the same may be said of those few who only think of and engage in sexual activities with those of their own sex—who are 100 percent homosexual. Instead, sexual preference can more realistically be viewed as potentially changing over time for most normal men and women, who may have thoughts or experiences of same-sex interests at some point in their lives.

A recent study of persons with homosexual and heterosexual preferences found that most of those who identify themselves as homosexual reported that they had also experienced heterosexual intercourse; approximately one-fourth of them stated that it had occurred within a year of the interview.[15] Not only might the same individual change behaviorally over time—from same-sex play in prepuberty to heterosexual or bisexual behavior as an adult—but the strength of the preference also can vary from person to person. For instance, one who may feel very attracted to a person of the same sex or who fantasizes about a same-sex partner may never act on those feelings. On the other hand, the person who may have little overall attraction to members of his or her own sex may engage in homosexual behavior occasionally because willing opposite-sex partners are not available.

It appears that sexual preference does not always fall neatly into two discrete categories—heterosexual or homosexual—but instead that most men and women have their own unique thoughts, feelings, and behaviors that lie somewhere between these two preferences and that may change with time and with the situation. *Most* people exhibit heterosexual behavior *most* of the time, but we cannot say clearly whether or not most prefer that behavior because social (and even legal) sanctions against any other behavior have been enforced. Until 1978, for instance, "homosexuals" routinely were denied military or government service; even in 1980, two women out of a total of eight who were tried by the Navy were discharged because it was claimed that their lesbian activities were interfering with their duties. In 1981, a United States congressman was forced to resign his office after it was reported that he had performed a homosexual act. No one asked whether that was his exclusive sexual preference or inquired how homosexual activity disqualified him for his work.

Identified "homosexuals" are still the object of public ridicule and prejudice more often than they are accepted. Religious groups have usually condemned same-sex preference and have used as their rationale the argument that such behavior undermines the family unit. Until recently, a single parent who admitted homosexuality was usually deprived of the right to have custody of his or her children even if such a person had established a stable home by living with another person. The courts considered such a person incapable of providing a "proper" home.

Although there may be a growing tolerance and acceptance of an individual's rights to his or her sexual preference in the United States, it will probably be a long time before men and women with anything other than exclusive heterosexual preference will feel entirely comfortable and free of the stigmas that have prevailed in our society.

The debate continues over whether one's sexual preference is primarily learned or is at least partially, if not mostly, due to biological causes. Most of the literature leans toward the explanation that sexual preference is learned; more research is needed, however. The case for learned behavior stems from studies indicating that homosexual behavior as viewed in different societies has a visibly strong cultural influence. It seems to be influenced by peer groups and by how the individual with same-sex preference is treated in his or her family. Most studies on homosexuality indicate that the first such experience occurs at a relatively early age. Studies have shown that the boys and girls involved are less physically interested in the opposite sex during adolescence and have received less information about sexual interaction from their parents and peers.[16]

Other, less direct arguments for the position that sexual preferences are learned are built on the fact that human sexuality—especially female interest in sexual activities—is less controlled by hormones than is that of animals. The

fact that many nonhuman female animals are sexually receptive only during a part of the estrous cycle (when they are often aggressive as well), whereas human females are capable of being sexually aroused at any time, is cited as evidence that hormones play a different role in humans from that in animals.

Some recent research has led to speculation that homosexuality might be determined to some degree by the effect of androgens on the fetal brain.[17] Attempts to pin down the cause of homosexual behavior may be a waste of time and effort, since any discovery of a way to control sexual preference is likely to suggest action incompatible with our democratic principles. If indeed our aim is to permit freedom in sexual preference rather than to limit freedom, it might be wiser to decide that such research is not urgent.

Summary

■ Sex preference may be for sexual interaction with the opposite sex (heterosexuality), with the same sex (homosexuality), or with both sexes (bisexuality).

■ Current research indicates that very few people have always been either 100 percent homosexual or 100 percent heterosexual. Many have had at least some limited experience (usually in early sex play) with persons of both genders.

■ Hypotheses about the determination of sexual preference have focused primarily on learning. There is also some speculation that homosexuality may be partially caused by the effects of androgen on the fetal brain. Although more research might answer such questions, the motives behind this type of research may be suspect.

Masculinity and Femininity

Every society attempts to define what characteristics are desirable for males and for females. Usually an ideal type is constructed for each sex against which men and women can measure themselves. Anthropological literature indicates that societies vary considerably with respect to which traits are socially appropriate for males or for females. However, there do seem to be two sets of "core" characteristics—one for masculinity and one for femininity—that are socially approved throughout much of the world. In traditional China, for instance, masculinity and femininity were viewed as contrasting but complementary sets of characteristics.

In most societies these clusters of traits lie at opposite ends of a continuum, so that the approved characteristics for males are specifically *not* approved for females. Similarly, feminine traits are taboo for males. In this way, masculinity and femininity are seen as bipolar opposites. For instance, if it is considered masculine to be aggressive, a woman who is aggressive would be judged to lack femininity because of her exhibition of this masculine trait. Additionally, the feminine cluster might include modesty and submissiveness as desirable traits, a situation that would further deny the possibility of a woman's being both aggressive and feminine.

A man judged truly masculine would have no feminine traits but would hold those considered explicitly *nonfeminine*. Women who adhered closely to the ideal type of femininity would be unlikely to have any of those traits specifically associated with ideal masculinity. Child psychologists have noted that from early in a boy's life he is often trained to be as different from girls as possible. Assertions that "only girls cry" or that "only girls play with dolls" warn him against developing feminine behavior. In fact, his early definition of what it means to be a boy often seems based more on avoidance of femininity than on positive instruction or modeling for what is considered masculine. It is not entirely clear why this is so. A possible explanation that most experts stress is that, unlike girls, boys must break their early identification with their mothers in order to be able to learn the masculine patterns.

To encourage little boys to break their identification with their mothers—unlike their sisters, who can continue comfortably in this pattern—the advantages of being a male must be spotlighted. When a little boy is told to give up the comfort that tears may bring and to "stop crying—act like a man," he needs to believe that to "act like a man" is important. Schools have sometimes reinforced these definitions in subtle ways, as through sex-segregated play areas and the requirement that boys play different games from girls. Occasionally, boys are reminded explicitly of the undesirability of associating with or behaving like girls. Teachers may punish mischievous boys by making them play in the girls' area or sit at a table with all girls, as though this were truly a humiliating fate.

The bipolar notion of masculinity and femininity has been so widely accepted that nearly all research in the behavioral sciences indicates the sex of subjects or respondents and compares the findings for the two as if results were always likely to be different for men than for women. The stereotypes that have developed around each ideal type remain entrenched in much of society. It is not uncommon, for instance, to hear a man say that "all women are emotional" or for a woman to respond, even more sweepingly, that "men are all sexists."

In the past, stereotypes of masculinity and femininity were often so rigid that any man who showed traits considered peculiarly feminine—such as passivity or sensitivity—was considered a "sissy." A woman who was competitive or dominant—traits relegated to the masculine end of the continuum—often was said to be "castrating" or to have unresolved dilemmas about her gender.

A recent study has questioned the assumption that the emotionally healthy and socially well-adjusted male is one who strongly exhibits the stereotypical masculine traits—aggression, dominance, toughness, nonemotionality—and has suggested that a better model may be the man who is able to integrate

gentleness, warmth, and other non-"macho" qualities into his personality. In the same study, women who were stereotypically feminine (that is, dainty, sweet, submissive, and dependent) scored lower on measures of social and emotional adjustment than did women whose personalities included some "masculine" traits. Cross-sex characteristics were found more often in men and women who were judged more secure with their genders, who had higher self-esteem and higher competence, and who got along better socially.[18] The term used to describe the male or female who combines masculine and feminine traits in his or her personality is **androgyny**. Androgynous persons seemed freer of the usual constraints of masculine or feminine stereotypes but were not considered abnormal or peculiar by others despite their nonconformity.[19]

Critics of the research on androgyny have suggested that the methods used have not always been objective but instead have been biased toward linking sameness of the sexes with good mental health. It is suggested by some experts that it would be more constructive to emphasize that masculinity and femininity are different but should be equally valued. This is not to imply that there is only one model for men and one for women to follow. Instead, the critics of androgyny research believe that there are many ways to be masculine or feminine that are acceptable in our society but that we must not lose sight of the fact that good mental health is not necessarily dependent on being a middle-of-the-road man or woman.

New and different patterns will continue to emerge as the social realities of our times change. As more women enter the labor market, for instance, it may become an acceptable feminine trait to be assertive—perhaps even aggressive. As more men involve themselves with child care, nurturance should cease to be exclusively a feminine activity.

In a poll of 28,000 men and women, the majority of whom were well educat-ed and politically moderate to liberal, the participants were asked to describe the ideal man and the ideal woman, using both personality traits and behaviors as criteria for judgment.[20] The ten traits rated the highest for the ideal woman by women themselves and by men are as follows.

Ideal Woman

As Men Describe Her	*As Women Describe Her*
1. able to love	1. able to love
2. warm	2. stands up for beliefs
3. stands up for beliefs	3. warm
4. gentle	4. self-confident
5. self-confident	5. gentle
6. fights to protect family	6. intelligent
7. intelligent	7. fights to protect family
8. romantic	8. romantic
9. soft	9. sexually faithful
10. sexually faithful	10. soft

The descriptions by men and women of an ideal woman are almost identi-cal—over 75 percent of both men and women agree on the first five attributes, and over 55 percent agree on all ten. Other traits and behaviors were men-tioned but received many fewer votes. With few exceptions ("self-confident," "intelligent," "stands up for beliefs"), the description does not sound very different from that of the ideal woman of the 1950s or 1960s. Only 41 percent of the men and 60 percent of the women mentioned being successful at their work as a criterion for being "ideal."

The ideal man was also described by women and by men themselves.

Ideal Man

As Women Describe Him	*As Men Describe Him*
1. able to love	1. able to love
2. stands up for beliefs	2. stands up for beliefs
3. warm	3. self-confident
4. self-confident	4. fights to protect family
5. gentle	5. intelligent
6. intelligent	6. warm
7. fights to protect family	7. gentle
8. successful at work	8. successful at work
9. romantic	9. romantic

The men's and women's lists for the ideal man not only are very similar to each other but also are surprisingly close to the lists for the ideal woman. Those polled evidently value almost the same attributes in both men and women.

We have said that we are born male or female but that we learn concepts of masculinity and femininity just as we learn other cultural definitions. Such learning begins in ways that parents may be unaware of fostering in their children. For instance, research shows that girl babies are picked up more quickly when they cry than are boy babies, even though newborn males in fact cry more and sleep less than female babies.[21] Boys are held as much as girls, but they are held differently and are played with more boisterously than are girls. Although too young to label such differential treatment as "how boys are treated" or "how girls are treated," children may come to consider the distinction made by the parents familiar and "normal."

Small children watch their parents closely and often model their behaviors on those of the same-sex parent. Their attitudes about what is "good" and what is "bad" are reinforced by the rewards and punishments that are attached to their behaviors. Parents and teachers pay more attention to boys when they are aggressive, whereas girls are rewarded for being sweet, looking pretty, and keeping quiet. They may be told that "little girls don't (or can't) do that," a statement that reinforces their dependency. Eventually children develop a concept of what it means to be a socially approved male or female child in our society.

Summary

■ Masculinity and femininity have been pushed to opposite extremes in our society. Men who have many feminine traits may be considered "sissies," and women who are not totally "feminine" are often believed to have trouble with their self-definitions as women. These definitions begin early in childhood and are taught directly as well as subtly.

■ Stereotypes of masculinity and femininity have been questioned by recent research results suggesting that men who are rigidly "macho" or women who are very passive and dependent score lower on social and emotional adjustment scales. Thus, androgyny has been suggested as the compromise between the stereotypes.

■ Critics of the proponents of androgyny suggest that masculinity and femininity are useful concepts but that there is no one way to conform to either. Instead, there are many models for what is a "good" man or a "good" woman.

Learning Gender Roles

It is sometimes confusing to try to sort out attributes of masculinity and femininity from the behavior that results from these self-concepts. We start with the facts that biology affects behavior and that behavior can also affect biology. These ideas are central to what has been called the **biosocial** approach to ex-

plaining human behavior and are especially germane to the development of the
concepts of masculine and feminine.

The biosocial approach acknowledges biological differences between males
and females that affect the likelihood that sex-appropriate learning will take
place later. In other words, biology sets certain limits within which social learning operates to define masculinity or femininity. The second important fact is
that how one views oneself is also determined by how one behaves. It is not
easy to divide these two facts into discrete segments. Each affects the other, and
each is vital to our understanding of male-female differences and similarities
that are at the core of sexual interaction, marriage, reproduction, and gender
roles in our society.

Gender Roles

The customary behavioral differences between men and women in a given
society and the positions that customarily may be assigned either to males or to
females include tasks considered appropriate for each sex. Collectively these
become the gender roles that are assigned or assumed. In every society, as a
part of their growing-up process, children are taught directly what they may do
at any given time or may be expected to do in the future. The learning experiences that ultimately lead to the development of gender-role behavior come
under the collective heading of **socialization**, which is the process by which
children learn to interact effectively with others in their society. In this process
children learn the socially approved ways to behave according to their gender.
The principal methods of socialization for sex roles, in addition to direct
teaching, are imitation and identification.

Imitation

Children are great imitators of parents, peers, adults in the community, and
media figures. They observe much more closely and carefully than adults may
realize. They adopt a bit from one source and a bit from another, mixing and
matching until they form a style of their own. Children can often be seen
playing at roles as though they were "trying on" what it is like to be a fireman,
an angry neighbor, or a nurturant or busy parent. Children are very selective
about whom they imitate, and research has identified some of the variables that
influence them in choosing models.[22]

One of the most important and perhaps least complicated factors influencing which observed behaviors children will adopt has to do with reward and
punishment. It is clear that children are more likely to imitate behavior that
prompts a reward and to avoid behavior that elicits punishment. When parents
reward what they consider sex-appropriate modeling and punish what they
consider inappropriate imitation, children learn quickly what is expected. If,
for example, a little boy imitates his mother by putting red polish on his nails,
he may get a negative reaction that quickly lets him know that his parents

consider this modeling behavior inappropriate for him, although the same behavior in his sister may be approved or at least tolerated.

Reward and punishment have another equally important effect on children's behavior. When children observe others whose actions are either rewarded or punished, they are more likely to imitate those who receive rewards.[23] There is also a good deal of evidence that children are most likely to imitate those with whom they have positive relationships. Thus a child is much more likely to model him- or herself on a parent, a teacher, or a coach, for instance, if the adult in question is accepting, warm, and supportive.[24]

Other studies have shown that children are well aware of which adults have the power to reward and to punish and are much more likely to imitate an adult in such a position. The parent who is dominant in the home is more often imitated than the less dominant parent. When the parent seen as powerful is also warm and supportive, the likelihood of his or her being imitated is increased even more.[25]

Several experts on gender-role typing have proposed that children more frequently choose to imitate those with whom they feel a similarity or a kindred spirit. One of the most influential similarities seems to be sameness of sex—males imitate other males and females imitate other females.[26] In practice this usually means that boys imitate their fathers and girls model themselves after their mothers. Thus the maximum amount of imitation should be facilitated by a warm, supportive parent of the same sex who is also seen as the purveyor of rewards or punishments. There is considerable evidence suggesting that this is the case. Since fathers are viewed as more powerful in many families, it can be anticipated that boys will be likely to imitate their fathers and that girls will be likely to imitate both parents to some extent. As it now is, girls are less likely to be teased, shamed, or punished for imitating their fathers than are boys for imitating their mothers.

It appears that parental attitudes and parental treatment of children are more often closely related to children's learning of masculine or feminine traits than are the actual masculine or feminine behaviors of the parents whom the children imitate.[27] For instance, a father who himself might not fit the stereotyped notion of "masculine" might still insist that his son conform to standards the father deems "masculine." Studies have indicated that fathers have stronger influences than mothers on whether or not their daughters develop highly feminine traits.[28] Although girls imitate their mothers, fathers appear to be the most insistent parents in expecting gender-typed behavior of children of both sexes.[29]

Studies have found that, when there is no father in the home, there can be effects on the psychosexual development of both boys and girls different from those evident in father-intact homes. Father-absent boys have been shown to identify more with their mothers or to have a confused gender-role identity unless there has been another male adult with whom to identify.[30]

Girls are less affected by father absence in their early years, but differences show up in adolescence when father-absent girls display attitudes toward males that differ from those of girls whose fathers have been present.[31] Girls whose fathers were absent because of divorce sought more attention and praise from males and were more often described as "boy crazy," whereas those whose fathers had died tended to avoid males. Therefore, the parents' presence in the home and their sex-role definitions and behaviors become crucial to the ways children learn to behave. The more "traditional" the parents, for instance, the more the children may use this behavior as a model and grow up believing that this is the "right" way to be.

In the United States, "traditional" gender-role behavior varies greatly between different ethnic, religious, and social-class constituencies. Puerto Rican, Mexican, Japanese, and African family traditions can be very different from each other and from those of other ethnic entities; so are Mormon, Orthodox Jewish, Buddhist, and Unitarian traditions; so are the customs of Boston "Brahmins," Dallas suburbanites, and St. Louis ghetto residents.[32]

Identification

Most theorists distinguish between imitation and a more complex process called **identification**. The term *identification* has been used to connote a variety of processes, including the child's belief that he or she actually possesses some of the same characteristics as the one being imitated. In a review of the literature on identification, it has been noted how often the term is used interchangeably with *imitation*. Among those who distinguish between the terms, there is sometimes disagreement on just how they differ.[33] Most definitions agree that identification is a broader concept but that imitation plays a central role in the identification process.

Freud's theory of identification (which changed throughout his career) has been very influential in defining gender identity. Freud believed that children develop strong emotional bondings with and dependencies on nurturant parents. Their dependency makes them want to be as close as possible to their caretakers; as a result, they attempt to take on various personality characteristics of one or more of these adults.[34]

Many aspects of Freud's theory have been criticized, although the basic notion that children often incorporate traits of their parents (particularly of same-sex parents) finds little disagreement. Whether identification and imitation are too closely related to require differentiation may be an academic argument better left to those who want to pursue it. For our purposes, each is seen as a process by which children learn gender identity and sex-appropriate behavior.

In explaining the process in which children come to understand how to play appropriate gender roles, it is important to acknowledge a distinction between the gender-role model of parents and the gender-role model of peers. An adolescent male, for instance, may see his father as a responsible, hard-working authority figure and disciplinarian but may rarely see him in the masculine role defined by the adolescent's peers—sexually potent, physically strong, attractive to females, competitive, and athletic. Likewise, the gender-role model an adolescent female gets from her peers is quite different from the model supplied by her mother. The adolescent female is likely to see her peers anticipating a role of sexiness and romanticism—quite the opposite of the model, emphasizing nurturance, understanding, and success, that she learns from her middle-aged mother. The notion of the sexy, romantic female is reinforced by the mass media and usually is restricted to those who are well below middle age.

The impact of peers has been demonstrated in research from early childhood to adolescence. Three-year-olds in nursery schools have been observed to reinforce each other for gender-appropriate behavior. In one study boys criticized and ostracized other boys whom they judged not to be behaving appropriately.[35] In another study adolescent boys who, as a result of early childhood experiences, appeared to have confused or weak gender-identification in many instances showed exaggerated "masculinity" in an effort to conform to the model of a "real man" described by their adolescent peers.[36]

Summary

■ The behavior that results from cultural beliefs and concepts of masculinity or femininity based on biological differences between males and females gives rise to different gender roles for men and women.

■ Children are taught directly how to behave according to their genders. They also imitate others of their same sex with whom they relate positively.

■ Socialization is the process by which children learn how to interact effectively with others in their society; gender-appropriate behavior is a major focus of this process.

■ Children learn about gender roles from their peers as well as from adults. Peers become particularly influential in defining appropriate adolescent sexual behavior.

Can Genders Be Different Yet Equal?

How Gender Roles Mold Our Lives

Regardless of the theoretical bent of those concerned with socialization for gender roles, there does appear to be agreement that as gender roles develop, each individual will adopt a multifaceted self-concept. The gender role is not only multifaceted but also subject to change both over time and according to the particular situations in which behaviors take place. There is also a great deal of variation from one society to another with respect to what is considered appropriate for each gender.

In Margaret Mead's early studies of three societies in New Guinea, she found one society, the Tchambule, in which men's roles very much resembled those of women in the rest of the world.[37] In Madagascar, the Vakinankarata women are assigned the role of the dominant members of society and handle all community transactions, while the men enact roles more similar to the stereotyped patterns for females in our society.[38] Men are trained to be passive and dependent on dominant women; those who are gentle and polite are highly regarded.

In the United States, there is also great variation in how men and women of different ethnic, religious, and social-class backgrounds enact gender roles. In most people's minds, however, there is no question about which behaviors belong to each sex. The following are descriptions of two individuals who should not be difficult to assign to their genders.

J. is an engineering student who is now attending a prestigious technological institute on the East Coast. J.'s parents knew from the time J. was a toddler that the child had mechanical ability, since favorite toys were always ones to take apart and put back together. As J. progressed in school, favorite subjects were math and physics. All was not work, however; there were also honors in football and baseball. J. decided to work on a construction crew in the summer to keep fit for sports during the school year. Now that college studies are so time consuming, J. is worried that life is going to be more work than play.

L. is a major in Foods and Nutrition. As a small child, L. always liked to be in the kitchen, helping to cook. Petite and very attractive, L. receives much attention from the opposite sex. Working with children, teaching them crafts and games, has occupied L.'s summers. All these activities have been voluntary, following a family tradition of helping out with charities and groups that cannot afford to hire such services. L. also works on Saturdays as a volunteer in the local hospital, reading to patients and running errands for them.

There is little doubt that J. is a male and L. is a female. Of course, some girls do grow up to be engineers and to work on construction crews. Even in the 1980s, however, this is still the exception rather than the rule. Even less likely is that a male would be described as petite or would have spent his early years following his mother around or helping her fix dinner. There are still enough differences between the ways males and females behave that such distinctions are not difficult to make.

Men and women sometimes seem to operate on different wavelengths. For instance, several research studies have found that the two sexes have quite different ways of speaking and writing—that the same words frequently convey different concepts to each. Women tend to use more nouns and descriptive adjectives in their conversations; men tend to use more verbs that convey movement and action. These differences may be traceable in part to the encouragement that boys receive for doing things and to their more aggressive natures and that girls, often the more careful observers, receive for being more passive.[39]

Studies have shown that even at a very early age, boys are more interested in objects and in seeing how things work than are girls. When very young, boys demonstrate spatial orientation, depth perception, and a sense of direction superior to the analogous capabilities of girls. These aptitudes facilitate the learning of mathematics, mechanics, engineering, and other disciplines related to stereotypical "masculine" occupations.[40]

On the other hand, young girls seem attuned to human relations from their earliest months of life. They smile earlier (some studies report that females smile more throughout their lives), talk earlier, and pay more attention to people than do boys. They learn early to rely on social cues and, as their verbal ability develops, seem more aware than boys of verbal behavior in others. Research has shown that before their first birthdays, little girls recognize pictures of familiar adults and respond to familiar voices (even on the telephone).[41]

A sampling of sociological and psychological studies on male-female differences shows various claims.

1. Women tend to attribute their success or failure in projects to external circumstances and to good or bad luck, whereas men more often feel that they have internal control over what happens to them.[42]
2. Men tend to have higher self-esteem (even to overrate their abilities), whereas women tend to underestimate most things about themselves except their physical attractiveness.[43]

3. Women are usually more "intuitive" and "accommodative" and consistently better than men at interpreting nonverbal cues.[44]
4. Women are more expressive of their emotions than are men, who early learn to suppress many of their feelings.[45]

The notion that many gender-role differences reflect a polarity between kinds of family responsibilities is widely accepted. Parsons and Bales characterize these polarities as "instrumental and expressive."[46] Men traditionally have been thought to be the instrumental persons in representing the family to the community and the world of work, whereas women have taken care of the nurturance of the family by tending to its members' physical and emotional needs. Therefore, men managed their families' economic interests through having access to the exchange of assets outside the family. Women, on the other hand, controlled men's access to affection, sex, and nurturance. The polarity hypothesis implies that if men were powerful and dominant agents of the family in its interface with the world, then women could not be. Similarly, if women were dominant in controlling the affectional resources of the family, then men could not be.

In the Parsons and Bales theoretical model, men could gain power in the family by withholding (or threatening to withhold) money; women could gain power by withholding (or threatening to withhold) sex. At present, court decisions and state laws are much more likely to restrict men's power in this model than women's. Recent decisions and recently passed laws generally support a wife's right to withhold sex from her husband but deny a husband's right to withhold financial support from his wife.

A perspective on marital gender roles that differs from the structural view of polarities, taken by Parsons and Bales—a perspective that is reminiscent of conflict theory—is the more functionalist view of a marriage as a system based on gender roles that complement each other. From such a perspective, the system can be said to have survived because a man and a woman living together believe that the way they enact their roles will express their values and enable them to achieve their goals. If each partner believes that both instrumental activities (exchange of assets with the outside world) and expressive activities (affectional satisfactions within the family) are important, then their gender roles should evolve in a direction that will maximize this achievement.

In the nearly three decades since the Parsons-Bales position was announced, gender roles have changed considerably. In particular, a good deal of attention has been paid to changes in the roles of women. There have been many shifts in the positions women hold and in how men view women, women view men, and both view themselves.

Some have called the 1970s the decade of women. If nothing else, the increase in the number of middle-class women who are working outside their homes has forced some revision of gender stereotypes. Changes have occurred both in the workplace and in home life. Women have slowly begun to realize that as childbearing and child rearing require a smaller proportion of their lives, they as well as men can be responsible for extrafamily economic activities when they are no longer needed at home full time.

Many women who are in their child-rearing years also work outside the home to help support the family unit. As a result, middle-class women have been reexamining gender roles, and some are beginning to challenge the traditional notions of femininity that they have been socialized to believe—especially those that suggest that homemaking and child rearing are primarily a woman's obligation, whereas earning a living is the province of males.

A recent survey of family-relations professionals indicated that they consider the shift in women's roles and the greater involvement of women in extrafamily activities among the most significant changes ever to affect the American family. Typical of the comments about the impact of women's changing gender roles were: "Influence of the women's movement encouraging growth of women leads to discontent with the status quo when it is seen as oppressive"; "More women are ready to be independent"; and "Women in their relationships have become much more demanding." [47]

When women change their definitions of femininity and of sex-role behavior, men must also change, and vice versa. There are no signs that men and women today are any less involved with each other than in the past; thus, changes affecting one sex must necessarily lead to changes for the other. Some observers of men's reactions to the "new woman" have noted that some men find it difficult to accept the changing definitions of femininity and even more difficult to adjust to women's new roles. Some men reacted with anger to the early feminists who seemed to feel they could improve their position only at the expense of men.

Men who have taken their responsibilities of supporting a wife and children seriously and have worked long hours to this end have understandably resented being labeled "male chauvinist pigs." Still others felt uneasy when their capability of carrying out the role of family decision-maker appeared to be questioned. Many were at least somewhat confused by the demand that they denounce the "masculine" roles taught to them by their parents and adopt "feminine" roles taught (often painfully) to be inappropriate for them. The demands of the traditional male role, involving sole responsibility for earning a living, made some men wonder whether or not they would be shirking their moral responsibility if they transferred part of the financial burden of supporting their families to their wives in return for a chance to spend more time with their children.

"Men's liberation" has become a popular topic in recent years as men and women have begun to change their gender roles. Special issues of professional journals have been devoted to examining changing male roles critically and sensitively.[48-50] Research provides evidence that the American male is in transition—partly clinging to his old, familiar behaviors and partly adjusting to new values, with some men leading the way and others holding tenaciously to traditionalism. It has been proposed that men's roles currently fall into one of three general patterns:

1. The *traditionalist* feels most comfortable when the differences between masculinity and femininity are clear. He may be upset with women who wish to deny him what he sees as his morally imperative role and puzzled by men who accept traditional feminine roles.
2. The *liberal* tries to respect both old and new values. He is likely to favor liberalized legislation and to be strongly in favor of equal rights for women. However, he sometimes has difficulty dealing with his emotions over changes that affect him personally—the feeling that he is inadequate if his wife earns more than he does, for instance, or the feeling that he is risking his job security (and indeed at the present time he may well be) if he stays home with a sick child as often as does his working wife.
3. The *changing man* has a strong sense of what equality means and attempts to make changes around him that will eliminate sex-role stereotyping. Sometimes he has been active in consciousness-raising (CR) groups of men who discuss men's concerns, issues of **sexism**, and the challenge involved in changing their definitions of masculinity.[51]

Betty Friedan, whose book *The Feminine Mystique* became legendary in the 1960s, recently stated:

> *I believe that American men are at the edge of a tidal wave of change—a change in their very identity as men. This is a quiet movement, a shifting in direction . . . a searching for new values, a struggling with basic questions that each man seems to be going through alone. At the same time, he continues the outward motions that always have defined men's lives, making it (or struggling to make it) at the office, the plant, the ball park—making it with women— getting married—having children—yet he senses that something is happening with men, something large and historic, and he wants to be a part of it. He carries the baby in his back pack, shops at the supermarket on Saturdays, with a certain showing-off quality.[52]*

We believe that the changes in gender roles are evolving slowly enough that, although many men and women have some private doubts about the "rightness" of alternative gender-role behaviors, they are finding constructive ways to adjust. The changes taking place are exposing them to unexplored parts of themselves that offer the potential for expansion and greater fulfillment—but, of course, at a price. People often resist change because it leads to uncertainty. The old ways, even when they are undesirable, are at least familiar, whereas the prospect of the unknown can produce anxiety. Changes of the magnitude currently expected of men and women do not occur quickly or without some pain.

Some deeply ingrained beliefs and behaviors will be slow to change despite

the best intentions, desires, and efforts. As marital therapists, we see one problem so often that it bears mention: a learned difference in the way most men and women deal with their feelings. Boys are generally taught by women as well as men to suppress any feelings that may convey "weakness"—anxiety, fear, hurt, perhaps even open acknowledgment of warmth and love.

When a boy grows up and marries, he may handle his emotions with stoicism, silence, repression—what has been called the "stiff-upper-lip" attitude. Typically, this attitude will have been reinforced by the significant women in his early life; it cannot be dismissed simply by his hearing from another significant woman that it is undesirable. This may puzzle his wife, who as a woman may feel free to cry when she is upset and to acknowledge her feelings more openly, as she has done since her girlhood. She often complains that in her relationships with men there is no sharing of feelings. Many women report that men not only fail to share feelings but also seem distressed when women exhibit emotions.

A marriage and family therapist conducting a call-in radio program in Los Angeles once asked the male audience what each man would consider a plus if he could be transformed magically into a woman. Ninety percent of the men who called said they would be relieved to be able to express freely their feelings of love, hurt, and anxiety, as women do. (Women answered the corresponding question by referring to the greater freedom they believed men to have in pursuing an occupation without being bound to home and children as their exclusive duty, and to the greater control and autonomy men seemed to have.)[53]

Despite male-female differences in gender roles, the similarities found in most human traits shared by both men and women are striking. All men are not alike, nor are all women. Some women may exhibit more typically "masculine" traits than some men do. Roles must fit the individuals filling them as much as individuals must mold themselves to role descriptions. Too often we have seen men and women lose sight of who they are as individuals in the pursuit of roles defined by society to fit "the average person" (who in reality does not exist at all). Perhaps the most important "revolutionary" development of the past two decades has been the growing acceptance of the notion that both men and women must create life-styles that suit them as individuals rather than adapting themselves to prescribed roles.

Summary

■ In our society males and females have been socialized to believe that masculinity and femininity are at opposite poles in definition. The presence of traits of one has automatically meant the exclusion of traits of the other.

■ In this century, particularly since 1960, there have been trends toward more egalitarian ideas about gender roles. Middle-class women's roles have changed most noticeably, but because women and men are so involved with each other, men's roles have had to change in order to keep pace.

■ "Women's liberation" and "men's liberation" have caused confusion and uncertainty about the new roles and about how men and women can be expected to relate to each other.

■ Both men and women will need time to accept change and to adjust to new styles of masculinity and femininity. Instead of adopting rigid new roles to replace the old ones, men and women may need to design their own roles, tailoring them to individual needs.

Glossary

Androgens Male sex hormones.

Androgynization A condition in which excess androgen in prenatal life affects a female fetus in such a way as to produce masculine characteristics.

Androgyny The state of having both male and female characteristics.

Biosocial Dealing with both biological and social phenomena simultaneously; sometimes refers to social effects attributed to biological causes.

Bisexuality Sexual attraction to members of both sexes. Bisexual persons may alternate between male partners and female partners or may seek mixed-group sex.

Chromosomes   Bodies in the nucleus of reproductive cells that carry the genes for heredity.

Estrogens   Female sex hormones.

Fallopian tubes   Passages to the uterus through which ova are transported and in which fertilization normally occurs.

Gender identity   The knowledge and awareness, whether conscious or unconscious, that one belongs to one sex and not to the other.

Genitalia   The organs of reproduction, especially those that are external; the penis-testicles-prostate system in human males and the vulva-vagina-uterus-ovaries system in human females.

Gonads   The primary sex organs; the testicles in human males and the ovaries in human females. (See Appendix A for more complete discussion of gonads.)

Hermaphroditism   The condition in which an individual has some physical sexual characteristics of both sexes while those of neither are fully developed.

Heterosexuality   The preference for sex partners of the opposite sex.

Homosexuality   The preference for sexual activity with partners of one's own sex.

Identification   The process by which a person, often a child, incorporates certain behaviors or characteristics of another person, often a parent, and makes them a part of his or her personality.

Lesbian   A woman whose sexual preference is for other women.

Neural   Pertaining to nerves.

Ovaries   Female organs that produce egg cells (ova) and certain hormones.

Puberty   The beginning of biological sexual maturity, when the capability of creating or supporting a pregnancy develops and secondary sex characteristics (for instance, pubic hair, breasts, beards) begin to appear.

Sexism   Prejudice or discrimination based on gender alone.

Sexologist   One who specializes in the study of sexual behavior, particularly that of humans.

Socialization   The process by which persons learn to interact effectively with others in their society.

Testes   Male organs that produce sperm and testosterone.

Testosterone   An androgen responsible for the male sex drive and also for secondary male sex characteristics such as facial hair and lower voice.

Transsexual   A genetically male or genetically female person who, at odds with his or her own sex, is mentally and emotionally of the opposite sex.

Transvestism   The practice of dressing in clothing of the opposite sex, especially for the purpose of attaining sexual excitement.

Uterus (womb)   The structure within the female body in which the fetus develops.

Sex is by no means everything. It varies, as a matter of fact, from only as high as 78 per cent of everything to a low of 3.1 per cent of everything. The norm in a sane, healthy person should be between 18 and 24 per cent.

—James Thurber and E. B. White, *Is Sex Necessary?*

3 · Human Sexuality

Human sexuality is both an individual and a social matter. In every society children are taught how to view their sexuality and how to behave sexually. This socialization takes place in precisely the same way as does learning about any other important aspect of children's lives—through direct teaching from adults and peers, through observation and imitation, and through personal experience. As a result, children grow up with a blend of accurate and inaccurate information. As adults, we keep learning about our sexual selves and about our partners'. Earlier influences affect adult attitudes and behaviors—sometimes in limiting ways. Warm, loving experiences later on, however, often can help us overcome earlier misconceptions and enable us to achieve new levels of sexual understanding and enjoyment.

Over half a century ago, Mark Twain wrote:

> *Adam and Eve entered the world naked and unashamed—naked and pure-minded; and no descendant of theirs has ever entered it otherwise. All have entered it naked, unashamed, and clean in mind. They have entered it modest. They had to acquire immodesty and a soiled mind; there was no other way to get it.*

—Mark Twain, *Letters from the Earth,* Letter III

Mark Twain's commentary on the kind of attitudes toward sex American children learn points to the common knowledge that many children grow up with distorted sentiments about sex and a distressing range of sexual problems. Sentiments are learned in many ways—by modeling on others with whom a person is trying to identify, by very precise indoctrination, and by conditioning. Often they are learned through emotional responses to the behaviors of important others—parents, family, and close friends. Everyone brings sentiments to a system, and sexual systems are no exception. The following section deals with sentiments about sex that are learned in childhood.

Before we begin a discussion of early sex education, it is probably worthwhile to review some of the ideas that both children and adults may associate—often in confusing ways—with the notion of sex. These include ideas about excretion, reproduction, and social **taboos** related to sex.

1. *Ideas, terms, and behaviors associated with excretion:* The first association many children make with their genitals is that they are the point of exit of urine for males and seen as near the point of exit for females. When adults are teaching bathroom hygiene, they do not always make clear to children whether it is the sex organs themselves or their excretory products that are "dirty." When an adult tells a child that it is important to keep his or her genitals concealed from public view, the child will usually associate them with excretory organs and conclude they are both, at the very least, unattractive or obscene, and, if not actually shameful, so provoking that they may cause trouble. Often the parent seems visibly distressed by the child's exposure. A child who experiences pleasant sensations in the sex organs is likely to view these feelings as a secondary rather than a primary function of those important, attention-getting parts of the body.

Sometimes adults fail to "grow up" sexually and continue to find something "sexy" or **erotic** about urination. However, well-adjusted adults are able to distinguish clearly between the eliminatory and the sexual functions and feelings of their genitals.

2. *The reproductive process:* Technically, the human reproductive process is a sexual one; that is, it begins when a female sex cell is fertilized by a male sex cell. This fertilization may or may not be the result of an encounter that is erotic for both a male and a female: one does not have to enjoy sexual intercourse to become pregnant. Rape is certainly not an erotic event for normal women, despite some popular myths to the contrary. **Artificial insemination** is not necessarily an erotic experience. It is also obvious that not all erotic encounters result in reproduction. Yet "sex education," particularly at the elementary school level, is likely to be concerned exclusively with reproduction, including the menstrual cycle, leading children to believe erroneously that **coitus** always causes conception or that "grown-ups" have intercourse only in order to conceive.

Four- or five-year-olds may comprehend very well the erotic properties of their sex organs, even to the point of recognizing differences between the erotic quality of sex play with boys and that of sex play with girls.[1] The child may also know that babies grow in mother's abdomen, that they make their exit from her body by means of a "special passage," and that they originated there because the father put "seeds" in the mother; but it is unlikely that from such a description the child will see reproduction as very "sexy."[2]

Actually, most adults are not excited sexually by thoughts of reproduction. They may make sentimental associations between childbirth and sexual arousal, but for most people these sentiments are very different. Occasionally a man may have a strong conscious urge to make a woman pregnant, but he is probably not thinking of doing so by means of immaculate conception or artificial insemination. If the reproductive organs (the uterus, the **prostate gland,** and so forth) seem "sexy" to an adult, it is because they are associated with the notion of two persons giving each other pleasure by joining their sex organs. That is the distinctive theme of erotic sex as opposed to reproductive sex.

It is true that when **contraception** was less effective than it is now, a couple's engaging in regular coitus usually would result in pregnancy sooner or later. However, the confusion of sex with reproduction has affected the sexual attitudes of many people. A child may come to believe that whatever coitus his or her parents may have experienced was a solemn ritual, endured once for each baby and totally unrelated to the excitement of the child's own secret games and sensations.

3. *Social taboos:* Finally, there are social taboos of one sort or another that somehow come to have a sexual connotation, emotionally at least, for some people—and often especially for young children. Perhaps it is because they are forbidden that such acts become associated with sexuality. Persons who deal with social deviants report apparent connections between disapproved behaviors and erotic stimuli, associations that most of us cannot understand. A police officer reported having picked up an adolescent who told him that he had achieved **orgasm** while stealing a bicycle. According to common rumor, many bullfighters achieve orgasm at the moment they thrust the sword home into the bull. Pyromaniacs often report that they become orgasmic watching the fires they have set.

Sexiness may be confused with elimination, reproduction, sex-identified objects, or taboos. Sex education as conceptualized in this book, however, has nothing to do with excretory behavior; it is not focused on reproduction; and it is in a completely different category from social taboos and deviations.

How Children Learn about Sex

Peers provide children with a kind of education about sex that is very different from the lessons taught by their parents. Children have a lore and a language that are passed on from child to child in songs, games, and rhymes. Words that are taboo around adults are used, and certain terminology common to the peer group is learned early.

An important function of children's sex lore is that it establishes a compartmentalized social group distinct in that part of its microculture from the family group. The bonds of trust (reinforced by secrecy) are formed, and children learn to respect affiliations of their own choosing as opposed to those thrust on them. Adults are sometimes astonished to learn that their children are telling the same jokes and using the same words that they used at a particular age. It becomes clear that children pass on this lore to other children quite independently of the adult society.

At least half a dozen explicit and unmistakable terms are used by children to describe coitus, as well as dozens of euphemisms that convey the idea adequately. Males who use euphemisms may say "screw" or "punch"; females may "make love" or "do it," just as poets "pluck blossoms," "touch souls," or "become one." Children readily acquire the taboo terms at such an early age that most of them cannot remember where they first heard them. By the end of the fourth grade, any child who does not know what these words mean is thought by his or her peers to be either poorly enculturated or else overprotected by parents.

Two additional ideas have also usually been conveyed: first, that "nice" girls and boys must not be caught doing it by adults but, second, that it is a very exciting thing to do. This relieves parents and teachers of several painful chores. They do not need to tell a child who is ten or older that sexual intercourse exists: the child already knows. They do not need to tell children that sexual intercourse among children is subject to the disapproval of adults: the children already know. They do not need to tell children that sexual intercourse can be exciting: the children have already learned this (unless they have somehow been so conditioned that they are repelled by the idea, which happens rarely to boys but not infrequently to girls).

**Role
of Adults**

What, then, should a parent or teacher tell a child about sex before puberty? Some important things can be taught in the "facts-of-life" talks that many adults dread but consider a duty. An important function of these talks can be to make clear by both words and actions the conceptual distinctions discussed at the beginning of this chapter. Ideas, terms, and behaviors associated with excretion, the reproductive process, menstruation, and other areas so often confused with sex need to be clarified and distinguished from sex but also related to sex appropriately.

Through words and actions, it can be made clear that the parent or teacher and his or her sexual partner have a warm and physical relationship. Sex therapists Masters and Johnson have said that the best sex education a child can receive is to see his or her Dad give Mom a pat on her "fanny" and to see her smile and enjoy it.[3] Adults can make clear through words and actions that sex is a normal, pleasurable, mutual activity. There are also many bits of information that parents and teachers can convey to children in order to guide them, enlighten them, or make them feel more comfortable with their own sexual propensities or activities. Replacing misinformation received from peers and other sources with factual data discussed in an open and relaxed manner can go far in helping young people grow up with healthy attitudes toward sex.

Parents and teachers can provide warnings that sex can be the source of some diseases, just as other contacts are, and that a child who suspects that he or she has contracted such a disease should get it treated immediately, just as with any other disease. Terrifying children about **venereal diseases** serves no useful purpose in the long run but only reinforces the notion that sex is dirty. Venereal disease is a serious health problem—just as measles and mononucleosis are—to be avoided and, if contracted, to be treated by professionals.

Children should be told that it is unfair for an individual to engage in any kind of sexual behavior with another person when that person is unwilling or is ignorant of what is taking place. This approach may help a child to define appropriate sexual behavior and to respond more rationally and calmly to sexual aggression. Emphasizing mutuality and responsibility in sexual activity goes a long way toward teaching morality and the ethical notion that what is obscene is exploitation—not sex itself.

Parents and teachers can convey the idea that sexual feelings (that is, erotic feelings) are normal and healthy and that not only young people have them— so do adults, even grandparents. It should be pointed out that erections of the penis are normal, that all boys have them, and that erections can occur from just thinking about sex or even for no apparent reason at all. That information

seems fairly obvious; yet many boys grow up with feelings of guilt about their erections, and most girls are somewhat misinformed on this subject. It is not at all unusual for an otherwise sophisticated woman to believe that erections are under a man's voluntary control and that a man should be able either to produce one at will or to keep himself from doing so.

Girls, too, need assurance that their feelings of sexual arousal are normal. They should know that sexual excitement causes wetness of their genitals and that this wetness is not urine but rather a clean secretion that indicates they are growing up. This secretion, rather than menstrual fluid, is analogous to a boy's first pleasurable **ejaculation** in heralding the beginning of adulthood.

Although boys and girls should learn how to wash their sex organs when they bathe, parents should explain that these organs are no dirtier than any other parts of the body. It can be pointed out that urine is a natural fluid that does not contaminate the sex organs and that is less likely than other body products (for example, saliva or feces) to contain bacteria in a normally healthy person.[4]

Girls sometimes believe that males urinate into females during intercourse and may be relieved to learn that this is not so. This common carry-over from the early childhood confusion about the use of the penis both as an excretory organ and as a sexual organ, if not cleared up satisfactorily, may cause a young woman to dread her first sexual encounter.

Although most children begin sexual self-stimulation at a very early age, the way they feel about it is often determined by the attitudes of peers or of their parents and siblings. Occasions may arise for supportive counseling from both parents and teachers that can aid children in socializing this normal activity. Very young girls and boys frequently touch their genitals or **masturbate** simply because it feels good. It may be embarrassing to their parents or to others if it is done in public, but it is basically harmless to the little child unless an emotional issue is made of it. As a normal child grows older, this pattern may disappear for several years. After puberty, however, masturbation in solitude often returns and is a lifelong activity for most individuals.[5]

Although children of both sexes are capable of achieving orgasm before puberty, relatively few actually do. Self-stimulation without orgasm is likely to be intermittent in both sexes before puberty and is certainly harmless. Once orgasm has been achieved, however, masturbation normally becomes regular and frequent unless repressive instruction by peers and elders has led to unnecessary guilt feelings.

There may be occasion to explain to a child that one cannot "use up" one's sexual capacity and that, if anything, regular sexual activity tends to prolong one's effective sexual life span. Much has been said about "excessive masturbation" in the absence of a definition of "excessive." Such phrases sometimes reflect a fear that masturbation will cause one to lose energy or to become a victim of uncontrollable sexual desire, but more often they have mysterious moralistic overtones. Adults can help to put masturbation in a sensible perspective for children and to reassure young people that it is physically harmless. A few religious groups still consider self-stimulation a "sin"; children who are taught this will continue to face the dilemma of reconciling their religious upbringing with the frequent urge to masturbate.

It seems important for children to know that there is not always a one-to-one relationship between sexual intercourse and pregnancy. Children should not be surprised at the thought that their parents or other adults engage in intercourse fairly regularly with no desire for pregnancy to occur. As a corollary of this principle, children may be told about contraception as a typical practice for people who want to have intercourse but who do not want to have babies. It might even be added that contraception is a special blessing for people who wish to plan the sizes of their families—an advantage that people of past generations lacked. Often children know how a baby is conceived long before they realize that not all sex is for procreation. Again, certain religious groups still teach the one-to-one relationship between sex and procreation and view contraceptive use as sinful.

It may be explained to children that it is not uncommon for unmarried women to become pregnant, even though contraceptives are easily obtainable. Such a conversation might lead to a discussion of the reasons for and the possible outcomes of such a pregnancy. It may also be pointed out that once a couple begins having sexual intercourse, it is sometimes difficult for them to discontinue without discontinuing their relationship entirely. This should be offered as an observation, not a threat.

Sex is usually an emotional issue. Furthermore, it is a rare parent-child relationship that is not an emotional one. Therefore, it is as unlikely that parents can comfortably undertake the total sex education of their children as that a physician will undertake the total medical care of his or her own children. Few parents have escaped their own childhood sex training free of all emotional "hang-ups." Parents certainly can provide support, add some factual knowledge, and impart their own values about sex; but because of parents' own sexual problems it is likely that the overall task can be carried out better by a detached, qualified professional over a reasonable period of time. For this reason, a well-planned curriculum taught by specially trained teachers is probably the best method of providing children's sex education that is currently available.

Role of Peers

Peers can exchange certain facts and feelings about sex, but they often lack the necessary resources for providing accurate information. They may fail to make the conceptual distinctions described earlier. They often exaggerate the social humiliation and parental anger that will result if sexual activities are discovered. It is even possible that some suicides of teenage girls occur because the girls believe the disgrace of pregnancy will be too much to face.

Several studies have been conducted to determine the ages and the sources that are the best for imparting sex education and other kinds of information about sexuality to young people.[6,7] Generally speaking, the data indicate that young people are most interested in sex education between the ages of twelve and fifteen years and that peers are their most frequent source of information.[8]

Same-Sex Peers. In the contemporary United States it is not unusual for adolescent boys to have a history of sexual activities with other boys. They often engage in genital exhibition and examination, mutual masturbation, and other forms of sexual behavior, usually in the company of same-sex peers and sometimes in the presence of girls. This activity is usually "secret," and some males report having to perform sexual exhibitions as a condition of membership in boys' "clubs" or gangs. Sex organs may be measured; the number of ejaculations produced in a fixed time or the number produced without losing an erection may be carefully counted. Although such activities are unquestionably erotic, they are not considered indications of any proclivity for homosexuality. They can best be described as a combination of "playing" and learning one's sexual potential. They are usually boisterous rather than passionate, "fun" rather than serious.[9]

About five times as many boys as girls engage in such social sexual behavior before adolescence.[10] The reasons for this double standard are not entirely clear. Experts do not agree about whether boys and girls act differently because they have learned different feelings about sex—feelings of rightness or wrongness, for example. There is also the possibility that boys' testosterone levels are much more nearly constant than are girls' estrogen levels, which are cyclical, and that the levels of these hormones are directly related to tensions that can be satisfactorily relieved only by orgasm. It may even be that the constant sexual tension of boys is comparable to that experienced by girls for only a few days each month. The evidence either way is far from conclusive, however; it does appear that in humans social and cultural constraints on sexual behavior are more powerful than hormonal ones.

Cliques of early adolescent girls may talk about sexual behavior and circulate books on the subject; but there is apparently less same-sex erotic play than among boys. Exhibition and examination of genitalia by other girls may be the extent of sex "play." It is not at all unusual for an adult woman never to have seen female genitalia—not even her own in a mirror. Breast exhibition is a different matter, however. Early adolescent girls seem to be just as aware of the breast development and dimensions of the members of their cliques as boys are of the penis size and growth of pubic hair of the members of theirs.

Kinsey reported that the homosexual behavior that does occur between early adolescent girls involves for the most part kissing and general body contact, with genital techniques coming later, if at all.[11] Although there may be some boisterousness in breast play comparable to that of boys' penis play, girls' homosexual genital contacts, when they do occur, seem to be "serious" rather than fun and perhaps more predictive of adult homosexuality than the penis play of boys.

According to Kinsey, older women who have had homosexual contact report that adolescent homosexual activity was more satisfying than coitus, while older men report the opposite. Kinsey noted that women with a history of early homosexual experience usually report an intention to have it again but that no such intention is reported by men.

As the clique disappears into the heterosexual crowd around or before midadolescence, patterns of same-sex activity among boys disappear except for the relatively small fraction of boys who will continue homosexual or bisexual behavior in adulthood. The data for girls are not as clear, but it appears that the fraction engaging in active homosexual behavior—always smaller than the fraction for men—continues to increase until well into middle age.[12]

By late adolescence most males regard their earlier homosexual behavior as a developmental phenomenon, consider it childish, and are not disturbed by whatever recollections they have not forgotten or repressed. It should be noted, especially in view of the extensive work done by Broderick and others, that most male sex play with other males during early adolescence is accompanied by joking, conversation, recounting of experiences, plans for the future, and fantasies about heterosexual activities with particular girls or with girls in general. Thus, although the *behavior* is homosexual, the **ideation** is heterosexual.[13]

Cross-Sex Peers. Most studies on the subject report that the number of boys engaging in various forms of heterosexual activity during adolescence greatly exceeds the corresponding number of girls.[14] The number of boys reporting that they engage in sex play with girls during adolescence is from five to seven times as great as the number of girls who report engaging in sex play with boys during adolescence. This discrepancy might be reconciled—incorrectly—by means of a simple explanation that those adolescent girls who do engage in sexual behavior with boys are very active and each have, on the average, contact with five to seven times as many boys as boys on the average have with girls. However, in all studies, the average adolescent girl who has engaged in heterosexual sex behavior reports contact with fewer boys than the number of girls with whom the average boy reports contact. Nor does frequency of contact help to solve the dilemma; on the contrary, girls typically have reported less frequency of heterosexual contact than boys.

In 1978 it was reported that 56 percent of all college women reported having coital experience before age eighteen. Less than one-fourth (23 percent) had coitus with more than five different partners (compared with 22 percent in 1968), which suggests that the pattern is not changing very rapidly.[15]

It has been established that girls who report that they are currently in love tend to discount their earlier experiences as "not really love" more often than do boys. In a similar vein, it is possible that as girls progress to more effective and more satisfactory sex experiences with boys, they tend to discount their earlier experiences as being somehow less than sexual. Both explanations are within the realm of possibility. On the other hand, it is difficult to overlook the likelihood that girls—especially girls aged sixteen or over—will be introduced to sexual activity by males who are older than they are. This prevailing norm should result in a higher, rather than a lower, rate of sexual activity for adolescent girls than for adolescent boys.

Most men and boys can recall their first orgasms in some detail. Male orgasm is a definitive event; there is no question whether or not it has occurred. When a boy experiences an orgasm while engaging in any kind of activity with a girl, it is immediately clear to him that the experience was a sexual one, regardless of how the girl may have interpreted it. His criterion for defining an experience as sexual is reasonably stable from the moment of his first orgasm on.

Girls, on the other hand, are likely to have many heterosexual contacts before they ever achieve orgasm. Of sexually active women aged nineteen or younger, 51 percent have reported no experience with orgasm.[16] Even though each earlier contact might have been clearly defined as sexual in the girl's mind at the time, the absence of orgasm might later call for a redefinition of her criteria. If orgasm did not occur, in reflection she might be likely to discount the experience as truly sexual. Thus it is entirely possible that an adolescent boy may perceive an encounter as sexual because he achieved an orgasm as a result of it, whereas his female partner may not consider the same contact overtly sexual, especially if she recalls it at a later date, when she has become much more experienced sexually.

Non-coital heterosexual behavior is usually graded as "necking," "petting," or "heavy petting." Necking is usually defined as hugging and kissing. Although necking is unlikely to cause even a sexually experienced girl to reach orgasm, it may easily excite an adolescent boy to orgasm. A certain amount of necking is anticipated by boys and girls from the beginning of adolescence on. During early adolescence there is a good deal of concern about effective sexual procedures and limits, although the intentions usually precede the establishment of sufficient confidence to carry them out by a considerable period of time.

Petting involves hugging and kissing but also includes caressing and exploration of the entire body. "Heavy petting," if it is distinguished from petting in general, refers to the continuation of stroking, caressing, and kissing various parts of the body (especially erogenous areas) until orgasm is achieved by the boy and sought, if not achieved, by the girl.

As with necking, petting is usually preceded by a period of rehearsal through fantasizing by boys, who almost invariably take the initiative in actual behavior, even though girls may make elaborate arrangements to make it possible. At least until midadolescence, the petting activities of boys might more accurately be described as exploratory ventures, with a twofold purpose: (1) to find out how girls are constructed anatomically and how they function physiologically, and (2) to determine the extent of permissiveness of particular girls.

In early adolescence, boys generally expect resistance to petting from girls and often are rebuffed on their first attempts. As a rule, at this age "nice" girls seldom go beyond making themselves available or easily accessible for explorations, kissing, and hugs. There is a widespread belief among boys, probably not without empirical support, that if a girl aggressively grasps or fondles a boy's penis, he "has it made"—that she then expects him to continue intimacies until she achieves orgasm and that she expects him to achieve orgasm too, either coitally or non-coitally.

The cross-sex activities of adolescents leave little question of the existence of a double standard at this age. A boy may use sexual exploitation to enhance his self-esteem and self-confidence in an area that is almost totally free from parental interference, since it is usually thoroughly compartmentalized by the boy and quite irrelevant (as he sees it) to the social organization of his family. Although some view this with alarm, it is probably an important developmental stage in the establishment of identity and self-sufficiency, particularly in young adolescents. The gratification that comes from establishing leadership and strength in a social relationship completely free of parental or other adult domination cannot be achieved very often in many other legitimate areas for this age group.

Adolescent girls, on the other hand, experience a transfer of sexual permission from the parents or other restrictive adults to themselves. A girl alone must make and enforce her decision about how "far" to let particular boys "go." She may consider it a tribute to her attractiveness if she can achieve and maintain the interest of boys while denying them access to sexual privileges, although in fact her shyness about exhibiting her body or her inexperience may be a greater factor. The ultimate decisions that she must make when she is alone with boys are hers and not her parents'. For her, too, learning to manage her compartmentalized heterosexual activities is an important feature in the development of a sense of adequacy and self-sufficiency.

In the "game" of heterosexual relationships between adolescent boys and girls, as Udry describes it, the boys win points by increasing their exploitative and exploratory behaviors with girls. Girls, on the other hand, win points by getting boys involved with them emotionally and lose points by being increasingly permissive of the exploratory and exploitative sexual behaviors of boys.[17]

There are three scales involved in our understanding of Udry's "game": a status scale, a sexual intimacy scale, and a commitment scale. The comparison-level scale of the relative statuses of the boy and the girl is based on the

social desirability of each as a partner, as estimated by each of them. The athletic stardom of a boy is the most widespread determinant of his high "market value." The status of girls seems to be more closely related to the social class background of the students involved. The higher the social class of the students in the school, the more likely are girls who are leaders in activities to be highly valued; the lower the class status of the school, the more likableness makes a girl "most popular." Of course, in every school there are minority cliques who evaluate boys and girls on different dimensions—physical attractiveness, scholarship, parental status in the community, dress and grooming, car ownership, religiosity, morality, and available spending money, to name a few.

The second scale used in the adolescent "game" measures the degree of sexual intimacy permitted by the girl. Probably the most elaborate scale is suggested by William R. Reevy.[18] Reevy's scale, developed from the sex histories of college women in Pennsylvania, does not necessarily apply to young women of other socioeconomic categories or in other regions. He listed twenty-four items that seemed to fall more or less in order of intimacy level:

1. kissing on the lips
2. close embracing
3. "tongue kissing"
4. dancing "close" with a man or boy
5. fondling of breasts through clothing
6. pressing breasts against boy while dancing
7. pressing vulva against boy while dancing
8. touching a man's or boy's penis through clothing
9. being bitten as a part of sex play
10. having bare breasts fondled
11. permitting vulva to be caressed through clothing
12. permitting bare breasts to be kissed
13. lying together with a man or boy while fully or partially clothed and going through the motions of intercourse with him
14. permitting vulva and/or vagina to be caressed but not removing underpants
15. touching a man's bare penis
16. masturbating each other
17. undressing completely for a boy or man
18. lying still with a boy or man with his bare penis resting on or touching bare vulva without movement or penetration of vagina
19. kissing a boy's breasts on the nipples
20. holding a man's or boy's penis between the thighs but not in the vagina while he makes the motion of sexual intercourse to achieve orgasm and ejaculation
21. not wearing or removing underpants while otherwise fully dressed and permitting vulva and/or vagina to be caressed underneath the skirt
22. permitting the nipples of the breast to be sucked for long period of time
23. permitting penetration of the vagina by the penis of a man or boy who achieves orgasm and ejaculation inside you (having complete sexual intercourse)
24. having vulva and/or vagina kissed by a man or boy, penetrated by his tongue, or otherwise stimulated orally

Because the average boy in the United States discovers orgasm at an earlier age than the average girl does, boys' reasons for wanting to engage in coitus may be somewhat different from those of girls. For the adolescent boy, experiencing orgasm during coitus often is a goal in itself, although it may also signify both a social accomplishment and an affirmation of his masculinity. For the adolescent girl it is often a means to achieve a different goal—to satisfy her curiosity; to please the boy (since girls are often socialized to associate sex with love, and pleasing a boy may be seen as bringing the two together); to show that she is "grown up"; or to prove that she is "sexier," warmer, or "more of a woman" than her competitors. For most adolescent boys and girls—at least at the conscious level—conceiving a child has little or nothing to do with their motivations for having coitus. Whether they wish to propagate the human race or not, apparently boys are more likely to anticipate physical rewards in coitus, whereas girls more typically anticipate social rewards.

Adolescents who are experiencing active levels of sexual interest in a society with many inhibitory sanctions often feel caught between their urges and adult values. As one observer of this conflict remarked:

> *To whatever extent a youngster has been molded by middle-class values, he is "damned if he does and damned if he doesn't." There is the double burden of attempting to suppress his increasingly urgent sexual desires and the weight of guilt when he almost inevitably fails to do so. Where the attitudes of middle-class culture have determined a child's rearing, they make healthy adolescent use of any sexual outlet very nearly impossible.*[19]

The commitment scale involved in the "game" adolescents play estimates two dimensions of the relationship: duration and power. The duration dimension is concerned with the length of time the partner intends the relationship to last—for the rest of the summer, for "as long as it's fun," until graduation, or forever. The power dimension of commitment estimates the amount of energy, time, and resources a partner can be expected to devote to pleasing one or carrying out one's expressed or unexpressed wishes.

Put together, the three scales of the adolescent "game" can be interpreted by exchange theory or by equity theory as the interaction of two adolescents, each seeking a favorable (exchange) or fair (equity) balance of costs and rewards in a relationship. Costs and rewards are measured subjectively by each partner.

Having a relationship with a socially desirable partner is usually considered to be rewarding by persons with high self-esteem but may be considered costly by persons with low self-esteem who might develop feelings of insecurity and anxiety about the partner's attractiveness to others. A high degree of sexual intimacy is likely to be seen as rewarding by nearly all males and by some females, although females socialized to view sexual interaction as a gift or a concession on their part rather than a mutual sharing may see it as a cost. Finally, both one's own and one's partner's commitment to the relationship may be viewed as either costly or rewarding, depending on whether it is interpreted as a loss of personal freedom or as a gain in personal power.

The adolescent "game" will probably have vanished by young adulthood (between the ages of eighteen and twenty-two) for most persons. Pairing and the satisfaction of intimate interpersonal communication and understanding usually will have superseded the early "explore and exploit" pattern. Although the *quantity* of cross-sex sexual activity may provide reassurance for a minority of young adults, most will be more concerned with the *quality* of interaction with one person of the opposite sex. This generally means the establishment of a more or less durable petting-to-orgasm relationship with a particular member of the opposite sex or with a sequence of such partners over a period of time. For some, there will be abstinence from any sexual contacts other than necking until later in adulthood or until marriage.

As a rule, young adults rarely regress from the point they have achieved on the intimacy scale. For example, once a male has established a pattern of mutual masturbation leading to orgasm on his part, he is less likely to be interested in a relationship with a partner who permits him less intimacy. Similarly, females are unlikely to regress from whatever level of intimacy has been achieved in young adulthood, tending instead to resume the maximum intimacy permitted with a former partner shortly after committing themselves to lasting relationships with new partners. Both males and females, once they have had pleasurable intercourse, rarely stop seeking such sexual experience in later relationships.

Legal Institutions and Law Enforcement Agencies

It is clear that some sexual behaviors are subject to legal regulation. Not only does every state in the United States recognize this in its statutes, but also law enforcement agencies commonly are empowered either formally or informally to warn, cite, and arrest persons for a number of sexual behaviors under statutes of a general nature. "Contributing to the delinquency of a minor," juvenile delinquency, public indecency, vagrancy, loitering, and a wide variety of other offenses named in state or local laws are sometimes defined broadly. In practice, their specific meanings are likely to be defined by police officers who seek out or apprehend offenders (or, on the other hand, ignore them) according to their personal moral judgments. For instance, a child enticing another child to go swimming in the nude in a country stream might be apprehended by a police officer on the grounds supplied by any of the above-named offenses (one of the authors attended precisely such a hearing in juvenile court). On the other hand, an officer coming across a male having intercourse with a seventeen-year-old female (a felony in all but three states) on a public beach (an additional violation) may simply look the other way, especially if the woman's age is doubtful and she appears to be consenting.

In some jurisdictions, precisely defined sexual behaviors of adolescents may be specifically forbidden by statute. In other states, probation departments or juvenile courts are permitted to inquire into the sexual activities of juveniles and to take steps toward the prevention of any sexual behavior patterns that they consider improper or harmful. This latter kind of supervision terminates as early as age sixteen in some jurisdictions and as late as age eighteen in others. Although these age distinctions may appear arbitrary since they do not seem to take into consideration the different rates of individual development, legal codes universally regard chronological age as appropriate for distinguishing between the acceptability and the nonacceptability of a wide variety of sexual behaviors.

The American notion that children under a certain age should be "protected" from exposure to sexual ideas or behaviors has a history that extends far back into the roots of Western civilization. This kind of thinking is not universal; it is absent in the histories of many societies, especially in the islands of the Pacific and in Africa. Once the idea that sex is "evil" has become established in a society, however, the citizens may feel that there should be laws to repress, prevent, or punish numerous sexual behaviors.

Influence of the New Morality

Such magazines as *Playboy* and *Penthouse* have prospered financially by selling sexual stimulation. Lately, magazines for women have been published with centerfold pictures of nude males. In some communities there are bars that feature nude male performers and are patronized by women. It is not certain whether females are being reconditioned to enjoy such visual stimulation or whether they have always secretly appreciated such opportunities but only now feel free to express their interest in sex. In either case, there does appear to be a recent change in females' interests in seeing nude male bodies.[20]

It is only a step from socially acceptable erotic stimuli to those that are socially considered "improper." Erotic enjoyment of the sight, feel, or smell of underwear, shoes, sweaters, boots, leather clothing, and a host of other articles may or may not be considered "normal" depending on the contexts in which such articles become exciting.

Some authorities consider almost anything "normal" that gives sexual pleasure, providing it does not offend one's partner.[21,22] Others find anything "normal" that ultimately leads to a healthy heterosexual experience. Still others limit what is "normal" to whatever leads to a heterosexual experience with no attempt to prevent conception. Thus, being sexually aroused by leather clothing would be seen by many as abnormal if the result was always self-stimulation or homosexual activity, but the use of leather as a stimulant in a heterosexual encounter with one's spouse without using contraceptives might be considered "normal." What is "normal" is, at best, controversial, and this can be very confusing to a young person who is trying to learn.

It is probably safe to say that adults generally succeed in passing on not only their good feelings but their sexual prejudices and guilt feelings about sex to their children and that adults themselves either live with these biases or spend years trying to recondition themselves. However, despite the adolescent struggle with sexual conflicts, most young people reach adulthood without devastating sexual problems or at least, as adults, are able to overcome them somewhat. Surely, if this were not so, far fewer adults would report that their sex lives are reasonably satisfactory.[23,24]

Summary

■ Children often confuse attitudes about sex with other ideas based on generalizations that have an emotional quality. For instance, children frequently believe sex is "dirty" because they associate their genitals only with elimination processes. For many children sex and reproduction are paired so completely that for years children may not know that making babies is not the only motivation for coitus.

■ Children learn about sex as they learn about everything else that is emotional—through direct teaching, imitation, and experience. They learn from adults—both parents and other teachers—who can convey either that sex is normal and healthy or that it is sinful and dirty. Most parents probably convey both messages from time to time. Parents may have their own "hang-ups" and, in addition, may be so emotionally involved with their children that they find it difficult if not impossible to be the sole providers of sex education.

■ Peers, both same-sex and cross-sex, are the most common source of sex information (often inaccurate) for young people. Many of the sexual attitudes of young people are formed in early discussions and experimentation with their peers. About five times as many boys as girls engage in social sexual behaviors before adolescence—much of it with same-sex peers.

■ By mid- to late adolescence, heterosexual relationships are the rule. Girls still report less frequent encounters, fewer partners, and fewer orgasms than do boys. This is largely due to differences between socialization patterns for males and those for females, according to which early sexual activity is more highly approved for males. In addition, females may typically underreport their activities, whereas males may overreport. Much of this early activity is non-coital—"necking," "petting," or "heavy petting."

■ Laws, the media, and the so-called new morality also affect young people's sexual attitudes. It is often confusing and difficult to define what is "normal." Despite the struggles involved in growing up sexually, however, most individuals manage to overcome their early socialization well enough to report satisfactory sexual adjustment as adults, although many do grow up saddled with guilt and make poor adult adjustments.

Sexual Sensations

The state of knowing something is the result of brain activity. However, responses to many kinds of bodily stimuli do not pass through the brain in the same way other stimuli do. Some sensations that may be identified as sexual do not. In other words, stimuli to nerve endings in various parts of the human body may produce responses in both primary and secondary sex organs that are not consciously associated with sex but that are nevertheless defined as sexual. An infant's penis or clitoris becomes erect when it is stroked or when a stream of water plays on it, even though the infant cannot *think* about what his or her nerve endings are sensing or interpret these sensations as sexual.

In contrast to unwilled and unknowing reactions of the sex organs to stimuli, humans also interpret as sexual any stimuli (including memories and fantasies as well as present sights, sounds, scents, touches, and tastes) that produce erections of the penis, clitoris, and perhaps nipples, as well as lubrication of the vagina, secretion of preejaculatory fluids, and all the other symptoms of being "turned on" or "horny."

Sensations are interpreted *after* they have been sensed. Just as bodily feelings of anger or happiness are at first simply physical responses (which we later learn to label and to judge as "good" or "bad"), so are many sensations later interpreted as sexual and judged to be good or bad by standards that are learned rather than innate.

Zones of the body that are associated with sexual responses are called **erogenous** zones. Although some of these connections are **subcortical**—that is, they do not have to be interpreted as sexual by the brain in order for the response to occur—most of them do involve either awareness or conditioning. As one woman put it, "When I was a teenager, my whole body was an erogenous zone!"* What she undoubtedly meant was that if she interpreted a situation as sexual, then almost anything she sensed would increase her sexual response.

The context of an interaction is very important to the interpretation of sensations as sexual.[25] For example, usually there is a vast difference between a woman's reactions to a pelvic examination by a gynecologist in a hospital and to heavy petting with an attractive male, even in terms of physical responses such as clitoral erection and lubrication, although the parts of the body touched or pressed may be the same.

There are also individual and cultural differences in the interpretation of sensations as sexual. One woman may find that nursing her baby stimulates strong genital responses; another may report that she cannot stand to have her partner touch her breasts during the months she is nursing her baby because "he's invading the baby's territory; my breasts are not to be used for sexual approaches then."* Kinsey reported that better-educated persons typically are much more likely to interpret oral stimuli (French kissing, **cunnilingus, fellatio**) as sexually arousing than are less well educated persons—undoubtedly a cultural difference.[26]

What is sexually arousing in humans can be expected to vary not only from person to person, but also from one time period to another and from one situation to another with the same person. Some women have heightened sexual responses during their times of ovulation, others during their menstrual

---

* Clinical record.

periods, and some during the period between these events.[27] It seems unlikely that such differences are genetic.

One of the main reasons that enduring sexual relationships seem to be preferable to "one-night stands" is that maximum satisfaction in sexual activities depends in part on getting to know what pleases one's partner. Since what turns each person on seems to grow out of personal experiences and usually seems "natural" to that person, guessing what someone will find sexually stimulating is probably less satisfactory than the knowledge that comes from having experienced that person in a variety of contexts and having had open communication with him or her over an extended period of time.

The Process of Orgasm

Once a decision has been made to engage in sexual activities and erection of the penis or clitoris has occurred, continued stimulation leads to the establishment of a "plateau" level of sexual tension. At this plateau level, the sex organs have reached certain recognizable physical conditions (see Appendix A). The ridge (the **corona**) that separates the head of a penis from its shaft usually increases in circumference, as does the head itself (although in some men this may not happen at all and in others it may occur sometimes). The outer third of the vagina (the inner sheath of a woman's sex organ, which is not usually visible) decreases in size, becoming "tighter"; its diameter shrinks to as little as 50 percent of what it is in the relaxed state.

As sexual stimulation continues during the plateau, males secrete anywhere from two drops to a cubic centimeter of glandular fluid, which, although it is not **semen**, may contain some **spermatozoa**. In the plateau phase, interior "sweating" of the vagina diminishes, but secretions begin from glands in the vulva (the outer, visible part of a woman's sex organs). Near the end of the plateau phase, the clitoris appears to go upward and backward, and the little lips within the **vulva** turn bright red (in women who have never borne children) or a deeper burgundy color (in women who have). Once this change in color has occurred, continued stimulation of the clitoris will produce orgasm.

In males, the plateau phase ends when orgasm begins. The man feels a sudden contraction of the internal sex organs, which is a signal to him that an ejaculation will begin within two or three seconds and is no longer under his control. At this "point of no return" he is likely to make a forward thrust and "freeze," pausing briefly until involuntary contractions of his prostate (an internal gland that spurts out most of the fluid in an ejaculation) begin.

At the conclusion of this "period of inevitability," two or three strong contractions occur through the major pelvic organs at intervals of approximately eight-tenths of a second, followed by a series of lesser contractions at progressively widely spaced intervals. The first strong contraction causes the ejaculation to occur. The peak of pleasure for the male probably comes just before and during this first spurt of semen, although the ejaculation may continue through several contractions.

Normally, the release of tension in the muscles and the relief of congestion in the sex organs of the ejaculating male is so great that his penis quickly becomes flaccid. He experiences such total relaxation that he may soon drift into sleep or lie still for several minutes in a trancelike state. Occasionally, however, particularly among the relatively young, a man may be able to maintain his erection and return to a plateau level immediately.

Masters and Johnson documented the case of one male subject who maintained sexual stimulation through three ejaculations in a total of ten minutes from the beginning of sexual stimulation.[28] Normally, however, even in young men, the resolution of tension is so complete and so relaxing that a satisfactory erection will not be regained for at least twenty minutes.

The female orgasmic experience differs from that of the male in several ways. First, the two- or three-second "freeze" between the plateau phase and the onset of the contractions of the uterus (womb), which constitutes the beginning of orgasm, is not present. In fact, for a female to experience complete orgasm, it may be essential for her to have continued rhythmic stimulation, not just until the orgasm has begun but until it is quite advanced, if not finished.

For females, orgasm begins with anywhere from four to eight contractions of the uterus and squeezes of the outer third of the vagina at intervals of eight-tenths of a second, followed by three to four contractions at irregular intervals and with diminishing force. Like males, females also experience two to four contractions of the **anus** at the same eight-tenths-of-a-second interval.

Resolution of muscle tension and pelvic congestion occurs more slowly in females than in males, requiring up to several minutes after orgasm. No doubt it is partly because of this difference that women can experience orgasm several times during coitus. If stimulation continues, some women are capable of achieving *status orgasmus* lasting from twenty seconds to as much as sixty seconds, during which they experience either rapidly recurring orgasms or a single long, continuous orgasmic episode.[29]

The orgasm is the fastest and most satisfying resolution of muscle tension and congestion resulting from sexual stimulation. If orgasm is not achieved, the length of time required for resolution is roughly proportional to the length of time that stimulation has continued. In both sexes, frequent stimulation without orgasm may lead to discomfort and even to chronic inflammation and pain resulting from unrelieved congestion.

The experience of orgasm is exquisite. Having once experienced it, people generally desire any subsequent strong sexual stimulation to continue to orgasm if circumstances permit, and may remain quite tense until the sexual stress is relieved. This tendency may seem to be considerably stronger in men, possibly because it usually has been effectively reinforced by "wet dreams" if no other outlet intervenes. Because male and female sentiments and socialization patterns are different, it may be difficult for a woman who has never experienced orgasm in any way to understand the attraction that coitus holds for most males or females who have experienced orgasm.

It is often difficult for those who have established an orgasmic response pattern to discontinue sexual activities altogether for any appreciable period of time. Losing a partner, for whatever reason, with whom one has established a pattern of orgasmic release may be particularly difficult. For those who have never learned to achieve orgasm through self-stimulation the discomfort may be even greater.

Masturbation

Awareness of the importance of masturbation usually precedes adolescence. Ordinarily, it begins when a boy or girl realizes that touching his or her genitals produces unique sensations. Boys who have not experienced the sensations of masturbation directly—by handling their genitals during bathing, by exploring their own bodies with their hands, or by allowing someone else to manipulate them—will almost certainly learn about it from their peers by the time they reach puberty.

The practice is reportedly much less common among girls and women.[30] Kinsey, in his extensive reports on human sexuality, estimated that by the time of marriage the average male has experienced slightly over 1,500 orgasms, with about 330 of those occurring during intercourse.[31] He estimated that the average female, at marriage, had experienced a total of 223 orgasms, with only 39 of them occurring during coitus.[32] As discussed earlier, the sexual activity of boys, whether coital or from self-stimulation, is probably more closely related to the number of orgasms they have than is the sexual activity of girls. The number of orgasms that girls report undoubtedly underrepresents the amount of sexual activity in which they have engaged to a much greater extent than is true of the number of orgasms boys report.[33]

For obvious reasons it is difficult to obtain totally accurate data, but the best estimates from research on the subject are that nearly all males and about two-thirds of females practice masturbation sometime during adolescence.[34] It is unrealistic to think that a person who has begun masturbating will stop voluntarily without some replacement activity, particularly once orgasm has been achieved in this way. There seem to be no satisfying substitutes for orgasms, which provide a unique kind of pleasurable satisfaction. Since every physically and mentally healthy adolescent has all the physical equipment necessary to produce orgasms, the only likely reason that girls report a lower incidence than do boys is either that fewer of them have actually learned how to induce orgasm or that girls have learned stronger taboos than have boys. As the sexual double standard declines, it seems probable that girls will feel freer to report such activity and that frequency of self-stimulation and orgasm will more closely approximate that of boys.

In research on college students, nearly 90 percent of males and over 60 percent of females reported that they masturbated mostly between the ages of nine and sixteen.[35] The end of a period of frequent masturbation seems to be closely tied to the beginning of coitus, although this is not to say that those who have active sex lives do not continue to find interest in self-stimulation.

Research has indicated that nearly all males continue to masturbate throughout their lifetimes, even though the incidence is highest in adolescence and early adulthood. Women too, both married and unmarried, feel that masturbation is a positive aspect of their lives.[36] Those with the highest feelings of self-esteem and with high sex drives are also more likely to masturbate.[37]

Females report that the orgasms achieved through masturbation often are more intense than those experienced through intercourse. Some report that they alleviate menstrual symptoms (backaches, cramps) by self-stimulation.[38]

Sexual Fantasies

Whether or not stimuli are considered sexual depends on the interpretation given to them. This interpretation in turn depends on individual experiences and includes "imagining"—constructing a context of ideas about situations that do not actually exist and including these in the interpretation of what does actually exist. The point at which interpretation becomes fantasy may be much less precise than the terms suggest. It is clear, however, that the most important sex organ in the human body is the brain and that how one thinks about sex can enhance one's experiences greatly.

Those who are making their first sexual approaches to each other have some interpretation of the meaning of that behavior as well as some images or fantasies about the behaviors that will follow, even though these have not yet occurred. How they feel at the moment—anxious, joyous, frightened, content, sexually stimulated—depends to a great extent on their expectations of events that have not yet actually occurred.

Few people feel at any given moment that they have all the qualities, possessions, or relationships they would like. Nearly all persons find that inadequacies, rules, frustrations, or powerful people stand between them and their hearts' desires. A small boy can sometimes escape the reality of his powerlessness by visualizing himself as a powerful person such as a professional football player; a little girl can blot out her musical ineptitude by imagining herself up on the podium, conducting the New York Philharmonic. An adult can respond to current needs or frustrations by fantasizing about past achievements, about potential capabilities or attributes, or about personal goals that may or may not be possible: wealth, power, love, sexual attractiveness, potency, and fulfillment, to name a few.

Probably few adults feel as powerful or as attractive as they would like to be. For most men and women, the prospect of being able to exert power over others is exhilarating; the prospect of being desired sexually by attractive persons is itself sexually arousing. The fear of defeat or rejection that may be present in the real world can be set aside in the world of fantasy.

For the most part, men's sexual fantasies involve freedom from restrictive rules about sexual behavior, which they often see, consciously or unconsciously, as having been set down by their mothers and other women.[39] Men tend to fantasize that they are free to choose their own sexual activities and their own sexual partners, although a very small minority are stimulated by fantasies of being enslaved or humiliated by a woman.[40] Men also seem to fantasize about actual persons they know or have seen or heard about.

Women are more likely to fantasize about faceless persons, mysterious strangers, fictional characters, or other unattainable individuals. This "double standard" of fantasy is probably related to the notion in our culture that women "give" sexual favors and that men who receive them should see themselves as specially privileged or chosen over other men to receive these valuable gifts. Women, on the other hand, have not traditionally felt special because they were wanted sexually by a particular man but, rather, because they were wanted by many men in competition for them.

Although women's fantasies (which, according to Nancy Friday, are often "the strongest foreplay of all") have the same chief quality as those of men, they seem much more likely to involve power than freedom.[41] Many women fantasize being overpowered by men or other women who force them into sexual acts; others fantasize that they are the powerful persons—that either their aggressive behavior or their irresistible seductiveness commands others to carry out their sexual wishes.

Since no one can foretell the future accurately, most persons fantasize to some extent whenever they base their behaviors on what they believe is going to happen. If the prospects are happy, they "feel good"; if bad, they feel depressed. Most people have spent many years fantasizing about what certain sexual experiences will (or would) be like. Even when they are engaging in sexual activities, they may be comparing reality with anticipation—but the anticipation may already have been defined in part by their ideas of what the mysterious reality will be like.

No one knows exactly what another person is feeling, let alone what another person will feel. Fantasies help to establish what one will feel. For example, fantasizing that one's partner is having sex out of a sense of obligation, or only to satisfy a selfish desire, is certainly possible but is not very exciting. On the other hand, fantasizing that one's partner is having sex because one is special and attractive, even irresistible, can be sexually stimulating.

Because sexual behavior is intimate and private, there is no need to be judged by other people's standards or realities. If a couple wishes to imagine during their sexual activities that they are in a pine forest, on a desert island, or in the tenth or the thirtieth century, or that they are Romeo and Juliet, they need answer to no one else.

Sexual Scripts

A script is a set of directions that actors follow to convey the writer's story or message. It includes the words that must be said and the actions that must be taken to create a mood and enact a story line. Nearly everyone has in mind a script that will define his or her sexual character to others. This is usually conceptualized as the way to behave in order to achieve certain outcomes. People who have very different sexual scripts may not be able to establish an enduring relationship.

Of course, having the same script does not mean that the actors play the same roles; rather, in most scripts the roles are complementary or reciprocal. *Complementary roles* are demonstrated when each actor enacts a role that "fills in" the parts that are not enacted by the other(s). *Reciprocal roles* are enacted when each actor's role is developed through an ongoing response to that of the other(s).

Let us suppose that Jane's sexual script, which she has constructed from communication with parents and friends and from the mass media, defines sexual intercourse as necessary for making babies and for fulfilling her needs to be a mother, but as something personal and private, never to be mentioned to others—especially not to her parents or children—and not to be entered into lightly, since babymaking is a serious matter. She sees her vagina as being constructed as it is in order to enable sperm to be deposited to fertilize her egg cells and to permit the birth of her babies when they come to term. She views the complementary function of her husband as providing sperm to fertilize her egg cells. The role of her breasts is to provide milk for her babies. Jane's sexual script could have been written by students in a sixth-grade sex education course in many schools.

Karen's sexual script is very different from Jane's. Karen views sexual intercourse as a natural step in growth toward intimacy. People who are attracted to each other enjoy physical contact with each other. A person who holds your hand likes you and wants to be your friend. If he kisses you, he wants to establish some sort of relationship. If he has intercourse with you, he wants that relationship to be special and intimate. For Karen, pregnancy and marriage are separate issues from sexuality.

Laurie's sexual script is different from either Jane's or Karen's. Laurie enjoys experiencing orgasms. Although she can achieve orgasms by herself, she enjoys them more when they are produced by a skilled and willing partner. She intends to marry and to have babies but does not see marriage and conception as the primary goals of sexual activity. Sex should be gratifying for its own sake; relationships and babies might as well be associated with good sex as with poor or mediocre sex.

Diana has still a fourth sexual script. To Diana sexual intercourse is a gift (or perhaps a sacrifice) that she gives to someone in exchange for love or commitment. It has nothing to do with babies, intimacy, or pleasure—although all of these may result. Sexual intercourse is something you do because your partner wants or expects it. If you love him, you will give it to him because he wants it.

Of course, these scripts are not given in detail and are grossly oversimplified here. Not only are there other sexual scripts for women, but also most women have some elements of more than one such script. Men also have a wide variety of sexual scripts.[42] Scripts mediate between us and our social context. They tell us how to interpret the behavior of others and how to structure our own behaviors meaningfully and properly. Our scripts tell us how to make interaction turn out "right" and what to do when things aren't going as we wish.

Scripts may change through time, of course, but they seldom change very rapidly once adulthood has been reached. Most people seem to believe that the sexual script of all "normal" people either is the same as theirs or ought to be; therefore, it is not unusual for a couple to fail to recognize the source of discord in their relationship as the incompatibility of their scripts. A skilled counselor or therapist usually can spot such incompatibilities quickly and can confront the couple with the need to resolve their differences in order to reduce the discord.

When an adult couple or group engages in behaviors that they jointly perceive as sexual, what does it mean to them or about them? What does it say about two people that they have slept in the same bed overnight? For that matter, what does it mean if two adult men are seen embracing each other and kissing each other's lips? What does it mean if an adult married to someone else is invited to have sexual intercourse?

These questions have almost as many answers as there are people to answer them because there are almost as many sexual scripts as there are people. For one person, in one situation, intercourse means permanent bonding. For another it means rebellion; for a third, conquest; for still another, defilement. Sexual intercourse may be an affirmation of gender, of adulthood, of relationship status. It may mean reaching for immortality through producing children; it may mean fun and games; it may mean security and contentment; it may mean "restoring one's soul."

Whatever sexual intercourse means to particular persons, it is usually a landmark event. People do not ordinarily forget whether or not they have had sexual intercourse with particular others, regardless of the circumstances. Intercourse is also a matter of social interest and concern, as is evident from the number of laws about it and the amount of gossip it generates. At times it seems that the significance of sexual intercourse is exaggerated beyond reason. Relationships lasting half a century or more have been generated by it, and others lasting equally long have been dissolved because of it. People may be disgusted—or enthralled—to learn that two people are making love.

Whatever sexual intercourse may mean, we can conclude that it is one of life's most significant activities for most people. Whether that significance is rationally justifiable is beside the point, both for individual mental health and for the comfortable functioning of marital and family systems.

Summary

■ The context of an interaction often determines whether or not one interprets one's sensations as sexual. There are both individual and cultural differences in how people interpret sensations; these vary not only from person to person but also from one time to another with the same person.

■ Orgasm is the release of tension in the muscles and the relief of congestion in the genitals and pelvis. Those who have experienced orgasm are very likely in future encounters to follow sexual stimulation to an orgasmic experience.

■ Masturbation is often a replacement for sex with a partner. It is most prevalent between the ages of nine and sixteen but for most men and women continues throughout life, although at a lower frequency.

■ Sexual fantasies enhance most individuals' sexual encounters. Men's fantasies differ somewhat from those of women, but members of both sexes find them to be powerful arousal mechanisms.

■ Sexual scripts—what people think must be said and done—are usually both complementary and reciprocal. Scripts change over time, but some of their elements may be so fixed that two individuals with conflicting scripts can find difficulty resolving their expectations. Whatever *sex* means to a particular person, establishing a sexual relationship is usually a landmark event.

Sexual Preferences

Virtually all adults have sexual impulses. People who have such impulses may say that they need "outlets," or seek "sexual peace," or are trying to gratify an "urge" or "drive." However they are viewed, such sexual impulses must be channeled into patterns that not only are satisfying to the individual but also do not cause undue stress within the confines of society. Deciding whether or not to gratify these urges, either alone or in interaction with another person or persons, may result in a consistently repeated pattern or may depend entirely on the opportunities present in a particular situation.

What is considered a "sexual opportunity" differs considerably from one person to another. Some choices and opportunities are defined consciously; often the chooser sees them as his or her "natural" preferences and believes that few other satisfying possibilities exist for him or her.

Celibacy

Celibacy is a state in which one has made a choice—usually consciously—not to engage in sexual activities with any other person. Sometimes the term is also used to denote that a person has chosen not to marry (usually for philosophical or religious reasons), but such a choice may or may not have any connotations for sexual activities.

Celibate persons, such as priests and nuns, may take vows declaring that they do not intend to provoke in themselves any kind of genital sexual sensations or even to have thoughts of doing such things. Many celibate persons do not condemn sex as bad or wrong for everyone but aspire to channel their own sexual energies into activities and thoughts that are more valuable to them. If they are successful, their sexual glands and other organs eventually may atrophy—shrivel or become incapable of functioning—after which their aspirations become easier to achieve.

Celibacy may also be interpreted to mean that one confines one's sexual gratification to self-stimulation. This can be either a moral choice—a feeling that it is not right to engage in sex with another person—or a result of social ineptitude, shyness, or a poor self-concept. Celibacy is sometimes forced on people by their acceptance of the idea that physical disfigurements somehow disqualify them sexually; by their feeling that they have nothing worthwhile to offer any partner; or by their expectation of being so inept sexually that their partners would laugh at them or would be unsatisfied.

Obviously, the happiest celibates are likely to be those who have made a conscious choice to forego any sexual activity (or any sexual activity involving others) and who see themselves as gaining from that abstinence some more valuable reward. Such persons, if deprived of that choice, would be deprived of their right to human dignity.

Social Sex: Heterosexuality

The most common form of sexual preference in the United States at present, at least among adults, is generally believed to be heterosexuality. Most people consider "proper" only sexual activities that take place between males and females.

Feelings about the "correctness" of heterosexuality are often so strong that those who have them react strongly to any sexual attraction they may feel to persons of the same sex. Many men and women immediately deny or repress any hint of sexual feeling toward a person of their own sex. Behaviors that might be construed as homosexual are scrupulously avoided, and persons who appear to have homosexual inclinations are ridiculed or punished.

Virtually all kinds of erotic behaviors can be acted out both homosexually and heterosexually. Coitus, however, is exclusive to heterosexual couples by definition, since it is defined as the union that occurs when one person's penis is placed inside another person's vagina. For many people this is considered to be the ultimate sexual act—both in degree of intimacy and as an expression of love.

Because intercourse has such significance, it has a great deal of anxiety and surplus meaning attached to it, both by couples who are contemplating intercourse and by those who have been engaging in it for years. The refusal of a partner to engage in sexual activities of any sort is easily interpreted as rejection. Sometimes people are unwilling to urge their partners toward coitus in particular because the potential for feeling rejected threatens to destroy their self-esteem.

Social Sex: Homosexuality

Homosexual sex preference means that one prefers to engage in sexual activities with other persons of the same sex. Depending on how one defines *sexual behavior*, one might argue that homosexual behaviors are if anything more

"normal" during preadolescence than are heterosexual behaviors. It may be that a homosexual developmental phase is necessary for the emergence of a comfortable heterosexual preference later on.

Whatever the case may be, historically there has been great social prejudice and discrimination against adults known to engage in homosexual activities and, indeed, even against those who are merely suspected of homosexuality, often on insubstantial grounds. This has been particularly true for men.

The prejudice against females who may be engaging in homosexual behaviors has been less than that against males. One can only speculate about the reasons for this, but it has been suggested that the idea of two women holding hands, being otherwise affectionate to each other, or even living together has never had the same connotation as does similar behavior between two men. In our society women are allowed a wider range of physical contact with other women than men are with other men. In addition, women who choose other women as sexual partners usually have no more than one or two such partners. Men sometimes have many partners and may therefore call more attention to their sexual activities than do women.[43]

The "gay rights" movement has successfully combated some of the discrimination against persons who engage in homosexual behaviors or who express such preferences. With a few exceptions, when laws or policies that discriminate on grounds of sexual preference have been challenged in court, they have been repealed or annulled; even so, there is still a considerable amount of social prejudice.[44]

Social Sex:
Bisexuality

Since all sexual behaviors are transitory—that is, individual sex acts do not last forever—one might engage in homosexual behaviors on some occasions and in heterosexual behaviors on others, just as preadolescents do. Although this is popularly called *bisexuality*, that term suggests an enduring personality trait that may not actually exist. It is entirely conceivable, for example, that some men and women may during their lifetimes have warm erotic relationships with both those of the same sex and those of the opposite sex at different times or, perhaps, even at the same time.

Our avoidance of the words *homosexuals, heterosexuals,* and *bisexuals* as substantive nouns is in part an effort to avoid labeling persons, thereby legitimizing their treatment in some discriminatory way, on the basis of limited behaviors. People are *sexual*, and their sexual *behaviors* may be heterosexual, homosexual, or bisexual. Not everyone agrees with this distinction, however; there are those who identify themselves as "straight" or "gay" or "lesbian." There are also people who claim a true bisexual identity, although this definition is not completely clear. Some young people seem to have been influenced by media figures—rock stars, actors, and writers—who are self-proclaimed

*Billie Jean King,
shown with her hus-
band, Larry, admit-
ted at a May 1981
news conference that
she once had a les-
bian relationship.*

"bisexuals."[45] Some bars that once were exclusively gay now try to attract patrons who dance with persons of either sex.[46] Many of those who identify themselves as bisexual seem to believe that this somehow represents more "liberated" behavior than does exclusive heterosexuality or homosexuality.[47]

Types of Sexual Relationships

The term *relationship* usually implies a repeated interaction over an appreciable period of time, with some ordering of behavior by the two or more people involved. Thus casual sexual events do not necessarily constitute social relationships, since they imply only the briefest or most superficial ordering of behavior. In fact, the essence of casual sex may lie in the avoidance of commitment, ordering, or consistency. Such behavior may symbolize a desire not to be committed and may simply represent an experiential outlet or an anonymous release of sexual tension.

Establishments exist in which one may engage in sex with strangers. Some have darkened rooms so that the persons never see each other clearly. There may be a rule against using last names, or people may elect to use fictitious names. Some people choose to have sex with strangers whom they will never see again so that there can be no further involvement. However, few people are content to rely solely on casual sex for any extended period of time. This is too lonely and too unpredictable a life for most people. It can also be risky because it increases the likelihood of one's contracting venereal or other diseases or of meeting with physical danger. There appears to be an increase in the number of single persons involved in a succession of short-term relationships, however.[48] Many people deliberately choose a short-term emotional-sexual involvement because they want to avoid a premature commitment but are not content with casual sex. They may believe that all friendships have the potential for sexual contact but that circumstances can either encourage sexual involvement or, just as easily, terminate it.

A few marriages have incorporated understandings between the spouses sanctioning extramarital sexual activities, which often include short-term relationships. "Affairs" are often of this nature and duration. In one study, about half the married men reported extramarital experience. The wives of nearly a third of these men knew about it. In 20 percent of the cases, the men told their wives; in 3 percent, the wives found out by other means; and in about 8 percent, there was a prior understanding that extramarital sex was permissible in the marriage.[49]

Monogamous Relationships	At the opposite end of the scale from casual sex is the *monogamous relationship*. Such relationships usually function as marriages. The concept of marriage in our society assumes that there will be an enduring and mutually consenting sexual relationship. In fact, in some states a marriage is not valid until the couple has consummated it (that is, engaged in coitus).

Monogamy literally means "one mating." It can be interpreted to mean having only one sexual partner ever during one's entire lifetime, or having one primary sexual relationship during any long period of time. Many people practice each of these interpretations, and many more hold one or the other as personal ideals.

There are no convincing data on the number of persons in the United States who have sexual intercourse with one and only one partner during their entire lifetimes, including the periods before marriage and after widowhood. The conclusions of both Kinsey and Hunt suggest that the number of such persons is greater than less carefully chosen samples have indicated.[50,51]

A *Cosmopolitan* magazine study reported that only 9 percent of the sample had confined sexual activity to one lover and that two-thirds had had more than five lovers. However, the sample was composed of employed women between the ages of eighteen and thirty-four who lived in cities of over one million, selected from 106,000 volunteer respondents to a questionnaire printed in *Cosmopolitan*.[52] This kind of sample would be more likely to report more sexual activity than would respondents more representative of the general population.

Most research indicates that around half of the population will have only their spouses as sexual partners during marriage but that the number who will have had more than one partner before, between, and after marriages is increasing.[53]

The sexual intentions and expectations in a monogamous relationship are normally in a constant but gradual state of change. Because the sexual peak for men (in terms of potential frequency of orgasm) occurs in the late teens, whereas the sexual peak for women (in terms of actual frequency of orgasm) occurs in the early thirties, one would expect the greatest frequency of mutual sexual activity to occur somewhere between these two peaks. This usually occurs in the first few years of most marriages.[54]

It is more difficult both to collect and to interpret information on satisfaction with sexual behaviors over the span of a marriage than to collect data on the frequency of intercourse. The quality of sexual activities should improve steadily as the years go by. As couples overcome inhibitions and learn new and more effective skills in sexual communication and in sexual behaviors, at least the potential for increasing satisfaction exists.

One of the most thorough recent studies of marital sexuality has given evidence that there is a high correlation between the degree of marital closeness and the quality of couples' sex lives with each other.[55] This work generally confirmed the essential sexuality of Americans and showed trends toward wider acceptance and enjoyment of sexual activities that had often been considered deviant in the past. (For example, over three-fourths of all married couples reported engaging in oral stimulation of the genital organs of their partners.)

Most marriage experts agree that mutual satisfaction in a couple's sex life is a powerful factor in overall marital adjustment. Conversely, couples who report sexual maladjustment, may also have more general problems in their marriages.

Extramarital Sex

Probably more has been written on the subject of infidelity than on almost any other aspect of marital sex. The major reasons for engaging in **extramarital sex** seem to be a desire for variety and for the enjoyment of intimate friendships with others than the spouse.[56] An "inadequate sex life at home" and "other serious problems in the marriage" are rather low on the list. In fact, 80 percent of the middle-class men reporting extramarital sex in Yablonsky's study said that their sex lives with their wives were "good" or "excellent," and an additional 14 percent reported that sex life at home was "fair." Other research, however, has indicated that marital sex is not rated as high by those who have affairs as by those who do not.[57] Those who have extramarital affairs may bias their replies according to what they want the interviewer to believe or in order to justify their own feelings about their behavior.

It is interesting to note that of those who eventually divorced, any extramarital sex they had typically began early in their marriages. Half of those in one study reported that extramarital relationships began in the first year of marriage. For those who did not divorce, the average duration of the marriage before the advent of extramarital sex was between six and seven years.[58]

Although discussion of extramarital affairs with friends and interviewers appears to be much more open than it was forty years ago when Kinsey did his studies, Hunt notes that ". . . our data indicate that there is still a great emphasis on secrecy, based on the clear recognition that such extramarital acts will be perceived by the spouse as disloyalty, partial abandonment, and a repudiation of marital love."[59] Only one-fifth of both men and women engaging in extramarital intercourse believed that their spouses actually knew about it, and Hunt concluded that the "liberated" younger married people were just as secretive as the older men and women.

The debate continues over whether a middle-class person can have an extramarital affair and a healthy marriage at the same time. A spokesman for one point of view says that the long-term affair in particular is a form of neurotic behavior and a reflection of the immaturity of the person so engaged.[60] This point of view emphasizes the frustrations, disappointments, and expectations of the man or woman involved in a long-term affair. Another viewpoint is represented by this statement:

> *The most interesting question of all may well be whether or not extramarital intercourse is normal. I must answer with a somewhat qualified yes. It is normal in that sexually monogamous permanent marriage places an unnatural restriction upon the human animal's biologically normal desire and capacity for sexual variety. . . . It is equally true that any specific instance of infidelity may have its roots not in normal human tendencies, but in every kind and level of intrapsychic and interpersonal immaturity or emotional disorder. The existence of inappropriate motivations similarly cannot justify a blanket condemnation of sex outside an existing marriage.[61]*

Whether a particular extramarital relationship is healthy or neurotic, it seems clear that the incidence of infidelity is rising, particularly among younger middle-class couples. Some reasons offered for the increase are that life expectancy is increasing; that our society has become more mobile and urban; and that there are more middle-class women in the labor market, which maximizes extramarital opportunities for them as well as for men. Last, but certainly not least, is the existence of effective birth control methods, which has permitted the separation of sex from reproduction.[62]

Although it is impossible to determine the exact percentage of men and women who have extramarital sex, a conservative study reported that about 45 percent of husbands and about 35 percent of wives have one such encounter or more.[63] The Kinsey and Hunt studies show much higher figures. Other studies show that the first instance of sex outside marriage is occurring at a younger age for both men and women and that few stop after just one instance.[64,65]

It is clear that one of the major problems in research on extramarital sex has involved trying to classify all such incidences as belonging to one category. In fact, there is a variety of reasons for such behavior, as well as a range of marital agreements and degrees of marital secrecy that result in many meanings of sex outside marriage. "Open marriage," for instance, is a relationship in which fidelity is defined not as sexual exclusivity but, rather, as commitment of another kind to one's mate. There is open respect for the spouse's judgments and behaviors, including his or her own and the partner's extramarital sexual relationships.[66] There can be little doubt that open respect for the spouse's judgment sets up an entirely different climate from one in which there is secrecy, deceit, and feelings of betrayal of trust.

Summary

■ Celibacy is a state in which one refrains from engaging in sexual intercourse. Often this abstinence is chosen for religious reasons and is seen as a way of channeling sexual energies into more valuable thoughts or activities. Other celibates may limit their sexual activities to self-stimulation for reasons that range from morality to shyness.

■ Heterosexuality, homosexuality, and bisexuality are variations of social sex. Heterosexuality is the most frequently practiced preference and is considered "normal" by most persons. Homosexuality and bisexuality now are subject to less social stigmatization than was previously the case, although in the United States today there is still a generally repressive attitude toward these variations of sexuality.

■ Casual sex and short-term relationships are both prevalent forms of sexual encounters. The most popular form of social sex, however, is married monogamy. It is perhaps more of an ideal than an actuality for many reasons, however, since many have had sexual relations with other partners before they were married and still others have sex with partners other than their mates while they are married.

■ Extramarital sex ranges from that which may be agreed on in "open marriages," where there is spousal acceptance, to disapproved sex that can sometimes destroy a marriage relationship. One study estimates conservatively that approximately 45 percent of husbands and 35 percent of wives have at least one such encounter. Other studies show much higher figures. The numbers seem to be increasing somewhat, especially among younger persons.

Glossary

Anus The opening at the outer end of the intestine through which feces pass.

Artificial insemination The placement of sperm in a woman's uterus with a syringe or a similar device for the purpose of fertilizing ova. If the husband's sperm is used (as when he is incapable of completing coitus or he has had sperm frozen prior to vasectomy), the procedure is called AIH. If a donor's sperm is used, the procedure is called AID.

Celibacy Abstinence from sexual activities with another; sometimes used to denote the decision to remain unmarried.

Coitus Specifically, insertion of the penis into the vagina; does not include other acts (for example, homosexual behaviors). The term *sexual intercourse* often is used to include behaviors other than penetration of the vagina by a penis.

Contraception The act of preventing pregnancy; any method used for this purpose.

Corona The ridge on the penis at the base of the glans.

Cunnilingus Oral stimulation of the female genitals.

Ejaculation The rhythmic ejection of semen through the penis.

Erogenous Pertaining to those feelings, thoughts, and sensations that produce sexual arousal.

Erotic Sexually arousing.

Extramarital sex Sexual relations between persons who are not married to each other.

Fellatio Oral stimulation of the male genitals.

Ideation The process of forming ideas or thoughts about issues, people, or objects that are theoretical or conjectural.

Masturbation Self-stimulation of the genital organs, usually to orgasm.

Menstruation The monthly discharge of blood and unused tissue from the lining of the uterus, which occurs when no fertilized egg has been implanted.

Orgasm Sexual climax in which sexual tension reaches a peak and is reduced in a series of extremely pleasurable rhythmic contractions.

Prostate gland The male gland that supplies seminal fluid and produces hormones. The prostate is involved with the smooth-muscle activity present in orgasm.

Semen The fluid that carries the sperm cells.

Spermatozoa Male reproductive cells.

Subcortical Characteristic of that part of the brain, below the cerebral cortex and above the midbrain, that is particularly involved with emotions.

Taboo Behavior, thoughts, or feelings that are believed to be forbidden and punishable by social sanctions or metaphysical forces.

Venereal disease Sexually transmissible diseases such as gonorrhea, syphilis, and herpes genitalis.

Vulva External female genitalia.

As there are as
many minds as
there are heads, so
there are as many
kinds of love as
there are hearts.

—Leo Tolstoy, *Anna
Karenina*

4 · Love and Attraction

There is no question that from childhood on people are more attracted to some individuals than to others. Social psychologists have been intrigued by the questions of just what causes attraction—or rejection—and why some relationships based on attraction persist, whereas others fade. Exchange theorists agree that people are attracted to those from whom they feel they gain something and reject those who seem to cost them more. Gains and costs are not always easy factors to measure objectively, however, since each person may have his or her own unique needs and standards. Research shows that most people feel rewarded by those who are similar to them, who like them, who meet their needs, who make them comfortable, and who match their self-judgments.

Human beings are born with a potential to be loved and to love. Throughout one's lifetime, love is a much sought-after source of personal happiness. In the United States it is the basis for those intimate relationships that determine the nature of marriage and the family. In the past, love has been considered a mystery with no place in the world of scientific inquiry. Most informal analyses of love have been far from objective and have asked such questions as "How *much* do you love me?" or "How *long* will you love me?" In the 1970s, however, social scientists began to inquire about the processes and definitions of love: how it begins, how it grows, how it functions, and how and why it ends. Such researchers believe that any emotion that can bring so much joy and so much sorrow to so many people needs to be better understood.

Love

Do you remember the first time you gave any serious thought to the meaning of love? As a youngster you may have had a "boyfriend" or "girlfriend." You may have carved entwined hearts on a tree or scrawled them on a notebook. For many of you, the words "I love you" flowed easily during high school dating experiences, but the sentiment was unspoken or virtually unknown to others.

The authors can remember talking about love with our peers and wondering how we would know when it happened. At times we felt certain that what we were feeling was love—only to decide, in light of the broken romance, that it was just "infatuation." Occasional discussion with adults elicited a series of homilies about not letting the heart rule the head. A married cousin, perhaps speaking from experience, advised, "Never date anyone you wouldn't consider marrying." The point was clear: one might fall in love with someone inappropriate to marry. Parental words of wisdom ranged from, "It's as easy to fall in love with a rich person as a poor one" to "Don't worry about it. When love hits, you'll know it." None of this advice seemed very helpful.

Popular songs, films, and novels were just as confusing. Literature classes exposed us to the peculiarities of love as experienced, for example, by Dante and Beatrice—the love that inspired Dante's *Divine Comedy*. As a child, Dante saw Beatrice once and never recovered from the passion he felt. He married someone else and had seven children, but in his poems he mentions only Beatrice. In school, too, we read Shakespeare's love tragedies. Who will ever forget Romeo and Juliet, those star-crossed Shakespearean lovers?

Further back in history, in the fifth century B.C., Plato explained why people fall in love. In his *Symposium*, Plato proposed that there were once three categories of humans—men, women, and hermaphrodites. In a rage, the god Zeus, who was armed with thunder and lightning, cut all mortals in half. To become whole beings again, they had to find their other halves. Today, we sometimes hear someone say, "Without the one I love, I am only half a person."

Plato believed that love comes on us as we meet our other halves. A man needs a woman; a woman needs a man; hermaphrodites likewise seek those who match them in such a way that they become whole.

Homosexual love was considered as natural in Plato's time as was love between men and women. In fact, Plato seemed to favor homosexual attachments, although his definition of love has more to do with the essence of beauty and goodness within each person than with sex. This emphasis on mind and heart led to the concept of **platonic love,** a term that has been used through the ages to denote love that does not necessarily involve sex.

Sometime between the tenth and twelfth centuries in Europe, there was a merging of platonic love and sexual love in the concept of *romantic love.* In his

excellent treatment of the history of love, family sociologist Ira Reiss speculates about the reasons for the rise in romantic love at this particular time in history:

> *Surely it was in part the rediscovery of the Greek and Roman writings; in part, a reaction to the brutality of the age; in part a reaction to the scarcity of noblewomen in castles with many bachelor knights; and in part, perhaps an anti-church reaction. But whatever the causes were, the romantic love development of those centuries led to a tender, sexual relationship between men and women. . . . This is a very important historical event if we are to understand present-day love and sexual customs.*[1]

Today, the results of virtually every research study and poll tell us that nine out of every ten Americans consider love the most essential foundation of a happy relationship.[2] Indeed, when love is *not* the stated reason that two people decide to form an intimate relationship, the usual reaction is disapproval. For instance, marrying for security or because one is lonely is not considered healthy by most Americans. Love, then, is an emotion on the basis of which one is expected to make a major life decision. As the authors of *Styles of Loving* have written:

> *If we do not have it, we want it. If we have it, we want more of it, or a different version of it, or a different partner with whom to share it. If our love is*

unrequited, we are miserable. If we have it and then lose it, we seek to recapture it. Even those who admit to never having experienced love at all still agree that it does indeed, exist. And they, too, hope to find it.[3]

By the end of adolescence most of us have experienced the emotion of love. Before the average man or woman marries, he or she may have been in and out of love several times. Males usually claim to have been in love more times than females do. One study of this phenomenon suggests that females tend to see only the current love as "real love" and to regard past loves as "infatuations." Males, on the other hand, are more likely to describe all past serious involvements as "being in love."[4]

Family and Peer Effects on Our Love Lives

Family
Influence

The potential for loving and being loved is believed to exist from the moment we are born. The way our needs are met from the very beginning either conveys or fails to convey that love is an emotion flowing from parent to child.

At first an infant is intensely attracted to anyone who fulfills his or her needs. The noted psychiatrist Martha Mahler has proposed that for the first few months after birth, the baby and mother (or other principal caretaker) are linked as one social-psychological unit.[5] The infant's world revolves around interaction with this person, and the baby perceives the caretaker's world as centering on his or her limited orb as well. This perception is motivated by the child's need for survival; it is also the earliest form of love.

A baby's evident contentment when its needs have been met is pleasing to its parents. In that sense the infant is a source of love for the parents as well as a receiver of parental love. This interaction sets the stage for one definition of love: the desire to be close to another who will meet our needs. Mahler suggests that true emotional attachment develops by the age of five to six months. When a baby of that age is near his or her parents, he or she reaches out, touches, smiles, makes contented sounds. These gestures and body rhythms are the early language of love.

As soon as a baby can crawl and move away from its parents—as well as toward them—a certain amount of separation comes under the child's control. Until then, the parents have been the ones to leave and return. Separation may distress the infant until he or she begins to make some of the choices about how much togetherness there will be.

Even as adults, some of us feel fearful of being abandoned. One theory holds that for such people the gap was never bridged between the early dependence necessary for survival in childhood and the assurance that a certain amount of separation is both necessary and desirable. Such awareness is generally considered a significant step toward mature love.[6]

If one has never learned to be comfortable while separated from one's care-takers, it becomes impossible to choose a partner from any perspective other than that of a dependent, needy child. We often see whining, clinging children who seem panicky at the thought of any separation from their parents. As marriage counselors, we see similar behavior in many persons who are adults chronologically but who never learned that it is not catastrophic to be alone for a while. As children they somehow failed to make the transition from dependency to a sense of security when separated from their parents. One reason for this failure may have been that the parents were emotionally distant, making it virtually impossible for their child to feel secure. Another possibility is that the parents bound the child too closely, never allowing him or her to develop independence.

Most children do manage to become secure in the belief that love does not vanish when loved ones are out of sight. At first the child needs love substitutes while parents are away: a favorite sitter, a doll, or a pet. As adults we some-times carry love substitutes when we are away from loved ones: a picture, a letter, a ring. These are reminders that love is constant. They help us learn that separation is as important an aspect of love as is the initial bonding.[7] Learning to be apart teaches the valuable lesson that one can be intimate and yet retain a sense of self.

Overprotectiveness—"too much love"—is damaging in much the same way as is too little love. Overprotective parents usually convey the idea that life is filled with hazards with which a child cannot hope to cope alone. Such an attitude often has a lasting effect, producing an adult who does not trust his or

her capacity to be alone. With either too much or too little attention, a child can grow into an adult who finds it difficult to be independent and who frequently exhibits extreme emotional neediness. Such persons often seek a love that will fulfill their infantile yearnings—a partner who will satisfy all needs. The search is rarely fruitful, and the result is constant fear of being alone and helpless.

Another important influence in learning to love—other than how we are loved by our parents—is how they love each other. Children are keen observers and often learn more from watching what others do than from hearing what others say. Some parents are very loving to each other in front of their children. Others make no display of affection at all. There may be ample love in such undemonstrative marriages, but children are left to pick up indirect and often vague clues. Children, after all, cannot observe parents' feelings—only their behaviors. Love is a learned emotion, and it is best learned when a child has early opportunities to see loving behavior modeled directly.

Of course, there are what may be termed *love-poor families.* In such homes children neither see loving behavior between their parents nor experience sufficient love themselves. There are some striking similarities among such families. They tend to act as though loving behavior is unimportant and to emphasize material possessions as substitutes for relationships. Children from such families are far more likely to grow into adults who prize money as the avenue to happiness than are those who grow up in families that share and display love openly.

Children from love-poor families often comment that their parents provided everything they ever wanted materially but that they never got the parents' time, attention, and affection. As a result, these children learn to ask for more and more "things" to substitute for the love that has not been forthcoming. As adults they may even try to avoid situations and relationships in which love might be found. Many do not seem to know how to love.

In sharp contrast to love-poor children are those whose families, though financially poor, were rich in love, or those whose families gave love freely in addition to providing material resources. To be without love would be incomprehensible to such children. Material items could never compare with the love they received. Clearly, then, parents exert a powerful influence on how children learn to love and on what they expect from those they love and those who love them.

Peer
Influence

By the time a child reaches the age of six, peers are beginning to exert an important influence on his or her thoughts and emotions. Harry Stack Sullivan, an early and prominent psychotherapist, believed that the years of middle childhood provide children with experiences with others of the same age and sex that are invaluable to their later development of loving behavior.[8]

Sullivan was a **neo-Freudian** who conceptualized the period of same-sex friendships as one during which sexual feelings were quiet and children had no thoughts of love. Early literature in the field of child psychology emphasized that this is a time during which boys ignore girls and vice versa or they tease (but are repelled by) members of the opposite sex. This may be true in part, but more recent observations have indicated that children from six to twelve do have active thoughts and feelings of "love" for those of the opposite sex.[9]

"Boyfriends" and "girlfriends" are not at all uncommon in elementary school. Passing love notes in school, gossiping about who "likes" whom, and playing kissing games are all commonplace activities. The family sociologist Carlfred Broderick has made extensive studies of childhood romances.[10] Nine out of ten of the children he observed had "sweethearts" whom they claimed to "love." These studies seem to indicate that at least a large percentage of children do not have a sexually quiet period. What a young child means by saying he or she loves someone may be very different from what an adult would mean. But whatever children felt, Broderick says, "they behaved for all the world as if they had crushes on each other."[11]

Perhaps the greatest peer influences on concepts of love are felt during adolescence. As the young person's autonomy within the family grows, the influence of peers outside the home increases. Most young people begin to go out to parties in mixed-sex company—and often as couples—by the beginning of the teenage years. Most have fallen "seriously" in love by the end of adolescence.[12]

The eminent child psychiatrist Erik Erikson believes that the teenage years are crucial for learning how to love and to be intimate with persons outside the family system. "Where a youth does not accomplish such intimate relationships with others—and I would add, with his own inner resources—he may settle for highly stereotyped interpersonal relations and come to retain a deep sense of isolation."[13]

If the adolescent years are not used to learn how to achieve intimacy, a crucial juncture may pass, after which caring for and being close to another person may be increasingly difficult. If Erikson is right, parents who prohibit or unnecessarily delay dating during the teens may be doing a real disservice to their sons and daughters.

A young friend, for example, told us of her parents' rules: she could not date until her senior year in high school, and even then she was limited to a maximum of three dates with each young man. Her parents' intention was to keep any intimacy from developing. By her third date with one boyfriend, however, she was "in love," so the couple continued their forbidden love relationship secretly. In this case, parental interference failed, and the young woman and man eventually married. Sometimes, in fact, parental opposition actually intensifies the urge to be together. When peers are also encouraging the couple, the parents may be fighting a losing battle. One study has reported that the more

the parents interfere with their children, the more likely the children are to fall in love. This has been termed the "Romeo and Juliet effect."[14]

Adolescence, especially, is a time when songs, magazines, movies, television, and advertisements all have an impact on ideas about love. At this age the average young person begins to form impressions of what makes him or her feel loved or unloved. Adolescents know that what they feel, or what they think they are supposed to feel, is different from liking or from friendship. They know by observation whether other couples are in love or are just good friends.

Couples who are in love sit close together, lean toward each other, and spend a lot of time looking at each other.[15] In 1884 Sir Francis Galton documented those who were "inclined" toward each other: "When two persons have an inclination to one another, they visibly incline or slope together when sitting side by side, as at the dinner table, and they then throw the stress of their weight on the near legs of their chairs."[16] More recently, the social psychologist Donn Byrne and his associates completed research documenting that two people who are romantically attracted to each other will stand closer to each other than two who are not.[17]

One of the best known of the psychologists doing research on love and interpersonal attraction is Zick Rubin, whose studies reveal that those couples reporting that they are very much in love spend considerably more time observing each other—gazing into each other's eyes—than do couples who rate their interest in each other as lower.[18]

All in all, by the end of adolescence and the beginning of young adulthood, love is recognized as a basic element of meaningful relationships. Each person has developed his or her own unique definition of love. The definition may be incomplete, since future experiences undoubtedly will change anyone's understandings. However, current research suggests that elements of our early definitions of love run as threads throughout our lives.[19]

The persistence of early definitions of love may well account for the romantic affairs of couples in their later years who, having met and fallen in love, are as starry-eyed as they were in their youth. It is probable that they are adding years to their lives as well. Being with someone you love and who also loves you has been correlated with longevity and an absence of heart disease.[20] No matter how we define love, and whether or not our notions of love change with time, there is nearly universal agreement about its importance in our lives.

Summary

■ Love is the basis for marriage in much of the world today, although romantic love as a basis for an enduring relationship is a concept that emerged historically relatively recently.

■ Learning to love and to be loved begins at birth. Parents teach love directly and also serve as models of loving behavior for children. It has been said that we learn to love through the way we remember having been loved.

■ Siblings and peers are influential in helping children form a definition of love. All during childhood, boys and girls are aware of the idea of love, both from interacting with each other and from their interpretations of adults' behaviors. They play house, show affection to each other, and have "crushes" on each other.

■ By adolescence most young people have experienced feelings that they call "love." Teenage dating facilitates this developmental task, which is a necessary part of learning how to be close and, ultimately, how to achieve intimacy.

■ Each person, through unique experiences, develops his or her own definition of love, which is of great importance for intimate relationships, marriage, and family life.

Attraction

George Bernard Shaw once commented that love is an overemphasis on the difference between one person and all others.[21] Once we have discovered that all people are not alike, we begin to have different feelings about different individuals. We feel "better," "happier," or "more powerful" in the presence of some people than in the presence of others. We wish to spend more time with some and less time (or perhaps none at all) with others. We can actually sense changes in our bodies when particular people are near us. If those sensations are unpleasant, they can be called **antipathy**; but if they are pleasant and make us want to be near the other person more often, they can be called *attraction*. Since at some point relationships involve attraction between two people, it is important to understand this phenomenon.

There have been countless studies of the reasons that partners are attracted to each other. Among the most widely quoted is one in which a general framework was developed based on "equity theory," which encompasses four basic propositions:

1. We seek pleasure rather than pain.
2. However, we have to be able to give pleasure in order to receive it. The more we give, the more we receive.
3. We are most comfortable when there is a fair balance between what we give and what we receive. Having less than we deserve makes us resentful.
4. If the giving and the receiving are out of balance, we will work to restore a balance, either actually or in fantasy, or we will end the relationship.[22]

Walster and Walster found that couples whose relationships were more equitable were happier and more content with each other. Happy lovers were similar on a remarkable number of traits, such as physical attractiveness, popularity, emotional and physical well-being, although a "plus" in one area could offset a "minus" in another. For instance, a physically attractive person might not be hampered by lack of money, whereas one with neither good looks nor wealth might have to make up for the lack in other areas or settle for a partner with the same total social value. This theory is a variation of social exchange theory, which says, in effect, that one can predict which persons might fall in love by knowing what they have to offer each other.

A research psychologist who favors exchange theory is Bernard I. Murstein.[23] He, too, believes we are attracted to those who offer the best combination of rewards for the most reasonable cost. If the satisfaction is mutual, the relationship continues. Murstein has proposed a three-stage process by which attraction and love develop. First, there is the *stimulus* stage, in which physical appearance plays a large role. The second stage, termed *value comparison*, occurs when the couple tests their "fit" for each other. The third phase is that of compatible *ideal self* and *ideal other* images. These ideal images refer to expectations of how partners will feel, think, and behave. When all three phases are experienced successfully, romance can blossom.

Exchange theory has offered one of the most popular explanations of the process of falling in love with particular individuals. One criticism of the theory is that not all people are as logical and as able to evaluate themselves and others as exchange theory implies. Some relationships even seem to be based on altruism (unselfish love) that is concerned only with giving, not with receiving at all. The idea of mutually rewarding relationships is well entrenched, however, and there is more than a kernel of truth in it.

Sensing Others

Most people observe others for many of their waking hours. Humans have five senses with which to experience the world: vision, hearing, smell, touch, and taste. As people-watchers they "size up" others by observing physical features and behaviors and, if they are close enough, by listening to what people say and how they say it. They listen not only to language—the accents, pitch, rhythm, and content of things spoken—but also to sighs, wheezes, coughs, and giggles. If they are closer still, they may smell the other person, too, although in American society they learn not to say much about people's odors.

Touching is another way to gain information. Touching may occur in the form of a handshake or may imply intimacy and the existence or wish for some kind of relationship. The temperature and moisture of the skin, the soft or calloused texture of hands, even the locations on the person's body where he or she feels comfortable being touched—all provide information about a person.

Tasting a person is even more intimate and might be difficult even for lovers to discuss at times. Kissing another person gives one an opportunity to get information through taste, but usually this is overshadowed by other sensations and symbolic thoughts about kissing.

Visual (seeing) and auditory (hearing) sensations involve far less intimate contact with another person than do tactile (touching), olfactory (smelling), or gustatory (tasting) sensations. Uninteresting or negative visual or auditory impressions usually discourage people from getting close enough ever to use the other senses for attraction.

Only a person's physical characteristics and actions can actually be observed, of course. Everything else one person believes about another derives from memories of experiences with that person or with someone like him or her, beliefs about "that kind of person," or an identification with the person ("I know how he feels" or "I can understand why she did that").

Usually, one thinks of a person as a complete, self-contained being. However, the meaning we give to our observations depends largely on our own beliefs and feelings about people in general (or about people similar to the one we are observing). To be *attracted* to a person (or repelled), then, is a function of one's own mind as much as of the physical characteristics or behaviors of that person. "Beauty is in the eye of the beholder" is not an idle phrase.[24]

We learn who attracts through our **socialization**, which is the ongoing process of establishing ways of relating to others. A child usually begins the process of socialization within the family to which he or she is born. Of course, one cannot choose one's family members, with their particular ways of relating to one another and to persons outside the family. No child is asked whether he or she would like parents who are rich or poor, black or brown, residents of Chicago or Pocatello. Consequently, until later in life there is no alternative to learning the ways of the family to which one is born. Often these family patterns become deeply ingrained from early childhood and resist new learning later in life.

In a family, a young child learns various behaviors, such as making special kinds of sounds to affect the behaviors of others. Eventually he or she learns a language with which to communicate. The child also learns what others do when he or she smiles or frowns or hits or hides or kisses or cuddles. At the same time the child is also experiencing *feelings* about those with whom such interactions take place. These feelings, although not directly observable themselves, are often inferred by others from the child's behaviors.

Feelings toward others, such as love and hate or anger and comfort, seem to be so "natural" that we rarely analyze the ways in which they were learned as responses to particular people in particular situations. Furthermore, because it is easier to deal with a consistent and orderly world than with one in which definitions change from day to day (or even from minute to minute), people tend to generalize or stereotype their feelings toward particular others or groups of others. Whatever form this takes—"I love blonds," or "I hate women"—an overgeneralized feeling toward an entire category of people often leads to ineffective or inappropriate behaviors. Clearly, *all* members of any category are not going to be identical.

As misleading or ineffective as stereotyped beliefs may be, the behaviors based on them are nonetheless very real. Inaccurate generalizations about racial, religious, or social class categories often are responsible for "blind spots" in perceiving others. These blind spots may be the basis for rejection of some people, but they can also work in the opposite fashion to form the basis for attraction.

An early sociologist, Edwin Sutherland, proposed that the influence another person has on one's feelings and behavior is determined by the frequency, duration, intensity, and priority of social contacts with that particular person.[25] The facts that most of us are with our mothers and fathers over a long period of time, have strong feelings toward them, and place those relationships ahead of others in importance mean that parents are very influential in early socialization.

By the time a child begins to attend school, he or she has been socialized to have definite ideas about certain types of people. Sociologists say that children normally develop degrees of *social distance* toward whole categories of people (strangers, old people, children, boys, girls, teachers, racial or religious categories, nurses, police officers, and so forth) as well as toward particular individuals. Social distance varies from a minimum ("social nearness"), to a maximum ("social farness").[26]

Social nearness is expressed as a feeling of sympathetically understanding others, liking them, being comfortable with them, or loving them. Social farness is felt as being uncomfortable with particular people, disliking them, believing that it is impossible to understand them, or even hating them. Children usually accept their feelings of nearness or farness as valid without giving any thought to how they originated. It is well documented that adults do the same.

Human Hungers

Most studies of attraction have focused on the attributes of attractive persons. However, the idea of attractiveness necessarily involves two or more people; one cannot be attractive without being attractive *to* someone. The need to be attractive to someone has been called a *human hunger.*[27]

Why does a person "hunger" for interaction and relationships with other people? What kinds of stresses can best be reduced through interaction with another person? Obviously, tiny human fetuses need another human body to grow in (even "test tube babies" need someone to provide care for them if they are to exist for long). This is a survival need, just as air, water, and nutrients are for all humans.

Human interaction is a survival need for the first few years of life. Although it is not humane to conduct isolation experiments on children to see what will happen to them, nearly all the evidence from observation of cases of "natural" isolation suggests that infants who lack adequate interaction may develop a condition called **marasmus**, as a result of which they become sickly and may even die. If they survive, they may fail to develop many "human" characteristics.[28] In famous nonhuman experiments, Harlow and his associates have demonstrated that even though young monkeys may not die from lack of interaction with other monkeys, neither will they want to mate (or, if mating is forced on them, they usually relate poorly to their own babies).[29]

Do human adults also need contact with other humans? No one really knows how long an adult human can survive in isolation in a comfortable environment with adequate nutrition and freedom from illness or accident. Admiral Richard E. Byrd, a pioneer explorer of the Antarctic, wrote in his diary that after seventy-five days of isolation he no longer knew whether he was sane or insane.[30] One of the concerns about space travel has to do with the possible effects of long periods of isolation on astronauts. Most adults—even those who enjoy brief periods of time alone—have a limit to how much time they can spend without human contact. Some experiments report that each person has his or her unique threshold beyond which isolation becomes intolerable.[31]

Berne lists five "human hungers" that he has concluded are inherent in all normal people.[32] These help to explain the need for affiliation:

1. *Stimulus hunger:* the need for sensations to which the body can respond. Laboratory studies of sensory deprivation show that being immersed in water at 98.6 degrees Fahrenheit in a dark, soundproof place produces disorientation in human subjects within a very short period of time.

2. *Recognition hunger:* the need to have one's identity affirmed (or at least positively responded to) by another person. Studies of the **serial invalidation** of a child's self-concept indicate that this is thought to be a cause of mental illness.[33]

3. *Contact hunger:* the need to touch or be touched by another person. So far, the few experimental studies of this "need" have been inconclusive because ethical and practical considerations make this a very difficult area to study. We believe, however, that for many persons the need to be touched can be nearly as great as the need for food and is certainly as important as recognition is for others. This need seems to depend on whether one was raised in an environment in which touching was welcome. There appear to be "touchers" and "nontouchers." Touchers seem to have this hunger, whereas nontouchers may fail to comprehend its importance. Sometimes, however, nontouchers who are given permission to touch others in a safe environment such as a therapy group may overcome any antipathy they may feel, at least to the extent of being more comfortable in the presence of people who are touching each other.

4. *Sexual hunger:* the need for sexual contact. The emotional context of sexual intercourse in our society makes it virtually impossible to do laboratory studies to confirm or deny the validity of this concept. Certainly many humans go for long periods of time—even a lifetime—without sexual contact. Symbolic substitutes may be so personal that generalization is impossible or so well concealed (even from the persons who employ them) that they are inaccessible for objective study—or both.

5. *Incident hunger:* the need for "something to happen." *Happenings* may be personally defined: what is a "happening" for one person may be an ordinary experience for another. The exciting event may be cloning the wrong virus or discovering a new planet, having the new boy in school smile at you or seeing an old friend. Little research on incident hunger has been performed, but it is clear that such a hunger exists.

One explanation for the greater attractiveness to a person of some individuals than of others is that people may believe fundamentally that certain persons (or perhaps one certain person) can reduce the stress of all or most of these hungers. In infancy, that person is usually the mother. A mother's reliability in reducing stress leads her child to believe that she is a very strong person who can make everything all right. Her reliable appearance in stressful situations and her manifest concern for reducing her child's stresses are conceptualized by the child as her commitment to him or her.[34] The degree of reliability and commitment a child perceives determines the child's trust in the mother. According to this explanation, attraction is the identification of that special person one can trust to relieve the stresses of one's human hungers. Because people define attractive qualities according to their own childhood experiences, being attracted is thought to be partly subconscious on the part of the attracted one.

There is no doubt that we use certain filters in determining who is attractive. For instance, quite a bit of research has been done on the relationship of beauty to attraction. Psychologists Wilson and Nias comment, "In the course of being introduced, we are frequently so absorbed with the person's looks that we forget to register their names."[35] There seems to be considerable general agreement on who is good-looking in photographs. Two studies have shown good consistency on rankings of the relative beauty of women whose photographs were published in newspapers.[36,37]

The notion that "beauty is in the eye of the beholder" or that personality is more important than **physiognomy** in judgments of good looks seems to hold only after a person has had some experience with the one being judged. Even a brief direct experience with a person may alter an initial attraction based on physical beauty. Wilson and Nias point out that when judges see beauty contestants "walk, talk, sniff, blink and smile," their agreement is less consistent.[38]

The observation that campus beauty queens chosen by student election seem to be objectively less beautiful in small institutions than in large ones probably does not mean that the most beautiful women go to the largest schools. It is likely, instead, that in small schools the meaning of "beauty" is affected by personal interaction.

What people hear can also be a positive source of attraction, even quite apart from the spoken message. Devices have been developed for altering tape-recorded voices in such a way that the speaker's voice qualities are retained but the content of the messages is unintelligible.[39] Studies using such devices have indicated that the voice qualities alone conveyed to a listener whether he or she was liked or disliked, even when the words themselves could not be understood. One such study concluded that a person's tone of voice might be a better indicator of his or her like or dislike for another than a verbal statement.[40]

Pear, who did extensive research in England on listeners' reactions to radio voices, remarked that "social intimacy or distance, friendliness or enmity, interest or boredom . . . are usually expressed by an appropriate speech-melody, . . . by the way in which the voice goes 'up and down.'"[41] Van de Velde, a medical sex researcher, was almost lyrical on the same point:

> . . . *The sexual impulse is far more often powerfully stirred by the intensely personal medium of the human voice; of a special voice.*
> *The tone color of a voice, and the intonation of a single word—and it may be*

a word with no special meaning or association in itself—may excite incredible intensity of desire. . . .[42]

A negative factor related to language behavior was reported by Havelock Ellis:

One of my fellow passengers—another teacher, if I remember rightly—improved the occasion by flirting with a girl he had become acquainted with on the boat and sat with his arm around her for several hours; toward night, having evidently thus acquired all the satisfaction he desired, he generously introduced her, unasked, to me . . . and left us alone. We walked once or twice up and down the deck, and she remarked to me by way of opening the conversation: "Ain't the moon lovely?" Such a feeling of loathing rose up within me that in a few moments after briefly responding I said it was time to go below and wished her good night.[43]

Odors, too, play a positive role in attraction. Setting aside for the moment the current discussion of whether or not humans have **pheromones** (attractive odors given off by animals during periods of sexual receptivity), there do appear to be attractive—and repulsive—scents to breath, hair, and perspiration, although Van de Velde labeled these *idiosyncratic*—that is, differing widely in different individuals. "Cases in which the odor of perspiration is attractive from the first are relatively rare, but they exist."[44] He believed that the abilities to perceive individual differences of this kind "are less numerous in the Western-Atlantic civilizations than among Orientals and in the tropics."[45]

Desmond Morris commented:

Every human body is constantly sending out signals to its social companions. Some of these signals invite intimate social contact and others repel it. Unless we are accidentally thrown against someone's body, we never touch one another until we have first carefully read the signs. . . . We can often sum up a social situation in a split second. . . . This does not imply carelessness; it simply means that the computers inside our skulls are brilliant at making rapid, almost instantaneous calculations concerning the appearance and mood of all the many individuals we encounter during our waking hours. The hundreds of separate signals coming from the details of their shape, size, colour, sound, smell, posture, movement and expression, crowd at lightning speed into our specialized sense organs, the social computer whirrs into action, and out comes the answer, to touch or not to touch.[46]

Inferences from Behaviors

Since another person's feelings and thoughts cannot be observed in the same fashion as can actual behavior, they are usually inferred from observed behaviors or physical conditions. When a person says, "I like you," or "I love you," the one he or she is addressing must decide whether to doubt or to trust the accuracy of that statement. The decision may be based on previous experience with the speaker, on observations of his or her behaviors, or on a general tendency of the listener to believe or to doubt what people (or certain kinds of people) say. There is no way for the listener to observe the speaker's *liking.* Only behavior associated with liking can be observed.

Recently, social psychologists have been interested in how attraction to others is affected by the observer's interpretations of others' behaviors and by expectations of how others will behave. Thibaut and Kelley have developed a theory of attraction based on one person's **attribution** to another of behaviors and traits. Attribution is defined as an assumption that a person's behavior is attributable either to his or her will or to certain external conditions. The attribution made determines appropriate response behavior.[47] If Harry attributes Hildegarde's attraction to him as a result of her rational will, he may respond differently to her from the way he would respond if he attributed it to Hildegarde's mother's manipulation of her.

It is suggested that some history of experience with a person may improve the accuracy of one's expectations, although attribution does not actually require such experience. One may experience liking—or even love—"at first sight." It is not unusual for people to "judge the character" of others on the basis of a single observation. Once this has been done, even though the judgment may be inaccurate, a system of interaction develops between the two people based on the assumptions of each about the other. If their mutual responses lead them to be comfortable with their self-concepts and their predictions, the system will function for them and they probably will maintain their relationship. If not, they will experience disillusionment. This helps to account for the couples who decide after one meeting that they are in love, marry, and actually do live "happily ever after." It also accounts in part for the high divorce rate among such couples.

Inferences about the other's attributes also include predictions about how the other person feels or what he or she believes. Again, this may or may not be based on a history of actual experiences and observations. Berscheid and Walster believe that attraction occurs when others are believed to: (1) like us; (2) have the same views that we do on social, economic, and political matters; and (3) furnish emotional support to us if we are lonely, fearful, or under stress. In fact, what an individual believes to be true is usually much more powerful for determining his or her behavior than any objective measure of the situation or person is likely to be.[48]

We know that there is not only some general agreement about what is attractive—whether it is physical or behavioral—but also individual tastes that may be shared by few, if any, others. These unique tastes may be about specific characteristics no matter who exhibits them. For instance, one may believe that slender people have better self-concepts or that blonds have more fun. On the other hand, an idiosyncratic notion of what is attractive is specific to one person. A friend of ours who dislikes beards fell in love with a man who has a glorious one. When questioned, she said that on him it is attractive but that she still generally prefers clean-shaven men.

Most of the actions and traits that attract us to another person are attributed to choices that the other person makes more or less voluntarily. However, one fascinating research finding is that if a photograph of a young woman is retouched so that the pupils of her eyes appear to be larger, she will be rated by most men as more attractive than in the unretouched photograph.[49] Although humans have little or no control over the dilation of their pupils, the pupils have been shown to respond to excitement in general by enlarging. Thus larger pupils seem to suggest interest or excitement (presumably about the observer). The thought of this is attractive, even though the person's pupils may have enlarged because of stress or tension.[50] Dilated pupils and slightly moist eyes have been symbols of love for a long time. In the first century B.C., the Roman poet Catullus described his beloved as "cow-eyed," an expression that loses something in the translation to twentieth-century English.

The system of mutual attraction seems to be circular; that is, knowing that a person is attracted to us usually makes that person seem more attractive to us than we had previously noted. One's behavior usually reflects that fact, and the other person responds accordingly, thus generating another round of attraction. Research has shown that a person who appears to grow increasingly attracted to another becomes even more attractive to that person than does one who was highly attracted right from the start. The concept of *gain* in attractiveness evidently works positively, causing us to find a person increasingly attracted to us more attractive to us also.[51]

It is possible that, because of this "gain phenomenon," strangers and new acquaintances may always be more attractive to some people than are old friends and lovers. People for whom this is true seem to change partners frequently and to be seeking someone new and—they believe—more rewarding. For most persons, this is not the case, however. Aronson explains the continued attraction necessary in enduring relationships by the fact that the long-term relationships that generate the greatest attraction between two partners are those that have ups and downs: the occasional bad times make the good times look more attractive. Such a system minimizes the threat of a new person stepping in to lure a partner away. Couples we know who have been through many "ups" and "downs" together have reported that they find quite enough novelty with each other to keep life interesting and to ensure that their relationship remains alive.

Self-Concepts and Attraction

A number of studies report an association between one's degree of self-esteem and the tendency to find others more or less attractive. In a study of the psychological factors involved in attraction, it was reported that persons with low self-esteem are less likely than their counterparts with high self-esteem to

demand that their partners meet their ideals for what is attractive.[52] In other words, it seems that one's self-esteem influences who seems to be a realistic choice. For someone with low self-esteem, a highly attractive person may seem out of reach.

Social psychologists report that some people choose not to associate with others who upset their self-concepts.[53] A man who believes he is good-looking, for example, will be less likely to be attracted to (or to interact with) a woman who seems to act as though he is not good-looking, than to a woman who seems to confirm his self-concept. A woman who is confident in her ability to succeed in her chosen career will be unlikely to be attracted to people who imply that she will not succeed or to those who do not view her success in a career as a valuable trait.

The reasons that certain individuals are attracted to each other continue to prompt more questions than answers. However, social psychologists have begun to put the pieces of the puzzle together. The search is an important one for students of marriage and the family because each couple that eventually marries begins someplace on the continuum of mutual attraction. For some, attraction is instantaneous, whereas for others it may develop slowly over months or even years. Not all attraction leads to permanent relationships, of course, so we must search further to learn why some find love and eventually choose each other for mates.

Summary

■   Attraction can be one-sided, of course, but in that case it is not likely to develop into an enduring relationship. Relationships come from mutual attraction that reinforces each partner in a variety of ways. Mutual attraction is believed to result from beliefs each person has that the other satisfies certain human hungers.

■   Exchange theory and equity theory are also popular explanations for attraction. A relationship that both partners consider a fair exchange is more likely to continue than one in which either partner feels he or she is getting or giving very much more than the other.

■   Attribution theory has proposed that attraction is determined by one's inferences about another's behavior. If those inferences create a positive picture, attraction is more likely.

■   Self-concept has been the subject of considerable investigation to determine how attraction to others is affected by one's self-judgment. It appears that the self-concept influences each person's choices of friends and lovers.

Defining Love

Everyone agrees that love is a feeling about another person. As noted earlier, however, some people resist trying to understand what the feeling means to those who have it; others are confused about its meaning; and still others have concluded that the meaning is so personal that people cannot communicate about it.

In his presidential address to the American Psychological Association in 1958, Harry Harlow, whose pioneering work with primates is well known, defended his studies of loving behavior:

> *Love is a wondrous state, deep, tender, and reassuring. Because of its intimate and personal nature it is regarded by some as an improper topic for experimental research. But, whatever our personal feelings may be, our assigned mission as psychologists is to analyze all facets of human and animal behavior into their component variables. So far as love or affection is concerned, psychologists have failed their mission. The little we know about love does not transcend simple observation and the little we write about it has been written better by poets and novelists.*[54]

The sociologist William Kephart was still lamenting the absence of research on love nearly ten years later when he wrote in 1967, "It is strange that in a society in which romantic love presumably serves as a basis for marriage, love itself has been largely rejected as a topic for serious study."[55]

From our counseling experiences we learned that there was no scientific knowledge about the effect on a partner's self-concept or self-esteem when what he or she intended as loving behavior was challenged as being unloving. But we did observe conflict, distress, hurt, and disappointment over feelings of love or lack of it. We needed to know how people decided that they were in love or no longer in love, what kinds of behavior they expected from those who said they loved them, and how love manifested itself in their own behaviors.

At the same time that Kephart's article was published, love was being studied in at least a dozen locations in the United States, Canada, and England. Such research tended either to involve attempts to separate love from other similar emotions (such as liking, physical attraction, or infatuation), or to be aimed at identifying the common definition of love used by couples who said they were in love. Almost all the research was based on the assumption that there was one *true* definition of love that people who were *really* in love shared, and that whatever else they might experience was something other than love.

Rubin's report that lovers gaze into each other's eyes more than nonlovers do was a step toward cataloging the attributes of love. Rubin is best known, however, for his research studies that distinguished loving from liking. His efforts were not free of frustration. He remarked that "setting out to devise measures of love is like setting out to prepare a gourmet dish with a thousand different recipes but no pots and pans." [56] Despite the obstacles, he devised scales to measure two attitudes: the "Romantic Love Scale" and the "Liking Scale." He presented these scales to students at the University of Michigan in 1968 and 1969. The relatively simple tests proved to distinguish the two concepts quite clearly. His subjects evidently knew the difference between liking and loving.

Rubin stated that of all that he learned about liking and loving, perhaps the most important fact was that each has as much to do with what people *think* as with how they feel. In other words, sentiments consist of both feelings and thoughts (**affect** and **cognition**), so that the process of falling in love is to some extent a cognitive one. [57]

The sociologist Ira Reiss began his studies on love earlier than most of the researchers discussed here. He labeled his overall conception of how love develops "the wheel theory." [58] He proposed that love involves four major processes: (1) *rapport*—the extent to which two people feel at ease with each other; (2) *self-revelation*; (3) *mutual dependence*; and (4) *need fulfillment*. These are interdependent, and the growth or reduction of any one of them will affect all of the others. Reiss places them in a circle or wheel (Figure 4.1) indicating that the wheel will move forward or backward depending on the loading of each of the four quadrants. Thus love will increase or decrease with the flow from one process to the next.

Another scholar who set out to do research on love during this period was University of Bridgeport psychologist Dorothy Tennov. [59] She was particularly interested in romantic love—especially the sort that causes a considerable

FIGURE 4.1

Wheel Theory of
Reiss

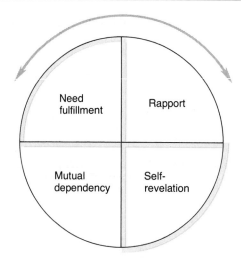

Source: From *Family Systems in America*, third ed.,
by Ira L. Reiss. Copyright © 1980 by Holt, Rinehart and Winston; 1976 by The Dryden Press, a
division of Holt, Rinehart and Winston; and 1971
by Holt, Rinehart and Winston, Inc. Reprinted by
permission of Holt, Rinehart and Winston.

amount of distress to otherwise normal people. She found that more than half
her subjects had been depressed at one time or another over a love affair and
that many had even considered suicide. (At the same time, she noted that
significant numbers of her respondents had never experienced the trauma connected with love at all.) She coined the term **limerence** to describe the extreme
highs and deep lows that accompany love for so many and that begin, as the
French say, with a *coup de foudre* ("thunderbolt"). "Limerence" is an emotion of
enormous intensity and is characterized by the following basic components:

- intrusive thinking about the lover

- acute longing for him or her to reciprocate

- mood swings attached to the lover's action—"walking on air" when
  things are good, "heartache" when there are troubles

- blindness to the possibility that anyone but the lover even exists as someone to love

- unsettling shyness or clumsiness around the lover because of fear of rejection

- preoccupation with and sensitivity to any act or thought (real or imagined) of the lover's, to the point of letting other interests slide

- inability to see any flaws in the lover and overemphasis on his or her strengths

Trouble seems to abound for "limerents," who tend to personalize all their partners' actions as "stop" or "go" signals. Thus a limerent person's actions are really reactions. If he or she does not come to realize that many people never experience such intense feelings and that a partner's less extreme actions may reflect a different but still loving relationship, love can be a miserable experience.

While all of these studies were appearing in the United States—including our own research, which is described in detail in Appendix B—questions about love were also being addressed in England and in Canada. At the International Conference on Love and Attraction in Wales in 1977, a group of people interested in love research met. Wilson and Nias, along with Murstein, emphasized physical attractiveness as an important preliminary to falling in love.[60] Although they acknowledged that beauty is in the eye of the beholder, they pointed out that there is considerable general agreement about who is or is not physically attractive.

Wilson and Nias's model for falling in love predicted the gradual unfolding of mutually held, similar attitudes that eventually serve to reinforce and sustain the initial attraction. An important mutual attitude, Wilson and Nias emphasized, is sexual attraction—the "chemistry of love." Although many studies take care to separate love from physical attraction, these psychologists believe that both sex and love are enmeshed in a total "eligibility score" that people assign to their potential partners.

Earlier, in Canada, sociologist John Alan Lee produced a comprehensive typology of love. He devised a scale for identifying a subject's "style of loving" based on the extent to which the person associated different meanings of love with particular feelings, thoughts, and actions. He distinguished eight different meanings commonly used by lovers. Using the analogy of a color wheel, he suggested that just as all colors are derived from the three primary colors—red, blue, and yellow—so there are several types of love derived from three primary ones:

1. *Eros:* romantic, sexual, sensual love, characterized by love at first sight
2. *Ludus:* a playful, challenging, nonpossessive kind of love
3. *Storge:* comfortable, affectionate, slow-to-develop but intimate kind of love[61]

Besides these three primary types, Lee proposed three secondary ones that are often mixed in varying degrees with either eros, ludus, or storge. The three are: *mania* (reminiscent of Tennov's "limerence" since it is possessive, jealous, and stressful); *agape* (an unselfish, altruistic love); and *pragma* (logical and sensible). In addition, Lee added two popular combinations—*storgic ludus* and *ludic eros*—for a total of eight different types of love.

In the meantime, our own work had been influenced by our growing recognition that, along with most other social scientists, we had uncritically accepted the popular notion that there was one "true" universal concept of love that had not been clearly defined. We began by examining the kinds of conflict that occurred when a couple used a common word—love—to talk about very different conclusions and behaviors.

We were especially interested in the definitions—the cognitive aspects—of love. Of course, we were also aware of a physiological component, ranging from changes in heart rate, skin temperature, breathing rate, blood pressure, and pupil dilation, to scores of reported sensations such as "butterflies in the stomach" and "stars in the eyes." However, we know from the work of psychologist Stanley Schachter and his colleagues that physiological reactions during one emotion can look deceptively like those of any other.[62] That is, people who display similar body symptoms might at that moment be experiencing fear, anger, excitement, or even love. Surprisingly, two people—both of them experiencing an emotion that they call love—might manifest very different physical symptoms.

In a pilot study we instructed our subjects to imagine an experience that made them angry (or to recall a real one). We measured their bodily reactions by using **biofeedback** equipment, which gave us information on their heartbeat rates, skin temperatures, blood pressures, and heightened skin resistances compared with corresponding measures in a normal state. After a rest interval we repeated the measurements, asking the subjects to imagine or recall both a fearsome time and an experience of love. The results confirmed those of Schachter, as well as indicating that a subject's definition of love made no reliable difference in his or her biofeedback responses. Persons with different definitions of love had similar biofeedback reactions; those with nearly identical definitions often showed very different bodily symptoms.[63] In other words, our bodies tell us we are experiencing some kind of emotion, but we use our minds to label it.

In Appendix B, we have described the six definitions of love that emerged from our research. Also included in Appendix B is the self-test that we used and that the reader can employ to determine his or her own definition.

Summary

■ Despite the acknowledged importance of love, it has defied serious study by social scientists until very recently. A few studies began in the 1960s, but only in the 1970s did love research come into its own.

■ Definitions of love range from those that call it a learned response to those that describe love as a dependent, addictive clinging to another person who holds promise of meeting one's needs.

■ In an attempt to bring more objectivity to the study of such a complex emotion, a number of love scales were developed. Most emphasized an intensity of feeling that must be present for love to be felt. Certain unique attributes were ascribed to the loved one as well. It became clear that loving and liking are two distinct phenomena.

■ In an effort to get away from attempts to stick to only one possible definition of love (which seemed artificial to many of those objectively exploring love), it has been proposed that there are several basic definitions used in various combinations to account for differences in both behavior and reported feelings of those in love.

Glossary

Affect A feeling or emotion.

Antipathy A dislike of or aversion to an object, person, or idea.

Attribution The assignment of motivations, emotions, and attitudes to others to explain their behaviors.

Biofeedback A process by which internal biological states are reported by instruments. An example is the use of an EEG (electroencephalograph) to measure brain waves.

Cognition Feelings and knowledges.

Limerence A term coined to describe the intense emotional highs and lows that sometimes accompany the state of being in love.

Marasmus A progressive emaciation found in infants, associated with the lack of consistent positive responses from parent or parent-surrogate figures.

Neo-Freudian A modernized version of Freudian theory that uses an approach combining the concept of the unconscious, one's childhood experiences, and one's conscious functioning in the present.

Pheromones Chemical substances exuded by animals that give off odors that elicit sexual responses from others of the same species.

Physiognomy The face of a person or object, especially when it is used to make judgments of characteristics not visible.

Platonic love A love relationship in which no overt sexual behavior and no erotic components are present.

Serial invalidation A condition that exists when one or both parents continually judge a child's behavior as wrong or inappropriate or when the child interprets their behavior as such a judgment.

I never wanted to
get married. The
last thing I wanted
was infinite
security, and to be
the place an arrow
shoots off from. I
wanted change and
excitement and to
shoot off in all
directions myself,
like the colored
arrows from a
Fourth of July
rocket.

—Sylvia Plath,
The Bell Jar

5 · Singlehood and Cohabitation

The single population in the United States has been growing gradually since 1970. Roughly one-third of all persons over the age of eighteen are currently unmarried, and 45 percent of those between eighteen and thirty-nine are currently single. Some have not married yet, but will; a few will never marry; some have been married and divorced. There is probably no such thing as a "singles life-style" because the population of unmarried persons at any given time is so diverse. Attitudes and behaviors with respect to unmarried sex have changed greatly over the past few decades, with about two-thirds of Americans accepting unmarried sex for males and nearly half believing that it is also permissible for females. If couples have an affectional bond, and especially if they are planning to marry, most persons now agree that it is likely that the couple will engage in coitus. With the liberalization of sexual attitudes and the growing phenomenon of singlehood, more and more couples are choosing to cohabit. Most of those who live together do so for very short periods of time, subsequently either separating or marrying each other. Thus for many couples, cohabitation seems to be part of the courtship system, a way of postponing marriage for the time being. Eventually, however, virtually all persons marry at least once; cohabitation shows no signs of taking the place of marriage.

The Choice to Be Single

Since 1970 an interesting change in single life has developed in the United States. There has been a gradual increase in the proportion of individuals who are single. In the past, when a man or woman remained unmarried past an age that parents and friends deemed appropriate, the judgment was sometimes made that no one wanted to marry him or her. Even today few people intend never to marry, although some predict that 8 to 9 percent of those currently in their early twenties will stay single. Of those who are now over forty years of age, only 4 to 5 percent have never married.[1]

In 1976, approximately 18 percent of those over eighteen years of age had not yet married—although many of them probably will marry. About one-third of those who had formerly been married were widowed or divorced in 1976.[2] Fewer than 5 percent never marry during a lifetime, but an increasingly large percentage of adults spend a significant amount of time single before, between, or after marriages. It should be noted that a disproportionately large number of these persons are black women, and that a disproportionately large number of those are the heads of single-parent families. Being single does not necessarily mean being childless.*

More research is needed on singlehood to understand all the variables determining how and why persons remain or voluntarily become single, but several studies indicate that many variables combine to explain it.[3,4] Other studies attempt to define the different types of single life-styles, exploring the ways that single people manage their lives.[5,6]

Why Singlehood Has Increased

One of the interesting reasons offered by some for persons remaining or becoming single is that sex roles have changed—in particular, that middle-class women's life options have expanded, along with their increased opportunities for education and employment. One study reported that during the 1960s not only did the women's movement change many women's views of marriage, but also of the 13.8 million new jobs that were created, two-thirds were classified by employers as "women's jobs."[7] Not coincidentally, between 1960 and 1980 there was a 43 percent increase in the number of single-person households.[8] A large number of these represented independent women working and living alone before marriage, between marriages, or instead of marrying.

---

* *Current Population Reports* (series P-20, no. 352, July 1980, p. 3) notes that proportionately over three times as many black families as white were one-parent families and that over fifteen times as many one-parent black families were headed by women as by men. The same report comments that for middle-aged white couples, "virtually the same description would have applied [as] in 1970 [p. 2]." Norms for the white population have changed very little.

Accompanying greater economic opportunities for women have come ideas of liberation from stereotyped roles for both men and women—roles that may have hampered freedom and personal goals. In one survey, single men and women, asked why they chose to remain single, frequently mentioned career opportunities, freedom for change and mobility, and psychological and social autonomy.[9]

The options that greater economic independence has brought to women, along with the desires of both men and women for a measure of autonomy, have led to more critical examination of marriage. Not only may singlehood be growing more attractive, but also, for some persons, being married may have become less attractive. Many young persons report disillusionment about their parents' marriages and wonder whether it is worth giving up their freedom for the sake of marriage. In one study, half of the single men interviewed reported that their parents had been unhappy in their marriages.[10] Of those who have ever been married, many are so disenchanted with the idea of marriage that they vow never to marry again. A considerable number of these nevertheless eventually do marry or remarry, but a few manage to do without marriage permanently.

What population experts have called the "marriage squeeze" has also contributed to the growing numbers of singles. The post–World War II "baby boom," which lasted from 1946 to 1957, followed a wartime period during which many fewer children were born. Thus, when those born in 1946 reached marrying age, a problem developed. Since women in the United States usually marry men two to three years older than they are, those born in the first two to three years of the baby boom found that the number of potential mates was much smaller than the number looking. Many women born in these early postwar years had to choose between postponing marriage and remaining single indefinitely. Of course, some of them voluntarily opted for singlehood. It is not accidental that those born from 1946 to 1949 reached the average age of marriage during the late 1960s and early 1970s, as the women's movement began to peak and employment opportunities for women increased. Another phenomenon of the 1960s was the development of the birth control pill, which helped to remove the fear of pregnancy for those single women who chose to have active sex lives. All these factors combined helped account for the rising number of single women.

Demographers believed that as the years passed the surplus of women of marriageable age would level off and that the rising number of single persons was therefore a temporary phenomenon. However, the leveling off took long enough that it merged with still another "marriage squeeze." This time, there was a shortage of available women, and there were too many men who were looking for wives. When males born during the last three years of the baby boom (1954–1957) reached marrying age in the late 1970s, they found that there were fewer females from whom to choose because the fertility rate had

begun to drop in 1958 and there were, therefore, fewer females two to three years younger than they were.[11]

As the number of single young persons has grown, so has the ease with which they are accepted in society. This is true not only because of the increasing number of other singles with whom to associate but also because being single has become more socially approved. Young singles have become a social force to be reckoned with. Advertisers have appealed to the young singles market as they became aware that they spend more than married persons on entertainment, travel, automobiles, clothes, and accessories. It was reported in 1974 that young single women spend over one-third more money on clothes than young married women do and that almost half the Porsches sold were bought by young singles.[12] The existence of 14 million young singles has given rise to apartments for singles, singles' bars and clubs, singles' vacations, and singles' magazines. The old notion of the lonely, socially isolated "spinster" or "bachelor" has given way in the media to a picture of the carefree life of the "swinging singles." Although in fact only a small percentage of singles live this "good life," the image has been well enough publicized to suggest an attractive alternative to marriage for millions of persons.

TABLE 5.1
Pushes from Marriage and Pulls toward Being Single

Pushes from Marriage	Pulls toward Singlehood
Restrictions within relationships: Suffocating one-to-one relationships	Career opportunities
	Variety of experiences and plurality of roles
Feeling trapped	Self-sufficiency
Obstacles to self-development	Psychological and social autonomy
Boredom, unhappiness, anger	Exciting life-style
Role playing and conformity to expectations	Mobility and freedom to change
Poor communication with mate	Sustaining friendships
Sexual frustration	Sexual availability
Lack of friends, isolation, loneliness	
Limited mobility and availability of new experiences	

Those who advocate the single life report advantages in terms of privacy, independence, and excitement. Table 5.1 was developed to contrast the reported negative features of being married (pushes) with the positive features about being single (pulls).[13]

Single Life-Styles

As we have noted, there appears to be a good bit of distortion in the popular view of "swinging" singlehood. Although such a carefree life may be possible for many men and women, this simplistic view does not fit the countless varieties of persons who are unmarried at any given point in their lives. Young singles who are merely postponing marriage, previously married men and women who have custody of one or more children, and older singles who have been divorced or widowed all present very different pictures from one another. Being single in a small town may be nothing like being single in New York City, Chicago, or Dallas. Affluent singles may avail themselves of the "good life" but those barely getting by financially lead a very different existence.

Perhaps among the most important factors in understanding the various life-styles of singles are whether or not singlehood is voluntary or nonvoluntary and at what age a person is single. For example, voluntarily choosing to be single for several years before marrying has become a respected and applauded attitude among family-life experts, many parents, and young people them-selves.[14] However, after a certain age—usually around thirty—pressure to marry may come from parents, friends, and even subtly from employers. Friends may begin to arrange meetings between "eligible" singles; parents may wonder aloud whether their son or daughter is "seeing anyone"; and employ-ers may have second thoughts about promoting single persons to responsible positions.[15]

In a thoughtful review of the life-styles of those who had never married, the following typology of singlehood was devised:

Temporary Voluntary Singlehood

1. young persons who have never been married and who are postponing marriage indefinitely
2. recently divorced or widowed persons who need time to be single but want a mate again eventually
3. older never-marrieds who have decided that if the right person comes along, they would marry, but who are not actively looking
4. cohabitors who will eventually marry either each other or someone else

Temporary Involuntary Singlehood

1. young persons who have never been married but who are actively seek-ing a mate
2. divorced or widowed persons or single parents who are lonely and want to remarry soon

Permanent Voluntary Singlehood

1. cohabitors who never intend to have a ceremonial marriage
2. formerly married persons who believe that once was enough
3. those who have taken religious vows not to marry
4. never-married persons of all ages who have no intention ever to marry

Permanent Involuntary Singlehood

1. older widowed, divorced, or never-married persons—most frequently women—who wanted to marry or remarry but have had no opportunities and have become reconciled to their single state
2. never-married persons who are handicapped in some way that has made them unavailable or undesirable as marriage partners (for example, those who are mentally retarded or grossly physically impaired)[16]

Another important difference has been noted between the single life-styles of men and women. Virtually every study has indicated that single women get along better without men than single men get along without women.[17] Single women of all ages are less lonely, have fewer mental health and adjust-ment problems, and are happier.[18,19] A significantly larger percentage of single women (61.2 percent) than married women (50.2 percent) are in the labor force, but a significantly smaller percentage of single men (70.7 percent) are in the labor force than married men (81.0 percent).[20] Single women also report a higher degree of satisfaction with their work than do single men. One explanation for the fact that single women seem to adjust better than single men do is that women seem more adept than men at establishing and maintaining close friendships with members of both sexes. Many men have problems of loneliness and feelings of alienation that seem to be less profoundly experienced by women.[21]

Racial differences in the proportions of men and women who live alone are remarkable. A 1981 census report comments:

> *Among people 45 to 64 years old in 1979, the majority of men (83 percent) and women (72 percent) lived with their spouses. . . . In addition, far greater proportions of White men and women lived with their spouses than was true of Black men and women . . . ; Black women were three times as likely as White women to maintain families with no husband present (28 percent versus 9 percent).*
>
> *Blacks 45 to 64 years old, especially men, were less likely to live in a family than Whites in this age group; 23 percent of Black men did not live in a family, while only 9 percent of White men did not live in a family. The percentages for Black and White women were 21 and 14 percent, respectively.[22]*

Figure 5.1 shows that middle-aged white men are almost twice as likely to be married and living with their spouses as middle-aged black women (85.3 percent versus 46 percent), six times less likely to be separated, eleven times less likely to be widowed, and less than half as likely to be divorced. Black men, on the other hand, are more than twice as likely as white women never to have married. The single life is much more typically a black than a white life-style.

Some family-life experts have proposed that single women get along so well precisely because they are free from domestic roles and from having to adjust their lives to the demands of husbands and children. They are, therefore, able to develop their potential for growth.[23] The results of several studies suggest that women may profit from marriage much less than men do.[24]

Another possible explanation is that men who do not marry may be the rejected ones, whereas women may be choosing to stay single. This explanation for differences between unmarried men and women had been proposed by sociologist Jessie Bernard, who coined the term **marriage gradient** to describe the tendency of lower- and middle-class females to marry men higher in economic and social status than they are, whereas middle-class men obviously do just the opposite.[25] Thus women of high status and high achievement have a smaller pool from whom to choose and are therefore more likely to remain single. At the same time, men of low status and low achievement are not chosen. According to Bernard: "As the marriageable men drop out of the single

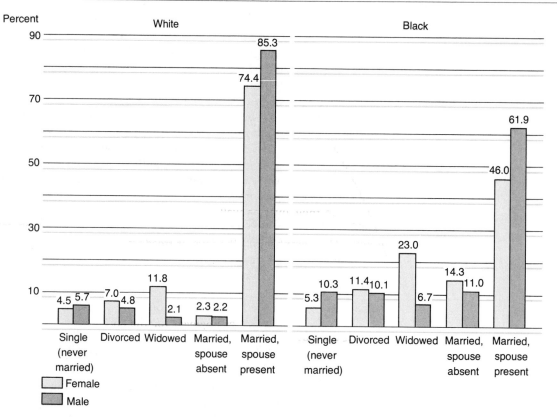

Percent

White

Black

FIGURE 5.1

Marital Status of Persons 45 to 64 Years Old, by Race and Sex: March 1979

Source: U.S. Bureau of the Census, "Social and Economic Characteristics of Americans during Midlife," *Current Population Reports,* series P-23, no. 111 (June 1981), p. 4.

population, those who are left show up worse and worse as compared with their feminine counterparts, so that [by] ages forty-five to fifty-four, the gap between them is a veritable chasm."[26]

Other studies, however, have noted that for younger men and women the differences in adjustment between the sexes is less pronounced, although, as one researcher says, "the truth is that there are more carefree spinsters and anxious bachelors."[27] Nonetheless, single men and women both report good and not-so-good sides to the single life. A recent article on singlehood said:

> *Living alone is an obscure blend of joys and terrors. I have never been able to decide whether I love it or hate it, nor have I ever known whether I actually chose to live alone or simply wound up there by default. . . . For myself, I know that I have a very active, independent life, good friends, am successful in my work and travel a lot, that I would never go to a singles bar, never have a computer date or even go skiing in the hope of meeting someone interesting.*

*The life I lead suits my character. And yet—like most people—sometimes I
wonder.*[28]

In an in-depth study of never-married, college-educated men and women
over the age of thirty, six life-style patterns were discovered:

1. *Professional:* These persons organized their lives around their work and
   identified strongly with their occupational roles. Most of their time and
   energy was spent in career-related activities.
2. *Social:* Individuals in this category had involved social lives and many
   personal relationships. They often enjoyed their work, but their friends
   clearly held first priority. They were "joiners" or pursued hobbies that
   put them in frequent contact with people. Family often played an important role in their lives as well.
3. *Individualistic:* Those with this life-style focused their attention on self-
   growth. They emphasized the joys of freedom and privacy. They liked
   living alone and having to answer to no one for their time. They pursued
   hobbies, took classes for self-improvement, and enjoyed reading and
   other solitary pursuits.
4. *Activist:* This group centered their lives around the community and political causes. They did not get involved for the social contacts nearly as
   much as for the sake of the issues. Their work was important, but most of
   their time and energy was devoted to working for what they considered a
   better world.
5. *Passive:* These were the loners who spent their free time at home alone or
   in solitary pursuits such as shopping or attending movies. They showed
   the least initiative of any of the six groups in shaping their lives cre-
   atively. They also had the most negative outlooks on life.
6. *Supportive:* Persons falling into this pattern filled their lives by giving
   service to others. Few persons reported this life-style, but the women in
   this category reported that they were highly satisfied with their lives.[29]

It is obvious from the research on single life-styles that there is great variety.
Some people live alone, some live with roommates or with their families of
orientation. Some want to marry eventually; others plan never to marry; still
others cohabit in a "semi-married" state. Some are affluent; others barely get
by financially. Some are young, but many are middle-aged or old. Some are
parents; some are grandparents; many are childless. One thing is certain, however: single persons are members of a rapidly growing minority group. They
are as individual as members of any other minority, but they also face problems common to any group of persons who voluntarily or involuntarily occupy
a minority status. Certain discriminatory attitudes and practices are still common, but as the numbers grow, singlehood not only should assume a more
attractive status but also should generate its own social support systems to
combat the social stigma that being single has often carried.

Summary

■   There has been a gradual increase in the number of men and women who are choosing to remain single for long periods of their lives. Most eventually marry or have been married.

■   Sex roles have been changing. In particular, women have more life options than ever before. With greater economic opportunities for women has come a degree of liberation from stereotyped sex roles for both men and women. Not only is being single growing more attractive, but also marriage is increasingly seen as restrictive, especially for those who have been married.

■   Demographers have called attention to the "marriage squeeze" brought about by the two cycles of rising and falling fertility rates in the United States. This has resulted in later marriages for many persons.

■   There is no one "single" life-style; instead, there are probably as many as there are single persons. Two major factors seem most important in determining how singles live, however: age and whether singlehood is voluntary or involuntary.

■   Women seem to fare better in singlehood than do men. Some family-life experts suggest that women profit less from marriage than men do. Another explanation is that men who do not marry may be the rejected ones, whereas women may more often choose to remain unmarried. The concept of the "marriage gradient" has been proposed to explain this phenomenon. Females tend to marry upward and males downward in terms of various measures of status. Consequently, when the most eligible men are taken, women of high status have so few partners to choose from that they often opt to remain single.

Singlehood and Sex

With a growing number of adults being single at certain stages in their lives—and some remaining single for extended periods or for a lifetime—unmarried sex has become an accepted fact for more and more persons. The later men and women marry or the longer they remain single between marriages, the more likely they are to become sexually involved. Bear in mind that those who never marry never have anything other than premarital sex. By society's standards, unmarried sex is very different for a forty-year-old, never-married person than for a seventeen-year-old. As single persons leave the teen years, more sexual experience and a history of more sexual partners is the rule. However, the reality is far from the picture of general promiscuity often drawn by the media or lamented by those who fear that changing sexual values mean a serious decline in the nation's moral standards.[30]

A study reporting on the sexual lives of unmarried young men and women during the 1970s showed that two-thirds of the women between eighteen and twenty-four reported having intercourse, but that the median number of partners was only two in one year. For single men under twenty-five, the median number of partners during the previous year was also two.[31] Sexual activity between marriages is much more widespread than is premarital sex. Research indicated that of divorced persons under the age of fifty-five, all the men interviewed and 90 percent of the women were sexually active, usually having several partners in a year.[32] In another study, 82 percent of the divorced women reportedly had engaged in sex during the first year after their divorces.[33] However, sometime after that first year, most divorced persons seemed to tire of sexual experimentation and to settle into more intimate relationships.[34] Although attitudes toward sex before and between marriages appear to have become much more permissive in recent years, the patterns of unmarried sex still appear to be operating largely "within the framework of our long-held cultural values of intimacy and love."[35]

Standards of Unmarried Sex

Approval—or even acceptance—of new sexual standards is far from unanimous, however. Religion plays an important part in molding more conservative attitudes for countless young people. Small towns, rural communities, and some entire regions may hold far less permissive opinions about sexual behavior for unmarried persons.[36] From a survey of the research on sexual attitudes and sexual behavior, four standards for unmarried sex have been proposed.[37]

1. *Abstinence*: restraint from nonmarital intercourse. In most cases this attitude is based on a religious, moral belief that sex outside marriage is sinful. Many fundamentalist religious organizations support this viewpoint, as do many conservative parents who cannot bring themselves to condone in today's young people what was forbidden in their own youth.[38] Often abstinence is the approved mode of behavior for women but not necessarily for men—an obvious double-standard tradition.

Recently, abstinence has found a new group of supporters who base their beliefs not on any religious or moral notions of right or wrong but rather on the need for sexual freedom. Advocates of this position take exception to the pressure teenagers seem to feel to end their virginity and hold that *celibacy* should be as respected as the freedom to have several partners. Virtually no research exists on those who voluntarily become celibate for long periods of time, although interviews with these persons suggest some information about their motives. Reasons vary considerably, but a common motivation is the need to shift one's energy and creativity to work, to self-assessment, and to an evaluation of relationships generally.[39]

2. *The double standard*: the idea that premarital intercourse is always more acceptable for males than for females. This standard was supported by approximately one-quarter of the college students interviewed.[40] Older men and women seem to favor the double standard more than younger persons do,

although in general all age groups are shifting noticeably away from the belief that males should be allowed more sexual freedom than females.[41] A variation on the double standard that has surfaced in the last two decades is that it is less acceptable for females to have several partners than for males to do so. That is, it is acceptable for women to have nonmarital sex only with a person with whom they are in love or whom they plan to marry, but males are not limited in this fashion.[42]

3. *Permissiveness with affection:* The double standard does not apply here; instead, the "right" or "wrong" of unmarried sex is tied to whether two people love each other (or at least are in a stable and caring relationship). This is not a new standard by any means; couples who are seriously involved with each other have always received less condemnation for unmarried sex—especially if they eventually marry.[43]

4. *Permissiveness with or without affection:* If two people are so inclined, then nothing more is needed to make sex acceptable. In other words, the decision should be mutual but need not (although it may) reflect love or even a stable relationship. Of those who hold this standard, some still may place a greater value on sex with affection. In our society more men than women are thought to hold this standard, but in certain other societies women too may engage in unmarried sex as freely as men do.[44]

Those who specialize in working with divorced, widowed, separated, and never-married men and women believe that sex is often a major source of frustration in a single person's life.[45] For the most part this frustration is the result of sheer unpredictability. As one book for singles says:

> *Overall singles complain that there isn't enough sex when they want it or more rarely, that there is an abundance available when they can't handle it. For most singles, it is either feast or famine. Though there may be long periods at the bare subsistence level, the sex life of singles lacks the predictability associated with marriage. And it is anything but the copulation cornucopia associated with the popular image of the swinging single.*[46]

**Common
Sexual Problems
of Singles**

The double standard still seems to linger among many single people. Women complain that men do not want a serious relationship but instead rush them into one that is sexual. Furthermore, they often note that men abandon the relationship very soon after it has become sexual. Men, on the other hand, claim that women lead them on by indicating that they are interested in them as sexual partners and then refuse to become involved on that level. Some men have difficulty with what they call "aggressive women" who make the first moves.

Psychologist Marie Edwards, who runs groups for single persons, says:

Women's liberation notwithstanding, traditional role playing cannot be reversed overnight. Since sex roles are no longer defined as they were just a few years ago, there is confusion for everyone. With traditional courtship patterns changing—a less extended pursuit, less clearly defined rules, the dropping of coyness and game playing—we often find men and women equally confused and uncertain.[47]

Because of the obvious physical hazards of having a variety of sex partners, most singles prefer to settle for a companion who also limits his or her sexual contact to a carefully chosen few. Venereal disease and pregnancy are two of the major concerns of the unmarried. In addition, singles often mention the problem of where and when to have sex. "Your place or mine?" has become a cliché, but singles often speak of the impact of family, friends, and neighbors who may not approve of an overnight visit. Getting up to go home in the middle of the night is not usually a good solution. If the relationship is not exclusive, couples may worry that another lover will call or drop in. Single parents with custody of their children usually do not like to be away from them overnight very often, and most will not have an overnight guest when their children are at home. Motels and hotels often have connotations that unmarried men and women dislike. Especially for older unmarried persons, parking in a car is unacceptable; for many younger singles as well, the dangers involved in being in an isolated area at night have become too great. Meeting for afternoon trysts, borrowing a friend's apartment, and taking advantage of weekends when the children are visiting the noncustodial parent all become modes of maintaining a sexual relationship.

Despite all these difficulties, unmarried sex is a growing phenomenon. Thus, not only have sexual values and sexual behavior been changing, especially among the unmarried, but the liberal trend is expected to continue in the future as well.[48] More unmarried men and women are likely to experience sexual intercourse and to begin at a younger age. During the 1970s there was a 30 percent increase in women under the age of nineteen who engaged in coitus, with the average age for the first experience declining about four months during this decade (from 16.5 to 16.1).[49] Sexual equality is expected to continue to increase, as is the belief that sex and procreation are separate issues. As one family sociologist has stated, "Sexuality will no longer be the primary resource to be used in negotiations toward commitment and marriage, but rather as an expression of emotions to be enjoyed."[50]

Summary

■ Unmarried sex has come to be accepted by more and more persons, especially by those who delay marriage for several years beyond the average age at which their peers marry. Sex between marriages also has become the rule rather than the exception. However, most unmarried persons who engage in coitus have only one or two partners in the space of a year and thus are far from promiscuous.

- Approval of and participation in unmarried sex is far from universal, however. There are still those who favor abstinence and those who choose long-term celibacy.

- The double standard is widely held in the United States. Even though women are gaining sexual equality with men in many ways, the notion that casual sex is less acceptable for women than for men is still common.

- Few men or women condone sexual permissiveness without some kind of relationship. Even those who feel that the sole prerequisite of coitus is mutual agreement between the individuals involved often believe that sex with affection is very different from (if not necessarily better than) sex without affection.

- Unmarried sex has its problems—venereal disease, pregnancy, unavailability of a propitious time and place for the encounter—but despite the difficulties, it is a growing phenomenon, which is expected to continue to increase in the next decades.

Cohabitation

Cohabitation is the term usually used to refer to unrelated adults who are living together and presumably having sexual relations but are not married to each other. Although the concept is reasonably clear, it is not as easy as it might seem to learn the extent of the practice. After reporting that about two million households consisted of two unrelated persons in 1979, the U.S. Census Bureau commented that:

> In addition to a certain number of what are generally termed "unmarried couples," these multimember nonfamily households include unrelated adults sharing a dwelling to reduce their individual housing expenses, two widows who are not related but are living together for companionship, or a landlord/landlady with several persons living in their home as roomers.[51]

Offsetting the effect of counting persons who are merely roommates, however, is the failure to count the unknown number of persons who maintain separate living quarters but who have an enduring sexual relationship, perhaps spending several days or nights a week together in a marriagelike relationship. They may appear in the census as householders living alone or with their families. The phenomenon of "living apart together" seems to be a growing one.

Not only does the U.S. Census Bureau have difficulty estimating just how many unmarried persons cohabit, but those doing research on such couples have even greater difficulty defining just what the term implies. A recent survey of the literature found that there were over twenty definitions in use, which varied around such factors as how long a couple must live together to be classified as cohabiting; how many days and nights of the week they must sleep in the same household to qualify; and, perhaps most important, whether or not the couple considered themselves cohabitors.[52]

The most controversial of the questions posed by those who have searched for a definition of a "cohabiting couple" is how long a man and a woman must live together in order to qualify. Some have suggested six months,[53] whereas several research studies have used the number of nights per week over a continuous period of time as their criterion.[54] It is very likely that this definition of cohabitation will include some persons who consider themselves merely roommates and will exclude many who consider that they are living together after only a few days because they intend that their relationship will be continuous.

Counting numbers of couples who meet the specifications set (unrelated, opposite sex, not legally married to each other, sharing a bedroom for a specified number of nights over a specified period of time) has resulted in the definition of a numerically small proportion of all couple households as cohabiting. This figure was placed at 3 percent in 1979.[55]

Although the percentage is low in the general population, best estimates are that it is growing rapidly. In 1970, for instance, the number was only half what it was ten years later; between 1978 and 1979, the increase was reported to be 19 percent.[56] Furthermore, although cohabitation is found in all age groups, its prevalence among college-aged young adults has grown even more rapidly than its incidence in the general population. Research suggests that approximately 25 percent of college undergraduates in the United States today have cohabited at least once; another 25 percent say they would do so if the right person came along.[57,58] Another study found that 18 percent of young men aged twenty to thirty had cohabited for six months or more.[59] Research has been carried out in all regions of the United States, and the percentages are comparable from region to region.[60]

About half of all cohabiting couples have never been married, but over 90 percent of college students living together plan to marry someone (if not their current partner) at some time in the future.[61] For them, cohabitation seems to be a part of the courtship process. The other half of all males and females who are cohabiting have been married previously or are married but separated.[62] Seventy-five percent of cohabiting couples have no other persons in their households, but a growing number of single parents with custody of their children are choosing this life-style.[63] In addition, more senior citizens are cohabiting—almost one-third of cohabiting couples are over fifty-five—seeking companionship without merging their financial assets or diminishing any retirement benefits that might be affected by marriage.[64]

The rapidly growing popularity of "living together" has been the subject of a good deal of speculation. Researchers are interested not only in the rapidity of the increase but also in the reasons for its occurrence at all. Possible explana-

"Honey, look who I ran into downtown—Bob Phelps, my old college roommate."
Drawing by W. Miller; © 1979 The New Yorker Magazine, Inc.

tions range from the high cost of living to the increased availability of reliable contraceptives, both of which seem well documented.[65, 66]

One of the most thoroughly discussed explanations for the dramatic increase in cohabitation deals with the liberalization of sexual attitudes. Traditional values with respect to virginity and waiting until marriage for sexual involvement have slowly given way to a widespread belief that being in love—especially with an intent to marry—justifies sex outside marriage.[67] In addition, adherence to the double standard condoning sex outside marriage for males but not for females has diminished considerably. Previously, most women believed (often correctly) that men did not want to marry a woman who had experienced sex before marriage. Since according to current estimates approximately two-thirds of American women have had intercourse by the average age of first marriage for women in the United States, that old admonition clearly has lost much of its meaning.[68]

As social attitudes have changed concerning sexual involvement between two persons who love each other, more permissive sexual attitudes have spread to include those who have limited commitment to each other. As values concerning sex outside marriage have changed, so has acceptance of unmarried persons living together.[69] Several studies have indicated that among the college population there is a generally supportive attitude toward cohabitation and, in fact, that college students may actually encourage each other to do so.[70]

Among cohabiting couples, there appears to be a wide range of commitment. Research has identified several types of cohabiting couples, ranging from those who are together for a few weeks to those who maintain a permanent cohabiting arrangement as an alternative to marriage. The following types of couples have been identified:

1. *Short-term relationships:* Often these couples are young and are looking for a sexual experience. One study reported that 82 percent of males and 67 percent of females under age twenty reported that their longest period of cohabitation was less than three months. Of those twenty-one or twenty-two years of age, 63 percent of the males and 48 percent of the females reported a three-month maximum.[71] Because of the large number of such short-term relationships, the rates of those who have "ever cohabited" are much higher than any estimate of those who are currently living together.[72]

2. *Longer-term love relationships:* These are primarily couples who have never been married. They have a definite degree of commitment to each other but are not ready to marry each other—or anyone else—in the foreseeable future. It is estimated that slightly over half of all cohabiting couples fall into this category.[73] In this sense, cohabitation has the effect of delaying marriage. In Sweden most individuals cohabit before eventually marrying someone. There, cohabitation is a step in the courtship process, and many suggest that something similar may be happening in the United States as the average age at first marriage rises. The Swedish sociologist Jan Trost has suggested that this kind of cohabitation in the United States is much more like the "going steady" aspect of courtship in Sweden.[74]

3. *Trial marriage:* A growing number of couples who have previously been divorced, and still others who have previously cohabited with one or more partners, state that they first want to live with any person they may eventually marry.[75] In this sense cohabitation is a variation of the engagement period, although there may be no public announcement of the intention to marry. It is estimated that between 10 and 20 percent fall into this category.[76]

4. *Permanent alternatives to marriage:* Since very few persons never marry, it is unlikely that more than 1 or 2 percent of all cohabiting couples fall into this category. Virtually all cohabitation either terminates or moves into legal marriage.[77] One major distinction between this type of cohabitation and all other forms is that the idea of having children is accepted.[78] Another important difference is that the family and friends of the couple in this category are likely to be supportive of the relationship.[79] In many states the legal system eventually recognizes such unions as nonceremonial marriages or common-law marriages.

In reviewing the research and talking to couples who were living together at the time, a recent study named four patterns of living together:[80]

1. *"Linus blanket":* Sometimes couples decide to live together because they are insecure and dependent. Many young persons who have recently left their families but who are not yet ready to live alone drift (or rush) into cohabitation in order to have someone to lean on. Pregnancy, parental pressure, or fear of abandonment may push such couples into marriage. Usually, however, these relationships end when one or both partners grow strong enough to move on. If one partner remains insecure and dependent while the other grows more secure, the one who no longer needs a "security blanket" may feel used or trapped.

2. *Emancipation:* Some young persons seem to use cohabitation to make a statement of their adult status and sexual freedom to their parents. Those in this category usually had a history of several short-term cohabiting relationships. The research turned up many females with this motivation who came from a very traditional, strict moral upbringing (a large number of Catholics was in this group). They seemed to be seeking a way to break out of their early patterns but tended to become so guilt-stricken or to face so much parental disapproval that they broke off the relationship.

3. *Convenience:* Some obviously exploitative cohabiting relationships were found, in which one or both partners were meeting selfish needs at the other's expense. The usual pattern was one in which the male openly acknowledged that he was in the relationship primarily for sex and often to have domestic tasks done for him. Females often hoped for eventual marriage but sometimes traded their services for financial support. In some cases women were seen as supplying sex and homemaking because the males were their emotional "security blankets." Since social exchange theory states that inequitable relationships will not endure for long, one must assume that relationships of this type will not last unless both partners are fulfilling some of their important needs.[81]

4. *Testing:* Relationships in this category are often labeled *trial marriage.* They usually begin with an established commitment and are set up for the purpose of determining whether or not living together confirms a couple's decision to marry. Couples who choose *not* to marry as a result of having lived intimately with each other usually report that it was a beneficial experience and that they are wiser for having done so.

Characteristics of Those Who Cohabit

Most research on the differences between individuals who choose cohabitation and those who do not has used college-aged students as the sample. Since nearly two-thirds of the cohabiting couples are older than this age group, it is obvious that the following information presents an incomplete picture.

In general, those who cohabit are fairly representative of other persons of similar ages. They tend to label themselves as more flexible and more liberal about life than they believe others to be, but the only objective evidence of this comes from some of their personal habits. For instance, they use marijuana and other drugs more often than noncohabitants.[82] They have had a greater variety of sex partners and report less guilt about their sexual behavior than do noncohabitants.[83] They report that they are not rigid about sex roles—males are more emotionally supportive than noncohabiting males, and females who cohabit are more assertive than are those who do not.[84] In addition, cohabiting couples report lower incidences of religious affiliation, although they perceive themselves as having many beliefs of a religious nature.[85]

A recent study has indicated that couples who live together before marriage have less formal weddings with fewer guests and are less likely to go on honeymoons.[86] The couples interviewed reported that while they were living together their parents had pressured them either to marry or to quit living together. Another interesting finding was that for cohabiting couples who eventually marry each other, there was a shorter time between their first date and their decision to marry. It is an open question whether this was the result of parental pressure or occurred because the two people involved were more serious about each other early in the relationship.

Couples who cohabit usually have friends who are also living together.[87] They report an openness of communication and an ease in establishing intimate relationships. One researcher sums up the profile of those who cohabit: "In general, those who take the opportunity to live together have no religious reasons not to, are comfortable engaging in nontraditional behavior, have had

considerable interpersonal experience, and want to increase the amount of time spent with the partner because they feel happier when with the partner.[88]

In spite of perceiving themselves as more liberal in nearly every way, most cohabiting couples nonetheless adhere as closely to the traditional division of labor as do their married counterparts. For instance, even more cohabiting females wash the dishes than do married females; the likelihood of responsibility for cooking and menu planning is nearly the same for cohabiting as for married females. The percentages of cohabiting males and married males who cut the lawn, take out the trash, and clean the garage are very similar. As with married couples, more cohabiting females than males are responsible for dusting, vacuuming, and doing the laundry.[89] Perhaps this is because the research has centered primarily on young couples who are still fresh from parental homes with their traditional role models. It would be interesting to determine whether older cohabiting couples follow the same patterns and whether or not those young couples who stay together evolve into more egalitarian relationships over time.

Cohabiting as a Predictor of Marital Success

There is still no definitive answer to the question of whether the chances for success in marriage are enhanced for two partners who live with each other before they marry. Cohabitors who do eventually marry each other usually report that living together was beneficial, although no objective evidence actually exists that they have better marriages than those who did not cohabit.[90]

As noted, there is a high breakup rate for cohabiting couples. It is quite likely that those that break up are the ones in which one or both partners were not seriously committed or were using living together as a way to avoid commitment.[91] Research that centered primarily on those who enter cohabitation as "trial marriage" and who marry ceremonially later might show a rate of success that was better than average. However, the factors involved in making marriages work are so complex that it seems doubtful that cohabitation would ever be the deciding factor. Perhaps the greatest benefit cohabitation affords the success of marriages in general is that it keeps some persons from marrying each other at an early age, having children, and later divorcing. As one study concluded: "The best divorce you get is the one you get before you get married."[92]

Breakup of cohabiting couples is not necessarily free of the pain and other stresses associated with divorce, however. For those who are highly committed, the breakup often resembles a divorce in its emotional aspects. This is especially true for couples who may have lived together for several years, making a home together and, in some instances, having a child together.

There are important legal differences between being married and cohabiting, of course. Research in both the United States and Sweden has indicated, for one thing, that commitment is greater in marriage.[93,94] Not only have married couples publicly announced their commitment, but they also have the

On April 18, 1979, actor Lee Marvin addressed news reporters briefly on the court's decision to reject Michelle Marvin's $1.8 million claim against him.

recognition of family and friends of their intention to make a life together.

Legally, of course, there are major differences between married and unmarried cohabitation. Although each state has different laws, in over one-third of them it is a crime for an unmarried couple to cohabit.[95] The laws are not enforced with great regularity, but some states provide for a penalty of six months imprisonment and a $500 fine.[96] Until recently, unmarried cohabitors had no legal obligations to each other. When they split up, they could both go their own ways, she taking her television set and he taking his stereo. However, several recent court decisions have changed the obligations and the property ownership of cohabiting persons dramatically.[97] These decisions have opened the way for legal enforcement of certain agreements made between unmarried cohabitants.

The landmark case involved actor Lee Marvin and Michelle Triola, a woman who lived with him for seven years and who took his last name, becoming known as Michelle Marvin. After they separated, Lee Marvin supported her for nearly two years. When the support ceased, Michelle Marvin sued, claiming that Lee Marvin had promised to support her for life and to share his earnings with her if she would drop her career as an entertainer and live with him. During the seven years they lived together (a part of which he was still married), they purchased no joint property and filed separate income tax returns. This later became an issue in the case because Lee Marvin's attorneys claimed that this indicated that he meant to keep his assets separate. Michelle Marvin was eventually awarded $104,000 in 1979 as a kind of compensation for the years that her career was set aside and as a fund to help her financially while she reestablished herself.[98] Although the decision did not award her either lifetime support or a share of Lee Marvin's earnings, she was the first unmarried person to win "equitable relief" similar to that offered to married persons by alimony. The term **palimony** was coined to describe this award, and since then several other cases were decided in a similar fashion.[99] In 1981, the California appellate court overturned the ruling, denying the award in the process. While Triola's attorneys are appealing once more, it is believed that the denial decision will stand.

Couples who cohabit are well advised to understand the laws of their states. Many lawyers advise unmarried cohabiting couples to draw up a contract specifying exactly how they want to agree on property and earnings. There can be a contract *not* to share or a contract *to* share. Lawyers often suggest:

1. Couples should list the major items each brought to the relationship.
2. Any property acquired while living together should belong to whoever paid for it, unless each partner's proportionate share of ownership has been spelled out at the time of purchase.
3. Any agreements to share earnings or property while living together or in the future should be put in writing.
4. Couples should keep separate bank accounts and credit cards and should keep names as they were before living together.
5. If large investments—for example, a condominium or a house—are made jointly, both names should be on the deed or mortgage and it should be stated clearly what happens to the property in case of a breakup. This advice is also applicable when the couple signs a rental or lease agreement.[100]

Cohabiting couples also face other important differences from married couples with respect to insurance and taxes. Automobile insurers, for instance, consider even a long-term cohabiting couple as two single persons. Not only does each partner pay premiums higher than those married couples would pay, but cohabiting couples also do not qualify for the discount usually given for a second family car. Health insurance plans cover the couple as though each were single, denying them the lower rate a spouse enjoys. In fact, one unmarried spouse may not even include the other as a dependent, but each must have his or her own coverage. In case of death of one partner, employee survivors' benefits often are only payable to spouses.[101]

The way taxes are levied on two unmarried cohabitors can be more advantageous than for married couples, if each has large deductions and both are employed. However, if one stays at home, in the nineteen states in which cohabitation is a crime, that partner does not qualify as a dependent (as a spouse or other relative would).

In his book, *Oh Promise Me but Put It in Writing,* civil lawyer Paul Ashley recommends legal agreements such as joint ownership agreements, partnerships, and other types of contracts whether or not the couples live in states where cohabitation is legal. He cautions couples in states where they are breaking the laws by living together to avoid mentioning this fact in their contracts, but encourages them nonetheless to have a "proper agreement."[102]

Homosexual Cohabitation

In recent years homosexuals have been more open about their relationships. Many homosexuals now live together openly and consider themselves "married." Some have marriage ceremonies similar to those performed for heterosexual couples. One of the main differences between such unions and heterosexual marriages, of course, is that homosexual marriages are not legally recognized. This creates a situation for homosexual couples nearly identical to that of unmarried heterosexuals who live together on a committed basis. There has been increasing research on same-sex intimate relationships as a type of family form. The studies have shown that there is a growing acceptance of stable couple units within the gay community.[103,104]

In a recent study of homosexuals, it was determined that nearly all those interviewed had been involved in an exclusive relationship that had lasted over a year and were currently leading satisfying personal lives.[105] Very few differences existed between homosexual couples as a group and heterosexual couples (not all of whom cohabited in either category). Caring for one another and relational adjustment were very similar for the two groups.[106]

Most homosexual couples are childless, but not all. One or both partners in a lesbian couple often have custody of children from a previous heterosexual union.[107] It is less common for a gay father to have custody of his children and to live in a "marriage" with another man, but this phenomenon may become less unusual as the numbers of both gay couples and custodial fathers increase.[108]

There has been little research on how children fare in a home with a gay parent and a gay "stepparent." In counseling such families, however, we have found that children generally adjust as well as the adults do to their life-style. In other words, if the parents are comfortable with their lives, the children also adjust well. These families have many of the same problems as other stepfamilies. In addition, however, they have certain other social adjustments to make that may be generated by the attitudes of their peers and of other community members. They may be subjected to teasing, criticism, or in some instances, ostracism. In many respects, the treatment of gay families resembles the treatment in some very conservative communities of families in which the adults are unmarried cohabitants.[109]

Summary

■ Although it is impossible to get an accurate count of the number of unmarried persons who cohabit, there is agreement that the numbers have grown dramatically in recent years among both young never-married persons and those who have been divorced or widowed. Beyond the problem of determining the numbers accurately, it also has been difficult to define cohabitation precisely.

■ About half of all cohabiting couples have never been married, but over 90 percent of young persons who cohabit plan to marry someone eventually. Thus cohabitation is not taking the place of marriage but appears instead to be part of the courtship process for many, as well as a way of delaying marriage.

■ Among the reasons that cohabitation has grown in popularity, one of the most discussed is the changes in sexual values that have made it unnecessary for couples to marry before they engage in coitus. As these attitudes have come to be shared by large numbers of single persons, social attitudes about living together have also changed for a sizable portion of the population.

■ Many levels of commitment are found in cohabiting couples, ranging from minimal commitment to an intention to live together for a lifetime. In general, those who cohabit are fairly representative of other persons of similar ages.

They are more likely to label themselves as liberal and less likely to report religious affiliations. Despite their generally less traditional appearance, young cohabiting couples seem to follow a very traditional pattern of division of household tasks.

■ There is a high breakup rate for cohabiting couples, perhaps because many are not highly committed to the relationship from the beginning. There is still no definitive answer to the question of whether living together helps a future marriage between the two persons involved. Perhaps studying only those who see living together as a "trial marriage" would give a better indication of cohabitation as a predictor of marital success.

■ Couples who live together must face certain legal problems. Lawyers advise unmarried cohabiting couples to draw up a contract specifying exactly how they want to agree on division of property and earnings.

■ Homosexual "marriages" have grown more frequent in recent years and are another form of unmarried cohabitation because they are not recognized as legal in any state. Most homosexual couples are childless, but some have custody of children from a previous heterosexual union. It is predicted that this type of single-parent home may become more common in the future.

Glossary

Marriage gradient A term coined to describe the tendency of lower- and middle-class women to marry men of higher social and economic status than they.

Palimony Court order to pay a former cohabitant support, civil damages, or a share of community property earned during the period of cohabitation, based on proof of intent to establish a household even though no valid marriage existed.

Sometimes I think
people were meant
to be strangers.
Not to get to know
one another,
not to get close
enough to damage
the heart
made older by each
new encounter.

But then,
someone comes along
and changes all that.

—From *Stanyan
Street and Other
Sorrows* by Rod
McKuen.
Copyright ©
1966 by Rod
McKuen.
Reprinted by
permission of
Random House,
Inc.

148

6 · Mate Selection and Getting Married

Even though in general there may be less pressure on young Americans to marry than there was in the past, marriage is still a life-course experience that nearly all people expect to have sooner or later. Very few persons (probably less than 4 percent of the population) actually live alone or with a member of their families of origin all their lives. The increase in the number of couples living together without marrying has not seemed to decrease significantly the number who eventually marry. Cohabitation may delay marriage, but ultimately nearly everyone walks down the aisle—a growing number more than once. Some are looking for "that special person" or a "marriage made in heaven." Others are just looking for *someone* and seek the best prospect through work, church, friends, dating bureaus, or even newspaper advertisements. Family specialists are interested in the process of mate selection and in how people successfully move from singlehood to marriage or to unmarried cohabitation.

In studying eighteenth-century America, one learns that early settlers sometimes sent across the Atlantic for unseen brides and met them for the first time when they arrived at the dock. Selections, although sometimes made by family members, might also be made by a ship's officer, who would deliver a marriageable woman for the price of her passage. In the nineteenth and early twentieth centuries, Chinese laborers in the United States ordered brides from the Orient from agencies that distributed pictures of prospective mates. Even today, Orthodox Jews in particular may seek the help of a "marriage broker"—either a professional or a nonprofessional—to help find a suitable marriage partner.

In other parts of the world, arranged marriages still occur. In Turkey, for instance, a recent study reported that three-quarters of the marriages were arranged by the families or their designated intermediaries.[1] In other areas the arrangement may be largely ceremonial, but couples are far from having the kind of free choice taken for granted in the United States. Young people may have a "veto" over parents' choices for them, but few would defy their parents by marrying someone of whom the parents disapproved.

In general, however, the trend for the world as a whole over the past ten years has been in the direction of more self-determination for couples in choosing their mates. The rate of movement toward freer choices seems to be related to industrialization and, in particular, to the growing role of middle-class women in subsistence level or higher income production.[2] In his review of the literature on mate selection in the 1970s, Murstein concludes:

> It can be speculated that, cross-culturally, the absence of economic means for the woman leads to early marriage and little individual freedom. The possibility of working leads women to avoid arranged marriages, enhances the possibility of love matches, and may slightly diminish the marriage rate.[3]

Although it is often difficult for contemporary Americans to understand, historically "love matches" have had very little to do with the choice of a life partner in much of the world. Most Americans firmly believe that it would be miserable, possibly tragic, perhaps even immoral to enter into a life partnership without being "in love." Yet in many present-day societies and in some cultural groups, getting married simply because one is in love is considered frivolous at best.[4]

Although the marriage of Edward VIII of England to Wallis Warfield Simpson in the 1930s delighted the hearts of romantics because he gave up the throne for the woman he loved, others (including his own family and especially the Queen Mother) saw his behavior as weak and irresponsible. In their opinion, anyone who thought that marriage should be based on love alone was insufficiently wise and mature to be king of England, especially when the woman involved had no royal ancestry and was divorced. "Love," for them, could not possibly compensate for these flaws. Whether Prince Charles and Princess Diana have changed the royal perception of love versus duty must be left to history to determine.

As young persons have moved away from the direct influence of their parents in choosing their mates, the trend has been away from "practical" criteria for selecting a partner and toward more emotional criteria and a greater concern with love as the basis for a lifelong commitment.

Although it may seem that in the United States we have as much free choice as possible to fall in love and choose a mate, there continue to be restrictions and factors that predetermine our choices. There are "automatic disqualifications" or filters for mate selection that occur upon acquaintance—or even before. These reduce the pool of possible eligible mates.[5] Thus, whether marriage partners are chosen by parents, family, or the participants themselves, there is a social context within which the choice is made.

Differential Association

One of the important determinants of whether or not the potential for mate selection ever develops is the social context within which the selection is made. Everyone spends more time with some persons than with others. The term for this selectivity is **differential association**; and it occurs for a number of reasons. One is simply that of physical availability or **propinquity**. A child is likely to spend less time with a playmate who lives a mile away than with one who lives next door. We associate more with our schoolmates or coworkers than with persons who live and work far away. Several studies have shown that the geographic accessibility of an attractive potential partner may make a big difference in whether or not a relationship persists.[6]

Geographic accessibility, however, although necessary, is by no means sufficient. We may never become friends with our next-door neighbors or with some of our coworkers. Another important factor in differential association, therefore, is the amount of time people spend together. Some of this is not so much the result of mutual attraction as it is a **functional involvement**. For instance, members of the same household usually find it more efficient to eat their meals in the same place and at the same time, to take vacations together, to visit relatives and friends together, and even to do some household chores together. People who go to the same school, work in the same place, attend the same church, or do the same type of volunteer work have to spend some time together in order to achieve their goals.

Propinquity, or nearness of physical location, and functional involvement are components of mate selection that play a powerful role in providing or denying the opportunity for selection to occur. Most people get together in one of the ways mentioned here, although some resort to dating services or advertisements to meet those whose paths they might otherwise not cross. Even the advertisements in a magazine such as *Intro*, however, typically indicate either the area in which the persons placing the notices live or the area in which they wish to meet people. Most people find enough attractive persons nearby or through their activities to make voluntary friendships or to choose special friends and lovers.

Negative and Positive Factors in Mate Selection

Negative Factors
in Mate Selection

Although there is general agreement on some of the factors involved in bringing two people together as a couple—propinquity and functional involvement, for instance—there are many other variables in attraction that are harder to explain. Obviously, one does not establish a relationship with every person of a suitable age who lives nearby or with every person with whom one is functionally involved. Neither does one establish a relationship with every sexually attractive person one encounters.

The pool of prospective partners is always reduced by factors that are often beyond our control—historical, cultural, social, and physiological features. Those factors that reduce the population from which one selects are called *negative factors* in selection. They determine those persons who may not be (or at least have little probability of being) chosen as partners. Since, as already noted, propinquity brings people together, geographic distance is thus a negative factor. A woman in Coos Bay, Oregon, is not likely to develop a love relationship with a person in Ullapool, Scotland, simply because she is unlikely to know that such a person even exists. A Northern Irish Protestant may be unlikely to fall in love with a Northern Irish Catholic—not because of geographic distance but because of the historic struggle between Catholics and Protestants in Northern Ireland. Similarly, negative factors may restrict the field of eligible persons by ruling out prison or mental hospital inmates, slum dwellers, college professors, vegetarians, "liberated women," or just about any category of persons about whom one might say "I wouldn't (or couldn't) marry . . ."

The sum of the negative factors in partner selection leads to a condition called homogamy—the tendency of persons to select as mates those who have several significant characteristics similar to their own. There is a common belief that people voluntarily seek out those who are like themselves. Sometimes this may be true, but it seems more likely that the choices of persons who are similar on the variables usually studied—social class, race, religion, educational background, and so forth—are the result of the failure of people to be attracted by those who are very different from themselves. In other words, they screen out persons dissimilar in some negatively significant way rather than looking consciously for those who are similar.

A Protestant male from Ulster (Northern Ireland) does not choose a particular mate simply *because* she is Protestant—after all, there are many Protestants from whom to choose. What is important to him is to avoid marrying a Catho-

Prince Charles and Lady Diana at Balmoral, Scotland, May 1981.

lic. He does not choose his mate *because* she is near his age but because she is neither "too old" nor "too young." He does not choose her *because* she is of his social class but because she is neither a snob nor a slob (unless he is either a snob or a slob).

Regulation of the potential pool of partners whom we do meet is accomplished by a variety of other factors that determine who is and who is not eligible for marriage. Two fairly common social regulations are **exogamy** and **endogamy.** Exogamy rules out large numbers of persons from the field of eligibles by requiring that mates be chosen from outside specified groups of people. For instance, in some tribal societies marrying a member of one's own clan or tribe may be prohibited. The best-known exogamy rule is that no legal marriages are allowed between persons who are close kin (incest) or who are of the same sex (homosexual). Endogamy, on the other hand, disqualifies those who are not within a certain set of boundaries that are socially acceptable.

Race is as good an example as any of endogamy. Although a few persons do choose mates who are of a different race, the majority do not do so. Interracial marriage accounts for only about 3 percent of all marriages in the United States.[7] In a decision handed down on June 12, 1967, the U.S. Supreme Court ruled that laws prohibiting interracial marriage were unconstitutional. Before that date, forty states had such laws at one time or another. In spite of the change in the laws, however, in many communities informal sanctions still operate to cause members of certain racial or ethnic groups to marry only within these groups.

All kinds of prejudices and antipathies lead to automatic disqualification of persons from consideration as partners for a long-term intimate relationship. Many are disqualifications on the basis of some personal characteristic, ranging from sexual orientation and religion to tastes in clothing and language habits. As discussed previously, disqualifying all but a relatively few in this way tends to have the effect of homogamy or similarity between those who finally choose each other. In other words, homogamy arises not from positive selection of those who are similar as much as from lack of interest in or sympathetic understanding of whole categories of people.

One of the most important disqualifiers of potential partners is age. While most persons prefer to choose marriage partners within a range of ages near their own, social pressures may be brought to bear on persons who "rob the cradle," "marry their mothers," or "find a father figure." There are no statutory upper limits to the ages of persons wishing to marry, but every state has statutes prohibiting persons below specified ages from marrying (see Table 6.2, pp. 164–165).

Kinship is another negative selective factor for most people with respect to partnership attraction. As with "age of consent" laws, every state has laws prohibiting incest. Typically, incest laws prohibit marriage to or sexual relations with ancestors, descendants, brothers, sisters, uncles, aunts, nephews, and nieces. Some states include first cousins as well as many specific other relationships (half-brother, steprelative, and so forth). These taboos are so well ingrained that the thought of dating someone who falls into one of these categories does not even occur to most people. They would quickly dismiss the thought even if they felt such an attraction. Such laws do not always prevent involvement, however, and there are exceptions to all of these general attitudes. Again, as with age of consent, laws cannot prevent attraction but can provide punishment for behaviors resulting from attraction. Incest laws probably reflect usual patterns of attraction rather than determining them.

Positive Factors in Mate Selection

Positive factors are those that motivate one to choose another in order to gain some value or goal or to enhance one's self-concept or general feeling of well-being, often expressed as, "I want to marry someone who . . ." Positive factors seem more likely to change through one's life cycle than do negative factors. At eighteen a woman may be attracted to a good dancer, at twenty-eight to a high achiever, at fifty-eight to a good companion. She may always find all these qualities desirable, but her priorities may shift.

A basic theory of homogamy is Fritz Heider's *balance theory*.[8] Generally, balance theory maintains that less stress is produced when one selects a partner who has the same beliefs, thoughts, and feelings about other persons, ideas, and events. People tend to like and to feel comfortable with others who think and feel as they do. They may have less to argue about, as well as more in common to talk about and enjoy together.

Suppose that one of Darleen's main satisfactions in life comes from knowing that she is intellectually capable and that she takes particular pride in her excellent academic record. While she is talking with Daniel and Joe at a college orientation meeting, Daniel remarks that he hopes he can make an "A" in his English course because he plans to try to get into one of the best graduate schools. Joe laughs at him and says that he (Joe) is not going to waste his time going to graduate school but intends to get out of college as soon as possible and become a salesman. All things being equal (which they never quite seem to be), according to Heider's balance theory, Darleen will like the academically motivated Daniel better than she likes Joe. She will say that she and Daniel have "more in common."

Being "too tall" or "too short," having a "bad temper" or a prison record, having children by another partner—all these are "reasons" that some people are disqualified as mates. A moment's reflection or a little research will reveal that such persons usually are chosen as mates by someone; we know of no hard data demonstrating that such choices are any less happy in the long run than others. The fact is simply that each person has a set of judgments about who is a suitable mate, and most of us tend to be as choosy as we dare. Murstein believes that we may more often *settle for* than *choose* a partner: ". . . only individuals with numerous interpersonal assets and few liabilities really *choose* each other. Those with fewer assets and more liabilities often *settle* for each other."[9]

Whether or not this is so, research on mate selection consistently shows that strong evidence of automatic disqualification is a force that moves those who are similar toward each other.[10] The term **assortativeness** is often used in the family literature to describe how traits or persons are distributed into similar groups or varieties. Assortativeness is well documented as a factor in mate selection in such categories as age, education, intelligence, socioeconomic status, race, and (to a somewhat lesser extent) ethnic background and religion.

It is possible that college admissions offices are among the most effective matchmakers in the United States. They screen for academic ability, give men and women of equal educational background an opportunity to meet each other, and provide a pool of eligible persons of similar age and socioeconomic backgrounds from whom to choose (or for whom to settle).

It is interesting how often marriage partners are from the same social class. While one study has reported that upper-class women "marry down" in socioeconomic class more often than men do, interclass marriage in the United States has been shown to be quite infrequent.[11] The high degree of consistency of the social classes of marriage partners is hardly surprising considering that social class is significantly related to education, occupation, values, attitudes, and goals. Two people with so much in common are much more likely to like each other and to want to spend time together: they "speak the same language."

**Interactive
Disqualifications**

Other ways in which endogamy regulates mate selection involve the system of interaction—the flow of responses—that develops between two persons. This kind of disqualification—often expressed as "we just can't get along" or more often as "I just don't like him"—may reflect a simple lack of social skills, chiefly in the area of communication but also often in a lack of **empathy**—an understanding of how another person feels. Lack of empathy is closely related to communication problems and usually produces the complaint that "he doesn't respect my feelings" or, more dramatically, "she doesn't treat me like a human being!" and is likely to disqualify the nonempathetic person as a potential partner.

Interactional disqualification occurs when people cannot communicate well. When they cannot share their feelings and meanings, each has to guess who the other is. The result is that each has a mental picture of the other that sooner or later will be inconsistent with the other's actual behavior. When that happens, expectations are not met and disappointment occurs. Although communication and empathy are never perfect, if they contribute to too many disappointments, they make it unpleasant to maintain a relationship.

Another kind of interactive disqualifier has been reported in some recent research showing that sex drive and sex interest are also assortatively selected. In other words, engaged couples have significantly greater agreement on their respective needs for sex than do others who are dating.[12] Murstein suggests that by 1990 marital choice may well be influenced more by such dynamic aspects of interpersonal relations than by the traditional sociocultural disqualifiers such as race, religion, and social class.[13]

Summary

■ Free choice of a mate is historically and cross-culturally a rather recent phenomenon. In the past ten years, however, the trend for the world as a whole seems to be in the direction of independence of choice that Americans take for granted. This increasing freedom has led to the growth of love as a basis for mate selection.

■ Homogamy (the tendency for persons in a relationship to be alike in many respects) is probably achieved more by elimination of certain persons than by seeking out those who possess particular characteristics. Whatever the reason, partners who are drawn to each other usually have characteristics such as race, religion, and social class in common.

■ *Positive factors* are those that draw one to another person. These may change over the life cycle as one's interests and values change. What attracts us to another person is ordinarily a behavior or trait that he or she has chosen, although it may be a behavior that is determined at an unconscious level.

■ There are certain automatic disqualifications employed in mate selection, some of which occur even before one meets a potential mate. Some of these are based on prejudice and others on various practical considerations. Factors of age, race, religion, ethnicity, and socioeconomic status are among those used as filters.

■   There are interactive disqualifications as well for mate selection. These depend on the system of interaction between two persons rather than from individual attributes. Empathy and ability to communicate, as well as sexual compatibility, are important factors in determining mate selection.

Theories of Mate Selection

Exchange Theory

Exchange theory may be the most widely accepted explanation of interpersonal attraction.[14] Chapter 4 described part of Murstein's stimulus-value-role theory of general attraction. This is an exchange theory which posits that "in a relatively free choice situation, attraction and interaction depend on the exchange of value of the assets and liabilities that each of the parties brings to the situation."[15] This theory holds that the basis for a continuing relationship between two partners is that each believes he or she will get as much or more from the relationship as it will cost. Exchange theory was not developed as a mate-selection theory, but it has interesting implications for understanding the way in which two people choose each other as mates. Since the theory implies that those who are looking for mates all have the same idea—to maximize their chances for a rewarding marriage—partners more often than not wind up being quite equal in their abilities to reward one another.[16] Those who believe they have a good deal to offer will choose someone who also has resources or traits that seem valuable. In other words, each person compares his or her assets and liabilities with those of a potential partner. Anyone above or below this *comparison level of exchange* is likely to be disqualified.[17]

A variation on exchange theory in explaining mate selection has been described as "equity."[18] In simple terms, equity is "fairness." Most people believe it is most fair to get benefits from a relationship in proportion to what they give to the relationship. Giving to a partner may be measured in ways that are complex,[19] and fairness is not the same as equality. For instance, an agreement that each partner will spend the same number of dollars on apartment rent may seem unfair if one partner's income is much lower than the other's even though both work an equal number of hours. It is just as uncomfortable to feel one is shortchanging one's partner as to feel one is being shortchanged; indeed the partner with the better deal may develop contempt for the other. Equity theory stresses that one is attracted by a "fair deal" rather than by a profitable exchange.

Fairness is partly psychological. For example, a campus beauty who dates the football captain may feel that the value of her prettiness should be judged by its scarcity, and that the relationship is equitable because football captains are also scarce. He, on the other hand, may feel that the value of becoming football captain should be judged by the amount of time and effort necessary to attain the position, and that since being pretty requires little effort for her, she should contribute something more than her looks to make the relationship equitable.

Even though the analogy of the market is often used to explain exchange theory, neither exchange theory nor equity theory should be understood in terms of objective monetary values alone. More often in interpersonal relations, intangibles like thought and effort are the primary considerations. For example, a person may feel that a handknit sweater either is or is not an equitable exchange for an expensive watch. If the person who knitted the sweater spent hours working on it but believes that the person who bought the watch spent no more than fifteen minutes picking it out and perhaps charged it to a parent, the knitter may feel that the inequitable exchange (in terms of energy, care, and time spent) lessens the attractiveness of both the watch and the watch-giver.

In equity theory, as described by Walster, Walster, and Traupmann, persons feel attracted to others from whom they get as much as they give.[20] As a corollary, we propose that at least for some persons the "getting" is no more important for attraction than equity of the *giving* on both sides.

It has been suggested that values involved in judging equity may include physical attractiveness, mental health, physical health, family background, family solidity, and popularity.[21] One can easily expand that list by adding items such as career expectations, potential income, political and religious status, sexual skill, and a host of other personal values.

Complementary Needs Theory

Family sociologist Robert Winch and others have explored attraction as a relationship between two (or possibly more) persons who could be said to have needs that the other *complements*.[22] Although most theories of mate selection propose that each partner believes his or her functioning in the relationship is dependent on the other's behavior, few make this as clear as Winch does in his concept of "complementary needs" in mate selection.

Winch as well as his followers and his critics has tended to limit his discussions to the attractiveness of complementary "personality" needs. He described two types of complementarity. In the first type, known as "Type I complementarity," a person with high needs in certain areas is attracted to a person with few needs in the *same* areas. For example, consider someone we will call Gary, who has a tremendous need to talk constantly, and Geraldine, to whom he is attracted, at least in part because she rarely feels the need to talk at all, thus giving Gary the opportunity to do almost all the talking when they are together. It pleases Geraldine that Gary talks enough for both of them. An example of Type I complementarity is that of the couple with one member who has hands large enough to grip and unscrew pickle jar lids while the other has hands small enough to reach inside the jar when it is opened. The result: both can enjoy the pickles!

"Type II complementarity" occurs when people are attracted to each other because each has *different* needs that the other can satisfy. This can be illustrated by the case of Fred and Frieda. Fred loves to eat, and Frieda needs to be appreciated. She also loves to cook (as most good cooks do), and Fred hates to cook. When they get together, their mutual needs ensure a satisfying time. Frieda cooks for Fred, who in turn gives her the appreciation she needs.

If the notion of complementarity seems to be contradictory to the theory of homogamy, it is probably because both have been overgeneralized. Most couples are likely to consist of two persons who are homogamous in several census-listed characteristics but complementary in many idiosyncratic ones. They may be alike in educational, religious, and family income backgrounds, for instance, but have complementary differences in certain areas of interpersonal, intimate behavior. They may be alike racially (homogamous) but of opposite, mutually gratifying sexual orientation (complementary). The roles played by two marital partners may be influenced by the fact that the two are very similar in consumer values, recreational interests, and economic goals, and also by their complementarity in that one enjoys daily responsibilities that the other finds tedious or distasteful.

So far, the possibility that complementarity is the main factor in mate selection for most people has not been demonstrated empirically. Complementarity is clearly neither the only process nor even the most important process involved in choosing a mate, but it does account for some kinds of attraction.

Psychodynamic Theory

Childhood interaction with one's parents or other family members is thought to affect mate selection because it is believed that a person searches for a partner who will help him or her to reenact earlier emotional experiences. Some have suggested that a woman looks for a man similar to her father and that a man seeks a wife who resembles his mother.[23] The song lyric "I want a girl just like the girl who married dear old Dad" reflects this belief. There is little current research to support this contention, however, although one study has shown that mothers' images often influence the marital choices of both their sons and their daughters.[24]

Psychodynamic influences include such explanations of mate choice as **imprinting**—an emotional attachment developed in the early months of life to persons with particular physical characteristics—which is reputed to cause a search for a mate whose physical appearance is just right. Studies of *birth order* are another attempt to find answers to why certain persons choose each other to marry.[25] Birth order refers to whether one is the firstborn, second, last, or only child. Some well-done studies have failed to support the original research,[26] and still others have shown that size of the family may have a more pronounced effect on personality than does birth order.[27] Other studies, however, support the notion that birth order does affect not only the way one perceives others but also other personality and behavior patterns.[28]

It has been suggested that an only child may be at a disadvantage in marriage because he or she has never experienced competition in intimate relationships and may also have an exaggerated sense of importance in relationships. According to the birth order theory, the oldest brother in a family of sons should get along better with men than with women. His aggressiveness and need to control suggest that his happiest choice of mate would be a woman who functions in a subservient manner. The youngest son in a family with all male children was reported to be imaginative but shy and awkward around females. His most compatible partner thus ought to be an oldest sister of brothers, provided that she is nurturant and capable.[29]

Such analyses can also be made for the oldest brother of sisters, the youngest brother of sisters, the oldest sister of sisters, and so on. The general conclusion is that people have better chances of happiness in relationships when they choose partners who allow them to enact the roles that they learned in their families of origin, and are therefore presumably attracted to such persons more often than chance would dictate.[30]

Although this is an appealing theory, which may in some instances be relevant to how men and women choose each other for marriage partners, any general application of the theory is unfounded. Perhaps the statement of one who has done exhaustive work on birth order sums up the implications of birth-order theory: "In marriage consider yourself and your partner as unique people, partially molded and trained in special ways of relating to others by the accident of your birth position."[31]

Process Theory

Mate selection is clearly a process of choice determined by a complex assortment of social and psychological factors that both restrict and enhance choice. Figure 6.1 shows a hierarchy of filters used to sort through all potential mates

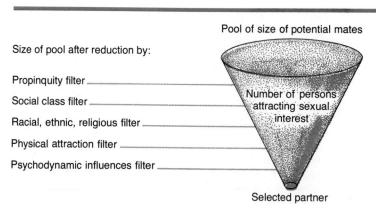

FIGURE 6.1

Filtering Process in Mate Selection

Size of pool after reduction by:

Pool of size of potential mates

Propinquity filter

Social class filter

Racial, ethnic, religious filter

Physical attraction filter

Psychodynamic influences filter

Number of persons attracting sexual interest

Selected partner

Source: David Klimek, *Beneath Mate Selection and Marriage: The Unconscious Motives in Human Pairing* (New York: Van Nostrand Reinhold, 1979), p. 13.

to the final choice of a partner. The filtering process has been called a "funnel" because the initially large number of possible partners is reduced by each filter until only a few eligibles remain for the final choice. Since two people are engaged in the same selection process, Broderick has called it "the double funnel."*

Process theories insist that there can be no single-principle approach but that instead there are many factors that determine marital choice.[32,33] Deciding whom to marry is a complicated matter for most persons, one that may vary not only from individual to individual but also for the same person over his or her life cycle. There is an increasing need for further research on the many variables involved in mate selection and on how men and women move from singlehood to marriage or unmarried cohabitation.

Summary

■ Exchange theory applies the logic of the marketplace to mate selection. People try to get equal value—or perhaps a bargain—when they "invest" themselves in a relationship, and they expect their chosen partners to seek an equal or profitable "return."

■ Equity theory emphasizes that the values in exchange are not necessarily perceived identically by the partners, so that *equity* is not necessarily the same as *equal exchange*. Personal values rather than market values determine what constitutes a profit.

■ Complementary needs theory maintains that people choose partners who are either low in needs in which they themselves are high (or vice versa) or who have different needs that can be satisfied by their chosen partners.

■ Similarity of chosen partners to opposite-sex parent and complementariness of birth order are examples of psychodynamics in partner selection. Insufficient empirical evidence is available to prove or disprove psychodynamic theories of mate selection on general populations.

■ Process theories stress that mate selection is a process determined by a complicated array of social and psychological factors. They insist that there can be no single-principle approach to mate choice but that a multivariate approach is necessary.

Life Cycle and Mate Selection

There is a relationship between one's location in the life cycle and the probability that one will choose a partner and "settle down." The usual statistic collected and reported to reflect this is the average age at first marriage. In the

---

*C. Broderick, lectures at the James A. Peterson Human Relations Center, Los Angeles, May 1981.

TABLE 6.1
*Age at First
Marriage*

Year	Women	Men
1790*	21.0	24.0
1890	22.0	26.1
1920	21.2	24.6
1940	21.5	24.3
1950	20.3	22.8
1960	20.3	22.8
1979	22.1	24.4

Source: B. Wilson, "First Marriages: United States," National Center for Health Statistics, series 21, no. 35 (September 1979).

*Approximately.

United States in 1979, the median age at first marriage for men was 24.4 years and for women 22.1 years.[34] These figures show that both men and women are about two years older at first marriage than they were in 1956, when the median age at first marriage was the lowest since statistics have been available for comparison.

The age at first marriage has been rising slightly for the past decade, and there is reason to believe that it will continue to rise slowly for the next few years (see Table 6.1). Age at first marriage fluctuates with a number of factors, such as the economy, liberalization of attitudes toward premarital sex, and changes in sex roles for both women and men. It is a common myth that in the early years of the United States couples married younger than they do now. Actually, the age at first marriage in 1790, 24 for men and 21 for women, was very close to what it is now.

Laws Related to Age at Marriage

Every state has a legal minimum age for marriage. Parental consent or court approval may authorize exceptions to those minimums. The laws defining minimum ages are probably based primarily on cultural beliefs, but they also have many intricate associations with the personal needs and capabilities of adolescents as well as with the social and economic organization of the states in which they have been enacted. For example, an old Iowa statute provided that persons under the age of twenty-one could not legally be sold any alcoholic beverages—unless the person was a married female, in which case there was no minimum age.

Presumably, for an Iowa woman, being "old enough to marry" was a more important criterion for being considered old enough to drink alcohol than attaining a specific chronological age. At the time that the Iowa statute was

Marriage Section
221 REGISTRY DIVISION

passed, the minimum age for marriage for women was sixteen years, but under "special conditions" it could be as low as twelve years. Almost certainly the "special conditions" in the minds of the legislature meant pregnancy. The logic apparently was that any woman who was old enough to become pregnant was old enough to marry legally and old enough to drink alcoholic beverages. In both Kansas and New Jersey the legal age for females to marry with consent is twelve years; in New Hampshire it is thirteen; and in several other states, fourteen (see Table 6.2).[35]

The logic that being old enough to create a pregnancy means being old enough to marry has not been applied as widely to males. Currently, the earliest age at which males can marry legally without being required to obtain court or parental consent is sixteen years (Utah). In most states the minimum legal age is eighteen for both males and females, but until the advent of equal rights legislation, the minimum age for men was often higher than for women.

The doctrine underlying the enactment of minimum-age-for-marriage statutes was undoubtedly concern about the capacity of the applicants to undertake the economic responsibility for support of the household, the couple, and their probable children. At the time the first of such laws were passed, there was no federal support for welfare programs. The misery created by the marriages and their propagation of societal dependents was obvious to all.

TABLE 6.2

Marriage Age with and without Parental/Court Consent, 1981

State	Age with Consent		Age without Consent	
	Men	Women	Men	Women
Alabama	14	14	18	18
Alaska	16	16	18	18
Arizona	16*	16	18	18
Arkansas	17	16*	18	18
California	18*	18*	18	18
Colorado	16	16	18	18
Connecticut	16	16*	18	18
Delaware	18	16*	18	18
District of Columbia	16	16	18	18
Florida	18	18	18	18
Georgia	16	16	18	18
Hawaii	16	16	18	18
Idaho	16	16	18	18
Illinois	16	16	18	18
Indiana	17*	17*	18	18
Iowa	16*	16*	18	18
Kansas	14	12	18	18
Kentucky	18*	18*	18	18
Louisiana	18*	16*	18	18
Maine	16*	16*	18	18
Maryland	16	16	18	18
Massachusetts	√	√	18	18
Michigan	18	16	18	18
Minnesota	—	16*	18	18
Mississippi	17	15	21	21
Missouri	15	15	18	18
Montana	15	15	18	18
Nebraska	17	17	18	18
Nevada	16	16	18	18
New Hampshire	14*	13*	18	18
New Jersey	—	12	18	18
New Mexico	16	16	18	18
New York	16	14	18	18

Source: Compiled by William E. Mariano, Council on Marriage Relations, Inc., 110 E. 42nd St., New York 10017. Data as of January 1, 1980.

*Minimum can be reduced with consent of parents/court.

√ If under eighteen, consent of parents and court.

TABLE 6.2 (cont'd.)

State	Age with Consent		Age without Consent	
	Men	Women	Men	Women
North Carolina	16	16	18	18
North Dakota	16	16	18	18
Ohio	18	16	18	18
Oklahoma	16	16	18	18
Oregon	17	17	17	17
Pennsylvania	16	16	18	18
Rhode Island	18	16	18	18
South Carolina	16	14	18	18
South Dakota	16	16	18	18
Tennessee	16	16	18	18
Texas	14	14	18	18
Utah	14	14	16	16
Vermont	18	16	18	18
Virginia	16	16	18	18
Washington	17	17	18	18
West Virginia	√	16*	18	16
Wisconsin	16	16	18	18
Wyoming	16	16	19	19
Puerto Rico	18	16	21	21
Virgin Islands	16	14	18	18

The responsibilities of men and women in nineteenth- and early twentieth-century marriages were assumed to be different. An adequate male was one who could provide an income; maintain the family's real property; protect the family from external perils; and represent the family in civic, political, and economic matters. An adequate female was one who could bear and rear children, maintain the system of interpersonal relations within the family, run a smoothly functioning household, maintain the family's standards of cleanliness and health, generally accept responsibility for the manners and morals of herself and her children, and be the family's social secretary and social leader. Although the marital responsibilities of women seem as heavy as those of men, it appears that those who made the laws believed that women could handle the role of wife at an earlier age than men could take on the role of husband. Perhaps the uncertain longevity of the parents of even an early teenager made legislators doubly anxious about her support in the event of the then irrevocable physical reality of her pregnancy.

Legislators must have recognized, consciously or unconsciously, that before a certain point in the development of the life cycle a child cannot carry out the traditional marital roles, even if they are fully understood, and that therefore the right to make the decision to marry before that point should be withheld. In states that permit marriage at an earlier age with parental consent, the implication is that either the parents are better able than a fixed chronological standard to determine whether the individual child is sufficiently mature, or the parents will assume some of the child's marital responsibilities because the child is a minor. As Table 6.2 indicates, only Florida makes no exception to the requirement that both parties be at least eighteen years old, allowing neither parents nor the courts to approve marriage at an earlier age.

Several questions come to mind concerning age requirements for marriage: Are the laws specifying minimum ages for marriage more or less necessary than they were in the past? Is it any of the state's business whether people are sufficiently mature to be good companions, affectionate partners, and adequate parents? If so, below what age should people be deprived of the right to marry? The evidence is mixed and is nearly all probabilistic. That is, the probability that age at marriage affects the outcome of the quality of the marriage is not based on a clearly established cutoff point that applies to all persons, but rather on the odds that marriage after a given age will endure.

Some first marriages at any given age last until one partner dies, but the fraction that endures increases with each year up until both bride and groom are in their late twenties. And those figures tell us only about endurance of the marriage. So far, there is no procedure for collecting direct, objective evidence on the degree of companionship and affection experienced by people who marry at various ages; however, there is some indirect evidence that sheds light on the subject. For example, in 1979 half the divorces granted to women were awarded to women no older than twenty-seven.[36]

Since a divorce is likely to be preceded by a period of separation and a required **interlocutory period**, it can fairly safely be estimated that most women who ever divorce will have experienced some kind of marital unhappiness by the age of twenty-five. From this, it can be concluded that the proportion of women who are not going to stay married is probabilistically greater for those who marry before age twenty-four (allowing a year for unhappiness to surface). Although many persons do remain in unhappy marriages, it appears that those women who marry before they are twenty-four years old run a greater risk of being unhappily married than those who marry at age twenty-eight or later.

Divorce rates are lowest for both men and women who marry for the first time at age twenty-eight or later. The chances for a stable marriage increase as both partners reach the age of thirty and then level off; waiting beyond that age to marry does not increase the probability of successfully avoiding divorce significantly. Couples who desire children have reason not to wait much beyond age thirty to thirty-five to marry if they want to have their children before the risk factor of late pregnancy becomes an issue. This knowledge has led to the conclusion that the maximum likelihood of success in companionship, affection, and procreation in marriage exists when marriage occurs between the ages of twenty-eight and thirty-four (allowing a year for conception if one child is planned), between twenty-eight and thirty-two if two children are planned, and between twenty-eight and thirty if three children are planned. If no children are desired, the age of the couple for parenthood obviously is not a consideration.[37]

Personal values differ, of course. If having a large number of children is more important than affection and companionship with one's mate, earlier marriage may be indicated. If childbearing is not a value, then marriage at any time after twenty-eight holds the greatest promise of lasting until the death of one of the partners.

On the average, men marry women two to three years younger than themselves. This most likely reflects the expectations that men's responsibilities to earn a living and provide for a family are better carried out when they are older. On the other hand, since the average woman lives several years longer than the average man, women can expect their later years to be spent as widows when they marry men who are older than they are. From this standpoint, the argument can easily be made that men should be younger than their wives so that both partners are likely to spend fewer lonely years at life's end.

On the average, an additional year could be added to the length of the marriage for each year the husband is younger than his wife. It has been found that men who marry older women also stay married to them longer on the average than men who marry younger women.[38] This is probably less a magic formula than an insight into the personalities of the participants. Since their age pattern is contrary to popular practice, the participants in an older woman–younger man marriage must value their personal relationship more than conformity to custom. In other words, their motivation to be married to each other may be greater than (or, at least different from) that of those who follow the usual pattern. Whatever the explanation, empirically, marriages are less likely to end in divorce if the bridegroom is younger than the bride than if the reverse is true. If length of marriage is an important value, then a man is most likely to achieve it by marrying a woman older than he is some time after his twenty-eighth birthday.

| Sex and Age at Marriage | Because we live in a complex social world in which sexual behaviors are subject to many social and internal controls, there are some issues that should be thought through carefully by those who consider deferring marriage until age twenty-eight. For instance, there is research indicating that the earlier in life a woman becomes orgasmic, the longer and more active her sex life will be.[39] If |

it is morally important to a woman to remain virginal until her marriage, then waiting until age twenty-eight to marry may well foreshadow a relatively short, and perhaps relatively inactive, sex life.

Various solutions to the dilemma of evaluating "best age to initiate sexual activity" as opposed to "best age to marry" have been proposed. It has often been recommended that there should be a "trial," nonprocreational marriage that would be legally distinct from a more permanent, childbearing marriage.[40,41] Such a trial marriage would have legal sanction but would not involve the same property, support, and inheritance provisions that characterize traditional marriages; therefore, it could be more easily dissolved. It would also be a marriage without children. Although social and personal acceptance cannot be legislated, those who propose such a plan believe that public acceptance probably would follow.

The formalization of a new legal status may actually be unnecessary. Although the relative percentage of such couples is still low, social acceptance of cohabitation (living together without marriage) is apparently increasing, with two-and-a-half times as many couples reporting that arrangement at the end of the 1970s as at the beginning of that decade.[42] For couples both of whose members are under the age of twenty-five, the increase was eightfold. In fact, it has been reported that the primary change in courtship behavior in the past ten years has been in the number of unmarried couples who are living together.[43]

In 1979 nearly half of those living together as unmarried couples had never been married, as noted in Chapter 5. For many such couples cohabitation seems a part of the courtship process. It is not meant to replace marriage, although it does have the effect of delaying marriage. In a recent survey, over 90 percent of cohabiting college students reported that they intend to marry eventually—if not the current partner, then someone else.[44]

Increasing acceptance of sex before and between marriages and particularly of unmarried couples cohabiting may be cause for distress among persons with traditional views of sexual behavior. It would be a mistake for us to insist that there is one right or wrong point of view about sexual behavior outside marriage because of the differing and sometimes highly emotional sentiments of contemporary potential marriage partners. Nevertheless, delaying marriage until the late twenties does seem predictive of greater success in marriage. Early sexual interest and activity (including self-stimulation) do seem predictive of a fuller and better lifetime of sexual adjustment. To delay both marriage and sexual activity creates a set of conditions very different from those that result from marrying early to legitimize sexual activity, or delaying marriage but being sexually active premaritally.

Social Maturity

Regardless of chronological age, some persons are always going to be more or less socially immature. Some eighteen-year-olds may be more ready for the commitment and the responsibilities of marriage than are others in their mid-twenties. At any given chronological age, a socially immature person often denies that there will be any problems in a close personal relationship such as marriage or believes that someone or "something" will prevent them or solve them if they do occur. The most painfully immature are those who plan to escape the problems and responsibilities they face in their parental families by getting married. Many socially immature people marry to get away from home. Many, unrealistically, believe that getting married will solve their problems or that they will have more freedom and less responsibility than in their families of origin.

More common than those who are running away from intolerable home situations, we believe, are those socially and emotionally immature young people who marry as one way to break away from their dependency on their parents. They almost seem to believe that two socially immature persons together can help each other grow up. Of course, this does occur sometimes. On the other hand, they may make unrealistic demands on each other, which neither is capable of fulfilling. Not infrequently these demands border on the expectation that the mate will function as a "good parent" or will give unconditional love and support in the face of any problem that should arise. Greater effort may be expended in trying to change each other to meet these demands, with disappointment and disillusionment as frequent results. Many experts are convinced that the high divorce rate among such young couples can often be traced to social immaturity.[45]

Ideally, marriage partners in our contemporary society should be two adults who are physically, socially, and psychologically capable of modifying their individualities into mutually acceptable patterns that will bring them more joys than sorrows in their lifelong relationship with each other. The ability to be social adults is probably more widespread among twenty-two-year-olds than among eighteen-year-olds and is almost certainly more widespread among twenty-eight-year-olds than among twenty-two-year-olds. Nevertheless, chronological age is far from a perfect index.

The meshing of personal identities into marriage and family life is a characteristic of social adulthood. Confidence in one's personal ability to overcome reasonable problems is also characteristic of adulthood. Although social adults typically have concerns and even doubts about how any new undertaking will work out, such awareness also typically will help them cope with marriage and family problems. They know there will be problems, but they also believe that they will find solutions.

Young people are often advised to try living independently on self-produced incomes for at least a year before marrying—worthwhile advice in most cases. One rarely hears married couples complain that they waited too long before they decided to marry. In fact, considering the research data on the optimum time to marry for the greatest success of a marriage in terms of both stability and reported satisfaction, many couples probably marry for the first time five to ten years before they would be ready to achieve their most satisfying and longest-lasting relationship. In many instances, had they waited, they would not have ended up marrying the persons they did marry.

Mate Selection in Remarriage

Even though about 60 percent of all marriages that end are dissolved by the death of one partner, nearly 40 percent are ended by divorce. First marriages, however, are less likely to end in divorce than are second marriages. The proportion of third, fourth, and fifth marriages ending in divorce raises the divorce rates significantly. Persons with multiple divorces and remarriages actually make up a small proportion of the population, however. Although over 95 percent of Americans who live past the age of fifteen marry at least once, only 3 percent have ever been married more than three times.[46] Such persons have received little attention from those doing research on divorce, but either their mate selection process or their ability to carry on a marriage seems questionable.

Of those women who are divorced before age thirty, 91 percent remarry within nine years of their divorces, most of them within three years.[47] It seems obvious that these men and women want to be married to someone but that something about their previous marriages was undesirable. Many apparently believe that the flaws lay in the partners they chose, not in the institution of marriage itself.

When people who have been divorced once choose a second mate, have they learned from this first experience? Are second mates better choices? Statistically, slightly fewer (56 percent) second marriages than first marriages last until one partner dies.[48] In other words, of the one-third whose first marriages end in divorce, about 44 percent will be divorced a second time, but 56 percent of them will be successful the second time around. Clearly, most do learn something about picking a mate and making a marriage work. For those who are unsuccessful the second time, it appears that whatever advantage may have been gained from experience at mate selection was canceled out by other complications of second marriages, such as stepchildren, support payments, and relationships with former spouses and in-laws.

Some persons seem to have a **repetition compulsion** in mate selection, repeatedly making the same kind of choice that has failed in the past. However, since so many second marriages last until death, it seems unlikely that there is a high proportion of remarriages in which one partner is the victim of repetition compulsion.

Summary

■ The age at first marriage for both men and women has been rising in recent years and is expected to continue to rise for at least the next decade.

■ Every state has a minimum age for legal marriage, ranging from a low of twelve years for females in New Jersey and Kansas (with court and parental consent) to a high of twenty-one years for both sexes (parental and court consent not required) in Mississippi.

■ Divorce rates drop off sharply for both men and women whose first marriage occurs in their late twenties. If the number of children desired is taken into consideration, later marriages have better chances to succeed than do earlier marriages.

■ Some authorities have recommended the establishment of more than one form of legal marriage to provide for the different needs and values of each of the partners. However, the present system actually functions quite well, with cohabitation serving informally in such a capacity for many contemporary couples.

■ Second marriages are almost as successful as first ones if divorce is used as the index for declaring a marriage unsuccessful. Multiple marriages are less successful, but they are only a small percentage of all marriages in the United States.

The Transition from Choice to Commitment

It is probably safe to say that for most people an ideal relationship is envisioned as one in which the persons involved are strong, have good self-concepts, perceive each other accurately, communicate freely and well, and feel secure in their relationship because each knows that they are together because they both want to be together. Such an ideal would satisfy virtually everyone except perhaps the rare person who would wonder if he or she could merit such a partner, who sounds almost too good to live with.

Relationships that measure up to this ideal are uncommon. However, the number of persons who want to believe that theirs is one of them is much larger than the number who will admit—even to each other—that it is perfectly all right for their relationship not to meet those high standards all the time in every respect.[49]

One of the stresses on a relationship lies in the naturalness—if not inevitability—of disagreement. This is stressful because the ideal of communicating freely and well conflicts with a strong belief many people have that open disagreement is "bad." Most people acquired this sentiment from unsettling childhood experiences with others (usually parents) who were angry with them. Since children are often punished for acting out their anger, particularly if the anger is directed toward parents, it is an easy step to believing that anger is "bad."

Free and unguarded communication therefore seems risky because it might lead to disagreement and conflict; it might hurt feelings or "damage" the relationship. The less secure one feels, the more risk there appears to be in open communication.

Some people may consciously or unconsciously believe that one way to reduce threats to a relationship is to avoid accurate and meaningful communication. Unfortunately, this tactic tends to lessen communication and to make misperception more likely. The net result is a vicious circle in which personal stress and insecurity in the relationship increase, making the relationship more insecure than ever.

One way of denying conflict or disagreement is to assume that one's partner shares one's important values, beliefs, or ideas about "right" and "wrong." The partner is idealized as a "good" person who wants to do good things, just as one is and does oneself, so disagreement cannot exist. When the partner eventually and inevitably behaves in a "different" way, the idealizer may respond with anger and feel betrayed. Since no two people are identical (not even so-called "identical twins," by the time they are born), it is unrealistic to expect any other person to have exactly the same goals, values, morals, and tastes as oneself. Thus idealization is doomed from the start, although it is still a major factor in some persons' choice of marriage partner.

A person can mentally construct an idealized picture of another and can identify with it even though it is not based on direct experience with that person. This is a problem in human relations for young people who are thinking about marriage. Schulman found that women are more likely to idealize their partners than are men.[50]

The idealization of sexual and marital partners is not different in its effects from any other kind of idealization. The greater the element of fantasy in the mental image of a lover, the greater the probability that expectations will not be met. Young persons who compared their own marriages with idealized pictures of marriage (perhaps drawn from conversations with unmarried friends, movies, or television) can expect to find many of their expectations invalid. Although idealization of marriage is a normal developmental phase, young persons are likely to experience considerable stress when their ideals cannot be met. This may be true even if the sentiments on which they have based their fantasies have been learned from their parents in childhood.

Why do people supply "facts" they cannot possibly know from any direct source to "fill in blanks" about others? To begin with, the very basis for thinking is recognizing objects as alike and putting them into categories that are usually represented by words. Because the actual information used to place an object or a person in a category is almost never sufficent to meet our actual needs for information, we generalize about the category from special cases we have known or sometimes from learned prejudice. Most of us come to believe that a very few clues about a person predict much more than they do. When we are right, it is efficient to believe this. When we are wrong, we may *make* it efficient by avoiding interaction with those who do not fit our **stereotypes**. That may be easier than giving up the stereotypes.

Some popular stereotypes are that beautiful women are more skillful sexually than plain women or that effeminate men prefer homosexual activities to heterosexual activities. The idealization of a prospective partner is much like stereotyping. Once one has become committed to another as a choice of mate, there is a strong desire to believe that one's choice was a good one. It becomes necessary, then, to reassure oneself of this by expecting any untested qualities of the partner to be "good." In the case of persons who had fantasized finding "Mr. Wonderful" or "the girl of my dreams," much of the stereotype was already prepared, waiting to be triggered by a few cues. Persons who are highly romantic often report that they had very precise images of what their lovers would be like before they ever saw them.[51]

Like stereotyping, idealization of a loved one may create a self-fulfilling prophecy. As early as 1902, sociologist Charles Horton Cooley observed that people tend to behave in accord with the expectations they believe others have of them.[52] If a person stays in a relationship very long, he or she will either begin to take on some characteristics the other person expects or will become uncomfortable in the relationship and perhaps end it. The peak of the idealization period usually comes in the early stages of commitment, or the "engagement" period. This is a very happy time for most couples. The partners are thinking positively about each other, mutually reinforcing their self-esteem.

Research indicates that idealization and expectations about partners are closely related to the definition given to a relationship by them.[53] For example, as one partner changes from boyfriend or girlfriend to fiancé or fiancée or to cohabitant or mate, both his or her expectations and the partner's behavior also change. We have only to listen to those couples who say that the day they were married, they both changed. No doubt, they did change—not only in behavior but also in the expectations that each held for how the other would behave in this new role.

As with all stereotypes, expectations are not always fulfilled when one person idealizes another. Usually by the second year of a relationship, unless the expectations of partners have come to match their behaviors to an appreciable degree, the relationship may be in for serious trouble. Most idealizations involve such high expectations that almost no one could measure up to them. Since a sufficient number of Americans marry persons with whom they have an idealized relationship, it is not surprising to find that the divorce rate peaks around the third year after marriage.[54]

More will be said about disillusionment after marriage in a later chapter. At this point, disillusionment should be mentioned as a phase in the life cycle of a relationship that is moving in the direction of a choice of long-term partners. If disillusionment arises early, it will probably lead to the termination of the relationship before it has really begun. In a recent study, it was reported that the three major reasons for breaking up are boredom, differences in interests, and the desire to be independent. Breaking up is rarely a mutual decision: 87 percent of the men and 85 percent of the women involved say that one person initiated the termination of the relationship.[55] All three of the reasons given are major ingredients in and reactions to disillusionment.

Disillusionment is the direct result of idealization. It occurs when one's partner's behavior fails to meet the other's expectations or when the relationship itself fails to fulfill some idealized image. Some degree of disillusionment seems inescapable, since no one can have completely accurate expectations for the future.

Commitment to a Relationship

In a very brief and generalized definition, *commitment* refers to a person's persistent willingness to be loyal to another and to give time and energy to achieve the goals of their relationship.[56] The process of moving from attraction to commitment in a relationship is called *courtship*. Courtship is an old-fashioned word that describes a process of great concern to contemporary family-life experts. In connection with commitment, it has a special meaning. In important ways, courtship is the pursuit of commitment from and to a loved one.

The psychological and sociological literature has identified five characteristics of commitment, although research has shown that most people do not analyze their own commitments but see them as a single characteristic. The elements described in the literature and reported in a recent study are:

1. dedication to continuing the relationship
2. rejection of competing or alternative relationships
3. limitation of one's personal activities to conform to the perceived social expectations for "a committed couple" or group
4. personal feelings of attachment
5. willingness to accept the behavioral norms that grow as the relationship develops[57]

A committed person gives time and energy to keeping the relationship going; does not get involved in other relationships that reduce the time, energy, or attention required for this "primary" relationship; gives up "selfish" activities so that others define him or her as committed; wishes to be physically close to the partner much of the time; and wants to work out patterns of behavior that are mutually satisfactory.

Schrader found that whether or not a couple believes they are committed to each other is more predictive of how long the relationship will last than any other variable that she studied, including the acceptance of their relationship by others, the couple's agreement on the definition of their relationship, or their homogamy.[58]

In her studies of commitment, Schrader found that men tend to believe that their partners define their commitment in the same way they do themselves—

that is, that their partners want to be involved in a relationship that is fun, provides good companionship, and respects the freedom of each partner (the right to make good decisions on his or her own). She found, however, that men are incorrect in this assumption. In fact, women define commitment primarily as sexual exclusiveness and dedication to the duration of the relationship. Unlike men, however, most women are aware that they define commitment differently than their partners.

Males tend to feel that their partners ought to show their commitment to a relationship by moving toward increased willingness to share and enjoy sex. Although females are fully aware that males have such expectations, their own commitment is actually to permanence of the relationship, with the intimacy of sex either irrelevant or of secondary significance. Schrader contends that "It is the women who are primarily pushing for a binding, exclusive, and committed relationship. They, more than the men, are holding to the traditional sex role ideology."[59]

Commitment was defined somewhat differently in another recent study.[60] Cohabiting and noncohabiting couples were asked to predict the probability of their marrying their current partners. Their predictions were then matched with whether or not they actually did marry within the period of the study. Women who were cohabiting estimated the probability of eventually marrying their current partners as somewhat greater than did men, apparently suggesting a stronger link between commitment and permanence of the relationship for women than for men.

Interestingly, cohabiting women saw themselves as at a greater power disadvantage in their relationships than did women who were "going together" with men but not cohabiting. The authors said, ". . . it may be easier for noncohabiting couples to achieve . . . an egalitarian relationship, than it is for cohabiting or married couples."[61]

Betrothal

Engagement to marry is still a customary preliminary to marriage in most of the world and is a public statement of commitment. Four concepts of betrothal have been described: Mediterranean, Nordic, Amerafrican, and contemporary American.[62] In the Mediterranean tradition, sexual access is viewed as an exclusive right of marriage partners. Coitus or the public statement of the intention to engage in sex is the moral equivalent of intention to marry, since coitus is not only improper but also socially disgraceful for women if it is not accompanied by marriage or at least by a promise of marriage. The Mediterranean tradition incorporates the double standard, however; premarital sex is considered permissible for men. **Betrothal**—a promise to marry—is a necessary prerequisite of indicating a desire for sex for a "socially acceptable" female. The Mediterranean concept of betrothal was prevalent in the United States in the late nineteenth and early twentieth centuries and continues today in some more traditional sections of the country and among some groups.

In the Nordic tradition, sex between unmarried persons is neither disgraceful nor improper but is viewed as a natural developmental expression of normal "falling in love." However, it is considered improper and disgraceful for a couple to become parents without at least an intent to marry. In the Nordic tradition, the discovery of pregnancy rather than the intent to have coitus is the appropriate occasion for betrothal. The Nordic tradition is apparent in the Scottish pattern of *handfasting* and the American colonial tradition of *bundling*. The seeming intimacy of both these customs seems almost shocking for their times until we realize that they had great significance for their societies. Bundling, for instance, was a courtship practice in the eighteenth century in which a couple would lie fully clothed, bundled in blankets (ostensibly to keep warm as well as to keep the young man from a chilly horseback ride home late at night). Often a board, as well as blankets and clothing, separated them; some parents added extra insurance by insisting that the young woman's legs be tied together. It is likely that another important purpose of bundling was to induce the couple to marry in order to legitimize any sexual arousal they might feel.[63]

Money describes "the Amerafrican legacy" in the United States as an absence of betrothal practice. The Africans brought to the United States as slaves came from so many different cultural backgrounds that there was no uniformity among them in betrothal or marriage practices. Further, the practice of slavery, the occasional separation of partners by sale, and the reputed practice of matings arranged to produce genetically superior slave stock are widely believed to be responsible for the general absence of betrothal. Neither coitus nor pregnancy indicated the propriety of a commitment on the part of either partner. Because of the absence of restrictions on coitus and the potential material value to the owner of each child, pregnancies began to occur soon afer puberty. Children born to any slave woman were the property of her owner and were typically reared by slaves who were too old to do heavy labor.

The contemporary betrothal patterns that have developed in the United States (but that still meet some resistance among more conservative members of the population) tend to be variations on the Nordic pattern rather than on the Mediterranean or Amerafrican patterns. The chief difference from the Nordic pattern is that births may be prevented by contraception or abortion by the partners. No public recognition of betrothal is necessary for initiating coitus or even for creating a pregnancy. Money feels that this concept of voluntary betrothal on grounds of commitment to a partner relationship (rather than a parent-child relationship) may eventually result in more mature patterns of mate selection, fewer divorces, and hence better homes for children, owing to the removal of the necessity to marry because of pregnancy or to legitimize sexual involvement.[64]

As an announcement of betrothal, formal engagement has been slowly disappearing from the American scene. Exceptions are found in certain regions of the country and in some upper- and upper-middle-class populations where engagement may function as much to reserve a date for the public celebration of a formal wedding as to indicate the nature of the current relationship between the partners. It is not a reliable indicator of whether the couple is having sexual relations or of whether a pregnancy has occurred, and hardly anyone expects it to be. (A substantial, though not particularly vocal, fraction of brides and grooms still follows the Mediterranean pattern of virginity until marriage, but this is generally considered a matter of personal preference rather than of social pressure.)

It may be that many couples avoid becoming formally engaged because of the high price of the diamond thought by many to be customarily given by a suitor to his fiancée when an engagement is announced. A diamond merchant told us recently that most sales of diamond engagement rings are chiefly to older couples entering second or third marriages or to upper socioeconomic couples.

The Wedding

The wedding vows that a couple takes represent a public statement—and one with great legal significance—of their mutual commitment to their enduring relationship. Regardless of cynical comments that the high divorce rate reflects a lack of commitment, it seems unlikely that very many persons actually enter into marriage without the intention of staying married. The very act of cohabiting out of wedlock is testimony to the seriousness with which people view the transition to being married.

The married state is of major social and psychological significance to the partners themselves, to their families and associates, and even to government

and other agencies. At present, for example, income tax legislation discriminates heavily against married persons both of whom are employed. Court policy is still being hammered out over the propriety of spouses testifying in court cases involving each other. The most profound effect of ceremonial marriage, however, is surely on the partners themselves.

Weddings, including wedding vows, are the public statements that two persons make of their intention to be husband and wife to each other and of their desire for social sanction of this decision. Some weddings are very private, with only the necessary officiant and witnesses present, but others are elaborate affairs with hundreds of witnesses. Many weddings are casual, nonreligious ceremonies; few brides today feel compelled to wear white to signify purity and virginity (although most do anyway). However, it has been estimated that three-fourths of weddings do have a religious base to them—that is, they are performed in a house of religious worship and/or the one who officiates is a minister, priest, or rabbi.[65]

Despite the facts that fewer brides and bridegrooms have had traditional courtships and engagements and that many have lived together for months or even years and that many are sexually involved with each other, when the time comes to make a legal, public statement about their relationship, most couples become somewhat traditional. Many have weddings that are not unlike those of their parents and grandparents.[66] One study reports that couples become traditional for their weddings because they realize the solemnity of adding a new family unit to society and intend to take their new roles seriously.[67]

Friends and relatives usually view a wedding as a happy occasion for the couple and give not only their good wishes but also, customarily, gifts to help the pair furnish their home together. Figures gathered from bridal magazine surveys and from related business sources reveal that 40 percent of the jewelers' business comes from wedding-related purchases: rings, attendants' gifts, silver, china, and crystal. One out of eight dollars spent on home furnishings and appliances is spent by engaged couples, newlyweds, or those buying gifts for them. Over $1 billion each year is spent on other wedding-related items such as clothing, cosmetics, and luggage, with nearly as much spent on honeymoon travel.[68]

After the wedding vows are spoken, whether they are read from the Bible or the Koran, or whether they are words composed by the couple themselves, the legal documents are filed and the relationship is formalized in a way that can be broken only by death or a court action. In all of the United States, marriage is recognized as valid only between those over a certain age who are not already married, who are considered capable of making a legal contract, and who are of opposite sex. Homosexuals may have a wedding ritual (and many committed homosexual couples do have such a ceremony and consider themselves married), but they are not married in the eyes of the law. Should they dissolve their relationship, no legal document of divorce or **annulment** is required.

The statutory requirements for marriage vary from state to state. The statutory definition of marriage spells out the rights and obligations of each partner. Couples may, if they wish, make additional informal or formal agreements with each other. Some couples draw up special agreements with each other in legal documents, which, if properly witnessed and filed, are valid as long as they do not in any way violate the laws or policies of the state in which the couple is married. For example, a contract that spells out conditions under which a couple might be divorced would not usually be valid, since the spirit of marriage is not well served by anticipating divorce. In other words, "public policy," which fixes the privileges and obligations of marital life, must not be subverted by individual contracts.

A kind of contract now allowable, but formerly not so, is one that might cover where the couple will live. Most states automatically used to change a woman's legal residence to that of her husband; if she had lived in North Dakota all her life but married a Texan, she automatically became a Texan, too, regardless of where she lived. When California had such a law designating a wife's legal domicile as her husband's legal residence, an acquaintance of ours who had always lived in California met and married a fellow student while at the University of California. Her husband was from Illinois, and she immediately was reclassified as a resident of that state, thus losing her claim to the much lower university tuition for California residents. A wife had to list her residence as her husband's; not to do so was considered desertion and thus constituted grounds for divorce.

Still another example of a customary understanding between marriage partners involves the name change that most women make. There is no statutory requirement that a woman take her husband's last name, but many couples never discuss other possibilities. A few women keep their maiden names; some couples use a hyphenated name. Most follow the traditional pattern of both husband and wife using the husband's last name.

Formal contracts drawn up before the marriage (**prenuptial** or **antenuptial** agreements) may not be enforceable if they in any way attempt to change "public policy" about marital rights or obligations. However, many couples do have agreements that are permissible in the state in which they are drawn and that deal with certain financial arrangements, child care, the education or religious training of children, household management, career decisions, and other issues that may be troublesome areas later if left to chance but that are not regulated by law. Of course, such contracts can always be renegotiated. Questions may be raised about appropriate penalties for broken marriage contracts if the partners are unwilling to renegotiate. Is a broken marriage agreement grounds for a civil suit? If so, how can damages be assessed? Should injunctions be ordered for violations of private marriage agreements? Is divorce an appropriate action when a contract concerning household management, career decisions, or child care is broken?

Perhaps in the future contracts will be used more than they are currently and will be subject to enforcement and arbitration. For now, most couples do not bother with formal agreements. Those who do often cannot depend on support from the courts should the contract be broken.

Summary

■ Courtship is the process of moving from attraction to commitment in a relationship. Five characteristics of commitment have been identified, although most couples tend to see their commitments as a single characteristic. A couple's belief that they are committed is more highly predictive of the length of the relationship than any other factors involved.

■ Betrothal (engagement to marry) is a customary and public statement of commitment. Expectations concerning betrothal differ in various societies, ranging from those who expect the partners (and especially the bride-to-be) to be virginal, to those who consider marriage necessary only when couples want to have a child.

■ Formal engagement as a preliminary to marriage appears to be declining somewhat in the United States. Some believe that cohabitation before marriage is being substituted for engagement by many couples. (Others believe that the cost of a diamond engagement ring has been a discouraging factor.)

■ The wedding is an even more definite statement of commitment—both socially and legally. Despite the informality of the courtship process among a growing number of couples, today's couples have weddings that are still usually traditional and often not unlike those of their parents and their grandparents.

■ Getting married implies both legal and extralegal contracts that vary from state to state. The extralegal ones vary also from couple to couple. An example of a part of the marriage customs followed by most American couples by tacit agreement is the changing of the wife's last name to that of her husband. Some couples may make this (or some other agreement about surnames) explicit; a few may put their agreement in writing. It is doubtful that many courts would award damages for breach of such an agreement.

Glossary

Annulment A court order declaring that what was assumed to be a marriage is not legal or valid because the participants were not competent to marry, because one deceived the other about an important fact, because coercion was used, and so forth.

Assortativeness The probability that particular persons select friends or mates from particular population categories or aggregates; the notion that one does not have an equal likelihood of marrying everyone in a population; non-randomness.

Betrothal The mutual promise partners make to marry each other or to live as husband and wife at some future time; often used synonymously with the word *engagement* in the United States.

Differential association The concept that a given person will associate with only a relatively small number of others and that relationships with those persons will vary in frequency, duration, priority, and intensity.

Empathy The quality of *understanding* how another thinks or feels; differs from *sympathy,* which *is* feeling what another feels.

Endogamy The practice of marrying within socially defined boundaries such as within particular religious or racial groups.

Exogamy The practice of marrying outside specific social boundaries such as kin groups.

Functional involvement Social contact resulting from the organization of people's individual activities, such as that arising from common work space or needs to obtain information, goods, or services by one person from others.

Homogamy Similarity of objective characteristics (social class, education, race, ethnic group, religion, interests, values, and so forth) between partners selected.

Imprinting A learning mechanism, highly resistant to modification and occurring at critical periods soon after birth, by which a newborn animal forms a bond to its species. Imprinting is critical to later species-specific behavior.

Interactional disqualification The process in which certain individuals are judged unsuitable for further association because their interaction is uncomfortable or counterproductive in some way.

Interlocutory period A legally required waiting period between the time a divorce action is filed and the time the divorce can become final.

Prenuptial or **antenuptial** Pertaining to any acts or contracts between two betrothed persons prior to their marriage; also used to describe anything pertaining to a couple before they marry.

Propinquity Geographical or physical nearness.

Psychodynamic Referring to the constantly changing psychological system underlying human behavior; the explanation of feelings or behaviors on the basis of a person's interpretation of his or her experiences, especially early life experiences.

Repetition compulsion A term used by Freud to describe the actions of those persons who seem compelled to repeat the same behavior over and over in the vain hope that the next time the results will be different.

Stereotype A belief that all the people who have a given characteristic are alike in a much broader set of characteristics.

A good marriage is
one which allows
for change and
growth in the
individuals and in
the way they
express their love.

—Pearl Buck, *To
My Daughters,
with Love*

7 · Being Married

As two individuals enter a marriage and begin to share their lives together, their psychological, social, and cultural differences are blended in a way that makes their marriage unique. In the past couples usually had the roles of husband and wife spelled out clearly. Today's couples have more choices and, for this reason, are more likely to have a marriage tailored to their unique needs, desires, and expectations. Communication is central to the way that couples learn to live harmoniously with each other. As two partners communicate, they share a system of interaction that undergoes changes as they progress through the stages of the life cycle, sharing emotions, children, good times, and troubled times.

"And they lived happily ever after" is the positive and romanticized view of life after the wedding. The transition to marriage is expected to be a happy one. For most couples, fortunately, it is, although usually not without some turbulence along the way. The negotiations necessary to blend two individuals into a couple almost certainly pose some basic dilemmas and create some problems.

Every marriage consists of two unique individuals. Each brings to the relationship a history of experiences, memories, and ways of behaving. Unique personalities have been formed since birth and have been influenced by genetic, physiological, psychological, social, and cultural factors. As a result, each partner brings personal meanings and unique ways of looking at life to the relationship. Individuals cannot be held personally accountable for their racial characteristics, their heights, or the colors of their eyes, even though one cannot deny that these and other genetically determined qualities—inherited diabetes, for example—may profoundly affect their self-concepts and their interactions with others.

There may be physiological differences in energy levels between two individuals in a relationship. There is also the well-known phenomenon of the

"morning person" married to the "night person." No two biological "time clocks" are quite the same, and some are so out of phase that two people may have serious problems trying to adjust to each other. Someone who likes to stay up late and who wakes up slowly in the morning may not understand a partner who gets up early but who grows sleepy early in the evening. It may be difficult for both to realize that these different energy patterns are interwoven with each individual's physiology—perhaps even genetically based—and are not totally a matter of will, even though they appear to be modifiable.

The psychological, social, and cultural uniquenesses of each member of a relationship are equally complex, beginning with the difference in gender, which is usually defined on genetic and physiological bases but which is also heavily influenced by social learning. Uniquenesses also lie in the heritages individuals bring from their family backgrounds, their communities, their peers, and their other sources of social and cultural learning.

All the traits, mannerisms, thoughts, and feelings that go into a unique human being make up what psychologists and sociologists refer to as "the person." Although there is no one agreed-on definition of "the person" or "the self," there is general agreement that each man and each woman has a concept of his or her uniqueness. Relating two of these distinct "selves" is the task of the transition to marriage.

Individuality and Marriage

No one remembers the early months of life clearly, but obviously they existed. Our minds and bodies have accomplished a great deal of business prior to our earliest memories, and much of that business affects our later lives. This notion is important because it suggests that from birth we have thoughts and particularly feelings that we may not understand. For instance, we may have feelings about our mothers long before we have any cognitive concept of "mother." Even in adulthood one may have physiological reactions to the physical presence of his or her mother without rational or intellectual insight into these feelings. Despite an apparent lack of understanding of what is happening to them, children do grow in these early months in awareness of themselves as unique and separate from others. This awareness is the beginning of the development of the **self-concept**.

Everyone has a mental picture of himself or herself. Part of this picture deals with specific traits—his or her eyes are brown, he or she has flat feet, he or she is intelligent, and so forth. People also have global estimates of themselves by which they compare their sense of overall worth or **self-esteem** with that of others. People have feelings about their specific traits: "I hate being shy," or "It makes me feel good to know that I am intelligent." They also have feelings about their global selves—pride and shame.

People like to think their behaviors are in harmony with their evaluations of themselves. Thus people seem to feel uncomfortable when their traits or behaviors—or, especially, others' reactions to them—do not match their pictures of themselves. Being "put down" by others—especially by those one loves—is painful; being highly overestimated by others can be embarrassing.

The identity and feelings of self-sufficiency of adults are important determinants of how they will live and love. Any relationships into which two adults enter can be no healthier than the two "selves" involved. Erik Erikson, who has written extensively on the concept of the "self"—recognizing that each person has many facets that correspond to the various relationships and situations that he or she meets in a lifetime—says:

> What the "I" reflects on when it sees or contemplates the body, the personality, and the roles to which it is attached for life—not knowing where it was before or will be after—are the various selves which make up their composite self. There are constant and often shock-like transitions between these selves: consider the nude-body self in the dark or suddenly exposed in the light; consider the clothed self among friends or in the company of higher-ups or lower-downs; consider the just-awakened drowsy self or the one stepping refreshed out of the surf or the one overcome by retching and fainting; the body-self in sexual excitement or in a rage; the competent self and the impotent one; the one on horseback, the one in the dentist's chair, and the one chained and tortured—by men who say "I." It takes, indeed, a healthy personality for the "I" to be able to speak out of all of these conditions in such a way that at any given moment it can testify to a reasonably coherent self.[1]

Others who have attempted to define the self focus on a "core-self" that remains essentially the same over time and that gives stability and continuity to an individual's personality. This core has been referred to by sociologist Ralph Turner as the "true self"—a subjectively held sense that people have of who and what they really are.[2]

Adulthood has been described as that stage of a person's life in which he or she has achieved a sense of self-sufficiency. This includes the ability to be one's own person, to function on one's own, and to enjoy the experience of autonomy. Marital therapists believe that this sense of identity is a vital ingredient in whether or not an individual will be successful in his or her intimate relationships.[3,4] Psychologist Laura Singer writes:

> In the early stages of marriage, couples inevitably discover certain things that can be very distressing. I often hear the dismayed reactions of people the first time they realize that they and their partners are separate individuals. Being dissimilar creates anxiety, and it usually stems from the unconscious sense that, "If we love each other, we should be the same. And if we're different, then something's wrong. Maybe we don't love each other."[5]

Until the sense of identity and the feeling of being able to depend on oneself develop, it is unlikely that a man or woman is capable of a truly intimate adult relationship. Until there is a sense of being separate and self-sufficient, there are barriers to the kind of intimacy that successful, sustained relationships need.

The barriers to being close to another are usually left over from childhood. As children, we are necessarily dependent and, consequently, extraordinarily vulnerable. This vulnerability often subjects children to fears of abandonment by those on whom they must depend. Even when children are content in their relationships with adults, these relationships are not ordinarily established by choice. Instead, from a child's perspective, adults must be present in order for children to survive. It is terrifying for children to imagine being abandoned by those who care for them—usually their parents. There is the pain of longing and deprivation that thoughts of rejection bring. The idea of separateness of any kind—physical or emotional—becomes frightening. In adults the fear of abandonment may surface from time to time and, if allowed to become too important, may interfere in relationships. Excessive demands on others for a total fusion with them hinder or prevent true intimacy.

The yearning for sameness and unity with another is a distorted concept that many people attach to the notions of love and marriage. Psychologists believe that the desire to "be as one" with a loved one is an attempt by those who have not achieved comfortable separation from their parents to relive the dependency, security, and warmth of the early mother-child relationship, if it was a good one. If it was not, then it is urgent for the new partner to replace feelings of rejection and neglect with feelings of security and to search for what was missing in the new relationship. Either way, the expectations of how a partner will fulfill needs, wants, and expectations is unrealistic and puts severe strains on the relationship. Striving to be the same denies the individuality of both partners and confuses the notion of intimacy with that of too much "togetherness" or sameness.[6]

For most children, a time comes when they usually—as young adults—separate themselves from their parents and establish their autonomy. This is a gradual process marked by adolescent struggle to redefine boundaries of the self and to discover ways to live separately from parents. This period is marked by intervals of distancing from "home base" that alternate with returns for emotional and financial refueling. At the end of this period, the adult personality emerges as a product of the successes and failures of childhood and adolescence.

The adult personality is characterized by greater security and integration and a readiness to establish intimacy with others. As one study on adult identity concludes:

> . . . *people must first begin to feel more secure in their identities; they then become able to establish intimacy with themselves (in their inner lives) and with others. This is the case both in friendship and eventually in a love-based*

mutually satisfying sexual relationship. In addition to establishing a mutually satisfying sexual relationship, the issues in establishing intimacy with another person involve learning to share financial goals, ideas, friends, and emotions. It is the successful establishment of this sharing that enables one to achieve intimacy. When people cannot enter wholly into an intimate relationship because of the fear of losing their identities, they may develop a sense of isolation.[7]

Unfortunately, some persons never have the chance to develop a sense of separateness. Those who marry young—in their teens or early twenties—often move directly from dependence on their parents to dependence on a partner who may also be less than autonomous. Neither of them may have had time to learn to depend on himself or herself. Once married, some may cling to each other, full of anxiety about being alone and giving each other room to be alone. Others may begin to feel trapped, as though they have missed some freedom that it is now too late to capture.

Some newly married persons experience a feeling of having been "engulfed." There is a terror that vulnerability and total togetherness will mean a surrender of the budding self. The very word *surrender* can cause acute anxiety in a man or woman who lacks a solid sense of identity. For such a person the only way to survive seems to be to resist intimacy out of the fear of being swallowed up. If both partners fear being engulfed by each other's needs and desires for closeness, they may view each other alternately as demanding or clinging and then as emotionally and physically distant. If only one partner avoids the vulnerability of intimacy, the other often experiences a chasing game—the more frustrated and distressed he or she becomes, the more the other runs away.

The fear of being engulfed and the fear of abandonment may seem at first glance to be opposites, but both actually stem from the same lack of inner self-confidence and sense of identity. Both are the result of a fear of true intimacy—one that intimacy will devour the insecure "self" and the other that the vulnerability that accompanies intimacy is a possible prelude to abandonment. Both feelings point to the fact that one cannot be intimate with another person unless one is secure enough to risk vulnerability.

Fears of vulnerability adversely affect the quality of the interpersonal experiences of those who have a poorly defined sense of self. Psychiatrist William Meissner has said of such individuals:

The poorly defined self establishes a relationship of dependence upon the other which tends to have a life and death quality. It is as though life and existence depend on the attachment to the important other. Often this attachment has a quality of hostile dependence to it, the "can't live with you, can't live without you" syndrome which is so familiar to clinicians.

As the person with a well differentiated and individuated identity enters into a relationship, he/she is able to enter into, share, and participate freely in the emotional life that takes place between and around the marital partners.[8]

Meeting Individual Needs in Marriage

A *need*, by definition, is something a person must have to stay healthy and sane. It is necessary and compelling. As noted in Chapter 4 on love and attraction, all human beings share basic physical needs: food, drink, sleep, elimination, and air. In addition, every individual has personal emotional needs. Some are common to nearly everyone, while others are unique. Recognition—having one's self-image validated by others—is thought to be an almost universal need, for example. To be accepted by those who matter and to be loved and cared for are also basic needs for nearly everyone. Needs that are less widely shared may originate from the different genetic or physiological backgrounds of a particular individual or from psychological, social, or cultural differences between his or her experience and that of others. As a result, what may be indispensable for one person may be less urgent for another. For example, some individuals need a certain amount of privacy or room to be alone with their thoughts and activities. They run out of "emotional space" and need time for themselves. Without room to recoup on a regular basis, they become upset and depressed and function very poorly. Carlfred Broderick has observed that "as emotional space approaches zero, one's repertoire of social responses is reduced to two: fighting or running."[9] Others do not need to be alone much at all, and some even find it stressful to be alone. They eagerly seek out company and often have little understanding of those who must have blocks of time by themselves to function adequately. As with so many other issues new couples face, how much privacy each needs must be defined, and some provision for it made—perhaps a compromise if their needs are very different.

Some needs can be met in an independent fashion—eating, sleeping, being free to make decisions—but some can be met only by another person. Affection, emotional support, and companionship require not only another person but a very special one at that. Reliance on another to meet such needs is the basis for dependency. The more one person has to have from a particular other, the greater the dependency. We have found that a great many couples are drawn to each other—and often stay together—because they become so mutually dependent that they believe that they could not survive apart. This may not be a problem if their relationship is generally a good one. Occasionally, however, couples are bound in mutual misery by their dependency. Each is afraid to let the other go.

Each individual brings his or her own set of needs to a relationship and hopes that a chosen partner will help to satisfy at least some of these needs. The amount of satisfaction a relationship brings is determined by (1) how well both partners meet each other's needs and (2) how much freedom their relationship allows both of them to meet their own needs. Self-analysis—finding out what one's needs actually are—is an important part of an individual's search for his or her self-image. The psychologist Abraham Maslow has proposed that needs can be identified by focusing on whether the absence of something in an individual's life causes him or her to have a chronic feeling of dissatisfaction, anxiety, or deprivation.[10] Satisfied persons are believed not to experience this kind of craving. Those who are not content in the deepest human needs—love, for example, or respect—may be frustrated, constantly seeking fulfillment, or may become defeated. Many of the disappointments registered in relationships stem from beliefs that needs that *ought* to be met by one's partner are not being met. Even the most loving partners may fail to meet each other's needs either because these needs have never been clearly defined or because one partner or both are unable to meet them.

Wants and Expectations

Although needs are basic and necessary to physical and psychological well-being, "wants" or desires represent a longing for something beyond fulfillment of needs. To be able to distinguish needs from wants is a significant step in self-analysis but often a rather difficult one. Because wants are often intense in nature, implying a strong motivation to attain the desired object or condition, they are frequently interpreted as essential to an individual's well-being and happiness.

Confusing needs and wants is a common failing. In therapy sessions, we often hear statements such as "I need to earn more money to feel successful," or "I need my husband to be more sexual with me," or "She needs me to tell her that I think she's beautiful." In each case, it is doubtful whether "need" is the real issue; more likely, needs are being confused with "wants." Just as with needs, each person brings to a relationship his or her own desires in life, and the health of the relationship may well depend largely on how well one's desires are met by the other. This is not to suggest that anyone ever gets everything he or she desires, but rather that a person's wishes must be acknowledged as an integral part of the self.

Not only do persons often fail to clarify to themselves the difference between their wants and their needs, but they also often fail to understand their partners' distinctions. One partner may project his or her own classification onto the other, believing that it is correct or proper for everyone. For instance, a man who *needs* validation of his sexual attractiveness to maintain his self-esteem may be treated by his wife as if that need were merely a selfish wish on his part. The same wife may *need* new experiences for personal growth in order to maintain her self-esteem, only to have her husband treat her need to grow as a selfish wish—perhaps an improper or frivolous one at that.

Along with everyone's needs and wants, there are also expectations about how others will behave, about one's own behavior in a given situation, and about the likely progress of each relationship. To have an expectation is to count on something happening (or to assume that something will not happen). Expectations are products of past experiences, values, goals, and dreams. They range from modest to monumental, from realistic to unrealistic. Unmet expectations are a common source of stress and frequently result in feelings of disappointment, hurt, and anger.

Psychologists use the term *scripts* as a label for the patterns of expectations that individuals carry with them into each relationship.[11,12] When the relationship is a marriage, the scripts are often based on the marriages of the partners' parents. Broderick points out that basing a marriage script on the marriage of parents "may be true even when the parental marriage style is consciously rejected in favor of a different kind of relationship. We may indeed achieve much of what we aim for; yet the parental model has a habit of sneaking up in the most unexpected places."[13]

Family therapist Leonard Friedman has devised an effective way to enlighten couples who do not realize how greatly their expectations are affected by their parents' marriages.[14] Each partner is encouraged to imagine a marriage between the father of one and the mother of the other. Through exploration of how these two people might get along in this fantasized marriage, and what it would be like to be a child in such a home, scripts often become more obvious. Often each spouse comes to a much better understanding of the other when he or she has gained insight into the other's script and into the influence of each set of parents.

Certain issues may be so basic to each person's script and, therefore, to his or her expectations for marriage, that one of them may jeopardize the marital commitment. Marital therapist Richard Stuart calls these central issues **core symbols**.[15] What may be a core symbol to one partner may seem relatively unimportant to another. For instance, Stuart cites the wearing of a wedding ring as a core symbol of marriage to countless men and women. Many would never consider removing the ring for any purpose short of terminating the marrriage once it has been put on during the wedding ceremony. Others, however, remove their wedding rings with no thought of violating their commitments; some even have more than one wedding ring and may wear them interchangeably or may not wear a ring at all except on special occasions. None of these patterns of behavior is objectively more right or wrong than any of the others. However, core symbols are seldom viewed objectively. If two people feel very differently about such a basic issue, conflict can easily arise that is not readily resolved.

Expectations are often fantasies that others will behave in ways that they have never agreed to do or that they may even be unaware are expected of them. These fantasies may attempt to minimize differences between the partners that one or both of those in a relationship do not want to accept. By expecting certain behaviors and then registering disappointment when they do not occur, a person may hope to ensure that, next time, the anticipated action

will actually take place. Expectations may even be translated into demands that the partner change.

Sometimes, persons believe that marriage will change their partners in specific ways—often to resemble *their* parents or some ideal couple. Such beliefs may be reinforced by platitudes, such as, "She'll settle down once she's married." The expectations that flirting, or drinking, or selfishness, or gambling, or "workaholism," or any other characteristic of a partner will change automatically and effortlessly during a wedding ceremony are, of course, fantasy. People will change, but a wedding alone is not a particularly good predictor of the kind, direction, or degree of those changes.

Many of the conflicts that arise in the first months of marriage can be traced to one or both partners' expectations of what marriage should or should not be. Most couples, however, do not share a uniform set of expectations. Consequently, both partners may have many unfulfilled expectations, which are likely to lead to marital disillusionment. Sometimes partners fix their expectations of each other during their courtship period. Often each partner has "put a best foot forward" to attract the other before marriage, and it is impossible to maintain that unnatural posture permanently. Once married, they may "relax," believing that courtship behavior is no longer necessary or even appropriate. Untidy habits reappear, little courtesies disappear.

In the earlier discussion of attraction and love, "idealization" was discussed—how we may not see the loved one as clearly during courtship as we do when we settle into a day-to-day existence with him or her. Unless the couple has lived together (and often not even then), there may be considerable disillusionment when both partners exhibit daily living habits (not picking up clothes, leaving wet towels on the floor, and so forth). These behaviors do not meet expectations that the two persons may have of married life.

The phrase "the honeymoon is over" often means that the unrealistic belief that one has married an individual with few faults (or that he or she will quickly change those behaviors that are annoying) is being reexamined. The "real" selves of both partners begins to come into focus and may not be accepted readily by either of them. A tug-of-war often ensues to get one partner to change to fit the pattern of expectations of the other. Unfortunately, some couples never get beyond this struggle; when they are unsuccessful in molding each other into a "suitable" pattern, they begin to think of divorce. The highest percentage of divorces occurs during the first few years after marriage.[16] Many divorce experts attribute this fact in large measure to the many unfulfilled expectations of the couple.[17]

Sometimes partners go into a relationship without fully understanding their own expectations. They somehow expect their partners to be mind readers who can figure it all out. If communication between them is difficult, expectations may not come out in the open until a residue of hurt, disgust, or anger has been built up. Such feelings, which are usually clues to unfulfilled expectations, can serve as paths to understanding when they do arise. For example, if one feels hurt or disappointed by a partner's behavior, there usually was an expectation that something different "should" have occurred. The question "What did I expect?" followed by "Did my partner know what I expected?" and "Did my partner agree with my expectation?" often points to a misunderstanding or to a disagreement about appropriate behavior. Partners often prove to be poor at mind reading, and once they discover each other's expectations, they may lack the resources to meet them should they want to do so. A great deal of conflict might be avoided if the way was opened early in a relationship for a discussion of each partner's preconceived notions of how the marriage should function.

Summary

■ Every marriage is composed of two individuals who are unique genetically, physiologically, psychologically, socially, and culturally. One's concept of one's uniqueness constitutes the "self." The relating of two unique "selves" is the process of transition from singlehood to marriage.

■ Often couples marry before one or both of the partners have a sense of identity separate from their families of origin. Marital therapists believe that this individuality and sense of identity is a vital ingredient in a successful marriage.

■ In the absence of a feeling of self-sufficiency, there is often a yearning for sameness and fusion with a partner that stifles the growth of both mates. The insecurity of dependency may cause a fear of abandonment or being engulfed by the intimacy.

- Since no two people are identical, each partner will bring individual needs, desires, and expectations to the relationship. The amount of satisfaction a relationship brings is determined by how well both partners meet each other's needs as well as by how conducive the relationship is to allowing each of them to meet his or her own needs.

- Expectations often are unknown to each person unless the partner fails to measure up. Hurt, anger, or disappointed feelings are often clues that one expected something that did not happen or did not expect something that did occur. Some expectations are known to one partner but not to the other. Since most human beings are poor mind readers, unfulfilled expectations are common. Expectations are often unrealistic since they are based on "idealization" of oneself, of one's partner, or of married life.

Communication

Communication in marriage has received a great deal of attention as an important determinant of how two people will get along with each other. In fact, studies of marital adjustment have indicated that "quality communication is central to a quality marriage."[18] Although there is probably no such thing as perfect communication, some guidelines to quality communication have been gleaned from several research studies and from family therapists.[19,20]

One of the most important factors in quality communication is the degree of *openness* that exists between two partners. The amount of self-disclosure and genuineness in intimate relationships has been shown to have a significant effect on the levels of satisfaction that partners feel with their relationship.[21] In general, the more open the two partners are with each other, the greater the satisfaction reported. The openness must be mutual, however. If only one partner offers personal and private information and the other does not (and perhaps is not even receptive to such disclosures), the relationship is not enhanced.

Openness allows a person to get to know another's likes, dislikes, thoughts, and feelings. It is basic to interpersonal understanding. This mutual understanding and awareness that each partner has of himself or herself and of the partner is an essential ingredient in marital satisfaction.[22]

An important aspect of openness is, of course, *honesty*. There is no doubt that for good communication to exist, the information exchanged must be believable. There is clear evidence that under most circumstances honesty and frankness are forces for good. Honesty helps clarify feelings, avert misunderstanding, and dissipate resentments. With so much emphasis on full and free communication as the basis for a satisfying relationship, it is easy to see how total honesty has come to be seen as a worthy goal.

There are times, however, when total "truth telling" may not be in the best interests of the relationship. Frankness may be a mask for hostility or for a need to "dump" one's fears or guilt or to seek reassurance for one's own opinions. In short, there may be such a thing as too much honesty—the kind that can cause conflicts and harm relationships. Family therapist Paul Watzlawick puts it well when he says: ". . . a large part of communication consists in knowing what one is *not* supposed to say, not supposed to think, not supposed to see, not supposed to hear."[23]

In a study made some years ago, couples reported that they felt the biggest difference between good and bad communication was whether a partner tended to say things that would be better left unsaid.[24] Honesty appears to be a two-way street, involving both the giving and the seeking of information but not the frankness that is intended to hurt or to bolster oneself at the other's expense.

Family therapist Richard Stuart uses the concept of "measured honesty" to describe the balance between honesty and frankness-for-the-sake-of-being-frank. He cautions couples first to ask themselves whether what they have to say will be *constructive* to the relationship and, second, whether it is *necessary* to a better understanding between them.[25]

In every successful relationship some things probably go unsaid in the interest of getting along more harmoniously. Criticism usually falls into this category. Successful married couples have usually learned to use criticism sparingly and never to hide behind "this is for your own good." Although the intent of criticism may be to help one's partner, it often is read as disapproval or even rejection. Apparent disapproval can lead to feelings of alienation and lack of support rather than to a sense that the criticism was "for one's own good." The implications of feeling rejected have been documented by family therapists who link **disconfirmation** and feelings of alienation with disturbances in marriages and families.[26]

Advice about honesty from marital therapists can be summarized as follows:

- Before you volunteer information or respond to a question, ask yourself: Is what I am about to say really true? Is it useful for the other person to know it? Will there be a more appropriate time and place to make this statement? Am I saying this to put myself "one up"?

- Be as certain as you can about the other person's emotional capacity to handle a frank answer or comment. In general, someone who is unwilling to level with you is unlikely to want you to respond frankly to him or her. At certain times or in certain situations, a person may be more sensitive or vulnerable than at other times.

- Be sensitive to the other person's values, and talk about matters you know are important to him or her with particular accuracy, gentleness, and tact.[27]

As surely as disapproval is correlated with unhappiness in marriage, endorsement and acceptance are correlated with happiness and satisfaction in the relationship.[28] This is not to imply that approval always works for healthy marital functioning. For example, approval that is not honestly felt—perhaps given to avoid an argument or for fear of hurting the partner's feelings—may set up an atmosphere of disconfirmation. Honest approval says, "You are right" or "I like you." Disconfirmation communicates, "You cannot handle what I might say" or even "You do not exist."[29] What is perhaps most important for quality communication and for marital satisfaction is that both partners agree on the definitions each holds about the other and about the relationship, whether approving or disapproving. For communication to be a quality experience, it is vital to have what one is, what one thinks, what one feels, what one does, and what one says confirmed by another. Experts on marriage emphasize that the amount of agreement about each other's good qualities couples have is predictive of their degree of intimacy.[30,31]

Having partners agree with each one's own self-concept and behavior is called **mutual validation**. It is a singularly important aspect of positive human interaction and of individual psychological well-being. Studies of communication indicate that marriages in which there are mutual validations have more realistic expectations and better communication.[32] As reported in one survey of marital communication, mutual validation "permeates all segments of the partners' lives together. It determines their style in managing such stock marital concerns as conflict, . . . decision making, . . . and affiliation."[33] When two people feel confident that their partners see them in the same ways that they see themselves, responses to each other are bound to be more appropriate and communication more open.

Most communication experts believe that the essential element in clear and open communication is not only in the actual words spoken but also in feelings and in the intent of the messages. In other words, it is not only what two people say to each other, but also how and why they say it. Couples in an intimate relationship attach personal meanings to both verbal and nonverbal behavior based on their experiences with each other over a period of time. These meanings may be quite independent of social and cultural meanings. The language with which they speak to each other is symbolic of their experiences together and provides a pool of meaning from which only they may draw. It is a unique combination of their individualities and of their interactions. They may "speak" without words—with only a glance, a smile, or a shrug of the shoulders. When two people have the same style (or recognize each other's meaning, if it is different), it increases comfort in the relationship and builds a foundation of security. It feels good to be understood. It is not so much a matter of what is discussed or even of how much a couple talk, although both are important. Instead, it is *how* they communicate that can make or break a relationship.

To facilitate mutual understanding, both partners must be aware—have a conscious recognition—of their interpersonal situation and must be able to *control the flow of communication* to produce constructive results. In other words, quality communication necessitates "the ability of marriage partners to control their communication rather than letting their communication control them."[34] Awareness results from the ability to listen actively and attentively. In a survey of marital therapists, it was reported that listening and being receptive to a partner's messages are vital to good communication and are important determinants of marital satisfaction.[35]

Listening is an active process, one that requires concentration. Unless both partners listen actively to each other, there can be no dialogue. Listening also requires that one be able to give "feedback" on what has been said. That is, the listener should be able to sum up what the speaker has just said, to the satisfaction of both. A recent study of couples who were having communication difficulties reported that the most frequent problem was that neither partner really listened to the other.[36] Common faults in listening are interrupting constantly, not paying attention, hearing selectively only the parts that one wants to hear, picking out points to debate rather than waiting for the complete message, and becoming emotional so that concentration is blocked.[37]

Because listening is often poor, *misinterpretation* is a common occurrence in communication. Misinterpretation, however, is just as often the result of the way the message is sent as of the way it is received. Quality communication depends equally on each partner's capacity to send and receive information. Communication problems often arise because of the vagueness with which a message is conveyed. Couples often report difficulty in conveying their ideas and, especially, their feelings to each other accurately. Sometimes, of course, the vagueness may be intentional—an effort to keep from communicating some message that may be controversial. At other times it may be the result of uncertainty on the part of the speaker. The listener can often help by encouraging his or her partner to fill in the gaps in the messages and by providing an understanding of the partner's difficulty in doing so.

Listening with empathy means that one tries to put oneself in another person's shoes and to understand what he or she is feeling. Several research studies have pointed to the positive effect that the ability to empathize has on marital communication.[38,39] Empathic listening shows a genuine interest and concern for what others mean: an empathic listener usually has to get beyond words or gestures to discover the *intent* of the message. This involves checking out assumptions and avoiding attributing meanings to what another says without trying to discover the other's intended meanings.

The intent of a *message* sometimes may be explicit and clear, but often it is only implicit and may also be ambiguous in comparison with the spoken words. For example, one partner may say, "You always choose the right words to say to make a person feel good." This could be a sincere compliment, or if said in anger, could be a cutting comment.

Meanings implied by and inferred from a message are often more important than the actual words or gestures. The simple message "I love you" not only has different meanings to different persons, but its meaning also may change through time for one person as a result of life-course experiences. Although intense interaction with another person over a long period of time is helpful in achieving shared meaning, it is no guarantee that two people will always understand each other. It may even stand in the way of consensus, if, for example, one partner clings to a meaning that is ten years out of date, no matter how valid the meaning may have been at that time.

"Talking about talking" is the way many family therapists describe the need to discuss meanings behind words or nonverbal behavior. The term **meta-communication** has been coined to label the messages that are often implicit in overt statements or questions.[40] Behind the actual words may be an intent or a meaning not always obvious to the listener. Two people who communicate well learn to read each other's implicit messages as they develop the ability to understand, for example, a tone of voice, a body posture, a choice of words that conveys the precise definition or intensity of the interchange.

Confusion is the typical symptom of misunderstood meaning and can, from this perspective, be a useful step in the communication process. It signals that the partners are conscious of something awry and of possible differences in understandings. This awareness is better than the assumption that an incorrectly understood message is understood, which can lead to inappropriate action. Studies have shown that couples who are more satisfied with their relationships with each other are better able to make the adjustments necessary to cut through confusion and misunderstandings. They more frequently feel understood by their mates because they know how to get their messages across.[41,42]

Styles of Communication

It has been suggested that "the ability to establish and sustain a smooth and easy pattern of interaction" is the essential element of quality communication.[43] Couples develop rules governing their dialogues with each other that may have the potential to make communication either more or less effective. Eventually these patterns become predictable and stable. Such rules are the result of the couple's continued interaction with each other and are related to their reported level of marital satisfaction. If the rules facilitate communication, the satisfaction level is high. If the rules impede communication, the satisfaction level is affected negatively.[44]

One analysis of types of basic communication styles among couples described three: complementary, symmetrical, and parallel.[45] It is believed that although most couples may use all three, there is a tendency to favor one of these modes of communication.

In the complementary communication style, each partner plays counterpoint to the other. For example, one may be verbal and expressive, but the other may be a person of few words. If both were as talkative as the one or as quiet as the other, their pattern would be symmetrical. A symmetrical pattern is often seen

Drawing by Levin; © 1978 The New Yorker Magazine, Inc.

in couples who compete with each other for center stage, each trying to outtalk the other. This may be their way of trying to influence each other or to win arguments. Members of silent couples, too, may use the silence to maximize their control of the situation.

The third style, parallel communication, is more flexible and emphasizes situational adaptability. In other words, those who adopt this as a favored pattern relate in a manner that seems most appropriate for the particular situation in which they are communicating. This quality is believed to be important to marital satisfaction; flexibility in both style and content is a factor in what couples consider good communication.[46]

Four different styles of communication have been described by other communication specialists. Each has a characteristic set of intentions behind it.

1. *Style I:* A casual, chatty conversation that is meant to keep things light and friendly. Many couples use this style to check in with each other at the end of the day or to talk sociably over breakfast or dinner. Often there is little content and few feelings are involved.

2. *Style II:* The intention of this style is to persuade or to give directions. Conversation is punctuated with the words *should* and *ought.* This style often is judgmental, blaming, and filled with unsolicited advice about how the other might behave differently. Often this style is high in emotional content.

3. *Style III:* This style is often speculative and explores alternatives. Many questions are asked in a search for thoughts and feelings; the implication is that others will ask questions too. Unlike Style II, which has "the" answers, Style III still is searching.

4. *Style IV:* This style emphasizes sharing of thoughts. Compared with Style III, less tentativeness and more personal statements are involved. A problem-solving approach is evident, which is explicit, responsive, accepting, and aware—based on listening to the other.[47]

Style IV is viewed as the most fruitful for the development and maintenance of a compatible relationship because this style allows for two people to resolve differences. In this type of interchange, couples share feelings and emotions and reveal their perceptions of themselves.

Another communication-style typology also defines four communication styles: controlling, conventional, speculative, and contactful.[48]

1. *Controlling:* Persons who exhibit this style discourage any disagreement and seek to have their own way. Often they show little awareness of their partner's opinions; even if they do, being right and "winning" is more important to them than affection or having a good relationship. Power in all decisions and issues is paramount for a person who is classified as controlling. Implicit is lack of trust of the partner's judgment or capabilities, or sometimes lack of respect for the partner's personal dignity.

2. *Conventional:* This style is similar to Style I or Style II described earlier. Those who communicate in this manner give the appearance of talking, but the topics are superficial and do not risk exploring issues that may be emotional or controversial.

3. *Speculative:* This type involves exploration of issues and openness to new ideas. This kind of person, however, is unable to self-disclose readily and may spend a good deal of time asking questions of the partner to avoid talking about himself or herself.

4. *Contactful:* Persons who exhibit this style not only are interested in their partners' viewpoints but are also self-revealing. They are similar to Style IV communicators mentioned earlier in that they emphasize sharing of thoughts. This type, followed by the speculative style, was ranked as the most positive communication style in the research that defined these four types.

Some couples seem to start out with a similarity of communication style. This may, in fact, have been an important reason that they were drawn together in the first place. Other successful couples have had to work at developing a good communication style because they have not always understood each other. Some couples seem to expect little communication with each other and are not disappointed by their lack of communication. Others discuss everything and would be unhappy any other way. Dissatisfaction evidently is experienced only when expectations are not met.[49] Good marital communication, then, is based on mutuality and shared understandings that allow couples to experience intimacy and security with each other. Communication expert Barbara Montgomery believes that this process is necessary to each couple's definition of marriage:

> *Within the marital dyad spouses are constantly sharing information about their individual conceptualizations of the relationship and then negotiating a mutually acceptable relationship definition. This process of collaboration results in a "custom-made" definition of marriage that is unique to the individuals involved.*[50]

Sexual Communication

We have said that communication occurs whenever two or more people arrive at the mutual conclusion that they have achieved the same idea or the same feelings about an idea as a result of their interaction. Of course, no one can ever know whether two persons' ideas and feelings are really the same because there is no way to observe another person's ideas or feelings directly. All that can be observed directly are behaviors or bodily changes believed to result from ideas and feelings—what a person says, what he or she does, what happens to his or her body. Some words, an action, a blush, or a tear give clues to another's thoughts and feelings.

Sexual communication is a special kind of couple communication. It is different from personal sexual satisfaction, although the latter may facilitate good communication and also may be facilitated by it. For people with a high degree of sympathetic understanding about their mutual sexual activities, intimacy and love may be more effectively communicated by actions than by words.

Some couples who report that they communicate well in other areas of their lives may find talking about sex to be troublesome. Many couples seem hesitant to comment on a partner's sexual behavior and equally reticent to speak of their own desires. We can only speculate that problems in sexual communication may pose special problems because of the emotional content of such messages and because in our society "sex talk" has not been present in most families of origin. Serious inhibitions and a great deal of sensitivity often surround such issues.

It may be difficult for some women to understand the penetration of another person's body as a loving act, even though the same women can accept a growing fetus within them with a loving feeling. It may be difficult for some men to understand the wish to be penetrated and impregnated as loving. It is probably easier for both men and women to understand the giving and receiving of pleasure in orgasm as loving. It is often easier, therefore, to feel in touch with one another about sexual behaviors that lead to mutual satisfaction from day to day than to agree on whether or not there are differences between the deep underlying sexual urges of men and women.

How do those in close relationships go about increasing sexual intimacy through good communication? Four important areas common to all quality communication are also, we believe, crucial for sexual communication: signals, meanings, feelings, and roles.

Signals vary in clarity and accuracy. Verbal communication is at its best when words are clearly spoken and used with shared meaning. Nonverbal communication is most successful when touches can be felt, sighs can be heard, and frowns or smiles can be seen. Only half the responsibility lies with the one who signals. The intended receiver must also be listening, watching, paying attention, and recognizing the significance of the signals.

Getting signals straight may be the easiest step in communication in most situations; however, in highly emotional sexual interaction, although crucial, it is not always simple: many people will not ask such questions as "What did you say?" or "Did you touch me there on purpose?" or "Did you pull away just now?" To confirm, deny, or elaborate on signals appears to be difficult for many persons. Some couples seem to believe that they should intuitively know what the signals mean and that clarification should be unnecessary. Often, however, partners do not read each other very well. In working with couples, we have found that most can improve their sexual communication by learning to understand each other's signals. The assumption that one person naturally understands the other's signals is an important source of sexual difficulty.[51]

As discussed earlier, _meanings_ behind words or gestures must be mutually understood to facilitate good communication. This principle is equally true in sexual communication. What meaning is intended when a woman slips her hand inside a man's shirt or when she straightens his necktie? What meaning is intended when a man takes a shower and shaves before going to bed? Are the meanings the same for both persons?

One couple reported that they had difficulty understanding each other's signals until the husband figured out that when his wife said, "I'm going to bed now. Are you going to be long?" she meant she was interested in sex and wished he would turn off the television set and come to bed with her. He had never caught her meaning before and had always interpreted her question as meaning that she was tired and hoped he would not stay up too late or disturb her sleep when he finally did come to bed. Meanwhile, she had been feeling rejected.

Exploration of meanings sometimes reveals hidden agenda; the outcome is not always desirable. In the previous example, the woman might actually have been tired; if her husband had followed her to bed in hopes of having sex, she might have considered him just as insensitive for not knowing that she really meant to go to sleep.

Feelings almost always accompany a couple's sexual behavior with each other. Two people who can be open with each other about their feelings usually gain useful information for increasing sympathetic understandings and for facilitating sexual communication. In general, listening to another's description of his or her feelings and granting that person the right to have those feelings, whether they are agreeable or not, encourage sexual intimacy. Occasionally one partner or both may have negative feelings about their sexual lives with each other. As painful as it is to talk about these matters, keeping silent is often a greater barrier to improvement. Dishonesty also blocks intimacy, because it makes it very difficult, if not impossible, for partners to develop shared meanings. Feelings are not always logical, but they are real nonetheless. Talking about them often puts them in a perspective that can enable the couple to deal with them. Unspoken, they remain troublesome.

Finally, a part of sexual communication involves a consensus about the roles taken by the persons involved. Whenever a person makes a sexual statement or gesture, he or she is assuming the existence of some kind of relationship with the partner. By assuming a role, one necessarily projects a reciprocal role on the person with whom one is interacting. For example, a woman who believes that men should always be the initiators of sex projects this role onto her partner. If he does not initiate sex, she may be disappointed but, having defined her role as one who waits to be asked and his role as one who initiates, will not make any suggestion herself.

Consciousness of the role one is taking is vital to good sexual communication. It is also necessary to let one's partner know what is expected and to determine his or her own consciousness of role. If one's partner does not wish to play out the role as expected, a mutually acceptable one can often be negotiated. In sexual relationships one finds the roles of "teacher," "learner," "critic," "judge," "adventurer," "martyr," and so forth—and a long list of ways that each role can be played.

An index of good sexual communication is a mutual feeling of closeness and intimacy. The cues between two people may be subtle—just a touch or a word—but easily responded to. Sexual communication may well permeate all aspects of a couple's life together.[52]

Summary

■ Research on marital adjustment has emphasized that quality communication is central to the health of a marriage. Factors in quality communication are openness, honesty, confirmation, mutual validation, and control of the flow of communication.

■ Listening is as important as is sending messages. Listening with an ear to understanding is called empathy. Trying to discover the intent of a message and the meanings behind the message is essential if good communication is to occur.

■ The unique styles by which couples communicate with each other are governed by certain rules that are also unique to each couple. This process results in a "custom-made" definition of marriage. What is important is that the couple share meanings and understand each other's style of communication.

■ Sexual communication is one of the most intimate and often difficult kinds of interaction between couples. Sexual signals and their meanings are often vague, yet highly emotional. Roles taken by or assigned to sexual partners also play an important part in sexual communication.

Marriage Styles

The quality of marital relationships is a popular topic for research. The results have indicated that when two unique human beings marry, they form a system of interaction with each other based on how they communicate, what their expectations are, and how they behave in relationship to each other. Their system of relating may bring out either the best or the worst both in each other and in themselves. They may get along with each other very differently from the way that they relate to others because of the intensity and the meaning of their relationship. We often counsel couples who are successful in all their other social endeavors but are failing with each other. They are puzzled by their behavior with each other since they behave in such distressing ways with no one else. Clearly, marriage brings out behaviors that are unique to the relationship.

Family therapist David Kantor believes that each relationship has its own behavioral repertoires or patterns of actions and reactions that are "steering mechanisms" for the relationship. He describes these as *strategies* developed specifically for each marriage or for each family system. The strategies are called on for decision making, problem solving, and crisis resolution—for living and working together. Kantor refers to the particular configuration that each couple or each family works out as its *signature*.[53] No two marriages (and no two families) are ever exactly alike. One of the tasks of each couple and of each family becomes to "tailor" their own unique patterns and style of being together.

Compatibility is an important factor in the way members of a system work out their agreements. Compatibility is measured by the efficiency with which those who make up a system such as a marriage or a family interact. Values, interests, behaviors, and other facets of their individual styles of living must be accommodated. The more mutually acceptable the behaviors of people are, the more compatible they are said to be. Many couples start out and remain in considerable agreement, but other couples may grow either more alike or more different from each other as time passes. Perfect agreement is largely unattainable, of course, and might be dull if it were achieved. However, a fairly high level of compatibility is a major source of satisfaction in marriage and family living. Those whose relationships are burdened with marked differences in their philosophies about important areas of living together report considerably less satisfaction and marital happiness.[54]

Learning to live harmoniously and intimately with another person for a lifetime, sharing in all facets of life—finances, emotions, sex, children, illness, criteria for assessing success and failure—is perhaps the most challenging task we ever face. One of the leading family sociologists in the United States has said: "The most popular—and the roughest—contact sport in the country is not professional football; it is marriage."[55] Although this statement may sound a bit grim, many couples who have struggled through problems of marital adjustment—successfully or unsuccessfully—may nod in agreement.

The difficulties of marital adjustment and of working out a marital life-style are compounded by the fact that most marriage partners do not know each other as well as they believed they did when they got married. In one study of couples in both successful and unsuccessful marriages, it was reported that virtually everyone interviewed had faced at least one postnuptial revelation about his or her spouse's habits or personality that came as a surprise. Usually there were several such revelations.[56] Often these surprises would have been fairly obvious had both partners had their eyes open a little wider. But being in love caused them to see selectively and even to disregard or mislabel what they saw. "The end result," the authors state, "is that, in varying degrees, everyone marries a stranger."[57]

Our own bias is that not much can be done to insure that two people who marry will know all that they need to know about each other in order to accommodate right from the start. Even if they do, both will change with time, experience, maturity, and certainly with the addition of children. Just about the time two people feel comfortable and settled, something changes in one or both of them or in the external environment that affects their definitions of themselves, their partners, or their relationship.

The essence of compatible marriage styles is not only acceptance of the habits and personality traits of partners but also the ability to be flexible and to accommodate to change. As the life span increases, more years will be spent in marriages. It has been predicted that by the year 2050, half of all men will expect to live to be over seventy. If they are married in their early twenties to women a year or two younger than they, their expectation of life together could be fifty years or more. Any photograph album records the physical differences between couples in their early twenties and those same persons in their early seventies. Personality changes are developed just as gradually as wrinkles and grey hair but these cannot be caught by a camera and frozen at two moments in time. Common sense tells us that we cannot expect to act and think the same when we are constantly changing physically and encountering new experiences.

A great deal of research has suggested that adults go through "stages" just as children do: the venturesome but trying twenties, the occupationally oriented and family-building thirties, the "middle-age crises" of the forties and fifties, the adjustment to retirement and the end-of-life adjustments that come in later years.[58,59] When two people are married, these adult stages affect each partner just as much as do the external happenings in their lives.

In addition, family sociologists have suggested that marriages also have "stages" that together form what is termed the *marital life cycle*.[60] These are not likely to be developmental in the same way that individual life-cycle changes are but are accounted for by life-course events—the birth of the first child, the school-age years of one's children, and the departure of the last child (creating the "empty nest") for instance. Further examples may serve to illustrate the impact of certain stages on husbands' and wives' marriage styles and compatibility:

- Parents of young children frequently report a marked drop in the amount of time they spend conversing with each other and a similar decline in social and leisure activities after the birth of the first child.[61]

- Couple interests and couple activities fall off as a man or woman becomes more involved in a career.[62]

- A husband's satisfaction with marriage increases during the empty-nest period, but a wife's satisfaction decreases slightly at the beginning of that period and rises just before retirement.[63]

These findings are important for an understanding of marital life-styles. They indicate to some extent the impact of life-cycle stages on a couple's interaction patterns. There are ups and downs—biological, emotional, and psychological cycles—even within each stage. All marriages have peaks and valleys. This flow of highs and lows must be expected regardless of differences in the economic or social backgrounds, education, personality, or habits of the couples. Certain stages of marriage are subject to potential difficulties no matter how the partners feel about each other.[64] Flexibility in adjusting to each other's changes, to changes brought about by the marital life cycle, and to changes in the external environment is the key to much of the success of marriage.

Marital Adjustment

There have been more studies of unhappy marriages than of successful ones. However, a few notable research projects have examined married couples who are judged to be happy and well adjusted. The outstanding finding of the studies on good marital adjustment is that there are many models of marriage that seem to work well. In one early study, over four hundred prominent people described their marriages in depth to the researchers. From the data, five separate successful marriage styles were delineated:

1. *Devitalized*: a placid match involving little if any conflict but also little if any passion. Whatever zest there had been in the early years of the marriage seemed to have faded.
2. *Conflict-habituated*: characterized by a great deal of fighting, which, however, was tolerated well by the couple, if not actually enjoyed.
3. *Passive-congenial*: a comfortable and convenient match with each partner involved as much or more outside the marriage as in it.
4. *Total*: characterized by constant togetherness and intensely shared mutual interests.
5. *Vital*: highly involved but not locked into restrictive togetherness. Couples give each other more room for personal growth than in the "total" marriage.[65]

The first three categories—devitalized, conflict-habituated, and passive-congenial—were categorized as *utilitarian* types. Couples considered representative of these three types judged their marriages to be good, functional ones. These marriages were often successful because the couples were allowed to meet mutually important goals: raising children, maintaining a certain standard of living, attaining a desired social status, and otherwise meeting their requirements for adult living.

The "total" and "vital" marriages were termed *intrinsic* marriages. These marriages were marked by the personal involvements the partners had with

each other. Partners shared many activities and had deep feelings for each other. The primary focus in life was on each other. Cuber and Harroff found fewer intrinsic marriages than utilitarian ones and concluded from their research that the norm for successful marriage in the United States is that the relationship be comfortable, functional, and of low intensity. Evidently, the kind of involvement necessary for intrinsic marriages is too great for most couples to sustain while they are busy building careers and raising families. As Cuber and Harroff comment: "People who live in this way place enormous stress on the personal relation—strains that are not present in the utilitarian marriage. . . ."[66]

Others who have engaged in research on successful relationships have approached the study of marital quality by acknowledging that there are a variety of models that work and that are considered successful by the couples interviewed. However, most such studies have used as departure points the traditional marriage on the one hand and the egalitarian marriage on the other.[67,68]

The types of marriages that fall near the *traditional* end of the scale tend to emphasize time-honored roles and expectations of husbands and wives that are more in keeping with the traditional sex roles. Division of responsibilities provides that the man be the principal provider and the woman the principal homemaker and child rearer. Most studies indicate that the more traditional the marriage, the more the husband defines the roles and is expected to be dominant, brighter, better educated, and somewhat older.[69]

Studies of marriages leaning toward the *egalitarian* model show that emphases are on communication, shared tasks, closeness, privacy, and caring.[70] These marriages are considered successful by those in them when there is comfortable personal interaction and when the emotional well-being of the partners is being met. Individual growth is also an important variable in the happiness of couples who are in more egalitarian marriages.[71]

As might be expected, the quality of marriages—no matter what the styles—seems to be highly correlated with how much agreement the husbands and wives have about how the roles are carried out.[72] "Role-fit" necessarily rests on how partners see both their own and each other's roles. Total agreement is not essential, however; most experts agree that good marriages leave room for individual differences. It is seen as vital, however, that there be a plan for reaching agreement when there is conflict.[73]

Marital Adjustment Scales

Over the past forty years, more than a dozen major inventories have been devised to measure marital adjustment.[74,75] Sophisticated statistical methods and computer capabilities gradually improved the adjustment inventories so that more variables can be considered and so that the interaction of those variables can be studied. As a result, it is now generally agreed that social, cultural, and personal variables all are associated with marital adjustment in a complex variety of ways.[76,77] Even so, the complexity of the relationship, the speed and variability of social change, and the richness of human experiences make valid findings scarce.

As we have noted, mutual validation, shared meanings in communication, and compatibility have all been shown to increase marital adjustment. One marital adjustment factor that is implied by these qualities is being comfortable with one's partner. A scale assessing the degrees of "feeling comfortable" determined that there were six factors basic to relationship comfort:

1. *Empathy:* the ability to put oneself in another's shoes, to try to understand how he or she might feel
2. *Spontaneity:* being able to be oneself without having to be guarded or otherwise inhibited
3. *Trust:* being able to count on each other and to know that honesty prevails
4. *Interest-care:* feeling loved and loving, cared for and caring, interested in and interesting to one's partner
5. *Respect:* having a high regard for and a belief in the other's integrity and right to be unique
6. *Criticalness-hostility:* a negative factor in feeling comfortable, indicating that individuality is not appreciated or respected.[78]

Almost all the marital inventory scales have attempted to ascertain the current state of the relationship by asking the partners to rate their happiness, satisfaction, or adjustment on a variety of factors. In recent years, however, a trend has developed to measure factors that are believed to contribute to the ongoing process of marital adjustment rather than to make a simple judgment of the quality of the current state. A recently developed measure of this type was designed to assess the quality of marriages and of the relationships of couples who may not be legally married but who live together as couples.[79]

The author states that the success of couples in adjusting to each other may be viewed in two distinct ways: (1) as a process that must be studied over the life of the relationship or (2) as a qualitative evaluation at any given period in which couples analyze their marriages. The latter approach is like taking a "snapshot" of a couple's compatibility at any one point in time. The process approach allows a relationship to be viewed both at a particular time and as a predictive measure of the probability of future adjustment. Such factors as

FIGURE 7.1 *Dyadic Adjustment Scale*
Most persons have disagreements in their relationships. Please indicate below the approximate extent of agreement or disagreement between you and your partner for each item on the following list.

	Always Agree	Almost Always Agree	Occa- sionally Disagree	Fre- quently Disagree	Almost Always Disagree	Always Disagree
1. Handling family finances	5	4	3	2	1	0
2. Matters of recreation	5	4	3	2	1	0
3. Religious matters	5	4	3	2	1	0
4. Demonstrations of affection	5	4	3	2	1	0
5. Friends	5	4	3	2	1	0
6. Sex relations	5	4	3	2	1	0
7. Conventionality (correct or proper behavior)	5	4	3	2	1	0
8. Philosophy of life	5	4	3	2	1	0
9. Ways of dealing with parents or in- laws	5	4	3	2	1	0
10. Aims, goals, and things believed important	5	4	3	2	1	0
11. Amount of time spent together	5	4	3	2	1	0
12. Making major decisions	5	4	3	2	1	0
13. Household tasks	5	4	3	2	1	0
14. Leisure time interests and activities	5	4	3	2	1	0
15. Career decisions	5	4	3	2	1	0

	All the Time	Most of the Time	More Often Than Not	Occa- sionally	Rarely	Never
16. How often do you discuss or have you considered divorce, separation, or terminating your relationship?	0	1	2	3	4	5
17. How often do you or your mate leave the house after a fight?	0	1	2	3	4	5
18. In general, how often do you think that things between you and your partner are going well?	5	4	3	2	1	0
19. Do you confide in your mate?	5	4	3	2	1	0
20. Do you ever regret that you married (or lived together)?	0	1	2	3	4	5
21. How often do you and your partner quarrel?	0	1	2	3	4	5
22. How often do you and your mate "get on each other's nerves?"	0	1	2	3	4	5

adaptability, communication, interpersonal tensions, and affectional expression are thought to be parts of the process of the marital life cycle that are not as likely to change from one time to another as are reports of whether or not the partners are currently happy and/or satisfied with their relationship.

The Spanier Dyadic Adjustment Scale is shown in Figure 7.1. In addition to using this scale to measure adjustment and to speculate about future adjustment, it may be interesting for a couple to complete it and compare how much

FIGURE 7.1 *Dyadic Adjustment Scale (Continued)*

	Every Day	Almost Every Day	Occa-sionally	Rarely	Never
23. Do you kiss your mate?	4	3	2	1	0

	All of Them	Most of Them	Some of Them	Very Few of Them	None of Them
24. Do you and your mate engage in outside interests together?	4	3	2	1	0

How often would you say the following events occur between you and your mate?

	Never	Less Than Once a Month	Once or Twice a Month	Once or Twice a Week	Once a Day	More Often
25. Have a stimulating exchange of ideas	0	1	2	3	4	5
26. Laugh together	0	1	2	3	4	5
27. Calmly discuss something	0	1	2	3	4	5
28. Work together on a project	0	1	2	3	4	5

These are some things about which couples sometimes agree and sometimes disagree. Indicate if either item below caused differences of opinions or were problems in your relationship during the past few weeks. (Check yes or no)

	Yes	No	
29.	0	1	Being too tired for sex.
30.	0	1	Not showing love.

31. The dots on the following line represent different degrees of happiness in your relationship. The middle point, "happy," represents the degree of happiness of most relationships. Please circle the dot which best describes the degree of happiness, all things considered, of your relationship.

0	1	2	3	4	5	6
•	•	•	•	•	•	•
Extremely Unhappy	Fairly Unhappy	A Little Unhappy	Happy	Very Happy	Extremely Happy	Perfect

32. Which of the following statements best describes how you feel about the future of your relationship?

  5 I want desperately for my relationship to succeed, and *would go to almost any length* to see that it does.
  4 I want very much for my relationship to succeed, and *will do all I can* to see that it does.
  3 I want very much for my relationship to succeed, and *will do my fair share* to see that it does.
  2 It would be nice if my relationship succeeded, but *I can't do much more than I am doing* now to help it succeed.
  1 It would be nice if it succeeded, but *I refuse to do any more than I am doing* now to keep the relationship going.
  0 My relationship can never succeed, and *there is no more that I can do* to keep the relationship going.

Source: Graham B. Spanier, "Measuring Dyadic Adjustment," *Journal of Marriage and the Family* 38 (February 1976), pp. 15–28. Copyrighted 1976 by the National Council on Family Relations. Reprinted by permission.

they agree on each of the thirty-two items. The scale has a possible total score of 151 points. Spanier's study of married and divorced samples reported a mean (average) score of 114.8 for married persons and 70.7 for divorced persons (see Figure 7.1).

Summary

■ Each marital relationship develops its own style based on unique behavioral patterns of actions and reactions that the partners make to each other. They develop strategies for problem solving, for decision making, and for living and working together.

■ Learning to live harmoniously with someone else is a measure of compatibility with that person. Marital adjustment is significantly correlated with a couple's compatibility. Learning to mesh individual traits is an ongoing process in marriage because rarely do two people know each other totally when they marry. Even if total knowledge were possible, people would still change over the life cycle, making adjustment a dynamic process that continues throughout the marriage.

■ Studies of successful marriages indicate that there are many styles that work well. The quality of marriages—no matter what their styles—seem to be highly correlated with how much agreement the husbands and wives have about how their roles are carried out.

■ Many marital adjustment scales have been developed over the years to measure couples' satisfaction with their relationship. Most inventories have asked for the current status of the marriage, but recently attempts have been made to measure those facets of marriage that are believed to carry over from one stage of the life cycle to others.

Glossary

Core symbols Words, behaviors, or objects that have such powerful meanings to those involved in a relationship that their use or abuse may be interpreted as a crisis in the relationship (e.g., putting on or taking off a wedding ring; sleeping in the same bed or in separate beds or rooms; denying coitus to a partner or having coitus with someone else).

Disconfirmation Denial or attack of a person's self-perception by another.

Metacommunication The messages behind actual spoken or written words; nonverbal behavior that may convey different meanings of or may emphasize overt messages.

Mutual validation The condition that exists when two people support each other's values, behaviors, or self-concepts.

Self-concept The mental picture one has of oneself; the feelings, attitudes, and values that each individual has with respect to his or her own behaviors, abilities, and worth.

Self-esteem The worth one places on oneself, usually based on comparisons with others or with some idealized self.

But one of the
attributes of love,
like art, is to bring
harmony and order
out of chaos, to
introduce meaning
and affect where
before there was
none, to give
rhythmic variations,
highs and lows, to
a landscape that
was previously flat.

—Molly Haskell,
  *From Reverence to
  Rape*

214

8 · Challenges in Marriage

It is through sharing that a marriage stands or falls. Sharing love, companionship, decisions, goals, and time together are essential to maintaining couples' feelings of closeness. Being adaptable to inevitable changes and flexible while maintaining the stability necessary for commitment may be a great challenge to every married couple. There are certain patterns that must develop in every successful marriage in the course of day-to-day living. Decisions must be made, power struggles overcome, problems solved, and conflicts resolved. Most couples want to make an already good marriage even better or to improve a marriage that is floundering. Skills, insights, and confidence are the ingredients necessary to make any relationship more effective and more rewarding.

In our experience and that of many other marital therapists, the quality of married life—adjustment, happiness, and satisfaction—is related directly to husbands' and wives' abilities to be flexible in their marital roles. This includes adaptability both in their rules for living together and in their goals as they respond to changing life situations while simultaneously maintaining the stability of their marriages. A balance between stability and flexibility appears necessary for marital development.[1]

All married couples face certain basic challenges in their relationships. These challenges are not unique to marriage: any long-term, close relationships (such as those of business partners or of parents and children) must also develop patterns of interaction that allow for change and growth. However, few relationships last as long as the average marriage or have the intimacy and range of common ground that marriages have. For this reason, meeting the basic challenges that we will describe in this chapter is central to the quality of marriage. As will be seen in a subsequent chapter, many couples run into serious difficulties with each other, and many marriages ultimately fail. Besides those couples who divorce, there are others who live together in quiet resignation or perpetuate a "cold war." We believe that in large part these failures are the result of inadequate management of several basic factors in a partnership.

A number of studies have focused on the qualities found in good marriages. We have already discussed good communication, intimacy and closeness, sexuality, and honesty and trust, all of which have been shown to be necessary to satisfying relationships. There are other important aspects of marriage that are also basic and must somehow be accommodated by every married couple. Four of these factors will be discussed in this chapter: decision making, conflict resolution, definition of mutual goals, and time management.

Decision Making

If two persons are to live together compatibly, one of the most important day-to-day skills they need is the ability to work out mutually agreeable and efficient ways of handling decisions. Most couples eventually develop one or more decision-making patterns, but these are often neither mutually satisfying nor particularly efficient. In fact, often these methods are actually self-defeating for the partners and may lead to open conflict. For example, one partner may make a decision without consulting the other even though the other partner is affected by the decision. Financial difficulties can often be traced to one partner's expenditures that deplete the family budget while the other partner worries about how to pay the bills.

Another flawed pattern for making decisions is actually based on *not* making decisions. "Decidophobia" is a word coined to describe avoidance of decisions until someone else—an outsider such as a relative, a lawyer, an employer, or even a police officer—makes the decision instead. Defaulting on decisions frequently creates a crisis, and some couples seem to live from crisis to crisis precisely for this reason. Essentially, "deciding by default" often reflects a fear of making choices on the part of one or both partners. One partner may defer to the other, or they may juggle the choice between them out of apathy or unwillingness even to discuss it.

Family experts report that the power balance between the partners is a key factor in how couples make decisions. The study of marital power and decision-making patterns has been the subject of much research, beginning with a study of 900 couples published in 1960.[2] Decisions such as which car to buy, where to vacation, and how to set up household budgets were analyzed. It was discovered that the partner with the most resources—earning power, education, information—made most of the decisions. The *resource theory of family power*, as it was termed, took into account many different kinds of resources: skills, social status, physical attractiveness, and other assets. The theory postulated that when one partner perceived the other as being more in control because of these assets, he or she usually gave in on decisions.

More recent studies of power and its relation to decision making have added to the resource theory by suggesting that possible bases for power might include what the couple consider an appropriate authority structure between husbands and wives.[3] There are various cultural definitions of who has or should have decision-making power. For example, certain religious doctrines designate husbands as the final authorities in any major or contested decisions. Decision-making patterns in certain racial or ethnic groups have also been studied. For example, the stereotype of the "black family matriarchy" has been shown to lack validity; a pattern of equality in decision making is more often the rule. In fact, black middle-class couples more often share power than do white middle-class couples.[4]

Another source of power has been shown to stem from each partner's respective level of dependence on the other or degree of involvement in the relationship.[5] A wife who is financially dependent on her husband may defer to his wishes more than she would if she had her own source of income. A man who loves his wife more than she loves him may back away from decisions that might cause her to become distant.

In addition to the effect of resources on the power balance and decision making in marriage, several studies have explored the techniques couples employ in their attempts to negotiate with each other or to gain control of the decision-making process.[6] These techniques include assertiveness, manipulation, persuasion, and a variety of other direct and indirect acts that influence the course of couples' decision-making patterns. One of the favored definitions of scholars who study the power balance between individuals in relationships is that *power* is the ability to produce intended effects on others. Thus power is viewed as a process rather than as a static concept.[7]

Many couples find that their marital happiness is eroded when they reach decisions on the basis of power. The partner who feels coerced or manipulated and who typically gives in can easily become frustrated and resentful. Couples who habitually deal with decisions on a win-or-lose basis often discover that winning a marital conflict can be an illusion. The victory can easily turn into an ultimate loss for both when angry and hurt feelings develop between the partners. The marriage is reduced to a power struggle as winning becomes more important for each partner than having a good relationship. Many couples who seek marital therapy are locked into just such conflicts. They argue over everything from household duties to their sex lives.

It is important to note, however, that power does not always have to involve conflict but, in fact, often functions to keep conflict at a minimum. The use of resources or techniques, for example, may be a way for husbands and wives to provide definitions of situations for each other or to utilize their knowledge or expertise to solve problems.[8] If a wife convinces her husband that she knows best how to handle a particular situation, her husband may, in fact, feel relieved that she has taken the matter into her own hands.

In addition to the resources and techniques used in "deciding who decides," it is important to look at decision outcomes. In other words, it is a question not only of how the decision is made and of whether one or the other "wins," but also of who decides which partner will ultimately carry out the decision. In a study of couples to determine which partner implemented decisions and which delegated authority, two types of power were distinguished: orchestration power and implementation power.[9]

Orchestration power is that in which one spouse makes the major decisions that determine the life-style, characteristics, and features of the couple's lives but does not bother with any decisions that infringe on his or her time or energy. The person who has orchestration power usually delegates what are considered mundane or time-consuming decisions to the other partner. In addition, **implementation power** may be delegated. For example, a husband may decide how much money his wife can spend for a new appliance, but she may be the one who actually makes the purchase. As long as she does not spend more than the decided amount or in any other way modify his decision, there is no conflict. The same study reported that orchestration power is most frequently held by the partner with the most resources.

The researchers used exchange theory to explain the bargaining power derived from controlling resources. Especially important was the fact of being "more in love." The spouse who reported being more in love was found to have less orchestration power, whereas those partners who believed that they were equally in love shared major decisions in the marriage. Women who had lower levels of economic resources were often able to gain in orchestration power when their husbands were the ones "more in love." It was as though they exchanged love for the right to make many of the major decisions.

Drawing by Ziegler; © 1980 The New Yorker Magazine, Inc.

Recent research seems to point to the fact that there is more to how husbands and wives make decisions than who controls the most resources and what each partner has learned about who should or should not make decisions.[10] For one thing, as more women are earning an equal share of the family income, their decision-making power has increased to the point that they often actually have *more* impact than their husbands do on decisions made.[11] It has been suggested that women who earn as much as their husbands are also as well educated, as intelligent, and in possession of as many or more personal skills and competencies; therefore, they may move into a position of greater power than their husbands. Some studies also point to the increased marital power currently being achieved by women as a major factor in divorce.[12]

Earlier studies suggested that marital satisfaction is greater in families in which women do not have greater marital power than their husbands do.[13] However, the simple conclusion cannot be reached that men are unhappy if they are not dominant or even that women prefer that their husbands be stronger. Although both conclusions may be true for some couples, it is more likely that the dissatisfactions were already present and that the resources of income, personal skills, and competence allowed the women to leave bad marriages by giving them the option of being able to support themselves. Another frequently mentioned explanation for greater marital discontent in husband-dominated marriages is that such marriages often fit a learned notion of the traditional pattern that couples may have seen modeled by their own parents.

Couples who share marital power equally are more likely to report high marital satisfaction.[14] The sharing of decision making reflects an important principle. Considerable research has indicated that when all parties affected by a decision have a part in making the decision, they are usually more satisfied with the outcome.[15] This fact probably also reflects the fact that these couples have achieved a cooperative relationship. It has been shown that in such relationships tasks and family roles are less traditionally assigned and are more often shared.[16]

No one formula for decision making can work for all couples. Some husbands and wives delegate decision areas so that each partner has his or her own territory. These different "spheres of interest" may be divided traditionally, according to "men's work" and "women's work," or according to interest, expertise, or qualifications unique to each couple.[17]

Two couples we have counseled come to mind as illustrations of the "spheres of interest" approach. In each of the marriages the wife was a bookkeeper for a large corporation. In one instance, the husband insisted on taking care of the checkbook and record keeping even though his wife was more skilled, and his wife concurred because in each of their own families of orientation the father had played that role. The other couple had the same arrangement, but in this case the wife asked to be relieved of the task because she spent over forty hours a week keeping books and said she would rather do some other task instead.

Many couples have concluded that not every decision needs to be a joint one or even agreed on by both partners. There is merit, for instance, in keeping a portion of one's life separate *within* the unity of the relationship. Some matters that affect the partners individually are resolved by each person independently, while those decisions having an impact on both members are made jointly. What one couple might consider suitable for an individual decision another couple might want to decide together.[18] Some couples agree that all major decisions will be made jointly (provided they can agree on just which ones are major). Usually major decisions have to do with place of residence; earning, spending, and saving money; children, friends, and relatives; and sex.

Decision-making patterns and power balances frequently change over the marital life cycle. For example, many marriages begin as egalitarian relationships, with both partners earning their livings and sharing domestic tasks. With the birth of children, roles may become specialized—the wife/mother decides household/child matters, and the husband/father specializes in producing income and making family financial decisions. As mentioned earlier, many experts believe that such specialization tips the balance of power in the husband's favor and so gives husbands more of a role in major decision making.[19] Later, when the children are older, wives may return to the labor market and find that they no longer have the interest or time to make all the household decisions. Once again contributing to the family income, they also may want a larger voice in other major decisions, including financial ones.

Marriage counselors often are called on to help couples correct faulty decision-making patterns or to change from one pattern that may have functioned well during a preceding period of their lives to a new one that fits their changed statuses. Restructuring decision-making processes usually involves the following steps: (1) exploring why the present method is not working; (2) sorting out which decision areas each partner believes are major and which minor; (3) deciding which decisions are to be made jointly; (4) examining the effectiveness of following through with decisions, including who implements them; and (5) developing a variety of techniques to be used depending on the situation, rather than getting locked into one set pattern.[20]

In addition to these guidelines, couples can draw on the well-known, orderly sequence of steps in making decisions that have been developed in business management and by social psychologists.[21,22,23]

1. *Define the issue to be decided.* Usually one partner brings an issue to the other's attention, although sometimes both are aware that something needs attention. The issues may, of course, be problems, but not all decisions involve conflict—often there are pleasant decisions to be made too.
2. *Gather relevant information and discuss the facts.* This step includes several

major issues. Perhaps as important as getting the objective data about the issue (if not more important) is determining how each partner feels about this issue. In other words, it is essential not only to discuss the facts but also to take the other person's feelings, priorities, and values into consideration in reaching a mutual decision. It has been shown that decisions made by considering only objective facts but omitting feelings are more likely to be regretted later.[24]

3. *Explore alternative decisions and select one.* Sometimes, when the issue is fully understood and each partner has had the opportunity to be heard, the decision is easy to reach. Sometimes, however, the decision is not what either person would have chosen if left to his or her own devices but, rather, a compromise that both can live with.

4. *Spell out whatever action is needed to implement the decision.* This step is important so that the partners are not working at cross-purposes. This may also include setting a future time to check progress to be certain that the plan is working and does not need to be amended. Some couples also set a timetable for taking action on the decision.

The follow-through is as important as the decision, of course. Many couples make a good decision and map a strategy for it but find that their downfall is that no one actually carries out what they agreed to do. Getting things accomplished and feeling good about it seems to be a powerful ingredient in most successful relationships.[25]

Summary

■ Flexibility in marital roles—which includes adaptability in rules and goals—is essential in dealing with the changes that are inevitable during the marital life cycle. There are basic challenges to every long-term relationship based on the need for partners to differ and to accommodate each other's growth.

■ Decision making is one of the most important challenges facing couples as they attempt to work out mutually agreeable and efficient ways of living together compatibly. Family experts report that the power balance between the partners is a key factor in the decision-making patterns that couples characteristically develop.

■ The resource theory proposes that the partner with the most resources has the most authority to decide how the couple will live. Resources may be financial or may have to do with skills, personality traits, self-confidence, or love and sex.

■ Techniques that couples employ in negotiation with each other have also been shown to affect the decision-making process. Power, therefore, lies not only in resources but also in assertiveness, manipulation, and persuasive abilities.

■ Studies of decision outcomes—who actually carries out the decision—reveal that there is power not only in who makes the decisions but also in the delegation of decisions and their implementation. As women are becoming more equal partners in financial matters, there is a gradual tendency toward equality between partners in both major decision making and implementation power.

■ Decision-making patterns and power balances frequently change over the marital life cycle. What works well during one phase may need revision at another. Flexibility in the day-to-day skills of getting along harmoniously, getting things accomplished, and feeling good about decisions is a powerful ingredient in successful marriages.

Conflict Resolution

We have said that not all decisions involve disagreements. When disagreements occur, however, they may lead to conflicts. Every marriage has conflicts from time to time, and most couples have developed methods to resolve them. If this were not so, the divorce rate would likely be higher than it already is. Conflict is so much a recognized phenomenon in relationships that many family experts use conflict theory to explain much of marital interaction.[26]

Conflict theory proposes that it is impossible for two persons who are products of unique experiences (one having been treated as a male and one as a female while growing up, for instance) to live together without having their

uniquenesses clash from time to time. It is through the resolution of these disagreements that growth in the relationship is believed to occur. Many marital therapists encourage couples to bring disagreements into the open so that they can experience the growth that comes from resolving them rather than simply avoid a fight.[27]

The amount of conflict varies from couple to couple, of course, and the amount that a given couple experiences may vary from period to period during the marital life cycle. In other words, some couples may argue throughout a lifetime as an accepted part of their interaction—they may even expect to disagree almost daily. Some even appear to enjoy a good argument and have developed a pattern of fighting unique to their marriage. Couples who develop this pattern of interaction have been described as "conflict-habituated" by some experts who believe these partners have a habituated need to do psychological battle with each other.[28] Other couples may go along smoothly for periods of time but have cycles in which they disagree much more than usual. These usually are periods of change in one or both partners that make it necessary to confront certain troublesome issues between them.

Change

Two kinds of personal change have been recognized in the literature.[29] *First-order change* is change that arises out of the natural stages of life. Such change comes gradually and seems to fit sensibly into normal life-cycle patterns. People marry and have children, children grow and adults mature, relationships deepen and fade away—these changes we can accept and understand. They are likely to occur for both partners over generally the same period of time, and couples can usually deal with such transitions together—or at least have a degree of understanding about what is going on so that they are able to weather the other's "natural" disruptions.[30] Sometimes these changes cause disagreements, but for the most part they seem to cause far less disruption than does the second variety.

Second-order change is the kind that seems to occur abruptly and unpredictably. Forces may have been at work for a long time to cause such change, but it often appears sudden and puzzling to both partners. For example, one partner may suddenly announce that he or she has resigned from a job. The idea may have been fermenting for weeks, or it may have been an impulsive action. To the partner who is caught off guard, it may be not only a surprise but a disruptive one at that.

Second-order change is often cause for conflict in a marriage. Even changes that both partners agree are desirable may disrupt their marriage equilibrium.[31] Such changes usually require transformation of attitudes toward the initiating partner's new status or new behavior. There may be a sense of discontinuity, strangeness, and frustration. Some second-order changes provoke anger, anxiety, confusion, or even a feeling of betrayal. Such changes frequently call for extensive alterations in the relationship and are therefore understandably unsettling.

The partner who makes a second-order change actually forces a change on his or her partner. For example, many former homemakers who enter the labor force and become enthusiastic about their jobs make changes in their marriages that cause resentment and confusion in husbands. Systems theory explains that when one partner in a system changes his or her behavior, the other partner necessarily must change in reaction.[32] For many persons, having to change in order to accommodate another's behavior is distressing, and their resistance is the basic element in the conflict that results.

Marital and family therapists are familiar with resistance to change and with the difficulties, in particular, of adjusting to what appears to be a sudden change in one family member. It is this difficulty with "evolving"—or being stuck in an outmoded way of reacting to a changed partner—that is at the heart of many marital problems. As one family therapist has written, ". . . the task of therapy should be to make available . . . the power inherent in all living systems: the ability to transcend the stuckness and move to a different stage."[33]

Most couples do not need marital therapy to accomplish the adjustments or "transcend the stuckness" involving their own and their partners' changes throughout the life cycle. Couples usually learn that communicating about the motives for the change and reassurance about its outcomes go a long way toward making it easier to understand what is happening. It is inevitable that two people will change. How each person adjusts to change becomes crucial to the success of their relationship.

Another kind of conflict involving change in relationships is the desire of one partner for the other to change. Conflicts in a marriage often are reduced to blaming the partner. Criticism of one partner by the other becomes a weapon; the clear message delivered is "If only *you* would change, there would be no problem." Criticism and blame are much less effective in negotiating change in another than is convincing the other person that he or she also will benefit from the change.

In recent years, behavior modification has become a popular method for teaching couples to change their own and each other's behaviors through the use of rewards for desired behaviors.[34] A husband may, for example, exchange an act his wife desires for a change he is requesting from her. For instance, he may agree to build shelves to store her papers and books if she will agree to keep the desk they share uncluttered. A contract such as this can prove useful in achieving specific changes, and most couples agree that it is more pleasant than criticism.

Three important steps involved in negotiating change have been suggested by family therapists:

1. *Communication.* Talking honestly about the behavior in question and the changes desired is important. Who seeks the change, why the other is

    resistant, and what goals the change would achieve need to be understood by both.

2. *Specific goals.* The partner who is asking the other to change can facilitate an understanding by being specific about what he or she wants the other to do. This includes spelling out the advantages of making the change.

3. *Request behavior change only.* Negotiating for change in what another *does* is far easier than trying to get him or her to modify feelings or even thoughts. In other words, one partner can ask the other to behave in a particular fashion but cannot demand that he or she enjoy it.[35]

Roles in Couple Conflict

It has been suggested that how each couple relate to each other during their disagreements is directly related to the roles each plays in their interpersonal system.[36] Four roles or "parts" frequently observed are: (1) a *mover*, the partner who defines or initiates an action; (2) a *follower*, who agrees with, supports, or continues the action; (3) an *opposer*, who challenges or goes against the action; and (4) a *bystander*, who watches what happens but who remains detached. One couple may, for example, be composed of two people—one a mover and one a follower—who coexist very peacefully and have little conflict. A couple consisting of one mover and one opposer, however, may have a great deal of disagreement. The bystander may remain aloof from the opposer or from the mover, causing frustration for either type of partner. The bystander also may give free rein to the mover and offer the opposer no one to oppose. A follower and a bystander married to each other may well become stuck in the decision-making or problem-solving processes.

Family-systems theorists believe that a marriage without a mover would be dull; a marriage in which neither partner ever follows cannot reach its goals; a marriage without opposers learns nothing new from within; and a marriage in which bystanding never occurs is likely to repeat unsuccessful problem-solving patterns. The flexibility of the partners in learning to play each of the four roles when appropriate is believed to be an important index of how well the couple functions in resolving conflicts.

An individual who is "stuck" in one of the four roles in a couple system—for example, one who is always an opposer or always a follower—limits his or her mate's options to change roles. If one always opposes *any* suggestions—no matter what their merit—or always complies with *all* suggestions—no matter how inappropriate—the couple's ability to change a troubled system is seriously impaired.

Many couples develop what may be called a *ritual impasse*, in which they typically become stuck at the same point in every effort to solve problems.[37] The stuck "bystander," for example, might always block any disagreement by predictably refusing to become involved. In that example, the ritual of withdrawal effectively terminates the problem-solving process and creates an impasse, no matter how serious the issue.

A set of attitudes that have been labeled **reality-oriented** and **defense-oriented** may be used to designate characteristic responses of persons to couple conflict. A reality-oriented person habitually directs his or her inputs to a conflict toward understanding and solving the underlying disagreement. A defense-oriented person habitually attempts to reduce the discomfort, tension, or disagreement by "explaining" behavior that appears to be causing it.[38]

Although defending one's position or behavior may reduce interpersonal tension, it is rarely useful in solving problems—especially marital problems—and can sometimes heighten conflict.

Typical defensive behaviors include, among others:

1. *rationalization:* giving reasons for one's behavior that make the action taken sound logical, but that have been made up after the fact
2. *intellectualization:* moving the focus to a discussion of higher principles of ethics, aesthetics, or philosophy and away from the concrete behavior
3. *denial:* insisting that what apparently happened did not happen at all, that perhaps it was misperceived
4. *suppression:* "forgetting" an agreement or a contract previously made on the issue
5. *Pollyannaism:* insisting that no matter how painful the situation may be, it is surely all for some future good or benefit

Most defense-oriented persons form distinctive defensive patterns that they use whenever anxiety is high as it often is in a conflict situation. However, defense-oriented behavior usually blocks the resolution of conflicts simply because defenses typically distort or deny reality—just as the user intends them to do. As long as one partner avoids reality, effective problem solving cannot take place, and serious erosion of a relationship may develop.

Conflicts are sometimes masked by what the psychiatrist Eric Berne has called marital *games*.[39] These "games" are used to sidestep real issues. Each partner in a game defends his or her position—usually a "basic truth" about the way things really *ought* to be done (what Berne calls a *script*)—while manipulating the other into a "wrong" position. Marital games take many forms—for example, "See What You've Made Me Do!" or "Look How Hard I Was Trying!" The common feature of games is that they distort or disguise the real issues that the couple may need to resolve in order to reduce conflict.

Reality-oriented persons may not always have solutions for their conflicts, of course; but when couples can keep their problems in focus, they stand a much better chance of discovering their areas of difference and working out a solution. Problem solving is impossible unless the problem can first be identified. Mutual agreement that a problem exists, what the problem is, and exactly how—and how much—each partner contributes to it may be the three most important steps to the marital challenge of conflict resolution.[40]

Types of Conflict

Conflict emerges in a variety of forms, ranging from minor irritations to serious and often complicated issues about which partners disagree. Marital therapists are familiar with couples who, after a fight, have trouble remembering what the original issue was. If they do remember, the issue often seems rather trivial in retrospect. The tensions couples experience often are not so much the result of major differences between them as of comparatively minor day-to-day irritations. Marital therapists probably hear as many complaints about trivial faults—leaving a messy bathroom or letting the gas tank run dry in the car—as they do about more serious problems such as poor communication or lack of trust.[41]

Minor irritations are often symptomatic of more serious underlying problems. One study of married couples found that when couples are experiencing stress in their relationship, they tend to find fault with each other and to interpret each other's actions and words more negatively than was intended by the mate.[42] Minor irritations also have a way of escalating into major conflicts; they may accumulate until they spill over to affect a couple's basic relationship. Even when the partners do not mention their irritations, an undercurrent of anger or disappointment can easily create a distance between them that erodes the relationship.

Couples can find an endless variety of things to disagree on. Virtually anything can become a problem.[43] In particular, couples who are engaged in a struggle over the balance of power between them can usually find an arena for disagreement. However, even couples who usually agree and who have little or no power struggle between them are bound at times to have differences between them that are important enough to fight for. Marital therapists stress that under the right circumstances fights can be productive and can bring partners closer together rather than pushing them apart.[44] The key to avoiding a destructive conflict, as we have noted, is to keep in mind that the goal is to solve the problem rather than to win the argument. Discussions that stick to the issues and avoid personal attacks have the best chances of producing positive results.

Studies show that partners who attack each other's self-esteem more often report being unhappy and dissatisfied with their relationships than do couples who manage their conflicts in ways that enhance each other's self-concepts.[45] Steps toward replacing fighting to win with constructive approaches to problem solving include the following:

1. Identify the subjects of the most frequent and most intense arguments. Cut through the surface disagreements to the emotional meanings underneath.

2. Avoid equating "losing" a dispute with losing self-esteem. Keep in mind that marriage is a cooperative enterprise, not a competitive one. The goal is *not* to decide who is right or wrong but, rather, to solve a problem.

3. Learn the art of effective and honest compromise. A compromise that works—even if it is not an ideal answer to a conflict—is better than a brilliant solution that one partner is likely to sabotage.

4. Try humor as a mood-changing technique. Humor may not solve the problem, but the atmosphere will be more relaxed if those involved do not take themselves too seriously.

5. Avoid turning disagreements into crises by overdramatizing or by using them to reopen more serious conflicts. Most often such tactics are used to win and thus are symptomatic of a power struggle.[46]

In a discussion of attitudes toward marital conflict and resolution, family therapist Israel Charney has written that "there is much to be gained from learning how to fight with one's spouse openly, saying what we feel but not promiscuously; sharing our angers but not overwhelming one another."[47] Conveying honest feelings openly and resolving differences of opinion constructively may be two of the most difficult obligations of marriage.

Summary

■ Conflicts are a natural phenomenon of marriage. They are not pleasant, to be sure, but marital experts believe that, if handled constructively, they may open the way for growth and positive change.

■ Change is one of the major reasons for conflict. First-order changes are those that come gradually and seem sensible as adjustments to normal life-cycle patterns. These do not usually cause the kinds of difficulties associated with second-order changes, which seem to occur unpredictably and usually catch others by surprise, often causing conflict in a marriage.

■ The attempt to evoke change in one's partner is another source of frequent conflict in marriages. Important steps in negotiating change are: communication, making the goals specific, and requesting behavior changes only.

■ Marriage partners often learn particular roles in dealing with each other during conflict. If they are not flexible in playing roles that are appropriate and constructive for problem solving, they may find that they usually wind up in an impasse.

■ Conflict emerges in a variety of ways, over major issues and minor irritations. In particular, couples who are engaged in a power struggle may disagree on an almost unlimited number of issues. Learning constructive approaches to conflict resolution is one of the major challenges in marriage and may also be one of its most difficult obligations.

Mutual Goals

With the current emphasis on individual growth and satisfaction, marriage is no longer identified as an institution into which men and women must fit as in a mold. Instead, marriage is seen as a union that enables partners to meet their needs. Thus a good and satisfying marriage is a relationship that allows for enough freedom and enough separateness for each partner to grow and to pursue his or her own goals in life. In this respect, marriage is no different from any other relationship—whether with a friend or with a group in which one is involved. Social psychologists report that greater value is placed on a relationship or a group that facilitates meeting one's goals. On the other hand, when a relationship, such as a marriage, or a group, such as a family, limits individual freedom, one tends to become dissatisfied.[48] In other words, if a marriage is to be rewarding, it must not severely inhibit either partner's need fulfillment or growth.

We rather routinely ask couples in marital therapy this question: If you could be doing anything you want, anywhere you want, with anyone you want, how would you like your life to be five years from now? This apparent exercise in fantasy can be useful in revealing potential goals. More important, if each partner's "five-year plan" includes the spouse, this is one of the best predictors that a relationship will continue to thrive. Partners whose individual plans include the other have set themselves up for what social psychologists term *mutual interdependence*.[49] They need each other in order to accomplish their goals.

Individual and Mutual Goals

One of the most important tasks of any two persons in a partnership or of members of a group (such as a family) is linking individual goals with mutual goals.[50] If good marriages provide room for the attainment of individual goals, then it is equally important that there be enough closeness and cooperation that couples can also achieve mutual goals. From years of working with couples in troubled relationships, we have become convinced that the lack of mutual goals is often a warning sign that a marriage is in serious trouble. Research indicates that working cooperatively as a team toward mutual goals leads to greater feelings of attraction to each other.[51] Evidently, everyone likes to be on a smoothly operating team that is getting the job done. Cooperative behavior is rewarding in and of itself, since it moves the couple toward their desired goals. As partners aid each other, make constructive suggestions, and share the load, they come to value each other more.

Differentiating individual goals from mutual goals is not always as easy as it may seem at first. Early analyses proposed that mutual goals are merely composites of the individual goals of the two partners.[52] It soon became obvious, however, that partners' individual goals not only may be quite different from each other's but may actually be in conflict. For example, a husband may wish to save money for a new car, but his wife may want to spend money now for landscaping the yard. This is an example of a conflict between a long-range goal and an immediate goal as well as an example of a conflict between goals: saving for one means that the other is denied.

Mutual marital goals that are a composite of each partner's individual goals are made possible by a cooperative effort to include what each partner desires when possible so that a mutual goal is the end result. Individual goals that do not become mutual continue to influence each partner's behavior and often may be achieved simultaneously with joint endeavors. The degree to which both mutual and individual goals can be achieved by the same activities helps to determine how satisfying a marriage becomes.[53]

Early studies in social psychology were instrumental in showing how two persons become interdependent by developing mutual goals.[54] These studies found that when one of a pair completed a task that both wanted done, it affected the other partner as if he or she had completed it. In other words, once a couple establishes mutual goals, completing them (even if only one partner actually performs the task) has the same effect as if both had accomplished a personal goal.

It is easy for some couples to identify their mutual goals because they have discussed them and have agreed on them. Saving to buy a home, working to build a business, or planning for a special vacation are frequent joint marital ventures. However, many couples, if asked to list their mutual goals, would be at a loss to reply. They may never have thought about articulating their goals. Couples vary greatly in the extent to which they are aware of their mutual goals, and some seem truly to have none. Research has indicated that those couples who are aware of and can articulate their goals show greater interdependence between the partners.[55]

Variations between married couples are found in the extent to which they accept stated marital goals. Disagreement is particularly common in marriages with many goals because the question of priority frequently arises. When two people cannot agree about which goal takes priority, there is the risk of a power struggle and of diminishing cooperation. If, for example, a couple has agreed that they both want to save for a new car and also want to buy new furniture, they can be said to have two mutual goals. However, since both goals require the same resources for fulfillment, it is essential that the couple agree on priority as well. If buying the car is a top priority for one partner but buying furniture ranks higher with the other, the stage is set for the transformation of mutual goals into two personal goals. This sets up a competitive situation that undermines interdependence.[56] When both partners accept a goal, accord it the same level of priority, and work toward it together (even though one partner may be more responsible for its achievement than the other), interdependence and satisfaction are maximum.

Cooperation versus Competition in Marriage

A *cooperative relationship* has been defined as one in which the goals of the participants are so linked that either partner can attain his or her goal if, and only if, the other also attains his or hers.[57] For example, a newly married couple might mutually desire to buy a condominium that is more expensive than either partner could afford alone. Thus both must agree to work and to contribute to the cost of the condominium. Neither of them can reach this goal without working cooperatively toward it. Competition, on the other hand, results when goals are linked in such a way that one partner can reach his or her goals only if the other does not. For example, if one partner wishes to go to Hawaii for vacation and the other wants to use the vacation money for investment, the one who "wins" does so at the other's expense.

Cooperation is not defined only in terms of shared goals, however. Although working toward a joint goal is obviously of primary importance in cooperation, the *means* by which couples go about reaching their goals are also important. In fact, as marital therapists we probably hear as much disagreement about the means to the goals as we do about the goals themselves. It is not unusual for two persons to fail to reach a goal that both want very much because they cannot agree on how to get there. Husbands and wives may agree, for instance, that they want their children to be well behaved or to do well in school, but may argue about how to achieve these goals. Agreement on ways to achieve shared goals is vital to the cooperative effort because in a cooperative marriage each partner must facilitate the other's contribution. Without agreement, this is not possible.

There are several ways in which couples disagree about means to ends. They often attempt to duplicate each other's efforts because one does not like the way the other performs. If they have agreed that one will cook the dinner while the other sets the table, for example, each may instead attempt to redo what the other has done or may criticize the other's efforts. Both behaviors often can lead to breakdown in cooperation.

Sometimes there is unequal participation in working toward a goal, so that one partner may believe that the other is not facilitating movement or does not want the end result as much. Problems occur when both partners agree on a goal, but one gives it only halfhearted effort. Although it is true that a mutual goal, when reached, is as rewarding to the inactive spouse as to the one who actually accomplished it, the active spouse may feel a lack of support and be less willing to repeat the effort.

Studies comparing the means by which couples work together with the extent to which they agree on their goals reveal that the most satisfactory relationships occur when couples share ways of getting to goals but that it is even more important that they agree on where they are going.[58] As long as two people do not work against each other by setting up a competitive situation, it is possible for them to work independently or to pursue their mutual goals quite differently and still work out a satisfactory solution. If, for example, two people decide to redecorate a room in their home, not only might they work independently at different tasks (the husband may paint, the wife may sand the floor), but they also could have very different approaches to their work (he working ten hours each day over the weekend, she doing a little bit every evening for several weeks).

Cooperative behavior appears to be facilitated when partners communicate their intentions to each other—usually, the more they communicate, the greater the cooperation.[59] Married couples with a history of successful communication have been shown to be more cooperative on joint ventures assigned to them in research projects than are couples who have no such history.[60] Although laboratory research is far different from studying couples working together at home in real-life situations, the importance of communication for facilitating goals seems to be a well-established fact. Our experience and that of many other marital therapists is that helping couples increase and improve their communication with each other leads to less competitive and selfish behavior and to more cooperative and considerate interaction.

Other research has indicated that cooperation often hinges on the *trust* two people feel for each other.[61] Trust is a basic link that holds two people together and a constant thread that runs throughout the fabric of a marriage in the ordinary give-and-take of living together. Partners trust each other to be reliable, to be honest, to be caring. They must be able to count on each other dozens of times a day. A frequent complaint in troubled marriages is that one partner has failed to be there for the other at a time when cooperation was necessary. Many couples complain, for example, that their cooperative interaction breaks down during a crisis. They seem unable to give each other the support both need to make and implement constructive decisions.

Building marital trust—and, in particular, repairing broken trust—can be a slow, gradual, and often anxiety-producing process. Without trust, however, two people remain isolated from each other. A marriage empty of trust is likely to foster loneliness and feelings of alienation.

To trust another person, one must be able to trust oneself. Being able to count on one's inner strengths—self-reliance—makes the vulnerability involved in trusting another less frightening. Knowing that one can handle whatever comes along makes it less important to control all the marital decisions, marital goals, and means of achieving those goals. Trust between marital partners, at the simplest level, may be the antidote to most power struggles and competitive relationships that hinge on being "right" or "winning."[62]

Time Management

The fourth challenge to couples in adjusting to each other over a lifetime together lies in finding time both for each other and for themselves as individuals, while balancing busy schedules with heavy demands from outsiders.

"Time to talk or to be quiet, time to play together or to work side by side, time for sex, time for solitude, time to be a spouse, parent, lover, but also time to be one's self—all of these 'times' are vital ingredients of marriage."[63]

Most studies of time management in marriage support the notion that marital satisfaction depends largely on the quality of time spent together (rather than on the quantity) and on whether the partners agree on how their time is allocated.[64] For example, there are countless couples who spend every evening together but who complain of being bored with each other or who may feel lonely and alienated. Other couples spend much less actual time together but find their moments rewarding. One partner may believe that "time together" includes time spent reading or independently watching television, but the other may count only time spent together while interacting in some enjoyable activity.

Major interferences with quality time together as a couple come from many sources. When both partners fill their days with too much activity, shared or otherwise, they may find that tension and fatigue undermine their enjoyment of each other. Couples frequently give their best efforts and energies to their work, to children, or to outsiders. Home may become a refuge from outside pressures—a place to relax—with the result that the partner gets what is left over—perhaps only a nervous and exhausted mate.

Patterns of overactivity that keep couples apart, however, are not always the result of poor scheduling or of too many demands. Keeping too busy to spend time with a mate often is a way of avoiding intimacy. In that case the difficulty is not one of time management but of a deeper level of conflict in the marriage. One of the important clues to a marriage that is in trouble is that one or both partners begin to withdraw from contact.[65]

For those couples who do want to spend more quality time together but are caught in a "time bind," the dilemma of how to carve out that time for themselves when most of it (or all of it) is already spoken for by children, family, friends, bosses, and coworkers in civic and community affairs becomes a central issue. On top of these demands come what family sociologist Arlene Skolnick describes as "the horde of seemingly irrelevant trivia—missing buttons, lost keys, dental appointments, PTA meetings, broken washing machines—that determine the time, energy, and moods" a couple have to give to each other.[66]

In working with couples who present time management as a problem in their marriages, we have found a number of techniques useful for helping them satisfy the essential claims of "outsiders" while still finding time for themselves as couples.

1. *Find out exactly how time is spent.* Many couples have only a vague idea of how each day is spent. Keeping a fairly detailed log for at least two weeks may reveal several extended telephone conversations that could have been shorter

or unnecessary errands that could have been consolidated. Some couples discover that by finding exactly where their time goes, they become able to make constructive changes that can help ease their time problem.

2. *Compare calendars.* Two busy people can easily discover that when one has free time, the other does not. Although it may seem peculiar to try to schedule time to be together rather than let it happen spontaneously, the fact is that otherwise they may never find time for themselves as a couple. It may help for them to think of these calendar comparisons as a way of making sure they do not make individual schedules that *prohibit* them from having time together.

3. *Learn to say "no."* There may come a time in the overcommitted lives of any couple when they must face the fact that if they take on one more obligation, it will mean that something else must go undone. Too often what is sacrificed is time either with a partner or alone. Often spouses and children are asked to be tolerant so that outsiders can be served. Most people find it difficult to turn down invitations or other kinds of requests until they realize that they are giving other people higher priority than those at home.

Every marriage needs nurturance and quality attention if both partners are to be satisfied with their relationship. Although time spent together may not be the most important ingredient in a happy marriage, it is perhaps the base on which the other factors must rest. It is very difficult to become intimate companions, love each other, make joint decisions, and reach mutual goals without spending sufficient time in interaction to accomplish these tasks.

Summary

■ Couples whose marriages give them room to meet their individual goals place greater value on their marriages. When each partner facilitates the other's plans, they have what is termed *mutual interdependence.*

■ Good marriages must find ways to link individual goals to mutual goals shared by the partners. Research indicates that working cooperatively as a team toward mutual goals leads to greater attraction between partners and to greater satisfaction with their marriage.

■ Cooperation is not only defined in terms of shared goals, however. The means by which couples seek their goals is also important. Not only must there be mutual interdependence in goals, in other words, but there must also be interdependence in the means of achieving goals.

■ Cooperation often hinges on communication. The more couples communicate, the more they facilitate cooperation. Communication without trust, however, does not help move couples toward their goals. Trust must be present before cooperation becomes the rule.

■ Time management is another challenge that can facilitate a marital relationship or, if handled poorly, can create serious feelings of distance and alienation between the partners. Most studies of time that couples spend together emphasize the quality of the time rather than the quantity. However, the quantity must be sufficient to satisfy both partners in a reasonable fashion.

■ Major interferences with quality time for couples come from a variety of sources: too many activities, demands of work and other activities or of children, family, friends, and other "outsiders." Couples with busy schedules would do well to compare calendars and to schedule time for themselves as they do for others. This may entail learning to say "no" as they give their marriages a higher priority than many of the activities or persons who previously may have taken precedence.

Glossary

Defense-oriented   Pertaining to behaviors, thoughts, or feelings that deny or distort reality for the purpose of reducing personal anxiety.

Implementation power   The right or responsibility of a person to whom tasks are delegated to make the decisions necessary for carrying out those tasks.

Orchestration power   The right or responsibility of a delegated person to decide who will carry out organizational tasks so that the necessary activities to achieve family goals are effectively articulated.

Reality-oriented   Pertaining to a condition in which an individual perceives his or her environment in substantially the same way that it is objectively measured or is seen by most other persons.

Many will still
decide, for all sorts
of personally valid
reasons, that
parenthood is not
for them, but
others, remembering
their own joyful
childhoods, will be
eager to participate
in such an
experience again, as
parent now instead
of child.

—Bernice Lott

9 · Family Planning and Birth Control

Throughout most of the world for most of human history, women have been expected to be either pregnant or nursing babies from adolescence until menopause. Civilization brought with it a restrictive morality about childbearing, although before the Christian era ways of enjoying sexual intercourse without causing pregnancy were devised. Motives for limiting the number of pregnancies began to change in the nineteenth century. Since that time contraceptive procedures have advanced technologically with growing speed.

This chapter deals with the contraceptive methods currently in use, their advantages, their drawbacks, and their relative effectiveness. It also deals with abortion as a means of limiting births, the methods by which abortions are carried out, and their effects. Finally, there is a section on the remedies for involuntary childlessness.

Undoubtedly early humans saw pregnancy as a normal developmental event for women, occurring first in adolescence and recurring until menopause (or, in most cases, until death, since few females lived to reach menopause). As civilizations advanced, ruling classes in particular controlled lines of descent by restricting sexual access to women, demanding virginity at marriage (or concubinage), and allowing sexual access only to the husband after marriage. This evolving social system made it desirable to find ways to have sexual intercourse without causing pregnancy.

Although earlier efforts at preventing pregnancy are believed by some to have been designed primarily for the benefit of men, Marie Stopes in England and Margaret Sanger in the United States became especially concerned with the effects of uncontrolled conception on the health and welfare of women.[1] A century before Stopes and Sanger, Thomas Malthus argued for the limitation of births for economic reasons, urging premarital chastity and late marriage for the upper classes and, for the lower classes, starvation as a means of control.[2] Even though these procedures were acceptable under the ancient moral code, Malthus fared little better than Stopes and Sanger in his public relations, being called "dismal" by his fellow scholars and sometimes suffering physical abuse from the working class as he walked through the streets of England.

As a result of improved nutrition, better methods of refrigeration, better maternal and infant care, and better control of contagious diseases, the survival rate of babies and the prolongation of life caused an unprecedented population boom in the twentieth century. In the United States this coincided with the movement of the bulk of the population from family farms to urban industrial areas. Dependent parents and children no longer contributed to the family economy but instead became a severe financial drain. The limitation of reproduction became necessary for survival.

Differences among various moral codes about limiting childbearing are by no means resolved today. The Roman Catholic and Mormon churches have official doctrines that encourage large families by banning "artificial" methods of birth control. Some ethnic groups also encourage large families. Even so, a substantial fraction of the adult population—including members of virtually all religious, racial, and ethnic groups—practice some form of birth control, primarily for personal rather than ideological reasons. As contraceptive use has spread, for the first time in history it has become possible for most persons to choose when to have a child, how many to have, or whether to have any at all. The result has been that many Third World countries that formerly had high birth rates have been able to curb the growth of their populations.

As a result of the use of contraceptives and abortion, the United States is now near or even below "**zero population growth**," meaning that the average woman is having 2.1 or fewer children who will grow to be old enough to replace themselves in the population pool. A low of 1.8 was reached in 1976.[3] Considering that 5 percent of married couples will have no children and another 5 percent of women will remain unmarried and probably childless, our

FIGURE 9.1

Changes in the Components of Fertility: 1970–1975 and 1975–1980

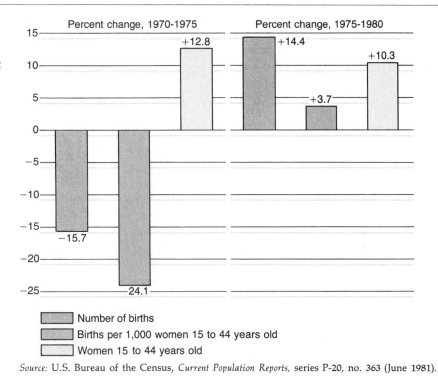

Number of births

Births per 1,000 women 15 to 44 years old

Women 15 to 44 years old

Source: U.S. Bureau of the Census, *Current Population Reports*, series P-20, no. 363 (June 1981).

population size may even begin to decrease at some time in the future, although probably not until well into the twenty-first century. At present, there is a modest increasing trend (see Figure 9.1).

The fertility rate for 1976 was the lowest in recorded United States history; the 1978 rate was the second lowest. The rate for women aged forty to forty-nine had increased about 9 percent by 1979.[4] Postponement of childbearing is credited for this increase: over 12 percent of the women over age thirty were having their first baby and nearly 7 percent their second.

As they near the age of thirty-five, many American women believe that their time to reproduce is running out. They have noted research showing more maternal and infant deaths and more birth defects when older women conceive. The most frequently diagnosed defect is Down's Syndrome (mongolism), which has a risk factor of 1 in 1,500 live births to mothers under age thirty that escalates to 1 in 130 for mothers between the ages of forty and forty-four and to 1 in 20 for women over forty-five.[5] Consequently, women in the thirty to thirty-four age group who have postponed having children may decide they cannot safely wait any longer.

In the United States, there is a distinction made between children born to married women and those born to unmarried women, while in some countries no legal distinction is made. In Sweden, for instance, the notion of **illegitimacy** is not an important one, especially in matters of support or inheritance from the biological father as well as from the mother.[6] In 1975 the European Convention on the Status of Children Born out of Wedlock suggested that the concept of illegitimacy be dropped. The point was made that children born to a married woman are not considered illegitimate even if a man other than her husband is the biological father. The question became, "Why is the child of an unmarried woman singled out for discrimination?"[7]

In the United States there is beginning to be a shift toward doing away with legal distinctions between legitimate and illegitimate births. One reason for this may be that a growing number of single women are freely choosing to bear children. These are often somewhat older women who decide not to marry but who nonetheless want to be mothers. There are also formerly married women who bear children while they are between marriages. Ten percent of births occur after a woman's divorce and before her remarriage.[8]

Although earlier data are often incomplete and unreliable, it is known that in 1940 there were only 17 illegitimate births recorded in the United States for every 1,000 unmarried women over twenty-five years of age. By 1977 that figure had more than tripled to 57 for every 1,000 unmarried women over the age of twenty-five.[9] Since it is known that nearly all women over the age of twenty-five have been exposed to knowledge about the use of contraceptives, it is believed that a large number of the conceptions may be deliberate. The idea of an older woman choosing to have a child even though she is single gives us quite a different picture of illegitimacy from that of a teenager who gets pregnant (intentionally or unintentionally) and who thereby may create a problem for herself, the child, the father, her parents, and often for taxpayers.

The women maintaining families in 1978 were generally younger, more likely to be divorced or never married, and more likely to be black than their 1960 counterparts.[10] Forty-four percent of all black children under the age of eighteen were living with only one parent in 1979, nineteen of every twenty of them with their mothers.[11]

Teenagers account for nearly 50 percent of all out-of-wedlock births. This is very likely one important reason that illegitimacy continues to bear the stigma that it does. An unplanned birth can make a very young mother and her baby vulnerable to economic, social, and psychological problems. In his comprehensive work on family planning, Arthur Campbell has stated:

> The girl who has an illegitimate child at the age of sixteen suddenly has 90 percent of her life's script written for her. She will probably drop out of school, even if someone else in her family helps to take care of the baby. She will probably not be able to find a steady job that pays enough to provide for herself and her child; she may feel impelled to marry someone she might not otherwise have chosen. Her life choices are few, and most of them are bad. Had she been able to delay the first child, her prospects might have been quite different assuming that she would have had opportunities to continue her education,

*improve her vocational skills, find a job, marry someone she wanted to marry,
and have a child when she and her husband were ready for it.*[12]

A wealth of research has attempted to explain why the fifteen- to nineteen-year-old age group has such a high rate of illegitimacy. One factor is that females are sexually active at an earlier age than ever before. By age nineteen, 55 percent of all females report experiencing intercourse.[13] It is unlikely that sexually active teenagers will be married: only 24 percent under the age of nineteen have ever been married; less than 3 percent under the age of seventeen have ever been married.[14] Therefore, any children conceived by sexually active females in this age category are likely to be born out of wedlock. As a result of better diets and a general increase in health, American girls today begin to menstruate nearly a year earlier than their grandmothers did, indicating the possibility of earlier pregnancy.

There are two other important factors in teenage pregnancies. First, teenagers are likely to be less well informed about both reproduction and contraception than are older persons. This situation seems to be improving somewhat as more sex education courses are being offered in high schools. Unfortunately, many of these are actually focused on reproduction—on how babies grow in the uterus rather than on why they get there in the first place. In the 1976 National Survey of Young Women, 70 percent of the single fifteen- to nineteen-year-old females reported that they had taken such a course and that it had included instruction about the menstrual cycle and pregnancy.[15] Our impression, however, is that the necessity for the use of contraceptives if pregnancy is to be avoided is often underemphasized in such courses and that the necessary social skills for discussing contraceptive use with a partner are likely to be totally ignored as a topic.

A second factor accounting for the current number of teenage pregnancies is that learning about contraception in a classroom is a far cry from purchasing and correctly using such devices. Particularly when they first begin sexual activity, many young women report that they resist the idea of going on a date "prepared" since this eliminates spontaneity and causes them to feel calculating. Of those who do want to use contraceptives, many report that they are embarrassed to buy them or to ask a physician for them.

Although we have not seen any concrete figures on this subject, we speculate that very few young women plan their first sexual intercourse or are prepared with contraceptives in advance. As one young woman told us:

*It is important in our school not to have the reputation of sleeping around and
being easy. Even though it is well-known that you had sex with the last guy you
went out with steadily, the next one needs to believe he is special and you have
to make him wait at least a while before you have sex. To carry a diaphragm
around in your purse looks like you are ready anytime. It has to happen as
though you were swept away by the moment—not as though you were planning
it.*[16]

TABLE 9.1

*Percentage of Sexually
Active Women Using
Contraceptives*

Age	1971	1976
15	30%	52%
16	38	56
17	45	63
18	47	70
19	55	69

Source: M. Zelnik and J. F. Kantner, "Sexual and Contraceptive Experience of Young Unmarried Women in the United States, 1976 and 1971," *Family Planning Perspectives* 9 (March–April 1977), p. 62. Reprinted with permission from the authors and *Family Planning Perspectives*, Volume 9, Number 2, 1977.

Two national studies have determined that many teenagers are sexually active for as long as a year before they begin to use any kind of contraception.[17] As young women get older, there is an increase in their use of contraceptives. There has been a significant change from 1971, when the first of the National Survey of Young Women studies was done, to 1976, when the second one occurred (see Table 9.1).

The American Public Health Association has indicated that the age of first intercourse is related to current use of contraceptives. Those aged fifteen or younger when they first have intercourse are significantly less reliable users than persons who are older at first intercourse.[18]

Shah and Zelnik have studied the effects of parental and peer influence on the use of contraceptives by unmarried fifteen- to nineteen-year-old women. They report:

> The premarital pregnancy experience of young women by parent and peer influence is consistent with their contraceptive use status. Black women with views like their parents' have the highest rate (50 percent) of premarital pregnancy. This group also has the highest proportion (52 percent) of those who never use contraception. White women with views like their parents' have the lowest rate of premarital pregnancy (22 percent); this group also has the lowest proportion of women who have had unprotected intercourse. The association between parent and peer influence among whites is not surprising; those influenced by parents are less likely to have a premarital pregnancy than those influenced by friends.[19]

The increased knowledge and use of contraceptives by teenagers is encouraging to those who would like to see teenage pregnancy rates drop. It should follow that the availability of contraceptives will lead to a decrease in the number of children born to women who are not yet ready to be mothers. However, this has not been the case. Although some of the more than 500,000 births a year to unwed mothers in the United States may have been planned, it is safe to say that the majority probably were not.

Ninety-four percent of single mothers elect to keep their babies.[20] In their extensive study of premarital pregnancy, Zelnik and Kantner reported that 9 percent of those women fifteen to nineteen years old who became pregnant married shortly after their baby was born. Eighty-five percent of teenaged unwed mothers spent a longer period of time as single parents.[21]

One study reported that one year after their babies were born, 75 percent of the young mothers reported that they were responsible for the babies' care. The figure dropped to 60 percent after two years and to less than 50 percent in a subsequent follow-up. After one year, nearly 20 percent of the mothers had lost contact with the fathers; after five years, 37 percent of the fathers had not been heard from for over a year. The main source of assistance the young mother had was her own family.[22]

Eventually, most of these young women married someone and made an adjustment. It may be that the most serious drawbacks to an illegitimate pregnancy are short term. In the long run, with the help of their families, many young women manage to overcome some of the bad personal consequences of their premature motherhood.

Summary

■ It is more possible now than at any previous time in the history of the world for people to control the conception of children. Improved hygiene and medical care have reduced the infant mortality rates in Third World countries, so that limiting the number of births may be the only way for populations to live within their food supplies.

■ Although there has been a long-term decline in fertility rates in the United States, there has been an upward trend since 1976, especially among women aged thirty to thirty-four.

■ There has been a sharp rise in recent years in the number of births to unmarried women, 50 percent of whom are teenagers.

■ Although more sex education courses are being offered in high schools, our impression is that they tend to focus on the physiology of menstruation and reproduction rather than on contraception and the social skills needed to avoid unwanted pregnancies.

■ Although an increasing number of sexually active teenagers are using contraceptives, nearly one-third do not.

■ A half million babies are born to unwed mothers each year, and 94 percent of their mothers keep them.

Why People Have Children

The reasons for creating pregnancies differ from person to person, of course. Couples who are deliberately trying to produce a pregnancy do so for a variety of reasons, and indeed any person, married or not, may have unique reasons for wishing to become a parent.

Unintended or even unwanted pregnancies may occur simply because a male or female or both together have a compelling urge to have sexual intercourse. They need not have any enduring relationship; in fact, the "compelling urge" may be acted out in prostitution or rape between total strangers. The pregnancies resulting from such acts produce children just as surely as ones for which the parents have planned for years. There is no way of knowing how many babies are born simply because a sexual encounter was so overpowering that one or both of the participants were not really concerned with the consequences. The Emory University Family Planning Program issued a report stating that of every hundred sexually active women who left the consequences of intercourse to chance, ninety actually became pregnant in the course of one year.[23] Their findings are shown in Table 9.3, p. 267.

The Commission on Population Growth reported in 1972 that 44 percent of all births to married women in the United States between 1966 and 1970 were unplanned.[24] It can be assumed that these babies were conceived because having intercourse was valuable to the couples—or at least to one of them—for whatever reason, and that there were varying degrees of concern (either positive or negative) about whether a pregnancy would result.

Studies of motives for having children have revealed that there are nine basic values that are often reported as important reasons for conceiving children:[25,26]

1. to prove that one is an adult
2. to have some personal expansion of oneself and perhaps of one's ancestors that will last beyond one's own lifetime
3. to satisfy certain standards set by one's family or religion
4. to create an intimate, affectionate living group larger than the couple alone
5. to experience the adventures of childbearing and child rearing
6. to create a new person
7. to have someone to take care of who is dependent and can be molded
8. to demonstrate that one can accomplish something that others long to do
9. to have another family member to share in the family's work and to count on in old age

A review and modification of this list may suggest further rational motives that many persons actually have or, at least, are aware of having. Although a wish to have children that is separate from the wish to have sexual intercourse may not qualify as an "urge" or a "drive," there does seem to exist in some persons a longing to have one's own children that has no rational component. Many couples may well ask why they must have a reason—they just want to have children, and it is not a decision they spend a great deal of time debating.

Voluntary Childlessness

Although many couples are deciding to have children, a slowly growing number are currently childless. Until relatively recently, if a woman did not bear children, it was assumed that she could not. Those few who chose to announce bravely that their state was voluntary were often subjected to harsh judgments about their mental health or their lack of femininity. Kinder friends or relatives might have tried to make them see the error of the decision.

The effectiveness of the considerable social and emotional pressure that was often applied is evident in surveys made by the Bureau of the Census that asked women how many children they planned to have. During the twenty-one-year period from 1946 to 1967, only about 3 percent of American women said that they expected to be childless.[27] In the 1920s and 1930s the figure had been much higher: about 20 percent of the women surveyed expected to remain childless; however, many of those may simply have been acknowledging their own or their husbands' infertility. With improvements in diet, general health, and medical care (especially treatment for infertility and the acceptability of artificial insemination), more women knew they would be able to conceive if they wished to, and that may have accounted for some of the change.

Once involuntary childlessness decreased, the number of women who remained childless dropped from 20 percent to 5 percent, where it stayed until the "baby boom" that followed World War II (1946–1957). As families were reunited after the war, there seemed to be an urge to get the country "back to normal." Most couples evidently wished to have children: part of normality, evidently, was "nest building" and filling the nest with babies.

The trend toward large families lasted until 1957, but the general idea of having some children continued to be popular for another decade. Not until the birth control pill was mass marketed in 1966–1967 was there a marked gain in the number of women who wanted no children at all. Even then, the increase was only enough to bring the percentage back to 9 percent.

As recently as 1973, a Gallup poll found that only 1 percent of the population believed that being childless was preferable or that childless couples had a better life.[28] It may be that many of those who are childless at any given time are either involuntarily so or will change their minds eventually. Since 1977 there has been a slight but steady increase in the number of married women

who expect to remain childless. The most recent census report shows that the figure is now slightly above 5 percent.[29]

Educational attainment is related to the proportions of women who expect to remain childless. Expectation of childlessness is most common among women who have attended college, less common among high school graduates, and still less common among those who have dropped out of school (see Table 9.2).

A fact that is related to the figures on education and childlessness is that women who are (or intend to be) successful in careers for which education has prepared them are those who are least likely to want children.[30] At the same time, school- and/or college-aged women who have babies are surely less likely to continue in school than those who do not, regardless of whether the pregnancy was intentional or unintentional. In a recent study carried out in the Midwest, childless married women were asked why they had chosen not to have children. Eighty-one percent responded that children would interfere with their jobs or careers.[31] Some of the other reasons cited were also related to work goals: 90 percent mentioned that opportunities and freedom would be hampered by children; 48 percent listed economic concerns; and 43 percent mentioned managing the work load with both a job and children. Clearly, women with career goals are concerned with the impact of children on their

TABLE 9.2

Married Women Who Expect to Remain Childless

Total (18–34 years of age)	=	14,940,000
College: 5 years +	=	14.3%
4 years	=	7.5%
1–3 years	=	7.3%
High school graduate	=	4.9%
Non–high school graduate	=	2.6%

Source: U.S. Bureau of the Census, *Current Population Reports,* series P-20, no. 341 (1977), p. 27.

lives. Even though fathers are taking a more active role in parenting in the 1980s, women evidently still believe that responsibilities demanding a substantial amount of time and energy will fall to them.

White women are somewhat more likely to remain childless if they are college educated than are black women (7.5 percent of white women compared with 6.6 percent of black women).[32] Never-married white women are far more likely to remain childless than never-married black women. By the completion of childbearing years (age fifty to fifty-nine category), every 1,000 such white women had borne seventy-two children in 1979, but 1,000 such black women had borne 1,644 children.[33] Although we do not have comparable data for other racial and ethnic groups, a report issued on women of Spanish origin in Los Angeles would lead us to believe that the proportion remaining childless would be significantly lower. Women of Spanish origin have a much higher fertility rate than American women as a whole. This is attributed to their desires for larger families rather than to the failure of their family planning efforts, which have been found to have the same rate of success for them as for other American women.[34]

Making the Decision to Remain Childless

Researchers have addressed several questions about people who decide not to have children. In recent years well over a hundred studies have addressed themselves to: (1) how couples make the decision to remain childless; (2) when they make this decision; (3) whether it is a mutual decision or one more heavily influenced by the wife or husband; and (4) how couples who aspire to childlessness compare in terms of marital satisfaction with couples who decide to have children.[35]

It has already been mentioned that women who are contemplating lifelong careers are among the foremost advocates of voluntary childlessness. It appears from this that couples' decisions would be dominated by women, since it is women who are most affected by having to balance their children with their jobs. Most of the research on this topic has indicated that, indeed, wives are much more likely to make the decision in nearly all instances. One study found that half the husbands who agreed not to have children admitted that if their wives should change and want a baby, they would agree.[36] Not one of the wives said that if her husband had a change of heart, it would affect her feelings on the subject.

It is very possible that the general finding that women have the greatest influence in the decision of whether or not to have children would not hold for some populations if separate data were compiled. The data for college-educated women, upper-socioeconomic-class wives, those with formal religious ties, and those with careers are not known; women in some of these categories may be more strongly influenced by what their husbands want.

According to one study of childless couples, most of them talked about whether or not to have children for months or even years before they made their decisions; most reported a minimum of two to three years.[37] Further, most of the couples studied reported that the decision was made after their marriage, not before, and was attributed primarily to the wife's employment and the couple's subsequent commitment to a childless life-style. Having more time for each other as a couple and enjoying travel and leisure time together were important considerations. In another study, only 29 percent of those replying to the question of why they were remaining childless mentioned feeling that they would not be good parents or that they did not like children.[38]

A recent study has identified some women who make the decision to remain childless relatively early in their lives, long before they marry.[39] These women were compared with women who made the decision after marriage. Significant differences in family background between women in the two categories were found. Those who decided early to remain childless had been socialized to accept more autonomy and were more likely to describe themselves as independent of social pressures. In addition, they were high achievers and had surrounded themselves with a support group of other achievers who approved of their choice to remain childless. This study refutes the notion that social pressure always aims to get women to decide to have children. Women who prefer not to have children also seek each other out for support.[40]

Marital Satisfaction of Voluntarily Childless Couples

Most of the research comparing the degree of marital satisfaction of childless couples with that of those who do have children has reported that children often have a negative effect on marriages.[41] However, rarely have the reasons behind the childlessness been considered. Marital satisfaction may be more closely related to whether or not couples who want children have them and those who do not want children do not have them than to the mere presence or absence of children. Couples who want children and have them may be more satisfied than couples who want them but do not have them. Similarly, couples who do not want children and do not have any may report higher marital satisfaction than do those who do not want children but have them anyway.[42]

In a carefully designed study that distinguished the marital adjustment of voluntarily childless women from that of women who were postponing conception or who were involuntarily childless, a small but significant trend toward greater adjustment was found for those women who intentionally chose not to have children.[43] The fact that the difference was not large has led to speculation that the major factor in marital satisfaction may not be having or not having a child but, rather, that childless couples often have more resources, more time to be together, and more flexibility in their schedules. This points to the need for more research to control for the factors of education, employment, religion, and resources including money, household help, and family support.

It is reasonable to assume that populations who do not value large families, who are well educated, and who have access to effective means of contraception will have lower reproductive rates than their counterparts in other groups. In 1979 the average family with a college-educated head under forty-five years of age had 1.95 children under eighteen years of age; their grammar-school-educated counterparts had 2.49 children.[44] Whether this is due to a positive wish to have more children on the part of less well educated persons, to lack of knowledge about or access to contraceptives, or simply to indifference about birth control probably varies from couple to couple, if not from person to person.

Most men and women who use contraceptives do so because they want a specific number of children at certain intervals. Very few use contraceptives for the purpose of remaining childless throughout their lifetimes. Only one married woman in twenty dies or reaches menopause without ever having been pregnant, as compared with figures for 1790 of one in three who were never pregnant in their lives. The number has declined steadily over the years and is continuing to do so as a result of improvement in the general health of the population and better methods of increasing fertility. Therefore, even though substantially more couples are choosing to be childless—citing overpopulation or their personal wishes not to be parents as reasons—the decrease in involuntary childlessness has offset these numbers. Consequently, the total number of childless couples remains low.

Although most women have at least one child, millions of women are postponing the births of their first children. In the last ten years the number of women under the age of thirty who are still childless but who eventually want children has increased dramatically.[45] A variety of explanations have been offered, but the most likely is that women have occupational goals to achieve before they become mothers and that financial conditions for most young couples necessitate that they have two incomes for several years if they are to be able to afford a family.

As today's couples face the real choice of whether or not to become parents, the pros and cons of parenthood have come into sharper focus. Couples should consider their desire and ability to be parents as well as whether they are genetically fit to reproduce. Some genetic conditions have a strong likelihood of being passed on, and couples with such an inheritance should weigh the risks and their implications. Some couples seek **genetic counseling**, which can detect whether or not the parents are carriers of certain diseases or abnormalities before they conceive. Other genetic screening may be done during the pregnancy to determine whether the fetus is affected. This can be done by a process called **amniocentesis**, which will be discussed more thoroughly later. Some couples choose abortion if they discover through such a procedure that a fetus will have a serious abnormality.

Summary

■ Pregnancies normally result from acts of sexual intercourse. Intercourse may occur because of its intrinsic value to one or both members of a couple or because it is intended to achieve some other value, including causing a pregnancy.

■ As recently as 1970, about nine out of every twenty births to married women were unplanned. The motives for having babies intentionally are varied and often complex.

■ Voluntary childlessness by means other than abstention from coitus is a relatively recent possibility. In 1978 only about one married American woman in twenty wanted to be childless, down from one in five during the 1920s and 1930s.

■ The decision of married couples about whether or not to have children is almost always made by the wives. The reasons most frequently given relate to the wives' work and career decisions.

■ The average number of children born into a household with a grammar-school-educated head (either male or female) was about 25 percent higher than the average number born into a household with a college-educated head in 1979.

Birth Control

Birth control is used to decrease the probability that coitus will result in pregnancy or to influence the likelihood that pregnancy will occur at a particular time. Considerations of whether or not and when to become pregnant involve such issues as the ages of the parents, their financial security, religious and family pressures or customs, the career stages of each partner, the number (if any) of previous children (of this or previous marriages), and even the kind of neighborhood or housing in which the prospective parents currently live.

The physical health of both mothers and children is believed to be adversely affected by pregnancies that are spaced more closely than two years apart.[46] An increasing number of couples recognize this fact and also wish to give themselves a breather between children for reasons of finances and fatigue. Fifteen percent of couples now wait more than five years after marriage to begin to have children (as opposed to only 9 percent a quarter of a century ago), and more couples are putting two or more years between births.[47] It is impossible to determine definitely how many of these shifts represent changes in the values of particular persons, how many represent changes in knowledge about and proper use of contraceptives, and how many represent changes related to other factors such as economic or housing problems.

Whether people wish to remain childless while enjoying an active sex life or simply wish to plan the timing of their pregnancies, most want a reliable contraceptive procedure. Since the average woman is fertile for approximately three decades and theoretically is supposed to ovulate once every lunar month (13 times a year or, on average, 390 times in her life), it is unlikely that she would want as many children as she might have if she did nothing at all to prevent pregnancy. Even more unlikely is the notion that a man might want to fertilize as many ova as he is capable of doing since, theoretically, he could easily impregnate one or more women every day. Consequently, some form of birth control is desired by most people who have wanted sex without pregnancy ever since the first human realization that intercourse and pregnancy are related.

In some societies pregnancy was believed to be caused by a spirit that entered a woman's body; in others it was believed to result from exposure to the wind or from eating some special food or potion. Even where the association of sexual intercourse with subsequent pregnancy was known, its nature has not always been well understood. Some explanations centered around the phase of the moon or the tides. Some societies believed that each time a member of the group died, another was created.[48] Others believed that males exuded microscopically small human beings in their semen, and that these grew to birth size in women.

Conception has a fascinating history. Early literature shows that in ancient times, when a woman wished to prevent or to postpone pregnancy, she had a choice of several methods. Women were advised to place feathers or small sponges in their vaginas to absorb the sperm or to use hollowed-out lemon or pomegranate halves to cover the cervix. Some women believed that they could prevent conception by jumping up and down after the man had ejaculated or holding their breaths during orgasm.[49]

The notorious lover Casanova viewed contraceptive efforts as a way of avoiding the social responsibilities of pregnancy and devised methods by which men could protect themselves from unwanted paternity. He described his use of animal skin condoms tied with a ribbon. He also recommended the use of a gold ball inserted in the vagina as a contraceptive plan for women he loved. In 1798 Thomas Malthus suggested abstinence from premarital intercourse, followed by late marriage, as a birth control plan. He reportedly had never engaged in coitus by the time he married at age forty.

The issue of birth control has been the cause of much social conflict. In the United States in 1873, opponents of birth control were successful in securing an act of Congress, the Comstock Law (named for the secretary of the New York Society for the Suppression of Vice), that made it unlawful to disseminate birth control devices or information about them through the mail. Many states enacted further legislation that forbade the sale or dispensing of such devices by doctors or druggists or in any store. These laws were in force in many areas of the United States until very recently. Not until 1966 was the last state law banning the sale of contraceptives repealed.

In 1915 Margaret Sanger (who coined the term *birth control*) in the United States and Marie Stopes in England began attempts to overturn the Comstock laws. Applying skills she had learned in England, Sanger opened a birth control clinic. She published a newsletter and initiated research aimed at developing reliable methods of controlling fertility. Sanger went to jail for her efforts, which were primarily to help women whose health was threatened by pregnancy or who lacked the resources or the strength to care for more children.[50]

Until Stopes and Sanger began their activities on behalf of women, men had generally taken the initiative in contraception, usually as a way of enjoying sexual intercourse while reducing the probability of the social or financial responsibilities of fathering a child. Stopes and Sanger introduced the idea that

Margaret Sanger

women as well as men were entitled to the right to prevent pregnancy. However, they were probably more concerned with women's health and financial welfare than with their right to enjoy sex whenever they chose.

Slowly, over the years, laws and sentiments about contraception have been changing—but the controversy has not totally ended. Many American Catholics, including some members of the clergy, are beginning to question the banning of contraceptives when it is a matter of record that the majority of Catholic women use some form of birth control. In a speech delivered before the United States National Conference of Catholic Bishops in September 1980, Archbishop John Quinn said that in view of published studies reporting that 76.5 percent of American Roman Catholic women are using birth control and that 71 percent of Catholic priests in the United States do not believe that birth control is immoral, a new church doctrine of "responsible parenthood" is needed.[51] This position, however, was almost immediately denounced by the Vatican, and the conflict goes on.

Even today, strange as it may seem, some opposition is still directed toward making contraceptives available to sexually active unmarried teenagers. The logic of the opponents seems to be that allowing teenagers access to contraceptives will encourage premarital sexual activity. Still others believe that sex outside of marriage is a sin and that sinners should be punished by having to live with their mistakes—meaning any resulting pregnancy, any resulting social disgrace, any financial burden. The old saying that "the penalty for an hour of pleasure is a lifetime of regret" seems appropriate to this belief.

Some persons argue that teenagers should not be allowed to obtain contraceptives without parental consent. Here the logic seems to be that parents should know what their teenagers are doing sexually so that they may be able to prevent such activity (or perhaps somehow supervise it). The problem with this belief is that most teenagers do not confide in their parents about their sex lives—any more than parents confide in their children—and if they were forced to do so to gain access to contraceptives, most would opt to do without.

The picture in the United States currently is one of relative contraceptive freedom, with 92 percent of married women who do not want to become pregnant (including the nearly 30 percent who have chosen sterilization) using some form of contraception.[52] Teenagers are currently legally free to receive contraceptive advice without parental consent. Some physicians reportedly still refuse to give contraceptive assistance to unmarried teenagers because of their own personal religious or moral beliefs. Planned Parenthood clinics across the United States, however, give advice and make referrals for any person who needs them, possibly recognizing that the younger the potential parent, the more urgent the need.

The last stronghold of opposition to freely available contraceptives seems to center around the issue of who pays for them. Many taxpayers resent subsidizing birth control clinics and contraceptives for those who cannot pay. The logic seems to be that making such help available provides an easy way out of the risk of pregnancy at the taxpayers' expense and perhaps encourages illicit sexual activity. Ironically, it is often those who can least afford to support their children who are prohibited from securing contraceptives by their inability to pay for them. Instead of paying for birth control clinics and contraceptives, taxpayers may well end up paying for prenatal care, childbirth, and eighteen years of support for some out-of-wedlock children.

It is interesting to note that those who wish to prevent any pregnancy, if they are well informed, have a higher success rate than do those who are delaying birth or spacing children.[53] This is evidence of the importance of motivation in the use and success of contraceptives.

In their analysis of contraceptive use, Diamond and Karlen give three rules, to which we have added a fourth:

1. Any method is better than none.
2. Two methods combined are better than one.
3. No method is perfect: all have failures or side effects.[54]
4. Always provide for *your own* contraception, no matter what your partner does, if you want to be absolutely certain that precautions are being taken.

We have added the fourth rule to the foregoing list because we believe it eliminates any tendency to blame one's partner for a contraceptive failure; because, ironically, people may engage in sexual intercourse and yet feel embarrassed about discussing contraception; because all too often people *assume* that their partners "know enough to be on the Pill," or "know enough to withdraw before ejaculation" without checking their assumptions; because the best way to be sure of the quality of contraceptives is to buy them yourself after an informed discussion; and, most of all, because we believe that people who are old enough to be risking pregnancy are old enough to take full personal responsibility for any and all of their behaviors, including the decisions they make and the persons whose advice they take.

With these thoughts in mind, we turn to a discussion of the various methods of contraception.

Surgical
Intervention:
Sterilization

The word *sterilization* is not a neutral one to very many people. For some it threatens the very essence of their self-concepts as males or females. For others, it may be controversial from a social or a religious perspective. There has been evidence of involuntary sterilization of persons on welfare, prisoners, and minority-group members who do not understand that they are being given a choice about whether or not to be sterilized.[55] The first recorded intentional surgical sterilization in the United States was performed in 1897 on a woman who was judged mentally deranged and who already had several children. In that same year vasectomies were given to prison inmates in Illinois.

The Department of Health and Human Services has attempted to prevent any future injustices such as those that have occurred in involuntary sterilizations by issuing guidelines that forbid any patient in a federally assisted medical program from being sterilized without having received complete information in a language that he or she clearly understands. In addition, there is a mandatory thirty-day waiting period between the time the person signs the consent form and the date of the operation. No doubt some sterilization still occurs that is not truly voluntary; however, with heightened public awareness, the amount of such action seems to be diminishing.

The religious objections to sterilization have remained fairly constant over the years. The major argument against sterilization on religious grounds is that any means of controlling pregnancy other than abstinence or the rhythm method is against the will of God unless the sterilization occurs as a byproduct of surgery for other purposes. For instance, a papal encyclical of the Catholic Church in 1968 approved hysterectomies as necessary for certain gynecological reasons and therefore sanctioned the resulting sterilization as well.

Some arguments against sterilization have come from members of the medical professions, who in many cases have set themselves up as judges of whether or not a man or woman has a right to be sterilized. Such criteria as age, number of children, marital status (persons under twenty-five with no children and unmarried persons have been routinely turned down by many physicians) have been used as factors to restrict such surgery. Successful lawsuits have been brought in court, and currently sterilization is rarely refused (except in Utah, where medical necessity still must be proved).[56]

In spite of opposition in some quarters, sterilization is now the most popular form of contraception in the United States for those couples who have already had their desired number of children. Recent figures indicate that 15 percent of all adult females and 11 percent of all adult males have been sterilized.[57]

The usual procedure for male sterilization is called **vasectomy**. The physician cuts and ties off the tube (*vas deferens*) that carries sperm from each of the testicles. Over 50,000 such operations are performed each year. A vasectomy affects only the delivery of sperm, not their production nor the production of male hormones. After vasectomy, sperm produced are resorbed into the bloodstream rather than being ejaculated with the seminal fluid (which continues to be produced by the prostate and other glands). Since the production of androgens is not affected, neither interest in sexual activity nor secondary sex characteristics should be changed. This surgery is considered minor; it is usually performed in a doctor's office with the patient under a local anesthetic; discomfort is usually not great, although there are rare exceptions.[58] Most physicians recommend the resumption of normal sexual activity in two weeks.

The success rate for preventing pregnancy by vasectomy is almost perfect. Any pregnancies following surgery usually are due to the resumption of intercourse before the seminal fluid has had time to clear itself of sperm left between the ligation and the end of the penis at the time of surgery. Ejaculate usually is sperm-free after approximately fifteen ejaculations (or in six weeks or so) but must be checked microscopically to be certain that this is so.

Vasectomy is generally considered a permanent sterilization since attempts to reconnect the vas deferens, though fairly successful with new microsurgery techniques, do not necessarily result in resumption of fertility. One complication seems to be that following vasectomy, many men seem to produce **antibodies** that will kill their own sperm. The most serious negative effect of a vasectomy is its association with atherosclerosis later in life, resulting in proportionately greater numbers of heart problems in men who have had vasectomies than among those who have not.[59]

Sterilization for women (**tubal ligation**) is more complicated than vasectomy since the tubes that must be severed and tied are less accessible than the male's vas deferens. One type of tubal ligation procedure closely approximates the simplicity of the vasectomy, however, and its popularity has been growing. This process, called a *minilaparotomy*, usually is performed on an outpatient basis, under only local anesthesia in most instances. The procedure involves two small incisions near the pubic hair line, which make the fallopian tubes accessible to be tied or cut.

Many physicians use an instrument called a *laparoscope*, which they insert through an abdominal incision (often at the navel so that no scar shows) both to see the instrument at work internally and to perform the operation. This procedure is called *laparoscopy* and, since the incision is so small, has been referred to popularly as "band-aid" surgery.

An older and more traditional method is performed in the hospital under general anesthesia because a larger incision is made in the abdomen and the process (*laparotomy*) is considered major surgery. Women who are obese or who have a history of pelvic infections or certain other health problems are candidates for this procedure rather than for the simpler ones.

Both the *laparoscopy* and the *laparotomy* can be performed through the vagina. This is less commonly done but is favored by some women since it leaves no visible scars.

Tubal ligation works by interfering with the progress of eggs, which cannot pass through the fallopian tubes after such surgery. It has no other known physical effects. The eggs disintegrate and are absorbed by the body. It is generally considered permanent sterilization, although the minilaparotomy is believed to have some potential for reversibility.[60]

A **hysterectomy** (removal of the uterus) is not routinely used for sterilization purposes because it is major surgery and necessitates a long recovery period. However, since large numbers of women need such surgery for other gynecological problems (it is the third most common female operation), it is also a source of sterilization for these women.[61] Hysterectomy often has negative effects; Masters and Johnson report that the uterus is important for a woman's orgasmic response and should never be removed unless it is absolutely necessary.[62] Nevertheless, thousands of women make good recoveries and since ethical physicians perform hysterectomy only to alleviate serious problems, the complications are usually not as bad as the original complaints were. The resulting sterilization is usually seen as a bonus for a woman who wants no more children.

Psychologically, some persons report feeling better as a result of sterilization. This is attributed to the lack of worry about unwanted pregnancy and a feeling of freedom from the constraints of other types of contraception. On the other hand, some men and women are bothered by the removal of the ability to reproduce. Those who associate their masculinity or femininity with their fertility may report a decreased interest in sex once they realize that this fertility is gone. In a recent study of 200 men who had had successful vasectomies, 1 percent regretted that they could father no more children, and 3 percent reported "sexual problems." However, 8 percent reported that their sexual performance was more satisfactory than before the surgery. The majority reported no regrets and no changes in their sexual performance or satisfaction.[63]

Chemical Contraceptives

Chemicals are used for contraception in two ways: (1) to stop the production of eggs (as with the birth control pill) and (2) to create a destructive environment for sperm (as with spermicides). It is estimated that one-third of all women of childbearing age in the United States use oral contraceptives. About eighty million women around the world are users.[64] The popularity of "the Pill" has been based on its effectiveness (among those who use it exactly as directed, fewer than 2 percent become pregnant each year) and on the fact that taking contraceptive pills is independent of the sex act and thus does not interfere with spontaneity.

The Pill works to prevent ovulation by increasing hormones (combinations of estrogens and **progesterones**) to the levels found in pregnancy. It also acts to thicken the mucous plug in the cervix, which inhibits sperm penetration, and to change the lining of the uterus so that even if the first two effects fail, a fertilized egg is not likely to implant. As extra benefits, some women find that menstrual irregularity, cramps, heavy flow, and premenstrual tension are diminished or eliminated by the use of oral contraceptives.

Recently, there has been a decline in use of many varieties of the Pill, although it is still the most popular nonpermanent contraceptive method.[65] This drop is almost certainly due to current information about possible side effects of oral contraceptive use. The contraceptive pill causes changes in body chemistry and, consequently, affects nearly all the organs of a woman's body. Serious complications are rare, however, and the risks to most women from oral contraceptives are much lower than the risks from pregnancy and childbirth. Nonetheless, many women are leery of tampering with body chemistry in this way, especially when other types of contraception are available.

A "minipill" has been developed that does not aim at stopping ovulation but does slow down the rate of movement of eggs in the fallopian tubes. It also thickens the mucous plug to inhibit sperm entry at the **cervix**. Since this pill contains no estrogen (which some studies suggest is related to cancer and blood clots), risks are minimized. The contraceptive ability of the minipill is as good as that of the older varieties, although some women experience irregular menstruation and more may develop infections with this type of contraceptive pill. It is clear that no pill has yet been developed that is both effective and free of all complications. Pills are, after all, medication; any medication may produce undesirable effects and must be medically managed.[66]

Chemicals that have been banned for use in the United States, usually because they have not yet been tested thoroughly enough to satisfy the Food and Drug Administration, are being widely used as contraceptives in some countries. One of these is Depo Provera, an injection of progestin that lasts for three months. Under-the-skin implants of time-released capsules of progesterone that remain effective for years are also being tested and used outside the United States.

The so-called morning-after pill is sometimes used in this country, although infrequently. An injection or a three- to seven-day series of pills containing high levels of artificial estrogen speeds up the progress of ova to the uterus so that they arrive before the lining of the uterus is prepared for implantation. These high estrogen doses are a shock to the system, however, and many women report unpleasant effects, such as nausea. More seriously, the artificial estrogen (diethylstilbestrol, or DES) has been linked to the presence of cell abnormalities in the cervixes of daughters of women who have been given this drug to prevent miscarriages. The sons of such women also often show testicular abnormalities.[67]

Some male birth control pills have been tested and are in use in other parts of the world, often on an experimental basis. These pills are reported to produce such undesirable effects (impaired liver function, cardiovascular problems) that they are not recommended by the World Health Organization. However, recent reports are encouraging and acceptable male birth control pills may be developed in the future.

One of the most promising avenues of research on contraception is reported from China, where a substance made from cottonseed has been found to interfere with sperm development. Other experimenters are attempting to produce antibodies to sperm like those that develop in many men after vasectomy.[68]

Spermicides are the second major type of chemical contraception. These have a history that dates back at least as far as the ancient Greeks, who inserted vinegar or lemon juice mixed with honey into the vagina to destroy sperm. Dried pigeon, elephant, or crocodile dung soaked in sour milk has also had wide usage over the years in various societies. Various other acids—including boric acid and even fruit beverages—have been used, since an acid environment is not healthful for sperm.

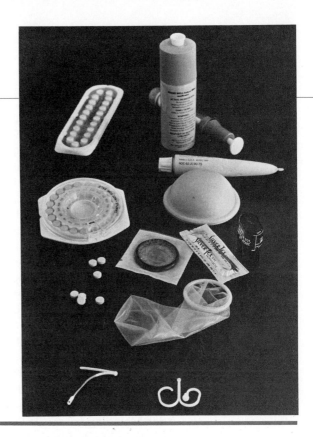

*Chemical and Barrier
Contraceptives*

Men have coated their penises with pastes containing an acid combined with cedarwood oil, fig pulp, and other such exotic substances in an effort to kill their sperm. One of the recently developed spermicides based on these earlier techniques is widely used in Switzerland. It can be used either by men (on the penis) or by women (in the vagina). It is a postage-stamp-sized filament called C-film that is melted readily by body heat and is an effective spermicide.[69]

The best-known commercially produced spermicides are jellies, creams, foams, and suppositories inserted into the vagina shortly before intercourse. Although these are less effective than oral contraceptives, they provide protection when they are used according to instructions and renewed for each act of intercourse. To be highly effective, they must be used in conjunction with a condom or a diaphragm. A few persons may have mild allergies to particular brands. Some couples complain that they cause more lubrication than they want, although others consider the additional lubrication an advantage. In addition, some spermicides may incidentally afford protection against various venereal diseases and vaginal infections. They are not designed as prophylactics, however, and one should never assume that they provide adequate protection against contracting syphilis, gonorrhea, or herpes from infected persons.

Barrier
Contraceptive
Devices

At one time the most popular contraceptive was the vaginal occlusive diaphragm used with a spermicide. Commonly called simply "the diaphragm," this thin rubber sheet is surrounded by a flexible spring. When diametrically opposite points on the circular spring are held together, the diaphragm (ideally well coated with a spermicide) can be inserted quickly and easily through the outer opening of the vagina. Once past the muscular entrance, the spring resumes its circular shape, with the supple vaginal sheath adapting to its configuration. When there is nothing in it, the vagina has no empty space within its periphery; it is completely collapsed. When the dome-like diaphragm is tucked up behind the pubic bone in front, the cervix is beyond the rubber barrier: sperm ejaculated against the front of the diaphragm would have to journey through the spermicidal jelly and around the perimeter that is snug against the vagina to reach the entrance to the uterus. Statistics demonstrate that few sperm ever make it.

Because the measurements of women differ, the size of a diaphragm should be selected by a trained health-care professional. Because women's measurements typically change with weight gain or loss, pelvic surgery, childbirth, and sexual activity, the fit should be checked at least once a year routinely, immediately following any changes suspected from the above list, and a few weeks after beginning coitus for the first time.

In the 1940s and 1950s about one-third of American couples practicing birth control favored the diaphragm for contraception. Its popularity began to wane when other successful methods became available that did not have to be used just before or during the sex act (oral contraceptives and the intrauterine device, or IUD, for example). Recently, however, use of the diaphragm has increased as reports of adverse effects have raised serious questions about the newer methods. Studies have shown that, properly used, a diaphragm plus a spermicide is very nearly as effective as the best oral contraceptives.[70]

A device that is very popular in Europe and is somewhat similar to the diaphragm is the *cervical cap.* It is smaller than the diaphragm and fits directly over the cervix, held there by suction. Certain varieties can remain in place at all times except during menstruation, although others must be removed every two or three days to prevent irritation. A recent model has been developed with a one-way valve that allows menstrual fluids to flow out but prevents sperm from entering.[71] Although hollowed-out lemon halves were used as cervical caps in the Roman Empire, the cervical cap is currently considered "experimental" by the U.S. Food and Drug Administration and is not widely available in the United States because of restrictions by that agency.

The *condom* ("rubber," "safe") has been in wide use since it was first developed after the mid-nineteenth-century invention of vulcanizing rubber (which also made the diaphragm possible). Earlier, men had covered their penises with skin from animal intestines, fish skin, or linen.[72] Currently, condoms are the most popular contraceptive method in Japan, Sweden, and England. They are marketed in a variety of textures, colors, and shapes; however, most women report that they cannot feel the textures, and all four of the dyes reported to be in use are prohibited by the Food and Drug Administration—the black dye actually contains known carcinogens. The safest for all concerned is the reservoir-end, plain, uncolored condom.[73]

It is estimated that 15 to 20 percent of American couples use condoms to prevent pregnancy.[74] As with the Pill and the diaphragm, if condoms are properly used, the success rate is high. Proper use includes: (1) putting the condom on before there is *any* contact of penis with vulva or vagina; (2) making sure there is no air between penis and condom, but a little space to receive semen at the end; (3) making sure that the vagina is well lubricated, preferably with natural fluids and *never* with any petroleum product (hydrocarbons disintegrate rubber); and (4) being careful to withdraw the condom while the open end is still at the base of the penis, especially if the penis has become flaccid after ejaculation.

Some men object to condoms because a loss of sensitivity is caused by the covering. Other men report that they are able to maintain an erection longer before orgasm because of the decreased sensitivity, which may be appreciated by women who are slow to reach orgasm or who wish to have several orgasms during coitus. This points to a recognized fact about contraceptives—that each person must decide for himself or herself just what suits best.

One of the major advantages of the use of the condom for the male is that he can be more certain that protection actually exists. As one unmarried male told us: "I am never sure when a woman says she is on the pill that she remembers to take it every day. Sometimes diaphragms might not fit right or get dislodged. I know I put the sheath on right and I can check to see whether it comes out still in place."

Besides being highly effective in preventing pregnancy, properly used condoms are the most effective method of preventing the spread of venereal diseases. Strange as it may seem, **herpes II** (which is now epidemic in the United States) has no known cure. The use of the condom for protection against this and other venereal diseases may be its most important function.

A final and considerable advantage of condoms is that they can be very inexpensive and are readily available to anyone who wishes to buy them. There is no research indicating that expensive condoms are any more effective than inexpensive ones. Pharmacies and drugstores stock them without prescription. Any brand will fit, and they are sometimes accompanied by instructions, if needed, for their use. When the advantages and disadvantages of methods of contraception—especially for unmarried persons—are weighed, the condom usually ranks high. For those who have infrequent or unexpected sexual contacts, especially with new or different partners, the condom seems unexcelled.

The *intrauterine device* (IUD) became widely available in the 1960s, although the idea of putting a foreign body in the uterus to discourage pregnancy dates back centuries. Items of glass, ivory, ebony, gold, or platinum have been used; Hippocrates described such devices over 2,000 years ago. It is well known that camel drivers who were concerned that their animals not become pregnant on long trips across the desert inserted pebbles into the camels' uterine cavities.

No one is absolutely certain why intrauterine devices work, although there are some widely held theories. A popular explanation is that the foreign body causes a constant mild irritation of the lining of the uterus (the **endometrium**), rallying white blood cells, which destroy sperm. Special types of modern plastic IUDs work in additional ways. The copper wire used to wrap one model is believed to change the chemical balance of the uterus in such a way as to foil implantation. Another model is treated with progestins, which are slowly released in the uterus, affecting implantation of ova and increasing the mucous plug of the cervix as a barrier to sperm entry.

The IUD is highly effective in preventing pregnancy. It is now the leading contraceptive method in many countries of the world. It is estimated that approximately five million women in the United States are users, although recently many have grown skeptical because of the incidence of infection (which sometimes leaves scar tissue that can block the fallopian tubes, leading to possible inability to become pregnant later); heavy menstrual bleeding; and increased likelihood of anemia. Most physicians acknowledge these risks but believe that the IUD is generally a good and safe contraceptive that can always be removed in case of serious side effects.[75] New research on its side effects may cause these opinions to be modified, however. The problems associated with the IUD will be discussed later in this chapter.

Other Techniques

Other contraceptive techniques include the *rhythm method,* which has been widely used, with varying success, depending on the knowledge and regularity of the female's menstrual cycle. Generally this has not been a very reliable method because a woman is unlikely to ovulate at exactly the same time each month for a variety of reasons, including emotional and physical stresses. It has been estimated that two-thirds of all women are too irregular in their menstrual cycles to depend on this method.[76] In addition, many women are either uninformed or careless about keeping track of when they are in a fertile period. Even when women keep accurate records, some experts believe that there is no absolute "safe period"—not even during menstruation. This is true because some women seem to be "reflex ovulators" who ovulate at odd times as a result of high levels of excitement or anxiety.[77] For women (and partners, too) who enjoy frequent or spontaneous intercourse, reliance on the rhythm method alone has the serious disadvantage of several sequential days' abstinence from coitus. This is especially distressing for persons who restrict their sexual interaction to coitus exclusively.

The rhythm method is the only method of birth control officially sanctioned by the Roman Catholic Church and some other religions. Others use it because they dislike ingesting chemicals or using devices that are not "natural." Recent modifications and implementations designed to enhance the rhythm method's effectiveness have begun to result in improvements. One development has involved the use of the basal body temperature to gauge the time of ovulation. Twelve to twenty-four hours before ovulation, the body temperature drops slightly, and rises again as soon as ovulation has occurred. Another improvement in the rhythm method requires that a woman learn to detect changes in the mucous discharge from her cervix. That discharge becomes clear and slippery (rather like raw egg white) when she ovulates. Some women experience recognizable breast tenderness and a special ovulatory pain called *Mittelschmerz* (cramps in the middle of the month). Recently devices have been developed to measure the viscosity of the mucus, to give accurate temperature readouts, and to measure changes in body rhythms that accompany ovulation.[78] None of these procedures (called "sympto-thermal" and "natural family planning") should be attempted without competent professional guidance, however, unless the persons involved are prepared to accept the responsibility for a pregnancy.

When properly used, the new devices to simplify keeping records and to reduce the human error in accomplishing birth control by the rhythm method may make it more reliable than it was in the past. Some recent studies have indicated that effectiveness rates for the rhythm method are at an all-time high of 89 percent in selected samples.[79]

A problem with depending on the rhythm method that has received little attention is that there is considerable variation in the length of viability of male sperm. Part of the sperm's vitality is associated with the chemical conditions present in the female reproductive tract, but part of it is inherent in the spermatozoa themselves.

Although most sperm will die within two or three days in the reproductive tract, live sperm have been recovered as much as seven days after they were deposited.[80] Most rhythm computations allow no more than four days in estimating the probable occurrence of ovulation. If even three days were allowed for the life of the sperm, and four days allowed for error in estimating when ovulation might occur, then intercourse would need to be limited to the first nine and the last ten days of a twenty-eight-day menstrual cycle. Couples who do not have intercourse during menstruation would be further restricted.

Withdrawal (coitus interruptus) is an old and relatively widely used but not very effective method of preventing pregnancy. Part of the problem with coitus interruptus is that it is difficult for many men to exert the necessary control to withdraw when orgasm is imminent. The greatest trap, however, is that, as noted earlier, the preejaculatory fluid easily can contain enough sperm to cause fertilization.

Hyperthermia—the application of heat to the testicles—has long been thought to kill sperm. Shepherds reportedly have used a method to decrease the size of their herds that involves wrapping the rams' testes in pouches to keep them unusually warm in order to destroy the sperm. Some fertility experts have recently questioned whether or not men's tight-fitting underwear and pants might not keep their testes so warm that they act to kill sperm. Hot baths and saunas may interfere temporarily with sperm life, but most experts do not advise hyperthermia as a primary means of birth control.

Some contemporary researchers are investigating the use of ultrasonic waves as a hyperthermic contraceptive procedure.[81] This research is based on the knowledge that in rare cases of undescended testicles, sperm are less likely to mature because of the higher temperatures that exist where they are housed in the abdomen. Descended testicles hang outside the body, where the temperature is lower, and that fosters sperm development. It is also known that extremely high fevers over a long period of time often cause temporary—if not permanent—sterility, as in some cases of mumps.

Douching to flush out the vagina with some form of liquid is very ineffective as a contraceptive even if the liquid used is highly acid (vinegar and water). Some sperm usually will have reached the cervix long before douching can take place, and the circulation of the liquid may actually help to force others through the cervix.

The relative effectiveness of the various contraceptive methods is shown in Table 9.3.

Abstinence is the only completely reliable method of contraception. It is widely used, particularly during periods of presumed fertility. Sexual play can take the place of intercourse at these times. However, many of those who use abstinence as a means of contraception do so because their religion prohibits any other means. Those same persons may find that certain alternative forms of sexual activity (oral sex, anal sex, or masturbation) may also be forbidden to them.

Summary

■ Birth control is used to permit sexual intercourse with a minimal risk of causing pregnancy. The goal may be for a couple to remain childless, or it may be to control the time or spacing of births.

■ Sterilization is surgical intervention that prevents conception without interfering with the capacity to have intercourse. The process is usually carried out by vasectomy in males and by tubal ligation in females.

■ Chemical contraceptives are used either (1) to inhibit the production of ova or (2) to destroy sperm. Douching is the least effective of these.

■ Mechanical devices consist of barriers to sperm (diaphragms, condoms) or devices that inhibit implantation (IUDs).

TABLE 9.3
First-Year Failure Rates of Birth Control Methods

Method	Lowest Observed Failure Rate*	Failure Rate in Typical Users**
Tubal ligation	0.04	0.04
Vasectomy	0.15	0.15
Injectable progestin	0.25	0.25
Combined birth control pill	0.5	2
Progestin-only pill	1	2.5
IUD	1.5	4
Condom	2	10
Diaphragm (with spermicide)	2	13
Cervical cap	2	13
Foam, cream, jelly, and vaginal suppository	3–5	15
Coitus interruptus	16	23
Fertility awareness techniques (basal body temperature, mucus method, calendar, and "rhythm")	2–20	20–30
Douche	—	40
Chance (no method of birth control)	90	90

* Designed to complete the sentence, "Of 100 women who start out the year using a given method and who use it correctly and consistently, the lowest observed failure rate has been _____."

** Designed to complete the sentence, "Of 100 typical users who start out the year employing a given method, the number who will be pregnant by the end of the year will be _____."

Note: Many of the failure rates in the second column of this paper (failure rates in typical users) were derived from "Contraceptive Failure among Women in the United States, 1970–1973"; B. Trussell Vaughn, J. Menken, and E. Jones, *Family Planning Perspectives* 8:81–86, 1976.

Source: Contraceptive Technology, 1982–83: R. A. Hatcher, M.D., and G. K. Stewart, M.D.

■ The rhythm method is intended to enable partners to avoid sexual intercourse at times when conception is likely.

■ Coitus interruptus is intended to prevent spermatozoa from being deposited in the female genital tract by withdrawing the penis from the vagina during intercourse so that ejaculation occurs outside the female.

■ Abstinence is refraining from having intercourse and is widely used on a periodic basis for contraception.

Abortion

**Legal Status
of Abortion**

Half or more of all pregnancies are unplanned, and it is estimated that about 30 or 40 percent of those who do not want any children (or who do not want a child at the time they conceive) will seek an abortion.[82]

Whether a healthy woman has a right to end her pregnancy may well be the most controversial topic in the marriage and family field today. In a 1972 Gallup poll, 64 percent of the respondents supported the notion that a pregnant woman and her physician should determine whether or not she could have an abortion. In 1973, the Supreme Court handed down a decision that reflected the sentiment of a growing number of people in the United States that women have a right to choose whether or not to bear the children they have conceived.

The 1973 Supreme Court decision decriminalized abortion and allowed the termination of a pregnancy to be performed by qualified medical personnel. It was believed that as a result of this decision the complications and possible deaths of women undergoing such procedures could be kept to an absolute minimum. Although the sentiment of the majority still seemed to be that preventing undesired pregnancy in the first place was far preferable to terminating one already begun, the decision seemed to be necessary to safeguard the health of hundreds of thousands of women who were resorting to illegal abortions.

Hardly had the decriminalization of abortion been announced, however, when "pro-life" groups across the country voiced objections, arguing for the rights of unborn children to live. These groups cited both legal and religious reasons for their opposition to abortion, whereas those favoring legalization of abortions stressed physical and mental health reasons that some women should not have unwanted children.

In the years since 1973 the voices for and against abortion have not been silent. Laws have been passed, and new laws have overturned previous ones. Recently there has been conflict over who will pay for the abortions for women who want them but cannot afford them, particularly those on welfare. In keeping with a 1977 Supreme Court ruling, Medicaid, the program that provides combined state and federal medical payments for low-income persons, has ceased payment for abortion. Before that, nearly one-third of all abortions were paid for by Medicaid following the decriminalization ruling in 1973. Under the later ruling, exceptions are made if a woman's health is in jeopardy as a result of pregnancy or if her pregnancy is the result of incest or rape.

In a recent look at "abortion politics," Stewart and Nicholson report that states are funding fewer and fewer abortions as the federal courts have established a minimum use of Medicaid funds for such purposes. The result has been that poor women must either resort once more to "back-alley" abortions or continue their pregnancies and, often, ultimately end up living on tax-supported welfare for themselves and their dependent children.[83]

The United States is not the only country in which there has been controversy over abortion. In a recent article on abortion in the developed nations of the world, Field has reported that many nations have recently liberalized their laws on the termination of pregnancy, but not without considerable dissent:

> *This variation appears to be linked—at least in the short run—to several political/ideological differences across nations including differences in the proportion of the Catholic population, the presence of governing Socialist parties, the type of regime, and the nature of non-electoral policy-making institutions.*[84]

As Field suggested, certain religious groups provide strong opposition to abortion. The Catholic Church is an interesting case in point. Until 1869 abortion was permissible by Catholic canon law for the first ninety days for a female fetus or forty days for a male, at which time the soul was thought to enter the fetus. (It is not clear how the sex of the unborn child was determined, since this is a rather recently developed technique.) However, in 1869 Pope Pius IX took the position that all abortion is murder; and for slightly more than a hundred years, this has been the Catholic position.[85]

The Mormon Church also maintains that induced abortion is a sin: "As a church we oppose legalized, nontherapeutic abortions. . . . We consider such actions among the most grievous of sins. As in other areas, we receive some helpful counsel from modern scripture in which we are instructed not to kill, 'nor do anything like unto it.'"[86]

Statistics on the number of abortions and characteristics of the women who have them have been kept only since 1969, when enough states had adopted liberalized laws to allow for relevant data collection. For earlier periods, there are only estimates of the number of abortions that occurred, except for the few legal ones performed (when the mother's life was clearly in danger from the pregnancy or the pregnancy was due to rape or incest). The estimate was that one million illegal abortions occurred every year before 1973.[87]

In 1977, 1,270,000 legal abortions were performed—a small increase over the previous estimated number of illegal abortions but one that signified a large change in the quality of care. Approximately 75 percent of the legal abortions involved unmarried (including divorced and widowed) women, with two-thirds of the women being under the age of twenty-four. Teenagers accounted for 400,000 abortions.

Abortion is now the most common surgical procedure in the United States—in fact, in the world. The variety of techniques used to terminate a pregnancy are reasonably standard in modern societies. In some Asian and European countries abortion is much more prevalent than in the United States. Hungary, Czechoslovakia, Poland, Rumania, Denmark, and Singapore all have higher rates than does the United States. Cuba has the highest rate of abortions for women aged fifteen to forty-four.[88]

Reasons
for Abortion

The decision to have an abortion is usually motivated by such practical considerations as finances, job and educational goals, age, and the lack of support of
the father and of family and friends. Reasons most frequently given are: (1) "I
am not married" (34 percent); (2) "I cannot afford a child now" (31.5 percent);
(3) "A child would interfere with my education" (22 percent); (4) "I feel unable
to cope with a child now" (22 percent); (5) "I have enough children already" (16
percent); and (6) "I think I am too young to have a child" (14 percent). Most
women asked gave more than one reason.[89]

Women from all backgrounds and of all ages seek abortions—women who
are married or unmarried; Catholic, Jewish, or Protestant; black or white—and
15 percent of them have more than one abortion.[90]

When abortions were illegal, women were cautioned that repeated abortions
might create serious problems in later pregnancies. Repeated terminations
were associated with later low-birth-weight infants, miscarriages, and premature deliveries. However, the risks were considerably reduced when the legalization of abortion made back-alley abortions almost a thing of the past. It has
been reported that some women have had as many as twenty abortions under
careful medical care without known problems resulting. However, recent research indicates that although some of the risks have been lowered in multiple
abortions, they still may damage the uterus and interfere with later implanta-
tions, making miscarriages more likely. Repeated abortion does not seem a
desirable alternative to contraception for these and many other reasons.

Recent legislation prohibiting the use of public funds to pay for abortions
for those who cannot otherwise afford them may cause an increase in illegal
surgery, which will probably result in poorer care and more deaths.[91] Unfortunately, it is difficult to gather data on illegal activities, and figures on injuries
and deaths resulting from such activities are always questionable.

The great majority of women who make decisions to have abortions do so as
soon as their pregnancies are confirmed. One study reported that nearly 10
percent had decided even before they became pregnant that if pregnancy did
occur, they would certainly terminate it.[92] Most women who have had abortions say that they made the right decision; follow-up studies consistently show
that most of them continue to feel that their decisions were correct.[93] Even so,
others are troubled by their abortions at the time, and some have regrets later,
especially if fertility problems occur.

An exception to early decisions about abortion is found in the case of
women who have had amniocentesis. This is a procedure in which cells drawn
from the amniotic sac surrounding the fetus are collected and examined. Careful analysis of the cells can detect damage to the fetus caused by such events as
German measles in the mother, as well as major chromosomal and other types
of genetic abnormalities. Amniocentesis cannot be performed successfully
until after the fourteenth week of pregnancy, and the most valid results cannot
be obtained until the seventeenth week. Learning that there are no likely defects can be tremendously reassuring to a couple who have been in doubt. If

there is great risk or certainty that the fetus will have an abnormality, many couples decide at that time to have an abortion.

Abortion Methods

For those who believe that having an abortion is preferable to having an unwanted child, the first indication for abortion is confirmation of the suspected pregnancy. Once a menstrual period has been missed, this may be accomplished by pregnancy tests given as early as the time of the first missed period.

There is a home pregnancy test on the market that a woman can use one week to ten days after a missed menstrual period, with a repeat test a week later as an added precaution, to determine whether or not she needs to consult a physician. False negative results from these tests (indications that a woman is not pregnant when in fact she is) are quite common in the early stages of pregnancy; consequently, many physicians wait until the second menstrual period is missed before performing a test for pregnancy. By this time the woman is six to eight weeks pregnant.

Recently tests have been developed to check for the presence of HCG (a hormone produced by the placenta) in the blood. As soon as the **placenta** begins to grow, this substance, which shows up in the blood first and in the urine a bit later, can give an accurate reading of a pregnancy. Accurate assessment of pregnancy by these methods can come within the month following conception. For women who do not want to be mothers, this is usually a time of high anxiety, during which they must decide whether or not to terminate the pregnancy.

If a decision is made to have an abortion within the first few weeks after conception, there is ample time for the most commonly used technique— *vacuum aspiration.* This method is used from seven to twelve weeks after the most recent menstrual period and is usually performed in a clinic on an outpatient basis. A local anesthetic may be used because there is some discomfort, but the operation is relatively simple. The duration of the procedure is usually no more than fifteen minutes, although preexamination, counseling, and a stay in the clinic for several hours to be certain that there are no complications may take the better part of a day. Any anesthesia affects the mind-body system; some time may be needed to restore comfortable functioning as well as to discharge the emotions heightened by the pregnancy. Usually a few days' time suffices.

The procedure for abortion by vacuum aspiration is to dilate the **cervical os** gradually, either by a series of graduated dilators or by use of *laminaria digitate* (a seaweed stem), which works to draw moisture from the cervix and thereby to pull the os open gently. A tube is inserted into the uterus, and the contents are withdrawn by suction.

In one method of inducing abortion, a curette (curved scraper) may be inserted into the uterus following dilation and the contents removed by scraping them loose. This is called *curettage*; it is also a common operation for women who are not pregnant but who have some need for treatment because of menstrual difficulties or infection. The operation is widely known as D&C (for dilation and curettage) and usually calls for a general anesthetic.

After the twelfth week of pregnancy abortion becomes much more complicated. The walls of the uterus have become increasingly thin, soft, and spongy. They can be perforated more easily; inserting objects into the uterus is more likely to cause damage. Also, as the fetus grows larger, suction removal becomes less and less possible. From the twelfth to the sixteenth weeks, however, some physicians will perform what is termed *dilation and evacuation* surgery, which takes longer than the other procedures described and is done under general anesthesia in a hospital. This method uses both vacuum and curettage.

Generally, between the twelfth and the twenty-sixth week (some physicians will not perform abortions after the twenty-fourth week), the safest method for terminating pregnancy is inducing a kind of premature labor and forcing a miscarriage. The further along the pregnancy, of course, the more like a full-term birth the procedure is. Women who choose abortion following amniocentesis at the seventeenth week will undergo this process. There are two accepted methods used in these later pregnancies. One is to remove an amount of the amniotic fluid from around the fetus with a syringe, replacing it with a saline solution. The uterus will react to the saline solution by contracting and will expel the fetus and placenta within a day of the procedure.

An alternative method of inducing a late abortion is to insert a hormonal substance called **prostaglandin** into the amniotic sac, either by injection or in the form of suppositories. This procedure usually causes a miscarriage to occur more quickly than does the saline injection; however, many women complain that they suffer side effects such as diarrhea and vomiting. In addition, both the saline solution and prostaglandins cause the painful contractions associated with birth, which may last from eight to fifteen hours.[94]

Eugene Sandberg, a professor of gynecology and obstetrics, comments: "Abortion, although undesirable, is sufficiently inexpensive and safe to be accepted as a legitimate escape from an undesirable situation and, in many minds, is not an undue price to pay if sensual gambles fail."[95] But women who have been through an abortion usually do not want to repeat the experience. Only a small proportion of women have subsequent abortions; it is probable that they have learned that abortion is not to be taken lightly and that contraception is a far better way to postpone motherhood until the time is right.

Summary

■ The right of a healthy woman to interrupt her pregnancy legally was upheld by the United States Supreme Court in 1973.

■ A Supreme Court ruling in 1977 held that federal funds may not be used to pay for voluntary abortions except in cases of incest, rape, or undue risk to the mother's health.

■ Catholic and Mormon authorities hold that abortion is a sin. Other religious groups and "right-to-life" groups also have strong opposition to abortions.

■ Well over a million legal abortions are performed each year. Unmarried women account for approximately three-quarters of them, and teenagers figure in about one-third.

■ Early abortions are most often performed by vacuum aspirations; an alternate method is dilation and curettage. Later abortions are performed by dilation and evacuation, still later ones by the injection of a saline solution or prostaglandins.

Involuntary Childlessness

Since there are more couples attuned to preventing conception than concerned with being unable to bear children, it is understandable that the distress caused by infertility has often been overlooked. Nonetheless, it is estimated that 10 to 15 percent of American couples cannot conceive without medical help; for many such persons this is a very deep disappointment. Some have no hope of ever being able to conceive—a condition called *sterility*. Others have low fertility—a condition that may lend itself to treatment.

The cure for low fertility is sometimes as simple as learning new coital techniques. Certain positions in coitus increase the likelihood of fertilization. The man-above, face-to-face position is particularly recommended, especially if the woman raises her hips after her partner's ejaculation so that the semen stays inside. A rear-entry position with the woman on her knees and elbows is also highly effective.

Another simple cause of infertility is timing. Although women usually ovulate 13 times a year, it is easily possible for a couple to miss each occasion, especially if one of them has low sexual interest or vitality that results in infrequent coitus. Couples who have coitus fewer than three times a week may need to use basal body temperature charts to pinpoint the time of ovulation. Such charts may also show lack of ovulation, which can often be remedied by the use of a drug such as Clomid.

Those with more serious infertility problems must seek medical help and sometimes even surgery to find a cure. Both sterility and low fertility have a variety of causes, including hormonal imbalances, infections or other types of illnesses, anatomical defects, anemia, and even psychological stress. Some authorities on infertility believe that fertility problems are on the increase as a result of the use of modern methods of birth control and of the epidemic rise in venereal disease, which can lead to blockage of the fallopian tubes.

The birth control pill is believed to stop ovulation permanently in some women with a history of irregular menstrual periods and ovulation problems. The chemicals in these pills are known to depress the fertility hormones that are released by the pituitary gland, and the suspicion is that this effect may be permanent even though use of the Pill is discontinued.

The IUD (intrauterine device) has been cited as the cause of pelvic infection and tubal blockage in many women. Both of these are causes of infertility in women; the woman is believed to be the partner with the infertility problem in 60 to 70 percent of the cases.

It is estimated that since 1970 well over a million women have suffered from acute pelvic infections caused by the use of IUDs. Of that number, nearly one-quarter either are already sterile or have had their fallopian tubes damaged to such an extent from the infections that they stand almost no chance of getting pregnant. The fallopian tubes may become so scarred that they can no longer function to transport eggs from the ovaries. In many cases the tubes are completely blocked by scar tissue that was laid down as a result of infections. Surgery can sometimes remove the scar tissue, but often the damage is not correctable.[96]

In men (who have the infertility problem in 30 to 40 percent of infertile marriages) fertility problems are usually due to some deficiency either in the sperm count or in sperm activity. A healthy sperm count is between 60 and 100 million sperm per cubic centimeter, with 60 percent of these being observably active.[97]

In a long-range study of men conducted over the past fifty years in the United States, it has been discovered that sperm counts are dropping. In 1929 the median count was over 90 million per cubic centimeter; in 1974 the median count had dropped to 65 million; and in the most recent study (in 1979), the median was 60 million, or just at the low edge of normal. Twenty-three percent of the subjects had sperm densities of 20 million or less, a level generally agreed on as a functional definition of sterility.

Although it is not clear just why the sperm count is dropping, Ralph C. Dougherty, a chemist who reported this research at the meetings of the American Chemical Society, has said: "It is possible that toxic substances in the environment may be partially responsible for this apparent shift. The chemicals enter the body through the food chain where they usually accumulate in fatty tissue."[98]

At an international conference in Jerusalem in 1980, Paolo Parisi, a geneticist at the Mendel Institute in Rome, suggested that industrial pollutants, especially pesticides, may be what is damaging sperm and noted that the effect is worldwide.[99] Research done with laboratory animals in Bulgaria found that exposure to loud noise (100 decibels) for a period of one year resulted in sterility in 80 percent of the animals.[100] It may well be that as industrialization and resulting environmental pollution increase, sperm counts in males will continue to decrease. As previously mentioned, some fertility experts report that they have had good results in increasing male fertility by getting men to change to loose underclothing and pants. Close-fitting underwear and jeans interfere with the natural process that drops the testes automatically away from the body when they become too warm for sperm to stay healthy.

The choice of whether or not to have a child is taken for granted by a majority of couples. When that choice is removed by sterility or diminished by low fertility, the realization can be a painful one. Couples usually consult a physician who evaluates the cause of the problem and attempts to correct matters when possible. A series of tests may be indicated, usually beginning with the male since his sperm count is fairly easy to determine from a specimen of his ejaculate. A widely used assessment technique employs multiple-exposure photography, which provides quick information about the number of sperm, the percentage of them that are motile, and their velocity. If the count is low or if the sperm are less active than normal, various remedies can be tried. One option is to determine as exactly as possible the time that the woman ovulates and to plan intercourse to coincide. The male will be advised to refrain from ejaculation for forty-eight hours beforehand so that as many sperm will be available as possible. Sometimes, the administration of Clomid will increase sperm count.

In cases in which it is determined that the woman is fertile but her partner's sperm count is low, his semen may be collected and saved by freezing it over a period of many ejaculations. Ultimately, it may be thawed and made into a concentrate that can be used by placing it directly into the uterus during the woman's time of ovulation. This process is one of the means of artificial insemination and is called AIH (which stands for "artificial insemination husband") if the husband's semen is used.

Artificial insemination is becoming increasingly accepted as a technique to enable couples with low fertility to have children. A controversial form of artificial insemination uses a donor other than the husband as the source of sperm (AID, for "artificial insemination donor"). When the husband is sterile, this is an option that allows his wife to conceive and to bear a child in a normal fashion. Although he is not the biological father, he is of course the parent in every other way—just as he would be with an adopted infant. A variation of this procedure involves mixing the husband's semen with that of a donor.

A few religions prohibit artificial insemination generally, although they may allow some variations. The Roman Catholic Church, for example, has approved what it calls "assisted insemination," which involves marital intercourse followed by the use of an instrument that pushes the semen into the cervix.

In addition to freezing sperm, researchers are working toward the day when ova can be frozen as well. The now famous Cambridge University team of Robert Edwards and Patrick Steptoe, who succeeded in the first *in vitro* fertilization ("test tube baby") are planning to freeze embryos and may at some later

"Baby Louise" Brown and Her Parents, September 1979

date be able to transplant these fertilized eggs into a woman in a sterile marriage. They are being aided in their research by David Whittingham of Britain's Medical Research Council, who has successfully accomplished such an implantation from a frozen embryo in a mouse.[101]

The first *in vitro* baby, Louise Brown, was born in July 1978 with the help of Edwards and Steptoe, nearly ten years after they first succeeded in fertilizing a human egg outside of a woman's body. In June 1980, in Australia, the procedure again resulted in the successful birth of a child. As late as 1981 no births had yet occurred in the United States in the *in vitro* fertilization clinic, the first of which was at Eastern Virginia Medical School, although several fertilized eggs reportedly had been implanted. The clinic received applications from 2,500 couples in the first year of its existence. A maximum of fifty couples a year can be treated, at a cost of approximately $4,000 each.[102] It is to be assumed, considering the successes in England and in Australia, that it is only a matter of time until the first birth from an *in vitro* fertilization takes place in the United States.

Tests to determine the fertility of women are usually more complicated than those for men in that they are concerned with imperfect or damaged fallopian tubes, cervix, or uterus. Failure to ovulate or improper development of the reproductive organs are possible causes, as are imperfect ova or hormonal imbalance. Many of the tests used to detect these problems can be time consuming, but most women who genuinely want a child persist.

It has been estimated that about half the childless couples who seek medical aid eventually will have children. For those who must accept their sterility, there can be many strong emotional reactions. Couples who have spent months preoccupied with temperature charts and ovulation schedules in an attempt to have intercourse at exactly the right moment and who have endured repeated tests may understandably respond angrily to the innocent query from friends, "When are you going to have a baby?"

The discovery of sterility often sets up what has been called the "infertility syndrome" by David Rosenfeld, professor of obstetrics and gynecology at Cornell Medical College, who has counseled hundreds of infertile couples. The syndrome is the "emotional trauma couples experience during the process of establishing their infertility and then the gradual, painful task of accepting it and incorporating this unwanted reality into their lives."[103] Such couples have a series of predictable emotional stages through which they pass:

1. *Denial:* "It's really not happening," they say. "We're probably just not having sex enough."
2. *Self-blame:* They accuse themselves, asking, "What did I do to make this happen? Is God punishing me?"
3. *Communication gap:* Husband and wife don't admit to each other that there is a problem. It is very difficult for one or the other to say, "Hey, there's something wrong. Let's see a doctor."
4. *Anger and depression:* When infertility is confirmed, the partners experience tremendous anger, alternating with depression. They are angry with everyone—themselves, their spouses, and their physicians.

The only option left to infertile couples who want to rear their own children is adoption. This may not be easy, since traditionally there have been far fewer desirable infants available for adoption than prospective adoptive parents. This ratio is becoming even less favorable because of the widespread use of contraceptives, the availability of abortion, and the fact that single mothers often keep their babies.

Public and private agencies provide state-regulated systems for adoption. These agencies employ screening processes that provide the best assurance possible that a baby will be placed in a home that is appropriate. However, the procedure is necessarily a lengthy one, and prospective parents may face a very long waiting period even though the process has been modified considerably in recent years to make it less arduous.

In an attempt to hasten the time when a child will be available for them, many couples turn to private placement. In such cases they often know little if anything about the child's natural parents, nor have they undergone a pre-placement investigation of themselves as potential parents. Often there is an intermediary between the biological mother and the adoptive parents—a physician, an attorney, a friend, or a relative—who makes the arrangements. This is illegal in some states, however, and is prohibited in still others if any money changed hands.[104]

Because children who are matched to the adoptive parents in terms of racial, ethnic, religious, and educational background of the natural parents are in such short supply, more and more couples are adopting children who are very different from them, are older than the infant they originally desired, are handicapped in some way, or for some other reason are classified as "hard to place." Such children must wait for adoption, and although statistics are inexact, it is estimated that there are about 100,000 of them at any given time.[105]

Much has been written about the pros and cons of cross-cultural and cross-racial adoptions. In an excellent review of the variables and opinions involved, Jones and Else note that such adoptions are much better for the child than institutional or long-term foster care. What is really important, other than love and security, is "the ability of the adoptive parents to provide a bicultural or biracial socialization" for the child.[106]

Summary

■ Involuntary childlessness results from sterility or low fertility, both of which have a variety of causes, including hormonal imbalances, infections, psychological stress, and anatomical defects.

■ The sperm count of American men has been dropping for the last fifty years, a phenomenon that is believed by many to be a prime consideration in many cases of low fertility.

■ Artificial insemination (using either the husband's semen or that of a donor) may be used to facilitate pregnancy. Although this has been a controversial topic, it is gaining in acceptability in the United States.

■ It is now possible to implant an already fertilized egg into a woman's uterus and have her carry it to full term. This method resulted in the birth of the first "test tube" baby in 1978.

■ About half the couples seeking medical aid for childlessness are actually helped. Of those who do not conceive, many choose to adopt a child, although infants available for adoption are far fewer than couples who wish to adopt.

Glossary

Amniocentesis A technique for checking cells in the amniotic fluid to determine the state of the fetus, especially with respect to potential birth defects.

Antibody A substance found in the blood that destroys particular kinds of cells or that counteracts the growth of foreign bodies.

Cervical os The opening in the cervix connecting the uterus with the vagina.

Cervix The neck of the uterus, which protrudes into the inner end of the vagina.

Endometrium The lining of the uterus, which thickens with tissue and blood each month in preparation for the implantation of a fertilized ovum.

Genetic counseling Professional advice on family planning to potential parents, based on their ancestral histories.

Herpes II A sexually transmitted disease (*herpes virus hominis* type 2) that is fast becoming the most common form of venereal disease.

Hysterectomy The surgical removal of the uterus.

Illegitimacy The state of having been born to an unmarried woman.

Placenta The organ, attached to the umbilical cord of the fetus, that provides for the exchange through the uterine wall of nutrients to and waste material from the fetus.

Progesterones Female hormones secreted by the ovaries to prepare the uterus for the implantation of a fertilized ovum.

Prostaglandin A drug that can stimulate a fertilized ovum to be released with the menstrual flow any time from conception to one month after conception.

Tubal ligation A procedure in which the fallopian tubes are cut, cauterized, and/or tied off to prevent the passage of ova to the uterus or sperm to the ova.

Vasectomy A process in which the two tubes (the *vases deferentes*) that normally carry sperm from the testes to the seminal vesicles are cut and tied to prevent the passage of the sperm through the penis.

Zero population growth A term used to describe a birth rate that is at or below a population's replacement level—one baby (or fewer) born for each person who dies.

The value of
marriage is not
that adults produce
children but that
children produce
adults.

—Peter De Vries

280

10 · Pregnancy, Birth, and Transition to Parenthood

The birth of a child transforms a married couple into a family. Although today couples have more of a choice than in the past about whether or not to become parents, very few remain childless. Family-life studies have given special attention to the birth of the first child, which is seen as having more impact on the parents than do subsequent additions to the family. Not only are both pregnancy and birth brand-new experiences with the firstborn child, but also the couple's familiar way of life becomes that of a "three-person system" that is infinitely more complex.

Couples are much better prepared for pregnancy and childbirth than they are for taking the baby home to begin family life. With the firstborn, this transition can often be difficult as new parents attempt to balance demands on their time, energy, and financial resources. A family system—mother, father, and children—may change over time but does not end. Parents are parents forever; even if their marriage does not endure, there is almost always contact for a lifetime through their children.

Anne Bernstein, a social scientist, has asked children, "How do people get babies?" She finds that children go through six basic levels of understanding about birth and sex.[1] The first level is common to those under five years of age: "You go to the hospital to get one." The second level, which shows confusion about "constructing" a baby, is common to children in kindergarten and the first grade. They believe that babies are manufactured somewhere before they are ready to be picked up at the hospital. Level three shows some understanding of growth inside the mother as a result of a "seed" being placed there by the father.

However, the facts of reproduction are not clear to most children until level four, which reflects an understanding of sperm, eggs, and penile penetration. Level five is marked by a more complete understanding of the process of conception and of how the fetus grows and is born. The sixth level, which occurs sometime around the age of twelve, shows the influence of reading and teaching and of responses to children's questions about cause and effect.

By twelve most children have a fairly clear picture, which persists until they learn more of the details as teenagers or young adults.[2] Much, of course, depends on the accuracy of the information children originally receive. Unfortunately, some of the adults who answer children's questions may have some

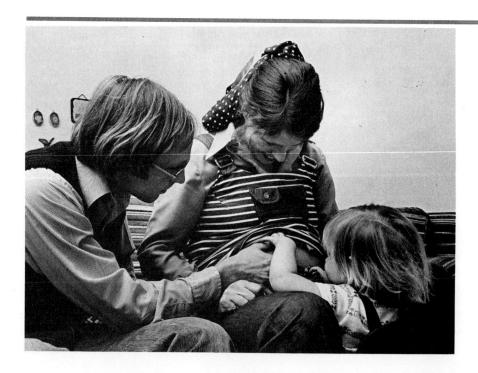

FIGURE 10.1

A Sperm Cell and an Egg Cell

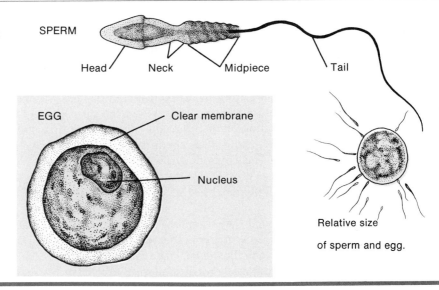

misguided notions themselves. Many children at level six, therefore, have a clear but not necessarily accurate picture.

By early adolescence most children begin to have their inaccurate ideas about pregnancy and birth corrected by knowledgeable adults. Many schools have courses or units of study on reproduction. The quality of instruction has steadily improved over the past decade, so that by the time that the average individual reaches adulthood, he or she knows that every cell in the body contains twenty-three pairs of chromosomes, which hold genetic information carried by the genes. Young adults also generally know that when the sperm cell of the male and the egg cell of the female unite, they combine their sets of chromosomes.

An adult understanding of conception involves the knowledge that a sperm cell has a head that contains chromosomes, a neck and a midsection that seem to guide the movement that is energized by a whiplike tail propelling the sperm forward after ejaculation. Sperm are produced in the testicles and are carried in glandular fluid called *semen*—the Latin word for seed—through the penis by muscular contractions during ejaculation. The tube through which semen is ejaculated (called the urethra) is the same tube through which urine passes; however, when a man's penis becomes erect, the same processes that cause it to get hard automatically block off any urine input and cleanse the urethra, by means of a neutralizing fluid, of any acid that might be present. A more detailed discussion of the anatomy and physiology of the genitalia appears in Appendix A.

Semen collects from the **seminal vesicles**, the **bulbourethral glands,** and the prostate gland. Each contributes substances necessary to the strength and motility of the sperm. The prostate, for instance, gives the seminal fluid its milky color and its characteristic odor; it provides nourishment for the sperm with acid phosphatase. In cases of rape, it is the remains of the acid phosphatase that constitute evidence of intercourse.[3]

The bulbourethral glands release the cleansing and lubricating fluid that is seen collecting on the tip of the penis during sexual excitement. Because this fluid is alkaline, it helps sperm survive during ejaculation by neutralizing the otherwise acid environment of the urethra.

The clear preejaculate fluid sometimes has enough sperm in it, either from the swelling seminal vesicles or from an earlier ejaculation, to cause pregnancy. This may happen when a couple have touched penis to vagina in foreplay but have believed they were safe from impregnation since actual ejaculation had not taken place. Sperm in the clear fluid can travel through a lubricated vagina, the cervix, and the uterus, into a fallopian tube to reach an ovum and penetrate it. Sperm can easily reach a fallopian tube in such a short time that it is impossible to stop them by douching or similar means once they have entered the uterus. If an egg is waiting in the tube, fertilization may take place.

During each cycle one or more eggs move in fluid through a fallopian tube to the uterus. If the egg is not fertilized during the approximately three-day journey through the tube, the uterine wall, which has been preparing for the implantation of the fertilized egg, sloughs off about two weeks later and leaves the body as menstrual flow.

What keeps pregnancy from occurring more frequently than it does in healthy, fertile women who are sexually active is that their ovulations theoretically happen only once a month. However, irregular ovulation (more or less often than once a month) is so common among women who have never been pregnant that it is also considered normal. It is not unusual for any woman to ovulate twice or even more often in a month from one or both ovaries. Fraternal twins and some other multiple births usually are conceived in just that way— if a woman is having daily intercourse without contraceptive barriers, there are always plenty of spermatozoa to fertilize as many ova as can possibly be present. In fact, a typical ejaculation contains thousands of times as many spermatozoa as would be needed to fertilize all the eggs that any woman could ever produce in a lifetime.

The released egg (or eggs) lasts only a few days before it disintegrates. The next month the entire process begins again. Women have some 400,000 primitive eggs **(oogonia)** present at birth. These lie dormant until puberty, when hormones begin the maturation process for the eggs one by one. Only about 400 will ever become mature enough to be released.

If fertilization does take place, cell division begins about twelve hours after the sperm has penetrated the egg. Cell division continues as the fertilized

FIGURE 10.2

Conception and Implantation

The process of conception is depicted. Released from an ovary, the ovum is shown entering the fallopian tube and being fertilized by a single sperm. The cells of the fertilized ovum repeatedly divide as it moves into the uterus. The ovum develops into a hollow base of cells (blastocyst) and becomes implanted in the endometrium. The elapsed time from ovulation to implantation is about seven days.

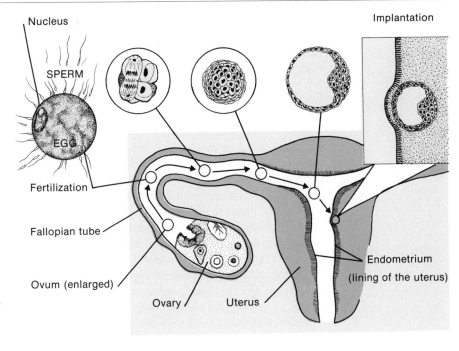

egg—now called a **zygote**—travels to the uterus. Already, genetic materials are determining just what this baby will be like, including its sex.

Human cells can be classified as body cells or germ cells. The body cells are the living "building blocks" of which body tissues are constructed and by which they are maintained. The germ cells are the sperm and ova that are stored and/or produced in the gonads. The nucleus of every normal human cell contains forty-six chromosomes (twenty-three pairs), each containing groups of genes that instruct the cells how to grow into tissues.

Two chromosomes in each cell carry the genes that direct the reproduction of germ cells and the development of sex organs and sex-linked characteristics. In females both these chromosomes are quite similar and are called X chromosomes. In males the two chromosomes are quite different; one is like the X chromosome in females, but the other—called Y—is peculiarly male.

Soon after the union of a sperm and an ovum, the cell nuclei merge following a complex process that has already separated each pair of chromosomes; twenty-three chromosomes from the sperm pair up with the corresponding twenty-three from the ovum to form a new set of forty-six necessary for human growth and development.

No matter which of the original pair of sex chromosomes from the ovum splits off and joins with the sex chromosome supplied by the sperm, it will surely be an X—ova have no Y chromosomes. There is almost (but actually not quite) a 50-50 chance that another X chromosome from the sperm will join the X from the ovum. If that happens, the new conception is instantly programmed to develop with female body cells and female sex cells. If the sperm's Y chromosome joins the ovum's X, an XY pair—the male program for growth and development—is established.

Thus a child's genetic sex is set at fertilization; some time after the twelfth week of pregnancy, the sex of a fetus can be determined by tests. For every 100 females conceived, there will be between 120 and 150 males, although only about 104 will actually be carried to full term and born alive.

Men are capable of producing mature sperm soon after puberty and can have a reproductive life of over seventy years. Theoretically, men can father an almost limitless number of children in a lifetime—possibly even thousands without artificial insemination.

Women first become fertile approximately one year after menstruation (at an average age of about twelve years) and are fertile until after menopause, which begins between about forty-five and fifty years of age on the average. Theoretically, then, a woman might be able to supply a maximum of 550 mature ova for in vitro fertilization but not more than about forty for normal pregnancies.

The *Guinness Book of World Records* lists the youngest documented mother (a Peruvian girl) as being five years, eight months old. In July 1980 a nine-year-old girl in Johannesburg, South Africa, gave birth by **caesarean delivery**.[4] In the United States, gross population statistics often posit that the fecund years of a female's life are, on the average, fifteen to forty-four. Births to mothers younger than fifteen and older than forty-four do occur, of course, but are not common enough to fall within the normal range.

Childbearing

The birth of a child still seems miraculous. The sense of wonder has not been destroyed by scientific knowledge of conception, pregnancy, and birth.

For parents, the addition of a child to their family almost always leads to important changes. Until recently, however, research into the dynamics of these personal and interpersonal changes has not kept pace with that on the physical aspects of conception and birth.

Recent studies finally have begun to shed some light on the important psychological and emotional effects of the emergence of a new family system. The research began by exploring various dimensions of motherhood, reflecting the traditional attitude of both men and women that pregnancy and birth are a

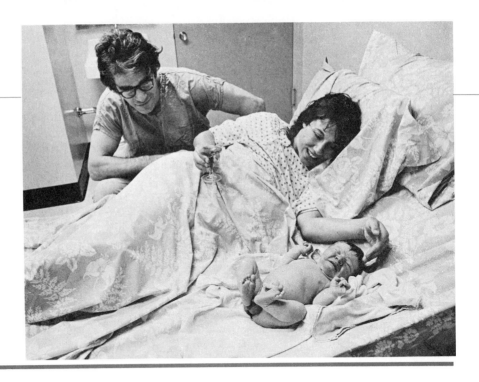

woman's domain. Gradually, however, researchers have gone on to include inquiries into the impact of parents on children and, finally, to focus on effects on fathers, on marital relationships, on siblings, on stepparents and stepchildren, and on grandparents.

As we discuss each of the stages in the emergence of new human beings, we need to be aware of the social and psychological significance of each step for those other family members whose lives are altered by the addition of a new member to the family.

The birth of the first child has received special attention because it is credited with having greater impact on the parents than do subsequent births. It has been described as a "period of 'metamorphosis' when a two-person group suddenly changes into a three-person one."[5] It requires that new parents make major adjustments; their success or failure in making these adjustments may set the stage for the challenges of childbearing and the quality of their later family life.

Even though couples today are more successful in preventing conception than ever before, most of them ultimately will have one or more children. More than ever before, married women who become pregnant are likely to have planned the pregnancy; approximately two-thirds of women are married at the time the child is conceived, and an even larger fraction (81 percent) are married when the child is born. For most couples there is a relatively short interval between marriage and the birth of their first child, although couples are waiting longer now than in the past. Of couples who marry before they become pregnant, 42 percent have their first child within three years of marriage, 43 percent within three to five years, and 15 percent after more than five years.[6]

Reasons for Having Children

Those men and women who want children want them for various reasons. There have been many investigations into the factors motivating the desire for children. One recent study of unmarried, childless women asked those who stated a preference for children why they wanted to be mothers.[7] Three equally important reasons given were:

1. that she wanted to experience the honesty and freshness of children
2. that she wanted to participate in the miracle of birth
3. that she thought she could be a good parent

The last of these seemed related to other findings of the same study showing that positive memories of the young woman's own childhood and of her parents' loving care were important variables in determining whether or not she wanted children.

To give love, to enjoy children, and to be a good parent are generally conceded as positive motivations. Unfortunately, other reasons that are frequently mentioned are questionable at best as motivations for becoming a parent. Couples often mention pressure from outsiders to conceive—perhaps their own parents want a grandchild or an heir to carry on the family name or dreams. Sometimes the pressure comes from religious beliefs that not only discourage contraception but actually encourage having several children. Some men and women report that they want to have a child because all their friends are having babies. Still others hope that a baby will improve a troubled marriage or be proof of virility or femininity. They may believe that the child will fill a need for companionship or love, or will keep them from loneliness now or in old age.

Financial Aspects of Childbearing

Whatever the reasons—good or bad—for wanting children, pregnancy is a process that is not only miraculous and wonderful but also anxiety producing. One of the chief anxieties about whether or not to have children and, if so, how many, has to do with finances. More and more couples are worried about the cost of living and the increasing expense of providing for a family. Unless they are totally supported by public welfare, many express concern about fees for prenatal medical care, hospitalization, and delivery of a child. Although the Pregnancy Discrimination Act enacted in 1979 mandates that health plans for employed persons must offer maternity benefits, partial coverage or coverage only for uncomplicated births is the rule.[8]

The costs to parents paying from their own resources of having a baby and supporting it for its first year must include:

- mother's maternity wardrobe
- medical expenses: prenatal care, delivery fee, hospital bill for normal delivery, and three-day hospitalization (or additional costs of alternative home care)

- pediatrician's examination in hospital plus six follow-up visits and required immunizations
- baby's clothing, bedding, linens, bibs
- diapers: cloth, laundered at home, diaper service, or disposable diapers; diaper bag
- nursery furnishings: bassinette, crib, bathtub, stroller, highchair, chest, wastebasket, night light, toys
- baby's food and vitamins
- supplies: bottles, swabs, tissues, powder, baby soap, oil, medications
- baby sitters

It is clear that *someone* must spend at least $5,000 for each baby born at current (1982) prices. Although a great deal more than this may be spent, the total can be cut significantly only if there are "hand-me-downs" of maternity wardrobe or of clothing and bedding from other children in the family, if the baby is breast-fed, or if friends and relatives help out. Baby showers and birth gifts may help to relieve some of the financial burden. Baby-sitting can be an especially valuable gift from friends or family members; it may well determine whether or not the new parents can afford to have the necessary time alone to keep their couple bonds intact.

Of course, medical and hospital insurance can help immeasurably if parents-to-be have such coverage. Some medical plans cover expenses only if the insurance was in force well before the pregnancy began. Other plans pay only a percentage of the total costs, and still others pay what the insurance company deems a "reasonable" charge, which may be much less than the actual cost. The costs for those on welfare who choose to become parents are covered by tax-supported government programs.

Pregnancy

Once a couple have conceived and are aware of the pregnancy (especially the first pregnancy), their lives begin to change. Their adjustment depends on a variety of factors—whether or not the child is wanted; their physical and mental health; their financial circumstances; their ages; and, most important, their mutual support and the support of significant others such as their families of origin and their close friends.

Traditionally, pregnancy has been treated by both men and women as a woman's experience even though men have usually been emotionally intensely involved with the children they father—as projections of themselves or their dreams, as heirs, or even as adversaries. Traditionally, men have been supposed to be supportive of their partners during pregnancy but have not been expected, as have been women, to let the experience disrupt their careers. This is not always the case now, however.

Jokes are often made about men who are jealous of the attention pregnant women receive. Very occasionally one learns of men who show symptoms of pregnancy such as morning sickness or backache. Some become depressed and share the "baby blues" after the delivery. These symptoms constitute what is called the "pregnant-husband syndrome." Some estimates are that nearly half of all expectant fathers are affected by the pregnancy to some degree, either emotionally or physically.[9] The syndrome is ritualized in some societies in which husbands even take to their beds and simulate birth in the belief that they will lure evil spirits away from the mother.[10] This practice is termed *couvade*.

However unusual (or even amusing) we may find the idea of couvade, child psychologists tell us that when a father-to-be is completely involved with his mate in a pregnancy, he is more likely to be an involved father. When an expectant father takes part in preparations for the birth (as in childbirth education classes) and when he takes the opportunity to participate in prenatal care and in the birth itself, he is likely to enjoy fathering more and to do a better job of it. Many fathers have been shown to spend as much of their time alone with infants in touching, talking to, and looking at the babies as do the mothers.[11]

In the Hopkins Study, a pioneering piece of research on couples having their first child, it was reported that fathers who had been present in the delivery room had very positive feelings about the experience. Furthermore, if a man reported that he had been deeply involved and interested in his wife's pregnancy, he was more likely later on to be an active parent to the baby (holding the infant, for example, or picking up a crying baby). There was also a correlation between how much husbands shared in housework during a pregnancy and how much they held and diapered their babies.[12] There is an encouraging trend toward more involvement of fathers in pregnancy and childbirth; the change is welcomed by most women, and, for those who experience it, it seems bound to change the emotional nature of pregnancy and childbirth for both parents and to have an effect on later family life.

The duration of an average pregnancy is a little over nine calendar months, or 280 days (for most women, the equivalent of ten menstrual cycles; the baby's birthday is estimated by subtracting three months from the first day of the mother's last menstrual period and adding ten days). Pregnancies can be a month or more longer or as much as ten weeks shorter. Late babies are often easier to care for immediately after birth; the chances of survival of a baby born earlier than seven months after conception are greatly reduced.

Pregnancy is divided by obstetricians into three-month periods (*trimesters*). For many women the first trimester may be well along before they know they are pregnant. About 20 percent of pregnant women continue to have periodic vaginal bleeding, which they believe to be menstruation; they do not have the clue most women use—a missed menstrual period—to alert them to their pregnancy. Some do not have (or may not notice) other first-trimester changes, such as breast swelling and tenderness, increased frequency of urination, unusual drowsiness or tiredness, or nausea. They may not notice the darkening of the area around the nipple (areola) or Montgomery's tubercles (like big goose bumps in the area). They may attribute any unusual sleepiness to fatigue or to illness. Most women, however, do notice one or more of the clues; a visit to a physician can confirm their pregnancy by tests or by pelvic examination.

Meanwhile, whether the mother-to-be knows it or not, in the first trimester the fertilized ovum (zygote) has undergone cell division and has passed into the uterus, where after approximately three days it implants on the uterine wall. It is now called an **embryo** and begins to grow at a steady rate, supported by life-giving tissues centered in the placenta. The placenta, connecting the uterine wall to the embryo by the **umbilical cord**, exchanges nutrients and oxygen for the waste products of the embryo. The placenta will be expelled soon after the baby has been born.

During the first trimester, the head, nervous system, internal organs, skeleton, and limbs of the embryo are formed. Between the ninth and twelfth weeks of pregnancy the embryo takes on a human appearance, and from this time until delivery it is called a **fetus**. It is during this important developmental period that many potential birth defects can be caused by drugs taken by the mother, by her exposure to radiation, or by transmission of a virus or contagious disease.

FIGURE 10.3
The Development of the Human Embryo in the First Eight Weeks (both actual size and enlarged for detail)

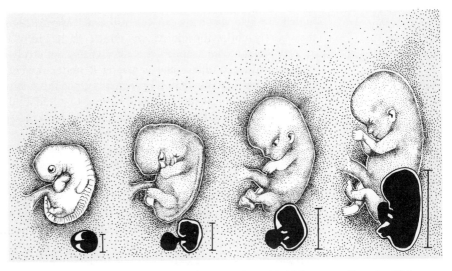

29 days 5.0mm   37 days 8.0mm   6 weeks 12.0mm   8 weeks 23.0mm

Since anything that finds its way into the blood of a pregnant woman crosses the placenta into the fetus, women who might be pregnant should guard against ingestion of potentially dangerous substances and exposure to infectious diseases or to environmental hazards such as radiation or air pollutants. Probably there will be no harmful effects (only 3.5 percent of babies are born seriously damaged), but simple precautions taken by each pregnant woman can decrease her chances of contributing to that statistic.

Tobacco, caffeine, and alcohol can affect the healthy development of the fetus. Nicotine and carbon monoxide from cigarette smoke restrict oxygen supply to the fetus and increase the likelihood of miscarriage, stillbirth, and low birth weight. Women who are heavy smokers have more distress after birth. Some research indicates that pregnant women who do not smoke can still be affected if they are subjected to others' smoking in their presence. Caffeine (which is present in coffee, cola drinks, cocoa, and chocolate) and theophylline (which is found in tea) are both stimulants that will pass through a placenta to a fetus. Although they rarely cause serious damage to the fetus, moderate or no intake is advised as a precautionary measure. Birth abnormalities associated with heavy alcohol consumption ("fetal alcohol syndrome") are considered the third most frequent cause of mental retardation in newborn babies; pregnant women should stop all alcoholic beverage consumption.

German measles (rubella) and syphilis used to be the diseases most dreaded for their effects on the fetus. Although both are still dangerous, there is now a prepregnancy vaccination against rubella, and syphilis can be diagnosed and successfully treated during pregnancy. This is also true of a less well known but equally dangerous disease called **toxoplasmosis**, which is caused by a parasite carried by cattle, pigs, and sheep. Cooking meat until it is well done can kill the toxoplasmosis parasite, although contact with live animals—including cats, which are also carriers—can cause the disease. Although a pregnant woman may barely notice the illness, the effects on her fetus can be serious.

Any woman who suspects that she is pregnant is advised to stop all medication immediately unless she is taking it under medical supervision and her doctor knows that she may be pregnant. Once the pregnancy is confirmed and she is under medical care, she will be told to avoid all drugs (unless medically supervised), to avoid radiation (including any kind of X-rays), and to take extra health precautions in diet, rest, vitamins, and hygiene to minimize any dangers.

By the end of the first trimester, most women feel well and have worked through any early feelings of depression or anxiety they may have had about their pregnancies. For some women, being pregnant takes getting used to. A woman may have to contend with drowsiness and morning sickness. The pregnancy may have been unplanned, or the mother-to-be may have doubts about the effects of the pregnancy on her career or about how she will manage as a mother. Not all women are excited about being pregnant, and some are quite depressed. A woman's depression or anxiety may be related to how the father-to-be is adjusting to her pregnancy and to the prospect of fatherhood.

FIGURE 10.4

The Development of the Human Fetus from Week Ten to Week Sixteen (actual size)

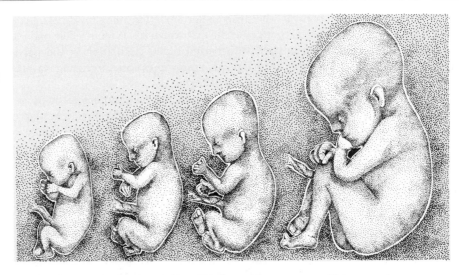

Ten weeks   Eleven weeks   Twelve weeks   Sixteen weeks

The second trimester is marked by the beginning of the mother's awareness of fetal activity (quickening). The fetus is about five-and-a-half inches long at sixteen weeks and may reach more than a foot in length by the end of the second trimester, with a weight gain from a few ounces to as much as two pounds. The fetal heartbeat can now be heard, and the eyes are open. The mother-to-be now looks pregnant and usually begins to wear maternity clothes. Some women begin to complain about feeling unattractive or clumsy, but most complaints in the second trimester are relatively minor.

By the second trimester, pregnant women begin to gain weight (much of which is accounted for by the combination of the weight of the amniotic fluid surrounding the fetus and their own breast and uterine enlargement). One of the most frequent concerns of pregnant women is about weight gain. Many women gain more weight than is good for them because they use pregnancy as an excuse to go on eating binges. Usually a weight gain of twenty to twenty-five pounds is considered advisable. Recent research indicating that any weight gain of less than fifteen pounds may be harmful to the developing fetus has lifted the burden of striving for minimal weight gain from most pregnant women. (Thirty years ago women were cautioned to keep their weight gain to no more than fifteen pounds, which was thought to be double the weight of an average baby at birth.)

During the second trimester the fatigue and malaise of the first trimester have ended, and the woman usually has renewed energy. As a result, there often is a renewal of sexual interest which may have decreased for a variety of

reasons—because of her anxieties, her drowsiness, or other physical or emotional changes of the first trimester. If renewed sexual interest occurs, it may be
due in part to increased blood circulation in the pelvic area. Pregnancy en-
hances normal pelvic **vasocongestion**, increasing warmth, lubrication, and sensitivity during sexual arousal.

Not all women find themselves more interested in sexual activity in the
second trimester than they were in the first. The degree of sexual interest is
heavily dependent on the symbolism of the pregnancy, of course; and just as at
any other time, it is heavily dependent on the interaction with potential sex
partners.

Deep-seated attitudes about sex may be intensified during pregnancy.
Women who feel that sex is dirty or sinful may now feel that they have extra
justification for rejecting their husbands; women who feel that sex is symbolic
of love and unity may find security in it; women who feel that sexual interaction is a natural, delightful game may intensify their flirtatiousness.

The way a woman thinks of her body during pregnancy has just as much of
an effect on her sexual interest as it has at any other time, too. Is her body
distorted? Is it fulfilled? Is it "cute" and special? Is the woman glowing with
good health, or is she sick?

The way people feel about their sexual selves is always dependent on their
interpretations of potential partners' responses to them, and being pregnant
does not alter this important rule. A woman who believes (correctly or incorrectly) that her partner does not find her sexually attractive will respond by
either depressing her interest in sexual interaction or finding a partner who
does find her sexually attractive. Traditionally, "proper" pregnant women will
do the former. If her partner seems more interested in the baby than in *her*, she
may respond by taking a mother role rather than a lover role.

Most pregnant working women continue on their jobs until the end of the
second trimester. A few continue throughout the nine months, although many
women want time to prepare for the birth. Some women are obliged to quit
working because of fatigue, which can become an increasing problem because
of the added weight they are carrying. Some experts believe that persistence at
work is an indication of good health during pregnancy. The president of a
chain of maternity clothes shops has reported that sales rose 21 percent from
1979 to 1980. He attributed this to the growing number of pregnant working
mothers who want to be fashionably dressed and who have more money to
spend on clothes than they would if they were not working.[13]

In the third trimester the fetus grows gradually to its full size (twenty inches,
seven-and-a-half pounds, on average, although the first baby is usually
smaller). Its skin has smoothed out from its earlier wrinkled state and is covered with a creamy coating (*vernix caseosa*) for protection. Hair, fingernails, and
toenails are obvious.

The fetus is literally surrounded by fluid that protects it from infections, acts
as a temperature regulator and a shock absorber, and serves as a medium for

collecting fetal wastes. From the beginning of the third trimester, the fetus displaces an increasing amount of the fluid in the **amniotic sac**; the fluid is either absorbed by the fetus or discharged through the placenta into the mother's system.

Early in the third trimester of pregnancy the woman's pelvis begins to widen in order to accommodate the passage of the fetus through her pelvic girdle, causing her leg bones to rotate slightly outward in her hip joints. This results in the "duck waddle" walk characteristic of pregnant women. Urination is more frequent in the third trimester of pregnancy because the bladder is crowded by the growing uterus. This crowding makes some pregnant women urinate involuntarily when they sneeze, cough, or laugh.

At one time some doctors recommended that sexual intercourse cease during the third trimester of pregnancy in the belief that some damage might occur to the amniotic sac, if not to the fetus itself. Others feared that infection might result if the male's mouth, hands, or penis was not properly clean. Today, such precautions are advised only if there has been any vaginal bleeding, leaking of amniotic fluid, or a history of premature births.

Nevertheless, sexual activity generally declines near the end of pregnancy. Most women report that there is no physically comfortable position for coitus. There are, of course, many ways for couples to give each other emotional support and satisfying sexual pleasure other than coitus. Many women report a sharp decline in sexual interest late in the third trimester, and this can be a problem unless they are willing to help their husbands to reduce their sexual tensions or unless their husbands find some outlet (such as masturbation) which does not involve them.[14]

Near the end of the third trimester the fetus shifts lower in the abdomen, normally head first, as a signal that birth is approaching.

Summary

■ A couple's first pregnancy, whether it is greeted with delight or with apprehension, requires major adjustments. Financial plans are necessary since pregnancy, childbirth, and the baby's first year may cost $5,000 or more. Life as a couple will change as partners take on the roles of parents. Nearly every survey reveals that the birth of the first child has significant effects on the couple's marriage.

■ Pregnancy and childbirth have traditionally been viewed as a woman's experience, although in certain societies men ritualistically participate. More informally, the pregnant-husband syndrome, in which fathers-to-be show certain symptoms associated with pregnancy, is not at all uncommon. Men who become highly involved in their wives' pregnancies and who take part in the actual birth may be better fathers than those who leave it all up to the women.

■ Pregnancy lasts for nine calendar months or approximately 280 days. Clinically, the term is divided into three periods called trimesters. During the first trimester, the fertilized egg undergoes cell division and implants on the uterine wall. During this period the embryo takes on a human appearance and thereafter is referred to as a fetus. It is during the first trimester that birth defects are especially likely to be caused by the mother's exposure to radiation, viruses, diseases, and harmful drugs or other toxins.

■   The second trimester of pregnancy is marked by the beginning of the mother's awareness of fetal activity. Weight gain is noted and is often a cause of concern for pregnant women. Most women feel healthy and may continue a normal schedule of activities, although they clearly appear pregnant and, in most cases, begin to wear maternity clothes during this trimester.

■   In the third trimester the fetus completes its growth. Near the end of this period, the baby usually shifts to a head-down position, ready to be born. As the last stage of this trimester ends, uterine contractions begin as the time for birth approaches.

Childbirth

No two childbirths are quite alike. Not only is the experience different for different women, but each woman also will find that each of her birth experiences is unique. For one thing, labor, the first stage of childbirth, usually is longer for a first child. In addition, the size and position of the baby, the mother's muscle tone, and her general physical and mental health all cause variations in the experience. Despite the dissimilarities, however, births also have similarities that form a recognizable pattern.

During the last weeks of pregnancy, changes take place in a future mother's body that may indicate to her that birth is approaching. Some women feel the baby's descent into the pelvis—"lightening," or "engagement"—as the baby gets into position for birth and the uterus readies itself for labor. They may notice the loss of the mucous plug or "bloody show" which has served as a barrier to infection in the opening of the uterus, or the cervix. There may be increased pressure and backache as the baby shifts lower and exerts more pull on the ligaments supporting the uterus. They may also feel contractions, tightenings of the uterine muscle that help get the uterus ready for labor while actually making some of the changes that will occur in labor.

Labor

A normal pregnancy ends with labor, the process by which two census units become three. The *first stage* of labor is marked by dilation (opening up) and effacement (thinning and flattening out) of the mother's cervix. These changes must occur for the baby to be ready to leave the uterus and begin moving down the birth canal.

Three phases can usually be identified during the first stage of labor: latent, active, and transition. During the *latent* phase, the mother's cervix usually effaces completely, and dilation begins as a result of uterine contractions. Initially, contractions may be felt by the expectant mother as cramps, abdominal tightening, backache, or even indigestion. But, unlike the other times she may have experienced these symptoms, during labor they will come and go, usually at increasingly shorter intervals as time passes. In addition, she will note that these sensations gradually become stronger and last for longer periods of time, with shorter rests in between. Although she is "in labor," she may find it perfectly possible to continue her normal activities during this latent phase, only pausing to time her contractions in an effort to help her determine whether or not active labor has actually begun.

During the *active* phase of labor, the incipient mother's contractions often become more regular. Certainly they are stronger and last longer. These contractions accomplish further dilation as the baby moves even deeper into the pelvis. The woman may now find it difficult to relax, and control of her responses begins to be less voluntary. If she has participated in childbirth preparation classes, she finds that the help of her labor coach can be invaluable in seeing that she is comfortable, as well as in helping her utilize the breathing patterns and relaxation techniques that she has learned in her childbirth classes. Most women go to the hospital or to an alternative place that has been chosen for the birth during this phase.

Transition is the last and most intense phase of the first stage of labor. The mother's contractions may last from sixty to ninety seconds each, and she may have as little as thirty to sixty seconds rest between them. A variety of other symptoms may occur during transition: nausea; increased sensitivity to heat, cold, lights, or sounds; back- or leg-aches; trembling; rectal pressure; and others. Because of the intensity of what she is feeling, she may want to give up and go home: she may become angry, discouraged, and fearful, and she may need all the support her coach can provide to get through her contractions.

Although it is the most intense, this phase is also the shortest. For mothers having their first babies, labor averages between ten and sixteen hours, although there is tremendous individual variation. Transition for many mothers lasts only half an hour to two hours. During this phase, dilation of the cervix is completed—to ten centimeters, or about four inches. If it has not already done so, the amniotic sac ("bag of waters") will break or be ruptured by obstetrical attendants. While this is not a painful procedure, since there are no nerve endings in the sac, the contractions that follow are usually felt more strongly, since the "shock absorber" provided by the fluid is gone.

It may be during the transition phase that the mother will be offered medication to help her cope with her labor. Although many women find that they are able to handle labor without medication, there are instances of tension and fatigue in which medication or anesthesia will help the labor move along more quickly, with the mother in greater control of her contractions. General anesthesia is rarely used today for normal vaginal births; most mothers prefer to be awake and aware during the birth of their babies.

Some women receive two or three drugs during labor; a few are so sedated that they are not at all aware of the actual birth. In the Hopkins Study reported earlier, it was determined that the more drugs a woman was given during delivery, the worse she felt physically and emotionally immediately after the birth. In the ninth month, half the women interviewed who eventually had normal deliveries had hoped "to be awake and feeling everything," but only 50 percent of them actually were. Nearly as many (43 percent) expressed the desire to be "awake but numb." Only half of them were. About 30 percent were numb or sedated to the point that they were not aware of what was going on at all, which was not what any of them had said they wanted.[15]

Delivery

The *second stage* of labor, expulsion, begins when dilation is complete and the baby is beginning to leave the uterus and start the journey down the vagina or birth canal. This calls for active participation by the mother and her coach, as the mother begins to work with her contractions to push the baby down and out. Most women, especially those who have not had anesthesia, experience an urge to push, which results from the pressure of the baby's head toward the pelvic floor. For many women it feels satisfying to push, although it is probably the hardest work they have ever done. Expulsion usually takes about an hour for women having their first babies, although there is wide variation. Once the head is visible, the woman is prepared for the birth by the persons who are in attendance.

Fortunately, most childbirth is fairly uncomplicated. On occasion, however, a baby will be too large to pass through the pelvis. Sometimes women who are small and who have narrow pelvic structures choose fathers for their babies who are big physically. This does not necessarily lead to trouble, but it may, since the baby may be large and difficult for the small mother to deliver.

If the baby's head and shoulders are so large that they threaten to tear tissues or muscles at the external opening of the vagina, a small surgical incision (an **episiotomy**) is made to enlarge it. Then the baby can emerge without permanent damage to the mother. After an episiotomy, a few pushes will usually complete the delivery and sutures can easily close the incision.

In some births a vaginal delivery is not possible. Either the baby's head is too large to pass through the pelvis or there are other delivery complications. For example, the baby may be in *breech presentation* (that is, not positioned head downward, and impossible to rotate). Sometimes an infection such as herpes simplex II (a virus that spreads easily and could infect the baby) is present in the genitalia. Sometimes labor fails to progress as it should. In such cases, a caesarean delivery is performed to bring the baby through an incision in the walls of the abdomen and the uterus. A caesarean procedure involves major surgery and the use of general anesthesia. The mother usually requires as long

FIGURE 10.5

The Birth Process

(A) Near the end of pregnancy, the baby is in the most common fetal position.
(B) The contractions of early labor cause effacement and dilation of the cervix.
(C) With complete dilation, the second stage of labor begins. The baby has rotated and begins the descent into the birth canal.
(D) The baby crowns upon beginning to emerge from the birth canal.
(E, F) Following the emergence of the head, the baby again rotates to release first one shoulder and then the other.

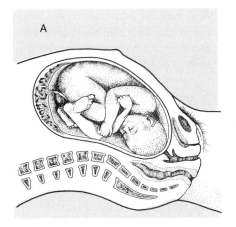

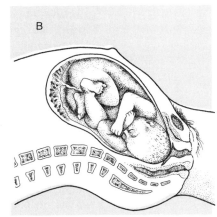

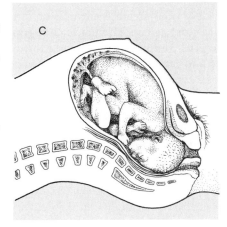

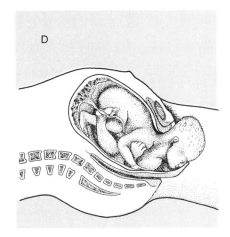

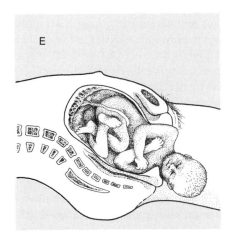

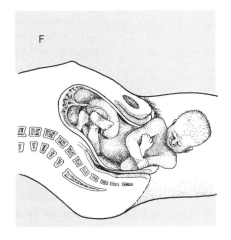

a recovery period as she would for any other major surgery. Some women have histories of more than one caesarean delivery, especially when there is a problem of pelvic size or herpes (for which no known cure exists). If the problem is simply one of improper positioning of the fetus, the chances for a vaginal delivery in the future are good.

A minority of births are considered to require caesarean deliveries. The procedure is actually performed in approximately 12 percent of all births, with some teaching hospitals reporting an even higher rate—up to 20 percent.[16] There is considerable controversy about whether or not the problems in such a high percentage of deliveries warrant this kind of intervention; on the other hand, both male and female obstetricians are reluctant to risk neurological damage to the baby from a difficult vaginal delivery, or a herpes-infected baby, or the malpractice suits that might result from either. In the Hopkins Study nearly 18 percent of the mothers experienced caesarean deliveries. Only one of these was anticipated prior to the start of labor.[17]

The *third stage* of labor occurs with the expulsion of the placenta. After the delivery, the umbilical cord is cut. The placenta begins to separate from the uterine wall as the uterus continues to contract. Most women, excited by the birth of their babies and fatigued from the labor, pay little attention to this stage of labor, since the contractions will not feel nearly as intense as the earlier ones. As the placenta separates, the coach may simply ask the mother to bear down and push with a contraction to expel the placenta (the "afterbirth"). This process is usually completed in about half an hour.

The *fourth stage* of labor is the onset of involution of the uterus. It is sometimes described as the immediate post-partum period when the mother is monitored carefully to make sure that her blood pressure is stable, her uterus is continuing to contract, and her bleeding is within normal limits.

Assuming that the baby was examined in the delivery room and was found to be in good health, many parents who deliver in facilities that stress family-centered maternity care are able to spend the next couple of hours in the recovery room getting acquainted with their new family member. Contrary to earlier suppositions, newborn babies are often very alert and responsive in the first hour or two of life.

In a small number of cases the newborn (**neonate**) has need for expert medical attention supplied by hospitals and birthing clinics. For instance, a premature birth occurs in about 7 out of every 100 babies born and is most likely to occur with a firstborn.[18] Premature infants have more difficulty making postnatal adjustments in breathing, temperature regulation, and ability to suck. They are more vulnerable to infection because of their small sizes and relatively underdeveloped neurological systems.

Blood incompatibility between the mother and the baby is another cause for medical attention in a hospital. When the mother's blood does not contain the **Rh factor** (a substance present in the blood of about 85 percent of the Caucasian population), she is classified as Rh negative. If the father does have the Rh

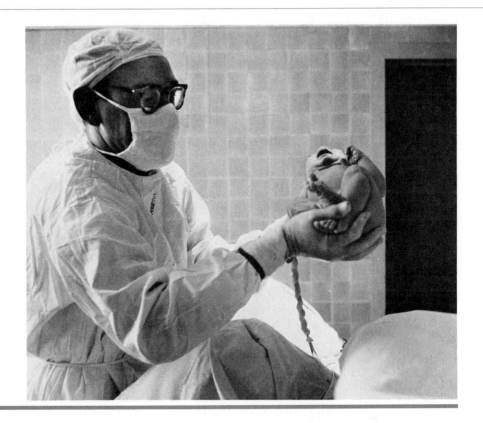

factor (and it is very likely that he will), he is classified as Rh positive. Prenatal blood tests of the mother and father can determine their Rh status and can warn of impending problems.

The Rh factor is dominant genetically; consequently, the child of an Rh-positive father will almost always also be Rh positive and will have blood factors that are incompatible with those of an Rh-negative mother. The mother's blood will develop antibodies against the alien Rh-positive blood of the fetus and will begin to destroy its red blood cells. Usually the firstborn is not affected, since the antibodies are not transmitted in great enough quantities to do damage until the birth process ruptures the placenta and fetal blood gets into the mother's system. Future fetuses, however, will have been left a legacy of antibodies in the mother's blood, and they must contend with them from the moment of implantation.

An Rh-immune globulin has been developed to administer to the Rh-negative mother during the twenty-eighth to thirty-second weeks of pregnancy or immediately after the birth of her first Rh-positive baby in order to prevent further buildup of the mother's antibodies so that her future conceptions will

not encounter an inhospitable and dangerous environment. The globulin acts as a kind of vaccine, and many hospitals routinely administer it to Rh-negative mothers following the birth of an Rh-positive child.

Multiple births usually call for medical intervention. Because these babies are often born two to three weeks earlier than full term, they are usually small. Also they may be positioned unusually for delivery, and caesarean procedure is more often desirable. Twins occur about once in every 85 to 90 deliveries. They may be **monozygotic** (one fertilized egg splits, giving each twin identical genetic material) or **dizygotic** (two eggs, each fertilized by different sperm cells). In the latter case the twins, who will be no more alike than any other two siblings, are called *fraternal twins*.

Triplets are born only once in 8,000 or 9,000 deliveries and quadruplets only once in 500,000. Quintuplets or sextuplets are even rarer, although increased use of fertility drugs such as Clomid (which stimulates ovulation of more than one egg) has been resulting in more multiple births recently than had occurred in the past.[19]

The maternal and infant mortality rates in the United States have dropped considerably in recent years, largely as a result of the availability of competent and immediate medical care for births that are not routine, such as caesarean deliveries. Hospitals, advanced medical techniques, and lifesaving equipment are probably essential for very few childbirths. It is estimated that 90 percent of deliveries need no more than routine medical intercession in the normal birth process.[20]

Many of the hospital procedures so necessary in emergencies are thought actually to interfere with normal births. For instance, when the mother-to-be lies flat on her back during labor, she is working against gravity, which can be detrimental during the second stage of the birth process when the baby is emerging. Before the mid-nineteenth century in Western civilization—and still in many societies—women sat or squatted during labor to take advantage of the pull of gravity.

Queen Victoria of England is credited with the first use of a drug (chloroform) to ease the pain of birth. Since that time drugs have been given routinely to women before and during delivery, with a variety of problems resulting. It is not that anesthesia is not welcome in many cases to relieve the discomfort of labor—and of course it is humanely absolutely necessary in certain situations, such as caesarean section. There is, however, the issue of comparing the advantages and the risks to both mother and baby. Most research shows that drugs given before and during delivery affect the delivery process itself. Some may lengthen labor; others lower the blood pressure and heart rate; certain drugs inhibit the mother's urge and ability to push during labor; and still other medications affect the baby's respiratory system and oxygen supply.[21]

Fetal heart monitoring has been of great importance in high-risk pregnancies, but its increasingly routine use in normal deliveries has been roundly criticized by some feminists as a major interference in the birth process.[22] When the monitoring is done by attaching electronic devices to the mother's abdomen by straps, she is required to lie very still, flat on her back, for long periods of time. This can be uncomfortable and can cause breathing and circulation problems that may in turn decrease the oxygen supply to the fetus.[23]

Finally, the use of forceps (tong-shaped instruments), which came to be needed as an aid in pulling the baby out in a slow or difficult delivery, is still common when medication either reduces the strength of the contractions or the mother is not sufficiently awake or motivated to push. Because of the risk of injury to the baby, the use of forceps is not routine. They are no longer used so much to pull the baby out as to direct the baby's route and to guide the head and shoulders through the passage.

Recent critics of the "medical model" of childbirth (in which the mother is treated as a surgical patient) have encouraged a return to the natural birth process. European countries began the movement toward a combination of natural childbirth with standby emergency procedures. This has resulted in a complete change of atmosphere and attitude in childbirthing clinics that use trained midwives for delivery with physicians on call if needed.[24]

Although only about 2 percent of all births in the United States occurred in hospitals in 1920, 98 percent did by 1960. Since then the movement away from routine hospital births has been slow. However, birthing clinics are beginning to appear. In many of them an expectant mother can have family and friends present, if she chooses, and the atmosphere is more like that of a home than of a hospital. In some states certified nurse-midwives may attend deliveries although a majority still require that a physician be in charge of institutional delivery rooms.

Although changes in the delivery process itself have been slow, there has been a growth in popularity of *prepared childbirth*—the best known and most widely used being the **Lamaze method**. Mothers and fathers attend regular classes prior to the birth of their babies to learn what will happen during the birth process. Childbirth preparation emphasizes prebirth exercises that will strengthen the mother's muscles; breathing techniques that will supply more oxygen to the muscles that will be working so hard; and ways of relaxing during labor to keep the pain from being magnified by tension.

In 1932 a British physician, Grantly Dick-Read, began to question the widespread use of anesthesia to modify pain during childbirth.[25] He attributed the extreme pain suffered by many women during the birth process to fear, which made them so tense that their pain was increased. He believed that as a result women often hindered the birth process, sometimes prolonging it, and certainly magnified their discomfort. He pioneered a method of "natural childbirth" based on the philosophy that if a woman understands what is happening to her during childbirth, she will be less afraid and tense and, consequently, will experience less pain. She will need little if any anesthesia and will be much more able to participate actively in the birth process.

A strong argument for natural childbirth over anesthetized delivery is that there is a great deal of evidence to suggest that early contact between mother and infant is extremely important in affecting how the mother grows to feel about the child. Placing the newborn in an alert mother's arms or on her abdomen is thought to release feelings in her that strongly favor her maternal attachment.

A recent study compared infants who had immediate contact with their mothers after birth with those who were treated in a standard fashion. Babies who had the contact—holding, vocalizing, rocking, kissing—cried less and smiled more.[26] Other research has shown that newborns respond to sound and to movement. They are especially responsive to touch and to nursing at the mother's breast; the warmth of the mother's body and her rhythmic heartbeat and breathing are comfortably familiar.[27] The mother's alertness and readiness for such stimulation following delivery can be seriously impeded by anesthesia. Also, newborn infants may be drowsy if they have been exposed to anesthetics and thus may be less able to take part in this earliest of bonding experiences.

The mother who has been awake during the delivery, along with her husband or other labor coach, will have shared the moment of birth, witnessed the child's first breath, and heard the first cry. They will now be able to touch and hold the child and begin an enduring relationship as they begin to know each other as a family.

Since 1932, preparation for childbirth has slowly been accepted by parents-to-be. In the mid-1960s there were still relatively few couples availing themselves of such classes, and physicians and hospitals were frequently reluctant to cooperate with those who did. Things are very different today, however. Childbirth preparation has become fashionable. The expectant father's (or other coach's) participation is strongly encouraged as he or she is taught how to help with the pregnant woman's relaxation, proper breathing, and comfort. He or she is intended to be present during labor and delivery for physical and emotional support that is usually much appreciated.[28]

The traditional hospital routine following a standard delivery goes something like this. First the infant is checked carefully to be certain that air passages are clear (the old favorite technique was to hold the baby upside down by the feet and slap its back to elicit crying). The umbilical cord is tied and cut. Tests for vital signs—muscle tone, body color, heart rate, respiration, and reflexes—are administered. A rating scale (called the Apgar scale) is used to rate each of these conditions as zero, one, or two.[29] A total score lower than three would be cause for great concern. A score greater than seven is considered to indicate a normal, healthy baby. Silver nitrate or an antibiotic is then dropped into the infant's eyes to counter infection (especially gonorrhea). An identification bracelet—still traditionally pink for girls and blue for boys in some hospitals—is snapped in place, and a footprint is taken to insure that no mistake can be made about who this baby is. The baby is weighed; measured; shown to the mother (if she is awake); wrapped in a blanket; and taken to the nursery, where the father gets his first look at the new arrival through a closed window.

In an attempt to humanize this method of hospital delivery, which has been prevalent for the past 50 years, birthing clinics and many hospitals have made significant progress toward family-centered maternity care. The infant is given to the mother to hold even before the umbilical cord is cut. The sensations of this skin contact usually act to increase her uterine contractions so that she can more quickly dislodge the afterbirth. The father is present and is involved in welcoming the baby to the outside world after so many months in the dark, protected uterus.

After the cord is cut, a routine examination is made, and the necessary identification processes take place. Then mother, father, and baby are taken to a room where they can all be together. "Rooming-in" allows the mother and father to hold and care for the infant from the beginning. As we previously noted, child psychologists believe that even the first few minutes after birth make a difference not only in how the mother and baby bond, but also in later father-child adjustment.

Research by Klaus and Kennell has demonstrated the importance both to parents and to babies of the initial period of bonding, or attachment. Parents allowed to remain with their babies during this period can touch, hold, talk to, and establish eye contact with their new babies; mothers have an opportunity to begin to learn the art of breast-feeding if the couple chooses.

The bonding process is a continuous one. It is not limited to the first hours after birth. But many new parents feel that it is important to begin it early. Indeed, Klaus and Kennell indicate that there can be long-range effects on the parenting behavior of both mothers and fathers when early interaction with their newborns have been rewarding.[30]

A recent variation on this new treatment of the birth process focuses on the neonate and was pioneered by a French physician, Frederick Le Boyer. His method attempts to make the transition from the womb less traumatic for the baby by the use of gentle handling, soft lights, lowered voices, immediate skin contact with the mother, and a warm bath.[31]

Breast-Feeding

Since breast milk does not begin to flow until one to three days after delivery, a woman may ask to be given hormones to prevent **lactation** (the production of milk) from occurring. Many women choose to do this because they want to return to their jobs; others want their partners or others to share the feeding responsibilities—especially during the night. Some fear that their breasts will sag; still other women (and men) consider the breasts sexual organs, and they are uncomfortable with the idea of redefining the breast as a source of food.

As interest in the natural birth process has grown in the United States, however, so has interest in breast-feeding. Many women are considering the positive aspects of breast-feeding for both themselves and the baby.

The advantages of breast-feeding for a baby are enormous; there are positive aspects for the mother and father as well. The drawbacks also do not loom so large when the advantages are considered. Mother's milk is nutritionally perfect for the baby. It is not high in fat, thereby keeping excessive fat cells from being laid down in the child's body and, possibly, helping to prevent later obesity. In addition, both breast milk and the clear fluid called **colostrum** that the breasts produce just before lactation begins contain antibodies that effectively protect the infant from a variety of diseases. Breast milk is always ready (provided the mother drinks enough liquid and gets proper rest). There are no bottles to be sterilized or warmed at 2:00 A.M., and breast milk is free—which may be a real boon for couples on limited budgets.

Breasts do enlarge during breast-feeding; however, a good nursing brassiere can eliminate sagging. Uterine contractions induced by nursing help the uterus return to its normal size more quickly. Breast-fed babies are much less likely to have digestive upsets than those who are bottle-fed; their bowel movements have less of an odor (which for first-time parents can be an advantage since changing soiled diapers is a new and often difficult experience until they get used to it); and breast-fed babies have fewer allergies and respiratory infections.[32] Some studies indicate that sexual interest returns sooner in women who breast-feed. A number of women find nursing erotic; some report achieving orgasm while nursing; and others report that orgasm during sex triggers milk ejection.[33]

One of the most important findings about mothers who breast-feed is that they report feeling maternal earlier than do other mothers. Maternal feelings are far from automatic, and some women report that it takes several months before they really begin to feel like mothers. The Hopkins Study reported that the average time was about six weeks. Half the women who engaged in successful breast-feeding reported feeling maternal after one week.[34] This development may be due to the fact that it is not possible for breast-feeding mothers to avoid protracted intimate flesh-to-flesh contact and cuddling. The reality of the baby and its dependence on her cannot be denied.

The La Leche League is an organization that offers information and support to mothers who want to nurse their babies. They provide individualized assistance and have been of great help to countless mothers who have questions and who need encouragement about breast-feeding.

Summary

■ Although no two childbirths are ever exactly alike, there are enough similarities to form a recognizable pattern. Four stages can be identified during labor: (1) dilation, (2) expulsion of the baby, (3) expulsion of the placenta, and (4) the onset of involution.

■ Labor usually lasts from ten to sixteen hours altogether for the firstborn and less than half that time for subsequent births.

■ The first stage of labor ends with transition, in which the cervix reaches complete dilation. As the second stage begins, the baby enters the birth canal, and the mother-to-be is called on to help to push the baby out. The second stage ends as the baby emerges.

■ The third stage of labor involves separation of the placenta from the wall of the uterus and the placenta's expulsion. In the last stage, the uterus begins its return to its nonpregnant size—about that of a fist.

■ Most childbirths are fairly routine. Drugs, caesarean delivery, and other obstetrical interventions may be used under unusual circumstances. Multiple or premature births, unusual positioning of the fetus, maternal health problems, and fetal distress may be cause for medical intervention in this otherwise natural process.

■ Early contact between mother and infant is facilitated by alertness on the part of the mother and infant following birth. With the increase in requests for family-centered maternity care, hospitals and medical staffs are becoming more frequent participants in natural childbirth, less medically oriented delivery processes, and "rooming-in."

■ Breast-feeding is on the increase as an accompaniment to the growing interest in the natural birth process. The body contact of mother and child and the nearly perfect food that breast milk is for the infant are two advantages to encourage mothers who may have some reservations about breast-feeding.

Adjustments to Being Parents

Enormous adjustments must be made after the birth of a couple's first child. Although a growing number of couples are prepared for pregnancy and birth, few are prepared for what being parents means. Not many have had any experience with infants, and most new parents grossly underestimate the time and work involved and the change of routine that a baby necessitates. In addition, it has been reported that fathers often overestimate the mothering capabilities of their wives, whereas women believe that men will be more help than they actually are.[35] Experts believe that inexperience as parents and romanticization of parenthood are major sources of stress in the emerging family.[36] Often relatives who might be counted on for advice and support live far away or may be unable to help for other reasons. The couple are left pretty much alone with a copy of "Dr. Spock" to learn about baby care.

The birth of the first child has frequently been described as a crisis or a trauma for the new parents.[37,38] Although many couples do not seem to be severely enough disrupted to use such extreme terms in describing the impact of the first baby on their relationships, the shift to parenthood rarely occurs without some marital conflicts.[39] In a thoughtful analysis of the dynamics of the emerging family, McGoldrick writes:

> *Some couples find the level of responsibility required in having a child a great burden. They are able to handle the responsibility of living with another adult, realizing they are not responsible for the other's survival, or even for being emotionally available more than a certain amount of the time. There is a qualitatively different level of commitment to parenthood than to marriage. As everyone knows, marriage vows can be broken. Parenthood is forever.*[40]

In an early article on the transition to parenthood, sociologist Alice Rossi cited four basic reasons that becoming parents for the first time is often difficult.[41] She pointed to the duration of the responsibility one assumes in becoming a parent as a crucial realization. There is nothing in the rest of life comparable to the awareness that with the birth of each child, a minimum eighteen-year contract of responsibility for the physical, mental, and social welfare of that child is put in force. Just facing that fact is often difficult because short of abandonment or putting the child up for adoption, there is no turning back. As one graduate student remarked a few weeks after her first son was born, "You have the baby in the hospital and you come home the next day and you go, 'Wow, this is my responsibility for a long, long time.'"[42]

The second stress of parenthood is that of role change. Rossi believes that women experience more difficulty in this area than men do because women usually become the primary parent to the small child. Also, many women leave an outside job to stay at home after the birth of a child. They add the role of mother and either give up the role of worker or try to balance the two roles in what many view as an almost impossible combination. Legally and socially, an infant's needs take precedence over its mother's job; she may feel torn between her desire to be at home with her baby and the necessity or desire to resume working.

A recent study revealed that after the birth of their first child, women tended to reduce the number of children they had previously desired and to lengthen the time interval they had thought was desirable between children. Their husbands generally showed no change in either, suggesting that there may be more maternal than paternal stress. Couples reported that deciding on the number of children they would have was more often an issue of disagreement after the first child's birth than before.[43]

Many, if not all, women suffer from some degree of depression following the birth of a child (*postpartum depression*, or "baby blues"), which can range from passing moods and fears to severe emotional disturbances. Most mothers who seek treatment for it do so within the first month after delivery. Although all women who suffer from postpartum depression do not follow a predictable pattern, there are several characteristics that they frequently share. Almost without exception, the woman involved was under some psychological stress before delivery, and the added responsibilities of motherhood make her feel overwhelmed. Usually she feels confronted with an impossible array of unfamiliar and demanding situations; being a new mother makes her feel helpless.

Instead of reaching out for help (if it is available), a depressed mother may become withdrawn and feel drained of energy. She may feel guilty and upset with herself for not being a "good mother" and may try to hide her feelings and to deny that she is in trouble. She often cries a great deal, has trouble sleeping, and is joyless. Suicidal thoughts are not unusual, and these only intensify her fears and feelings of despair. These severe symptoms are temporary, fading as the mother realizes that her child is thriving despite her self-defined "inadequacies." Sometimes, however, hospitalization is required. It has been estimated that such cases make up 10 percent of the female patients in mental hospitals.[44]

The third area of transition to parenthood that Rossi identifies as troublesome is the abruptness of the change from being part of a two-person unit to being part of a larger group. A great deal of help is available during pregnancy and birth itself, but little has been done to prepare the average couple for the impact of adding a baby to their unit and for understanding what this will do to change their lives together. In many ways it is as though the couple had applied for a job, were trained and aided in all the steps needed to be hired, and were then abandoned on the first day of work. One parent may be more or less anxious than the other, more or less fatigued, more or less nurturant, more or less flexible; but both are usually novices in their efforts to change from a couple to a family.

Couples are usually unprepared for the changes that cause disruption because they generally have focused on how a baby will add to their lives. The notion that children improve a marriage has been around for a long time. "They will keep us young" or "they will cause us to settle down" are familiar and perhaps often true statements. Family-life experts acknowledge that a child serves as a link between the parents and that having a baby is often a stabilizing effect on the relationship. However, having a child is not a path to marital happiness; in fact, it is likely to increase dissatisfactions that the partners feel with each other.

Even before the birth of a child—while the future parents are happily (or anxiously) anticipating the arrival—the problems may begin. Lovemaking may become awkward or nonexistent, for instance. The father-to-be may be jealous of the attention his pregnant wife receives or resentful of the demands she makes. She may have backaches or leg cramps for her husband to massage; she may not feel like cooking, or she may have cravings for special foods. She may feel tired often and ask for extra help from an already overworked husband.

After the child arrives, "settling down" may seem like a trap to both parents. One childless couple reported that they have more in common with their single friends than they do with married friends who now have a baby. "We keep forgetting that we can't suggest an impromptu weekend camping trip. And when we stay at their house past midnight, they suggest it's time for us to leave; one new father even fell asleep."[45]

The birth of a child changes the daily routine tremendously. The reason parents fall asleep at midnight may be that they have been awake continuously since 5:00 A.M. If the baby is small or sick, they may also have been up two or three times during the previous night. Children demand time and emotional energy that childless couples often cannot even imagine.

It is estimated that the amount of time a mother must spend on her children and the housework is at least double that of a childless wife. The amount of time she and her husband spend in conversation is often cut in half. It has been proposed by some that as marriage grows more and more into a companionship arrangement and as couples wait longer before having a child (and so become more "set in their ways"), the birth of the first child will increasingly become a crisis for the marital system.

Before pregnancy there is a two-person system (or *dyad*). After the child arrives, there is a three-person system (a triangle), but the number of interactions has grown in a geometric fashion (see Figure 10.6).

It is clear that the addition of even one more member to a two-person system increases the number of possible interactions enormously. The system

FIGURE 10.6

*The Impact of the
First-Born Child on
the Marital Dyad*

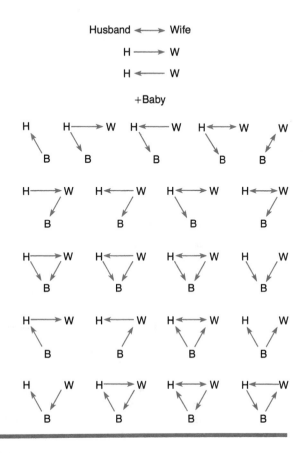

Possible dynamics of the dyad
(original two-person system)

Possible dynamics of the new
three-person system

must change to accommodate its new member. The parents must change to facilitate their added roles of mother and father without losing the roles of husband and wife.

An unstable mother-father-baby triangle immediately replaces the stable dyad. As one parent draws closer to the baby, the other may feel left out and distant. Much has been written about the mother-child closeness that often pushes the father to the outside position. The necessity to work longer hours often increases the father's distance from both wife and child, but the mother's responsibility for the child almost invariably increases the bond between her and their new baby.

The dynamics of the triangle in a family system is a major interest of family therapist Murray Bowen. He sees "triangulation" in families in this way:

In periods of calm, the triangle is made up of a comfortably close twosome and a less comfortable outsider. The twosome works to preserve the togetherness with one of the others, and there are numerous well-known moves to accomplish this.

In periods of stress, the outside person is the most comfortable and in the most desired position. In stress, each works to get the outside position to escape tension in the twosome. When it is not possible to shift forces in the triangle, one of the involved twosome triangles* in a fourth person, leaving the former third person aside for reinvolvement later.

When tensions are very high in families and available family triangles are exhausted, the family system triangles in people from outside the family, such as police and social agencies.[46]

Triangles frequently explain the dynamics behind feelings of jealousy that new mothers and fathers may have when they are the ones left out. Children learn at an early age to use the triangle by alternately shifting demonstrations of closeness from one parent to the other, thereby increasing any feelings of jealousy or alienation that one parent (or both) may have.

New mothers in particular often feel that their husbands' normal, healthy sexual interests are of secondary importance in the newly organized family. In the traditional sexually repressive family, steps may be taken even when the children are very young to conceal any evidence of sexual activity or interest. It is a short step for the husband to begin to blame his sexual rejection on the new competitor and an equally short one for the wife to see his sexual attraction to her as a demand that she devote time and energy to him that she should be giving to the much more important baby.

The new arrival changes the family triangulation patterns involving grandparents since he or she has membership in both paternal and maternal families. In periods of stress for the new mother, a frequent triangle formed is grandmother-mother-baby. New fathers may retriangulate with their own parents once more to overcome their feelings of distance from the wife-baby dyads.

Rossi's fourth troublesome factor in the transition to parenthood is that there are so few guidelines for desirable ways to bring up children in today's world. Young parents often believe that their parents' and grandparents' advice is outmoded. They may not be pleased with the way they believe they were treated as children and may have sworn to avoid the mistakes their parents made. Even if they approve of the way they were raised, they may believe that times are so different that the child-rearing techniques that worked twenty-five years ago to prepare today's successful adults will not be suitable for preparing children to live in the world as adults in the twenty-first century.

Research on families continually stresses the concern most parents have with being a good parent in a "confusing and dangerous world and in the absence of clear role guidelines."[47] The reading that they do seems to convince most parents of the powerful impact of the child's experiences in the first few

---

*That is, one parent in a parents-child triangle introduces a fourth person to the system (for example, a grandparent) to form a new triangle with the baby.

years on his or her later development. This often increases their anxieties.

In a discussion of how Dr. Benjamin Spock's famous book on baby care has become a bible of sorts to new parents, Reiss writes:

The very fundamental character of the information in Dr. Spock's book illustrates the tremendous lack of knowledge concerning infancy among new mothers. Spock, for example, resolves the mother's fears regarding the navel. The cutting of the umbilical cord at birth leaves a stub attached to the navel that takes about a week to dry up, turn black, and fall off. Many new mothers who do not know what the stub is are often anxiety ridden and fearful of excessive bleeding when it falls off. Spock comforts such mothers with his straightforward description and his playing down of the importance of this occurrence. Another source of anxiety is the soft spot on the newborn infant's head. The skull at birth is not fully formed (which helps allow for plasticity during birth). There is an area, triangular in shape, toward the top front of the skull which is only scalp, with no bone underneath. This soft spot is called the "fontanel," and many mothers are anxious about this also. Dr. Spock once more comes to the rescue with a simple, straightforward statement that the spot is stronger than it seems and will be gone in eighteen to twenty-four months.[48]

We might add to this that fathers and mothers often are needlessly upset by normal infant behavior that they do not understand (such as the infant's irregular breathing or sneezing to clear the nasal passages). Being a parent for the first time means having to learn a great deal very quickly. Fortunately, babies are generally sturdy and resilient. If given reasonably good care and love, they cope surprisingly well with their inexperienced parents in the first months of life. Being a baby for the first time means having to learn a great deal very quickly, too, but no baby has ever lived in a childless family to compare with his or her new family!

There is no question, however, that parents (particularly first-timers) need help with the task of learning to parent. Pediatrician T. Berry Brazelton has written of this need:

In other cultures that I have studied in Europe, Asia, and Africa, including [those of] many economically underdeveloped countries, young parents are cushioned from the beginning by a caring, extended-family system that not only nurtures them but also provides relatively clear guidelines for bringing up their children.

In my pediatric practice, behind every question a first-time mother asks me about how to bathe a baby or how to know if he "really" is upset, are ten or twenty more that she doesn't ask me. What she needs—and both she and I know it—is someone who has had the experience, who can answer each question as it arises.[49]

Couples experiencing the birth of their first children can expect to make important changes in their ways of relating to each other. An interesting analysis of the modes of change that emerging families choose has been proposed by family therapist Jack Bradt:

> *The environment into which children are born can be one in which there is no space for them, there is space for them, or there is a vacuum they are brought to fill. Many factors determine which context will be present in a family at the time of birth.*
>
> *As the work force becomes more evenly populated by men and women, there has been no comparable shift of men to the domestic sphere. . . . [This] leaves children often in a relatively adultless relationship. In effect, the outcome is that adults have less place in their lives for children.*[50]

Bradt believes that somewhere between the families that have no room for children and those that are overprotective is a kind of intimacy that represents a favorable environment for the flourishing of children and for the maintenance of the marital relationship.

With all the adjustments that must be made when a child is born, there seems to be a good reason to ask, "Why have them?" We have asked uncounted numbers of parents whether they would plan to have children if they could roll the clock back and begin their marriages again. Some replied that there were days when nothing went right and when their children's behavior would have tried the patience of a saint; on such occasions the answer would be a resounding "no." A few parents said that they always felt negative about being parents, an admission that points up the fact that not everyone is suited for parenthood. Most parents, however, reported that they had their highs and their lows; even with the problems of parenthood, once their children became part of their lives, they could not even imagine being childless.

Since most couples do have at least one child, perhaps the emphasis should be on how to minimize the negative aspects of adjustment. Few couples are sufficiently objective to be able to predict what their reactions will be to all of the crucial aspects of adjusting to parenthood; guidelines are needed to handle the emotional effects they will feel. Here are three we recommend:

1. Couples who have not yet had a child but are thinking about starting a family need to explore honestly how to restructure household duties, finances, and work schedules once the child arrives. Realism as well as honesty is important because too many couples have expectations for themselves that border on the unachievable ideals of "superparents."

2. Partners need to explore each other's attitudes toward various aspects of child rearing. One way to do this is to look back to their own childhoods and analyze how they were treated in their families of origin. Family therapists state that the agreement of parents on their philosophies of child rearing is one of the most crucial factors affecting the nature of later marital conflicts.

3. Couples should understand that firm boundaries must be established between their married lives and their parenting. Being a parent has a way of becoming all-consuming, and life can easily come to revolve almost entirely around children's needs, schedules, and demands. Couples must guard the primacy of marriage without abdicating as parents. In virtually every survey of what people want from marriage, companionship ranks at the top of the list. It is important that the birth of a child not create emotional distancing in the marriage and thus undermine companionship.

Eventually, nearly every marriage that endures will be again the dyad that it was in the beginning: just the couple. Parents must not lose sight of the fact that most married couples have far longer to live together without children in the home than with children in the home. We are reminded of a young couple with three children who told us of their infrequent weekends spent away from their children in order to reestablish their bonds as husband and wife:

> *As rarely as we go away, the children still seem to resent it and always make a fuss to go along. Finally, one day in near desperation over their whining, we hit upon an explanation that seemed to work. We told them that in only a few years they would be grown and would be leaving us. So we needed these weekends away to begin to practice being alone.*[51]

Summary

■ Although before it occurs few couples define the birth of their first child as an impending crisis, most new parents find that their lives change rather dramatically. Four basic reasons have been cited for difficulties encountered by new parents: (1) realization of the duration of the responsibility undertaken; (2) role change from husband to father/husband and from wife to mother/wife; (3) the abruptness of the change from a dyad to a three-person group; and (4) the lack of guidelines for raising children for tomorrow's world.

■ Triangulation is a frequent problem for new families. Family coalitions that leave one person out cannot happen in dyads; the feeling of being an outsider may be new and painful.

■ Some couples have trouble making space for the baby in their lives. Others may use the child to fill a void between them. All parents face the task of finding a middle ground that includes good parenting but also allows them to keep the marriage bond alive.

■ Eventually every enduring marriage will be a two-person unit again, just as it began. Because most married couples spend far fewer of their years with children in the home than without, the couple ties must stay strong.

Glossary

Amniotic sac   The fluid-filled membrane (impermeable except for the umbilical cord) that surrounds a fetus.

Bulbourethral glands (Cowper's glands)   A pair of small glands, situated adjacent to the male urethra, which secrete preejaculatory fluid in response to sexual excitement.

Caesarean delivery (caesarean section)   The delivery of a baby through an abdominal incision, a procedure restricted generally to cases in which vaginal delivery is impossible or undesirable because of the presence of infections or some other problem. The incision in the abdomen and uterus is called a caesarian section because Julius Caesar is said to have been delivered by such means.

Colostrum   The fluid secreted by a new mother's breasts before milk develops. Colostrum is high in protein and contains antibodies that provide an infant with immunities to certain infections during the nursing period.

Dizygotic   Produced from two fertilized egg cells; used to describe fraternal twins.

Embryo   The developing organism during the period from the second to the eighth week of pregnancy.

Episiotomy   Small surgical incisions made in the vulva/vagina during childbirth to enlarge the opening and facilitate the passage of the baby through the birth canal.

Fetus   The developing human organism from the eighth week of pregnancy to birth.

Lactation   Milk production.

Lamaze method   A method of "natural" childbirth in which labor and delivery proceed without anesthesia. The Lamaze method requires that the mother (and father or other birthing coach) be prepared in advance through instruction and practice for the mother in special breathing and relaxation techniques.

Monozygotic   Produced from one fertilized egg cell; used to describe identical twins.

Neonate   A term used to describe the newborn for approximately the first month of life.

Oogonia   Female germ cells at the stage of division.

Rh factor   Any of several substances in the blood that can cause reactions in a second or later fetus if the mother is Rh-negative and the father is Rh-positive (due to the mother's having developed antibodies to the Rh factor present in the blood of the first fetus).

Seminal vesicles   Saclike structures on either side of the prostate (the gland surrounding the male urethra) that produce prostaglandins and part of the seminal fluid.

Toxoplasmosis   A microorganism-transmitted infection, found in humans, in dogs and other mammals, and in birds, in which there is often extensive damage to the central nervous system.

Umbilical cord   The tube, connecting a fetus to its placenta, through which nutrients pass and waste materials are removed.

Vasocongestion   The engorgement of tissue with blood. In response to sexual stimulation, vasocongestion of the genitalia produces erection of the penis and the clitoris and transudation (lubrication) of the vagina.

Vernix caseosa   The creamlike coating on a newborn baby that has served as a protective shield during prenatal development; literally, "cheesy varnish."

Zygote   The cell formed when a sperm fertilizes an ovum.

There are only two
lasting bequests we
can hope to give
our children. One
of these is roots;
the other, wings.

—Hodding Carter

318

11 · Parenting: On Being Mothers and Fathers

Parenthood is usually a complicated undertaking. It transforms one generation automatically into the next as adult children become parents and their own parents become grandparents. The considerable research attention that the transition to parenthood has received has shown that most parents agree with family-life professionals that children do modify parents' lives with their needs for time, energy, and other parental resources. Not only do children change their parents, but there is also ample evidence that parents are major determiners of how their children grow up to be adults. The lack of training—other than "on-the-job" training—for parenthood leaves many parents ill prepared to meet the challenges of child care. However, the parenting process is of sufficient interest to parents and to nonparents alike that nearly everyone has developed a personal philosophy about "right" and "wrong" ways to bring up children. Every human society has some ways of assisting or even replacing parents if the physical or moral welfare of children is seriously threatened. This chapter is designed to help to evaluate philosophies, methods, and outcomes of parenting in the light of current knowledge in the fields of child development, psychology, and sociology.

Although there is no agreement among Americans on one best way to be parents, it is agreed that parents have a vital socializing influence on their children and that children play an active role in how their parents behave toward them. The many variations of parenting seem to have in common a strong conviction that parents must assume the basic responsibilities for child rearing, including ensuring their children's chances for survival, good health, an adequate education, conformity to the community's standards, social adjustment, and eventual self-sufficiency. Community members are on the alert for evidence of child neglect or child abuse, and school and religious groups encourage parents to meet their obligations. As a result, most parents soon learn what generally is expected of them (even though some may not always comply).

Idealization

The mental picture of a family that many people have is of a father and mother, married to each other for a year or more, who have given birth to a wanted child who is a product of their own conception. However, the parent-child relationship can begin with single parents of either sex; it can begin with parents in their late forties; it can begin with an unwanted child; it can begin with a homosexual couple. There is no end to the variations that can occur.

The mental pictures that people in a parenting system have of one another begin to take shape long before the first child is born or adopted. By the time a pregnancy or adoption has occurred or even when it is seriously contemplated, a process called *idealization* may have begun, which includes not only some thoughts about the physical appearance of the coming child, but also assumptions about his or her intelligence, health, affectional behavior, and even performance later in life. Idealization does not stop at birth or adoption. As long as they live, parents may continue to have mental images of their children that have varying degrees of accuracy. As the children grow older, they likewise form idealized images of their parents. By the time a child learns to talk, he or she has definite mental pictures of mother and father with special qualities that no others have.[1]

Family Roles

Besides idealizations about what a family should be, there are also usually ideas and feelings about the "rightness" and "wrongness" of actions for each specific person in the family. Although some of these ideas are unique to one specific individual ("David is always the first to clean his plate"; "Carrie is the family diplomat"), others refer to rules that are believed to be proper or improper for all families ("Mothers and fathers always put their children's welfare ahead of their own"; "Children shouldn't be allowed in their parents' beds at night after they are four years old"). Such rules characterize family roles—what persons in a family are expected to do or *ought* to do. The sources of these rules are varied and complex—observing other families, reading about how others live or believe life should be, watching television and movies, and so forth. For parents, perhaps the most important source of ideas about parent-child roles is their knowledge of how their own **families of orientation** functioned.[2] If the childhood home is remembered fondly, it may be emulated. If not, most parents probably hope to be better parents than their own were. Children, meanwhile, are learning from their parents how or how not to be parents themselves someday.

From these various sources, parents and children usually develop an idea of what a good outcome for their family would be if each member fulfilled his or her roles properly. The definition of "good outcomes" may differ considerably among family members, as may ideas about how to achieve them. To complicate family life further, family members' definitions are not always verbalized (sometimes they are not even consciously formulated) and, like other elements in the parenting system, are subject to change.

A mother may consider that a good outcome of parenting for her son would be his successful and happy marriage and subsequent fatherhood, whereas the son may define a good outcome as having his parents retire and turn over the family business to him. At another time a mother may consider as a good outcome for her son his becoming a priest, whereas the son may think of a good outcome as being "liberated" from his family responsibilities altogether.

Not only may ideas and feelings about the "correctness" of roles of family members differ at any given moment, but these ideas are also in a state of ongoing change for each person. Although this fact invariably creates some degree of disorganization and stress ("Connie, from now on you ought to earn your own spending money"; "Don't come in my room without knocking!"), it also is the way that such systems grow and adapt to ongoing changes in individual members.

In a family system, parent and child roles are *reciprocal*. In other words, a person cannot assume a parent's role unless another person assumes or accepts a child's role. Similarly, to define oneself as a child, one needs a parent. Systems theory has provided us with a unique way of understanding these interrelationships. The theoretical insights help us describe the effects of each member's roles on every other member and the energy and life of the system as a whole. If even one member is absent or behaving differently, the entire system will be altered.[3]

If and when family members give up their parent and child roles and relationships, the parenting system comes to an end. Every state has laws defining the age at which children legally become adults for various specific activities, but even within states the ages vary. A child may legally become an adult at the age of eighteen for purposes of registering to vote or of being subject to a military draft, for example, but may not legally purchase tobacco or alcoholic beverages in some states until he or she is twenty-one. The age at which child roles (and thus parent roles) end often has little to do with legal adulthood, however. Sometimes young adults who have given up the child role have considerable difficulty in convincing their parents to quit acting like parents. Parents too often have their share of difficulty in trying to persuade their grown children to give up childlike dependencies. A few parents and their grown children never give up their reciprocal roles even when the "children" are themselves parents. When family members disagree about whether parenting has ended or not, there is almost always stress, disorganization, and pain.[4]

A parent's demands that a child be an independent, self-sufficient adult (or a *"former* child") may seem to a late adolescent to be inconsistent with other parental demands that seem appropriate to a dependent child role.* For instance, parents often want a child to live on his or her own while at college but still want to impose limitations on with whom the child lives and other aspects of his or her life. The child's argument is familiar: "If I am mature enough to move from home to college to live, I am mature enough to live where I please and with whom I please!" On the other hand, parents may reply, "As long as we pay the bills, we make the rules!" Conflict over appropriate parent-child roles in a family system is very familiar in adolescence and may indeed be a necessary step in a child's redefinition of himself or herself as an adult.[5]

Changing Parent-Child Roles

One of the chief problems in defining parent-child relationships is that they are constantly changing. Although it is appealing to believe that persons in a social system of any sort are reliable and therefore predictable, such stability is rarely found. Paradoxically, in fact, stability in a family system may be less adaptive to a changing world and to changes in family members than a system characterized by "creative flexibility."

Change is inevitable in a family, if for no other reasons than the growth and development of the children and the physiological aging of the parents. Change is a necessary condition of any kind of growth, in fact. In addition, parents and children are always adapting to changes in other institutions—schools, churches, and government, to name but a few—in order to survive in a constantly changing world. There is a growing belief among family-life observers that understanding how families adapt to both internal and external change is an important source of knowledge about family strength and solidarity. Patterns of adjusting to change develop over time, and each family has its unique

---

* *Former child* is a term used by James Framo to describe an adult's relationship to his or her "former parent."

coping mechanisms. In a thoughtful appraisal of parents, children, and change, McCubbin et al. concluded:

Because the family is a system, coping behavior involves the management of various dimensions of family life simultaneously: (1) maintaining satisfactory internal conditions for communication and family organization, (2) promoting member independence and self-esteem, (3) maintenance of family bonds of coherence and unity, (4) maintenance and development of social supports in transactions with the community, and (5) maintenance of some efforts to control the impact of the stressor and the amount of change in the family unit. Coping then becomes a process of achieving a balance in the family system which facilitates organization and unity and promotes individual growth and development.[6]

As noted in the discussion on the transition to parenthood, when the first child is born, even the happiest and most well adjusted new parents must make drastic changes in their own behaviors and in their expectations of their partners. Budgets, leisure activities, household duties, even sleeping hours and sexual behaviors must be reorganized and redefined. Unless communication between the partners is good, there is a strong probability that each will be forced to engage in spontaneous decisions and behaviors that the other does not expect. New babies often create stress, although they also can be fulfilling and can strengthen the bond between the parents.[7] Whatever the direction—toward stress or toward fulfillment or both—change is the rule.

About the time that new parents have reorganized their behaviors and expectations in order to deal comfortably with the 2:00 A.M. feeding of the infant, the baby begins to sleep through the night. By the time all the breakable objects have been put away in cupboards, the child has learned to open the cupboards. Just when the family has adjusted to allowing the necessary space and facilities for bottle feeding, the child begins to drink from a cup. If anything is constant in the parenting process, surely it is change!

Roles and Family Size

The birth or adoption of any additional children also calls for reorganization of the parenting system. Relationships between brothers and sisters must be defined and redefined as the children grow up together. An endless series of decisions must be made—including who will make the decisions. Will Cindy and Michael share a bedroom? If so, for how long? Should they be consulted, or should one or both of the parents make the decision? The addition of each child changes the family structure. Not only does each sibling change the parents' relationship with each other, but the children's relationships with each other also undergo a change. A boy added to a family with girl siblings or a girl introduced into a home in which her brother has had all the attention produces a very different mix of emotions and behaviors from other possible combinations. Children who are widely spaced form family patterns that differ from those of siblings who are close together in age.

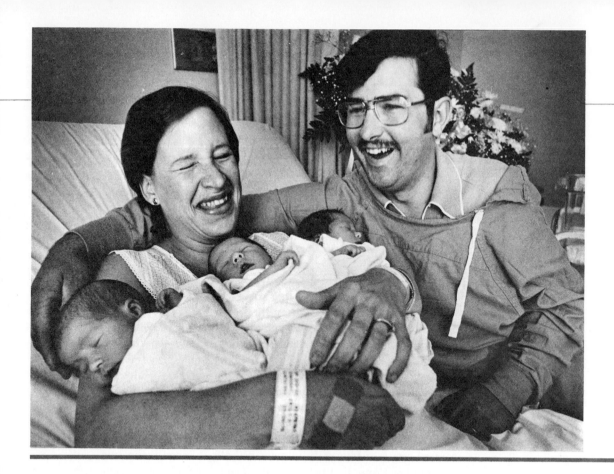

Studies of family size indicate that parenting roles take on different dimensions as the size of the family increases.[8] Particularly in middle-class families, parents tend to become more authoritarian in their attempts to modify or direct their children's behaviors according to predetermined standards of conduct. In one study, boys in large families reported greater parental control as family size increased than girls did.[9] It is not clear why parents exercise more authoritarian control over sons than over daughters. Perhaps the boys' behaviors evoked more concern in the parents, or perhaps it was simply that boys viewed control more negatively than did girls.

Parenting Styles

Parents, too, grow older, more mature, and different in their needs, wants, and expectations. They also change in response to their children's developmental stages. Some parents seem to enjoy babies more than older children. Others relate better to children who are old enough to be companions and find the infant stage burdensome. Parents may have different kinds of parenting styles and different ideals for the outcome of their parenting roles at different periods of the life cycle. An anxious first-time parent may relax as he or she becomes more experienced, for example. Adolescent behavior may increase parents' stress as they question their own and their children's values and behaviors.

One virtually inevitable outcome of the parent-child interaction is that children will develop their own styles and philosophies for relating to other family members. Some of these styles will be intentionally taught to a child by parents ("Always say 'please' when you ask a person for a favor and 'thank you' for any favor given to you") but many are learned by children from models set by parents (and others) without specific instructions. Not only may emulating parental behavior gain the child favor with the parent who is modeled, but children also seem to be gratified by being similar to parents who provide them with security and ways to gain a sense of mastery over their environment.

There is an old saying that children learn more from what their parents do than from what they say. Erikson has put it more bluntly: "Parents get the kinds of children that they deserve."[10] Besides being readily available for imitation, parents hold the keys to rewards and punishments and are therefore seen as worthy of being imitated. Furthermore, because parents usually offer security and love, children want to be like them as a way of being as close to them as possible.

It goes without saying that a parent cannot teach a child something that the child is not capable of learning. Successful parenting, therefore, involves parents' reasonable assessments of the **developmental levels** of their children. Newborn children are necessarily dependent on the activities of others for their satisfactions, pleasures, and comforts—even for their very survival. As a kind of social relationship, dependency means that someone must care enough about the dependent children to supply the materials, energy, and behaviors for their survival needs. Although a dependency state does not need to be taught, it obviously and definitely requires a very specific kind of social relationship that parents (or other caretakers) must create if children are to survive infancy. Studies have indicated that an atmosphere of interpersonal warmth (including reasoning and explanation) and acceptance of the child sets the stage for the child to learn to trust and to want to identify with his or her parents.[11]

As infants develop, they establish memories of events: a simple memory might be that hunger is reduced by the feeding process—nursing from a breast or bottle that produces food. Perhaps incidentally, the infant is exposed repeatedly to situations in which the breast or bottle appears when he or she cries. After a series of such occurrences, the child may remember that crying is followed by feeding. Cognitive and motor developments are now adequate for the appearance of a second level of social relationships. The child progresses from total dependency to a point at which he or she can manipulate certain facets of the environment.

In a manipulative social relationship one person deliberately engages in behavior intended to affect another person in a particular way. This new style of social relationship gives a child an alternative to dependency for survival and gratification. At this point, parent-child communication can be said to exist. The child has learned to express an idea ("I am hungry") through a motor activity (crying) that produces the same idea ("The child is hungry") in the mind of the parent. As the parent responds to the child's "statement" with rewarding behavior, the child learns the effectiveness of crying behavior in manipulating the parent.

The importance of the parent role during a child's development of manipulative capabilities cannot be overstated. The parent's responses directly affect the child's development of communication, secure attachment, and trust. A parent who responds immediately to a child's needs teaches the child to trust that his or her needs will be met. Parents who fail to respond communicate to the child that his or her needs are not important or that the parents' needs take precedence. If no caring adult ever consistently responds to a particular infant's activity, the child's motor activity becomes random, and cognitive development is impeded. Continued absence of adequate parenting beyond the fifteenth week of infancy may lead to a condition called marasmus, in which the infant is not only retarded in cognitive and motor development, but also falls behind in growth, weight, and physical health and has a much greater probability of dying during the first year of life than has the average infant.[12]

As a child's motor and cognitive capabilities continue to increase, the probability of being able to relate to others as a self-sufficient person also increases. As an illustration, the child learns to grasp and pull a blanket over herself or himself and develops the cognitive capabilities (1) to recognize that she or he feels chilly, (2) to remember that the stress of being cold is absent or reduced by being covered with a blanket, and (3) to *know* that she or he has the motor skills to pull on the blanket. With this increased capability, a child now has at least *three* options for reducing certain stresses or gratifying certain wishes: (1) "Let my parent decide what I need and provide it" (dependency); (2) "Tell my parent what I need and ask for it" (manipulation); or (3) "Do or get what I need myself" (self-sufficiency).

The impact of the parents' behavior on a child's self-sufficiency may seem less dramatic than how they respond to manipulativeness, for the child is not likely to die if self-sufficient development is frustrated. Nevertheless, the parent's actions are important at this step for enhancing the child's self-esteem and self-confidence. A child who is too rigidly controlled by autocratic parents has at least two "regressive" options: (1) he or she may resort to manipulating, from which a child may learn either assertiveness or seductiveness, according to the rewards received from each; or (2) the child may regress to the less mature option of dependency. (Manipulativeness is considered more mature because, unlike dependency, it demands both cognitive and motor capabilities.)

When children reach the self-sufficient stage, parents face decisions about guidance and punishment. Child psychologists have been interested in the mix between the support parents give a child in his or her struggle for self-sufficiency and the control that they attempt to exert to keep children compliant. The ratio of parental support to control has been shown to affect a child's later self-esteem and social competence.[13] The more affirmative that parents are, the better the child's evaluation of his or her self-worth.

Parental support is that quality in the relationship between parents and their children that creates a warm, positive environment in which the children are not afraid to show individuality. There is a mutual give-and-take that encourages a child to try new skills and gives positive feedback that builds self-esteem. Such support is believed to be essential to the development of **ego strength.** Essentially, ego strength is the capacity to choose between alternatives for dealing with the environment and to accept the responsibility for having chosen the alternative that one did.[14] Although for some persons this capability does not develop fully until adulthood (and for a few it never becomes adequate), a few children develop it by the time they are in elementary school—usually with the aid of their parents.

The parent's role in responding to a child's efforts toward developing ego strength requires the practice of an art, although it often appears to be intuitive. The parent must be extremely sensitive to the child's self-definition—sensitive enough to affirm or validate the child's accomplishment of his or her own goals or objectives. The criteria by which "accomplishments" are judged must be realistic enough that the child will achieve a fair measure of personal successes, but also challenging enough that he or she does not develop an inflated or unrealistic definition of his or her capabilities that may be shattered eventually by criticism from others.

Parental control can be coercive, with the parents demanding compliance and punishing any infraction. The affective climate of the home can easily become one in which the children feel dominated or exploited. Even when punishment produces compliance, it may also create hostility toward the punishing parents. A pattern of constant criticism and frequent punishment often leads to a condition termed serial invalidation, which is characterized by low self-esteem, lack of self-confidence, anger toward parents (and usually toward other authority figures), and erratic behavior patterns.[15]

The parent who encourages a child's self-sufficient behavior must also give judicious reassurance, approval of successes, and guidance about hazardous or potentially hazardous activities. An important part of the parental role is also self-restraint. A child's capability of carrying out a task cannot possibly be confirmed if he or she is not allowed to complete the task. Self-confidence and self-esteem grow through parental affirmation of their child's behaviors. In the absence of such positive feedback, the child may be unable to distinguish between socially approved and socially disapproved behaviors.

Summary

■ The notions that people have about parenting begin to take shape long before the first child is born or adopted. The "idealization" process that occurs includes how the baby will look, how intelligent the child will be, and myriads of other expectations.

■ There are also parental notions of "rightness" and "wrongness" of a child's behavior as well as of what parents "should" do. Many of these ideas are based on the parents' own childhood experiences—if good ones, to be emulated; if poor ones, to be corrected.

■ Parents go through cycles of "parenting" much as children go through developmental stages. Eventually, parenthood must end, although some parents find it difficult to give up that role, just as many adults find it difficult to quit being children.

■ One of the chief problems in defining parent-child relationships is that the life cycle mandates change. About the time that parents have adjusted to the new baby, for example, the baby changes. Then another child is born; then the children grow up and leave home. Parents, too, change over the life cycle, both as individuals and in reaction to their children's developmental needs.

■ Children learn from their parents both by direct teaching and by imitation. Children go through developmental stages from dependency to manipulation to self-sufficiency. Parents have the opportunity to contribute significantly at each level by creating a warm, supportive environment in which children can develop as individuals.

Parenting Styles and Children's Development

Parenthood is one of the few jobs in life for which there is little preparation other than "on-the-job" training. This lack of preparation is puzzling in view of the great concern evidenced generally about the welfare of children in the United States. It is almost as though couples believe that the big hurdles are pregnancy and childbirth and that the actual parenting will take care of itself. Many couples take classes in childbirth preparation, but relatively few take instruction in parenting. Of course, many read books such as Dr. Spock's *Baby and Child Care*, which was first published in 1945—just in time for the baby boom that began that year—and has been revised frequently since then.[16] Still, compared with nearly every other important task in life—many of which require licenses or degrees—parenting seems to suffer.

A recent poll of parents asked, "How much effect can parents have in determining how children will turn out?" Men and women did not give significantly different answers, but there were differences according to education and race. Of those who had a grade-school education, only 48 percent believed that parents have a strong influence, compared with 66 percent of those who were college educated. Blacks were less likely (39 percent) than whites (59 percent) to believe in parental influence.[17] The poll did not control for economic factors, nor is it clear whether college-educated blacks were more like all other blacks or more similar to college-educated whites. It appears from the responses that at least those who were well educated believed that there are cause-and-effect relationships between what they do and how their children grow up. College-educated parents may have had more training for parenthood and more resources to use in active parenting.

Countless studies have reported that parenting can be learned and that parents do indeed have an impact on their children's lives, whether they learn to parent well or leave parenting to chance.[18,19] Parent-training programs developed to teach more effective parenting procedures have had quite positive results. In a recent review of two types of training for more effective parenting, both **behavior modification** and **parent effectiveness training** were shown to be useful for reducing parent-child problems and increasing parents' knowledge of how to work with their children.[20] In behavior modification instruction, parents are taught systematic methods for modifying children's behaviors that they judge to be inappropriate. As a result of putting their training into action, deviant child behaviors have been reduced, and parents' perceptions of the problems have been altered. Parent effectiveness training, which focuses on communication patterns between parents and children, has been found to increase family cohesion and decrease family conflict.

Studies of various parenting styles and the results of each have provided information about basic approaches that are frequently followed. For nearly twenty years a study has been continued that began with observations of children of preschool age. Their behaviors were observed both at home with their parents and in nursery school classes. Follow-up studies were made when the children were between eight and nine years old, and the research is still in progress.[21] Three main parenting types were found, each of which had a different effect on the children:

1. *Authoritarian:* These parents valued obedience and believed in restricting the child's freedom. They did not encourage verbal give-and-take and expected the child to do as told. The highest value for these parents was found to be unquestioning obedience.
2. *Authoritative:* Such parents directed their children firmly and rationally. They focused on issues and set standards, but they also listened to their children's views and encouraged children to express their opinions. The children were allowed a certain amount of independence and could make many of their own decisions.
3. *Permissive:* This kind of parent gave the children little restraint and had little parenting philosophy other than giving children all the freedom they could handle, believing that they would naturally fulfill their potentials.

The second style, *authoritative,* was shown to produce the most responsible, self-reliant children. Parents of this type were responsive to their children, flexible in their roles, and apparently confident in their child-rearing practices.

In the follow-up studies these children were judged the most competent by their peers, significant adults, and the research observers.[22]

Authoritarian parents produced children who were obedient at home and often dependent and passive in other authority situations. They often displayed withdrawn behavior and were frequently distrustful and discontented.

Children from homes that were judged permissive often lacked self-control or self-reliance. Children raised under such influences tended to be afraid of new experiences, probably because they were unsure of what would be acceptable behavior in more authoritarian climates.

According to this research, members of different social classes viewed parenting differently. The authoritarian pattern has been described as more popular with blue-collar families; the authoritative style is more frequently favored by middle-class parents. Another study of four hundred families found that insisting on obedience, teaching children to control their impulses, and using physical punishment were most often characteristic of working-class parenting. Parents in the middle classes were more likely to be authoritative, prizing the child's individuality, explaining rules to the child, and emphasizing verbal discipline.[23]

In a comparative study of a working-class neighborhood, black, Mexican-American, and Anglo parents were compared.[24] Black parents were found to exhibit high levels of support, control, and open communication. Although they were strict, they also involved their children in decision making. Mexican-American parents were the most protective and were very consistent in rewarding and punishing their children. Anglo parents were less protective

than Mexican-American parents, were more apt to use guilt to control their children than were black parents, and were less apt to expect their children to obey at an early age than were black parents.

Actually, most children thrived (or at least were not seriously damaged) under all three parental styles (as they do under a variety of others). Perhaps more important than style is consistency and an atmosphere of caring. Lack of involvement with children or harsh, exploitative, and inconsistent parental behavior have been shown to be the most destructive parental qualities.[25] In their study of delinquent behavior of adolescents, the Gluecks studied several hundred delinquent boys. They reported that the families from which these boys came were generally unsupportive and unaffectionate, and that punishment was more likely to be harsh and physical than in families of nondelinquent boys.[26]

Some other common basic models of parenting have been described.[27] One is the *martyr* model. Parents with this style make sacrifices for their children and often seem to feel they must compensate for what was lacking in their own childhoods by seeing that their children want for very little. Such parents often are overprotective, regarding it as their duty to provide a "safe" world for the child. Often parents of the martyr type exhibit guilt over not doing enough for their children, as well as guilt when they take some time for themselves. For example, a mother who has not been employed outside the home while her children are small may suffer tremendous guilt when she decides to go back to school or to take a job for her own sake. Children often resent parents who overprotect. At the same time they are likely to feel angry when the parents' total availability for them is lessened. Some children rebel and break out of the overprotective environment (often a healthy move), while others are handicapped by having had too much done for them.

The second model described by LeMasters is the *buddy* or *pal* type. Parents often attempt to blur the boundaries between the generations by attempting either to become a part of the child's world or to make the child grow up too quickly to become an "instant adult." Research suggests that early marriages and young parenthood may have helped this model to develop. Many young parents and their children appear to be growing up together. When the children reach adolescence, their parents are still young and may have trouble visualizing themselves as parents of teenagers. A "buddy-pop" might tell his fifteen-year-old son, "Look, I'm only eighteen years older than you are, so I don't know a whole lot more about life than you do." Children whose parents adopt this model are often confused and may not know where to turn for the kind of parental expertise they need when they have problems.

A third model is the *police* or *drill sergeant* type. These are autocratic parents, versions of the controlling parents described earlier. They often appear more interested in the rules than in the child. Parents of this type fall on hard times when their children reach adolescence because teenagers are often ingenious in finding ways to avoid their parents and to get around the rules. Only when warmth and love are plentiful and obvious are such parents likely to succeed beyond the first few years of parenting. Sometimes a "benevolent dictatorship" can be developed, in which parents are very strict and controlling but their children tolerate them because they also feel loved and believe that their parents have their best interests in mind.

Another model is the *teacher-counselor* type of parenting. Here, the children's needs always come first, but within the tolerance limits of the family system. Parents set themselves up as experts. They participate in trying new techniques, read the latest books on child psychology, and are involved in most aspects of their children's lives. Such parents often report feeling anxious about making mistakes in their parenting and feeling guilty when they inevitably do.

The final model discussed by LeMasters is the *athletic coach* type of parent. This type often seems to have success since such parents evidently contain a good balance of cooperation, assertiveness, and concern for each member of the "team." This model involves being fit, knowing the rules, mastering skills, and developing self-discipline. Perhaps most important is the realization that the coach cannot play the game for the players—parents cannot live their children's lives—but are there for guidance, instruction, and emergency advice. The drawbacks are that there are fewer schools or training programs for parents than for coaches, and life is not as simple as a football game. Furthermore, coaches can select their players, and players can choose not to join a team. The coach gets a new team every year or so, but parents have the same players for twenty or more years.

Another interesting patterning of parental styles and values is taken from a widely used test called the *Parental Attitude Research Instrument*, which measures parents' implicit and explicit attitudes about parenting.[28] Points of view that were examined included the following:

1. *Parents know best.* Those who believe that this is true tend to expect their children to accept their opinions unquestioningly.
2. *Children's opinions should receive equal treatment with those of parents.* Parents with this viewpoint strive for an egalitarian relationship with their children.
3. *Children should have unquestioned loyalty.* Those with this perspective feel that children should never oppose their parents, nor should they ever doubt that the parents' word is to be respected.
4. *Deception is a legitimate part of parenting.* Sometimes parents believe that they must keep the truth from children since children do not always understand. (This is part of the notion that parents always know best and that children should trust them.)
5. *Children are demanding and bring occasional dissatisfaction.* This attitude implies that children are often a burden and that there is an annoying aspect to child rearing.

Still another look at parental models suggests that there are four major roles that parents play in shaping and molding their children: (1) the "potter," who shapes raw material into a finished product; (2) the "gardener," who provides the climate and nutrition for the child to grow; (3) the "maestro," who conducts the symphony of a child's life but lets the child develop into a fine performer; and (4) the "consultant," who is less authoritarian and serves as a guide and a mentor to the child.[29]

Although there are probably almost as many models for parenting as there are parents doing the job, parents clearly socialize their children by the behaviors that they themselves exhibit. Their own upbringing and their notions of right, wrong, good, bad, proper, and improper all mold their unique styles.

Punishment

Most parents use some form of punishment, of course, and children who come from families with no control at all often fare poorly. Evidence from most studies of discipline indicates that it is neither how much punishment is used nor what kind of punishment (short of real abuse) that makes a difference in the outcome for the child. Rather, it is the total pattern of parental control and the emotional climate of the home that really count.

A home in which there is positive support, love, and security is more effective for shaping children's characters than any one style of discipline. Rewarding behavior that parents favor and ignoring most other actions is probably the most effective technique. This is not to say, however, that occasional punishment is not needed for those willful acts of disobedience that happen from time to time. To let such acts go unpunished would be a form of reward for the behavior. If a child gets by with an act for which he or she expected punishment, this nearly always strengthens that response.

Punishment, however, does not need to be harsh to be effective. From a review of the research on punishment, the following facts emerge:

1. Punishment is most effective when it is closely associated in time with the undesired behavior.
2. Punishment should be accompanied by an explanation of why the behavior was wrong, and alternate behavior should be offered so that the child can be redirected.
3. The punishment should "fit the crime" as much as possible so that the child makes an association between the act and the punishment.[30]

Children generally accept discipline when it is rational and shows their parents' concerns for their welfare. Children who come from homes that are predominantly supportive and generally positive require less frequent punishment because they voluntarily conform more often to their parents' wishes. They also require less severe punishment because they are more sensitive to their parents' displeasure and respond to milder sanctions.[31]

American families today show a wide variety of life-styles, and children seem to be more aware than ever before that their own family living arrangements are but one model in a world of multiple models. Television and other media let children know that the world is much larger than their own homes or their own communities.

Family therapists believe that competent families, no matter what their values, rituals, or other cultural uniquenesses, have a number of similarities that distinguish them from families that function less well or that may even be in crisis regularly. Two similarities stand out as especially significant patterns of competent families: (1) the parents work cooperatively as a team, and (2) there are good communication patterns in the family.

Parental coalition is the concept that describes parents who stand unified and do not allow children to play one against the other. When the relationship between a mother and father is fragile, children may learn to use the rift between their parents as a means to achieve their own ends. Often couples with children are unable to form a parental coalition because of emotional conflicts between them. They may be unconsciously caught up in a fight for family power, for example, and children who sense the struggle may side with one parent or the other—perhaps with the one who offers the most. Compatibility of the parents' philosophies about child raising is one of the most crucial factors in parental coalition formation. Learning where they agree and working out compromises when they disagree helps them avoid many of the conflicts that lead to disharmony in families.

Parents are wise to establish boundaries between their married lives and their parental lives. The parents' marital fulfillment is important not only for their feelings of "being on the same team" but also because eventually the children will grow up and leave home. Maintaining the primacy of their relationship with each other helps to stave off the "empty-nest" syndrome and to give their marriage a vitality that only comes when partners have paid attention to each other all along the way.

Good *communication* patterns in families have been the objects of a great deal of family research. Family-life experts stress that effective family functioning necessitates clear communication channels between family members. A pioneer in the study of communication in the family, Don Jackson, remarked:

> *The family is an interacting communications network in which every member from the day-old baby to the 70-year-old grandfather influences the nature of the entire system and in turn is influenced by it.*[32]

Jackson stressed that in communication what is said is only a part of such influence. Just as important are how it is said and what the intention behind the communication is. Clear communication takes into consideration the levels of communication—from the first level, which is content, to the deeper levels involving tone of voice, body movements, inflections, emphasis, speed of the communication, and other nonverbal behaviors that give clues to various levels of meaning in the interchange.

Another of those who has emphasized clear communication as a necessary ingredient in functional, healthy families is Virginia Satir, who wrote:

> *There are four wrong ways people communicate. You can blame, you can placate, you can be irrelevant or you can be "reasonable." There's something incomplete about each way. The blamer leaves out what he feels about the other person, the placater leaves out what he feels about himself, the reasonable one leaves out what he feels about the subject being discussed and the irrelevant one leaves out everything.*[33]

Satir believed that each family develops its own rules of communication. In some, only positive comments are allowed and only good feelings may be expressed. An angry child is banished to his or her room or made to feel guilty about such feelings. No space is allowed for real feelings, and the family ceases to be a place where members can have their emotional needs met.

Successful families, on the other hand, foster an environment for growth in all dimensions of their members. Clear, open communication frees both children and parents to understand each other, support each other, and encourage each other to grow.

Summary

■ Parents do affect their children's lives, whether positively or negatively. Good parenting can be learned, and parent-training programs are proving to be highly effective.

■ Various parenting styles and the results of each have been the subject of numerous studies. Three styles that have been distinguished are authoritarian, authoritative, and permissive. Members of different social classes often differ with respect to which of these patterns is preferred. The authoritarian style was found to be more popular with blue-collar families. Middle-class families were more likely to be authoritative. Other types of parenting styles have been described as martyr, buddy, drill sergeant, teacher, and coach.

■ Most children do well with any of the types of parenting styles as long as parents are consistent, caring, and involved. Delinquent children most often come from homes where these factors are absent.

■ Punishment is often necessary but should be used judiciously. It is most effective when closely associated in time with the undesired behavior; when it is accompanied by an explanation and a suggestion of alternate behavior; and when it "fits the crime."

■ Family therapists believe that competent families have some things in common. Chief among these are that parents work cooperatively as a team and that there are good communication patterns in the family.

Father-Mother Differences

Studies of parent-child relations have typically been concerned with the influences of the mother on the child. Most of the early research placed a heavy emphasis on the mother-child interaction—almost as though fathers were hardly in the picture. In fact, the word *parenting* is of rather recent origin, having replaced *mothering,* which was used almost exclusively until recently.

Current research recognizes that fathers can play roles as significant in parenting as do mothers. As fathers spend more and more time with their children, their influence shows an increasing impact. Both parents can be blamed or praised for the way their children develop. Fathers have been declared "just as nurturant as mothers" and, given the opportunity, are as competent and enthusiastic about taking care of children as mothers are.[34,35] However, in most homes the father's role is as an important support for the mother, who is still usually the primary caretaker. The father is an occasional disciplinarian and, usually, the chief wage earner and financial support for the family. There has been a tendency in many families to assume that providing financial support is equivalent to being a good father.[36] Only recently has this notion been seriously called into question with the realization that earning a living has in fact frequently interfered with the father role.

A short time ago a research project explored men's family roles, including their participation in housework and child care. At that time (1975) it was found that men were involved in "family work" only between one and one-and-a-half hours a day, with child care occupying only a short period each day.[37] Men's work roles were to some extent blamed for their minimal involvement; but, more than anything, the authors cited "parental differentiation" as the cause. Women who did not work outside the home took the major child-rearing responsibilities, and men took the major financial responsibilities.

As increasing numbers of women are employed, many men are taking more active parenting roles. A recent study indicated that young children showed more desire to play with their fathers than earlier studies reported and that fathers showed more interest in their children—particularly their sons.[38] Fathers generally played more vigorously with children than mothers did, and children responded positively to this style of activity. It has been concluded that it may not be fathers per se that children prefer but, instead, the "physically stimulating, rough-and-tumble nonintellectual nature of paternal play."[39] Children whose fathers spent a substantial amount of time with them adapted more readily to new situations and were better able to withstand stress.[40] Active stimulation by their fathers seems to be one key to children's greater adaptability. Another is that the presence of two active parents caring for a child increases the child's diversity of responses.

In a comprehensive cross-cultural analysis of men and children, males were observed in their relationships with children in the United States, Ireland,

Spain, Japan, and Mexico.[41] These were not necessarily father-children observations since the observers made no attempts to determine kinship. However, the findings may well serve as an indication of "fathering-type" behaviors. Some of the major findings were that men in all five nations associated and interacted with children in very much the same manner. In general, the younger the child, the more likely the man was to touch the child. Men made no distinction between girls and boys, and in no instances did men interact less with children than did women who might also be present.

Some studies have suggested that fathers and mothers influence the development of their children differently. It has been reported that fathers respond to their sons more and that they tend to spend more time with them each day than they do with daughters.[42] The research is often contradictory, however, since most studies have not taken into consideration the total amount of time that fathers spend with their children. For instance, fathers who stay at home to take care of their children or who have primary care of them in single-parent households interact with their children much as mothers do.[43] When fathers spend more time caring for their children, they are believed to establish a nurturant relationship with them rather than the "pals" interaction that is often typical of many father-son relationships, in particular.[44]

Other studies have reported on the fathers' socioeconomic status and their parenting practices.[45] Fathers are thought to be instrumental in forming their children's lives by translating their socioeconomic values into behaviors toward their children. Higher-status fathers were reported to reward their children for thinking through problems and for being inquisitive about alternative approaches, and to tend to examine the children's motives and feelings more when they misbehaved. Lower-status fathers, on the other hand, tended to reward their children for unquestioning conformity. Deviation from the rules was more emotionally threatening for these fathers. Since children whose fathers were in the lower socioeconomic category were expected to conform to their fathers' values, they were also found to have identified their gender roles earlier in life and more narrowly than did children from higher-status homes.[46] Leisure activities were more likely to be sex-segregated in homes at lower socioeconomic levels than in upper-class ones, and being a "tomboy" or a "sissy" was a more serious violation of the rules.

Until rather recently most of the studies of children and adults either focused on mothers and children exclusively or gathered information about the father's role from the report of the mother. Since the father's role is defined in part by his relationship with his wife and how she sees his behavior as a father, her report of his relationship to his children was thought to be subject to bias. In his study of the role of fathers, Lamb not only confirmed this suspicion but also found that the child's perception of his or her father is influenced significantly by the mother's attitude toward the father.[47] A mother who warns the child, "Daddy will be tired and cross when he comes home, so stay out of his way," or "Wait until your father comes home and he will spank you," puts the father at a real disadvantage in relating well to his children. On the other hand, even when the father is absent from the home for extended periods of time (for example, for business or military duty), his picture on the wall and the anticipation of his letters, eagerly shared, can convey to children that their father is a very special person.

Fathers are not totally at the mercy of their wives' interpretations of them, however. Fathers' direct relationships with their children are more important and permit children to make their own judgments. It is true, however, that both mothers' and fathers' parenting behaviors are affected by the opinions of one another each conveys to children.

There is significant research showing that one parent's behavior is changed by the presence of the other during parent-child interaction.[48] For example, fathers talk to and touch children more when the mothers are also present. Mothers tend to respond to and play with girls less when the father is present. With boys, mothers smile and touch more when the father is also present than when they are alone with the little boys.[49] It might be concluded that fathers can enhance the mothers' interactions with their sons by being present during their times together. It is as though the father's presence encourages the mother to spend more time stimulating her son.

Since the evidence indicates that parents respond differently when they are alone with a child from the way they do when the other parent is present, understanding the true picture of *family* life requires that all members be seen in relationship to each other with other members also present. In their review of parent-child research of the 1970s, Walters and Walters have recommended that family studies focus on mother-father-child relationships and on mother-father-child-sibling relationships rather than (as has been done in the past) on mother-child relationships or, more recently, father-child relationships.[50] This is in keeping with the belief that families are systems in which each member affects every other member.

Influences of Children on Their Parents

Almost without exception, the literature on parent-child relationships has emphasized parents' influences on children. Until about ten years ago the powerful influences that children have on their parents were largely neglected. During the past decade a shift toward studying these influences has begun, although there is still relatively little research on the effects of children on their parents compared with those of parents' impact on children.[51]

The notion that children affect a marriage has been around for a long time. Family sociologists have reported that children tend to detract from rather than to contribute to marital satisfaction. Wives especially report that children have negative impacts on the quality of marriage.[52] On the other hand, in a study of couples with low levels of marital satisfaction, many reported that their children were among their only sources of mutual satisfaction.[53]

Most of the current evidence about the impact of children on their parents' marriages seems to support the notion that parents will manage to weather the child-rearing period if the marriage is intact and reasonably satisfying to both partners, although the drain on their time, energy, and economic resources may decrease their marital satisfaction. Children do not make marriages better but do not ruin them either.[54]

One of the advantages of parenthood is that it stimulates growth through new experiences. In their analysis of parenthood, the Rapoports comment:

> *Parents learn, through parenting, something about what kinds of persons they are. Many of their reactions and feelings in this new situation, tell them something about themselves and their attitudes and values to life as well as about their capacities in the specific role of parent. They see themselves exposed to experiences such as the handling of stresses and discomforts that may be new to them, and what they see may require a reappraisal of themselves as people.*[55]

One of the most complicated issues concerning children's impact on their parents has to do with how parents reconcile their personal needs with those of their children.

> *Parents are not only vehicles for the care of their children. They were persons before the child arrived; are persons while they are parents; and will be after the children leave. They were once told to listen to their parents. They are now told to listen to their children. They must, in addition, listen to themselves.*[56]

Parents' and children's needs do not always mesh. In the past, when children were often treated as ones who should be seen but not heard, parents' social needs came first. More recently, there has been a child-centered approach, with children's social needs coming first. The search for some balance seems necessary if family life is to meet the demands of individual family members and those of the outside community. Since the social needs of parents and children sometimes do not coincide, arrangements need to be made so that neither children nor parents suffer unduly. As the Rapoports state: "For the parent, no matter how devoted to the joys of parenthood, it is desirable—for the child's sake as well as the parent's—to avoid martyrdom. Arriving at compromises, exchanges, and settlements for families to achieve a tolerable degree of harmony is a major part of the work of parenting."[57]

Many of the discomforts and anxieties of today's parents and much of the unhappiness they reported as a result of trying to raise children satisfactorily seem to be directly related to how much the parental role totally eclipses the parents' individualities and their relationship as husband and wife. Too many couples seeking help for their troubled family relationships tell us that they "have nothing in common anymore except the children" or that they feel guilty if they take time for themselves, either individually or as a couple. When parents manage to find a balance between their own social needs and those of their children, not only do they become better parents, but they also report a greater satisfaction with their lives and their marriages.[58]

In a major cross-cultural study of parents' reactions to their children, it was found that parents ranked the emotional cost of having children as the most stressful disadvantage and ranked the psychological factors of happiness, love, and companionship that children bring as the main advantages of having children.[59] Sons were preferred—usually to ensure that the family name would be passed down to another generation. Also, some families believed that sons would bring more of the joys of parenting and might be of some economic help as well. In general, however, in the six societies studied, psychological reasons were the main motives for having children and also brought the greatest problems to parents.

Children with Handicaps

Parenthood at its best is rarely uncomplicated, but when a child is handicapped in some serious way, the effect on the parents' lives is often drastic. Whether the handicap is physical or mental, it is often very difficult for the parents to accept. Some parents become overly involved, devoting their entire lives to the child; others run the danger of rejecting the child as a result of their disappointment or feelings of guilt.[60] The parents may interpret the birth of such a child as the result of a flaw in their heredities. Sometimes the mother blames herself, believing that she may have been careless during pregnancy, that she failed to provide an adequate intrauterine environment, or that she is somehow being punished for some act or thought.

Although some parents may reject a handicapped child, overprotectiveness is a far more common reaction.[61] This was found to be so for children who suffered from blindness, congenital heart defects, Down's syndrome, and cerebral palsy. Excessive vigilance and restriction of both the child's and the parents' activities are often seen. It has been suggested that since our society places such emphasis on a child's development of independence, raising a handicapped child may cause greater stress for parents in the United States than in some other societies.[62]

Besides the obvious emotional factors involved in having a handicapped child, a considerable additional financial burden is often placed on parents. Family activities may be curtailed and other children in the family may feel slighted as a result of the parents' involvement with the handicapped child. The younger the handicapped child, the more the parents seem to be involved and the more the siblings are influenced.[63]

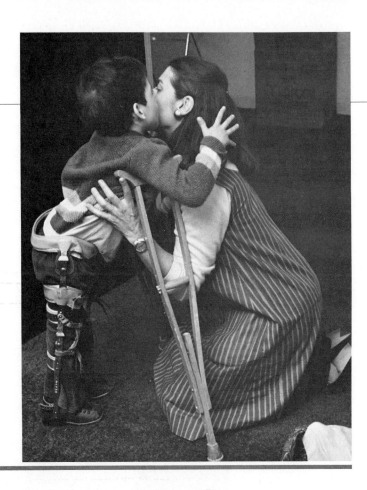

One-Parent Families

Children who are brought up in one-parent homes often are those whose parents have been separated or who are divorced. Most commonly the mother has custody in such cases. However, there are many children who have only one parent present because of a death or because they were born out of wedlock. A discussion of single-parent homes does not include those in which a parent is away for long periods of time as a result of job requirements. However, the problems may be very nearly the same except that the absent parent's financial contribution is very valuable. Children whose parents are divorced also may have financial help from the noncustodial parent. A later chapter will discuss the homes of divorced parents and their children. However, to cover the full range of parenting behavior, we must deal with those children who are brought up by only one parent (usually the mother, but sometimes—more often than ever before—by the father).

In the United States today there is a definite increase in the number of unmarried mothers who are choosing to keep their children. Over the last two decades, the Bureau of the Census has documented the number of families maintained by women with no husband present. During the 1970s this type of family had a higher rate of growth than any other type.[64] There were about 30.4 million households in the United States that had children of their own

A famous single parent—Liv Ullmann, shown with her daughter Linn

under the age of eighteen years present in 1979; 7.9 million of them were single-parent households.[65] The racial distribution of single-parent households is remarkable. While 85 percent of white households with children present were headed by married couples, and 77 percent of Spanish-origin* households were, only 51 percent—barely half—of black households with children had two parents present.[66]

Single parents tend to be less well educated. More than half the female heads of households in 1970 had not completed four years of high school; but paradoxically, as the population of single-parent householders has become more youthful, this percentage has decreased. In 1979, nearly 60 percent of women who were single parents were at least high school graduates, and 21 percent had attended college.[67]

It has been found that single-parent households have lower average incomes

---

*The Bureau of the Census notes that "persons of Spanish origin may be of any race."

than do two-parent homes; the median income of woman-headed households was slightly less than half the median income of two-parent households. Financial problems often are of greater concern than the fact that there is only one parent.

Besides their financial difficulties, single parents, who usually have full responsibility for their children, are generally overworked; fatigued; and lacking in the emotional, social, and material support provided by a spouse. Children brought up in homes with only one parent are more likely than children with two parents present to have behavioral problems.[68] However, the fact of having only one parent is not necessarily the primary cause of behavior problems. Rather, the many difficulties associated with having only one parent—lower income, parental stress, and social privation—may be the major factors.

Some single men and women adopt children. This is usually very difficult to accomplish unless the child is a relative or is difficult to place. In California, in 1974, the first single parent to adopt was apparently approved only because the child had handicaps and had been rejected by several couples. The adoptive parent was a male who presumably wanted to be a father but did not want to marry. Some single women who have not married also have adopted children. The new role of women and their increasing financial independence has enabled many who wish to do so to adopt children and continue to work, much like married men or women who have children and then divorce before the children are very old.

Single parents still report that they lack much of the social support given to two-parent families and that their children often are targeted as "different." They report occasional embarrassment in explaining that there is no father or mother present.[69]

Teenaged Parents

Sixty percent of the mothers who bear children in their teen years are married.[70] The partners of those who are married are, on the average, two years older than the mothers. If the young parents are still in school when their babies arrive, their educations usually must be interrupted. Studies show that men who marry in their teens are more likely than those who marry later to have unskilled, low-paying jobs. Even so, the father has a legally enforceable obligation to support his child for the next eighteen years.[71]

Having a baby in the teenage years tends to be related to having additional children in rapid succession. One-sixth of all mothers under eighteen who give birth to a child are, in fact, giving birth to a second or a third child.[72] This is especially likely to be the case if they are married. Several studies during the 1970s have indicated that teenage parenthood may be less disruptive if the parents do not marry, especially if the mother's family helps her and if she returns to school.[73]

Marrying and not returning to school usually result in a lack of the education that these young people need to secure the kinds of jobs that will enable them to support themselves and their child(ren). Unless the father is considerably older than the mother, the couple may be doomed to years of low income. A large nationwide survey found that of those who became mothers between ages thirteen and fifteen, only 11 percent ever graduated from high school. Of women who became mothers before age sixteen, 31 percent were living below the poverty level when interviewed.[74]

The divorce rate for couples who have a child in their teen years is about two-and-a-half times as great as that of those who wait until they are twenty-two or older.[75] Those couples who wait two years or more after marrying before having a child are less likely to divorce. Research findings imply that marriage and parenthood are likely to be more satisfying if couples do not hurry their "life schedules."[76] The following suggestions are given for a "life schedule" in which a person is more likely to develop a satisfying marriage and good experiences as a parent:

1   Complete an education.
2. Gain some work experience.
3. Find a person with whom you would really like to share your life and take time to become well acquainted.
4. Delay parenthood until the marriage has been tested for a couple of years.[77]

Summary

■ Early research on parenthood focused on mother-child interaction, but recently, as fathers have come in for study, it has been determined that they can be just as nurturant as mothers if they are given the opportunity. Typically, however, fathers have been defined socially and legally as support resources for mothers (who have had the primary responsibility for child care) and as wage earners for the family.

■ Fathers respond differently to children from the way mothers do and tend to treat their sons differently from their daughters unless they are in a primary care position (in which case they tend to interact with their children much as mothers do).

■ The role of father as culturally defined in the United States is affected by socioeconomic status. Since men are so often absent from the home during the child's waking hours, many mothers "interpret" the father role to the child. Parents tend to behave differently when they are in each other's presence. For this reason, it has been suggested that future parent-child studies should include all members of the family in interaction together as a system.

■ Children affect parents just as much as parents affect children. Research has shown that marriages are generally less satisfying after the birth of children, although parents also report that children bring satisfactions. Many of the dissatisfactions with parenthood that are reported appear to result from the pressure parents feel to subordinate their own needs to those of their children.

■ Children with handicaps present special problems for parents. The twin dangers are that parents may reject the handicapped child or that they may go to the other extreme and become overly involved to the detriment of their other children, their marriage, and their own needs.

■ One-parent families are a growing phenomenon in the United States. Traditionally single-parent families resulted from divorce or death, but the number of unmarried mothers has grown rapidly in recent years. There are a few single fathers, virtually all of whom are divorced or widowed.

■ Teenaged parents have a particularly difficult time because they so often quit school and settle for low-paying jobs. The divorce rate is high for such young couples. Recent research has indicated that a teenage pregnancy is less of a problem in the long run if the couple do not marry, if they continue school, and if their parents help out.

Glossary

Behavior modification The systematic attempt to change a subject's behavior patterns by responding to desired behaviors with rewards to the subject and by ignoring undesired behaviors (or by responding to them with punishment).

Developmental level The stage of the maturational process at which a child is currently functioning.

Ego strength The ability that an individual has to adjust to life, or the kind of character strength that he or she possesses; the ability to make decisions and the characteristic of taking personal responsibility for the decisions one has made.

Family of orientation The family in which one grows up.

Parent effectiveness training A program of instruction, developed by Thomas Gordon, in which parents receive guidelines for increased intimacy with children and for less authoritarian parenting.

There is in marriage an
energy and impulse of
joy that lasts as long as
life and that survives all
sorts of suffering and
distress and weariness.
The triumph of marriage
over all its antagonists
is almost inexplicable.

—James Douglas

12 · Outside Influences on Relationships

Every American family is subject to a host of outside influences. Some families passively accept what happens to them, and others react by attempting to change things when they can—sometimes constructively, sometimes not. One of the chief sources of outside pressures on families is the work life of the parents. Dual-income families have become the norm rather than the exception as a rising number of married women have entered the labor force. Child-care problems and overloading of time, energy, and coping strengths are still unresolved problems of this new life-style. Other sources of outside influences that affect the quality of marriage and family life are kin and friends. All hold the potential for being supportive and rewarding or for creating potentially destructive stresses and strains.

It is very important that marriage and the family be viewed in a broad context—not simply as parents and children with their own resources living in a relatively closed system, but rather as individuals who go outside the home daily to interact with members of the community at work, at school, in the neighborhood, at church, and at social functions. Kin and friends have an influence on the family unit as do the economy, politics, the weather, television, newspapers, and the educational system, to name but a few external phenomena.

Some outside influences are clearly under the control of the individual family members. They can choose whether to be receptive, indifferent, or hostile to them. They can turn off violent programs on television, choose certain friends over others, form a carpool or turn down the furnace to confront the energy crisis. Some outside influences are not as much a matter of choice, however. An individual cannot always change jobs easily if the old one becomes stressful, for instance. It may not be possible to move just because the neighborhood is changing or the air is polluted. One may have to put up with troublesome behavior from kin because they also offer some things that are valued. To change many of the outside influences on families often necessitates paying such a price that people choose to put up with them instead. Social exchange theory speaks of the **cost-reward ratio** and explains that although we may pay dearly in some respects for what we receive, as long as the rewards outweigh the costs, we will usually continue to pay the price.

Finally, some outside influences seem totally out of control. The most obvious are what are called "acts of God." These may be natural disasters—floods, fires, earthquakes—that can leave a family in a state of shock and near ruin. The recent eruptions of the volcano Mount St. Helens have reportedly caused unusual amounts of stress, anxiety, anger, and depression in the communities near the volcano. Physical abuse, suicide attempts, and calls to the community crisis line doubled, according to Washington State mental health authorities. Research on the effect of natural disasters on families has shown that to some extent the way the family defines the event is the most powerful determiner of how family members meet a stressful occurrence.[1]

Having the family home burn to the ground, with the loss of all their possessions, may be seen as the end by some families, but others—especially if they are well insured—may see it as a chance to rebuild. Not only the attitudes of family members, then, but also their resources account for the impact of a blow over which they seemingly have no control. Poor people and the elderly (who may also have low incomes) may be more severely affected by such traumas and are, in fact, more likely to be the victims. They are more likely to live in older, less adequate dwellings that are subject to fires or to flood or wind damage. Generally, however, natural disasters are not selective. The fatigue, anxiety, and worry that they cause provide fertile soil in which marital and family problems can grow.

Less dramatic, but also not easily within an individual family's control, is the state of the economy—depression; spiraling inflation; the rising cost of housing, food, and medical care—all these influence the family unit. In times of economic recession, for instance, mental health experts report increases in marital problems, drinking, child abuse, and suicide attempts.[2] Although the economy is not directly responsible for these difficulties, financial stress may cause those persons already predisposed to such actions to carry them out. It is as though the economic frustrations push people over the brink.[3]

Inflation, which now seems a permanent feature of the economy over which individuals have virtually no control, has profound implications on how a family makes its decisions. Changes may have to be made in standards of living. What was once taken for granted may be deemed a luxury in a few years. Women have gone to work in growing numbers to increase family incomes in order to stave off these cuts. Perhaps most adolescents also will have to work in the future to provide family resources or at least to help defray the cost of their own needs.

Rising mortgage rates, which keep families from buying homes at all or strap them financially if they do buy, have created enough financial pressure that mental health workers are reporting increases in family discord and breakup. In communities where rentals are scarce (New York City is reported to have less than one percent vacancy rate), it is reported that as families grow but cannot afford to move, crowding is becoming a serious source of stress.

In a now classic piece of research conducted after World War II on separations and reunions caused by war, Hill outlined a set of variables and their relationships that has served as the foundation for research on family stress ever since.[4] It is called the *ABCX* framework: *A* represents the event itself and

the resulting hardships, *B* the family's resources for meeting the problems, *C* the definition the family gives to the situation, and *X* the crisis that results. The process underlying the *ABCX* pattern leading to the family's eventual adjustment involves an initial period of disorganization followed by a period of recovery and, finally, a new level of organization.

Family-stress research has focused on the impact on marriage and family life of stressor events and has noted that families can be very vulnerable and may even disintegrate unless they can muster resources to help them to cope.[5] Three important areas must be considered in understanding the impact of outside influences on marriages and families: (1) resources of members; (2) the family's definition of the situation; and (3) the degree of stress present in the family at the time.

The first of these has to do with the *resources* of the family members. These include their coping skills, their personality strengths, their talents, their health, and their finances. Most families get through stressful times because they have learned to respond to any given situation in whatever ways the situation demands. They are usually versatile and flexible and are constantly adding to their repertoire of coping behaviors. In fact, some stress from external sources often has a positive effect on families. Family psychiatrist Jerry M. Lewis remarks:

> *There is something about being exposed to some stress that jolts the family into reevaluating its skills and characteristic ways of dealing with life. Assets that are hidden or little used may be discovered. The sharing can lead to deeper appreciation of each individual's humanness. Family stereotypes may be shattered and myths dissolved. Coping successfully with stress can lead to increased family confidence in the ability to deal with future difficulties.*[6]

Family-stress literature indicates that families cope with outside influences both by mobilizing these inner resources and by utilizing resources available from the outside.[7] The social structure in which family units are enmeshed has a powerful impact on them both by creating stress and by offering assistance to deal with it. Outside help from the community, friends, and kin comes not only through direct gifts of services and goods but indirectly as well through information, mediation, feedback, and validation of the family members' efforts to help themselves.

The family's *definition of the situation* is a second important variable in determining how they will respond to stress. Some families even choose a life-style that they know will be stressful rather than one that is lower in stress. Families who chose to move to Alaska to work on the oil pipeline projects, for example, endured long separations while fathers were working and often traumatic reunions when they returned. Mental health workers in Alaska reported high incidences of family disruption as a result.[8] Nonetheless, these families chose to stay in Alaska to work and to make their homes.

Military families have also been shown to be vulnerable to strains that other,

more conventional families may not experience. They endure frequent moves; separations in times of duty; and threats of injury or loss, especially during wartime. Loneliness, sexual tension, and dealing with children are major problems aggravated by military life. Although retention of military personnel is an acknowledged problem, attributable in part to family difficulties, there is still a large body of career military personnel who choose this life-style despite its hardships. Studies have indicated that although military wives rate their marital satisfaction lower than their husbands rate theirs, over half of the wives would be willing to have the men reenlist at the end of their terms.[9] A similar finding was made with army officers, over 60 percent of whom reported that their decisions to reenlist were influenced positively by their wives.[10] It is clear that either the advantages of some extremely stressful life-styles outweigh the stresses for many families or else these families do not perceive the disadvantages in the same way as do those who cannot cope.

Choice itself seems to explain a good deal of why some families are better able than others to cope with the stress imposed by their life-styles. When families view their life-styles as the best among the various alternatives for themselves, they tend to minimize the negative aspects and to view their situations more positively.[11]

The third important factor in how outside influences affect marriages and families relates to how many *other simultaneous sources of stress* exist in addition to what the family may currently be suffering. For instance, the father's loss of his job because of an economic recession will place great stress on the family unit. Most families can survive for a short period of time if they have other resources (savings, wife's earnings, unemployment benefits) to call on. However, if they also have the coexistent strain of a child being hurt in an accident, for instance, or the serious illness or death of an elderly parent to compound their problems, the overload may prove too much.

Under conditions of stress that are sufficiently severe or prolonged, even families who cope well under most circumstances can become very disturbed. It does not always take major stresses to push a family over the brink; often it is simply a series of incidents, each of which the family might be able to handle well, but which, when put together, add up to too much stress. Even minor stressful events can cumulatively reach unmanageable proportions. It may seem like a constant run of bad luck, one thing right after another—any one or two of which could be managed but which, taken together, cause such tension that the family unit begins to suffer.

Summary

- Marriages and families are not closed systems but instead interact daily with kin, neighbors, and community members. They are also affected by the economy, the weather, the media, and a host of other influences.

- Stress from outside sources can be as powerful an influence on marriage and family life as are internal stresses. Some stresses can be partially controlled, but many—such as "acts of God"—are not within the family's control.

- Three important areas to consider in understanding the impact of outside influences on family life are: (1) the resources of family members, (2) the family's definition of the stressful situation, and (3) how many other sources of stress the family is simultaneously facing.

Effects of Work

One of the most pervasive influences on the average family comes from the members' occupations. Sigmund Freud is reputed to have said that the two most important things we can do as adults are to work and to love. In an earlier chapter we had an extensive look at love, and now an exploration of the effects of work is important for understanding the impact of outside influences on

TABLE 12.1

Life Event	Mean Value
Fired at work	47
Retirement	45
Business readjustment (e.g., merger, reorganization, bankruptcy)	39
Change in financial state (a lot worse off or a lot better off than usual)	38
Change to different line of work	36
Change in responsibilities at work (promotion, demotion, or lateral transfer)	29
Change in work hours or conditions	29
Spouse begins or stops work	26
Trouble with boss	23

Source: Table from *How to Survive Being Alive* by Donald Dudley and Elton Welke. Copyright © 1977 by Donald Dudley and Elton Welke. Reprinted by permission of Doubleday and Company, Inc.

marriage and family life. Most of us work half or more of our waking hours each weekday. Jobs and those with whom we work are sources of some of the major satisfactions in life as well as of some major stresses.

In recent research on stress that uses a scale of items that cause stress in life, work-related events were found to account for one-quarter of the stressors in the average adult's life.[12] Some of the events are pleasant and desirable ones, but they may produce stress nonetheless. Each event on the scale is given a stress value, and research has indicated that when one accumulates 150 points within a two-year period, there is a strong possibility of an illness or accident resulting. Table 12.1 shows some of the work-related items and their values from the longer list of items.

Theoretically, if one were promoted (29 points) to a different line of work (36 points) with a nice pay raise (38 points), but with many more hours per week required (20 points), one would have 123 points—almost enough stress for trouble to be just around the corner. If, in addition, one or two other stressful events accompanied the foregoing—such as a move to a new location (20 points) and a traffic ticket (11 points)—a dangerous level of stress would be reached. Not only is there the increased possibility of health problems and accidents, but the tensions also may lead to more arguments with a spouse (35 points), sex difficulties (39 points), and possible separation (65 points). (The numbers in the parentheses are mean values, according to Dudley and Welke.)

When such a high score is reached, a downward spiral often begins, with the work-related stress spilling over into the marriage and family life.

Couples who seek marital and family therapy often are experiencing a great deal of stress at work or school in addition to having serious problems getting along with each other. It is easy to understand and to blame job stress when what is happening is obviously bad—such as being fired or demoted. However, couples may not realize that marriage-threatening stresses also result from good things happening at work. A sudden increase in income, status, or responsibility in one partner's job may place a tremendous strain on a marriage relationship, even though the couple would not want to change their good fortune.

We also know that relationships at home can affect work peformance; similarly, however, we do not usually recognize happy occurrences as stressful—even though indeed they may be. For instance, if one gets married (50 points), buys a condominium with a good sized mortgage (31 points), moves into it (20 points), and begins a new job (36 points), with one's mate also beginning a new job (26 points), the stress level is very high. Troubles with the boss might well begin (23 points), and consequently one might even receive a lateral transfer to another department (29 points) or be fired (47 points).

Since in more and more marriages both partners work outside the home, the chances for job-related stress to affect a marriage are very great. Only about 7 percent of the families in the United States fit the stereotypical model of a family in which the father is the sole wage earner for all the years the children are at home, while the mother remains at home, caring for it and for the children. In part this figure is so low because of the large numbers of single-parent households and of couples who have no children. Almost all single parents work outside the home, and virtually all married women who have no children work outside the home at some time during their childbearing years. Currently more than half of all married women with minor children are in the labor force.[13] Nearly half of those work part time—usually those with small children—but as their children grow older, they move to full-time employment in greater numbers. Mothers who work full time therefore are likely to be somewhat older and to have fewer children at home.

Dual-Worker Couples

The increase in the number of two-paycheck marriages is one of the most important changes that has taken place in recent years in the American family. At the turn of this century, only 18 percent of the labor force consisted of women, and 85 percent of those women who did work outside the home were single.[14] For over 150 years middle-class women were taught that their roles were concerned with the internal maintenance of the family and that their husbands' roles were concerned with the family's interface with the world outside the home.

The U.S. Bureau of the Census reports the present situation as follows:

The labor-force participation rate of women was close to 52 percent in 1980. In 1980, slightly more women were in the civilian labor force than were not in it. The civilian labor force participation rate for women rose from 37.7 percent in 1960 to 43.3 percent in 1970. By 1980, the rate had risen to 51.6 percent, passing the 50 percent mark set in 1978. (The labor force participation rate for persons of a given age is the proportion who are employed, looking for work, or laid off from a job.) For every 100 women in the total working-age population, there were 14 more in the 1980 civilian labor force than there had been in the 1960 civilian labor force.

With one exception (the rate for separated, widowed, or divorced women with no children under 18), labor force participation rates rose between 1960 and 1980 for women in each marital-status category, regardless of the presence and age of children. The rate increased the most for married women with husbands present and with children under 6; it went from 18.6 percent in 1960 to 30.3 percent in 1970 to 44.9 percent in 1980. Married women with school-age children only (6 to 17 years) also increased their participation rate from 39 percent in 1960 to 62 percent in 1980. In spite of these increases, however, the presence and age of children are factors still associated with relatively lower participation rates for married women with husbands present. For example, among such women of childbearing age (16 to 44 years), those without children under 18 had a participation rate of 79 percent in 1980, compared with 66 percent for those with children 6 to 17 years only and 45 percent for those with children under 6.[15]

Many women are postponing childbearing either because they want to keep jobs they enjoy or because they need the income. Once they have children, many women quit their jobs to stay at home for a few years before returning to full-time or part-time outside employment. The length of time women stay at home depends on the number and spacing of their children; the family's financial conditions; and whether or not they are in careers they enjoy or cannot leave except for a brief maternity furlough without great sacrifice (a law practice or a management position, for instance).

If women with young children return to outside employment, the most common pattern is one in which their family responsibilities are still paramount and the job is in an important second place. A recent article has suggested that women who have outside employment still assume major responsibilities for home and children.[16] Many women may thus have two full-time jobs—one at home and one outside—or one full-time homemaking job and one part-time outside one. One sociological study found that most working women believed that their husbands' careers were more important to the family than their own and that they would give up their jobs if they conflicted with family needs.[17]

An English study showed that the average wife and mother who also works outside the home in that country puts in a total of six more hours a week on

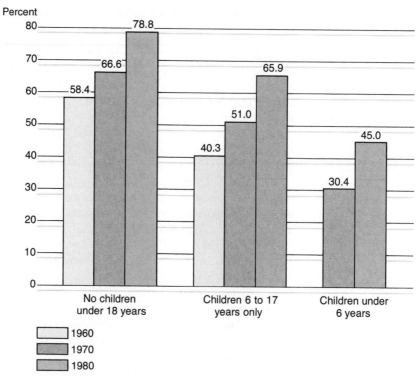

FIGURE 12.1 *Labor Force Participation Rates, for Married Women 16 to 44 Years Old with Husband Present, by Presence and Age of Children: 1960, 1970, and 1980**

*Data for 1960 relate to persons 14 to 44 years old.

Source: U.S. Bureau of the Census, *Current Population Reports,* series P-20, no. 363 (June 1981), p. 30.

both activities combined than her husband does on his job.[18] The same may be true in the United States.

Men who have traditionally borne the burden of family support often work at two jobs, too, or may put in a great deal of overtime to fulfill their responsibilities as providers. Nearly half of the men in the labor force do skilled or unskilled manual work requiring considerable physical effort. Thus work may take not only much of their time but also most of their energy.[19]

Working only part time enables many mothers to manage their heavy responsibilities. Part-time work schedules are easier to accommodate to school hours and to marketing, meal preparation, and other homemaking duties. Part-timers earn a much lower wage as a result, however—not only because they are employed for fewer hours but also because part-time jobs are usually at the low end of the pay scale and are not ones in which advancement is likely. Jobs that are available as part-time work often are ones that can be filled easily if the employee has to quit and consequently may not engender the kind of involvement that full-time jobs do. Research on job satisfaction indicates that it is positively related to hours worked and to fair pay. A recent study of employed married women showed that they are much more satisfied with their work when they have hours, salaries, and responsibilities equivalent to those of similarly employed men.[20]

The dual responsibilities of most working women as both homemakers and wage earners often means that they work part time or seasonally or as needed in a financial pinch. As a result, their pay stays at a level far below that of men who are consistently in the full-time labor force. Another factor in the lower incomes of women is that most full-time pay schedules recognize seniority, or length of time employed by the company or agency; since women are more likely to be employed intermittently or for fewer years at the same job, their pay is proportionately lower.

One in three employed women, however, earns as much as or more than her husband.[21] These women tend to be married to men located disproportionately at the lower end of the income scale (unskilled or semiskilled workers) or at the upper end of the income scale (in the case of two professionals, for example). In 1979 the average man in the United States who worked year round, full time earned $17,514, but the average female year-round full-time worker earned

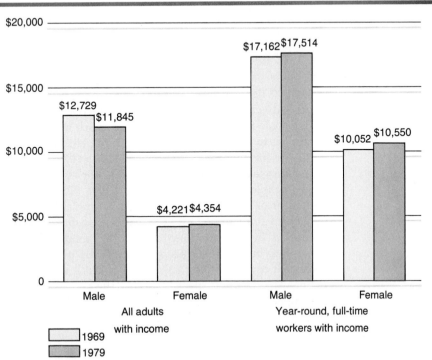

FIGURE 12.2 *Median Income, for Males and Females 14 Years and Over with Income, by Work Experience: 1979 and 1969 (in constant dollars)*

Source: U.S. Bureau of the Census, *Current Population Reports,* series P-20, no. 363 (June 1981), p. 40.

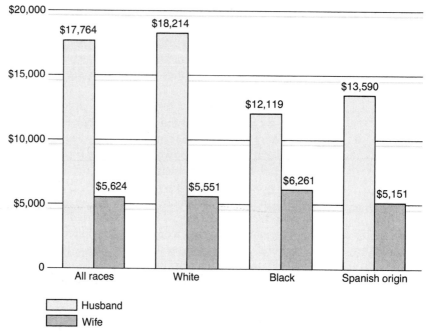

FIGURE 12.3 *Mean Income of Husband and Wife in Married-Couple Families: 1979*

Source: U.S. Bureau of the Census, *Current Population Reports*, series P-20, no. 363 (June 1981). p. 40.

$10,550. Between 1969 and 1979 the real median income for men declined by 7 percent, while there was a 3 percent increase for women.[22]

Female-headed households were much more likely than married-couple families to have low incomes. About 24 percent of families with female householders had incomes of less than $5,000 in 1979, compared with about 4 percent of married-couple households; at the other extreme, about 40 percent of married-couple families had incomes above $25,000 in 1979, but only about 9 percent of families with female householders had incomes in this range. In married-couple families, nearly all the husbands and 88 percent of the wives received at least some income in 1979 (about 30 percent of the wives had no earnings but received income from jointly owned assets or other sources): 89 percent of white wives, 83 percent of black wives, and 78 percent of wives of Spanish origin. The black wives had the highest mean income in 1979—$6,260, compared with $5,551 for white wives and $5,151 for wives of Spanish origin.[23]

Child Care

Child care is one of the biggest problems facing parents who must work outside the home.[24] Unavailability of high-quality care is one of the main reasons that, if they can manage financially, many women do not return to outside employment until their children are in school. Both parents appear to feel responsibility for parenting their children, but if satisfactory child care is not available, it is rarely the man who stays at home. Many experts believe that the unresolved problem of child care may be the biggest deterrent to equality in employment in the United States. Other countries have tried innovative methods that permit both parents to work while still caring for their children. For instance, in many families in Sweden both mother and father hold part-time jobs and share home responsibilities. **Job sharing** is being tried in some other countries, as are flexible schedules that enable the parents to pick the hours they would like to work. A father, for instance, might choose 9:00 A.M. to 5:00 P.M. so that he can get the children off to school, but the mother might choose 7:00 A.M. to 3:00 P.M. in order to be at home when the children return from school. Parents in this country sometimes work different shifts to gain flexibility in child care. However, split shifts create their own stresses on a marriage.

In the United States, flexible scheduling is easier on some jobs—such as those in which the worker is self-employed or is not confined to an office or factory. Usually, however, the hours are set by employers, not employees, although some companies are cooperating in "flextime" for some of their valuable employees who might otherwise look for some other job that allowed them needed family time. Some companies have tried a ten-hour, four-day work week, which can help if husbands and wives choose to take off different fifth days. For most couples who are finding an inflexible work schedule difficult to reconcile with family responsibilities, however, employers are doing little to help them work out solutions.

Job sharing is a small but growing phenomenon in certain professions in the United States. Usually two women share one position, each working half time; very few men share one position. There are a few job-sharing couples—usually professionals who can live on one salary (two halves) but who both want to work and to share household and child-care duties. Faculty positions at colleges and universities are occasionally filled by a husband-wife team, for instance. Most employers still resist the idea of job sharing because they have a negative attitude about the "half-time effort" they believe will result. Actually, recent research has shown that job-sharing couples typically put in more than half time each, so that their combined efforts result in increased productivity for the employer.[25] "Job sharing" in another form, of course, has often been expected by employers. Many men have jobs that require the active participation of their wives even though there is no direct wage for that contribution. This has been termed the "two-person career," in which the nature of the work demands a backup person. The clergy is one such occupation, as is a political career or any job that requires entertaining for business as a part of the wife's responsibilities.

Some couples have attempted their own time management by working split shifts—one on the day shift and one on the night or swing shift. There are very real advantages to this pattern, of course, since the children have twenty-four-hour coverage and each parent has time alone with the children and for himself or herself. However, the partners' time together as a couple is necessarily extremely limited. In a recent study of such couples, the uniform complaint was of no time to talk, to do things together, or for sex. One couple reported seeing each other only about forty-five minutes each day. The husband worked as a plant foreman from 5:00 P.M. to 1:00 A.M., and the wife was a nurse on the 7:00 A.M. to 3:00 P.M. shift. She got home at 3:30 P.M. after picking up the children from school, and he left at 4:15 to commute to work. Their sex life was restricted to weekends, although they reported that each took an occasional day of sick leave or vacation so they could have extra time together.[26]

There are six million working women in the United States whose children are too young to be in school while they are at their places of employment. Most working women with children must arrange for paid, full-time child care—in their own homes, in the home of a sitter or of a relative, or in a day-care center. Each plan has its merits and its drawbacks. If a child is ill, he or she cannot be taken where other children are—and young children have frequent fevers, colds, and earaches. On the other hand, a sitter can become ill, too, often at the last minute when a replacement may be impossible to find. The financial costs are about the same—day-care centers and schools vary in price a great deal, generally running from $40 to $100 a week depending on the hours the child stays, the age of the child (infants cost the most), and how many children the parent leaves. Some centers are publicly supported and charge according to ability to pay. Home care costs from $1.00 to $3.00 dollars an hour on the average (thus a forty-hour week would range from $40 to $120).

Over 25 percent of all children of working parents are cared for by a relative, often an older sibling, while their parents work. Another one-quarter take care of themselves until one of their parents returns from work (primarily older children, although some younger school-aged children also fend for themselves) and are sometimes called "latchkey" children. The remaining 50 percent are cared for in some other type of child-care arrangement, most commonly by one parent or the other (as in split-shift families); with limited help from a sitter or older sibling; or by using part-time day care. Most working parents use a home environment (either their own or the sitter's) for child care; only a small percentage use day care as their principal means of help.[27] The school-type settings (day care, nursery school, before- and after-school programs) that are popular in much of the rest of the world are used by only about 10 percent of the working parents in the United States for child care. Some critics of day care argue that parents obviously do not like such arrangements; otherwise, they would be more popular. On the contrary, however, the waiting lists for good facilities are long, and many communities have few, if any, licensed programs available—especially ones that take infants. Thus parents are forced to make other arrangements.

Tensions over child care are among the most severe that working parents face. They must work, or prefer to, but also want to be certain that their chil-

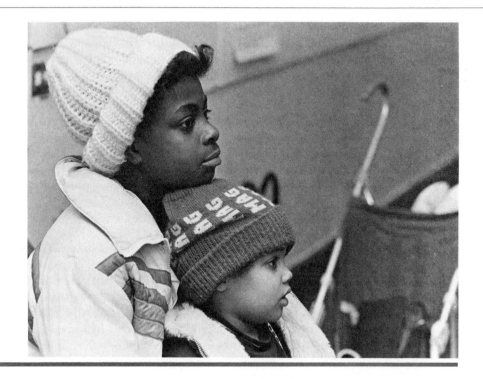

dren have good care. Leaving and returning to a happy child each working day relieves much of the stress that dual-worker couples already feel. Child experts have determined that *where* the child receives care is less important for his or her development than is the quality of the care received.[28]

Studies have reported that having both parents employed outside the home is usually stressful to the children only if the parents are suffering from stress about it. In an important study of the effect of the mother's outside employment on her children, Hoffman concludes that ". . . the working mother who obtains satisfaction from her work, who has adequate arrangements so that her dual role does not involve undue strain, and who does not feel so guilty that she overcompensates is likely to do quite well and, under certain conditions, better than the nonworking mother."[29] Hoffman's conditions add up to a tall order for working mothers, and few studies have located enough parents who meet all of these specifications to reach any definite conclusions about the effects of dual-worker parenting. It appears that there are too many other variables involved, beyond the fact of the mother's employment, that affect the adjustment of children. Anything that affects the stress level of the parents is likely to disturb their children. For instance, if the parents disagree about the mother's employment, the stress level of either or both parents may affect their children much more than does the simple fact of whether or not she is employed.

What is certain for many is that it is increasingly necessary for both parents to contribute to the family income and that trying to manage child care is one of the most difficult problems couples face.

It is comforting to know that no research has yet found any significant developmental differences between children whose mothers are employed outside the home and those whose mothers are not.[30] Working parents need more than reassurance, however: they need all the help they can get. Rather than answers to the question of what inadequate care does to children, parents need support in the form of flexible work hours, job sharing, day-care centers, and subsidized child-care programs for employees' children that are provided by business and industry as fringe benefits.

Overload

A major source of strain on modern dual-worker families is that of having far too much to do in much too little time. Fatigue, irritability, and "burnout" are commonly reported accompaniments of the increased volume of responsibilities and activities dual-worker families face. Particularly where both partners are working an eight-hour-plus day outside the home and where there are children, there is nearly always a strain in trying to get everything accomplished. In their study on working couples, the Rapoports have suggested four conditions that affect the issues of overload.[31]

1. *The emphasis placed on the degree of family life desired:* Parents not only have internalized standards about what a family is and how involved good parents must be with their children, but many also are subject to outside pressures from relatives and the community to conform to a socially approved family structure. Insinuations that they are not good parents if they do not get involved in the PTA or serve as Cub Scout den parents or Little League scorekeepers can cause guilt and even more stress for the parents.

2. *The standards the couple hold for housekeeping and other domestic living:* The fact that both parents are employed outside the home does not relieve them of the responsibilities for the daily tasks necessary to run the household. These duties are generally handled as "overtime," and much of the literature emphasizes that women pick up the lion's share of them.[32] Less than 10 percent of the families have paid household help. Instead, most parents report that they get up extra early in the morning, stay up late at night, and spend time on weekends to finish the house and yard work. Most complain that they really never finish and that they are not satisfied with the standards they keep. Most have learned to compromise their standards—to live with some untidiness and with quick meals—while others use some of their extra income for time- and effort-saving appliances, permanent press clothing, or eating out. Outside social pressures (real or imagined) often cause couples to feel guilty about these compromises even though they find them necessary.

3. *The degree to which tasks are evenly divided and accepted by family members:* Although the average working wife is seen as helping her husband support the family, most people still consider it the man's responsibility. Conversely, men help with what both partners usually view as the wife's job of homemaking and child care. The involvement of children in home duties varies with their ages and the parents' attitudes about their help.

Some experts have suggested that when mothers feel guilty about working outside the home, they are likely to ask for less help from the children. Such guilt seems to occur most frequently in women who do not have to work for financial reasons but who choose to be employed for personal reasons. Women who must seek outside employment to help out financially seem more likely to insist that children carry their fair share of the workload, especially if the mother feels her employment is not a matter of choice but one of necessity.[33]

In her recent article on dual-worker families, *Ms* magazine editor Letty Pogrebin said: "Housework is not trivial on any level. It even has an impact on future generations, for how the work is divided tells children how valuable males and females are and what their time is worth."[34] In other words, both boys and girls learn from their parents to place a value on housework as well as on outside employment. In the United States, although we pay lip service to the importance of homemaking, the truth is that housekeeping is low on most occupational status rankings. Pogrebin goes on to list two basic tenets for division of household responsibilities in dual-worker families: (1) tasks should not be apportioned with respect to who earns more or less, since each partner's *time* is equal; (2) no task should be seen as inappropriate for one partner or the other by virtue of sex. Work should more fairly be divided in terms of who is capable and who currently has the time and energy.

Some couples report that they are their own worst enemies in accepting these new standards because of their internalized values about masculinity and femininity—that men and women "should" do only certain tasks. Departure from these values can produce embarrassment or guilt. Others' expectations that couples behave in traditional ways also are cited as sources of strain. Social pressures often are equal to or greater than those that couples put on themselves. Some dual-worker couples, for example, report that they rarely entertain, not because they are too tired or do not have the time, but because their housekeeping standards have slipped so that they are embarrassed to have family and friends visit.

4. *The degree to which the couple can minimize the physical, social, and psychological strains:* Couples use a variety of techniques to manage work-related stress reduction. One frequently mentioned strategy is to compartmentalize work and family roles as much as possible. Most employers expect or even demand that employees give full attention to their work without interference from spouse or children (frequent telephone calls or visits, for instance, are usually discouraged). A bigger problem seems to arise in leaving work behind at the end of the day so that it does not interfere with family time. Many dual-worker couples believe this is important since their time with the family is so limited that they want it to be quality time.

Another way that dual-worker couples manage to minimize some strains inherent in their life-styles is to change the nature of their social lives. They are likely, for instance, to have friends who are also dual-worker couples. They avoid persons as friends who do not approve of their way of life or who make friendship demands on them that are impossible or uncomfortable to meet. Dual-worker parents often prefer to spend leisure time with their children or alone with each other. They are also less likely to go to functions together than are couples in which the wife is not employed outside the home. Many of the functions they attend are related to their jobs (business entertaining, a baby shower for a coworker, or a retirement dinner); since both partners work, there are double the number of functions for each if they go as a couple.

Many of the strains of dual-worker overload may be explained by the fact that only recently have many middle-class families begun to follow this pattern. In the past they would have been subject to significant social disapproval, as has often been the case for minorities who change traditions. With little in the way of social support, dual-worker families have had to battle the overload inherent in having both parents working outside the home in addition to that caused by criticism of their life-style from outsiders.

Marital Satisfaction in Dual-Worker Couples

Many studies have focused on the level of marital satisfaction that exists when both partners are employed outside the home.[35] The findings are that any outside influences that produce major strains usually have a negative impact on husband-wife relations. Employment is no exception. One of the earliest studies of the effect of the wife's employment on marital happiness determined that the marital relationship suffered by comparison with couples with nonworking wives only when the couple had preschool children. Once the children were of school age, however, those couples in which the woman was working by choice and liked her work reported better marriages than did either those couples in which the wife disliked going to work or in which the wife was not employed outside the home.[36] The woman's choice of employment and the pressures of child care for very young children were the two factors that made the difference in stress and, therefore, in marital satisfaction. Other studies have pinned the source of any marital upheaval caused by both partners being employed more specifically on major overload and on stresses involved in working out a life-style based on nontraditional roles.[37]

Six national samples of employed and unemployed wives were made between 1971 and 1976 to study marital happiness and other overall life satisfactions of these women and their mates. The general conclusions were that "both work outside the home and full-time housewifery have benefits and costs attached to them; the net result is that there is no consistent or significant difference in patterns of life satisfaction between the two groups."[38] In other words, these studies report that women who work outside the home have neither greater satisfactions nor greater dissatisfactions in their lives generally or in their marriages than do women who work full time as homemakers. These studies, however, did not divide the women into categories separating out those with preschool children—a factor that has been shown to make a difference. Nor did they ask the women whether they chose their occupations willingly and liked what they were doing—whether the job was homemaking or something else. Most important, perhaps, no consideration was given to the women's income or educational levels.

Other studies have shown that women from lower socioeconomic levels who are homemakers report less stress and more marital satisfaction than do women from the same background who are working outside the home.[39] It has been hypothesized that husbands may be less helpful and supportive at this lower socioeconomic level so that women not only have outside work but also nearly all the responsibility at home. A low income (below the national average) earned entirely by the husband seems to enable the wife to be more satisfied with her marriage than if he earns only a portion of it and she must also work just to meet minimum standards.

Some studies have been done to determine the effects of his wife's employment or lack of employment on the husband's satisfaction with marriage. One study revealed that men whose wives are employed experience no more marital discord and are under no more stress (although perhaps different kinds of stress) than men whose wives are homemakers. Many, in fact, reported that the extra income relieved a great deal of stress.[40] One study in particular made the interesting discovery that there was likely to be more stress in dual-worker families if the wife had worked less than one year at the time of the interview. There was also more stress if she was a housewife at the time but had previously been employed.[41] Perhaps the transition from one role to the other for her and the adjustments her husband had to make were the real stressors.

It has often been hypothesized that there will be a strain on a husband and resulting marital dissatisfaction if his wife has a better job or earns more money than he does. He may be proud of her and pleased with the money, but questions have been raised about his feelings of envy or loss of self-esteem. Research so far has found no evidence to indicate that marriages are any worse off or that husbands are particularly unhappy about being married to women who make more money or who have more prestigious jobs.[42] Again, however, few data were collected about the socioeconomic backgrounds of the couples, although it has been determined that of the two million or so women who earn more than their husbands, most are at either the upper or the lower end of the salary scale. Little mention is made of their occupations, ages, or educational levels, all important factors to consider. No doubt some men do resent wives who are more successful, and others may suffer loss of self-esteem. Some women feel envious and resentful of their husbands' successes as well.[43] We often hear a woman refer to herself as "just a housewife" or say that her economic contribution as a homemaker is scanty compared with that of her husband.

The one distinguishing feature of the marital relationship of dual-worker couples that has been found consistently is that women who are also earners typically have more say in family decisions. They assert themselves more readily, and their "bargaining power" increases.[44] This phenomenon has been explained by the obvious fact that when women earn enough money to support themselves (even if not at the level to which they are accustomed), they no longer believe they must give way to husbands who provide the family resources. This view may be too simplistic, however. It is more likely that employed married women take a more active part in the decision-making process not just because they are earning money. Instead, their new financial status may be a reflection of their upgraded feelings of competence and self-worth and of their increased awareness of how other couples balance the power between them.[45] Changes in the way a husband and wife relate to each other as a result of the wife's employment can create stress if the couple fail to reach a balance which allows them to view themselves as a cooperating team rather than as adversaries in a power struggle.

The key to whether dual paychecks will result in more or less marital satisfaction seems to lie in whether or not the couple is capable of working as a team. Qualities such as open communication, mutual respect, sensitivity to each other's feelings, and the ability to be fair and supportive are qualities of a functioning team that appear to compensate for the overload and other stresses inherent in such a life-style.

Summary

- Jobs and coworkers provide many of the rewards and also many of the stresses in the lives of the average couple.

- One of the significant changes in married life in the past two decades is the rapid increase in the number of middle-class women in the labor force. Dual-income marriages have become the norm rather than the exception.

- Child care is a major source of stress for most two-paycheck families. Mothers still bear the major responsibilities for children, although fathers are becoming more involved. The United States lags behind much of the world in offering support to dual-worker families by providing adequate child-care facilities.

- Overload is another major source of stress for working couples. Many attempt to keep up the household standards that were possible when the wife was a full-time homemaker. Often these pressures come as much from outsiders as from the couples' own expectations for themselves. Until recently, the middle-class working wife was generally denied social approval.

- Marital satisfaction of dual-worker couples compared with that of traditional couples depends on many factors other than the single variable of whether or not the wife works. The key seems to lie in whether or not the couple is capable of working as a team to compensate for the strains of child care, overload, and social pressures.

Dual-Career Marriages

A small but important segment of dual-worker couples are those who have careers. A *career* is defined as a self-selected identification with a lifelong occupation. Most careers involve years of schooling and training. Demands on time and energy are great and often are self-determined rather than set by an employer, and the work week may be as much as sixty or seventy hours. Usually, because of the self-dedication, the nature of the job, and the hours spent, the pay is good and job satisfaction is high.

Studies have indicated that dual-career partners are usually competitive individuals who need recognition and are achievement-motivated. In addition, they are ambitious and have high energy levels.[46] Such couples report almost all the stresses that dual-worker couples do (although more money may be available to buy services that can ease some of the strains), but they typically have additional stresses as well.

A problem often mentioned by both husband and wife in a dual-career marriage is that of one or both being "overinvolved" in the job. Not uncommonly, an all-consuming involvement in the career takes over, making family obligations difficult to fit in. Children usually get first call on whatever time is left, so it is the spouses who are apt to feel the most neglect. It is not surprising, then, that marital strain is often reported. Tension may occur if either partner's involvement makes the other resentful—particularly if both partners are overinvolved in careers.[47]

The **"workaholic"** has become a familiar figure among career-oriented people. Such a person's work life takes over almost to the point of obsession, with the result that family life and, often, physical and emotional health suffer. Workaholics have what the psychoanalyst Karen Horney has called the "tyranny of the should." It is difficult for them to enjoy even weekends and holidays because they think they "should" be working. Often the employer encourages this attitude and may even demand such dedication as evidence that a promotion or a raise is warranted. As a result, such intense job involvement usually does lead to high achievement and a successful career. Rewards keep the workaholic pressing on. This success may contribute positively to marital adjustment, of course, besides being a source of strain. Success usually brings financial gain, more material advantages, and a generally higher standard of living accompanied by a solid sense of security and of achievement.

Dual-career couples usually expect and understand each other's need for dedication, although the extreme cases still cause marital dissatisfaction. Women report more difficulty as a result of their high job involvement than men do.[48] Part of their problem, no doubt, is that neither they nor their husbands can totally rid themselves of notions of sex roles that usually place a heavier domestic responsibility on wives. Although many women accuse men of resisting full equality for women, it is also often a factor that women feel they "should" assume more homemaking and child-related duties. In addition, the new freedom to be away from home, meeting new people, traveling, and not being available when husbands want time with them, all can create dissension between husbands and career-oriented wives. Most of the research on dual-career marriages reveals that even when husbands are supportive of their wives' careers, they tend to accord them less importance than their own (and often so do the wives).[49] Clearly, even among dual-career couples the old traditional sex roles still have a foothold. Several studies of such couples have revealed that the women, on the one hand, compromise more in their career ambitions than the men do in order to relieve stress in the marriage, and, on the other, work harder at their careers than do other women who hold similar positions.[50,51]

A strain found particularly in dual-career marriages arises from pressures for geographic relocation. Transfers within a company or lucrative job offers outside the company that require moving to another location are real threats to a dual-career marriage. While the average working wife may take it for granted that she will move with her husband, a woman with a career knows that relocating to accompany her husband usually means starting all over at a lower position each time she is forced to move. Many couples agree always to live in a large city where both can engage in their careers with ample opportunity for mobility within that city. Others agree that a move will be made only if both partners are able to relocate in jobs equal to those they currently hold. This is often impossible, however, because of the types of work involved. There may be few openings, or every move may hold the inevitable risk of losing seniority, benefits, and the network of contacts built up over the years. Other couples take turns accepting relocation for job upgrading. A few live apart in what have been called "dual-residence" marriages, with one partner commuting on weekends or, in rare cases (usually when there are no children to care for), both partners taking turns commuting. This obviously is expensive, and typically these are couples with high incomes. According to one report, some such couples spent $10,000 each year on commuter travel.[52] Business and industry are beginning to try to help relocate the spouses of highly desired career personnel. In many instances, however, couples either pass up the opportunities, if both cannot successfully relocate, or else one sacrifices to aid the other. Women still seem to be the ones who sacrifice, either by moving or by not accepting positions that require them to relocate, more often than do men.[53]

In a large-scale study conducted on dual-career couples, it was determined that sacrifices for the sake of work are likely to be made in the early years of a career.[54] After partners become more established and have more career security, they can afford to devote a greater proportion of their time to family interests than they could at earlier periods. Family demands may also decrease as children grow older. It was also found that two careers are likely to be less stressful if both partners are in similar fields, although there is also an increased possibility of competition between them. Being in similar occupations seems to give husband and wife an understanding of the pressures and duties the jobs entail. Listening and being sympathetic is easier when the nature of the mate's job is at least familiar. Mutual support seems to be the key to making most dual-career marriages work.[55]

Although the stresses are even greater in some respects on those with dual careers than on dual-worker couples, the rewards seem to be greater as well.[56] Studies have shown that the relationship draws strength from the fact that each partner is economically self-sufficient. An important point is that both are more likely to be in the marriage by choice rather than from necessity, since each is capable of earning a good living independently. There is usually more money to ease financial demands and to spend for items and services the couple value. However, the biggest reward seems to be in the freedom each has to pursue what he or she most wants to do occupationally.[57] A man is freer to change from a less desirable position to one he really wants when his wife also provides an income. He is free from total responsibility for financial support and consequently is able to get out of a job that feels like a trap. A woman in this situation, too, has the freedom to develop her potential and to choose her occupation rather than to accept a role that society has assigned to her.

It means the couple must plan and negotiate, argue and compromise, deal with a host of unexpected feelings and reactions. But those couples who are already finding it a good way to live report that the gains are worth the troubles. When you have real and free choices, you can no longer blame each other for unhappiness or frustrations. [58]

Effects of Friends on Marriage and the Family

Stress from friends, neighbors, and coworkers is one of the other outside influences that have received attention as sources of marital difficulties. Research indicates that problems are likely to occur in several areas. The first centers around friends who relate only to one of the partners. These may be either old friends from before the marriage or new friendships maintained outside the marital relationship. Such friendships are especially likely to pose a problem when they involve opposite-sex friends. Most couples seem to have difficulty accepting that a husband can have a close woman friend or a wife have a close man friend without at least some jealousy or anxiety. Dual-career couples seem to adapt to the idea of male-female friendships more easily than most couples since they are used to the idea of work colleagues of both sexes. There may still be problems, however, if the spouse feels excluded or threatened by the closeness between his or her mate and a third person.[59]

Jealousy is one of the most difficult emotions to cope with and is nearly always directed at an outsider who is believed to be intruding. Studies of jealousy have shown that the emotion goes hand in hand with a feeling that one's partner might easily find someone else better for him or her and with a feeling of such dependence on the relationship that the threat becomes almost an obsession.[60] Some family sociologists believe that marital jealousy is declining as the notion of marriage as a possessive "ownership" of the mate changes. As women become less dependent and as the balance of power between mates equalizes, it is argued, human beings will have less reason to experience jealousy.[61] However, jealousy often can be an almost irrational emotion rooted in long-standing feelings of personal (as opposed to financial) insecurity. If this is true, then the problem is much too complex to be solved merely through male-female equality.

Outsiders can contribute to marital stress when a couple makes new friends together. It is typical for women to be more sociable and to initiate contacts, usually with other women. They then attempt to integrate the men so that they can be "couple friends." Not only must the men like each other, but each woman also must like the other's husband and each husband must like the other's wife—but not too much. The complexity of such relationships often leads to stress when one or more of those involved proves unable to participate or to be accepted. If there are children, they, too, can be a source of conflict if socializing involves families. Sometimes children do not get along, and often there is a problem between one set of parents and the children of the others.

On occasion a couple becomes intensely involved with another couple. The four persons may spend so much time together that they lower their horizons of experience and even stifle their growth as individuals. Such closeness has the potential to overwhelm a marriage. If something goes wrong between any two of the parties, it can create a serious problem for the others. In one case, two closely linked couples, who spent most of their leisure time together, who usually took their vacations together, and whose children were also best friends, ran into serious difficulty when one of the men became sexually aggressive with the other woman. "My feelings for him cooled at once," she reported. "I couldn't tell his wife why and risk hurting her and if I told my husband, he would have done something so she would know anyway. Besides, he and my husband really like each other and have some business ventures together."

A third stress that couples report involves those outsiders who make demands on the couple that interfere with their marriage and family life. This is of particular importance to dual-worker families who often already feel over-burdened. These demands may come from friends, from neighbors, from the community, or from adults involved with children of the couple. It is easy to find most of a family's extra time spoken for by those whose requests, taken individually, seem reasonable and are not easy to turn down. Collectively, however, when added to an existing overload, these demands produce stress by devouring all of a couple's leisure time. Often the time to be with friends, to collect for a charity, or to be a club officer is taken at the expense of the couple's time to be alone with each other. Some studies have indicated that, as a result, dual-worker couples may spend less than an hour a week in conversation and intimate contact with each other. Often what time together they do have deteriorates into problem-solving sessions rather than time for intimacy. Some couples complain that communication is all but nonexistent except for routine matters and discussion of problems. Sex may be infrequent because there is so little time as a result of outside demands. Some couples, of course, let outside demands detract from their time together as a device to avoid being together. Patterns of overactivity may be a sign of trouble in the marriage if the partners desire to spend as little time as possible with each other. However, many dual-worker couples, even those with conflicts between them, seem serious in their desire to find more time to spend with each other.

The Impact of Kin and In-Laws

When you fall in love or marry, you think you are involved with just the other person. But you are not. You are involved with your partner's family—with their traditions, attitudes and ways of living. Similarly, he or she is involved with your family. And each of you also brings to the relationship all of the feelings, acknowledged or repressed, you have about your own parents.[62]

This statement by a marital therapist concerns the most widely discussed "outsiders" in any couple's relationship—in-laws. One partner's in-laws are, of course, the other's kin. They can be wonderful and highly supportive; they can be distant and rarely (if ever) in contact; or they can be critical and interfering. Whatever behavior they choose and however the husband and wife choose to react to them, in-laws will have an impact, directly or indirectly. Each of us is a product of his or her past, and there is no more important influence on us than our families of origin. If we have not been positively molded in their pattern, we may have chosen to be negatively influenced by being as different as possible. Either way, what we are is measured by some yardstick drawn from our roots in that family.

The family unit in the United States has been described as an **"isolated nuclear" unit** (living apart from and in infrequent contact with kin).[63] Many family sociologists have taken exception to the "isolated" notion by demonstrating that most families and their kin have frequent contact.[64] Other studies have shown clearly that in most cases parents and their grown children live remarkably close to one another and maintain frequent contact. In the United States a large percentage of older persons lives either with a grown child or within a few minutes' distance.[65] In one study, about half the parents living apart from their children reported having seen one or more of them within the twenty-four hours previous to the interview, and 78 percent had visited within the previous week.[66] A recent poll of married women under the age of thirty-five reports that 70 percent live within one hundred miles of their in-laws and approximately 50 percent live in the same city.[67]

Even when there is a geographical separation between adults and their parents and siblings, surveys show that there is frequent contact by mail and telephone and occasional visits from parents to grown children, from adults to their parents, and between grown siblings. As longevity increases, there is a greater likelihood of several generations being alive and in contact. Married couples may have parents and their grandparents, children, and perhaps grandchildren to consider as family. These statistics would fit many families:

- age 90: great-grandparents (married at age 22 in 1914)
- age 66: grandparent (born two years later in 1916)
- age 44: grown child (born twenty-two years later in 1938)
- age 22: grandchild (born twenty-two years later in 1960)
- age 6 months: great-grandchild (born twenty-two years later in 1982)

This affords some idea of the size of the family kin network that one might have and that one's partner would inherit with marriage. There will be siblings, parents, grandparents, uncles, cousins, and their in-laws. In a study completed several years ago, Adams asked respondents how many relatives (not their in-laws) they would recognize if they saw them on the street. The average was thirty for women and twenty-six for men.[68] Adding in-laws could possibly double that number.

In-laws have not enjoyed a good reputation in the folklore of the family. There does seem to be evidence of a fair amount of troublesome interference. Marital therapists list in-law problems among the most common marital complaints. Even when they are not the primary problem, they are mentioned by a sizable percentage of those couples who seek marriage counseling as incidental to their troubles. Even "Dear Abby" says that in-law problems rank second only to romantic troubles among her readers.

Mothers-in-law have been especially singled out as the source of trouble, probably because women are more likely than men to be involved with each other in a direct, emotional way, as a result of women's more social role. They are usually charged with the responsibilities of maintaining ties to parents and to siblings. Wives generally keep the social calendar and handle family correspondence. Family sociologists have noted that women usually maintain closer ties to their own families of origin than they do to the husband's parents and brothers and sisters.[69] Interestingly, though, the source of contact—no matter whose side of the family it is on—is usually from woman to woman. Consequently, the wife will have the most frequent contact with her own mother and sisters, followed by her mother-in-law and sisters-in-law. This situation may account for the fact that twice as many women as men complain of in-law interference.[70]

The influence of kin and in-laws is felt in several ways. The first of these is direct interference, which may take the form of criticism or of attempts to influence the couple. This behavior is not difficult to recognize; when an in-law makes critical remarks to or about the member related by marriage, it is at least out in the open. However, other direct interference may be less obvious—for instance, behavior that is "too helpful." This more subtle type of interference couched in helping behavior is generally harder to combat. For example, the father who gives his daughter money because he does not feel her husband earns enough can be a source of great frustration and anger to his son-in-law. The mother-in-law who takes over in the kitchen or cleans house for her employed daughter-in-law in order to "help" may easily convey to her the criticism that she is not a good homemaker. Overruling parents' discipline or regulations when grandchildren visit is a frequent source of trouble. Sometimes in-laws criticize in the guise of "helpful" suggestions—for example, the mother-in-law who says to her daughter-in-law, "Bill looks so thin and tired. Have you thought of trying to get him to go on a little vacation by himself?" or the father-in-law who remarks to his son-in-law, "Sue has had that car since we bought it for her in college. I'm worried it will die on her one of these days. It seems like a good time to replace it." As irritating as such comments may be, they are hard to combat because the in-laws will claim to be misunderstood— they are only trying to be helpful.

A second major source of in-law and kin stress is direct but does not involve an intentional effort to stir up trouble. For instance, this is often the case with responsibilities toward aging parents and grandparents, which is of growing concern as the life cycle is extended. In the United States in 1900 there were only three million people over the age of sixty-five. Today there are more than twenty-two million, and it is estimated that by the year 2000 there will be over thirty million.[71] There is considerable evidence that kin—primarily grown children—are the primary source of support for the elderly. In a recent study of over 2,000 adults to determine their major areas of stress in life, it was found that, after their own mental and physical health, "parent-caring" was what worried them most.[72]

Women traditionally seem to bear the principal burden of the physical care of older family members, but men are the primary source of the financial support, whether of their own parents or of their in-laws. When the care is for in-laws, there may be conflict between the daughter-in-law and her husband or the son-in-law and his wife. A daughter-in-law may resent having to run errands for her in-laws or having to drive them to the market or to the doctor because her husband is too busy. She may also resent his siblings, who may not do as much for their parents as she is doing.

When the issue is the money used for the parent's support, the child-in-law may resent the expense. When their own family expenses are high, having to send money to parents may be a hardship. As one woman told us, "Just when we got our children through college and saw a chance at last to do some long-postponed travel, we now have to send money to my mother. And my father-in-law has to be put in a nursing home. We love them, of course, but it hardly seems fair that we end child responsibilities only to take on those of our parents."[73]

Some adults find they have angry feelings at their aging parents' dependence, feelings left over from the anger they felt when they themselves were the dependents: "Why should I be good to them when they were so rotten to me?" If the aid goes to in-laws, the angry feelings may be directed at the spouse: "Why should I send money to your parents when you aren't giving me what I want?"

Of course, kin and in-laws, besides being sources of stress to couples, can also be of great help. Studies have shown that support goes both ways—from parents to adult children and from adult children to parents. In a recent report on black families in the United States that covered a period of eight years in the lives of the families studied, the mutual aid between generations was clearly determined.[74] Those interviewed were usually a part of a multigenerational, interdependent kinship system with a definite sense of obligation to relatives and generally guided by a dominant family figure.

Similar research has shown that the extended family plays an important mutual-aid role in Mexican-American, Chinese-American, and Japanese-American families as well. Adams concluded that "minority status tends to result in residential compounding, and in strong kin ties for the sake of mutual aid and survival in a hostile environment."[75] A recent look at family circles and cousins' clubs of New York City Jews of Eastern European background shows an innovative way that these family members have developed to stay in touch in a large urban setting. Clubs composed of "cousins" enable even distantly related members of the same generation to stay in touch and to be supportive of each other. Older generations of cousins give a helping hand to younger ones as they make their way in establishing their occupations and families.[76]

A major influence of kin and in-laws may actually have little if anything to do with these family members directly. Instead, the influence comes indirectly from the ways in which families of origin still affect their grown children. The influence comes from the old (and often unacknowledged) feelings each partner has about his or her own parents. Basically, these unresolved feelings are of two types—both sides of the same emotional coin—unresolved dependence on

parents, on the one hand, and unresolved hostility toward them on the other. Younger couples are more likely to have one or both of these unfinished ties to their parents, although age alone does not necessarily resolve the feelings that seem to keep some men and women forever children when they are in the presence of their parents.

Dependence may send one spouse running home to parents every time there is a disagreement—if not literally, then at least figuratively. There may be interminable long-distance telephone calls or relayed advice from absent parents about what the couple should do to solve their conflicts. Men as well as women may remain so attached to their parents that their mates feel in competition with the parents for attention and affection.

Unresolved hostility toward one's own parents also may cause difficulty. It may be projected onto in-laws who themselves are innocent of any wrongdoing but who nonetheless become targets of the angry feelings. Sometimes these hostile feelings are actually ones toward the mate that cannot be expressed directly. For instance, a man might say he hates his father-in-law because his wife is always comparing the business acumen of the two men, or a woman might say she dislikes her mother-in-law because her husband thinks his mother is perfect. The in-law may not even know the comparison is occurring.

Often the comparison of the two families is the focus of indirect in-law interference. Without their being aware of it, parents-in-law may be cast by their married children into competing roles. Gifts, financial aid, and even affection may be the source of conflict, whether they flow from parents to children or from children to parents. Thus the arguments may be more *about* the parents than directly *with* them. Sometimes in-laws give costly gifts as a way of showing love and do not realize that they may be conveying to their children or grandchildren a message they do not intend. For example, a daughter-in-law may resent her in-laws' aid or gifts in the belief that the in-laws are competing with her own parents who either cannot or will not do as much for her. Or a son-in-law may believe his wife gives too much of her time, energy, or financial support to her parents because she does not give as much to his. In each case the in-laws may have no knowledge of their role in the conflict. The couples, however, use the in-laws as a focus for disagreements with each other.

In spite of stresses and strains produced by in-laws, a recent magazine survey of 300 young married women (eighteen to thirty-four years of age) representing a random, nationwide sample of almost 19 million such women, revealed that in-law relationships are generally quite good.[77] One reason seems to be that both in-laws and their married children are leading busier lives, particularly the women, who are more often employed or busy with volunteer work. This keeps them from being too intensely involved in each other's lives. The arrival of children reportedly strengthened the in-law bonds as both grandparents and new parents were reminded of the continuity of the generations. Another reason given for improved in-law relationships was that there has been a general increase in our society in tolerance for one another's differences, a tolerance that seems to be extending to in-laws.[78]

Summary

- Dual-career marriages are a relatively new, small, but significant outgrowth of the past two-and-a-half decades—a result of the women's movement, of family planning, and of more women being as well educated as men. Dual-career marriages have many of the same stresses as do dual-worker marriages, as well as others resulting from the dedication and motivation a career demands. There are high rewards for dual careers, however, the chief of which seem to be the opportunity for women to be as free to pursue a rewarding career as men are and the relief men receive from the total burden of family support.

- Friends, neighbors, and other community members can also exert influence on marriage and family life—both supportive and stressful. Problems arise, for example, in making "couple friends," maintaining friendships that do not include the partner, avoiding jealousy, and dealing with the time and energy demands of friendships.

■ In-laws and other family members have come in for their share of attention as influences on marriages and families. Usually, the implication has been that they are often more trouble than help. However, recent surveys have reported that families interact helpfully much more than has been realized by family-life experts in the past. As the life cycle lengthens, grandparents and great-grandparents are becoming more numerous, with the implication that multigenerational contacts will likely become more prevalent. As more women enter the labor force, some experts predict that "mother-in-law problems" may diminish since women will have less time to be so intensely involved in each others' lives.

Glossary

Cost-reward ratio The balance between what one gains from any given transaction and what the transaction costs—including the costs of time, energy, emotion, or anxiety.

Isolated nuclear unit A term used to describe a family unit that resides apart from extended kin and that is not in frequent face-to-face contact with them.

Job sharing Usually, the division of a job between two people, each of whom works half time.

Workaholic An individual whose work consumes his or her life to the point of seriously interfering with relationships and personal, mental, and physical well-being.

Jane Cox Vonnegut and I, childhood sweethearts in Indianapolis, separated in 1970 after a marriage which by conventional measurement was said to have lasted twenty-five years. We are still good friends, as they say.

Like so many couples who are no longer couples these days, we have been through some terrible, unavoidable accident that we are ill-equipped to understand. Like our six children, we only just arrived on this planet and we were doing the best we could. We never saw what hit us. It wasn't another woman. It wasn't another man.

We woke up in ambulances headed for different hospitals, so to speak, and would never get together again. We were alive, yes, but the marriage was dead.

—Kurt Vonnegut, *Palm Sunday*

378

13 · Troubled Relationships

Living together intimately for a lifetime is difficult for many couples and apparently an impossibility for the growing number who eventually divorce. Most marital and family therapists are equally adept at working with couples to resolve their marital problems and at providing divorce therapy to help couples end their troubled relationships as peacefully as possible. Although divorce may be the best solution for some couples, it is rarely an easy path to take, particularly when there are children involved. The number of divorces in the United States has risen steadily, and countless families are affected. The period leading up to a divorce is a traumatic period for the couples and their children alike. Both parents and children must face financial and emotional issues. Postdivorce adjustment is likely to be equally difficult for some divorced individuals, although those with the most resources—youth, money, friends, self-confidence—have an easier time of it.

"Marriage has been called the most difficult—if not impossible—social enterprise. Considering how poorly most people are prepared for it, and how immense their expectations of it are, the description more often than not unfortunately proves correct."[1] From the beginning, virtually all couples want their marriages to succeed. However, marriages often run into trouble, and not all couples manage to salvage their hopes and dreams.

Origins of Marital Problems

Marriage experts have long puzzled over why two people who love each other when they marry can turn so distant, so angry, so hurtful to each other that they want to end their relationship. What are the "irreconcilable differences" that lead to marital dissolution? The reasons couples give for wanting to divorce—adultery, poor communication, lack of similar values—never can describe the complexity of the demise of a marriage. The problems are never so simple and clear-cut. They rarely are entirely the fault of only one spouse, with the other totally innocent, as traditional grounds for divorce have so often implied. By the time two people decide to part, whatever conflicts they have are bound to have grown and to have spilled over into nearly all facets of their relationship.

Some troubled couples seek professional counseling for their marriages and succeed in getting them back on the right track. For some, however, counseling comes too late or is not an effective solution to their problems. Other couples manage to work things out for themselves. Why some couples succeed in staying together and others do not seems to depend on a number of factors rather than on any one simple cause. A look at some of the marital climates that hold the greatest risks for divorce and that indicate the need for professional help shows that there are several that are particularly hazardous.

**Marital
Danger Signals**

A problem that may be less obvious and certainly less dramatic than some other marital danger signals, but that is perhaps the most common, occurs when conflict has gone on so long that it has hardened into rigid confrontation, and the two partners seem unable to budge from their inflexible positions. Their viewpoints may be as unrealistic as they are resistant to change. Each may assume that only he or she sees the truth and that the other is an enemy. The struggle for power between the two may make it impossible to compromise or to cooperate. When, in addition, there is a definite imbalance of power between them—that is, one partner has the most resources—and the more powerful partner takes advantage of this position to "win" by intimidation, the relationship is usually in danger, if not already lost. Resources in power struggles may be sexual, financial, social, or psychological—whatever gives one partner an edge in controlling the other.

Sometimes one or both partners in a marriage have a need to hang on to a past hurt and to use this in an ongoing battle. They may not want to forgive the past but instead continue to punish each other and to seek revenge. They may be completely blind to any part they have played in causing the painful episodes. The past is alive for them, as though past events had just occurred. Often such couples are afraid of intimacy or commitment and therefore actually sabotage any attempt, either their partner's or their own, to settle any differences.

Fear of intimacy may be of long duration, even predating the present relationship. Usually in such cases couples consistently have what is called the "conversation of divorce." Accusations, insults, and threats all become increasingly ugly and wind up with talk of ending the relationship rather than with suggestions for solving the problems. Sometimes a partner becomes desperate enough to make a dramatic gesture such as moving out or seeing an attorney. Others may be driven to the point of threatening or even attempting suicide. Should any of these happen, there is no question but that professional help is needed, although the partner who needs it the most may not be willing to seek it. In such cases the other spouse is encouraged to go alone. It is valuable to know how to react to such behavior so that it does not escalate in seriousness.

Couples can find themselves in a particularly difficult situation when the conflict they are experiencing is deeply rooted in or inextricably linked to neurotic personality patterns of one or both partners. These can include character disorders such as compulsive gambling, constant lying, or lack of impulse control leading to suicidal tendencies, severe depression or acute nervousness, and deep feelings of insecurity or inadequacy. These are problems that may have been present before the marriage occurred or that may have given strong warning signals.

Often individuals who marry those with character disorders or with severe psychological problems either have serious but complementary disorders of their own or believe that they will effect miraculous changes in their disturbed partners. The psychological problems of one or both partners subsequently may either cause, or at least get in the way of solving, their controversies.[2]

Family Violence	A most damaging problem resulting from lack of control over impulses involves physical abuse. Family violence has been a target of much research recently, after having been virtually ignored by the public and by professionals for years. Family violence—including wife abuse, husband abuse, child abuse, sibling abuse, and parent abuse—has probably always been with us. It has played a part in many divorces.

The growth in both research and public interest in family violence has largely come about since 1970. The picture today is one of changed cultural norms. Since family violence is not considered acceptable behavior in the United States today—even though it has been in other places and at other times—what to do about physical abuse has become a topic of major concern.

It is known that one-quarter of all the murders in the United States begin with domestic quarrels. Love triangles account for another 7 percent. In California, for instance, it is estimated that well over half the women murdered have been killed by a husband or lover.[3] Wives kill husbands and lovers too. According to FBI statistics, in cases of homicide involving one spouse murdered by the other, there is no difference between the percentage of wives and that of husbands who are offenders.[4]

Battered spouses have become the focus of much social-problem research. An estimated 5 million women are victims of such abuse annually. Studies of couples now living together indicate that 3.3 million wives and over 250,000 husbands experience severe beatings from their spouses.[5] If we were to add to this the violence between partners who are separated but were formerly married, or that between unmarried persons who are living together, the total would be much higher. Even more devastating is the statistical evidence that in physically abusive couples these attacks happen several times a year. Financial analyst Sylvia Porter reports that abuse-related absenteeism on the job results in an estimated economic loss of $3 to $5 billion annually. Medical bills add another $100 million or more to that bill.[6]

Child abuse is even more prevalent than spouse battering as a form of family violence and is often an issue in a troubled marriage, although it seems to be more common in single-parent families. Very young children often suffer such abuse. Although accurate statistics on the incidence of child abuse are extremely difficult to obtain, estimates range between 1.5 and 2 million cases each year. Approximately 3 percent of children are kicked, bitten, or punched or have been threatened with a gun or a knife.[7] In 1974 Congress passed the Child Abuse Prevention and Treatment Act; as a result, all fifty states now require that persons knowing of abuse report it.

The psychological damage to children who are victims of abuse is of almost as much concern as is their physical danger. Likely outcomes to the children have been shown to be negative self-images, difficulty in relating to others, failure to trust others, and poor ability to handle their own aggressive impulses. The latter is of special importance in view of the fact that adults who abuse children very commonly were themselves abused as children.[8] Thus abused children are likely to repeat the pattern when they become parents.

Violence between siblings has been slow to be recognized as the severe problem that it is. Many parents accept acts that would be considered cause for intervention if they took place between husband and wife or between parent and child as "normal" when they occur between siblings. For instance, it is estimated that 138,000 children use a gun or a knife on a sibling each year. Eighteen percent of families report that siblings have beaten up each other; 5

percent of child abuse is at the hands of a brother or sister; and 3 percent of child homicides are committed by a sibling of the victim.[9] Although brothers hit, push, and throw things at each other more than sisters do, the greatest amount of physical violence occurs between brother-sister pairs.[10]

Abuse of parents has only recently begun to be recognized as a problem. Although there are often instances of adolescent children physically abusing parents—usually mothers—and occasionally murdering one or both parents, the most typical parent abuse is of elderly, dependent parents. This is a growing problem, in part because of the increasing numbers of old people in our society who, forced to retire from jobs, often become dependent on their grown children.

Of her recent study of battered parents, Steinmetz remarked: "It may well be that the 1980's will herald the 'public' awareness of the battered aged—elderly parents who reside with, are dependent on, and battered by their adult, caretaking children."[11] The problem is also a recognized one in England, where one study reporting on violence to the elderly concludes: ". . . individuals exposed to a high degree of physical punishment as children are more likely to resort to family violence as adults."[12] Children reared in an environment of violence tend to batter their children and spouses and in turn may find themselves exposed to violence later in life from their own children—who, of course, have been brought up by violent parents.

Sexual Abuse

Sexual abuse is usually separated in most persons' minds from the physical violence that goes on in families. However, even when physical damage is not a major concern, the psychological damage of such abuse can be very great and the fear can be overwhelming. Sexual abuse is usually linked to the abuse of children by adults—often parents, stepparents, or other relatives. Such acts are considered criminal offenses, and the adult, if convicted, faces the possibility of imprisonment. In reality, however, most such acts result in probation with the stipulation that the offender seek counseling. In addition, contact with the victim is forbidden for a specified period of time—often indefinitely. Needless to say, when a parent or stepparent sexually abuses a child, the marriage is usually in serious jeopardy.

Another kind of sexual abuse has gained attention recently. Research on marital violence has found evidence that many men have forced or threatened to force their wives to have sexual intercourse—**marital rape**—on at least one occasion. Some of these cases have been brought to trial, and several states have adopted legislation protecting women from coitus by force or threats of force.

Effective prevention programs are needed to aid families who are identified as high risks for violence. It would probably help if the mass media—radio, television, and newspapers—offered more education about family life and its stresses. It would also be useful if programs for aid to the abused and to abusers were increased. Crisis lines and protective agencies need to be identified so that people can know where to look for help at all hours. Meanwhile, victimized family members are advised not to remain in the home with any person who has an impulse control problem of this nature.

When treatment is either refused or is unsuccessful, divorce is seen as the only ready answer in many abuse cases. It is believed that violence is the underlying cause of thousands of divorces each year. Some states still list "physical cruelty" as a basis for divorce, but in most states, in which the usual reason given for marital dissolution is "irreconcilable differences," it is difficult to determine exactly how many divorce cases involve physical abuse.

Substance Abuse

A serious problem that affects millions of homes each year and is at the root of countless divorces is substance abuse, including alcoholism and abuse of other drugs.

In the past, most of the literature on "problem drinking" focused on the husband and viewed his wife and children as the victims. More males than females abuse alcohol; however, many women also are problem drinkers. It has been estimated that at least 20 percent of the five million alcoholics in this country are women.[13]

A family with a drinking problem is always a family in trouble, although outsiders may be unaware of it unless the drinker creates a disturbance that arouses the attention of neighbors, employers, friends, or the police. In most homes with a problem drinker, both the drinker and the spouse are likely to "cover up" and to distort the facts to excuse the drinking behavior. Specialists in the treatment of alcohol abuse believe that covering up is a serious mistake that can lead to even more serious problems such as physical abuse, financial difficulties, and eventual breakup of the marriage.

Among the complaints reported in a study of couples whose marriages were in trouble, alcohol abuse was mentioned in nearly one-fifth of the responses. Alcoholism occurred in about 6 percent of the spouses.[14] Although alcohol abuse was less frequently mentioned than some other marital complaints, it was often a facilitator of the most common ones—constant arguments, sexual dissatisfaction, communication problems, and financial disagreements. Marital therapists report that couples who seek professional help may cover up both alcohol abuse and the physical violence that often accompanies it. Only when directly questioned by the therapist will many couples reluctantly admit either of these as a problem in their lives.

Not every problem drinker is necessarily classified as an alcoholic. Alcoholics not only drink excessively but also are unable to control their drinking and, in many cases, do not recognize that it is out of control. Obviously, they harm both themselves and those whom they love. Problem drinkers, too, drink so excessively or in such a pattern that their relationships necessarily suffer. The diagnosis of alcoholism may be important from the standpoint of getting help for the alcohol abuser. In terms of whether or not there are marital problems, however, any drinking behavior that creates discord is a serious problem, whether or not the drinker is labeled alcoholic.

The best-known treatment plan for alcoholics is that of Alcoholics Anonymous (AA). Al-Anon Family Groups work with families of alcoholics. The AA plan has been highly successful and has served as a model for many self-help programs for problem drinkers. Other treatments that have been successful may use drugs to alter the effects of alcohol or behavior modification to retrain the drinker to avoid alcohol. The best treatment depends on the personality of the drinker and on his or her motivations for drinking. The most widely successful treatments combine elimination of all alcohol use with helping the alcoholic handle his or her life stresses and anxieties in other ways.

Since many of a problem drinker's difficulties may involve his or her family, family treatment is important. This treatment approach recognizes that the family is a system with each member influencing every other member. The goal is to change the system in which the problem drinker lives while helping him or her and the others involved to understand the illness. Family members must be encouraged to deal with their problems of living together in such a way that alcohol is not automatically blamed for every problem they have. "If only you didn't drink, everything would be fine" is not true for most of these families. However, not until alcohol is eliminated can they begin to focus on just what their problems are.[15]

Professional Help

Once a decision has been made to seek help with marital or family problems, it is often difficult to know how to find the most effective guidance. Counselors and therapists provide help by means of various methods that are available to them. Such counselors come from a variety of training backgrounds. The intervention of a professional person in problems as intimate and crucial to one's life as are most family difficulties is cause for careful consideration. Persons contemplating therapy may be filled with anxiety. However, there are guidelines that can be followed for seeking the best help possible. These involve knowing where to turn for a referral to a qualified therapist and what questions to ask of the person one is considering.

Referrals are made in two general ways—informal and formal. Informal referrals are generally by "word of mouth," either by having heard others speak highly of a therapist or by asking family, friends, or others for suggestions. Sometimes persons will suggest a therapist they have seen personally; sometimes they know someone else who has gone to a particular therapist. A therapist's good reputation with past clients is usually an indication of competence, although it is not always enough to ensure that he or she will suit you personally.

In addition to recommendations of friends and family, we suggest that the informal referral be combined with a more formal one made by reputable professional organizations representing family therapists. Some organizations that give referrals to highly trained therapists who work with individuals, couples, and families include:

- American Association for Marriage and Family Therapy
  924 West Ninth Street
  Upland, Calif. 91786

- National Council on Family Relations
  1219 University Avenue, S.E.
  Minneapolis, Minn. 55414

- Family Service Association of America
  44 East Twenty-third Street
  New York, N.Y. 10010

- American Family Therapists Association
  15 Bond Street, #107
  Great Neck, N.Y. 11021

- National Association of Social Workers
  49 Sheridan Avenue
  Albany, N.Y. 12210

- American Psychological Association
  1200 Seventeenth Street, N.W.
  Washington, D.C. 20036

- American Psychiatric Association
  1700 18th Street, N.W.
  Washington, D.C. 20009

One can also ask a clergyperson; a physician; or the psychology, psychiatry, social work, sociology, or family-life departments of a nearby college or university for referrals.

Once a prospective therapist is found, a telephone inquiry about methods, fees, and other pertinent matters can be made. It is especially important to determine that the focus of the therapy will be on the relationship and the interaction between the partners and other family members rather than on one particular member of the system. This does not mean that partners or other family members may not have individual sessions when the therapist believes that these will be beneficial. It is important, however, that the therapist believe that the actions and reactions of any individual are at least in part determined by the persons with whom he or she is interacting. This is especially so in a marriage or in a family, where change in the behavior of one member can easily cause change in that of other members. Counseling both partners together or all family members as a unit has been shown to be considerably more effective than working with only one member of the unit. The reasoning behind systems therapy is that—at least a majority of the time—the cause of problems between two or more people lies in their relationship rather than in the actions of any one of them alone.

Marital therapy can help; many couples credit it with saving their marriages. For those couples who want to work out their problems and who still love and respect each other, the rate of success is high. However, counseling does not always head off a divorce. Often, one or both partners really do not want to make the effort it will take to improve matters. They seem to find it easier to blame each other or some outside source than to look at their own contributions to the conflicts. Since not every marriage is destined to survive, many couples use the help of a professional as a kind of "predivorce" counseling that enables them to weigh the issues and to make a rational decision to end their marriage.

Summary

■ Many marriages have serious problems. Some right themselves, some require that the couple seek professional help, and some end in divorce. There are certain marital climates that are recognized as having great risks and that commonly lead to divorce. There are marriages in which conflict has become a way of life and partners have hardened into rigid, uncompromising positions. Sometimes there is stony silence, sometimes bitter arguing that results in "the conversation of divorce."

■ Sometimes marital problems are rooted in neurotic personality patterns of one or both partners. Psychological problems that may have been present before marriage can interfere with a couple's ability to solve issues between them.

■ Violence is one of the greatest problems facing many families today. Over one-third of all murders in the United States are believed to involve domestic or lovers' quarrels. Millions of women and men suffer beatings from their spouses every year. Child abuse, sibling abuse, and parent abuse add to these statistics. Sexual abuse of children by parents or stepparents and sexual abuse of wives ("marital rape") also are major factors in divorce.

■ Alcohol abuse is another serious problem affecting millions of homes each year. Although problem drinking in itself may not always lead to divorce, behavior resulting from drinking, such as fighting or sexual problems, may foster serious conflict.

■ Professional help from specialists in marital and family problems is often a wise move to head off a divorce. It is recommemded that a therapist be located not only through informal "word-of-mouth" referrals but also from reputable professional organizations representing therapists or from other knowledgable therapists. Not all marriages can be saved, and some perhaps should not continue, but therapists can help in those cases also, through "predivorce" counseling.

Divorce

Most thoughtful persons realize that not every marriage should endure. Some have not been good from the beginning, and others have reached a state in which the relationship is destructive to both partners. Because all societies recognize that a certain number of marriages will not succeed, virtually all societies provide ways of ending them.

Divorce rates in a large number of countries are higher than in the United States, often reflecting the ease and social acceptability of ending marriage contracts in those countries. For instance, some Islamic societies have permitted a man to divorce his wife by repeating "I divorce thee" three times. In societies in which divorce may be very difficult to obtain, there are fewer legal divorces but often a higher rate of separation and desertion: the husband or wife simply leaves. Desertion for a specified number of months or years is grounds for divorce in many countries; where it is not, however, the parties may remain legally married for the rest of their lives, even if they never see each other again. Many marry again illegally. Bigamous marriages can easily remain undetected if the couple moves a sufficient distance away from friends, families, and original spouses. It is impossible to know how many such marriages exist.

Changes in
Divorce Laws

For generations the United States made divorce difficult to obtain. In the northern colonies of pre-Revolutionary America, it was not unusual for a divorce to require an act of the legislature, if it was granted at all; as a result, there were very few. The southern colonies had no provision for divorce; couples could only separate from "bed and board." All states now sanction divorce, but until 1966 New York State granted divorces only in cases of proved adultery. Many other states had very few acceptable grounds. Beginning in 1970, states began to liberalize divorce laws by granting **dissolutions** on the basis of testimony that the two partners could not resolve their differences. The effects were predictable. From the trends in the United States it is readily apparent that as laws have been liberalized, the divorce rate has steadily climbed. Wars and depressions also clearly affect the rates—wars are followed by sharp increases, and depressions lower the rate—but the overall trend has been upward over the years (see Table 13.1).

TABLE 13.1

Year	Number of Divorces
1920	171,000
1930	196,000
1940	264,000
1950	385,000
1960	393,000
1970	715,000
1980 est.	1,140,000

Source: National Center for Health Statistics, *Monthly Vital Statistics Report* 28, no. 12 (1980).

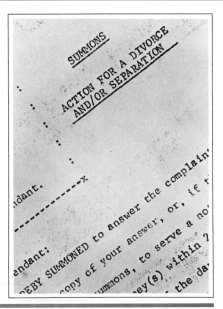

The upsurge in numbers of divorces is, in part, due to the increase in population during the years that divorce statistics have been kept. The more people there are, of course, the more will marry. More marriages provide more potential for divorces.

Divorce Rates

Divorce statistics can be quite misleading if one counts only the increase in numbers over the years. A more meaningful figure to look at is the number of divorces per 1,000 population. In 1920, for instance, the number of divorces per 1,000 population was 1.6; in 1970 the rate was 3.5 per 1,000; in 1976 it was 5.0 per 1,000; in 1979 it was 5.3 per 1,000; it is estimated that in the 1980s the figure will stay around 5.0 to 5.5 per 1,000.[16] There appears to have been a leveling off for 1976 and 1977 and, since then, a very slow yearly rise in the divorce rate. This leveling off may have been due to the economic recession or to demographic factors such as the trend toward later ages at marriage—which usually give marriages a better chance of success. Another factor contributing to the leveling off may well be that more unmarried couples reported living together without marrying. Should they break up, there is no divorce to add to the statistics.

The dramatic rise in the number of divorces in the United States came between 1963 and 1976, a period of other radical changes in our society. It was generally a time of affluence, of improved availability of birth control, and of the women's movement. In 1978 the upward climb resumed slowly, with a 4 percent gain registered nationally. The one exception was in the western states—formerly those with the highest divorce rates—where the rate in 1978 actually dropped slightly. It is anybody's guess what the 1980s will bring, but it appears that, although the divorce rate will continue to be high, the period of rapid gain may be over.

Even the method of calculating divorce trends by the number per 1,000 population can be misleading unless one looks at other factors affecting divorce statistics. For one thing, general divorce statistics include all divorces whether they are dissolutions of first marriages or sixth. First or second marriages, however, have a much lower likelihood of divorce than do third, fourth, and subsequent marriages.[17] Another factor that causes variation in the meaning of this divorce statistic is change in the relative size of age categories. An increase in the population under the age of fifteen, for example, would add to the population base but would not add a number of divorces proportionate to the number in the total population.

Certain population categories have higher divorce rates than do others. For instance, there are more divorced persons in urban areas than in rural ones. Western states have three to four times more divorces than do the states in the Northeast, which have the lowest rates. The North Central states are the next lowest, and the South ranks second to the West. Obviously geographical area does not make a difference per se; however, the attractive climates of the West and South are probably factors in their recent rapid growth, and family sociologists are aware that rapidly growing areas have less stable social environments and that couples who migrate may have less stable marriages with fewer support groups to aid them.[18]

Age at marriage is related to the likelihood of divorce, particularly if the partners are both teenagers when they marry. Teenaged couples who marry have nearly twice the probability of being divorced that those who marry later do. It has been suggested that age itself is not the only reason for their high divorce rate, although inexperience and immaturity can be real detriments to marital adjustment.[19] Teenagers who marry usually interrupt or discontinue their educations when they marry; thus they must often settle for unskilled jobs that pay less, a situation that puts stress on their marriage. They are more likely than older couples to have married despite parental opposition. Often very young couples marry because of pregnancy, and that frequently involves hostility of one or both sets of parents toward one or both of the couple, and perhaps guilt, blame, and anger between them. In a five-year study of teenaged mothers, it was reported that over 50 percent of those who married when they became pregnant were divorced within four years.[20] No matter what the age of a couple when they marry, if they have these limitations, they may be in trouble from the beginning.

College-educated couples usually have a much lower divorce rate than those with less education, but they also tend to marry several years later than the average person. More education affords them a higher standard of living; they

TABLE 13.2

Divorce Rates for Endogamous and Exogamous Catholics

Religious Combination	Age at Marriage	Divorce Rate	Average
Catholic-Catholic	Below 20	11.7 ⎫	
Catholic-Catholic	Over 20	0.6 ⎬	6.1
Catholic-Other	Below 20	39.7 ⎫	
Catholic-Other	Over 20	9.0 ⎬	24.3

Source: I. Reiss, *Family Systems in America,* 3rd ed. (New York: Holt, Rinehart and Winston, 1980).

are less likely to marry because of pregnancy or against parental opposition.

The only exception to the generally lower divorce rate for well-educated persons is that of women with seventeen or more years of education; they have a slightly higher average divorce rate than women with only four years of college. The reason may be that well-educated women are more likely to have professional careers and to be financially independent. Both factors have been blamed for marriage breakups, for (1) a self-supporting woman usually has attractive alternatives to remaining in an unhappy marriage, and (2) the complexity of the lives of two-career couples may be distressing to some.[21] Men who are married to such women may feel freer to divorce if their marriages are unhappy, since they are less likely to feel wholly responsible for their wives' financial support.

Interfaith marriages (which have increased since 1900) have been thought to have a higher failure rate than do marriages in which couples share religious beliefs. However, once again other factors intrude to make the findings more complex than they first appear. The ages of an interfaith couple at marriage makes a significant difference in the probability of survival of their marriage, for instance. Age at marriage, as we have seen, is related to educational level and to social and economic status, and these are highly correlated with the likelihood of success or failure of a marriage. An example of how these factors operate can be seen in divorce rates for Catholics who marry Catholics and for those who marry non-Catholics, considering the age variation (see Table 13.2). It can be seen that the rate of divorce is considerably higher for younger couples whether they are of the same faith or not, although Catholics who marry non-Catholics have a greater risk generally. Research has indicated similar findings for other religious groups.[22]

Early research found that divorce was more likely for couples whose parents had been divorced. One study reported that when neither set of parents were divorced, there was only a 15 percent chance a couple would divorce. This figure rose to 24 percent if one set of parents was divorced and to 38 percent if both sets of parents were divorced.[23] There appeared to be a logical explanation for this intergenerational effect. If one's parents had divorced, any strong family opposition to divorce had already been tested. The couple had a model from their own parents of how to solve difficulties through divorce. However, once again matters are more complex than they may seem from the findings. Educational, social, and economic variables were not controlled. More recent research has shown that although there may be some truth to the foregoing arguments, divorce may be "contagious" in some families more because the parents and their married children share other factors that increase the likelihood of divorce, such as being of a lower social class, having less education, and marrying at an early age.[24]

Likelihood of Divorce

For those couples who have troubled marriages, the first few years hold the greatest risk of divorce. There are more separations during the first year of marriage than at any other time. Because divorce usually is not completed for several months after the couple part, the divorce rate peaks somewhere around the third year. Although divorce naturally can occur at any time during a marriage, and the median duration of marriages ending in divorce is six-and-one-half years, at no time does the divorce rate again reach that of the first three years. One of the later peaks is at seven to ten years after marriage, another at eighteen to twenty years after marriage. Both of these coincide with "life-cycle crisis" periods that may cause discontent with many facets of life, including the marriage.[25]

Since the average person marries in his or her early twenties, seven to ten years later that person will be somewhere between twenty-eight and thirty-two years old. Studies have determined that many people experience dissatisfaction with themselves, their work, and their marriages at this time. Some decide to change jobs; others decide to change spouses or to try being single. This phase has been dubbed the "seven-year itch" by those trying to explain the upheaval in the marital relationship. It may, however, be better named the "thirty-year blahs" to indicate a general disspirited attitude.

After eighteen to twenty years of marriage, the average spouses are forty (give or take a year or two). Their children may be away at college or working, and the two partners may decide that although they are not old yet, they are not getting any younger either. In taking stock of life, they may decide that they do not want to live the rest of their years without realizing more of their hopes and dreams. They may blame each other for their failure to succeed or may believe that having a different partner or being single will help them to find what is missing. Therefore, a number of persons end long-standing marriages in their early forties although nowhere near the number who end marriages of three or four years' duration when they are still in their twenties.*

---

* The Bureau of the Census made an effort to find evidence of an increase in divorce rates as the youngest child approaches maturity, but found none [series P-20, no. 312 (August 1977), p. 12].

Each year, millions of couples decide to divorce. Over one million of them actually carry it through. Often, when one partner is reluctant to dissolve the marriage, the other initiates the final action. Sometimes the conclusion is reached jointly after a long period of unhappiness and tension. The couple may have separated and then reconciled. They may have sought professional help for their problems. They may have had loud arguments, or they may have carried on a "cold war." Finally, somehow, one or both make the decision and contact lawyers.

Many couples end their marriages only to regret it later. In a recent investigation of postdivorce adjustment, it was reported that two years after their divorces fully 25 percent of the women and 20 percent of the men expressed strong feelings of regret that they had not worked out the problems rather than divorcing.[26] It seems clear from this and other similar findings that legal divorce is not always the same as psychological divorce. Meyer Elkin, a long-time court of conciliation counselor, commented, "Every year we bury thousands of marriages that are still very much alive."[27]

Stages in the Divorce Process

For those who do not regret their divorces, one can only conclude that an adjustment has been made in the period since the divorce that is seen as an improvement over the troubled marital relationship. However, there is no smooth road from the time of decision to the time of feeling good about the action.

Most experts believe that resolution of a broken relationship takes a minimum of one to two years following a legal divorce decree. In the same study that surveyed couples after a two-year interval, it was determined that there was great difficulty in letting go of the ties the couple had to each other. In the two months immediately following the divorce, 70 percent of the wives and 60 percent of the husbands said that should a personal crisis arise, the first person they would call would be the ex-spouse.[28] The higher percentage for women may reflect the dependence they feel if they have child custody. It also may imply that women are somewhat more distressed by a divorce than men are, as other research has also indicated. However, a recent study has reported that men have a much higher need of psychiatric help following a divorce than do women.[29] It is probably safe to say that divorce is not easy for either of the partners.

Men seem to have a tendency to keep their feelings to themselves and to be less likely to discuss problems with relatives and friends than women are. Interviews with divorced men have shown that they often deny they are having difficulty in adjusting and, in general, seem to have a poorer grasp of why the divorce actually occurred than do women.[30]

Stages in the divorce process have been proposed by nearly a dozen family sociologists.[31] Although every divorce is unique, most couples seem to follow certain general patterns. A look at these stages may help to shed light on the coping processes couples use to get through the traumatic months following a divorce. Very few escape the depression, the sense of personal failure, and the diminished ability to function that follow the breakup of the long-standing emotional bonds of a marriage.

The most traumatic effects of divorce usually occur when only one partner wants to end the marriage and initiates the divorce. It is never easy to be rejected; when, in addition, one's whole life is upset against one's wishes, the results can be devastating. The responses to such a loss are very similar to those noted in persons who have been victims of natural disasters, have lost a loved one by death, or are facing the prospect of their own deaths. They go through a period of denying reality. This is followed by a period of despair and confusion. The repression of their feelings may cause them to develop psychosomatic disorders or other types of problems that lead them to professional help. Typically, anger follows, along with a feeling of betrayal. Finally, realistic planning and adjustment to the situation gradually begins to take over.[32]

In viewing the stages of the divorce process that have been proposed in the literature, it may be helpful to put them into two broad categories: (1) adjustments to the end of the marriage, and (2) adjustments to a new life-style.

Adjustments to the End of a Marriage

Nearly all those who have carefully studied the divorce process concur that the period during which the partners actually separate is one of the highest points of stress—far greater than the time of the legal divorce. In a study comparing recently separated men and women with those who were married and those who were already divorced, the separated showed the highest levels of stress and depression.[33]

In a comprehensive look at the divorce process, family sociologist Paul Bohannan used six overlapping phases to explain the complexity of divorce. The first five are useful for examining the early adjustments that divorcing persons must make. The sixth (the psychic divorce stage, in which individual autonomy is regained) deals more with the development of a new life-style.[34]

The first of Bohannan's "six stations of divorce" is the *emotional divorce,* which centers around a deteriorating marriage. Research on this phase has been aimed at determining the causes of marital strife that ultimately lead to divorce. Specific problems—finances, alcoholism, extramarital affairs, and poor communication—are often blamed. However, most experts agree that these problems are not the real causes of divorce but only the visible symptoms of an unlivable situation that gradually worsens over time. Kessler has divided this stage into three phases: disillusionment, erosion, and detachment.[35] Couples first concentrate on each other's weak points and blame each other for unhappinesses that may actually lie within themselves. Finally one or both

395
*Adjustments to the
End of a Marriage*

decide to move to the second stage—the legal divorce—knowing well that the marriage may have ended emotionally months earlier.

The *legal divorce* begins with the decision of who will file and what grounds will be used. In the past this was a far more difficult step than it is today. Until recently, it was necessary for one spouse to prove that the other was guilty on some grounds recognized by the court, such as adultery, mental cruelty, or impotence. Today almost all states have some form of "no-fault" divorce that allows partners simply to agree that they have "irreconcilable differences" or an "irretrievable breakdown." Some states have other grounds as well (such as insanity or long-term separation), although these are only infrequently used. Even if one partner disagrees with the decision, the other's word that there is an unresolvable difference holds. The logic is that if two spouses disagree about whether there is or is not an irreconcilable difference, their very disagreement makes it so.

Most persons turn to a lawyer at this juncture. Lawyers perform a number of important functions during the entire time of the divorce, but in this phase they are particularly valuable as sources of information about laws and rights. If two people can agree on grounds, support, custody, and visitation, a lawyer may serve only to review their decisions for fairness and legality and to make sure that proper legal procedures are followed and that various forms are completed and filed. A couple in some states, it they have limited assets and there are no

issues involving children, can secure a marital dissolution simply by filing a request for one.

The _economic divorce_ is the third phase. This is a crucial period filled with negotiations about child support, alimony, and property settlements. A thoughtful analysis of this phase has proposed that how well or poorly the negotiations proceed is a function of four primary factors: the emotional state of the divorcing partners, their ability as negotiators, the assets to be divided, and the power base from which each is operating.[36] Emotions often get in the way of rational settlements, as powerful feelings of anger, guilt, and vengefulness interfere with sensible negotiations. With couples who are divorcing, finances and children seem to be the topics that arouse the most passions.

In no-fault decisions, child custody and child support are decided separately from such financial issues of the divorce as property division and spousal support. In reality they often become confused with each other since money paid to children is often viewed by the noncustodial parent as payment to the parent with custody. Thus children, alimony, and child support often become intermingled as emotional issues in the minds of divorcing parents. If there are no children, then obviously property and spousal support have clearer boundaries. Since large numbers of divorced couples also are parents, however, confusion often arises.

If any issues between divorcing partners call for mediation, in many states they may call on the services of the court to settle matters, rather than hiring two lawyers to begin a legal battle. In many family court systems, trained mediators are available to guide the divorcing parties to an equitable and effective solution to their differences. The couple can avoid costly proceedings and may have a better chance to part on amicable terms than if they go through a prolonged legal fight during which, too often, the ex-spouses abandon all communication except through their respective attorneys. "We try to help people close the book gently," says Meyer Elkin, a pioneer court of conciliation counselor.[37]

Property and Support Agreements

Property distribution is most often done on an equal basis; hence, any advantage held by one who is a better negotiator is eliminated. Some states have legislation mandating _community property_, which means that all assets and debts accumulated since the wedding date will be divided equally unless the partners had a prior legal agreement to some other distribution. In other states, fault (grounds for divorce) still may decrease the share that the "guilty" partner (the one who is deemed at fault) is awarded. Usually, a parent who retains child custody is given some advantage in terms of maintaining a home for the children. The house, the furniture, and often a car are awarded when possible to the custodial parent. In community-property states, however, homes frequently must be sold to balance out the debts and assets equitably.

397
*Adjustments to the
End of a Marriage*

Spousal support is money paid regularly to one spouse by the other in addition to any child support that may be due. **Alimony,** as distinguished from spousal support, is a kind of restitution for "damages" or for "loss of marketable assets." Alimony is almost always a fixed amount, which the court may order to be paid in monthly installments or as a lump sum, due whether the partner remarries or not. Spousal support, in contrast, is usually a fixed stipend to be paid monthly until the partner remarries; dies; or, sometimes, has time to become self-supporting. Spousal support is intended to permit the spouse who may be left with the fewest resources to live in a manner that is not drastically different from that of the married years. Usually, however, both partners have to lower their standards of living substantially, since rarely is there enough combined income for them to maintain two households at the same level at which it was possible to maintain a joint one.

In recent years, alimony has been ordered less often by courts, especially when there is no evidence that the marriage has "taken the best years" of the spouse's life. It is rare for alimony to be awarded in addition to support. Usually the husband is ordered to pay his ex-wife either alimony or spousal support, either because she has been a homemaker or because, if she has had outside employment, it has been less continuous than his, and she has therefore earned less. If she earns as much as the husband does, usually no award is made to her. A growing number of courts are requiring a woman to pay support to her ex-husband should her income be greater than his and should he need such assistance.

Spousal support is based on both partners' abilities to earn, their standard of living during the marriage, the number of years they have been married, and the growth of their assets since they were married. It is considered that both have contributed to their financial prosperity by fulfilling whatever contract they made when they were married. Among high-income couples support can be a very complicated issue, with significant tax implications. The one who pays spousal support or alimony can deduct payments from his or her income tax totals, although child support is not deductible.

Couples who have not prospered or who are too newly married to have accumulated assets are more likely to avoid arguments about spousal support. Some courts view the age of a woman who has not had outside employment for years as a factor in her ability to support herself. If she is young, she should be able to work; but if she is older, her "marketability" may be doubtful. Her health and her job skills are also taken into consideration. Studies have shown that women who receive support from ex-husbands report less satisfactory postdivorce adjustment.[38] Continuing to depend on an ex-husband financially may be detrimental to a divorced woman's feelings of self-worth. However, it seems more likely that more traditionally oriented women (who would be most likely to receive support, since they would not have been employed) report a lower level of postdivorce adjustment (because their roles have changed more drastically) than do women who have held outside employment. Those who are in the labor force report better adjustment.[39]

Spousal support usually is ordered for a specified period—until the supported partner remarries or until his or her income reaches a specified amount. Support may be jeopardized in some states if the supported partner lives with someone on a more or less permanent basis and it can be shown that the other person is also contributing to his or her support. Usually, this becomes an issue when a man who is paying his ex-wife support learns that she is living with another man who is supporting her or contributing significantly to her support.

Child
Custody

The fourth of Bohannan's phases of divorce has been termed the *coparental divorce.* This phase deals with issues of custody, visitation, and child support. Traditionally, custody decisions following a divorce have awarded children to the mother. The practice was, until very recently, so commonly followed by the courts that 90 percent of the judgments placed children in the mother's care. A number of factors influenced this tradition, but probably none so powerfully as the notion that mothers and children somehow need to be together as a part of the natural order of things. There was even a "tender years" doctrine in the courts, spelling out the belief that a young child's interests can best be met by his or her mother.

As with all widely accepted beliefs, this one contained a kernel of truth around which the argument was built. Traditionally, most mothers took a more active role in child care than did fathers because mothers had primarily been homemakers and therefore were more available to the children during their waking hours. Consequently, for young children especially, the mother was usually the primary attachment.

Knowing that mothering would be their major role in life caused women to accept that they were the better "nurturers" and to have strong sentiments that they must have custody if they were to define themselves as good mothers and good women. It did not matter much that many times the father was the better parent or that the children preferred to be with him. The reasoning was that unless the father was happily remarried, he could not make as good a home for the children as their mother could since he would be away all day at his work. Therefore, if a father gained custody of his children, the assumption was that the mother was out of the picture (dead, a runaway, or institutionalized) or that she was otherwise unfit for motherhood.

Historically, being "unfit" often was related to a mother's past or current sex life. If it could be proved that she was living with a man (or, in the case of a lesbian, involved in a sexual relationship with a woman) or was entertaining partners sexually while the children were in the home, her ability to be a good parent was considered to be impaired. However, "living together" is becoming

399
*Adjustments to the
End of a Marriage*

more acceptable in the eyes of the courts, and some judges even take the view that another responsible adult in the home is an advantage rather than a negative factor for the children.

An important traditional reason for awarding mothers custody involved the nature of the divorce itself. Only recently have divorce laws been changed in most states to eliminate the notion of guilt or innocence over the breakup of a marriage. Under the old system, one party sued the other by bringing charges that were grounds for divorce. If those charges were proved and if the divorce was granted, the one who sued was the "innocent party" and often was awarded the children as well as a larger part of the property. It was not that women were usually "innocent" but that since women were expected to get the children anyway, they were the ones most often delegated to sue. In addition, many people believed that it was more "chivalrous" for a man to allow himself to be found "guilty" in a public trial than to "besmirch the character" of a woman by accusing her of wrongdoing, especially when she was to have custody of their children.

Child custody award practices have changed somewhat in recent years, however, and the prediction is that more and more fathers will retain custody of their children or, at the very least, will share custody. Shared custody may take the form of *joint custody,* in which both parents retain legal custody just as they had while married to each other. Where the child or children actually reside is termed *physical custody* and often is determined by the courts when the parents cannot agree. Usually a parent with legal custody also has physical custody. When more than one child is involved, each parent may be granted physical custody of one or more of the children. Another form of shared custody is shared physical custody, whereby the children live, for example, half the year with the mother and the other half with the father. One divorced couple we know worked out the physical arrangements by switching every two weeks. They lived in the same school district, and each parent maintained a room, clothes, and toys for each child.

The myth that mothers are able to stay at home to care for children while fathers must go to work is also being exposed. In almost all cases divorced women must work outside the home, so that their lives are as fragmented as a custodial father's would be. In 1977, 77 percent of divorced women were employed outside the home.[40]

Custodial Fathers

More and more men are speaking up about the issues of parenthood and the injustice of losing custody of their children. Many have seen child custody awarded to their ex-wives despite their knowledge that they would be the better parents, only to be asked at a later date to let one or more children come to live with them. Mothers and sons in particular seem to have problems after a divorce, and mothers often ask for help from the boy's father.[41] Occasionally, when a mother remarries, her new husband does not get along well with her children, and the move is made to have them live with their father.

Research on custodial fathers has been meager, but most existing studies show that such fathers adjust as well as mothers do. They provide somewhat different but equally good care for their children. Once fathers obtain custody, they utilize grandparents, baby-sitters, day-care centers, and schools to help with child care while they work—just as custodial mothers do. Custodial fathers report personal growth and increased sensitivity to others as a result of assuming greater responsibility for their children's needs.[42]

A recent study of the effects on children in father-custody cases compared with those in mother-custody cases has shown that children can fare well no matter which parent has custody. However, boys seem to do better with their fathers and girls with their mothers.[43] This observation may be the effect of sex similarity resulting in a greater understanding between same-sex persons or, conversely, of male-female antagonism—whatever the reason, however, there does seem to be ample evidence that the courts should perhaps reconsider the usual judgment that brothers and sisters should not be separated in custody decisions.

A growing number of fathers are becoming organized to protest the traditional custodial process. They resent giving up legal rights to be fathers to their own children. Presently there are more than eighty groups of divorced fathers in the United States—Fathers for Equal Justice, United Fathers' Coalition for Fair Divorce and Alimony Laws, and Male Parents for Equal Rights—attempting to change the father's chances to share in custody of his children after a divorce.

Joint Custody

Since being a single parent after divorce is often difficult, a trend toward shared custody seems to hold promise. Although many questions about shared custody remain to be answered—such as how two parents who got along so poorly that they divorced can now cooperate in a joint custody arrangement—there are distinct advantages. It is estimated that approximately 35 percent of divorced parents in the United States have some form of shared physical custody (considering the number of teenagers living with their fathers). This fact has emerged as a topic of major interest to the legal profession and to divorce therapists.[44]

The most common arrangement for joint custody is for childen to live the nine months of the school term with one parent and the three summer months plus other vacations with the other parent. Both parents have an equal voice in decisions about the children's welfare, education, and other important matters. If parents are willing to live in the same school district, blocks of time with each parent can be arranged during the school year as well. Parents usually like the shared responsibility and the opportunity for more personal freedom. Child

401
*Adjustments to the
End of a Marriage*

therapists believe that the close contact with both mother and father is especially valuable.[45]

One of the most important effects of shared custody is that it necessitates cooperation between the parents if it is to work. It eliminates custody battles (devastating to children and parents alike) in which children's loyalties are constantly at stake. Parents who have made joint custody work report that the process of negotiating the arrangements was a positive factor in achieving an amicable divorce. For instance, the father who has more contact and decision-making power with his children is more likely to be willing to help pay for their support. It is well known that many fathers who fail to pay child support say that they withhold the payments because the mothers are not allowing them to see their children on a regular basis.

Visitation

Most fathers are "part time" and see their children only as arranged by the court's visitation orders. This may be, for example, every other weekend, alternate holidays, and one month in the summer. Sometimes the court inserts the words "reasonable visitation" into the order, but too often bickering ex-spouses have difficulty deciding what "reasonable" is. Thus visitation is usually spelled out, taking into consideration both parents' wishes and the best interests of the children.

Many fathers report difficulty in making their visits with the children normal and easy. There is a temptation for the father to try to make every minute count in order to reestablish himself with his children as a "good guy." Fathers may try to do only things that are fun to make up for all of the pain of the divorce and to ensure that times together with their children are good. Visitation may be spent as a vacation would be—no set bedtimes, eating out, no homework—especially in the first months after the divorce. Custodial mothers complain that the children come home confused and resenting the discipline and responsibilities demanded of them. As one mother put it, "Daddy looks awfully good, taking them to the movies and to the ball game. Then they come home to a regular routine, plus taking out the garbage and picking up the dog's mess, and they scream that they want to live with their dad."[46] In California and Florida, this has been termed the "Disneyland-Dad syndrome" since every weekend the amusement parks hold many such fathers and children.

Over half of divorced fathers remarry within three years of their divorce. The new wife may have children of her own, to whom he becomes a live-in stepparent. He may begin to see his own children less often as he involves himself with his new family. Visits may be difficult because of crowding or of poor relationships of either the father or his children with stepsiblings or of the children with the stepmother. The children's mother may also have remarried, so that there is now an "in-house" stepfather to fill many of their needs. The result is often an emotional distancing with the noncustodial parent. Sometimes there is a geographical move away as well, often because employment demands mobility among many men and women in our society. Visitation rights are not lost by moving, but if the distance is great, they may be very difficult or inordinately expensive to exercise frequently.

Recent studies have indicated that the patterns and levels of contact between children and their noncustodial parents vary widely among divorced families. Some fathers see their children several times a week and have telephone contact at other times. Boys see their fathers more frequently than girls do and for longer periods. Some children spend enough time with their fathers to be a part of their lives and their households, which become like their second homes. When children are seen as part of two households, whether or not the parents share legal and physical custody, they are said to belong to *binuclear families.*[47] They are given responsibilities and are not treated as guests. This is in contrast to other children who see the noncustodial parent rarely and with little, if any, predictability.

A rather surprising finding of most research is that the frequency of visits is not the major factor in the quality of father-child relationships. The nature of the time spent together is what gives the child a secure feeling of a primary bond with the father. The studies conclude that relationships between noncustodial fathers and their children have a good chance to be maintained even when busy schedules, mother's preferences, business demands, and geographical distances interfere with frequency.[48]

Child Support

Fathers who do not have custody complain that they can go to jail for nonpayment of support but that nothing happens to ex-wives who make visitation difficult or even impossible. They are accurate in saying that they could be imprisoned, although most courts believe that such action only compounds the problem. Extreme measures are used only when a father who has the money to pay is willfully disobeying orders to support his children. Again, there is a kernel of truth around which can be built the argument for a law to enforce payment of child support. The financial situation for millions of mothers with custody of their children is perilous. A great part of the problem is that it is difficult to make ends meet today even with two incomes for one family. When divorce occurs and the total income must now support two households, there is often just not enough money to go around. Most women report a sharp drop in their standards of living following a divorce.

It may be difficult for fathers to pay child support regularly, especially if they remarry and begin a new family. Since money is at a premium under such conditions, many begin to lag behind. Nonsupporting fathers are sometimes arrested at work and may even be jailed, as mentioned earlier, although this is at a high social cost.[49] Not only is it usually impossible for a father who is in jail to continue to earn money, but the stigmatization and the alienation also are a great price to pay.

A federal child-support enforcement program became effective in 1975. It requires that absent parents (usually fathers) be located and required to help support their dependent children if they have failed to do so. Social security numbers and Internal Revenue Service records can be used to track down these delinquent parents. There is a minimal cost to the custodial parent unless she or he is on welfare; then it is free, since locating a paying parent has the potential to cut the cost of Aid to Dependent Children payments. Some states have a payroll deduction law for child-support payments. In those states, support payments are withheld from the parent's paycheck by his or her employer and paid directly to a support collection agency.

In most states child support continues until a child is eighteen. It is usually figured on the basis of both parents' incomes, the number of children involved, and their former standard of living. Most courts will not permit a noncustodial spouse to have more of the necessities of living than do the dependent children. In many states, this is translated to mean that the noncustodial parent shall contribute up to 40 percent of his or her net income to the children's support (depending on the income of the custodial parent).

As we noted previously, many noncustodial parents confuse the concept of child support with that of spousal support and refuse to pay for their children's support because they resent the divorced spouse's having access to the money. Finances are often used as a weapon to continue the battles that led to the end of the marriage. Children are the innocent victims. "I will quit my job and move out of the state before I will give her one dime," said one bitter husband whose wife left him for another man.[50] A woman whose husband was awarded custody in a contested suit was so angered when she was ordered to pay child support to him that she kidnapped their children and fled out of the country. The "economic divorce" is one that may take years to come about.

Other Relationships

The fifth stage of divorce described by Bohannan deals with *friends and community, which* affect every divorced person. We have often heard the remark that when we marry, we choose not only a mate but also his or her family and friends as well. An insightful analysis of the changes in relationships with kin and friends is provided by family sociologist Robert Weiss.[51] He stresses that it is not unusual for the decision to divorce to be postponed because the thought of telling family and friends just cannot be faced. Telling one's parents seems to be the hardest, perhaps because it is difficult to face disappointing or upsetting them.

In our clinical experience we have known couples who, living apart prior to a divorce, make a great show of still being together for the sake of their kin. They call family members regularly, never mentioning the split. If relatives are planning a visit, they temporarily reconcile in order to keep the secret a bit longer. Although their greatest fears of condemnation by family members may come true, most kin rally around after asking questions about what went wrong and offering advice for how to reconcile. Their reactions depend on how they evaluate the reasons for the divorce. If violence, alcoholism, gambling, or another lover has been in the picture, sympathy usually goes to the spouse who is seen as the victim. Parents may be critical of their own sons or daughters who have misbehaved and may side with their in-laws, at least at first. The old adage that "blood is thicker than water" usually proves true in the long run, however, and blood relatives eventually pull together.

Sometimes a divorced man or woman moves back to the parental home. This is far more common among relatively young divorced persons and more commonly it is the woman who has small children who seeks such refuge. Although this may be her only good choice, moving back with her parents often is distressing. Parents—especially white, middle-class parents—may treat grown children as if they were adolescents when they return. It is as though their "parent buttons" are pushed again by the dependency of the returned child. Although such an arrangement may be practical for a short time, it is usually temporary for that reason.

A custodial parent usually maintains some relationship with his or her in-laws. Since grandparents are blood relatives to their grandchildren, they are usually concerned about losing touch with them. If the divorce has been a bitter one or if the children live some distance from their grandparents, contact may be confined to times when the children are visiting their noncustodial parent.

Women usually have established stronger bonds with their in-laws than men have. This is probably because women traditionally plan family functions, keep up correspondence, buy gifts for special occasions, and see that children keep in touch with their grandparents. However, some men who are not close to their own families of origin may "adopt" their in-laws. If they are involved in a family business with in-laws, changes in relationships can be upsetting. Divorce may mean more than losing a family—it may also mean losing a job.

A divorcing person often has trouble continuing relationships with friends. He or she may feel let down or rejected at the very time when support is needed. Often friends have been primarily attached to one partner; after the divorce, they quickly lose touch with the other. They may take sides, blaming one spouse for the divorce. In the days before no-fault divorce, friends were often called on to testify for the "innocent" party who was suing for the divorce. Such testimony was a clear case of taking sides that understandably alienated the spouse, usually irrevocably.

Sometimes couples' friendships are based on their marital status—as in couples' bridge clubs or square-dance groups—so that a divorce terminates relationships with other couples for both of the divorced persons. When one's friends divorce, anxiety about the state of one's own marriage may be aroused. Some married couples try to avoid friends who are divorced, as though it might somehow be contagious. Newly single women in particular report feeling unwelcome at gatherings of their married friends. They may be anxious about being seen as threats to the other women, who may not trust them or may mistrust their own husbands around them.

Friends can, however, be very helpful and supportive in the months following a divorce. Eventually, ex-spouses usually begin to make new friends who know nothing of their past troubles or who themselves are divorced and trying to make a fresh start. Until this happens, there can be a time of loneliness ameliorated only by those friends who rally to one's support.

Summary

■ Virtually all societies recognize that some marriages are better ended and therefore provide ways to end them. In the United States, until relatively recently, divorce was difficult to obtain.

■ As a result of liberalized divorce laws, a lessening of social stigma attached to divorce, the ability of more women to make their ways financially, and other social variables, the divorce rate in the United States has increased steadily. Not all marriages are equally vulnerable to divorce. Age, geographic location, education, income, religion, and marital status of a couple's parents are all factors affecting divorce.

■ Adjustment to divorce follows a series of stages for most individuals as they face the inevitable changes necessary when a marriage has ended. Many divorce experts believe that the process of deciding to divorce and the actual physical separation create the greatest stress in the divorce process. This stage is termed the emotional divorce.

■ A legal divorce involves attorneys, courts, and arguments over support and custody issues. The legal and economic issues are heavily dependent on the emotional state of the divorcing partners, which affects their ability to negotiate, and on the assets and liabilities to be divided. No-fault divorce legislation has helped reduce the likelihood of one ex-partner taking advantage of the other.

■ Parental issues are difficult to decide. Traditionally, when divorces have occurred, women have received custody of children and men have paid child support. The picture is beginning to change gradually as more men are receiving custody of one or more children or are sharing custody with their ex-wives.

■ Family, friends, and the community can be important sources of either stress or support for a divorcing couple. Reactions depend on how these outsiders evaluate the reasons for the divorce. They are usually supportive to the partner who has been "wronged," although in the long run kin tend to side with their own blood relatives.

Adjustments to New Life-Styles

As difficult as it is to get through the emotional turmoil of ending a marriage and to live through months of legal negotiations and radical changes, many divorced persons report that starting over is in many ways an even bigger problem. Bohannan calls this stage the *psychic divorce*. It can be a rewarding period, in which growth begins to take the place of destructive forces and autonomy replaces dependency.

Adjustments to the divorced status usually involve problems of finances, companionship, children, and self-concepts. Those who have the most difficulty developing a new life-style are likely to be those with the fewest resources (and therefore, the fewest alternatives), whether in money, friends, custody decision, and child care, or in inner resources of self-confidence. Young childless couples who divorce generally blend back into the young singles scene relatively easily. Parents with child custody, particularly if there are several children, have a much more difficult time adjusting. They often have little time, energy, or money to go out; yet having visitors in the home may prove troublesome for the same reasons. In addition, children can be very difficult when they are asked to make room in their lives for their parents' friends. Older divorced men and women also have their special adjustment problems. Older men, of course, are often at a premium since there are so few of them compared with the number of older women.

**Problems
of Women**

Often women are at a distinct disadvantage after a divorce because they may be expected to make the most drastic changes with the fewest options open to them. A woman who has few marketable skills except those needed for home-making may now have to earn a living working in industry or in an office or a store. This is particularly difficult for mothers of young children who married at an early age and have little or no work history.

Immediately upon separation, divorced women who have worked little, if at all, outside the home must face child care problems and a transition from the financially dependent status of "wife" to that of "head of a household" with responsibility for making many unfamiliar decisions. Many such women moved at an early age from dependency on their parents to dependency on their husbands. They did not have time to experience the self-sufficiency that comes with living alone and supporting themselves for a few years or, in some cases, even a few weeks. It is not uncommon to find that a woman who has been married for several years does not know how to file a tax return, for instance, or when or how to buy new tires for the car.

Middle-aged or older women who have spent their lives as homemakers and mothers have an additional set of problems. They not only may have no way to earn a living except, as one woman put it, "as a maid in someone's home,"[52] but they often suffer from lack of confidence and from the fear that their social value has vanished with their youth. Again, the grain of truth is that many employers and personnel officers (both male and female) do give preference to female applicants with youthful appearances. In recent years, however, many large corporations have been forced by both union pressures and court decisions to give up age discrimination. Still, older women may feel too old to be trained for a job and unsure, if they find one, that they can compete with younger women.

Problems of Men

Many men have severe problems in starting over after divorce, although they may have more alternatives than their ex-wives. The hardest part for many men may be moving away from a home they have valued highly; men who have never lived alone may feel relatively helpless about domestic tasks that have always been done for them—first by their mothers, then by their wives. Psychiatrist Robert Robertiello says: "Divorce is one of the most highly traumatic things a man can go through. Men whose wives have left them are shattered, and they really do withdraw."[53] Learning to be alone after many years in a family may be the most difficult adjustment a man has to make. Often he is struggling financially to pay child support; if he did not want the divorce in the first place, he may be bitter as well. Many men fill their lonely hours by work or television, or haunt singles' bars looking for a series of "one-night stands" in an attempt to begin to feel attractive and to fill time.

Social Life

Beginning to date is not an easy task for either a man or a woman who has not done so for years. The average newly divorced man is thirty-two years old and the average woman almost twenty-eight. They have been closely related in the processes of courting, being married, perhaps raising children, and divorcing for nearly seven years. The longer they have been involved with each other, the more things will seem to have grown different in the singles' world—and, of course, the more the man or woman has changed from the young, relatively immature person he or she was in previous dating experiences.

Seventy-five percent of divorced persons begin dating within the first year after divorce; by the end of the second year, all but 10 percent have done so.[54] Those who find dating the easiest, again, are the ones who have the most resources—youth, good looks, money, self-confidence, and know-how.

A major difference in the "world of the formerly married" that is often a surprise to a man or woman is how early in a new dating acquaintance the topic of sex is raised. The assumption seems to be that both individuals are sexually experienced, both have sexual needs, and the games of teenage flirtations are a waste of time.

In a recent survey, six out of ten women reported that most or all of the men they had dated made serious sexual approaches on the first or second dates. Nearly three-quarters of the men and nearly two-thirds of the women had sex on this more or less casual basis. Of those who had been divorced for a year or more, only one man in twenty and one woman in fourteen had not had sexual intercourse. Nearly all reported that the effects were generally beneficial in terms of restoring their self-worth and enabling them to believe in love again. The Hunts comment, "Good, bad, or indifferent, the early dates of the formerly married are a virtual laboratory, an environment in which to observe behavior, perform tests, and make a number of discoveries about others and them- selves."[55]

Some men and women receive professional help during these months of transition to a new life. One study of divorced persons in 1960 found that 22 percent of the men and 40 percent of the women had sought some kind of professional help.[56] The percentage appears to have increased with the wider acceptance of counseling and therapy since 1960. Many divorced persons at- tend seminars or join self-help groups to meet others who are involved in similar struggles.

There are many organizations for those who are divorced. Perhaps the larg- est is Parents without Partners (7910 Woodmont Avenue, Suite 1000, Washing- ton, D.C. 20014), which has over 1,000 chapters and which organizes social and educational events for parents and their children. Churches, universities, and men's and women's organizations are all beginning to offer special interest groups for divorced persons. Newspapers routinely carry notices of meetings and events for singles (often specifying age groups that might be most welcome). These events range from social activities or trips to lectures or discussions about problems of adjustment. Studies of postdivorce adjustment report that the more divorced persons participate in social activities, the better is their adjustment.[57] Of course, the argument could be made that those who have the best adjustment are the most likely to feel like going out. This is no doubt the case, but dating and companionship do tend to relieve the pain of rejection and to reassure the person that he or she is socially acceptable and perhaps likable or even lovable once again.

Divorced persons have a tendency to find each other for support, and groups for postdivorce adjustment can help them come together. Experienced divorce counselor Esther Fisher, editor of the *Journal of Divorce*, believes that group support is one of the most valuable paths to adjustment following a divorce. As she states, "Post-divorce adjustment includes a variety of goals; namely, a reduction in feelings of bitterness and hostility; more understanding and acceptance of self, children, and ex-spouse, and of society generally; a return to work and social activity; and better management of personal affairs and the ability to handle the new problems that follow divorce."[58]

The Psychological Costs of Divorce to Children

Currently over one million children each year must face the divorces of their parents. In 1979, 49 percent of black families with children at home were maintained by only one parent.[59] It is predicted that by 1990, one-third of all children under eighteen years of age will have lived with a divorced parent at some time. Some of the children will have been through the experience more than once.[60]

It is difficult to determine exactly how much damage children suffer as a result of the traumas they may have suffered before a divorce occurs and how much can be attributed to the actual separation and postdivorce adjustment. Most experts believe that the accumulation of a long series of traumatic experiences causes some children to develop unhealthy reactions, but others adjust quite well. Child psychiatrist Richard Gardner says, ". . . the younger the child when the loss occurs and the longer he is exposed to the loss, the greater will be the harmful effects."[61]

Adjustments following their parents' divorces are difficult for all children. The range of reactions is wide, however, and the time needed to recover is variable. Some adjust well in a relatively short period of time, but others never quite recover. Parents who belong to Parents without Partners have estimated that their children take from one to three years on the average to adjust. Approximately 9 percent reported that even after many years, a child had not recovered.[62] Those children who have personality and behavior problems even

before their parents divorce usually suffer the most serious adjustment difficulties. Often they must receive professional help for such problems as antisocial behavior, serious school problems, and personality maladjustments. The most common reaction is depression. One recent study concluded that "divorce may now be the single largest cause of childhood depression."[63]

The first year following a divorce is typically filled with great stress and disorganization for the children, which may prompt negative behavior—nagging, whining, dependency, demanding behavior, rebelliousness—that causes the custodial parent to become cross and restrictive.[64]

The most distressed children are those who are caught in the crossfire of their parents' battles and whose parents themselves are having the most difficulty adjusting. Another important variable in a child's adjustment has to do with the financial condition in which the custodial home is left. Most intact families have a difficult enough time making financial ends meet in this time of escalating costs of living. When a family divides, there is often economic hardship. Income is a key factor in the adjustment of divorced couples and of their children.

A classic study of children and divorce was conducted in California. The age of children at the time of a divorce became an important clue to how the children went about adjusting. Preschool children typically react with denial and may ask, "When is daddy coming home?" They often talk and act as though nothing has changed, although on deeper investigation it is shown that they may harbor fantasies that the separation has occurred because they have been bad. Many children of this age believe that they have somehow caused the problems between their parents.

Somewhat older children (seven or eight years old) are less able to use denial than are younger ones. Their reaction is often one of sadness and withdrawal. Parents report the most difficulty in getting children of this age to talk about how they feel. Tears are common, but the children are unable to verbalize their emotions.

Children of nine and ten are often very angry and may blame one or the other parent (sometimes both) for the distress they feel. They may resent having to help more and become unpleasant about financial hardships. They often report feeling ashamed of what their parents have done.

Older children, particularly adolescents, realize the impact and finality of the divorce and may need to make sense out of why the marriage ended. They may take sides and withdraw emotionally from one or the other parent. They, more than younger children, will base their reactions on how the parents respond to their questions and on how the parents resolve conflicts.[65,66,67]

Although most children recuperate from the effects of divorce within a year or two, there are two basic differences found in later life between those who have experienced a parental divorce prior to age sixteen and those who have lived in intact families. First, those from divorced homes have a greater tendency as adults to identify childhood or adolescence (or both) as the unhappiest period of their lives. The exception to this is among those who have also been divorced themselves, in which case their own divorce may take precedence. The experience the child had when his or her parents divorced becomes a kind of yardstick by which to measure future misery.

The second major difference in adults whose parents divorced is that they are more likely than children from intact homes to experience later events as ones that produce high anxiety. This is especially true for males.[68] Interestingly, this finding is similar to other research suggesting that girls adjust to their parents' divorces sooner than boys do. Until 1976 children whose parents had divorced were also more likely to have sought professional help for their anxieties and personal problems than were those from intact homes.[69] (In 1976 the trend was for more people in general to seek professional help for their problems; this ended the disproportion in the number of clients whose parents had been divorced.)

When adults who experienced parental divorce as children are compared with those who did not, the differences in reports of childhood happiness and current anxiety levels are statistically significant. However, recent research has shown that experiencing a parental divorce, though traumatic in the short run, is in the long run one that most adults outgrow. Many come to believe that their parents made the right choice in parting. The parental divorce tends to remain as a subtle influence helping to shape the child's views of adult life roles.

What is significant in understanding the impact of divorce on children, in both the short run and the long run, is that for children the threat of divorce and the problems following divorce are determined by how the parents adjust. Since most parents have readjusted (and a sizable number have successfully remarried) within one to three years following divorce, it is not surprising that most children also have made a good recovery within a similar period of time.

Most studies of readjustment involve the reactions of the mothers, since the overwhelming majority of children of divorced parents have been placed in the custody of their mothers. Children and adolescents who live with mothers who have remarried have been shown to have self-concepts that are much better than those of children whose mothers have not remarried.[70] The mothers' readjustment seems to be the most important key to the children's readjustment. In fact, a recent study of schoolchildren showed that emotional problems evidenced by children depend on the amount of conflict experienced in the home, regardless of whether the parents are divorced, still married to each other, or remarried.[71] A stable single-parent home is more conducive to a conflict-free childhood than is a two-parent home filled with turmoil. The fact that most children show a good adjustment when their mothers remarry is thought to be a direct result of her good adjustment.

Although most divorced parents eventually remarry, children may live in single-parent households for a number of years. At any given time, it is estimated that over one-third of all children will spend some time in a single-parent family before age sixteen because of marital disruption.[72] A 1980 census report indicated that in March 1979 about four-and-two-thirds million children were living with a divorced parent who had not remarried. Most such families face major difficulties—finances, fatigue, unfamiliar tasks usually performed by the other parent, added child responsibilities, sibling quarrels brought on by stress and uncertainty—but with effort, these families do survive and most of them thrive.

Most single-parent families are headed by women—just over 90 percent—although there are some recent indications that this may change as a result of joint custody trends. Even so, experts believe that although the number of children living with their fathers may double by 1990, the change will amount to only 1 or 2 percent.[73] Many fathers who are single parents report that their jobs suffer because employers do not expect men to have demands made on their time by children. The 1979 film *Kramer vs. Kramer* dramatizes the plight of the father with custody. The father is depicted as an executive who must learn the hard way how to be a father. Many women who saw the film were unsympathetic, wondering aloud in newspaper and magazine editorials why fathers

A Scene from
Kramer vs. Kramer

learning to be "mothers" were being heralded when mothers have had to be "fathers" for generations. For either mother or father, it is a difficult task to care for children alone, to work, and to survive as a human being with a life of his or her own.

Annulment

Under special circumstances an annulment may be granted to a couple to end their relationship. Annulment is a legal process used in only about 3 percent of the cases of legal breakup, but it is interesting because of the conditions under which it is allowed. An annulment actually decrees that a marriage never really existed because for some reason it was not legally contracted. The grounds for annulment are quite uniform in the United States and are similar to the grounds for declaring any legal contract invalid.

Some of the reasons for the judgment that a marriage was not legally contracted involve the "competency" of either or both parties to enter into the agreement in the first place. For instance, they may have been below the legal age to marry. Approximately 25 percent are granted for this reason. One or both partners may have still been married to another person. This happens fairly often, in fact, whenever couples remarry before a final divorce decree is granted from previous spouses. However, it does not usually become an issue since the couple generally does not elect to end the current marriage before the last one is legally ended (or, if they do, would probably choose another divorce rather than an annulment).

The marriage contract may be void if it is determined that the parties are blood kin to some degree that is against the law for marriage. A few cases of "incompetency" to marry have been recorded in which one party was drugged or drunk or judged to be temporarily insane and therefore unable to consent to the legal agreement to marry. This happens only rarely because most states require a waiting period from the time the license is taken out to the time of the ceremony, and it is not likely that such an "incompetent" condition would go undetected for several days. However, there are states in which a couple could meet and marry within one day—even within a few hours—and lack of competency might be a possibility.

A second major determination of whether or not an annulment can be granted is the proof that one party has "defrauded" (misrepresented or concealed important information from) the other. It is surprising that more annulments are not granted, considering the range of information that is considered important when withheld: pregnancy of the bride without the groom's knowledge, or a claim that she is pregnant when she is not; concealment of impotence or knowledge of one's sterility; misrepresentation of one's intentions to have children; concealment of prison records or other illegal acts that may affect the spouse; concealment of debts or deliberate misrepresentation of income or assets; or misrepresentation of one's intentions to consummate the marriage (to have sexual intercourse). In addition, the use of force, threat, or other coercive measures to make one person marry the other constitutes grounds for annulment.

Should an annulment be granted, it takes effect immediately since the marriage is judged never to have existed. This makes annulment attractive to those for whom a divorce is an impediment to remarriage—for example, adherents of religions that do not recognize divorce. It should be noted, however, that legal annulment and religious annulment are two separate processes. For instance, one may have a church annulment following a legal divorce.

Some couples who have been married for years and who have children are granted annulments. However, there are some serious questions about the consequences. Their children are technically illegitimate since it has been decreed that a marriage never existed, and in some states this may affect inheritance and child support. Community property rights and spousal support may also be affected. However, some persons choose this route despite the problems.

Summary

■ Adjusting to the status of "divorced person" can be nearly as difficult as the separation process. Adjustments are easier for those who have the most resources: youth, money, friends, know-how, and self-confidence.

■ Both men and women report problems in beginning a new life-style. Women, however, are usually asked to take on the responsibility of child custody. Since most divorced women must work outside the home, those who have not previously done so may find the transition to be dramatic and demanding.

■ By the end of the second year after divorce, nearly all men and women have started to date again. They often have to relearn how to behave in the courtship process. Those who have been previously married also have different dating norms, particularly with respect to early sexual involvement.

■ Professionals and organizations for divorced persons can assist individuals who are making the adjustment to single life again. There is a tendency for divorced persons to group together to support each other through the adjustment process.

■ Adjustments to their parents' divorces are difficult for all children, although most research indicates that in the long run all but a small number adjust well. Those who have personality and behavior problems before the divorce seem to have the most serious adjustment problems. The key to the children's adjustment appears to lie in that of the parents.

■ Annulment is a legal process sometimes used to end a marriage when it can be proved that there was some defect in the union. There is also religious annulment, which is granted for reasons comparable to those for a legal annulment and which may be useful to those whose religions prohibit remarriage after divorce. An annulment decrees that the marriage never existed.

Glossary

Alimony Court-awarded payment to a spouse upon separation or divorce. Alimony, which should not be confused with support payments, is paid for restitution of losses or for remedy of wrongs done.

Child abuse Violence against or extreme neglect of a child.

Dissolution The formal, legal termination of a valid marriage by any means other than the death of one or both spouses.

Marital rape Coitus between married persons that is accomplished by force or the threat of force by the male partner.

After a divorce, and to an even greater extent after a remarriage, many individuals experience the insecurity of sharing children and sharing parents. Compassion and understanding can lessen the hurt, and aid the healing process. Individual growth can then occur, bringing with it an interpersonal warmth and a deep understanding of other human beings.

—Emily E. Visher and John Visher, Step-Families: A Guide to Working with Stepparents and Stepchildren.

14 · Remarriage and Stepparenting

As the number of divorces has grown in the past two decades, so has the number of remarriages and resulting step families. Couples who divorce clearly are not disillusioned with marriage—only with the person to whom they are married. Most divorced persons remarry, and rather quickly at that. Second marriages fare quite well and give strong evidence for the belief not only that divorce may be the best solution for some troubled marriages but also that some couples who divorce do learn how to succeed better the second time around.

Of the approximately 40 percent who divorce a second time, their chief complaints vary considerably from those that caused them to divorce the first time. Conflict in remarriages usually centers around finances, in-laws, ex-spouses, and stepchildren. Step families—sometimes called "blended" or "reconstituted" families—offer great challenges for both the parents and the children. With over fifteen million children living in step families, the blended family is no longer an oddity. In some communities, children who live with both natural parents seem to be hardly more numerous than those who have a stepparent.

Remarriage

Eventually, the desire to marry again arises in nearly all divorced persons. Even those who loudly proclaim "never again" at the time of their divorces find that as time heals most of their wounds, they begin to feel the desire for companionship and for someone with whom to share life. Furthermore, the social expectation that one ought to have a successful marriage usually leads people to "try again." Four out of every five divorced persons eventually remarry; most within three years of their divorces. In 1977, 32 percent of the total marriages in the United States were remarriages.[1]

Divorced men are more likely than divorced women to remarry, although the difference is not great (three of four women and five of six men).[2] The reason is probably that older women's chances of remarriage are diminished because there are many fewer men in their age range. (See Table 14.1. Men are usually older than their wives, but die several years younger than women on the average.) There is also some evidence that a woman with several children at home is less likely to remarry. By the time her children are grown, she may be in the pool of older women and have a limited choice of partners. A recent national survey of divorced women between the ages of fifteen and forty-four found that whether or not a woman remarries is determined primarily by her age at divorce, her educational level, and her race. The younger she was when divorced, of course, the greater the likelihood she would remarry. College-educated women were less likely to remarry, as were black women.[3]

The average interval after which divorced persons remarry has changed from approximately four years from the time of divorce in the 1950s to the current average of three years.[4] It is interesting to speculate about the reason for this. One factor may be simply that there are more divorced persons from whom to choose than there were previously. Since those who are divorced tend overwhelmingly to marry other divorced persons (just as never-married people tend to choose other never-marrieds and those who are widowed usually select others with the same histories), the increased availability of potential partners may also increase the speed with which they can be located. Perhaps another reason for the shorter time span from divorce to remarriage is the change in attitudes about the morality of divorce and subsequent remarriage. Rather than viewing either divorce or remarriage of divorced persons with the alarm that was common even one or two generations ago, most people view divorce as preferable to years of unhappy marriage, and remarriage as more desirable than celibacy and loneliness.

As life expectancy has lengthened from about forty-five years at the beginning of this century to well over seventy years currently, the period of adulthood has almost doubled. The average length of married life has increased accordingly. With the increase in the number of years that couples *can* be married and with the consequent decline in the proportion of child-rearing years to years with no children in the home, a reconsideration of the morality

TABLE 14.1
Males per 100
Females:
1970 and 1979

Age	1979	1970
All ages	95.0	95.9
0 to 9 years	104.5	104.0
10 to 19 years	103.7	103.5
20 to 24 years	101.4	101.2
25 to 34 years	98.8	98.0
35 to 44 years	95.4	95.7
45 to 64 years	92.1	91.7
45 to 54 years	94.3	93.3
55 to 64 years	89.8	89.7
65 to 74 years	77.0	77.7
75 to 84 years	60.4	65.9
85 years and over	44.7	53.2

Source: U.S. Bureau of the Census, *Current Population Reports,* series P-23, no. 111 (June 1981), p. 3.

of divorce is appropriate. Although there is a sadness at the pain and personal losses that occur in divorce, most people are no longer outraged by it. Most believe it would be cruel to force couples to stay married for forty or fifty years because of an error in judgment or unexpected situational or personality changes. The fact that over 30 percent of all marriages are remarriages has done much to reduce the former stigma associated with divorce and remarriage. Divorce is seen not as a sign of disenchantment with marriage itself but as a temporary state until a more satisfactory mate can be found.[5] It does not take as long as it did in the past to recover from a divorce and to turn to the possibility of making a new life.

Some divorced persons (over 15 percent) marry as soon as the divorce is final, often only a few months after they were first separated from their ex-mates.[6] This has led to speculation that many marriages end "so that one or both parties may be free to marry a person already selected."[7] However, there are indications that other factors may account for this statistic, at least in part, since some couples remarry quickly to persons they did not know before the divorce. Marital therapists have found some divorced persons have a strong need to convince themselves and others that they are capable of a successful marriage. Often they blame their ex-spouses for the breakup and need to show them as soon as possible that other partners find them desirable.

Most divorced persons move cautiously, however, as they sort through their doubts about whether they are likely to pick carbon copies of their mischosen ex-mates or whether their own faults might contribute in a similar fashion to still another troubled marriage. In their study of hundreds of separated and divorced men and women, Hunt and Hunt reported that prior to a remarriage most formerly married persons

> . . . have one or more relationships of some emotional intensity or importance. They are not all major love affairs: most, in fact, are trial runs or experiments: skyrocket infatuations that flare and burn out in a few weeks; dating relationships that gradually grow close and loving, then, unaccountably, waste away; friendships—with sexual intimacy—that are comforting and pleasing but never more than that. For most of the formerly married, such trials are an essential part of the process of self-discovery and development; the typical man or woman has three imperfect or abortive love relationships before entering one that is deep enough and "right" enough to seem like a realistic basis for remarriage.[8]

Psychologists and marital therapists have long been concerned with the question of whether or not divorced persons tend to choose new partners who are similar to their ex-mates. No doubt some do, although others go to the other extreme, picking someone diametrically opposite to the former spouse. In either of these situations, however, the new partner will possess qualities unique to him or her. As a result, the quality of interaction of the couple will be different from that of the former marriage. For instance, even if the new spouse has a bad temper, just as the ex-mate did, he or she also may have redeeming qualities that were missing in the former mate. In a recent survey of remarried couples, not one reported having married a carbon copy of an ex-spouse. In fact, many reported ending love affairs because they recognized troublesome traits similar to those of their divorced partners.[9]

Not only counselors but also most divorced men and women wonder whether they are likely to commit the same mistakes in a future marriage or whether they have learned something from the divorce experience that will make the next marriage better. Although many may marry before they finish analyzing their own roles in their divorces, it appears that most have gained increased awareness of the realities of marital relationships and are more mature socially and psychologically.[10]

Because there is no such thing as an easy divorce, no one comes through the experience unchanged. Most divorced persons, having recovered sufficiently to want to make new lives for themselves, see themselves as starting all over again. As one man put it, "I'm back to square one." But no one can really go back to the beginning. Every divorced person is more experienced, has different inner needs, has new perspectives on life.

The following wedding ceremony was written by a couple, each of whom was remarrying, and reflects their increased awareness of the vows they were taking:

> We are both entering a new intimacy with each other, but one which must inevitably bear the burdens of a first sundered intimate relationship with other partners. We bear scars and wounds unknown to other brides and grooms:

fears, doubts, and weaknesses of which only we are aware. But in these is our mutual strength to be found. Our love has gradually healed the wounds, calmed our fears, and established trust like a strong rock at the center of our mutual lives.[11]

Obviously, a divorce cannot create whole new persons; basic personality traits remain essentially the same. Even so, new partners are unlikely to react to those traits precisely as the ex-spouses did. Since each partner is affected by the actions and reactions of the other, the new relationship will be different.[12]

Remarriages usually involve people who are fairly close in age. If both parties have been previously married, their age difference is, on the average, four years. If a bride has never been married before but her new husband has, he will be, on the average, six years older than she. If a man has never been married but his bride has, the average difference between their ages is only a few months. Contrary to popular myth, very few divorced men marry women who are a great deal younger than they are. Only one divorced man in twenty-five marries a woman twenty years or more younger than he is. It is even rarer for a divorced woman to marry a man significantly younger than she.[13]

The success rate of second marriages has become a topic of great interest in light of the increasing number of them in recent years. Almost all studies have concentrated on partners who have both been previously married. Many have gone right to the point and have asked couples how the new marriage compares with the old. It is not surprising that an overwhelming number report that the present marriage is much better, since the former marriage was obviously not too good. But three-fifths report that the present marriage is better than those of other couples they know, and 67 percent report the current marriage to be even better than they had expected.[14]

The figures on the marital happiness of remarried persons may be inflated because of the tendency of couples to report positively on themselves and the tendency of couples who are having serious problems not to report at all. However, other national surveys have also indicated that second marriages are as satisfying and as successful as first marriages and have a very good chance to last.[15] In fact, there is a greater probability that a second marriage will end by the death of one spouse than that it will end in divorce.[16] The fact that the average couple is older undoubtedly contributes to this effect. Because most first divorces occur when the partners are still in their twenties or early thirties, there is a good chance that many second marriages will last to celebrate a golden wedding anniversary.

The average age for a second marriage for men is approximately thirty-four years and for women nearly thirty-one.[17] The obvious fact that couples are older on the average at the time of a remarriage than are couples marrying for the first time is one factor in favor of these marriages. Immaturity plays a large role in marital dissatisfaction and discord. We have already seen that those who marry young have a higher divorce rate.

In 1975 Norton and Glick estimated that one in three first marriages of younger persons (aged twenty-five to twenty-nine) will end in divorce (34 percent) and that 38 percent of second marriages will.[18] Since other research reports that those who decide to end a second marriage do so because they have less tolerance for a poor marriage and therefore will end it sooner than they did their first one (by an average of two years), it is even more likely that the success rate of second marriages means that those couples profited from the mistakes made in their first marriages.[19]

The United States Bureau of the Census refers to those who have been divorced more than once as **redivorced.** In 1975 there were over a million such persons, and the number appears to be growing steadily. Since 75 percent of persons redivorcing are under fifty years of age, they have plenty of time to marry again at least once. Although statistics are not readily available on multiple marriages because until now there have been too few cases from which to generalize, it is known that the risk for divorce grows with each remarriage.[20] The U.S. Census Bureau reports: "Few persons marry more than twice. About 3 percent of all persons 40 to 75 years old who have ever married have married more than twice." That figure includes remarriage after a former partner's death.[21]

It is not altogether clear why a first divorce makes for a relatively successful basis for remarriage, yet redivorces do not have the same effect. We can hypothesize that most first divorces are granted to those who married too early to have chosen wisely. A second marriage allows them a more mature choice and thus is more likely to be successful. Perhaps those who redivorce choose their partners poorly, have personal problems that keep them from relating well, do not understand what it takes to make a successful marriage, or have unrealistic ideals or expectations about married life. Remarriages (especially those involving children) necessitate different adjustments on the part of the partners from the adjustments faced in most first marriages. No doubt, many remarriages are disrupted over such issues as stepchildren, ex-mates, and support payments, to name but a few.

Couples who report significant difficulties in a remarriage following divorce usually cite quite different problems from those they list for their first marriages. Infidelity, loss of love, physical abuse, alcohol, and communication difficulties—all major factors in troubled first marriages—are much less often mentioned as problems in remarriages. Instead, financial problems are most often stated to be the single biggest trouble area in remarriage. Others are problems with in-laws, conflicts over children, and involvement with former marriage partners.[22] Further research is needed on multiple marriages before we can fully understand their complexity.

In her classic study of remarriage, family sociologist Jessie Bernard determined that the most important variable in whether or not a remarriage succeeds appears to be how much support the couple receives for their marriage from persons who are significant to them—children, in-laws, ex-spouses, and friends.[23] Remarriages appear to have no clearly defined patterns of behavior about many social and emotional issues that arise as the result of the complicated intertwining of past and current relationships. At any rate, remarriages after divorce seem to have different sets of problems from those that first marriages encounter.

Financial Problems

Financial strains are felt by nearly all American families today, but in remarriage these usually involve the added burden of helping to support two households. The husband may make child-support payments to his own children who live with their natural mother, or he may have one or more children living with him. He may also pay spousal support to his ex-wife if she has not remarried. His new wife may have children he is supporting or helping to support. Her ex-husband may not keep up support payments once she has remarried, or he may be able to afford very little as a result of his own remarriage.

In a survey of **step families,** it was discovered that 69 percent of stepfathers fully supported their stepchildren, receiving no money for child support from the natural fathers or from their mothers' employment.[24] For women who actually received child support from the children's fathers, the average amount received was less than $2,000 per year. Over 40 percent of the mothers never were awarded support for their children at all, and of those who were supposed to receive support, less than half received the full amount due.[25] A remarried couple may have additional children together and, because they are older on the average, are more likely to have elderly parents who have become dependent. All in all, a family formed by remarriage frequently feels a financial pinch.

Financial problems may not always have to do with hardship. For instance, the stepfather may resent that he is solely responsible for children of a man who contributes little or nothing to their support. Or he may feel guilty that his own children cannot have more support from him because of his responsibilities in his new marriage. A wife in a remarriage may understandably grow resentful if she is working to earn money that is sent on to an ex-wife who chooses to stay at home with her children. Although she may not object to working, she may object to doing without the things she could buy with that money. If the ex-wife or her new husband can provide luxuries for the children, the new wife may resent *any* gifts to them if she perceives that her own children are less well off. As one remarried mother said, "He took *his* children to *Disneyland* on his visitation day, but he complains about the cost every time we take mine to the movies."[26] No wonder studies consistently show that higher incomes are extremely favorable to the success of remarriages!

An interesting aspect of the financial condition of remarried couples is that men who remarry have higher incomes on the average than do men in first

marriages. Of course this is due in part to their being, on the average, somewhat older. They may have many more expenses as well, but they also have more money coming in. Women, on the other hand, tend to have lower family incomes in remarriages than in their first marriages. This has been explained by the fact that divorced women with children may feel an urgency to remarry that puts them at a disadvantage, so that they often "marry down" financially. Women in remarriages also report being less happy than women in first marriages do, but men in remarriages report being happier than men in first marriages say they are. Men in remarriages report being significantly more satisfied than their wives do.[27] Perhaps the finances are the key, or perhaps women who have settled for a lower standard of living than they would have had by staying in the first marriage consider this a cause for discontent.

Equally important to the inadequacy of income in creating discord in remarried couples is the *emotional* aspect of family finances. Transmission and discussion of money continues to tie ex-spouses together, especially when there are children. When there have been financial conflicts in the recent divorce, men and women become wary and often hesitant to pool their resources again in a remarriage. In her study of remarriage, Messinger reports:

> *Many remarried men were reluctant to speak freely about their financial assets and remarried women were often secretive about monies they had brought into the marriage. . . . Some women confided that they felt it necessary to keep some*

money aside in the eventuality of yet another divorce . . . some men appeared reluctant to revise their wills, insurance, and property assets.[28]

Some couples who remarry draw up prenuptial agreements to state how money and property will be handled in the marriage. Each can agree to keep separate any property or money they bring with them to the marriage. Unless the agreement violates existing state laws, they can agree on how to hold title to any property and earnings acquired while they are married. This can ensure that property and earnings will be kept unentangled if a divorce occurs—a comforting safeguard, especially when a partner has children by a previous marriage. However, because such precautions may make it seem that one or both partners are not fully committed to the marriage, some couples are hesitant to draw up such agreements.

In-Laws

After problems with finances and children, couples in a remarriage rank outside family (kin) as the third major problem they face.[29] Where there are children, grandparents may have played an active role following the parents' divorce. They may not wish to give up this new closeness and may oppose the remarriage. They may not be able to accept their stepgrandchildren, or they may favor their own grandchildren to the point of causing conflict. They may interfere with already touchy discipline controversies in the new home.

Typical of the sensitive situations that can develop is one that occurred in the home of a divorced man who gained custody of his two children. His retired parents moved in with him to help with family responsibilities. They were very fond of the children and in the three-year period before he remarried had established themselves as prime parent substitutes for the busy father. After the newly married couple returned from their honeymoon, the grandparents moved to a house a few blocks away but dropped in daily to be certain that the children were being cared for properly. Their father was grateful for all they had done for him and felt very close to his parents. His new wife, however, was resentful of their mistrust of her parenting abilities. The children adjusted poorly because their grandparents had sympathetic ears for even the most minor complaints. It took family therapy for all three generations to unravel their tangle of problems with each other.

Ex-in-laws sometimes are the source of problems in a remarriage, although they may not actually *cause* the problems. Most often the problems lie in the reaction of a new spouse to his or her mate's ex-in-laws. Just as some stepparents feel resentful or jealous over the constant reminders of a former family that stepchildren generate, so ex-in-laws in the picture may also be seen as threatening by the new spouse.

Divorced men are more likely than divorced women to end their relationships with their in-laws, partly because they usually do not have custody of
their children—who serve as the link to the in-law grandparents. Most such
men mention no hostility toward former parents-in-law (only 18 percent do),
but they report that there does not seem to be any reason to keep in touch or
that it is geographically difficult.[30]

Women who are divorced, on the other hand, interact more with family
members of their ex-husbands. Children are an important reason that custodial
mothers maintain contact with their children's paternal kin. Many mothers
report feeling some obligation to allow the grandparents and grandchildren to
have access to each other. However, divorced women report that the chief
reason they maintain contact is for affection, whether they have children or not.

Women have been shown to be the chief source of kin contact both with
their own families and with those of their husbands. When such contact has
been positive, that commitment seems to work to minimize disruption with the
in-laws after a divorce. In fact, over 40 percent of the women in the Spicer and
Hampe study reported seeing their ex-in-laws as much or more than they did
prior to the divorce. Only 17 percent of the men saw much or more of their
ex-wives' families.[31]

Ex-Spouses

One common stress in remarriage comes from the necessity for frequent contact with ex-spouses. As one ex-wife and writer on remarriage has said:

> The majority of ex-husbands and ex-wives seem not to like each other, even
> when it's all over and when they could presumably be friends again. There is
> something about being an ex- that, very often, causes any interaction to become
> extremely difficult and exacerbates any problems that may arise.
>
> When one remarries, one is never alone with a new mate. One lives with
> vibrations of other people who were part of one's old life and the new partner's
> former life. There are constant reminders of the past spent with others—
> portraits, photographs, monograms, laundry marks, furniture, tastes, hab-
> its—living ghosts that go along with every remarriage.[32]

Most of the problems that arise with ex-spouses have to do with children—
visitation, custody, child support. These are all issues that the divorcing couple
considered to have been settled in divorce court. It is not at all unusual for
divorced parents to go back to court again and again for postdivorce litigation
over such issues. Although there may, of course, be legitimate cause to file for
change of custody, to seek increased or decreased support payments, or to ask
for a ruling on disputed visitation rights and responsibilities, marital therapists
believe that there are usually underlying dynamics between the divorced

spouses that cause them to keep upsetting each other. In a study of 300 such cases, certain psychodynamics underlying conflicts between divorced spouses were found to exist in varying degrees and combinations.[33]

1. Divorce frequently does not end feelings of anger, hurt, rejection, and vengefulness. Some persons are "hostility junkies," who hang on to the divorced spouse by displacing this anger onto matters concerning their mutual children. As long as the bitterness can be focused on the ex-mate, no self-analysis need take place.
2. If one partner remarries, the single ex-spouse may feel jealous, especially if he or she had not wanted the divorce in the first place. The battles may actually represent a conscious or unconscious wish to get revenge by causing trouble so that the new marriage has less chance of success. The need to hold on to the ex-mate may be so strong that there is no acceptance of the reality that the marriage is over.
3. Occasionally, the new spouse is resentful of ongoing needs of the divorced parents to communicate about the children. He or she may cause trouble between the parents or between the children and the noncustodial parent. Children who refuse to visit their noncustodial parents are often acting out the custodial parent's problems. Often these stem from the knowledge that the contact necessary for a visit will anger the stepparent.

On occasion, the battle between divorced parents results in **"child snatching,"** which occurs when the noncustodial parent does not return the children from a visitation or when he or she picks them up at school, for instance, and then leaves for parts unknown. It is reported that there may be as many as 100,000 child stealings every year in the United States—one child stolen by a parent for every twenty-two divorces nationwide.[34] The rivalry between divorced parents that allows such action is so intense and so bitter that an attorney often must be appointed to represent the best interests of the children against their battling parents. Until recently there has been no interstate mechanism to help locate the children. Even when they have been found, there has been a good chance that the case would be heard in the state in which the children have been relocated. A Parental Kidnapping Prevention Act is currently before Congress; if passed, it will establish federal penalties for taking abducted children across state lines and will expand the use of the Federal Parent Location Service.

Not all problems with ex-spouses directly concern children. Other difficulties stem from the trouble some couples have in separating spousal and parental roles. These roles may have overlapped greatly when they were married. Studies have shown that in addition to continuing to relate to each other as parents, most divorced persons also keep in touch on non-child-related subjects. The most frequent topics they reportedly discuss, other than their own common problems, were news of their respective families and of their mutual friends. Most of the contact came when a noncustodial parent picked up or delivered the children or during telephone conversations. However, these friendly "news reports" were cited as the cause of trouble in their remarriages by a large number of couples.[35]

Research indicates that relationships between former spouses usually are not well defined and that couples seldom know how to respond appropriately to each other once they are divorced. Even less well defined is how the current wife should behave toward the former wife and how the current and ex-husbands should relate, if at all. The "divorce chain," as Bohannan calls it, gets even more complex when the ex-spouses of the remarried couple have also remarried.[36] They form a new kind of extended kinship system, and an etiquette for proper social relationships is often nonexistent.

To gain insight into the types of relationships that remarried persons maintain with their partners' ex-mates, couples who had been remarried just under a year were interviewed.[37] For 86 percent of the men and 87 percent of the women in the sample, this was a second marriage; for 11 percent of the men and 13 percent of the women, it was their third marriage; and for 3 percent of the men but none of the women, it was a fourth marriage. Men and women showed general agreement that they and their current spouses should be courteous (should say "hello" in public places, for example) to each other's ex-spouses. They also agreed that they should inform them of any serious illness or accidents either to the ex-spouses or to the children.

The agreement of recently remarried persons to exchange information on sickness and injuries is in keeping with other research findings that crisis situations increase communication and social solidarity, whether the crisis is a neighborhood emergency or a health-related problem in the family.[38] There seemed to be little agreement on other relationship issues by current wives about ex-wives, current husbands about ex-husbands, wives about current husbands, or husbands about what current wives should do concerning ex-mates. On each issue, however, there was distinctly more social distance preferred by wives toward ex-wives than by husbands toward ex-husbands.

Goetting suggests that an explanation of the distance desired by ex-spouses lies in social exchange theory. Exchange theory would predict that the more unpleasant a past marriage and divorce had been, the more contact with anyone connected with it would be avoided.[39]

Several studies have indicated that women have the most stressful time adjusting to divorce and stand to lose the most both in status and financially.[40] This may account for the greater social distance women prefer to keep from their husbands' ex-wives. Perhaps one could generalize to say that if the past marriage was "punishing," both women and men might vote to keep more distance from ex-spouses. At any rate, there are great individual differences in what is considered appropriate behavior for remarried persons and their ex-spouses. Some socialize comfortably, while others do not even speak. Most ex-spouses relate in patterns between these two extremes.

Friends

Integrating old friends from the past into a remarriage is often a source of difficulty since these persons may very well have been friends of the ex-spouse as well. Many of them may still continue to see both divorced partners, and this situation can be a source of discomfort to new spouses. A recently married woman spoke of her husband's friends left over from his past marriage:

> *I hate it when I know that people are also friends of my husband's ex-wife. Sometimes they let something slip into the conversation about her. Or they forget and start to reminisce about old times. One man even called me by her name once. I feel like a real outsider usually and I sometimes wonder if they are comparing me to her. I'm afraid I might say the wrong thing and they'll let it slip around her just as they get careless around me.*[41]

An especially difficult situation seems to arise when a remarriage takes one partner to the other's home town or neighborhood. Remarrying women often move from their previous residences to join their new husbands and face the decision of whether or not to make friends with people who were friendly with both him and his ex-wife. When a woman has custody of her children, they often attend the same schools as do their stepsiblings, who may live with their own mother in the same town or neighborhood.

Men who have been living in apartments often move into the new wife's home where she has been living with her children. The new husband, too, must make his way with neighbors and tradesmen who may be uncomfortable with this new man in the house. The very fact that the couple seem so happy and satisfied with their new relationship may create anxieties in those friends whose marriages are not doing so well. Many remarried couples report that they moved to a neighborhood or city new to both of them or changed churches to avoid contact with mutual friends from their previous marriages. They find it easier to make new friends than to face the problems created by maintaining old friendships.

Many remarried couples join discussion groups or attend workshops that focus on the special problems of remarriage. These partners may make new friends and develop a support group of understanding peers who can offer advice on, and serve as models for coping with, difficulties that may arise in remarriage.

Summary

■ Four out of five divorced persons eventually remarry—some as soon as the divorce is final, some many years later, with the average interval being about three years. Approximately one-third of all current marriages are remarriages.

■ Although many persons divorce and remarry more than once and are called the "redivorced" and the "multiply married," most people move cautiously from divorce to remarriage. As a result, second marriages are more often successful than not. There is a good chance that the second marriage will last until ended by the death of one spouse.

- Couples who report problems in a remarriage often are plagued by troubles that differ greatly from those of their first marriage. Financial difficulties, conflicts over stepchildren, and involvement with ex-spouses and with former in-laws seem to be the most troublesome issues in remarriages.

- Financial strains come not only from too little money to go around but also from emotional issues over sending and receiving monies to and from ex-spouses, supporting stepchildren, and having children of their own to support.

- In-laws, especially grandparents, may interfere with the new marriage and family life either by directly causing problems or by innocently being the source of emotional reactions of the new spouse and stepchildren. Women, who are usually the ones who maintain contact with kin, often want their children and the paternal grandparents to stay in touch. This may have its problems, however.

- Ex-spouses are often a source of trouble in a remarriage, particularly where there are children. Support, visitation, and continued conflict from the divorce often create trouble in the new marriage. Relationships between former spouses and between former and current ones are poorly defined, and problems often arise over what is acceptable behavior.

- Friends from the past who may also be friendly with the ex-spouses often are the cause of trouble in a remarriage. When the new spouse moves into the other's "territory" and must daily confront people from the mate's past married life—even the ex-mate—conflict often arises.

Stepparenting

Couples in a remarriage almost invariably report that integrating children into the new home is of major concern and is a source of frequent conflict. It is also the consensus of those who study remarriage that stepparent-stepchildren relationships are crucial to the success of the new marriage and vice versa. It is reported that over fifteen million minor children now live in step families, with an increase of nearly a million every year. Over half of all divorces involve children.

Of course, not all step families are the result of divorce. Each year approximately 400,000 children experience the death of a parent. Also, roughly 400,000 babies are born annually to unwed mothers. Many widowed parents remarry,

of course, and most unwed mothers eventually do. But the estimate is that 750,000 stepchildren each year owe their new statuses to divorce.[42]

The bulk of the stepparent homes (often called "blended" or "reconstituted" families) involve a stepfather whose new wife has custody of her children (nearly nine times more common than the case in which the husband has custody and the stepmother moves in*). The children become a part of a "remarriage package," usually through no choice of their own. Usually the mother and her children have been in an established single-parent home for months or even years prior to the remarriage. (The term *single-parent home* is used even though the children's other parent may be quite actively involved with them. It has been suggested that the term *single-custody home* may be more appropriate.) Whether a stepfather moves in with them, they move in with him, or they find a new place to live, major adjustments must be made. The longer a single-parent home has existed, the more difficult it will be for a stepfather to become a part of it. Research indicates that on the average it takes from one-and-a-half to two years for the adjustment to take place. The process goes more smoothly if the children are young.[43]

---

* About seven times more common for white persons, twenty times more common for black persons.

Stepfathers who have no children of their own may be very inexperienced at parenting. The founders of the Stepfamily Foundation of California comment: "While the mother has been filling many roles, the divorced man has had little family life. The mother may be feeling overwhelmed by all her parental responsibilities, particularly those of discipline, and imagine that the new husband will help her with all of her problems—financial, personal, and parental."[44] It will be very hard for any husband to live up to such a role, especially if he is coming into an ongoing system. Understanding the behaviors of children may be difficult for a man who has lived only with adults previously. Perhaps the most troublesome area will involve their discipline. Studies of step families have reported that the touchiest point in all such families is how discipline is handled.[45]

In her study of discipline in homes with a stepfather present, Stern reports that unless a new husband has been accepted into the family before he tries to become a disciplinarian, there will be serious problems: "The stepfather who moves slowly and attempts to make a friend of the child before moving to control him has a better chance of having his discipline integrated into the sentimental order of the family."[46]

It is easy for a stepfather who disciplines too soon and too harshly, or just differently from the mother, to cause a rift between himself and the children and often also between himself and his wife. Of course, this is also true for stepmothers who move too quickly to become disciplinarians to stepchildren. Children in such cases often play a "divide and conquer" game that leaves the stepfather or stepmother an outsider. One study has reported that the most glaring problem of the reconstituted family is "freezing out" the stepparent.[47]

Although a stepfather who has no children of his own may be at a real disadvantage because of inexperience, he still may have an easier time of it than does a man who is separated from children of his own. He must deal with his feelings of being a "live-in father" to his wife's children but only a "visiting father" to his own. His role may be poorly defined with both sets of children. When his own children come to visit, does he take them to the park or the ball game separately, or does he make them a part of his new family? If he succumbs to the temptation to devote all his time to his own children, since he sees them infrequently, how will this affect his stepchildren and his wife?

A new stepfather may find that it is less stressful for him to see his own children often and for long periods of time than when he was living alone because he, as a remarried person with stepchildren, now can provide a family setting in which his own children can visit. His wife may resent the additional time he spends with his children. The stepsiblings may have a hard time understanding their status and may resent the "intruders." On the other hand, the problems of having his children visit may be so great that the stepfather sees them less frequently. In that case, his guilt may mount.

Fathers who become stepfathers often have high expectations for themselves and also often report trying harder to live up to their responsibilities than they did in their first marriages. Since there are no established guidelines, they try one set of behaviors after another, looking for a formula that will work. As a result, stepfathers view themselves as less successful parents than do fathers living with their own children.[48]

However, stepfathers seem to fare better than stepmothers. Most stepmothers do not have their stepchildren living with them, but even the children's visits may be difficult. A stepmother may notice competition between her husband's children and hers. When hers are away visiting their father, she may have to take care of his or help entertain them. "You'll soon find that you cannot get rid of everybody, all at the same time. Consider school vacations, a grand time for your wife's ex-husband to take his kids for a week or two," writes father and stepfather Owen Spann, "but that's exactly the time that you inherit yours from your ex-wife."[49]

Stepmothers seem to get along better with stepchildren who are not teenagers, and younger stepmothers (under forty) seem to have better relationships with stepchildren than do those over forty.[50] Generally, however, stepmothers report that they find their roles stressful. Perhaps the reason is that stepmothers are traditionally more directly involved with the daily care of children than are stepfathers. They often report that their involvement with and attempts to care for their stepchildren are interpreted negatively by the children, as though they were asking them to be disloyal to their "own" mothers.[51] Virtually all children have been exposed to a long-standing myth that natural mothers instinctively care more and better for their own flesh and blood than anyone else does or ever can. It has been suggested that stepmothers step into the role with two strikes against them because of the images of wicked stepmothers in children's fairy tales.[52]

One stepmother wrote of an experience she had when she was driving her young stepdaughter and a little friend home from a birthday party: "Suddenly the friend asked, in a crystal English voice, 'Is that your stepmother?' The answer came, slightly shaky: 'Yes.' There was a pause. 'Oh. I always thought a stepmother was something like a witch.'"[53]

Perhaps in an effort not to be stereotyped, many stepmothers make noble efforts to love the husband's children and to be good to them. In her work with stepmothers, family therapist Sardanis-Zimmerman has found that most stepmothers begin with a "honeymoon" stage not only with the husband but also with his children.[54] They often deny problems that exist—as well as their own feelings—because they do not want to put their husbands in a position of divided loyalty. Many women report feeling trapped because they are afraid to complain and are even more afraid to act on their negative feelings.

A stepmother's own children often notice how differently she treats them when the stepsiblings arrive for a visit (or when her own come for a visit, if she is the noncustodial parent). She may be nicer to all of them, or she may hold the line with her own while treating the stepchildren as guests. Many stepmothers are aware that they make this distinction but report that their own

Cinderella with Her Wicked Stepmother and Stepsister

children know they are loved, but their stepchildren must be convinced that they are. The belief that a woman must immediately love her stepchildren and that they must return her love has been labeled "the myth of instant love."[55] Stepmothers report feeling they have somehow failed when these expectations do not materialize. On the other hand, they may blame the stepchildren, consoling themselves that their own efforts have gone unrewarded. Commenting on the problems of love in a step family, Roosevelt and Lofas say:

> Feeling obliged to love a stepchild and getting withdrawal sprinkled with hostility, a stepmother may tend to resolve the discrepancy by constructing an emotional brief of . . . her stepchild's faults and inadequacies. Who, her thinking goes, could ever be expected to love this child? . . . The stepchild finds his original negative assumption confirmed ("I always knew she was mean").[56]

Problems such as these above are cited by stepmothers who have custody of their own children and whose husbands' children also live with them. As one expert on step families has commented: "There is no more disunited a nation than the step family which assembled his and her children under one roof."[57]

As more fathers obtain custody of their children or share custody with their ex-wives, the "blended" family is gaining in visibility. Since custodial fathers are still in the minority, little is known concerning whether they are atypical in their relationships with their children. Perhaps they are men who were more involved with their children before their divorces than were noncustodial fathers. It may also be the case that they select wives who are different from those that noncustodial fathers would choose. More research in these areas is needed to answer the many questions about blended families.

Although it is easy to be pessimistic about the success of a blended family—and the issues are complex—there is a positive side. Both parents not only have their own children living with them, but each also has an experienced partner to help out. Each has a better basis for understanding what is happening to the other. Although there is a distinct possibility of favoritism being shown, at least there are no "guest children" on weekends and holidays. Many of the problems that are attributed to this family form are found in other families as well: favoritism of one child over another, bad feelings between a parent and a child, sibling rivalry, and friction between the parents over the children.

Three models for stepmothers have been proposed by Draughon in her work with families in which the father has custody (usually because of the mother's death, abandonment, or incapacitation).[58] Traditionally, few fathers received custody except in such cases or those in which the mother was judged "unfit," but this is slowly changing. Since there are an increasing number of father-custody homes, and the stepmother may be the woman who is the most active caretaker of his children, these models take on more importance. They are:

1. *Friend:* This role seems to work best with those children whose natural mothers see them regularly and are active though noncustodial. The stepmother is the other responsible adult in the household but does not try to fill the role of mother to her stepchildren. In such an arrangement the children usually call her by her first name, and the friendship can range from very close to casual. Stepmothers in this role generally take a light hand with discipline. This pattern seems to work well with older children, who often resent a stepmother entering the family—especially if she attempts to be a disciplinarian. This role can be difficult for a woman whose own children also live in the same home. Being a mother to one set of children and an adult friend to the others can be confusing to all family members.

2. *Primary mother:* This role is most successful when the natural mother is permanently out of the picture or when there is a mother-child estrangement. Very young children often feel comforted after the loss of their own mothers by having a complete family again. They usually call the stepmother "mother." Without a biological mother in the picture, the question of divided loyalty occurs less often. There may be difficult moments when the child confronts the stepmother with, "You're not my real mother. You can't tell me what to do." However, since the children are not members of two households and have no "real mother" to turn to, such outbursts seldom last long.

3. *Other mother:* This may be the most prevalent stepmother role and is possibly the most confusing and troublesome. This model is ambiguous, and the children often feel a conflict of loyalty. They may threaten to return to live with their "real" mothers whenever the stepmothers cross them. They may appeal to their fathers, who do not want the children complaining to their mothers about their new wives. If a father tries to intervene, his present wife may feel that her feelings are less important to him than his children's or even his ex-wife's. Studies of step families reveal that children often come between the spouses in the "other mother" or "other father" situation. The couple must form a cohesive unit to withstand such pressure. If their alliance is strong, the chances for success of the step family greatly increase.[59]

Stepmothers who have no children of their own have the same problems of inexperience that childless men have in becoming stepfathers. The most stressful stepparent homes we have seen involve a father who has custody of his children and a woman who has never had children. It is difficult for a woman to become an "instant mother" and a new wife at the same time. Childless women often have careers that they resolve to give up to become homemakers and mothers. Making so many changes at once in their life-styles can place a great strain on them.

New stepmothers who continue to work outside their new homes may be overburdened and may fail to meet their own and their husbands' expectations for their roles as stepmothers. They are often upset by the amount of contact that their husbands and their ex-wives have to discuss matters of visitation and financial arrangements, especially if the contact seems friendly. Some new stepmothers are upset if they are asked to participate in these discussions; others are upset because they are not.

One stepmother told us that she had no idea what she was getting into when she married a man who had custody of his children and whose ex-wife was always in the background:

> I feel more like an employee hired to take care of his children than like a new wife should feel. Everything centers around their welfare, their activities, what they want to eat, where they need to go. But I not only don't get paid, I get criticized by the children and also by my husband for not doing a better job. At the same time, their mother is always ready to pounce on us to regain custody. That doesn't help me to feel secure.[60]

Having a child by her new husband to add to their family has been shown to help all family members adjust. Not only is the stepmother now a mother, but the stepchildren's father is her baby's father as well. The existing children and the new baby are blood relatives. The baby often acts as a link between the stepmother and the stepchildren.[61] The birth of the new baby may end the fantasies some stepchildren have of breaking up the new marriage so that their parents can reunite. Of course, there may be jealousy and anxiety about being displaced by the new baby, but these feelings are also common among children who are living with both natural parents.

Stepsiblings often have an easier time getting along with each other than with their stepparents. Young children in particular may develop strong bonds, although, as in natural families, there is bound to be rivalry, conflict, and some instances of real dislike for each other. The better the stepsibling relationships, generally, the better the reconstituted family adjustment.[62]

A problem that is being addressed currently in the literature on stepsiblings has to do with sexual activities between unrelated children who are now sharing a home.[63] Sexual activity between siblings (even sibling incest) is not uncommon, but sexual activity between stepsiblings is thought to be more common. The process of growing up together from birth seems to dampen sexual interest between natural siblings or to lead to its repression or sublimation. Sometimes it appears as hostility. However, teenagers in particular who suddenly are thrown together in the intimate atmosphere of a home by a parent's remarriage often report being sexually aroused by close contact with an attractive stepsibling. Although incest may have been defined as taboo or unattractive, this new relationship is often undefined. Even parents may be uncertain about the "proper" rules for tickling, wrestling, kissing, and nudity, especially if these rules have been casual for the natural siblings.[64]

When the sexual urgency of adolescence is growing and the consciousness of sexual activity is heightened by knowing that their newly wed parents are sexually active, the enticement of a stepsibling may be a temptation some teenagers cannot resist. No one knows exactly how many sexual relationships exist between stepsiblings, but the growth in numbers of step-family homes, combined with increasingly permissive norms for adolescent sexual behavior, seems likely to make for increases each year.

Summary

■ Integrating children into a "reconstituted" family may be the most difficult task of a remarriage and a source of frequent conflict. How successfully the blending takes place is crucial to the new couple's marital satisfaction.

■ Most step families involve a mother, her children, and a stepfather. All in all, stepfathers seem to fare better than stepmothers do. The most troublesome area seems to involve discipline. The stepfather who waits to be accepted by the children before he tries to be a disciplinarian usually becomes integrated into the family within two years. The process goes more smoothly if the children are young.

■ Stepmothers get along better with younger children and do better in general if they also are young (under forty). Most stepmothers report that their roles are stressful, largely because of their greater involvement in daily child care.

Stepmothers also usually have their own children living with them; balancing the job of mother and stepmother is often difficult.

■ Stepsiblings often have an easier time adjusting to each other than to a stepparent. Usually, the better the children get along, the better the parents' marriage is.

■ Having a child of their own often has a positive effect that solidifies the reconstituted family. It is not that a new baby improves a bad situation but rather that a child of theirs together makes each person in the family kin in a new way.

Remarriage after Widowhood

Although most remarriages follow divorce, thousands of widowed persons also remarry each year. Only as recently as 1973–1974 did marriages ending in divorce began to equal those disrupted by death.[65] It is true that most persons whose spouses die are older—and they are predominantly women. Consequently, the stereotypical widowed person is an older woman whose husband has died, leaving her to melt into the "never-to-marry-again" population.

A widow who is over fifty-five years of age when her husband dies has less than half the probability of remarrying that a widower her same age has.[66] A woman may wish to remarry but may find no available men since not only do women far outlive men, on the average, but widowers also often remarry somewhat younger women. Twenty percent of widowers over age sixty-five who remarry choose women ten or more years younger than they are. Fewer than 3 percent of widows marry men that much younger than they are.[67] So many more women become widows compared with men who become widowers that there is only the word *widowed* to describe the state following the death of a spouse. Although we speak of "widow" and "widower," there is no such word as "widowered."

The median age at widowhood is in the early fifties. Since this is a median, it means that half of the men and women who lose their spouses by death are younger. Many of them have minor children (approximately 400,000 minor children a year experience the death of a parent). These men and women commonly remarry, often to another widowed person. Since there are many fewer of them than of persons who remarry following a divorce, few research studies have been done to determine how similar they are to couples who remarry after a divorce. The small number of studies, however, has been offset by the high quality of those that have been done. Some of the best research has concerned itself with older women who remain widows—those three currently unmarried women to every currently unmarried man over the age of sixty-five. Fewer than one-fifth of such women even declare a wish to remarry.[68]

Younger widows and widowers received attention in a recent study emerging from the Harvard Laboratory of Community Psychiatry.[69] The subjects were men and women under the age of forty-five. There were interesting differences between the adjustment patterns of women and men whose spouses had died. The two sexes organized their lives differently following loss of a mate. Widowers tended to view the death of a wife as a loss of part of themselves. They had difficulty mobilizing themselves to work, were very lonely, and felt sexually anxious. They yearned for the dead spouse but seemed unwilling to display their grief openly and viewed self-control as strength. Widows, on the other hand, viewed their loss as abandonment—being left to fend for themselves—but felt a fierce loyalty to their dead husbands that temporarily inhibited sexual thoughts.

How quickly both men and women recovered from their bereavement seemed closely related to whether or not the spouse's death was anticipated. If the spouse had died suddenly and unexpectedly, the recovery took longer, and the thought of remarriage was viewed cautiously. The loss of a spouse without warning affected the eventual success of recovery and the length of bereavement for both men and women.

Many men whose wives died suddenly eventually remarried but usually harbored anxiety and personal discomfort at the blow that fate had dealt them. Men who anticipated their wives' deaths were able to recover fairly rapidly; they wanted to reestablish orderly lives for themselves and their children. They moved more quickly into dating and remarriage than either men whose wives had died suddenly or than widows in general. A few widowers began dating several weeks after the wife's death; by the end of the first year after her death, 50 percent had remarried or were in serious relationships. Those men who had not expected the death were as slow as or slower than widows to recover.[70]

Only about 18 percent of widows were remarried or seriously involved within one year after their husbands' deaths, according to the Harvard study. Nearly one-third would not even consider remarriage at that time, and for most it was three or more years before they could consider "being disloyal to their husbands' memories" by contemplating remarriage. Willingness to date developed gradually, and often with a considerable sense of guilt, some time after the first year of bereavement. By the end of the fourth year after their husbands' deaths, a good many women were remarried or in serious relationships (about one year later on the average than divorced persons remarried).[71] Even so, many widows reported having moments of grief and mourning for their dead husbands for the rest of their lives.

Men and women whose spouses die are often in better financial condition than are those whose marriages end in divorce. There are, of course, some widowed persons who face heavy debts due to medical expenses resulting from a spouse's prolonged illness or to strained family finances during the marriage. Medical and life insurance help immeasurably, and Social Security benefits for widows and for minor children allow many families to continue a standard of living that does not change drastically. There is no property to divide as in a divorce, and there are no attorney's fees for battles over custody and support payments. Some states are doing away with inheritance taxes so that death does not place that burden on the survivors in addition to the many others. Widowers seem to have an easier time financially because most continue in their jobs with steady incomes. Widows know that insurance money usually will not last long and that they must begin to earn an income, if they have not done so previously, but life insurance gives them a period of some financial security while they adjust.

The major adjustments for those who have been widowed seem to involve dealing with their own grief and helping their children deal with theirs. Psychologically, the death of a married man or woman puts a more final end to the relationship for both spouse and children than does a divorce. However, both adults and children have some tendency to revere the dead person, and children in particular may mourn the loss for a lifetime. This can make the addition of a stepparent to the home difficult if the remarriage takes place too soon after the parent's death. Neither the person nor the role enacted can be the same; it is a mistake on the part of everyone involved to expect or even suggest that the lost one is being replaced.

In a recent study on bereavement in families it was found that

> . . . the feelings of the child about his dead parent seemed deeply private to him, based on the treasuring of memories. The dead parent, unlike the divorced parent, was no longer in existence in a way in which he could be experienced by others. Strangers who were unable to share the child's perceptions and hadn't known the dead person were, in this context, also often viewed as an intrusion rather than a support.[72]

Even very young children sometimes resist a stepparent and feel angry at what they perceive to be the surviving parent's disloyalty to the dead one. The stepparent is often in the awkward position of being rejected by the spouse's children while feeling compassionate toward them because of their grief.

It is no wonder that the special feelings of bereaved persons often lead widows and widowers to seek each other out for remarriage. They have had similar experiences of grief and have suffered the slow process of recovery accompanied by pangs of sadness and feelings of guilt or disloyalty as they begin to love again. Their children, too, often feel a more kindred spirit with stepparents and stepsiblings who have experienced a similar loss. Although they have many of the same problems in adjusting that other blended families have, they do not have the real pulls of a noncustodial parent. On the other hand, they do not have the advantages of being able to rely on the absent parent as a backup.

Older widows and widowers whose children are grown may also remarry, although the chances for the older widow to remarry are not as favorable as

those for the widower. If a woman is widowed before age thirty, there is over a 90 percent chance that she will remarry within five years of her husband's death. If she is between thirty and forty, a 70 percent chance exists, and between forty and fifty a 40 percent chance. However, if a woman is over fifty, she has less than an 8 percent probability of remarriage.[73]

Research on the remarriages of older couples is scant, but one such study has revealed that these marriages are often quite successful. A widower usually remarries within a year or two of his wife's death, but a widow may wait several years (often until her youngest child leaves home).[74] Grown children often resist their parents' remarriages because of concerns over inheritance or out of loyalty to the dead parent. Also, many adult children assume that marriage (and particularly sexual activity) is appropriate only for people much younger than their parents. This may result in part from the typical concealment of parental sexuality from children in earlier years, when many parents have shamed or even punished their children for showing any interest in sex or erotic materials.

McKain reports that older couples who remarry after being widowed are usually only a few years apart in age. They typically come from similar educational, social, economic, and religious backgrounds. This similarity may account for the high success rate of their marriages. Another factor may be that they had long and usually successful first marriages that gave them experience with and insight into the problems of married life. Many of the couples studied had been acquainted for years; some had been friends as couples while they were still married to their now deceased spouses. In general, it has been found that those elderly widowed persons who remarry are in better health and have higher incomes than those who do not remarry.[75] Both good health and adequate finances in turn have a positive effect on marital success.

Summary

■ Remarriage following the death of a spouse has certain aspects that differ from those that follow divorce. For one thing, widowed persons are usually older and in better financial condition. For another, the previous marriage was more likely a good one than was one that ended in divorce. The dead spouse is physically gone—unlike the divorced one, who may be very much present—although there is a tendency to revere a dead spouse.

■ Those who have been widowed most often seek each other to remarry. They have shared more similar experiences than either has with those who are single or divorced.

■ Young widows and widowers show some differences from each other in how they organize their lives and eventually remarry. Whether the spouse died suddenly or the death was expected influences the length of the bereavement. It takes longer for a spouse to recover from the sudden death of a partner and to reestablish his or her life.

■ Fifty percent of the men studied had remarried or were in a serious relationship by the end of the first anniversary of their wives' deaths. Only about 18 percent of the women were so involved.

■ The children whose parent has died also adjust differently from those whose parents divorce. They have grief over never seeing the parent again and often resist a stepparent because they feel disloyal. If the stepparent and stepsiblings have experienced a parent's death also, however, they usually have more of a kindred spirit.

■ Older widows and widowers who remarry may have problems with acceptance from their grown children over such issues as inheritance or disloyalty to the dead parent. Most such children recognize, however, that companionship is positive for adjustment to old age and that their parents will probably be healthier and happier because of the marriage.

■ Most older couples who marry are similar in age, education, religion, and socioeconomic background. This similarity may well account for the high success rate of their marriages.

Glossary

Child snatching The kidnapping of one's own child(ren) from the custodial parent after a divorce.

Redivorced A term used to describe one who is divorced a second time.

Step family The family formed by the remarriage of a parent following divorce or the death of the children's other parent.

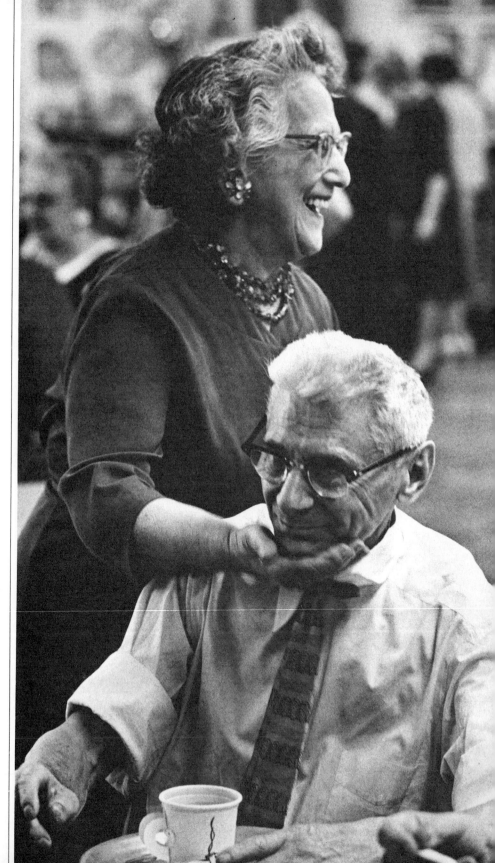

To see a young
couple loving each
other is no wonder;
but to see an old
couple loving each
other is the best
sight of all.

—William
Makepeace
Thackeray, *Fiery
Grains*

444

15 · Postparental Life and Aging

In 1990 there will be an estimated twenty-nine million men and women over the age of sixty-five. This represents almost a tenfold increase during this century. In an attempt to understand the needs and coping skills of the elderly population, the field of **gerontology** has become an important area of research. The prevailing negative view of aging has begun to change recently as people realize that, with luck, old age will come to all of us. Gerontologists have helped people find ways to cope and to make old age satisfying. To understand how we grow old, how to manage aging with grace and satisfaction, and what can be learned from those who are already senior citizens, research has concentrated on middle-age adjustments that are crucial for later adjustments when one is over sixty-five. Research on aging has looked at family relations, marital satisfaction, retirement, widowhood, loneliness, residential requirements, and other adjustment processes. More research is needed; we have just begun to scratch the surface.

FIGURE 15.1 *Average Years of Life Remaining at Selected Ages: 1977*

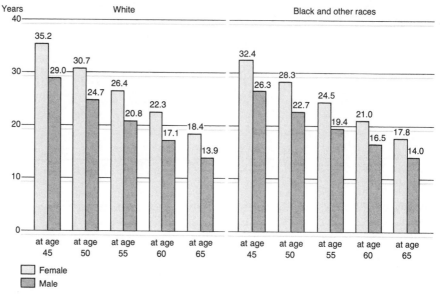

Source: U.S. Bureau of the Census, *Current Population Reports,* series P-23, no. 111 (June 1981).

In 1949 a survey of twenty marriage and family textbooks revealed that only two devoted more than a brief mention to aging or to how older men and women live and love. Of 10,697 pages of text that were analyzed, only 50 pages related to persons past middle age.[1] Much of the material in those 50 pages dealt with problems older men and women face and how their grown children must help them cope. Perhaps this was a reflection of the early years of this century, when fewer people lived past middle age than do so today and when those who did may not have been as healthy as today's older citizens. A baby born in 1900 had only a 39 percent chance of reaching age sixty-five. By 1970 the chances of reaching age sixty-five had risen to 72 percent, women having nearly a 50 percent chance of living to be eighty.[2]

The Growing Elderly Population

Much has happened in the more than thirty years since the 1949 survey. The older population in the United States has grown rapidly and is expected to continue to increase through the 1980s. Several factors are responsible for this growth—improved diet and health care have increased the chances of living longer; large numbers of children were born from 1900 to 1925 who are now in

TABLE 15.1

*Population of the
United States Aged
65 and Over*

1900	3.1 million
1920	4.9 million
1940	9.0 million
1960	16.7 million
1970	20.0 million
Projections	
1980	25.5 million
1990	29.8 million
2000	31.8 million

Source: U.S. Bureau of the Census, *Current Population Reports,* series P-23, no. 43 (February 1973), p. 2; series P-23, no. 78 (January 1979), p. 8; series P-20, no. 336 (April 1979), p. 15; and series P-20, no. 363 (June 1981), p. 9.

the aged population; and, perhaps most significantly, the great decrease in infant mortality and death from childhood diseases has allowed more babies to survive to grow old.

In 1900 only 4 percent of the population was sixty-five or older. In 1980 this figure reached 11 percent. This may not appear to be such a large gain until one realizes that the 1980 population on which the percentage is based is much larger than that of 1900. Perhaps the growth of the older population can be more clearly expressed by reference to actual numbers since 1900, as seen in Table 15.1.

Textbooks have taken note of the increased numbers and impact of our aged population. A survey of marriage and family texts in 1978 found that 50 percent gave good coverage to the issues of aging, although the focus was generally still on problems of retirement, poverty, illness, and widowhood. The other 50 percent gave token attention at best to the older population, and some clearly misrepresented the reality of aging in the United States.[3] Perhaps these omissions or inadequate treatments were carried over from the days when it was believed that college students were not interested in anyone over thirty—much less over fifty. Not only does this underestimate the awareness and intelligence of young people, but it also ignores the fact that classrooms are not populated solely with young adults. Even if they were, aging is a process that begins when we are conceived and, if we are lucky, will happen to all of us sooner or later. Irish playwright George Bernard Shaw, responding to the question of how it felt to be eighty, said that, considering the alternative, it was just fine.

A positive view of aging has unfortunately been missing in our society, and a negative attitude is reflected in our literature. A focus on problems has strongly devalued aging and has usually overlooked the fact that many older persons are leading satisfying and rewarding lives. This omission is reminis-

Maggie Kuhn,
Founder of the Gray
Panthers

cent of the ways racial and ethnic minorities were once portrayed in textbooks and led to the belief that the lives of few, if any, minorities had positive aspects. There are also still instances of misrepresentation of current sex roles for men and women, but these are being reversed systematically. It is time that our older population becomes represented realistically also, rather than suffering from the stereotypes that have surrounded aging in our society. Some activist groups have formed among the older population—the Gray Panthers, the National Council of Senior Citizens, the American Association of Retired Persons—and studies in gerontology have proliferated in an attempt to understand the physical, psychological, and social aspects of aging.

As a result, a new picture of the aging population—one that has both positive and negative qualities as well as all the other potentialities and drawbacks that any other age group faces—is beginning to emerge. The view of old age held by the elderly themselves seems to be an ambivalent one, as Shaw intimated. Family-life expert Gerhard Neubeck expressed this ambivalence in writing about his own aging process:

> *No, we are not charitable about old age. It is never in fashion, it is never desirable—political and economic movements such as the Gray Panthers not withstanding—at best it is tolerated. Mostly I believe it is so because, after all, it is the final stage before we die. A prelude to death . . . and who wants that!*
> *. . . the truth is that, for me getting older is a burdensome beast. . . . I will stop being in the not too distant future. I hate death for that reason, the brutality of having no control over prolonging my love for living permits me to enjoy this final phase of my life. My heart beats excitedly, my brain operates on both hemispheres and my loins will lie in lust. I am. That is why I would write this piece.[4]*

Older people, of course, have many problems that younger people usually do not have, such as declining physical strength and health problems, but they do not have many others that younger persons must face. They have raised their families and have done their lifework. Despite these differences, however, there are remarkable consistencies in life—things that change little over the years. Older persons are still social and sexual. Some are married, some are divorced, some remarry, others are widowed. Topics that are important in other stages of the life cycle are usually just as pertinent in the later stages of life.

The objective of this chapter is to explore what is known about the population of aging persons. First, *old* must be defined. Young adults often refer to their forty-five- or fifty-year-old parents as "over the hill" when the parents still think of themselves as young. The parents are seen as old because they belong to another generation and because to a person of twenty, even forty may look ancient. More important, however, their parents have finished their childbearing and child-rearing years and soon may become grandparents. When the third generation arrives, even if the grandparents are only forty, they are usually viewed as "growing old."

There is agreement among experts that middle age begins and ends and old age begins at different chronological ages for different persons. The United States Bureau of the Census uses the chronological age of sixty-five as the end of middle age and the beginning of old age. This choice is tied to the 1935 enactment of Social Security legislation, which up until the present writing has used sixty-five as the age for maximum retirement benefits to begin. Other countries use other chronological ages. Recently Congress passed a law that mandatory retirement for most employed persons in the United States could not be ordered on grounds of age alone until they reach seventy. It is likely that the arbitrary age of sixty-five as the beginning of old age will eventually be replaced by the arbitrary age of seventy. Also, as the life cycle lengthens and as older people remain healthy, vital, and young looking, the calendar calculation of old age may change. Family sociologist Ethel Shanas has suggested that we may need to divide our aging population into the "young-old" and the "old-old." Those who in 1900 might have been considered old may now appear to be "young-old" because at the turn of this century few people lived to be over eighty.[5] Currently there are over two-and-a-third million persons in the United States who are over eighty-five, and the number is growing.[6]

We all know people who are "young," spry, and alert but who, chronologically, are aged. There are also those in their fifties who look ancient and act for all the world as though life were over. The truth is that people age very differently. Some of the variation is due to genetic differences and some, surely, to physical health. Perhaps more than any other variable, however, gerontologists point to outlook on life.[7] A person's self-concept and understanding of relations with others depend on health, of course, and on whether he or she views his or her work as meaningful, on family and friends, and on finances.

TABLE 15.2

Percent of Women in
the Labor Force
(by age), 1979

Age	Percent
All women 16 years and over	51.0
16 to 19	54.5
20 to 24	69.1
25 to 34	63.8
35 to 44	63.6
45 to 54	58.4
55 to 59	48.7
60 to 64	33.9
65 and over	8.3

Source: U.S. Bureau of the Census, Current Population Reports, series P-23, no. 111 (June 1981), p. 8.

In a series of interviews with elderly persons, it was determined that patterns of social adjustment established in the earlier stages of their adult lives were related in important ways to their general life satisfaction in later years. Those who had been active in work, in hobbies, and in the community outside the home as younger adults were the most satisfied as they grew older.[8] This may account, at least in part, for findings from other research that women have a more difficult time in their later years than men do, since women who are now over sixty-five belong to generations in which many middle-class women believed that a woman's "place" was in the home. Perhaps future generations of women will have an easier time adjusting. About half of the women who are currently forty-five to sixty-four have spent some time in the labor force, and the trend seems to be in the direction of increasing participation. Table 15.2 shows the participation of various age cohorts.

Other reasons for greater adjustment problems for older women unfortunately have no such ready solution. One important factor is that there are so many more older women than older men, a discrepancy that increases with each advancing year. Women are therefore likely to spend their older years single and, as a result, are likely to have fewer economic resources. Half the women over sixty-five are single and live in poverty, with the bulk of their income coming from Social Security or old-age assistance.[9]

Most pension plans, whose benefits begin at retirement, are tied to full-time employment. Women usually have worked part time or have had work lives interspersed with periods at home and therefore have contributed less to pension plans. Women's lower salaries (partly due to lower pay scales for the jobs they are most likely to choose but often due to low seniority in equal–opportunity jobs—teaching, for example) also are reflected in lower pension benefits. Also, women not only typically retire earlier but on the average live longer after retirement than men do and thus have more years to survive on what may be smaller benefits than men. Some women have survivor's benefits from a deceased husband's pension, but such benefits may cease if they remarry. However, as today's young and middle-aged women spend more years in the labor force and accrue higher pension benefits, the number of retired women with incomes below the poverty line should drop dramatically.

Shanas believes that another important reason that older women report more difficulties in their later years than men do is that women are judged old by different standards from those used for men. Over twenty years ago Shanas asked a cross section of Americans, "When is a person old?" She reports that the findings still hold today. She found that no matter what a man's actual age, if he was active and energetic, he was not viewed as old. On the other hand, women were judged old according to their chronological age: "A man, then, is as old as his activities; a woman as old as her birthday."[10]

A definition of old age is incorporated in a description of who is young, middle-aged, and old that gerontology specialist Bernice Neugarten once gave. She said that when we are young we count our ages by how long it has been since birth. A time comes, however—usually between ages thirty-five and forty—when we also begin to contemplate how long we have left to live. When we begin to use both measures—time since birth and time left—we have entered middle-age. Eventually, she says, another milestone comes, when we no longer want to reckon with birthdays nor to think about how long it has been since the day we were born. Each day is counted as a blessing, but no plans for the future are made. When the focus shifts solely to how long is left, this marks the beginning of old age.

The mother of one of our friends, who is seventy-five, recently bought a very expensive piece of artwork. When her son asked why she had spent so much money this way, she snapped: "For an investment. Just think what I can sell it for in twenty years." By Neugarten's definition this woman is not old. She is planning for an active future and, we are sure, does not think of herself as old either.

Since one's adjustment to old age seems determined in part by events and experiences in the years preceding retirement, it may be useful to take a look at middle age as the precursor of old age. *Middle age* has been defined in as many different ways as has old age. This postparental stage begins some time around the age of forty or forty-five and coincides roughly with what the Bureau of the Census has for years somewhat arbitrarily designated as midlife (forty-five to sixty-four years old). For this reason, for many men and women the realization of their aging process begins in earnest with the launching of children and the onset of the postparental and grandparental years.

The Empty Nest

Much has been written about the "empty-nest" phase of life, which has been thought to affect women, primarily those whose lives have been devoted to their homes and their children. In our experience of working with women at this stage of their lives, for a good many of them the **empty-nest syndrome** has been considerably overemphasized. It is true, of course, that some women (and a good many men, for that matter) do have a difficult time allowing their children to establish independent lives away from home. We have known parents who became severely depressed and lonely when the last child left. Some have become pregnant again, if they could, or adopted a child or raised their grandchildren in an effort to recreate the years of the "filled nest."

However, it is not usually the departure of the children that is the upsetting factor. Instead, for women it is often a question of "Now what do I do?" There is new freedom to fulfill some of their own needs for a change, but often "retired" mothers are uncertain about what they want to do. More important, they are often unsure of their abilities to compete in a world of which they may not have been a part for twenty or more years. Going back to school may be attractive—but can they succeed? If they decide to work, they wonder who will hire them. How will husbands respond if they change their lives? These questions seem to be at the root of much of the turmoil attributed to the empty-nest stage for women.

Some women of this age believe that they are experiencing a menopausal depression and attribute their anxiety and lonely feelings to their physiological changes. Although there is no argument that physical changes do occur during menopause (in the late forties, on the average) and that most women notice some uncomfortable effects (hot flashes, dizziness, insomnia, headache, fatigue), only about 10 percent report severe distress.[11]

The psychological problems that occur simultaneously with menopause are not thought to be due primarily to the hormonal changes but more to the woman's interpretation of what is happening to her body. It is a forceful reminder that her childbearing years are over and that she is aging. It comes at the same time that her children leave home and that she must redefine her life. So many changes at once may easily be expected to produce psychological stress. As psychologists Hyde and Rosenberg have stated: ". . . any quirk in a middle-aged woman's behavior is attributed to the 'change.' It simultaneously becomes the cause of, and explanation for, all [her] problems and complaints. Ironically, idiosyncrasies in women of childbearing age are blamed on menstruation, while problems experienced by women who are past that age are blamed on the lack of it."[12]

Men miss their departed children too, but they are usually still actively involved in their work. The children's leaving changes little of that except to relieve the financial burden. However, when children leave home, the husband

and wife no longer have the distractions of parenthood to take their attention from each other and their marriage.

Some couples find that they are strangers to each other after their children leave. They have focused so completely on their children's needs that the parental role has totally eclipsed the marital one. They often have almost forgotten that they are husband and wife as they have submerged themselves in parenthood. They may even still refer to each other as "Mom" and "Dad." These emotional strangers, no longer linked together by the family responsibilities, may have serious adjustment problems that are far more complicated than merely adjusting to the departure of children. They may have to relearn how to relate on an intimate level and to direct to each other the love, support, and attention that were given for so many years to the children.

Most men and women, however, report that the postparental period is a time of improvement in their lives. They are still young (by their standards), many financial burdens have been removed, and they have more time to themselves. An overwhelming number of married couples report that their marital satisfaction returns to something resembling the preparenthood level.[13]

In a series of studies on postparenthood, couples report more shared activities and more companionship. In one particularly thorough research project, family sociologist Norval Glenn reported that married women's overall happiness was greater when their children left home and that marital happiness was generally higher for both men and women in the postparental stage.[14] Still other studies have indicated that when the children leave home, there is a return to sharing of provider and domestic tasks similar to the period before children were born. Couples over forty-five were shown to be twice as likely as younger couples to share earning a living equally, and only one-third of the wives over forty-five reported that they did all the housekeeping.[15]

Most couples also report that they are still in love and still sexually active with each other during their postparental years. Psychologically and physically, men and women in midlife undergo some sexual changes, of course, but most couples report that these changes are usually easily accommodated once they understand what to expect. Middle-aged men may experience some slowing down of sexual responses as the testosterone level begins to decline between the ages of forty to sixty (after which it stabilizes for the rest of life).[16]

Women may become more sexually responsive after menopause as a result of losing concern about pregnancy. They experience a rebalance of androgen and estrogen because of the decreased production of the latter. This rebalance may also serve to increase female sexual responsiveness. Some experts have suggested that the "out-of-phase" sexual interest on the part of men and women creates sexual problems for middle-aged couples. In our experience in counseling such couples, this is sometimes the case; more often, however, it is not a problem. It actually may improve the couple's sex life in cases in which the husband had a higher interest in sex than his wife did previously.

All in all, the middle years seem to be given a high rating by those in this stage of life as well as by professionals who have studied this age group. From her series of studies of more than 2,000 middle-aged subjects, Neugarten has concluded:

> *Despite the new realization of the finiteness of time, one of the most prevailing themes expressed by middle-age respondents is that middle adulthood is the period of maximum capacity and ability to handle a highly complex environment and a highly differentiated self.*[17]

Middle-aged persons seem to sense a renewal of interest in self-fulfillment that may have been almost dormant during the child-rearing years. Men and women seek fulfillment differently during these years, however, and often this difference becomes the source of marital strains. Some men, sensing that their financial burdens have been lifted considerably, may want to relax a bit, enjoy their new freedom, and pull back somewhat from the stresses of the work world. Other men who are less well off may decide that they must work even harder to achieve their goals. Some may acknowledge that they have reached a peak occupationally and that no amount of extra effort will change things. Many men begin to take better care of their bodies—through exercise, diet, and rest—now that they have it made and the family is raised. Others give up and settle into a complacency that may be frustrating to their wives.[18]

Women, on the other hand, often use their new freedom to seek self-fulfillment in increased activity. They may go to school or begin a serious work commitment. Just as her husband hopes to enjoy the fruits of his years of labor, so the woman wants to pursue interests that may block some of his plans. Both reactions to middle age reflect a growing awareness of the time left to live and to accomplish the goals not yet met. It is as though the middle-aged person is saying, "I'm not old yet but I'm not getting any younger, so I'd better do the things I've had to postpone or it may be too late."

Many men and women make major job changes in their midlives, spend more time on personal pursuits that had previously been postponed, and show certain other changes that are evident to those who know them. For instance, a man who has typically worn three-piece suits and driven a conservative car may buy a sports car and opt for open-necked shirts and gold chains. One woman lost fifty pounds, bought a youthful wardrobe, and learned to fly an airplane. Childless couples also experience this confrontation with the aging process, but for those who have had children, the transition takes on the added dimension of the end of a great many responsibilities and restrictions to their freedom.

The impact of middle age varies with each individual's reaction to the aging process. For some there are specific stresses and strains that have to do with the realities of aging, with the departure of children, with the push for self-fulfillment, and with the need to take stock of relationships (the marriage in particular) that have changed because of the changed roles that men and women play at this life period.

In general, the so-called "mid-life crisis" period seems to have been considerably exaggerated. Most persons see it instead as a time of increasing freedom, new options for both sexes, and a chance for a more intimate marriage than was possible during the child-rearing years. This is not to say that there are not doubts about aging, some regrets about missed opportunity, and the need for considerable readjustment to changed roles.

Summary

■ The older population in the United States has grown rapidly since 1900. Improved diet and health care and the decrease in childhood mortality have allowed more people to survive to old age.

■ A positive view of aging has been missing in our society. Instead, research and literature have concentrated on *problems* of aging such as poor health, poverty, loneliness, and impending death. Problems do exist, of course, but there are also millions of elderly persons living satisfying and productive lives.

■ There are many more elderly women than men. For this reason, much of the research has concentrated on women—particularly widows—who often live at the poverty level and are lonely. Most women over sixty-five who ever worked for pay at all were in the labor force for too short a time to earn pensions. Today, however, as more women are employed full time, it is likely that the poverty of elderly women will be eased somewhat.

■ Research indicates that adjustment to old age is determined in important ways by adjustment in middle age. The "empty nest" following the departure of children affects both men and women, but for women who have been homemakers, it raises the question of a mid-life "career" change. Men, on the other hand, usually have a continuous work history and do not face the question of "what to do now" until retirement.

■ The postparental years offer new freedom and allow husbands and wives to recreate the intimacy of their early childless years. Sexually, they are still active, although they undergo some sexual changes. Menopause is a landmark for women as they end their childbearing years. All in all, the middle years are generally given high marks by both family-life experts and those who are middle aged.

Grandparents

One of the most significant moments in the life of most middle-aged persons is that of becoming a grandparent. Margaret Mead expressed her wonder at this experience when she wrote:

> When the news came that Sevanne Margaret was born, I suddenly realized that through no act of my own I had become biologically related to a new

Margaret Mead and Her Grand-daughter

human being. I had never thought how strange it was to be involved at a distance in the birth of a biological descendant. The idea that as a grandparent one was dealing with action at a distance—that somewhere, miles away, a series of events occurred that changed one's status forever—I had not thought of that and I found it very odd.[19]

There is little research dealing with grandparenting, and what there is shows clearly that there is no agreement on a grandparent role. One family sociologist some years ago ventured to call grandparenthood a "roleless role."[20] One explanation for the variety of attitudes toward being grandparents lies in the fact that it is an event that occurs in middle age, when most grandparents are still busily engaged in their own pursuits. They do not fit the picture of the retired grandparents who have time to play with the children, go fishing, plant a garden, and feed the birds. The average man or woman in the United States first becomes a grandparent in his or her late forties or very early fifties.

It is the "old-old"—the great-grandparents—who may more closely resemble the stereotyped, beloved "gramps." Early studies on becoming grandparents emphasized how much more significant becoming a grandparent was for women and how men rarely became truly involved with their grandchildren until after retirement.[21]

As more and more women enter the labor force, the "new" grandparents may show little difference in involvement between men and women. With jobs claiming their time and energy until retirement, it is likely that grandparents will be classified into "young grandparents," who have little time for their grandchildren, and "retired grandparents," who will resemble the stereotype and who may also be great-grandparents. Since more four-generation families now exist than ever before, a new role of great-grandparent is coming into existence to fill the void created by the working grandmother.

Recent research on grandparents according to socioeconomic class indicates that in poorer families grandparents are more active with their grandchildren—especially grandmothers, who often are primary sources of child care for the grandchildren.[22] As we have noted, grandmothers have received more attention in the literature than grandfathers have, probably because, since women outlive men, there are more grandmothers. Also, women traditionally keep family ties alive and are likely to do the actual child care when grandchildren visit or come to live. A recent study of grandmothers categorized them into four types:

1. Seventeen percent of the grandmothers were somewhat older, usually widowed, and lonely. They saw their grandchildren as sources of company and aid and expected a great deal of contact.
2. About 28 percent of the grandmothers were concerned with doing what was right for the grandchildren and also with wanting to have a good relationship with them. These grandmothers were the most involved with their grandchildren—alternately spoiling them and being concerned with their manners and morals.
3. Another 28 percent of the grandmothers were remote and ritualistic in what little contact they had with their grandchildren (occasional visits and gifts, with most contact on holidays or birthdays).
4. About 26 percent were likely to be working (even more likely than the child's own mother was) and to be more involved in their marriages than any of the other women. They usually had strong ideas about family tradition and appropriate behavior. Their grandchildren were seen as extensions of the family tree and thus were thought to have certain roles to play. These grandmothers were usually busy in the community.[23]

Almost all grandparents actively enjoy their roles unless they feel burdened by having to reassume parental duties with their grandchildren. Even some who have this latter responsibility reportedly enjoy it. Grandfathers, who typically get more involved with their grandchildren after retirement, are often seen as teachers and as reservoirs of family wisdom. Grandfathers, like grandmothers, have different styles of grandparent behavior. Some are formal and leave parenting strictly to the parents. Others are informal and playful, totally enjoying the grandchildren. Another type is the distant figure who emerges infrequently and stays distant from the grandchildren. And there is the surrogate parent with whom the child may live or who takes over for an absent or ineffective parent.[24]

Most middle-aged parents enjoy becoming grandparents even though they may not always like to think of themselves as old enough for this to happen. Most of them remember their own grandparents as "old-old" and may be reluctant to put themselves in the grandparent category for fear their own

aging will miraculously speed up. The ways parents respond to becoming grandparents varies according to their personalities; their other satisfactions; and, of course, the relationships the new grandparents have with their grown children who are now parents.[25]

Retirement

Another fundamental role change that takes place as a part of the aging process is cause for what some experts term an "identity crisis." This change occurs upon retirement, which faces most workers and their spouses.

Retirement usually occurs between ages sixty and seventy and is often compulsory. Those who are self-employed do not have to face the mandatory retirement enforced by business and industry. There is the option of retiring gradually rather than with an unsettling suddenness. Nonetheless, when the chronological age for "old" is tied to retirement, even those who are still working at sixty-five or seventy may begin to judge themselves by Social Security standards.

Few issues have aroused as much controversy in the field of gerontology as the requirement that people who still want to work must retire from their jobs.[26] Some companies sponsor preretirement workshops to aid in preparation for what usually means a radical change in lifetime habits. Usually, however, men and women are left to deal with the impact on their own. Retirement is a complex phenomenon that can be very stressful because it requires a person to relinquish a meaningful status and, perhaps equally important, to accept a lower income. Of course, not everyone is sorry to retire; many workers look forward to retirement and plan for the enjoyment of more leisure.

The average life expectancy at age sixty-five is now 13.9 years for men and 18.3 for women, although it is predicted that by the year 2000, the average number of years following retirement will have risen considerably unless the age of retirement is raised. Since women on the average outlive men and also typically marry men older than they, they have a much longer life expectancy than their husbands after both retire. At present there are some twenty-one million men and women over the age of sixty-five who are classified as retired.[27]

Retirement is generally viewed as the milestone that marks the end of middle age and the entry into old age. In a review of studies on factors involved in retirement, the following five areas were identified.[28]

1. *Loss of finances:* Eighty percent of retired persons depend solely on Social Security benefits, with annual incomes of less that $6,000 (1976 figures). This is perhaps the biggest adjustment that retirement brings. In a recent survey more than half of those over sixty years of age reported that they were living only a "hand-to-mouth" existence, and 70 percent reported being very depressed about the effect of inflation on their retirement incomes. Three-quarters reported eating nutritiously, however, and over half were optimistic despite their hardships.[29]

Of those who are fortunate enough to have adequate income, retirement is often welcomed and enjoyed as a time to travel and to pursue hobbies or other avocations that have been put off until this time. Experts report that, by and large, most people retire just as soon as they have enough financial security to do so. Those who choose to work the longest are either those who cannot afford to retire or those who have absorbing work that they can do as long as they choose.

Current research has shown that responses to old age may be as crucially determined by social class and income as by any other factor. The higher the social class and the more resources the older person has, the more likely he or she is to view old age in terms of leisure, relaxation, and security. The less fortunate regard old age instead as a time of physical decline, lowered standard of living, and unhappiness.[30]

2. *Loss of self-esteem:* The role of productive worker is the equivalent of identity and status for many men and women. When they no longer feel useful and needed, they may lose a sense of self-worth. The exception seems to be the man or woman who is well off financially. Having money somehow acts as a symbol that "I was a success." Research findings are not uniform about the effects of retirement on self-esteem, but most agree that it depends on how comfortable the older person feels about life up to that point. If the retired person believes that he or she has been as successful as anticipated and has something to show for all the effort, self-esteem appears to suffer less.

3. *Loss of work-oriented social contacts:* Retirees often report missing the people with whom they interacted daily. Women who retire have been shown to take longer than men do to adjust and to get over their lonely feelings.[31] Many retired persons drop out of social organizations because of finances and have trouble finding new avenues to make friends.

4. *Loss of meaningful tasks:* As one observer of retirement puts it, "Marriages which have been stable for years can be shaken by a husband with retirement fidgets. On the simplest level, a great part of a man's adjustment to retirement involves filling the gap provided by the work situation."[32] Women feel this loss too. Some find homemaking waiting to keep them busy, although our preliminary research on aging couples is showing that women who have had busy careers often are not interested in resuming homemaking. They feel just as much of a sense of loss of meaningful tasks as men do—sometimes more. If both spouses are employed, the chances are very high that the husband (who is usually older) will retire sooner than his wife does. In couples whom we have interviewed, there is often a difficult transition as husbands pick up the domestic tasks while wives go to work each day. Should the husbands fail to do so, other kinds of problems result because wives often feel that they are carrying the greater burden. One of the major tasks of retirement seems to be to develop rewarding activities to replace work or to find new work to do. However, the activities need to please both partners rather than just the retired one.

5. *Loss of reference group:* Many workers—especially men—identify themselves by their work. It has been a way of life for them for all of their adult years. They now must adjust from having others think of them and refer to them as doctors, lawyers, teachers, contractors, plumbers, or bankers to being identified as retired (or simply old) persons. As more and more women have lifelong work roles, this will become an issue for them as well. A loss of identity with one's occupational status is often mentioned by those who say they would continue working after age sixty-five, if given the opportunity.

A recent study of the effect of retirement on morale of blacks, Mexican-Americans, and whites revealed that although morale is lower generally for all retired persons than for those who are still working, morale is based on so many factors that ceasing to work itself often is not the biggest issue.[33] Fifteen measures of morale were used to discover that there were significant differences in which factors affected morale in each of the three populations. Retired black men differed significantly from working black men in feeling less useful and in having less pep. On thirteen other measures there was very little difference between the two black categories. Neither feeling useful nor loss of pep was significantly related to age or status of the man's health, although lowered income was definitely related to feelings of usefulness (but not related to pep).

Retired white men differed significantly from working white men on three measures of morale: feeling lonely, getting upset easily, and feeling less useful. Mexican-American retired men had significant differences from Mexican-American working men on twelve of the fifteen measures of morale, with both income and health status related to their low morale. They were more apt to feel sad, to feel that life wasn't worth living, to worry so much that they could not sleep, to feel lonely, to get upset easily, to feel that things kept getting worse, to have little pep, to feel less useful, to feel that life was hard, to be unhappy, to believe things were worse than they had expected them to be, and not to foresee that they would be any happier in the future.

Retired black women also generally reported lower morale than did working black women. The primary factors in their low morale were worrying so much they could not sleep and not being happy. White women seemed primarily bothered that life was so hard after retirement. The lower morale expressed by Mexican-American retired women was related to five basic factors. They worried so that they could not sleep, felt afraid, got upset easily, were unhappy, and reported that each of these got progressively worse with age.

In all cases the study revealed that low income (as the result of not working) rather than loss of the worker role seemed to be at the root of the lower morale. Morale had rather different meanings across ethnic and sex groups, as the factors indicate. The feelings expressed by a retired black man, for instance, were not the same as those expressed by a retired Mexican-American man or by a black woman or a white woman.

Retirement, then, seems to be a matter of morale, of income, of health, and of family support. Not all members of the elderly population have resources in the same areas. Some have better health than others, for instance, but others have more money. The interrelationships between the areas of resources are complex. In his report on older persons in the United States, family expert Gordon Streib has examined five types of older families in terms of their major resources.

- *Type I:* "The golden sunset family" has all four necessary resources: good physical health, good emotional health, adequate economic resources, and good social resources.

- *Type II:* Those who are physically incapacitated but who are emotionally stable, have financial security, and who have family and friends for support make up this category.

- *Type III:* These are older persons who are both physically and emotionally unhealthy, but who have enough money and family resources to take care of themselves.

- *Type IV:* This type includes those who have only family to care for them. They are in poor physical and emotional health and have no money.

- *Type V:* This type is "the totally deprived family," who end their years in misery. These are the families that present the most serious problems in old age because many of them lack any of the four important resources.[34]

There are many other combinations of resources as well, but these five were found to be the most common for retirement adjustment.

Retirement, which releases men and women from their work roles, causes some older persons to disengage from other roles as well. The **theory of disengagement**, which was developed to explain why some persons withdraw, become preoccupied with themselves, and alter their relationships with others, has given insight into life experiences of the elderly.[35] From this research and that of the theory's critics, it is possible to conclude that for those who do disengage, it is not always a negative experience. For many, in fact, it is not a new or sudden adjustment process at all but, rather, a continuation of a lifestyle that had been one of modified withdrawal in earlier years. Such persons may enjoy a time for reflection and the opportunity to be less invested in others and in life's demands.[36] It has been proposed, however, that on the whole older men and women who remain active and who do not withdraw from the social system are essentially happier and better adjusted.[37]

Summary

■ Becoming grandparents is a significant milestone marking middle age. Most first-time grandparents are in their forties or fifties and do not match the stereotype of the retired, gray-haired person in a rocking chair. There is no grandparent role that suits all men and women.

■ Grandmothers have received more attention by family experts because there are more of them as a result of predominance of older women and also because women traditionally have been the ones to keep family ties alive. Grandmothers are not all alike by any means, but most report enjoying their grandchildren.

■ Grandfathers typically get more involved with their grandchildren after retirement and when the grandchildren are older. They, too, have varying styles of grandparenting but are often seen as teachers and as the reservoirs of family wisdom.

■ Retirement has been called an identity crisis. It is usually compulsory between the ages of sixty-five and seventy. Many workers still have good years left (over fifteen on the average) and it is predicted that, by the year 2000, this will increase by ten more years. At present, there are some twenty-one million retired persons in the United States.

■ The necessary adjustments to retirement seem to be greatest in the areas of income, morale, health, and social contacts. Those who are well off financially seem to fare the best. Many people retire as soon as they have the financial security to do so, but mandatory retirement unfortunately forces most persons to retire without such security.

■ Aside from finances and health, one of the major problems facing retirees is the need to develop rewarding activities to replace work. Those who stay "engaged" in work, community, and with family and friends seem to make better adjustments than do those who "disengage."

Old People and Their Families

Research indicates that most old people have a great deal of contact with family members—particularly their children—and about 8 percent of them have one or more children who provide significant social and psychological support. Furthermore, those children who do not live nearby usually keep in touch by telephone and by mail to keep their family bonds intact. Shanas has proposed that "socio-emotional distance" is a more significant factor in the closeness of adults and their parents than is geographical distance. Siblings of older men and women also are important, particularly when the older person has no children.[38]

In an article discussing the strength of family bonds, it was suggested that family relations are stronger and more durable than friendships because they are characterized by obligation rather than only by shared interests.[39] It is interesting to note that although family support has been shown to be one of the most important variables in how well older people adjust, older persons' adjustments toward aging, their health, their finances, and their living environment also influenced how well they got along with their children. It may not be easy, therefore, to distinguish cause and effect—the parents' adjustment causes a better relationship with their children, and a good relationship with their children facilitates the older persons' good adjustment.[40]

In his study of grandparents, parents, and their young married children, Hill reported that the grandparents received assistance from the other two generations, although some support and exchange of resources went to and from each generation.[41]

In a study of older married couples in the 1970s, it was found that those who had more extensive interaction with their grown children seemed more satisfied with their lives. However, this did not hold if they lived in the same household with them. It appears that being dependent on children is detrimental to morale of the elderly. Not only do many older persons feel demeaned by dependency on their adult children, but the children also often feel the strain of stretching their energy and income to help their parents. This stress spills over into their feelings for their parents, and many report developing negative feelings about their aging, dependent parents.[42]

This same research focused on the importance of an intact marriage to the adjustment of older persons. Eighty percent of all men over sixty-five and 50 percent of all women over that age are living with their spouses.[43] Since the average couple marrying today can expect to live to be over seventy years of age, they have a very good chance to have a marriage that lasts fifty years. We have become particularly interested in couples who have been married for more than fifty years. Of course, most of the couples we have interviewed have had one marriage that has lasted this long. However, we believe that there will be many second marriages that also will last for fifty or more years. Growing numbers of couples are celebrating sixtieth and even seventieth anniversaries.

Older Marriages

To date the world's record for length of marriage is held by a Bombay, India, couple married eighty-six years. Death ended their marriage in 1939. They had been betrothed as children. In England a couple were married seventy-eight years; in the United States, the record is eighty-three years.[44] In 1980 a California couple celebrated their seventy-first anniversary when they were ninety-four and ninety-one years of age respectively. They celebrated by going out to

dinner with their children, who are seventy and sixty—themselves "senior citizens." What is their advice to others who want their marriages to last?

> *"Don't stop on little things," says Mrs. R. "Be satisfied whatever happens. Ben didn't commit adultery, he's not a gambler, not a liar. . . ."*
>
> *"And not a drunk," adds Ben.*
>
> *"So what is there to complain about?" she concludes. Mr. R's advice is to "tell the truth. The main thing is to be honest. That way you have nothing to hide."* [45]

In a study of couples all of whom had been married over fifty years and whose average age was seventy-nine, all of them described their marriages as happy, and 93 percent said they would marry the same persons if they had to do it over again. [46]

There has been relatively little research on marriages in the later years—particularly those that have lasted more than fifty years. We have been intrigued by the few studies that have been done, however, because we live in a community that has a large retirement population. Our interest has been piqued by marriage in the later years as we have observed many couples who have been together for over half a century.

From the studies that have been done, we have learned that couples who have been married to each other for longer than fifty years generally report that it has been a very positive experience. [47,48] This is not surprising: we might expect that if living together for that long were not generally positive, the marriage would have ended (or at least, that it would be difficult to admit they had spent so many years unhappily).

It may also be that when couples are asked to look back over their lives together, there is a tendency to idealize the way it was or to convince themselves that since they did stay married all those years, it must have been generally positive. **Cognitive dissonance theory** would explain this phenomenon as the tendency to value something in direct proportion to how much one has invested in it. In a discussion of this theory as it applies to marital satisfaction over the life cycle, it has been proposed that by investing years of one's life in a relationship—time, emotion, energy, resources—and sharing so many of life's experiences together, older married persons may have a tendency to over-emphasize how good it has been and how satisfied they are.[49]

One exception to the reports of happiness of over-fifty-year marriages was a study recently reported by Friedman and Todd from interviews with couples who were married before 1930. These researchers found that many of the couples did not report satisfaction with their married years. In fact, many spoke of "surviving" but being disappointed that their expectations for marriage had not been met. The researchers reported that by current standards, they probably would have counseled divorce for many of the couples interviewed. The couples, however, reported that divorce was never an option for them since "it was not done."[50] Since couples who have married more recently do consider divorce an option, perhaps those who celebrate golden wedding anniversaries in the future will report even more satisfaction, since they will have stayed in the relationship by choice.

Why the couples in the Friedman and Todd sample seem at odds with the other couples interviewed is an interesting question. The couples were drawn from California and Israel, but we resist the notion that old people in California and Israel are so different from old people in general. Perhaps the explanation lies in the fact that the interviewers drew a different kind of sample or asked for different kinds of information from that requested by others who have done similar research, or that they interpreted the data differently from others.

The Friedman-Todd study began by asking couples who have been married over forty-five years for advice about what it takes to be happily married. The couples could not come up with any formula. They did report that they had worked out rules by which to share their lives that helped the marriage to continue. Both power and intimacy were related to their happiness. The spouses with the higher power were significantly happier than those with lower power.

Four patterns of power distribution were identified by Friedman and Todd: (1) *traditional*, in which the husband had more power; (2) *reversed*, in which the wife had more power; (3) *equal-high*, in which both received high power ratings; and (4) *equal-low*, in which both received low ratings. Husbands were happier in the traditional pattern, wives in the reversed pattern. Couples in the equal-high category both reported happiness, and couples in the equal-low category were the least happy.

For those old couples in the Friedman-Todd study who had lower power orientations, intimacy was the most significant factor in happiness. For spouses with high power, the importance of intimacy for happiness was diminished. Being happy, however, was not nearly as important for these couples as surviving in what they saw as a troubled world. It appears that the reports of dissatisfaction may have been more reflective of the older couples' reactions to their lives in general than to their marriages.

In a recent critique of research on marital satisfaction over the life cycle, one of the points made was that marital adjustment may actually be more closely related to individual partners' adjustments to life than to adjustments specific to their marriages.[51] It may well be, then, that marital adjustment in later years is a reflection of general well-being and life adjustment that allows partners to enjoy each other and to adjust to life together.

Marriages perceived as satisfactory in later years are also almost always perceived as having been satisfactory from the beginning. This finding is not surprising, of course, since satisfactory marriages should be expected to endure longer than unsatisfactory ones. Also, though not impossible, it is unlikely that a bad marriage in early years will turn into a really good marriage in later life. If, as many experts believe, well-adjusted individuals are more likely to report satisfying marriages, then these same individuals are likely to be more satisfied than the average person at any time in the marital life cycle. This is not to deny, however, that good marital adjustment contributes significantly to good personal adjustment in old age in a majority of cases, and love and companionship are reported to be valuable as contributors to morale.[52]

From other research on older persons' marriages we learn that even though most older couples consider their current marriage relationships to be as good as in their early years, lower-income couples report that their marital satisfaction has declined. They also report less satisfaction with life, more loneliness, and more worry. Again we see that low income has a damaging effect on the quality of life for older persons, which seriously affects their morale and their satisfaction in life, including marital satisfaction.[53]

Our own study of couples who have been married for over fifty years has tried to take into consideration the fact that not everything in any long-term marriage can be wonderful and satisfying. After all, these couples have been married through one major world war (perhaps two) and a severe economic depression. They are currently retired at a time when their incomes are being eaten away by inflation. These couples are special because both have survived (as have their marriages) to a record age for the United States. There are now hundreds of thousands of such couples, so that they are no longer quite the novelty that they were only a generation or two back.

We have been interested primarily in how couples (and their children and grandchildren) assess their marriages now and remember them from the past. This assessment includes satisfaction levels, communication roles, social adjustment as a couple, decision making, and sexual adjustment. We have attempted to adjust for selective recall, which is always a problem in attempting to remember the past. Family sociologist Reuben Hill has addressed this very point and believes that the longer ago the time period that is being recalled, the less trustworthy the memory. Hill said:

> *Certain behaviors simply may not be elicited back in time for such respondents: marital happiness, marital communication, value consensus, authority patterns and allocation of roles, parent-child and sibling-sibling relationships. On the other hand, from our Minnesota study, we have found residential histories, job histories, automobile and durable goods purchases, and family composition histories not impossible to obtain from our most aged respondents.*[54]

It appears that the very issues that are the most relevant in studying long-term marriages are also the ones subject to the most selective recall. We have come to believe that selective recall is one of the major reasons that most studies have found that older couples view their marital histories as positively as they do. To avoid the bias of selective recall as much as possible, studying couples from the beginning to the end of their lives together (a longitudinal study) may seem the only promising solution. However, since such a project would take over fifty years, it is not a practical undertaking for researchers, who may not complete their training until age thirty and who probably must retire at age sixty-five.

A number of family sociologists have been interested in methods to correct for selective recall, and various methodologies have been tried.[55] From the possible plans for research, we chose one that involves the children and the grandchildren of the couples we interviewed. Although we recognize that they, too, have selective recall as well as different perspectives from which they view life events, they have provided some checks on facts that we would not have had otherwise. In addition, when there were discrepancies, often one generation helped the others to correct their memories. Another bonus was that more information was made available because what one had forgotten, the others often remembered.

Marriages that last into postretirement years, although clearly not representative of marriages in general, are almost as varied in nature as marriages at any other time in the life cycle. However, there are two intractable facts about the life and marriage situation of older married people that do make them unique. Psychologist Clifford Swensen, who has done extensive research into the lives of retired men and women, says that the two differences are that "they have the time and opportunity to explore the joys and complexities of an intimate relationship with each other; [and] their time is limited."[56] These two factors give an urgency to their lives, since they know they cannot live forever, but also give them time to be together as a couple. For some men and women being together seems to be their paramount interest, and they grow closer with each passing day. Such couples have been called "golden sunset" couples as they walk hand in hand into the sunset. On the other hand, some older couples seem preoccupied with the feeling that time is running out. The ways couples cope with both of these factors seem to be an important factor in adjustment in later life.

Swensen concludes that when couples readjust their lives in the post-parental years, they do so with the same set of skills they have used to face other problems and to cope with other adjustments in the past. Patterns of coping skills are seen to be directly related to the level of personal maturity the partners have reached.

Swensen's research relied heavily on the conceptualization of the stages of ego development devised by Jan Loevinger, who proposed that personality is organized from the simple state of the infant to the highly integrated and complex state of an adult.[57] Loevinger proposed six stages, with transition levels between the fourth, fifth, and sixth levels. The first three stages are not of great concern to the study of retired persons because none of Swensen's respondents were still at these levels of maturity [(1) presocial, (2) impulsive, and (3) self-protective]. The last three stages plus the three transition stages, however, are important for understanding the adjustment of older men and women. Those in Swensen's study fell largely between the fourth (conformist) and the fifth (autonomous) states:

- *Stage 4.* Conformist: Believed to be the developmental level of most adults. Their concern is with doing what everyone else does, following the rules, and working for the approval of others.

- *Transition level A.* A greater self-awareness begins to take over. People at this stage still are conforming, but they often have reservations about what they are doing.

- *Transition level B.* Concern becomes more with personal values than with what others think. Conformity is still the rule, but more behavior is personally motivated.

- *Transition level C.* A much greater emphasis is placed on individuality, and there is a growing awareness of inner conflict between what others expect and what personal needs are.

- *Stage 5.* Autonomous state: Those who reach this level have an appreciation for their own and others' individuality. They cope with inner conflicts by recognizing and accepting the fact that everyone is unique and that there are several possible solutions to any given situation.

- *Stage 6.* Integrated state: This is the most complex and highly integrative state, in which one's sense of identity is accepted and consolidated.

Swensen applies these levels to the adjustment patterns of the aging population. When retirement comes, he says:

. . . for the first time in many years, the couple finds an opportunity to interact with each other as people without the disruption of others and they begin to realize the changes that have taken place within themselves and each other. The husband and wife have been doing different things. Their approach toward autonomy, or post conformity, has been by different paths—each has a job, or the husband has been so engrossed in his job that the wife has had to cope virtually alone with everything else in their lives, or there have been intrusive in-laws. In any case, renewed acquaintance for these intimate strangers may be frightening.

. . . there are several ways people can handle this. The most common way is to avoid the issue. I think this is what the typical conformist level couple does, so there is continued decline. They're stuck in a rut that they can't get out of and it's too disruptive to try. That's what happens in 50 to 60 percent of the cases.

The post conformist people, I think, face it, deal with it, and resolve it. That's where you get an increase in love expression and transcending of sex roles, the development of a relationship that uniquely fits each couple. Disagreements are rather interesting when there is that basic bond underneath for resolving them.[58]

Marital adjustment in later years and level of ego development are thought by Swensen to be closely tied together. None of his couples were more than a one-half level apart in ego development. Had they been, he believes they would have been living in "completely different worlds."

This research points up what may be the basis for differential findings in the quality of marriages of older persons. The 50 to 60 percent who are still at the conformist stage of ego development would be expected to touch on each other's lives in a way that follows the rules for living that they have always followed. Their satisfactions may come largely from interaction with their children, other relatives, and friends. For the other 40 to 50 percent, the post-conformist couples, there is the ability to go beyond established roles and to see and appreciate themselves and their partners as individuals. This may well account for the couples who report that marriage is better than ever and who have more intimacy as a couple in their postretirement years.

It is as though roughly half of older married couples see marriage as a given state in their lives that they have made work because it was expected of them or because they felt they had no choice. They are happy enough being married if they have good health, adequate income, and frequent contact with family and friends. If not, they are likely to report disappointment and a belief that marriage was one more ordeal of life that they have survived (as in the Friedman-Todd study).

The other half report greater rewards in their marriages. They seem to appreciate and enjoy life within the partnership increasingly as the years go by. They are very aware of the limited time left to them as a couple and want to make the most of it. One of the couples we interviewed, a retired United States Army general and his wife who have traveled the world, told us that they have never been happier and closer to each other in all their fifty years of marriage than they are now. The general said:

> *We have been everywhere, seen everything, and now we have time to hold hands and watch a sunset. There is an old story told of natives in India who could retire happily to their villages once they had gone out to see what lay between them and the next village. They often reported that they were happy now that they "had seen the elephant." Well, we have seen the elephant and we are considerably satisfied just to be together at home.*[59]

For the couples still in a marriage after fifty years, harmonious relationships seem to be a significant factor in successful aging. They often reminisce about past experiences and reflect on how their lives have progressed. This makes talking to older men and women a rich and rewarding experience. There is the ever present knowledge that each day is precious, since time may be limited. Although worries about one member's surviving the other may be on the couples' minds, for the most part the elderly seem less afraid of death than do younger people.[60] Perhaps it follows that if one has had a full and satisfying life, death has a meaning far different from that held by young people who have yet to experience most of the good things they hope life will hold— marriage, children, and satisfying work and friendships.

Older Remarried Couples

Of the nearly seven million married persons who are over sixty-five years of age, not all are in first marriages. Many have remarried after a divorce or after being widowed. A discussion of those who remarry after the age of sixty gives insight into a special aspect of aging in the United States. The number of older remarried persons has been growing as our aged population increases.

One hundred couples who married after the bride was past sixty years old were studied by McKain four to six years after their weddings. Certain factors were shown to be closely related to the success of these marriages:

1. The bride and groom had known each other for a long period of time.
2. The marriage was approved by their children and friends.
3. Both partners had adjusted well to other facets of retirement and aging.
4. The couple disposed of previously owned property and bought or rented a home for themselves.
5. There was sufficient income to live without economic hardship.[61]

McKain found a high degree of success in the remarriages. Seventy-four of the one hundred were judged to be successful on a five-factor scale (showing respect and affection for each other; enjoying each other's company; no serious complaints from either partner; partners were proud of each other; and they were considerate of each other).

Sex and the Older Person

There is no shortage of literature about the sexual behavior of the older population. There are many times more articles and books on the sex lives of older
persons than on marriages of persons over sixty-five. There is not a great deal
of scientific research on sexuality in old age, however, possibly because asking
older people what they actually do may have been a somewhat sensitive area
for younger researchers. The studies that exist report that most couples over
sixty-five are sexually active. There appears to be no cut-off age for sexual
desire and ability.[62] An enjoyable comment on this topic is reported by social
psychologist Carol Tavris, who received this letter:

> I am sixty years old and they say you never get too old to enjoy sex. I know,
> because once I asked my Grandma when you stop liking it and she was eighty.
> She said "child, you'll have to ask someone older than me."[63]

Yet the myth persists that older folks are no longer interested in sex. In our
practice we often encounter clients who wonder aloud if they are too old for sex
or who feel uneasy admitting their enjoyment of it. However, older persons are
often more comfortable about their sexuality than their children and grandchildren are about recognizing that the older couples are still sexually active.

Sexologist Sally Schumacher told a retirement group that "sexual activity
can help keep you young; it is a normal function to be enjoyed at any age, if
one is in reasonably good health. In fact, one cause of poor health among the
elderly is despondency resulting from a loss of interest in life. They feel that
everything of value, including physical love, is over for them. So they let themselves wither away."[64]

Our experience has been that older persons' perceptions of being sexually
active may not match what younger men and women use for criteria. We have
found much less emphasis on sexual intercourse and orgasms among our older
respondents and far more importance given to other forms of sexual expression. This does not mean that sexual intercourse is not an important part of the
sex lives of the elderly but, rather, that other sexual behaviors satisfy many of
their needs.

For the most part, those couples who reported greater activity and enjoyment in their earlier sex lives were the ones who remained the most active
sexually in their older years. Good health, energy, and physical activity are
much more evident in the current aged population than they were in previous
decades. A man or woman of seventy-five today may have sexual vigor and
interest on a level with that found only in much younger persons in 1900.
Although today's older persons may be less sexually active than they were at
thirty-five or even fifty-five, they are far from having reached the end of their
sexual lives.

Loneliness and the Elderly Single Person

There are approximately twelve million persons over sixty-five who are not married. The bulk of them are divorced or widowed (since less than 6 percent of the population never marry). There are four times as many women as men in this category—a plurality of approximately seven million women. Most of the research on aging single persons has centered on women and has found that loneliness is very commonly a problem.[65]

One study of over four hundred elderly widows in a rural area of South Carolina found that loneliness was tied more closely to unavailability of friends and "neighboring" than to lack of family involvement. Friends and neighbors provided avenues for daily activities such as meetings, shopping, or visiting.[66] The importance placed on friends and neighbors has its own problems, however. One of our widowed friends who is eighty-five remarks frequently that she has outlived most of her friends and that many of those remaining cannot be relied on because of their unpredictable health problems.

Another study of older rural widows also showed that social circumstances weighed the most heavily in determining whether or not loneliness was a problem. The basic element of social contact that determined loneliness was the quality rather than the number of such contacts.[67]

A widow's ability to adjust to her role as widow and to adapt her relationships accordingly may be closely related to Loevinger's level of ego development. Adjustment may also hinge on the widow's conception of her role in life. If she has seen herself primarily as a wife, the loss of this status may be more traumatic for her than for a woman who has other sources of identity—such as work—to give continuity and meaning to her life.

Other studies point to the impact of physical and mental health on whether or not the elderly are lonely. Several studies have shown that real or perceived poor health is an important factor in emotional and social withdrawal.[68]

Research on adjustment and loneliness of elderly single persons has revealed the importance of adequate transportation in facilitating their social involvement. Inability to drive, lack of access to a car, and the general unavailability of public transportation are often cited as major factors contributing to loneliness.[69]

Loneliness seems to be determined to a large extent by where and with whom the older person lives. It has been estimated that between 80 and 90 percent of an elderly person's time is spent at home. Retired persons seem to like to stay in their own homes even when they must live alone, as widows and widowers often do. Two-thirds of those over sixty-five own their own residences, and an overwhelming majority like living where they do, even though this may contribute to their loneliness.[70] There seems to be something comforting about being in familiar surroundings. In addition, many of those we have interviewed feel that once they give up their own homes, they will give up their autonomy, and they dislike the thought of being dependent.

Approximately 40 percent of the elderly live in older working-class areas near central cities. Nearly 35 percent live in the inner cities, and 25 percent live in rural areas.[71] Mobile homes often are favored by those who choose to leave a larger family home, while a few live in senior citizen apartment houses or hotels. For those who desire to stay in their own homes even after they are unable to care for themselves fully, having some form of home care is one possibility. This option is not without problems, however, because of the difficulty of finding and affording competent help. There are various services available to the elderly, such as visiting nurses, Meals on Wheels, volunteer drivers, and so forth; but coordinating the multiple services may be more than the old person can manage. As aging progresses, living independently in one's own home becomes increasingly problematic. When the decision is made to move, one of three alternatives is open—to live with a grown child or with other relatives or close friends, to move to a retirement community, or to enter a nursing home.

Retirement communities in various forms have attempted to meet the needs of the elderly. They have been particularly successful in dispelling loneliness since they facilitate social involvement. Often they also provide transportation, medical care, and readily accessible services and shopping.

Most elderly persons prefer the retirement community as a residence over a nursing home or a relative's or friend's home. Living with children connotes dependence, and children often cannot be relied on for a variety of reasons. Living with others is of growing interest as a possible solution for those who cannot or do not want to live alone. Sharing a home may meet the needs of many older persons who can help each other and provide needed companionship as well. In a study of a program called Share-a-Home it was reported that older persons form "families" not unlike natural families and that this does provide a viable alternative for the elderly.[72]

Institutional care seems to be a last choice for most older persons. Nonetheless, some 4 percent of the twenty-one million persons over sixty-five are in some kind of health care facility, including over 14 percent of those aged eighty-five and over.[73] Although many older persons need such care, the **nursing home** is usually viewed as "a place to go to die," as one elderly man told us. In a survey of the elderly in Southern California, it was determined that no matter how old, in what fragile health, and how poor they were, nearly all the respondents said they would not consider trading their personal independence for the relative security of a nursing home.[74]

A recent study, however, has looked at the positive aspects of institutional living and has soundly criticized the notion that institutional care exists only for the benefit of children who fail to support their elderly parents. The study found, for example, that in many instances the contact and support from adults to their aging parents increased after the parents went to a health care facility.

Many stresses and pressures on the grown children were relieved just by knowing that their parents were settled and receiving good care that could not be provided by any other means.[75]

Research findings are nearly uniform in demonstrating high satisfaction among those who have chosen to live in retirement communities. Their morale is higher, they enjoy more informal social contacts, and there is a decrease in withdrawal from life such as the phenomenon of *disengagement* discussed earlier.[76] Retirement communities first began in the warm climates of California, Florida, and Arizona; these states continue to be favorites of older persons who want to escape harsh winter weather. Such communities are generally located near stores and transportation, and many older persons enjoy the protected atmosphere with its absence of children, traffic, and crime. Medical care, recreational opportunities, and other services may make life easier for those whose energies may be waning.

Yet all older men and women are not the same, and some dislike the age segregation that a retirement community imposes. A study of black aged persons, for instance, found that twice as many of them as whites lived with relatives. They often helped the younger family members with child care and were quite likely to take their children and grandchildren into their own homes.[77] There seems to be no one formula that will suit every wish. There is a great need for research on types of living arrangements suitable for those who cannot maintain themselves independently but who do not need twenty-four-hour nursing home care either.

Much has been written about aging gracefully and about what factors go into the manner in which the crisis of aging is met. Most experts agree that being able to look back over one's life and believe that it was worth all the effort is the key. To feel content and at peace with the meaning of life has been described as a **developmental task** of the later years.[78] Gerontologists have noted the strong tendency most older persons have to be autobiographical. They may relive past experiences and do a mental "life review." Even their dreams are often of the past, and they enjoy talking about the good old days.[79]

One of the respondents in our study of fifty-year marriages told us her formula for making peace with her life and acknowledging that she had left a legacy:

> If you have planted a tree, built a house, written a book, and had a child, you have left the world a different place because you have lived. I have done them all and it feels good.[80]

Summary

■ As men and women begin their postretirement years, the support they give each other and receive from other family members seems to alleviate much of the stress caused by their transition. Most older persons maintain close relationships with their adult children and grandchildren.

■ Well over half of all men and women over sixty-five are married—many of them for over fifty years to a first spouse. Most research concludes that these marriages are satisfying and contribute to good adjustment in aging. For the most part, those marriages perceived as good in later years were also perceived as good from the beginning.

■ It is possible that good marital adjustment in later years is a factor of the personal adjustments of the husbands and wives. Those who have adjusted well to circumstances over a lifetime may be better able to use the increased time together during retirement to develop a new level of intimacy.

■ Most of the couples over sixty-five are still sexually active, although their criteria for satisfying sex may be different from what they were when they were younger. For the most part, those who are sexually active as older men and women report that they were active when they were younger as well.

■ Many older persons are single, and these are predominantly women who have been widowed. Poverty and loneliness seem to be their greatest problems. Loneliness is determined to a large extent by where and with whom the older persons live. Retired persons generally like to stay in their own homes even if they must live alone. However, this often cuts them off from social networks and increases their loneliness.

■ Relocating can be stressful for the older person. Living with their children does not suit many, although, of course, there are those who enjoy such a life. Institutionalization is closely correlated with poor health and inability to cope alone. For this reason, it is low in desirability for most older people. Retirement communities seem to be a favored relocation for many, although some do not like the age segregation that characterizes them.

Glossary

Cognitive dissonance theory   A social-psychological theory that holds that changes in attitudes or behaviors result from the effort to resolve conflicting perceptions.

Developmental tasks   Achievements or abilities that are expected to be accomplished at a given chronological age.

Empty-nest syndrome   A term used to describe the emotional problems experienced by some parents, usually mothers, when all their children have grown up and left home.

Gerontology   The study of aging and the elderly.

Menopause   Cessation of the menstrual cycle as a result of aging.

Nursing home   A medical care facility for those who need custodial and maintenance care for an extended period of time.

Theory of disengagement   A theory that postulates that the appropriate adjustment to aging is to withdraw from activities and relationships.

Appendix A •

Sexual Anatomy and Physiology

By the time they are old enough to start to school, nearly all children know what a penis looks like. Those who have not seen one in real life will have seen penises in photographs or in works of art of one sort or another. Because small children are likely to comprehend the penis only as an organ for urination, the value attached to its construction by either sex may be that it gives boys more (and sometimes better) options for locations and postures for urinating. This conceptualization may persist for a long time without serious critical review of its validity or implications. It may be years before the distinctive differences in construction between the male and female sex organs are understood to have the function of making reproduction of the species likely by making coitus highly pleasurable.

In contrast with the penis, female sex organs are much less likely to have been seen either in real life or in art by children of either sex. Sculpture and paintings typically conceal or omit altogether the genital cleft. In fact, in contemporary American society females of all ages are likely to see breasts as the sexually attractive features of women's bodies and to view their vulvas as serving excretory and reproductive functions.

This appendix is concerned, first, with the sex organs as they are experienced in real life and, second, with those glands, ducts, tubes, and other organs that are involved in sexual and reproductive behavior but are seldom seen or felt in day-to-day experiences.

Female Sex Organs

All that is likely to be exposed of the sex organs of a human female in ordinary postures or activities is the *genital cleft* in the *pubic mount* between her thighs. The cleft appears as a furrow or deep crease running from the pubic mount backward, usually appearing as continuous with the furrow between the buttocks in back.

The pubic mount (Latin: *mons veneris*) is a pad of soft tissue covering the forward part of the lower pelvis. At puberty, pubic hair begins to grow on the pubic mount, often concealing the genital cleft from view.

The soft tissue on either side of the genital cleft forms two smooth pillowy structures called the *large lips* (Latin: *labia majora*). When the large lips are spread apart, the vulva is made visible. Most women need the aid of a mirror to get an adequate view of their vulvas.

No two vulvas are quite alike.[1] Robert Rimmer has referred to vulvas as being as distinctive as faces.[2] Betty Dodson has drawn representations of the great variety.[3] The coloring of vulvas ranges from pale shell pink to deep plum and is independent of the race of the woman. Parts of the vulva change in color from time to time in response to both long- and short-term physiological changes. This change is quite normal and should be no cause for alarm.[4]

When the large lips of the vulva are parted, the most obvious structure visible is an inner mantle made up of a hood (*prepuce*) over the *clitoris* (the British colloquialism for which is "the little man in the boat," which seems decorous enough). The hood extends down and merges into the large lips just outside the two little lips (Latin: *labia minora*) that grow directly down from the clitoris.

The clitoris is usually, but not always, visible at its tip (*glans*); whether it is or not, its shaft can be felt through the hood as a small stem of erectile tissue. Like the nipples or the penis, it grows firm in response to gentle massage or erotic thoughts. The diameter of the clitoris when it is excited is usually no greater than that of a small birthday-cake candle. Only the glans can be seen; the shaft is completely covered by the hood. Sometimes only a small hole is visible at the top of the hood. In such a case the woman may wish to have this hole stretched so that the glans is visible and may be stimulated directly.

There is considerable variation in the reported sensitivity of the clitoris. For some women, direct contact with the glans is painful; others report that continued direct stimulation is the most pleasurable sensation they have ever felt. For most there is a range of pressure, rhythms, and moisture that provides varying degrees of pleasurable feelings, which change with the degree of sexual excitement being experienced at the moment. Because of these changing sensitivities, women who are unable to communicate their feelings and wishes to sexual partners may find that self-masturbation produces orgasms more readily than social sexual activities.

The structure, size, and coloring of the small inner lips of the vulva are responsible for the greatest differences in the appearances of vulvas. The lips range from little more than pale pink, semierectile ridges receding from the clitoris into the sides and bottom of the genital cleft to large, fluted, plum-colored, soft "curtains" (called "aprons" in some societies) that may bear a striking resemblance to a cattleya orchid. For some women, the latter configuration may make the small lips protrude visibly from the posterior end of the large lips even when they are closed. All these varieties are quite normal, and it should not distress a woman to find that her vulva is quite different from some other woman's, or a man to discover that one woman is remarkably different from another.

At the posterior end of the vulva is an opening (Latin: *introitus vagina*) that leads to the vagina. This appears as a small fold or slit, since the vagina itself is not actually visible. The entrance must be opened with an instrument (usually a *speculum*) or with the fingers in order to see into the vagina at all. If a woman's vagina has never had anything inserted into it, the entrance has an inner circumference of tissue called a *hymen* (English: maidenhead). This flexible tissue, like the other parts of the vulva, has a variety of possible configurations and thicknesses.[5] Usually the inner circumference of the hymen is large enough to accommodate a finger or a tampon; but if it is not, it usually can easily be stretched out and gently massaged until the insertion can be made quite comfortably. In those few cases in which the hymen cannot be stretched to a comfortable circumference, a small nick can be made surgically so that the hymen will stretch to the diameter of a tampon, a human penis, or several fingers.

Where the inner circumference of the unstretched hymen is smaller than a prospective partner's erect penis (and it almost always is), it can be stretched out by gentle massage by first one, then two, and finally perhaps three fingers (ideally, lubricated with vaginal secretions but otherwise with saliva or water-soluble surgical jelly, *not* with oil or petroleum jelly).[6]

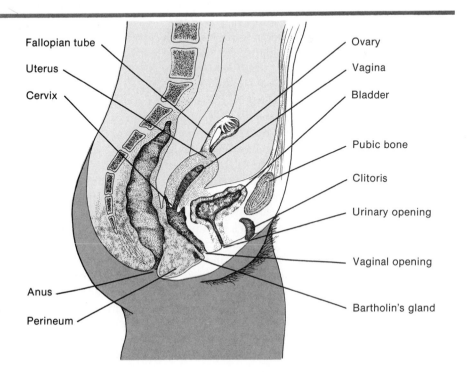

Fallopian tube

Uterus

Cervix

Ovary

Vagina

Bladder

Pubic bone

Clitoris

Urinary opening

Vaginal opening

Anus

Perineum

Bartholin's gland

Cross-sectional side view of the female pelvis, showing internal structures

The process of stretching a hymen to a comfortable entrance size may take no time at all, or it may take several weeks of frequent gentle massage. There is normally no great urgency, since the stretching-out process itself should be intimate, erotic, and pleasurable. If a partner is involved, knowing him or her well enough to ensure good communication is obviously desirable, as is the willingness and ability of the woman to communicate her sensations and wishes. The period can be a good one for learning to become sexually relaxed together and intimate. It is also a good time to discuss contraception, if it is likely that heterosexual intercourse is going to follow and if pregnancy is not desired.

Between the clitoris and the entrance to the vagina is the tiny slit (Latin: *meatus*) through which urine exits from the bladder through the *urethra* (urinary duct). It is quite separate from the vagina. Secretions from Skene's gland may come through this passage during sexual excitement, especially if the gland (which lies between the vagina and the urethra) is massaged. These secretions should not be confused with urine.

The part of the vulva that lies between the little lips is called the *vestibule*. It is kept moist by various secretions, some of which come from *Bartholin's glands,* the tiny, hardly visible ducts that open near the vaginal entrance. The warm, moist vulva may be subject to bacterial infection if it is not kept clean. In the past, unfortunately, confusion of modesty with discretion, and of sexual pleasure with shame, has prevented many women from ever being taught the necessity of and the techniques for cleaning these parts. Van de Velde recommended frequent washing with clear water, a function best carried out with the use of a bidet. Unfortunately, few North American bathrooms are equipped with bidets, and washing the vulva is likely to be done with less convenience and, perhaps, less hygienically.

Access to air for some part of the day is almost as desirable for keeping the vulva healthy or restoring it to health as is frequent washing. If underclothing is not of natural fibers (cotton, silk, or linen), it is more healthful to avoid wearing it all day long and all night too. Synthetic materials inhibit air circulation and are nonabsorbent compared with natural fibers. A woman who wears tight-fitting polyester pants, all-nylon pantyhose, close-fitting underpants of a synthetic material during the day, and nylon pajamas with close-fitting underpants of a similar material during the night is a prime candidate for vulval infection and has a poor prognosis for regaining health when infection occurs.[7]

Although breasts are classed as secondary female sex characteristics, their sexual symbolism and association with erotic sensations in contemporary American society lead many men and women to attach great sexual significance to them. Masters and Johnson have reported on the physiological linkage among the breasts, the brain, and the vulvo-vaginal parts.[8] They have observed that women's nipples (and many men's) become erect during the excitement phase of sexual response and that the total volume of the breasts of women who have never nursed a baby increases during the plateau phase. Conversely, about half of postpubescent females respond to nipple or breast stimulation with definite genital reactions, such as erection of the clitoris and lubrication of the vagina. It is difficult to know the extent to which such responses are affected by the cultural definition of breast play as erotic behavior. A common saying among sexologists is that the most important sex organ in the human body is the brain.

Male Sex Organs

The outwardly visible primary sex organs of the human male are the *penis* and the *scrotum*. Penises tend to be more alike in appearance than vulvas, but there are many differences in proportion as well as in size. The smaller the flaccid (soft) penis, the larger proportionately it tends to become when erect (hard).[9] Thus, erect penises tend to be more uniform in size than flaccid penises. For most men, the size of the flaccid penis changes during each day, responding to such variables as room and body temperatures, fullness of the bladder, degree of sexual excitement, and recency of sexual activity.

The visible aspect of the penis is a soft, loose-fitting, elastic tube of skin, covering a structure that somewhat resembles a mushroom with a thick stem and a small cap. In its flaccid state, the body of the penis is quite small, with a consistency roughly similar to that of a relaxed muscle in the forearm. When it is erect, the penile body is larger and has a consistency more like a flexed biceps muscle. The *glans* (Latin for "acorn"; English term: "head") is normally covered by the skin tube when the penis is flaccid but may be partially visible when the penis is erect. The skin covering the glans, called the *foreskin,* can easily be pulled back and caught below the raised ridge (the *corona*) at the base of the glans to expose the entire surface of the glans when the penis is either erect or flaccid. In rare cases the foreskin may be tight enough that it needs to be stretched in order to slip easily over the corona.

In the United States the foreskin is cut off the majority of the baby boys born in hospitals, in a surgical operation called *circumcision.* This is now done for cosmetic or religious reasons, although in the past it was believed by many to be hygienic. Masters and Johnson disproved the myth that circumcision had any effect on sexual performance.[10] In Israel and in Islamic countries circumcision is practiced for religious reasons. It is not customary in most other societies, with the possible exception of Canada, where it is estimated that as many as half the males born may have been circumcised in recent years, primarily as a result of the influence of United States customs.[11] The physical appearance of a circumcised penis is virtually the same as that of an uncircumcised penis with the foreskin pulled back and caught behind the corona.

The *scrotum* is a thin-skinned pouch that falls from the penis near the point at which it joins the pelvis. The outer skin of the scrotum is typically darker

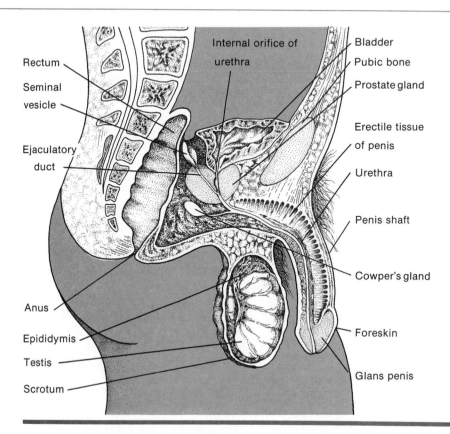

Rectum

Seminal
vesicle

Ejaculatory
duct

Internal orifice of
urethra

Bladder

Pubic bone

Prostate gland

Erectile tissue
of penis

Urethra

Penis shaft

Cowper's gland

Anus

Epididymis

Testis

Scrotum

Foreskin

Glans penis

*Cross-sectional side
view of the male
pelvis, showing
internal structures*

than the skin of the penis, just as the skin of the posterior surface of women's large lips is. Because a layer of muscles (the *dartos*) just beneath the scrotal skin responds involuntarily to temperature changes, touches to the skin of the adjacent thighs, emotions, and certain stages of sexual excitement, both the volume and the position of the scrotum are in frequent (if not constant) states of change. The scrotal skin of adult males has sparse, coarse hairs growing from it that are quite different from pubic hair.[12]

Although the two testicles (*testes*) are not directly visible, their shape, size, and position can easily be seen and felt within the scrotum. The testicles are egg shaped, about an inch and a half on the long axis and an inch on the short axis. They contain the tubules in which sperm are produced. One can also feel (but not see the form of) the *spermatic cords*, which carry sperm out of the scrotum. The testicles and the spermatic cords are extremely sensitive to pressure; anything more than a gentle touch may be very painful.

When the dartos muscles are relaxed, the left testicle hangs lower than the right testicle. This difference in position is perfectly normal and is no cause for alarm. The ridge that resembles a seam running from front to back at the center of the scrotum is called the *raphe;* it is a natural formation and should not be mistaken for evidence of injury or surgery.[13]

Fear, anger, cold, stimulation of the inner thigh, or sexual excitement cause the dartos muscles to contract. The contraction gives the outer skin of the scrotum a wrinkled appearance, and the entire pouch shrinks up against the penis in a full reaction. At the other extreme, the skin is smooth, and the testicles may hang as much as three inches below the flaccid penis. When the testicles are drawn up against the penis in sexual excitement, each increases about half again in size; as orgasm becomes inevitable, the testicles rotate within the scrotum.[14,15]

About 30 percent of males have nipple erections during sexual excitement, but in the United States the male nipples (unlike the female breasts) are not usually considered sex organs, even secondary ones.[16]

Hidden Anatomy

Although they may not ordinarily be seen or sensed in other ways, some of the hidden sexual and reproductive organs may affect interpersonal relationships and interactions. Since experiences with problems in this hidden anatomy are normally discussed with a physician on a personal basis, the discussion here will be limited to a few generalizations.

Gonads

Reproductive cells and sexually appropriate hormones are produced by the *gonads.* In women, the gonads are called *ovaries;* in men, they are called *testicles* (or *testes,* the Latin form).

The ovaries are located deep in the abdominal cavity, within the *pelvic girdle,* on either side of the *womb* (Latin: *uterus*). Each ovary is about the size and shape of an almond and weighs about one-quarter of an ounce in a young adult woman, although it normally shrinks after menopause. Each ovary has perhaps 200,000 tiny capsules (*follicles*), each of which contains an immature egg cell (Latin: *ovum,* Latin plural: *ova*), when a female is born. At puberty the eggs begin to ripen (usually, but not always, one at a time). The egg and its capsule enlarge as it ripens, and at *ovulation* (approximately once every twenty-eight days) a follicle bursts and ejects its egg into the abdominal cavity. The ruptured follicle then changes its form and color and generates the hormones *estrogen* and *progesterone* for a time.[17]

The testicles, which are located in the scrotum, have been described briefly. Cells in the testicles begin to divide and become mature sperm at puberty. Unlike the production of eggs in women; the production of sperm is not cyclic. It is relatively constant, although it may be affected by stress and possibly by other factors. Sperm production is estimated at several hundred million per day. The testicles also produce the male hormone *testosterone*.

Female Internal Organs for Gestation

Humans are born alive (*viviparous*) as opposed to being hatched from eggs outside of their mothers (*oviparous*); so the period between conception and birth, known as *gestation*, is spent inside the mother rather than in the outside world.

Even though a newly fertilized egg is completely separate from the mother, as are the *embryo* and, subsequently, the *fetus* into which it develops, the mother has a protective "nest" that enables her not only to carry the growing baby around with her, but also to engage in an intimate exchange of hormones, nutrients, chemicals of other sorts, viruses, and some disease germs.

The womb is the potential nest into which a fertilized egg is deposited if it is to develop normally. In its nonpregnant state, it is about the size of the woman's fist (perhaps slightly smaller in a woman who has never been pregnant). One may be able to feel the firm, muscular structure of the womb through the lower abdominal wall, behind the pubic bone, deep inside the pelvis. It also may be felt from inside the vagina, where its neck (Latin: *cervix*) can be reached deep within. It may feel somewhat like the head of an erect penis.

There is a central passage (Latin: *os*) in the neck of the womb through which a baby emerges at birth. The elasticity of the muscles in the womb can be appreciated by comparing the size of a newborn's head with what feels like a deep dimple. The volume of the womb itself is usually increased sixty-four-fold or more during a single-fetus pregnancy. Immediately following delivery, the process of *involution* begins to return the womb to near its prepregnant size within remarkably few days.

The opening in the neck of the womb is the passage through which the fluid of menstruation is expelled. This fluid is periodically expressed from the lining (*endometrium*) of the womb as it is influenced by hormonal changes.

The flexible sleeve that is connected to the womb at one end and to the vulva at the other, the *vagina* (a Latin word meaning "sheath") has both sexual and reproductive functions. Its mucous lining and its walls are quite elastic. It is not rigidly structured like the throat or the ear canals but is a soft, stretchable, and (except for its "anchors" at either end) easily movable connector between the doughnut-shaped muscle (the forward half of the *pubococcygeus* muscle) that closes it off from the vulva, and the womb. The sexual functions of the vagina are to provide lubrication so that a penis can be inserted comfortably through the muscular entrance and to confine the sperm ejaculated to the vicinity of the opening of the womb. Its reproductive function is to provide a connector between the womb and the outside world, closing off the abdominal cavity. It is not so much an organ of birth as a short, wide bellows between the womb and the outside world.

Sperm ejaculated into the vagina will swim against a current of fluid at the rate of one inch per hour; once they reach the womb they may be moved along much more rapidly by contractions of its walls. Sperm deposited directly at the os can easily fertilize a viable egg within an hour, especially if they are sped on by contractions of the womb occurring during the woman's orgasm.[18]

The anatomical feature that facilitates the fertilization of eggs and their delivery to the womb once they are fertilized are the *fallopian tubes* (Latin: *salpinges*). These ducts extend from the upper ends of the womb (one at either side) to the vicinity of the ovaries, sometimes embracing the ovaries but not attached to them. When an egg erupts from an ovarian follicle, it seems to be attracted by a force that is not yet well understood to the tiny slit at the end of one or the other of the tubes (it has been demonstrated that an egg from one ovary can migrate through the abdominal cavity to the tube on the other side).[19] Unfortunately, it is possible—although unlikely—for an egg cell to be fertilized and attach itself outside the womb to create an *ectopic* pregnancy in a tube or even elsewhere in the abdominal cavity. The fetus does not survive in such cases, and the consequences for the mother may be serious.[20]

Once the egg reaches the sperm (or vice versa), fertilization can take place. Any sperm that have been deposited within the previous three days or so will be ready and waiting for the egg when ovulation occurs; otherwise, the egg will probably be in a suitable condition and location to be fertilized for the next four days or so.[21] At the time of ovulation, the lining of the womb is in an optimum condition for *implantation* (*nidation*) of the mass of cells, clustered in a spherical shape, that have resulted from fertilization. By the tenth to the twelfth day after ovulation, any such mass will have burrowed firmly into the endometrium if it is going to be retained, with the result that the menstrual period expected about the fourteenth day after ovulation will be unlikely to occur.[22]

Male Internal Genital Organs

The male genital organs, like those of the female, have both sexual and reproductive functions; unlike those of the female, however, they are inextricably combined from the male's perspective. His reproductive function, in other words, *is* his sexual function.

A female may engage in coitus to orgasm without any reproductive consequences during more than two-thirds of her reproductive life span (usually arbitrarily put at thirty years); a male's coitus can create pregnancy at any time of the month for virtually all of adolescent and adult life. A female may ovulate without any sexual activity or any sexual sensation at all—indeed, with no awareness of her fertility. A male can, if he wishes, induce the ejaculation of viable sperm almost any time, and it is unlikely that even an involuntary ejaculation will ever go unnoticed.

Two functions make sex/reproduction possible for males: the erectile function and the ejaculatory function. The erectile function facilitates the delivery of semen to a location that makes fertilization of an egg possible; the ejacula-tory function delivers the sperm.

It is possible by means of special techniques or devices for a man to insert his penis into a woman's vagina without his having an erection. However, the natural collapsed state of the vagina and the elasticity of its normally closed entrance muscle make it mechanically more efficient and substantially more pleasurable for both partners if the penis is rigid. Erection makes it possible for the penis to push through the opening far enough that the corona is beyond the pubococcygeus muscle and can massage Skene's gland from inside the vagina and pull the little lips against the clitoris in the vulva.

Although erections may be caused by a variety of kinds of pressures and frictions, the overwhelming majority of them are purely involuntary responses to sexual excitement. A male can voluntarily expose himself to erotic stimuli or intentionally think erotic thoughts that would result in an erection, but he cannot simply decide to have an erection.[23] For that matter, he also cannot decide *not* to have an erection.

Mechanically, erections occur when more arterial blood is being pumped into the three spongy cylinders that make up the body of the penis than the amount of venous blood that is escaping. The result is analogous to the infla-tion of a football or a device for taking blood pressure. A system of valves (called *polsters*) permitting blood to flow freely from the arteries to the cylinders (two *corpora cavernosa* and one *corpus spongiosum*) are held nearly shut when the penis is flaccid; when the polsters relax in response to a spinal reflex, the penis "inflates" until similar valves controlling the outflow of blood to the veins balance the internal pressure at a degree of erection or flaccidity.[24]

Erection is the most delicate of the male sexual functions. Chronic failure, known as impotence, *can take many forms. The man may simply be unable to achieve erection under any circumstance or may only be impotent during some sexual activities or with some partners. . . .*

At one time or another every man experiences some loss of potency. . . . It is only when the problem is persistent that it is considered a malfunction.[25]

Sex therapist Helen Singer Kaplan writes of impotence:

On one level, the sexual dysfunctions . . . are caused by a single factor: anxi-ety. . . . [T]he physiological concomitants of anxiety are always the same, no matter what its source or depth or intensity, no matter what the relationship to conscious experience, and no matter what the level of insight.

. . . [A] man can lose his erection simply because he is worried that he will not perform that evening, an anxiety of which he is painfully aware, or because the sexual act with his wife evoked anxiety that derives from oedipal incest taboos acquired during early childhood, of which he is totally unconscious, or because he hears a burglar downstairs. On a physiological level the event is identical in all the cases and the penis does not know the difference. In all these

cases, the brain has "decided" that it is too "dangerous" to have sex. . . . [T]he blood will drain out of his penis instantly, producing impotence, no matter what the original stimulus was.[26]

Although Kaplan is surely correct about anxiety and erectile dysfunction, sex researcher Alfred Kinsey and his associates added a further cause:

Today most males . . . feel under some obligation to see that the female secures gratification comparable to their own in coitus. To such a male, the failure of the wife may seem an indication of some incapacity on his part and he, in consequence, may develop a sense of inferiority which, again, may compound the difficulties. Far from contributing to the solidarity of the marriage, the coitus then becomes a source of disappointment, friction, and more serious discord.[27]

Both Kaplan and Kinsey and his associates are correct. Feelings of inferiority, disappointment, fright, or anger can effectively prevent or terminate an erection.

The ejaculatory function of the male genital organs is to deliver sperm from the testicles to the outside of his body. The sperm, produced by cell division in approximately a mile of tiny tubes coiled within the testicles, are collected within a larger tube (Latin: *epididymis*) at the back of each testicle as they mature. The upward end of this latter tube becomes the *spermatic cord* (Latin: *vas deferens*) that carries the sperm through the lower abdominal cavity to the *seminal vesicles* on either side of the bladder. The spermatic cord can be felt through the thin skin of the scrotum. It is at that point, when a person is sterilized by vasectomy, that the spermatic cord is cut and tied. In the seminal vesicles, fluid is added to the sperm, increasing the volume and diluting it.

The prostate gland completely surrounds the urethra where it leaves the bladder to pass urine through the penis to the outside. A valvelike structure in the urethra between the bladder and the prostate closes off the urethra at that point during sexual excitement so that it is not possible for a male to pass any urine at all when he is sexually aroused.

As sexual excitement increases in men, a clear mucoid secretion is exuded through the urethra. This clear preejaculate neutralizes any acid in the urethra and serves to lubricate the glans penis. It probably comes from Cowper's glands, located at the base of the prostate.[28]

At orgasm the testicles are drawn up by a contraction of the scrotum, followed by contractions of the various tubes leading to the seminal vesicles; the strong muscles of the prostate begin a series of rhythmic contractions (with eight-tenths of a second between each peak) that draw the semen from the seminal vesicles through ejaculatory ducts into the prostate, and then eject it under considerable pressure together with more fluid added by the prostate into the urethra. Once in the urethra, the semen is moved along by a number of muscles that maintain sufficient pressure to expel it with some force at first—the first spurt sometimes being propelled several inches—with the pressure diminishing until the system is empty.[29]

Appendix B •

The Love Profile

We decided to try to find out what people meant when they said, "I love you," or "I don't love you any more." We collected literally hundreds of personal statements about the meaning of love and definitions from literary works, and especially from John Alan Lee's scholarly research.[1] By eliminating statements that appeared to be conceptual duplicates, the number of items was reduced to 144 that implied the presence or absence of specific behaviors, thoughts, or feelings of a person with reference to love. Next, we presented 220 subjects with the 144 items arranged as a true-false test. The subjects included a range of ages, religions, social classes, ethnicities, and races; but it cannot be claimed that they were representative of any particular large population. However, we later validated our findings on a much larger population.

By means of a statistical device called *item analysis* we were able to eliminate eighty-seven items from the scale because they showed no impressive relationship to the scoring patterns of the subjects; we later dropped seven additional items to pare the number down to an even fifty. At the suggestion of sociologist Milton Bloombaum at the University of Hawaii, we applied a technique called *smallest space analysis* to the remaining items and discovered that they separated into six quite distinct clusters.

We had confirmed Lee's finding that love means different things to different people, using a population a quarter of the way around the world from his and a different research procedure. We named the clusters of items after Lee's six primary and secondary love styles since they clearly fell into those patterns. It was then a simple step to construct scales for each of the clusters. Each of the six scales became an operational definition of a different kind of understanding of love: storgic, agapic, manic, pragmatic, ludic, and erotic. From the acronym for these scales we named their combined scores "The SAMPLE Profile."[2]

In still another replication of the SAMPLE research, Terry Hatkoff used a different procedure (called *factor analysis*) to study about 1,200 profiles from several different regions of the United States. She also reached the conclusion that the six dimensions were discrete.[3] We had cooperation from colleagues in the United States, Canada, South America, and Europe so that by the time we completed our research, literally thousands of subjects had contributed to the validation of our scale.

In our research and that of colleagues using "The SAMPLE Profile," the Greek and Latin names used by Lee were retained. For simplicity's sake, however, in 1980, in *Styles of Loving: Why You Love the Way You Do*, the six basic styles of loving were relabeled with popular colloquialisms. Storgic became *best friends*; agapic was translated as *unselfish*; manic was called *possessive*; pragmatic now was *logical*; ludic became *game-playing*; erotic was called *romantic*; and "The SAMPLE Profile" was retitled "The Love Profile."[4]

"The SAMPLE Profile," which follows, demonstrates clearly that there are many possible definitions of love. A person responding to these six scales may compare his or her profile with the profiles of others. Such a comparison can help a person know what kinds of behaviors make another feel loved. Not only are the behaviors that are intended to convey love not always perceived as loving by others, but often they may convey an unintended message of "I don't love you."

Instructions for Responding to the SAMPLE Scales

Each of the following questions is to be answered "true" or "false." Answer the questions in consecutive order, and *do not skip or omit any of them.* Some may seem ambiguous or out of your experience, and you may need to let your pencil choose your answer for no special reason. Remember that the test is a research instrument and that the profile was validated by the testing of thousands of men and women. It may help you to answer the questions if you think of your ideal or most memorable love relationship rather than a current one. Finally, complete the questionnaire independently of your classmates or your partner. There are no "correct" or "incorrect" answers to the items. Mark your responses on the answer sheet below or on a facsimile of it.

Answer True or False.

	T	F
1. I believe that "love at first sight" is possible.	☐	☐
2. I did not realize that I was in love until I actually had been for some time.	☐	☐
3. When things aren't going right with us, my stomach gets upset.	☐	☐
4. From a practical point of view, I must consider what a person is going to become in life before I commit myself to loving him/her.	☐	☐
5. You cannot have love unless you have first had *caring* for a while.	☐	☐
6. It's always a good idea to keep your lover a little uncertain about how committed you are to him/her.	☐	☐
7. The first time we kissed or rubbed cheeks, I felt a definite genital response (lubrication, erection).	☐	☐

	T	F
8. I still have good friendships with almost everyone with whom I have ever been involved in a love relationship.	☐	☐
9. It makes good sense to plan your life carefully before you choose a lover.	☐	☐
10. When my love affairs break up, I get so depressed that I have even thought of suicide.	☐	☐
11. Sometimes I get so excited about being in love that I can't sleep.	☐	☐
12. I try to use my own strength to help my lover through difficult times, even when he/she is behaving foolishly.	☐	☐
13. I would rather suffer myself than let my lover suffer.	☐	☐
14. Part of the fun of being in love is testing one's skill at keeping it going and getting what one wants from it at the same time.	☐	☐
15. As far as my lovers go, what they don't know won't hurt them.	☐	☐
16. It is best to love someone with a similar background.	☐	☐
17. We kissed each other soon after we met because we both wanted to.	☐	☐
18. When my lover doesn't pay attention to me, I feel sick all over.	☐	☐
19. I cannot be happy unless I place my lover's happiness before my own.	☐	☐
20. Usually the first thing that attracts my attention to a person is his/her pleasing physical appearance.	☐	☐
21. The best kind of love grows out of a long friendship.	☐	☐
22. When I am in love, I have trouble concentrating on anything else.	☐	☐
23. At the first touch of his/her hand, I knew that love was a real possibility.	☐	☐
24. When I break up with someone, I go out of my way to see that he/she is O.K.	☐	☐
25. I cannot relax if I suspect that he/she is with someone else.	☐	☐
26. I have at least once had to plan carefully to keep two of my lovers from finding out about each other.	☐	☐
27. I can get over love affairs pretty easily and quickly.	☐	☐
28. A main consideration in choosing a lover is how he/she reflects on my family.	☐	☐
29. The best part of love is living together, building a home together, and rearing children together.	☐	☐
30. I am usually willing to sacrifice my own wishes to let my lover achieve his/hers.	☐	☐
31. A main consideration in choosing a partner is whether or not he/she will be a good parent.	☐	☐
32. Kissing, cuddling, and sex shouldn't be rushed into; they will happen naturally when one's intimacy has grown enough.	☐	☐
33. I enjoy flirting with attractive people.	☐	☐

	T	F
34. My lover would get upset if he/she knew some of the things I've done with other people.	☐	☐
35. Before I ever fell in love, I had a pretty clear physical picture of what my true love would be like.	☐	☐
36. If my lover had a baby by someone else, I would want to raise it, love it, and care for it as if it were my own.	☐	☐
37. It is hard to say exactly when we fell in love.	☐	☐
38. I couldn't truly love anyone I would not be willing to marry.	☐	☐
39. Even though I don't want to be jealous, I can't help it when he/she pays attention to someone else.	☐	☐
40. I would rather break up with my lover than to stand in his/her way.	☐	☐
41. I like the idea of my lover and myself having the same kinds of clothes, hats, plants, bicycles, cars, etc.	☐	☐
42. I wouldn't date anyone that I wouldn't want to fall in love with.	☐	☐
43. At least once when I thought a love affair was all over, I saw him/her again and knew I couldn't realistically see that person again without loving him/her.	☐	☐
44. Whatever I own is my lover's to use as he/she chooses.	☐	☐
45. If my lover ignores me for a while, I sometimes do really stupid things to try to get his/her attention back.	☐	☐
46. It's fun to see whether I can get someone to go out with me even if I don't want to get involved with that person.	☐	☐
47. A main consideration in choosing a mate is how he/she will reflect on my career.	☐	☐
48. When my lover doesn't see me or call for a while, I assume he/she has a good reason.	☐	☐
49. Before getting very involved with anyone I try to figure out how compatible his/her hereditary background is with mine in case we ever have children.	☐	☐
50. The best love relationships are the ones that last the longest.	☐	☐

Tally.

1. *Circle the item number of each T (true) response on the scales to the right. Write the number of true responses per column in the space provided.*

S	A	M	P	L	E
2	12	3	4	6	1
5	13	10	9	14	7
8	19	11	16	15	17
21	24	18	28	26	20
29	30	22	31	27	23
32	36	25	38	33	35
37	40	39	42	34	41
50	44	43	47	46	
	48	45	49		

Total circled true

SAMPLE Profile

2. *Now fill in the histogram below by shading in each column up to the number of circles counted in the corresponding column in item 1, above.**

S	A	M	P	L	E	Percentile
						100
8	9	9	8, 9	8	6, 7	
		8	7	7		
7	8	7	6	6	5	90
	7	6	5	5	4	80
6						
						70
		5	4	4		
	6				3	60
5	4		3	3		50
	5	3				40
4			2	2	2	30
	4	2	1	1		20
3	3	1			1	10
2	2	0	0	0	0	
1	1					0

3. *The percentile reading on the right of the profile shows the proportion of the population that has less of the indicated trait than you have.*

S = Storge = "Best friends"
A = Agape = "Unselfish"
M = Mania = "Possessive"
P = Pragma = "Logical"
L = Ludus = "Game-playing"
E = Eros = "Romantic"

* We acknowledge the contribution of John and Betty Burnham in designing the Love Profile scoring device. It is reprinted by their permission.

S - 96
A - 100
M - 90

P - 93
L - 5
E - 83

You will have some "true" answers in several or, probably, all of the scales. Usually, however, two or three scales will have more "true" answers than others. If you have high percentiles in several or all scales, it does not necessarily mean you are a better lover—nor does scoring low in several or all of them mean that your love is in scarce supply. Instead, this is more likely to be a reflection of your test-taking attitude. Some people agree with a statement if it is true only once in a while, but others never answer "true" unless the situation always or almost always exists. The latter person is inclined to be analytical and cautious. Your relative lower and higher percentiles are more significant than your absolute scores.

The percentile numbers at the right side of the profile (page 495) indicate the percentage of respondents whose profiles have been studied who had lower scores than yours. After the first few hundred profiles had been recorded, these percentages became quite precise, and they have shown no tendency to change in subsequent studies.

We have never seen anyone who had "true" responses in only one column and none in the others. In other words, there are probably no "pure" types. Instead, most people define love as some kind of combination of several or all of the six definitions. There is an enormous number of possible combinations.

Your SAMPLE profile shows graphically how your scores on each of the scales blend into your own distinctive definition of love. There is no good or bad combination of scores for a person. Neither is one definition of love more or less mature than another.

Most people automatically assume that their own definitions of love are correct or at least "normal," although they may understand that others disagree with the meaning they give it. Social psychologist Daryl Bem has termed such unchallenged beliefs zero-order ones.[5] He points out that it is unlikely that a fish recognizes that it is wet, since it has known nothing else. If you have never been challenged before by the fact that there are as many definitions of love as there are people, you may want to defend the idea that yours is "real love" and others' are only infatuation or immature love. However, each person's definition of love is probably as correct to him or her as yours is to you. It is easy to see why, with such zero-order beliefs, partners with quite different styles of loving may have considerable difficulty in communicating their caring to each other.

The following descriptions of the various love styles are in alphabetical order to emphasize that no one style is more important or more popular than another. Further, they do not develop in a sequence from romantic to companionate love, as many believe.

It is important to understand that people do not always behave in accordance with their definitions of love, even though they believe that people who are in love ought to behave that way (just as persons sometimes tell lies even though they believe firmly that people ought not to lie). Most persons, although their feelings tend to overpower their intellectual definitions of whether or not they are in love, still expect others who are in love to behave according to those intellectual definitions! Such inconsistencies are not uncommon, and most people are able to rationalize their violations of their own rules.

Best Friends

The S (storge) scale on the SAMPLE profile is defined operationally by agreement with items 2, 5, 8, 21, 29, 32, 37, and 50. They indicate a belief that love is slowly growing to care for another person. Building a marriage on a close association over a long period of time together is usually important to those who define love in this way. A relatively high score on this scale (above the seventy-fifth percentile mark) usually means that there is the belief that two people who eventually grow to love each other should have begun their relationship by being friends. The initial rapport that Reiss mentions in his wheel theory clearly is seen as an important element by those who share this definition of love.[6] Rapport is based on mutual sharing; thoughtfulness; enjoyment of time spent together; and, particularly, having a great deal in common. Physical attraction and sexual urgency are seldom of paramount importance in "true love" for those with this definition.

Usually, persons whose ideas of love have a strong measure of best-friends meaning believe that sex ought to be deferred until after love is established (whether they defer it themselves or not)—that it should be a natural extension of the deep caring that has grown over time. These persons believe that people in love ought to acknowledge personal decisions of their partners as appropriate even when they do not agree with them. They believe that lovers ought to respect each other's personal dignity and do not see differences of opinion or arguments as threatening to a love relationship. They believe that those in love should not be anxious about a partner's temporary absence on business or on a family visit, for instance, and they also believe that lovers should have a concern about their partners in whatever they do, even if they do not always understand the partners' behaviors.

Those with high best-friends scores usually have difficulty accepting the idea of ending a relationship once it is well established. They expect feelings of caring to continue. In our clinical practice we have observed more than one person with a best-friends definition who after a divorce could not fully accept that the relationship was over and that the ex-spouse could think of marrying someone else. One ex-wife continued to ask for help with her income tax and for aid in choosing a new car. It made no sense to her that even though she and her husband were divorced, they should cease to be close friends.

Those with low scores probably distinguish "being in love" as very different from being "best friends." They may have difficulty accepting that people who feel as those with the best-friends definition do are really in love. They may see such comfortable friendship as "liking" but not as loving, although one with the best-friends orientation clearly knows the difference.

Game-Playing

This conceptualization of love is identified by high scores on the L (ludus) scale (items 6, 14, 15, 26, 27, 33, 34, and 46). The items that cluster together to define this conception of love operationally suggest that true love is viewed as risky, exciting, uncertain, and possibly fleeting. This definition assumes the need for strategies to keep the interaction interesting for both partners. Clinical experience indicates that one who holds this definition believes that "being taken for granted" is one of the worst things that can happen to lovers and might not even believe that one who treated a partner like an old shoe—comfortable and pliable—was truly in love. High scorers often feel that in "true" love partners must be self-sufficient and relatively independent. They do not believe that partners who are "clinging vines" are truly in love. They expect partners to make few demands on each other, not to dwell on one another's "responsibilities." True love is never dull. They expect lovers to provide novelty and adventure for each other. Pleasure in love should come from keeping a partner's interest high by playing the role of lover like a game. To them, a good lover must keep his or her partner somewhat uncertain about the future. As one four-time divorcee said, "When my marriage gets gray, I get out." High scorers on the game-playing scale tend to believe that sex, like love, should be adventuresome if a couple is *really* in love. Sex that is routine is viewed as boring by such persons, and they are more comfortable with the idea of withholding sex on occasion to heighten a partner's anticipation than with keeping to some kind of schedule. If both partners have high scores on game-playing, they usually can keep each other happy. However, if one partner does not define the give-and-take of a good game as being in love, there can be serious difficulties. High-scoring game-players are likely to believe that their partners no longer love them if they are "bored."

Persons with low scores on game-playing may not understand the apparent lack of commitment of game-playing lovers. How can it be love, they reason, if one needs a challenge all the time? A very low scoring woman might be embarrassed or annoyed if a few years after her marriage she received a bouquet of roses from a forgotten lover with a note: "I have missed you too long. Meet me at the Polo Lounge at noon on Thursday." If she showed up at all (and she most likely would not), she would feel suspicious and probably annoyed. A high-scoring woman, on the other hand, would be excited. If the man turned out to be her husband instead of an old boyfriend, she would feel very much loved.

Logical Love

Relatively high scores on the P (pragma) scale (items 4, 9, 16, 28, 31, 38, 42, 47, and 49) indicate a definition of love that is epitomized in rationality. The items that cluster together here suggest that those who understand love in this way believe that the core of every true love relationship is the practical capability of the partners to satisfy each other's goals, values, and wishes. Relationships that do not enable the partners to solve these practical problems are seen as foolish or are simply "infatuations," "physical attractions," or "immature"—they cannot be "true love."

When one with a pragma definition thinks about people falling in love, one thinks first of the candidates' qualifications. To logical definers, people should not even contemplate "unsuitable" persons as potential lovers. They consider it a waste of time for a person to get involved with anyone who fails to meet their standards. They think it is appropriate to have a series of filters through which a potential partner must pass. The idea of love at first sight makes no sense to those who understand love in this way. They reason that too many questions about the future remain unanswered until two people have done considerable self-revelation. A person with a high score on this definition of love believes that when a partner has failed to live up to his or her promise or has changed in some important ways, there may be a serious question of whether or not love can still exist.

A young woman we know who had a very high logical score married the "perfect" partner—one of the top students in an Ivy League law school, handsome, a good dancer. He entered a prestigious law firm, and the two of them were delighted at his immediate professional and financial success. But when their first child was born, her expectations of him as a father were unmet. His career absorbed his energy, and he refused to spend as much time with her and their son as she wanted. How could he love her, she thought, if he was unwilling to spend time with her and their child? Deciding he did not, she filed for divorce. Persons with high scores are more likely to weigh problem areas in their relationships against the good that exists. However, if something truly important cannot be worked out to meet their standards, there may be serious difficulty.

Clinical experience with persons who have high logical scores has shown that sex is not necessarily either more or less important than any of their other values. Although they tend to be "sensible," they are often far from calculating sexually. Finding the right partner allows such a person to relax, enjoy the relationship, and care deeply. A warm feeling of contentment comes from thinking about the partner's successes and suitability.

Persons with low logical scores may have difficulty believing that those with high scores can really be in love. Such "love" seems much too calculating and businesslike to them. The idea of measuring love by personal standards is foreign to one whose feelings of love are kindled by very different kinds of stimuli.

Possessive Love

Those with high scores on the possessive or M (mania) scale (items 3, 10, 11, 18, 22, 25, 39, 43, and 45) define being in love as an anxiety-producing relationship. As with the game-playing definition, they believe that a boring relationship is probably not love. In this case, however, uncertainty about the future of the relationship is considered threatening rather than exciting. Those with high possessive scores often expect Tennov's "limerent" experience for partners. They believe that people in love should alternate between peaks of euphoria and valleys of misery and depression ("The course of true love never runs smoothly"). A person who has a great deal of this quality in his or her definition needs much reassurance from a partner in the form of words, actions, time, and energy devoted to showing love.

A person with a possessive definition of love believes that no one should have to share a partner with anyone or anything else. People who are truly in love are "naturally" jealous. High scorers are likely to be emotional and intense in everything they do; loving is no exception. They see passion as a natural part of being in love and may even believe that the absence of such highs and lows is an indication that one is *not* in love. They usually stress the importance of sexual exclusivity in the relationship, and the thought of a partner even entertaining the notion that another person might be attractive may be quite unsettling. In fact, such persons may conclude that a relaxed, easygoing partner is not really in love since he or she does not get upset over such matters.

Those with low possessive scores usually do not relate a partner's jealousy to being in love and may even conceptualize it as a "sickness." One woman who scored low on the possessive scale described how the man she had been dating told her at lunch one day that he thought they had been seeing each other too much and should spend some time alone. He said he would call her in a week or so. She was puzzled because he had been very intense in the relationship and had appeared not to want her out of his sight. She agreed to his plan, however, as it seemed reasonable to her. She was awakened at 6:00 A.M. the next morning by her frantic lover asking, "Where were you last night? Who were you with?" He had tried to call and, when she did not answer, had alternated between worrying and feeling unloved because she had so easily agreed to their bargain. In her opinion, however, he was acting "crazy" rather than "in love," as he claimed.

Romantic Love

Eyes meet across a room and love at first sight occurs. For high romantic scorers the event is perfectly understandable. The variables on the E (eros) scale, which cluster to form this definition of love (1, 7, 17, 20, 23, 35, and 41), indicate that love is expected to include a strong physical and sexual component, an urgency, and an enmeshing of the partners.

Our impression of composite traits of persons with high romantic scores is that they expect people who are in love to be "on cloud nine." A total emotional interest is immediately in full bloom. The partner is expected to remember the moment of the first meeting in minute detail. High scorers expect their partners to want to know everything about them and to spend every possible moment with them. Great sexual urgency is expected, although it may not be acted out for various reasons. Sometimes, however, it propels the partners into marriage to legitimize the urgency.

Persons with high romantic scores usually expect their partners—and themselves—to be monogamous. If they become sexually involved with any persons other than their partners, they are likely to decide they have fallen out of love.

One who has a high romantic score expects a lover to commit himself or herself to a relationship quickly from the sheer intensity of the initial attraction. There is a conviction that "love conquers all"—that nothing else is really important as long as love lasts.

Many people believe that most love relationships begin with this definition and either dissolve when the partners' ideals are not met or "mature" into love under a different definition. Although this high level of passion would be difficult to sustain twenty-four hours a day for fifty years, and ideal images may not always be met, many couples who have been together for decades report that they still retain both their relationship and their romantic definitions. They still have moments between changing diapers and paying bills when smoldering passion and romance are again ablaze. On the other hand, scholars have blamed our high divorce rate on the "romantic fallacy"—the unlikelihood that the illusion about the partner can last more than two or three years. Those with low romantic scores tend to view candlelight and roses, or sentimental cards, as silly or juvenile. They see such things as being unrelated to "real" love, which they, of course, define in their own way. As one woman who scored very low said: "Roses fade, poems on cards are someone else's words. Give me a man who comes home every night, fixes the appliances, and gets along well with my folks. That's love."

Unselfish Love

It is characteristic of this definition of love that a person with high scores believes that true love is shown by caring more for one's partner's welfare than for one's own. The items that cluster to define the A (agape) scale conceptualization of love (12, 13, 19, 24, 30, 36, 40, 44, and 48) are centered about great respect and concern for one's partner's welfare and comfort. Love is not martyrdom but, rather, an unconditional caring, nurturing, giving, forgiving, and understanding of one's partner. One who is in love according to this definition is expected to experience love as a feeling of satisfaction and reward from knowing that the lover's needs are being met.

Clinical impressions show that high scorers enjoy sex to the fullest when the partner is pleased. As surprising as it may seem to some, mainland American men are more likely to incorporate this meaning into their definitions of love than are women (although in Hawaii the reverse was found to be true, and Lee reported that this definition was virtually nonexistent in Canada). The reasoning behind higher scores for men on the mainland may be that culturally, in the United States, men have been taught that loving women involves taking care of them. Perhaps in the future our changing sex roles will lead to a more equal feeling of responsibility for the other's welfare between men and women.[7]

Those with high unselfish scores usually do not view being in love as an exchange. They neither expect nor particularly want equity. True love for them is giving, forgiving, and doing what is best for one's partner. Benjamin Franklin's wife, Deborah, is someone who acted as we might expect of a person who holds this definition. While her illustrious husband interacted with intellectuals and politicians and charmed the royal courts of Europe, she managed their printing business and raised his illegitimate son. She apparently asked and got little in return for her sacrifices for love.

Persons with low scores on the unselfish scale fail to see behaviors characteristic of high scorers as having much to do with love. Instead, such actions and feelings may be viewed as anything from "parenting" to "being a doormat"—definitely not as a "turn-on." Those with low scores sometimes accuse high scorers of being masochistic. The accusers, of course, are quick to offer their own definitions of love, which typically are devoid of the unselfish quality.

Compatibility of Definitions

Whether the partners' definitions of love are similar is less important for the success of their relationship than that each understands what actions the other expects as evidence of being loved. Because many people find it difficult to say what they need to make them feel loved, their partners may be left to guess what to do. Most commonly, what they do is to behave according to their own expectations—doing what would make *them* feel loved. But this is one place where the Golden Rule does not necessarily apply.

In our experience in using "The SAMPLE Profile" in counseling hundreds of couples, whether married or not, partners who define love similarly or whose different definitions are accepted by each other find their relationships more satisfying than do those who are rigid in their different expectations—usually because each assumes there is only one type of "true love"—one that conforms to his or her own definition. Clear communication, respect for each other, and acceptance of the differences among people as a desirable fact are all much more important than demanding that a partner's definition of love be the same as one's own.

In a study carried out in California and Colorado, it was discovered that couples in marital therapy who spent six sessions examining their respective definitions of love showed a significantly greater change in their marital adjustment than did a matched control group of couples whose therapy did not include that experience.[8]

As Lasswell and Lobsenz state in *Styles of Loving:*

. . . the most important thing in life is to love someone, the second most important thing in life is to have someone love you, and the third most important thing is for the first two to happen at the same time . . . [and] that each partner understands what makes the other feel truly loved.

Despite the paucity of research into the parameters of love, most studies point to the same single factor as the critical one when a person decides whether or not he or she is in love: the belief that we understand the emotional motivation behind a partner's words and actions and that he or she similarly understands ours.[9]

Appendix C ▪

Handling Family Finances

Certainly there are lots of things in life that money won't buy,
but it's very funny—
Have you ever tried to buy them without money?*

—Ogden Nash

For many couples, near the top of the list in rating their marital compatibility is the matter of how money is earned, how it ought to be spent, and how much (if any) should be saved. Many marital therapists report that money problems are among the most frequently heard complaints in unhappy marriages.[1,2] However, disagreements about the management of money are likely to be seen by therapists as most often symptomatic of a couple's problems rather than as an underlying marital difficulty.

Money often provides a concrete focus for the expression of more general conflicts over values, goals, and life-styles. For some people the accumulation of money may be the only clearly countable measure of their worth to their families or to the world; for others it may be a measure of their self-sufficiency, which in turn may be seen as an index of their freedom.

Couples in every income bracket are represented among those who name finances as an arena for conflict. In fact, for most couples who disagree over how money is managed or who have difficulties in making financial ends meet, real lack of income is not the issue at all. High-income couples are often in as great distress over financial disagreements as are low-income couples.

Financial planning bogs down when one or both partners have strong emotional associations with money or its use. For example, one or both may use money emotionally, either as a weapon with which to control the other or as a way of compensating for inadequacies, guilt, or feelings of being unloved. Such

---

* From "The Terrible People," in *Verses from 1929 On*, by Ogden Nash. Copyright 1933 by Ogden Nash. By permission of Little, Brown and Company.

emotional associations are common; most of them probably come from parental responses to the loss, gifts, misuse, finding, or theft of money during the subject's childhood. Psychologists believe that the way an individual handles money is a good indication of how he or she functions in other more general ways.[3] Conflicts over money management may be symbolic of a couple's basic inability to resolve their other differences.

One family-life expert has stated that whatever is wrong with a couple's money management is a direct reflection of what is wrong with their marriage. Conversely, the ways many couples learn to agree on a money plan—taking into consideration their individual idiosyncrasies, goals, values, strengths, and weaknesses in financial affairs—can be a clue to how they manage the other differences in their lives.[4]

Messages received from parents about money are often anxiety-ridden. Ideas about who should handle the checkbook and pay the bills often involve deeply entrenched notions of rightness or wrongness learned from the ways such matters were discussed and handled in the parental home. Often the issue in the present is not which partner is the most competent or who has the most time to perform these tasks but whether one's father and/or mother seemed to attach emotional value to one or the other of them doing it.

There appear to be two opposite views about managing finances—"Live for today, it's only money" versus "Save for a rainy day." Both are perfectly good financial philosophies, and each has its loyal adherents. However, when two people who hold opposite views live together in an economic partnership, they often interpret the resulting disagreement as "trouble." If one believes in the short-term philosophy that there will always be more money coming in and hence it is better to buy now before inflation causes prices to go up, but the other is a long-range planner who wants to put money aside and believes in cash-only purchasing, then conflicts and arguments are virtually guaranteed. Couples who differ in their ideas of how money should be handled obviously must come up with a comfortable compromise to bridge their different philosophies, if they want to avoid constant bickering.

Since money has such different emotional and practical meanings for each person, it becomes crucial for husbands and wives to explore their meanings together and to be as mutually aware as possible of what money means to them. All the financial planning in the world cannot compensate for poor communication on this score.

Sometimes couples fail to recognize that their differences about saving and spending policies or consumer values may actually be a practical advantage for both of them. In the long run, the spendthrift is better off married to the person who squirrels away savings than to another spendthrift, even though the two spendthrifts might never argue about money. The squirrel, too, may enjoy some valuable experiences as a result of being married to a spendthrift, even though they argue. Complementarity of financial philosophies may mean that both partners will live better lives than they would if their philosophies were identical.

It seems extremely unlikely that any two persons will have precisely the same material values on every count. The extent to which their disagreements are seen as normal and inevitable and not as grounds for assaulting the partner's character or dignity will probably determine their compatibility level.

It is unlikely that anyone can state positively that any two goods are precisely equal; even the courts normally resolve such issues by reducing the value of the goods to money. Is $40 in a safe-deposit box equal to an afternoon spent getting a permanent wave? An afternoon on water skis? on snow skis? on a fishing barge? Dinner out at a fancy restaurant? A pair of shoes for one special occasion? A bet on a horse with good odds? It becomes clear that the search for an agreement on such questions cannot end with anyone's authoritative answer but depends on the establishing of each partner's rights to accept or violate the other's personal values.

Psychiatrist Edmund Bergler has given these guidelines for what he believes is a normal, healthy approach for couples to use in dealing with money matters:

1. Money is a means to the end of acquiring things one desires; do not make it an end in itself.
2. The fear of being taken advantage of in money matters should not be greatly out of proportion to the actual threat. One does not allow oneself to be taken advantage of, of course, and will be careful to avoid this.
3. One tries to make money as well and as much as one can. However, the process should not sacrifice health, love, hobbies, recreation, or contentment. Money should never become the center of one's life.
4. Spending money for necessities and for some luxuries should be taken for granted; it should not take a surgical operation to get a person to put a dollar in circulation. Hoarding of money, if a predominant motif in one's life, is a neurotic trait.
5. The phrase "I cannot afford it" is a simple statement of an objective fact and should never reflect a defensive way to punish oneself or another.[5]

Sound financial management and planning are necessities in today's world of spiraling inflation. A financially successful couple operate just as a fiscally sound business does. Both husband and wife should be completely involved in their finances, just as two business partners would be; marriage is in fact very much a business partnership. It has been estimated that the average old middle-class couple in the United States has passed over $1 million through their joint hands during their married life.[6]

In March 1981 a Gallup poll determined that the median amount that Americans believed was necessary to support a family of four was $277 a week ($14,404 per year). This figure represented a $27-per-week increase from 1980, and the 1980 figure was $27 higher than the 1979 figure. Inflation is looming as a greater and greater concern for American families. Seventy-three percent of those polled cited the high cost of living as the most important problem facing them and the nation. The cost of food alone—which most families agree is an item not easily pared down—has escalated dramatically since 1970—a staggering 56 percent.[7]

Life-Cycle Changes

Family finances are, of course, a constantly changing phenomenon. Young couples usually have only themselves to take care of and are usually both employed. In fact, it is rare today for a young wife with no children not to work outside the home. Eighty-two percent of childless married women aged twenty-five to thirty-four are in the labor force.[8] Sometimes, of course, young couples have very little money even though both partners are employed because they are in the beginning phases of their occupations. One or both of them may still be going to school, and they may be living in what has been described as "genteel poverty."

Young adult couples often are "broke" but know that things will get better as they accumulate assets and work their way up the occupational ladder. Usually their friends are at the same stage of life, and although they may often wish for the level of living once provided by their parents, they are not pessimistic about their current financial state. Some young couples manage to save money, to buy material items for their homes, and to afford a limited amount of travel and entertainment. Arguments over finances most often arise over how to resolve the earning, spending, and saving patterns brought from their families of origin; over issues of cash flow (income versus outgo); and over how to use credit.

Generally, the longer young couples postpone having children, the better off they become financially. The birth of children changes budgets dramatically. Not only do most women quit their jobs to stay at home with their young children, so that their incomes are lost, but also the expenses of having a child, of increased family needs, and possibly of the need for different housing all combine to change the financial picture (see Chapter 10).

A Gallup poll reported that a two-person household in 1981 said they needed $200 per week on the average to subsist; a three-person family needed $250; a four-person family needed $277; and a family of five or more could not get along on less than $300 per week. Food for an average couple ran $52 per week, for three persons $64, for four persons $77, and for five or more persons $98.[9]

Very few couples with growing families manage to save much during their child-rearing years. It has been estimated that it takes about three times an average earner's annual salary to provide for a child until he or she is eighteen years old. For most families, this translates to something between $40,000 and $90,000 for each child.[10] The cost of providing college educations for their children is seen as prohibitive by many parents. Others report that they borrow against their homes at this time when they would actually prefer to build their equity in them or to put money away for their own retirements.

Once their children are launched, some couples are able to spend more of their income for their personal needs and wishes unless they have aging parents who are becoming dependent at about the same time. This, unfortunately, is often the case. As a latent effect, this experience sometimes causes middle-aged couples to give increased thought to retirement and to investing wisely so that they will not be financially dependent on their children in their own old age. They may begin to save again instead of using more of their incomes for luxuries, for travel, and for long-postponed projects such as redecorating homes and buying new cars. A couple may even sell the family home and move to smaller or more convenient quarters.

Many women who have been full-time homemakers seek outside employment once their children are grown. The addition of their incomes to their husbands' (usually peak career) earnings means that the average middle-class, middle-aged couple today has more income than at any previous period in their married lives.

Lifelong instruction and encouragement to save money make it imperative that couples with surplus income review very carefully any investments to make certain that the taxes on the income from them do not reduce that income adjusted for inflation to a net loss. A clear example of such a misfortune would be the investment of $1,000 at 8 percent simple interest in a year in which the inflation rate is 8 percent or more. Not only is the $1,080 principal at the year's end worth the same as $1,000 at the beginning of the year, but the investor must pay $20 to the federal Internal Revenue Service (if he or she is in the 25 percent tax bracket) and often about $8 to the state tax collector. The investor is poorer at the end of the year than at the beginning! Passbook savings accounts that pay 5 percent or 5 $\frac{1}{2}$ percent interest leave the saver unable to buy as much at the end of a year as at the beginning if the inflation rate is 14 percent—the actual loss to the saver is about 9 percent of his or her investment, before taxes. These realistic figures need to be weighed carefully against sentimental pressures to save money in banks.

Finally, in retirement and old age, couples usually cut back on their spending to habits that resemble those of their newlywed days. Many draw on pension plans provided by their jobs; some have set up their own retirement plans in order to put away income that has not yet been taxed against the day when their retirement incomes would put them in a much lower tax bracket. They now can draw out this money as income for their retirement years. Unfortunately, as inflation rates continue to be high, many such plans have reduced the purchasing power of the money saved to far below the value of the original investment.

Most retired persons receive Social Security benefits that are paid each month upon retirement and, up to a fixed maximum, are based on the amount paid into the system over a working lifetime.

The average woman will outlive her husband by about ten years.[11] For this reason, she especially should know about the couple's economic status, be certain that they both have wills, and know the provisions of her husband's will and any estate plans. If they do not have wills, each partner's right to the property held by the other depends on the state in which they have legal residence at the time death occurs.

In community property states, a married person's property can be either separate or community. If it is separate, it is usually property owned before the marriage or received as a gift or by inheritance during the marriage. Community property includes all other holdings acquired during the marriage or separate property that is comingled (converted into community property, as in a joint home purchase). When a spouse dies, the survivor in such a state automatically retains his or her half of community property. Each can make provisions in a will to leave this half to anyone he or she pleases, including the spouse. If there is no will, some state laws entitle the surviving spouse to the entire estate. In other states, if there are children, they and their surviving parent are awarded specified fixed shares.

In states that have common-law marital property systems, the surviving spouse does not necessarily own a half interest in all property acquired during the marriage by both spouses. In these states all earnings and property accumulated by either spouse during the marriage may be his or her separate property. Often the husband has earned the most, although as more and more women enter the labor market this picture is changing somewhat. On the other hand, property or money acquired or inherited by a woman may become a "nest egg" rather than being dissipated in current living costs. This, plus various income and inheritance tax laws, bankruptcy laws, and a distribution of insurance beneficiaries strongly favoring women, results in the majority of inheritable wealth in such states being held by women.[12]

If a will is left, most states provide that neither partner can totally exclude the other. What share of the estate is awarded automatically in the absence of a will depends on state law. If no will is left, the surviving spouse's rights to the estate usually depend on how many other heirs there are. For instance, in Missouri the surviving spouse is entitled to the entire estate if there are no other heirs but to only half if there are children, grandchildren, parents, brothers, sisters, nieces, or nephews.[13]

In Oregon a surviving spouse is entitled to his or her late partner's entire estate if there are no children or grandchildren and to half if there are children and grandchildren. Arkansas adds the qualification that the couple must have been married for more than three years for this to apply, and Oklahoma specifies that a deceased husband's entire estate will be left to his wife only if it has been acquired by their "joint industry."[14]

It is probably safe to say that very few couples at any stage of the life cycle ever believe they have enough money. As income increases and tastes change, what was once considered a luxury easily comes to be viewed as a necessity. It is very difficult to retreat financially and to have to give up what one has become accustomed to having. Since there is nearly always some conflict between what people earn and what they spend (or would like to spend), couples—from the newly married ones to the retired—who have no consensual plan for money management are almost certain to face disagreements.

Financial Planning

Wouldn't it be wonderful to have an intelligent, flexible, workable plan for spending and saving money? Such a plan would calculate the amount available to spend and would keep records of what was spent. By knowing these two basic facts, couples could assess their financial status, plan for the future, and avert mishaps that might plunge them into financial difficulties. They could channel their cash flow into areas that would provide greater benefit to them than their immediate, often impulsive spending patterns might produce.

This sounds good until the name of the plan is mentioned—*budgeting*. The idea seems too restrictive to many, too complicated or boring to others. Yet there are certain things in life that one "should" do, and a budget seems to be one of them unless both partners are extremely good at managing money without one. Most people are not.

Budgeting can be very simple: what one earns from any source (spendable "take home" income) should equal or exceed the outlay. This is called the principle of *cash flow*. A budget should be simple and flexible. It will probably need to be revised fairly often to keep up with changes in earnings, unexpected changes in life-style, and needs to save. Unfortunately for those who abhor such work, budgets do necessitate record keeping. In our experience in working with couples over the years, however, in each marriage there is likely to be one record keeper and one who dislikes such details.

In a marriage in which both partners like to keep records, they may work cooperatively or take turns; if neither likes to do this job, they may be in trouble. They, too, may need to work cooperatively or to take turns. Some couples use a service that keeps track of their cash flow by computer for a moderate monthly fee. For couples who argue over budgets or who will not keep one at all since neither partner enjoys the record keeping, such a service may easily pay for itself by helping to avoid the pitfalls of emergency borrowing or excess interest charges on credit accounts.

For couples who want to set up a budget for themselves, there are several agreed-on steps to take: (1) It is important to get an accurate reading on fixed expenses based on past records (check stubs and old paid bills can give a good idea of past expenditures). These include those items that come due regularly, such as rent (or house payment), utilities, debt repayments, insurance, transportation costs, food, and household supplies. (2) These may then be subtracted from the fixed income.

Some fixed expenses are *nonnegotiable;* that is, there is nothing one can do to change them because they are set and controlled by someone else. Examples of these are home mortgage payments and property taxes; Social Security, state, and federal income taxes deducted from one's salary; insurance required by law or by lenders; minimum charges for water, power, and garbage collection; business, professional (if necessary for one's work), and driver's licenses; union, trade association, or professional association dues; sewer, street lighting, fire protection, and other assessments by cities or counties; any kind of interest, lien, garnishment, penalty, or fine that can cause one's eviction, imprisonment, or the loss or confiscation of one's property. The only alternatives to paying such minimums, dues, licenses, and taxes are to sell one's home, change one's occupation, declare bankruptcy, or (in some cases) petition for relief from the state legislature.

There is a necessary minimum for survival in some of the expenses called "fixed," such as food, rent, medicine, and medical care. That is, one can survive on a minimum diet, but cutting food expenditures below that minimum could lead to malnutrition. Fortunately, most people have enough income to fix their food budgets within a range that provides for more than a borderline starvation diet. Many can provide a good diet at less cost than they are currently spending, however, simply by planning their grocery shopping and menus more carefully and by paying more attention to nutritional values of foods, seasonal variations in price, and the relative costs of quantity buying (or sometimes of cooperative group purchasing of commodities that store well and are easily divided).

A federal interagency committee of the United States Government devised a formula based on the Department of Agriculture's economy food plan that reflects the different consumption requirements of families based on their size and composition, the sex and age of the head of household, and farm or nonfarm residence. It was determined that families of three or more persons spend approximately one-third of their incomes on food. Any income lower than three times the cost of a minimum adequate diet for families of three persons was considered to be at or below the poverty level.[15]

Persons living below the poverty level are usually eligible for a variety of cash and noncash forms of assistance with their finances. Noncash assistance may be in the form of food stamps, free or reduced-price school lunches, Medicare or Medicaid, public or subsidized housing, and other less common kinds of public assistance. Of the 79,108,000 households in the United States in 1979, 27,190,000 (about 34 percent) received one or more forms of this government aid. Of those, 6,925,000 were households living below the poverty level (just under 9 percent of all households). About three-quarters of the households receiving noncash benefits, then, have incomes above the poverty level—for example, 595,000 households receiving food stamps had incomes of over $15,000 in 1979, as did 177,000 households living in publicly owned or subsidized housing.[16] About one-third of the population of the United States has removed some fixed-cost items from budgets, or at least has reduced the fixed costs, as a result of public assistance.

When the fixed-cost items on the budget have been accounted for, any funds remaining can be designated *discretionary expenses*. If no money is left after expenses, then either cuts will have to be made or more income will have to be produced. It is obviously difficult to cut fixed expenses, although sometimes moving to less expensive housing, planning meals more carefully, or trying to cut utility bills (particularly telephone bills) can make the difference between a balanced and an unbalanced budget.

However, no one can live happily for very long without some of the items included in the usual list of discretionary expenses: entertainment, personal allowances, clothing, replacement of household items or furnishings, personal care, cleaning, costs associated with pets, vacations, newspapers, magazines, various contributions—and, for some persons, alcohol and/or tobacco. Each couple and each family will have its own list of items that they consider important to their own health and/or happiness.

Personal and Child Allowances

Enough should be included in each family budget (depending on resources) for each person to have some spending money that need not be accounted for. Whether one is an adult or a child, it is unpleasant to have to ask for every penny one needs or to feel guilty each time one spends any money on a personal item. Too often the one who keeps the family books becomes the family "comptroller" who doles out money on request. This is a situation reminiscent for most of a parent-child relationship in which the child (in this case, the wife, the husband, or a child) must justify money spent. Having an amount of pocket money that is allocated for personal items and does not need an accounting adds to one's feelings of independence and responsibility.

Children can be included in some financial discussions so that they develop responsibility and come to understand the family's cash flow. By the age of five or six a child can understand that a dime or a dollar buys an item; an eight- or nine-year-old can plan ahead, saving today's accumulated dimes for tomorrow's purchases. By middle childhood boys and girls are ready for an allowance—a fixed amount each week determined by their needs, the family's resources, and their peers' allowances.[17] When children first begin to manage money, they often make mistakes—spend it "foolishly"—just as some adults do. Child psychologists recommend that children not be given advances or gifts unless parents use these extra amounts to teach them about borrowing and credit.[18]

Some children earn their spending money. Other families believe that all spendable income is the family's and that children should get their fair share. These are two diametrically opposed points of view, each of which has its adherents. Each produces children with distinct views about money. Children who receive fixed allowances—amounts paid each week that are not connected with working—learn that family resources are shared. Such a child does assigned tasks as a member of the family and may be paid for extra jobs that ordinarily would cost the family extra (such as washing windows, washing the car, or doing yard work). The allowance is not withheld as a disciplinary measure because these parents do not believe it is wise to pay children to be good.

The other philosophy about money is that if children are paid a fixed amount, no matter what they do, they will not learn to work for a living. This approach emphasizes that children have certain tasks that are expected of them (such as keeping their rooms clean and picking up after themselves) but that they must earn any money they need. Tasks are posted with amounts of payment for each; children are expected to work for all amounts they are given.

Although few studies have been done to determine which method is the best, it is generally agreed that children who share in family resources and do not have to work for their money view money differently from children who earn the money they spend.[19] Some parents believe that since the family is the training ground for later life, giving children what they need—rather than making them earn it—is doing the children a disservice. Other families believe that income belongs to all family members and that the proper "work" of children is going to school and growing up: a child should not have to enter the marketplace at such an early age. Since there is no research to back up one side or the other, parents are left to their own sentiments on this issue.

Banking

Most people think of banks, credit unions, and savings and loan associations as safer places to keep their money than storing it at home in cash. That is true, of course, but these institutions also have other important functions. Perhaps the most important for most people is that they facilitate the transfer of money from one person or company to another without the actual cash being carried or sent. Banks always offer checking (sometimes called *commercial*) accounts, as do many credit unions and savings and loan associations.

Writing checks (orders to your financial agent to pay from your account) is not only more convenient and safer than carrying or mailing cash, but also provides a clear record of payment (and, when endorsed, constitutes a receipt by the endorser) and a set of memoranda from which an accounting of expenditures can be readily constructed.

Some banks and savings and loan associations pay interest on either the daily amount on deposit in a checking account or on the monthly minimum. Many have several kinds of service charges for maintaining checking accounts, with formulas based on minimum or average balances and/or on the number of checks written. Sometimes it is possible to arrange for a checking account that provides that checks written for more than one's balance are automatically covered by a loan from the financial institution. The interest charged for such an arrangement often runs as high as an 18 percent on an annual basis.

Banks, credit unions, and savings and loan associations make their money primarily by lending or investing the money of their depositors. It is obviously important for these institutions to lend the money available to them at interest rates higher than those they pay to the people who have accounts with them and to be sure that the money they lend will be repaid. Loans are *secured* by mortgages or liens on property, by savings accounts, or sometimes by the guarantee of a cosigner that the loan and its interest will be repaid. Since it usually takes a few days to process a loan, anyone who foresees that necessity should apply in advance.

Savings accounts are usually thought of as investments rather than as convenient ways to store money. Savings accounts may be simple passbook accounts to which money may be added or from which it may be withdrawn on demand (an institution may require thirty days notice for withdrawal, although few exercise this in normal times). Passbook accounts draw minimum interest. A higher rate of interest is usually paid on long-term accounts which sometimes require that the money be kept on deposit for several years if the full interest rate is to be paid, but this is not always true. Investors can choose the kind of account that best serves their personal needs.

Family members must decide whether they want their accounts to be joint or separate. Joint accounts have the advantage that withdrawals can be made or checks written by any of the depositors. This can be particularly advantageous in case of death, disability, or unavailability of the person who might otherwise have all the funds in his or her personal account. In the case of a minimum-balance checking account, a joint account might more often avoid service charges or draw interest than would two or more separate accounts. The chief disadvantage of joint accounts lies in keeping track of the balance in the account, particularly if more than one checkbook is in use.

Savings

There are long-range items that must be planned for in a budget. For instance, families with cars must plan for repairs and for upkeep. The same is true for household appliances and for home and yard maintenance. People sometimes get sick and need medical attention and drugs. There may be emergencies—a needed trip to visit an ailing parent or even to attend a funeral. There may be a layoff at work or an accident that damages the family car. Emergencies, as well as postponed purchases (furniture, cars, vacations, remodeling, children's college educations) all call for advance planning.

For these and other reasons, many families feel an urgency to put part of their income away for a "rainy day." When possible, it is wise to plan a budget so that it includes regular savings as a financial cushion and for larger-item purchases. It is usually recommended that 10 percent of spendable income be saved as a ready reserve for emergencies. In addition, many couples put aside another 10 percent for purchases they wish to make in the future (major items, vacations, holiday purchases).

Most couples who manage to save find it easier and more systematic to set aside a fixed amount each pay period. Some employers have payroll deductions to help employees to save regularly. In today's climate of high inflation, most couples keep only a minimum of their savings in low-interest accounts—just enough so that they can have ready access to them in an emergency. Other savings are put into higher-yield accounts like those in savings and loan banks that pay compound interest (interest on interest earned) on a frequent basis. For those who have a considerable amount in savings, certificates of deposit (like Treasury bills) that tie up their money for specified periods of time, such as six months or a year, pay still higher interest rates. Some people buy U.S. government bonds or municipal bonds. Many of the latter have the advantage of earning tax-free interest.

Investments

In contrast to savings, which put aside spendable income to be used when needed, investments remove income for longer periods, allowing assets to grow into even greater assets. Of course, the money can be removed by selling the investment properties, but the philosophy of investment is that the money will be left to grow on a long-term basis. The stock market is a favorite way to invest, judging by the report that one in seven Americans holds some stock. However, since the stock market fluctuates and is affected by general economic conditions, very few people who invest small amounts of savings make a great deal of profit. Some financial experts warn that it is not advisable to buy stocks if the money used is the only savings held.

In considering an investment, the watchwords are *safety*—if you cannot afford to lose some of what you have put in the market or the investment property, it is not safe enough for you; *growth*—the monies invested should be in investments that will increase in value; and *yield*—there should be some return on money invested (such as interest paid). The investment must be balanced: a safe investment that has no potential for growth or one that has a high yield but is very risky is not thought to be sound for those who have no base of security in other types of savings.

For most families, the biggest investment that they will make—and in inflationary times one of the best—is in *buying a home*. Real estate values have been increasing steadily in the United States during the past decade, so that the growth potential of property as an investment has been great in most parts of the country. However, the fundamental value of a home as an investment is in its value to the family that lives in it.

Unlike monthly rental payments, monthly payments on a house go partially toward an equity in the home, partly toward interest on the loan for the mortgage on the house, sometimes partly toward property taxes, and sometimes partly toward insurance, the latter two depending on the mortgage agreement. Since interest and taxes are presently allowable as deductions on income taxes, there is a saving at this level, too. Mortgage payments may be for a fixed amount for the duration of the mortgage, so that they do not fluctuate as rent is likely to do. Taxes and insurance, of course, will vary with the costs of living and with the increased value of the property. Some banks and loan companies currently offer *variable interest rate mortgages* that change the rate of interest the borrower pays on the loan according to the current rate of interest in effect. In another variation, young couples borrow at a low interest rate when their incomes are apt to be lowest, and the interest rate rises (as do their incomes, at least theoretically) over the years.

Financial experts suggest a formula for the amount couples can safely invest in a home. Two to three times the couple's yearly income is considered a reasonable figure. Obviously, other expenditures may make this amount unfeasible for some couples, but others may find that the amount is ridiculously low in relation to the price of property in their locale.

Most couples buying homes seem to base their decisions on how large a down payment they can afford (the requirement to secure a loan usually is from 20 to 30 percent down) and what monthly payments they can afford. Since most couples spend an average of one week's take-home pay for rent each month, this gives them some idea of what they can afford for a monthly payment on a home. However, since the prices of single-family houses and condominiums have risen much faster than rents, many families will be unable to buy homes even though currently there are distinct advantages to owning one as an investment. According to U.S. government figures, rents have risen 58 percent since 1967, but housing prices have risen 122 percent.[20]

Insurance

There are five major types of insurance: life insurance, property insurance, automobile insurance, medical and hospital insurance, and disability insurance. Insurance is a protection against future needs for money resulting from illness, a death in the family, an accident, a disability, a theft, or a loss of any other kind.

Life insurance is for the purpose of providing dependents with a sufficient amount of money to help them adjust in the event that a major part of their income ceases, as happens with the death of a breadwinner. The purpose of life insurance is to provide a continuing income until the survivors can manage to recuperate and to take care of themselves. It is important that both men and women who have children have such coverage. A wage earner needs to leave his or her family protected, and a homemaker should have coverage to pay someone to take over household and child-care responsibilities. It is generally advised that women take out policies on their husbands and that men take out policies on their wives in keeping with their estimates of needs and of the family budget. If each insures the other's life, neither will have to pay inheritance tax on the amount left as they might if it were left as a part of the estate.

The two major types of life insurance policies are *term insurance* (a policy written for a specified term—usually five years—and then reissued as needed) and *ordinary life insurance*—either that which one pays for throughout one's lifetime and which is collected by survivors, or that which has a specified period for payment.

It is advisable to shop for life insurance policies since not all insurance companies give the same coverage for the same rates. In considering employment it is wise to explore the fringe benefits, which often include various kinds of insurance and usually offer very competitive prices. Some companies pay all the premiums for the employees, but others require a percentage contribution from employees. In many cases, a smaller salary actually is more than compensated for by such fringe benefits, which are not paid directly to the employee (and therefore are not taxable) but which add immeasurably to the family's security. There are also group insurance plans offered by professional organizations or offered on existing loans, often at very attractive prices. The latter are paid if the insured dies and are used to pay off loans or mortgages that may be left outstanding. Typically, couples with children at home are advised to be insured for three to four times the annual take-home pay of one breadwinner in order to be well covered. For the average family approximately $100,000 of life insurance would be quite adequate in 1981.

Property insurance usually covers the home against damage or its furnishings against damage or theft. Sometimes families also insure their personal belongings and may take out "rider" or "floater" policies on very expensive items such as jewelry and silver which are often not covered by homeowner's policies. It is wise to keep an inventory of all belongings and to keep the record in a safe place such as a bank safe-deposit box. A record can be either written or put on tape by going from room to room and describing the property, or it can be made by photographing the property. After a fire or burglary such records, which serve as evidence of ownership before the loss occurred, can make the difference in whether or not many insurance companies will pay some of the claims. Most householders are likely to have trouble recalling details of missing or damaged items or may even fail to remember that certain items were ever owned.

Automobile insurance is essential for the financial security of most car owners. Many states mandate by law that there be minimum coverage for any damages the driver may cause. The two major categories of automobile insurance are *liability insurance* and *collision insurance*. Accident lawsuits can involve large amounts of money; liability coverage to take care of claims for both property damages and personal injuries should be in the hundreds of thousands of dollars to ensure protection. Although laws require a minimum liability coverage, the difference in cost between the minimum amount and larger amounts usually is not great. A capable general insurance agent adviser can find the range of coverage for a family that minimizes the risks without unduly burdening them financially. Collision insurance on one's own car is not mandated by law, although if payments are due on a car loan, the lending agency normally requires it. Most policies are not written to cover the full amount of any damage but have deductible amounts to be paid by the insured with the balance being paid by the insurance company. Many persons choose $100 or $200 deductible policies, although some financial advisors suggest $500 deductible, which reduces the amount of the yearly premium substantially in most cases.

A serious threat to family security is the cost of a prolonged illness or an accident that could result in hospitalization, large medical bills, and the inability of the sick or injured person to work. Among the important fringe benefits of employment is coverage for all these possible events. Such policies may cover a variety of medical, surgical, hospital, and major medical expenses, and may provide for some continued income for specified periods of time even though the wage earner cannot work. In addition, should the illness or injury be job related, workman's compensation can provide some income until the employee can return to work.

For those who are self-employed or whose employer provides no insurance coverage or only minimal protection, most families carry supplemental or total coverage privately. It is important to know what the policy will pay for, how much the coverage will be, how often payments will be made, and whether or not there is any choice of hospital and source of treatment. An insurance broker can be particularly helpful in coordinating comprehensive coverage or coverage supplemental to that provided by employers.

Tax-Sheltered Retirement or Pension Plans

Most companies have retirement plans that serve as a forced savings or investment for their employees' future. The money may be wholly contributed by the employer, or certain deductions from wages may be set aside before taxes. The government will collect taxes on the money only when it is paid upon retirement, by which time the employee will be likely to be in a lower tax bracket. Some plans allow an employee to draw out what has accumulated if he or she leaves the job before retirement. For those who do not have a pension plan through their jobs, an Individual Retirement Account (IRA) may be set up with a mutual fund, a savings and loan institution, or a bank. Fifteen percent of one's salary or wages (up to $1,500) may be saved each year in this way. Up to $1,750 may be put aside if one's spouse is included. If a person is self-employed, a Keogh Plan may be set up for retirement that allows up to 15 percent of the annual income, or $7,500 to be set aside before taxes. A careful investor in any of these plans must consider the probable effects of inflation rates as well as possible changes in income tax rates.

TABLE C.1
Tax Rate Schedules for 1980: Schedule Y for Use by Married Individuals Filing Joint Returns

Taxable Income	Tax on Column 1	% on Excess
$ 3,400 or less	$ 0	14
5,500	294	16
7,600	630	18
11,900	1,404	21
16,000	2,265	24
20,200	3,273	28
24,600	4,505	32
29,900	6,201	37
35,200	8,162	43
45,800	12,720	49
60,000	19,678	54
85,600	33,502	59
109,400	47,544	64
162,400	81,464	68
215,400	117,504	70

Income Taxes

Another consideration in any family budget is money taken from all citizens to run the government. The tax rate schedules for 1980 are shown in Table C.1. The taxes shown are federal income taxes and do not include state income taxes (which may be up to an additional 11 percent), municipal income taxes, or, of course, property, sales, or excise taxes.

The tax bite is considerable (it will be noted that family incomes above the poverty level will be taxed at least 25 percent on that amount by the federal government alone) and for most persons is automatically deducted from their paychecks and thus never considered as a part of spendable income. For this reason, the amount paid in income tax is sometimes not as well understood as if couples had to plan for payments (as many persons do who pay a percentage every quarter of a year) or who must pay an additional amount beyond their deductions when they file their yearly reports. Most people are either resigned to the inevitability of these deductions or hope that some of the amount may be returned to them because more was deducted than they owed. Many people are estimated to have overpaid their taxes each year because they do not consult a tax expert, and even more overpay because they file the short income tax form and do not take all their allowable deductions. A government publication entitled "Your Federal Income Tax," available from the Superintendent of Documents, Washington, D.C. 20402, explains how to itemize deductions and how to fill out the more complicated long form. This task, though not easy, should at least be attempted by couples to see whether the effort pays off.

Keeping careful records of purchases is a prerequisite for filling out the long federal income tax form since taxes already paid for items or for entertainment or certain luxuries may be deducted from taxable income. Interest paid on loans or on credit charges also is deductible. All past tax returns should be kept in a safe place—a fireproof, locked file is recommended. Other records used in preparing the tax return also should be saved for several years, as should any other important papers relating to taxes, for an indefinite period.

For future tax purposes, careful, permanent records also should be kept of any expenditures connected with the ownership, improvement, or repair of one's house. These expenses may eventually be deducted from the profit on the sale of the house on which capital gains tax will be levied. A capital gain is a profit made from a change in price of an investment asset. As the price of housing has been escalating almost daily in recent years, most persons who invest in property will sell at a profit and be subjected to capital gains tax (although reinvesting in a home of equal value can delay payment of such a tax).

Credit

With as many places as there are for the family dollar to be spent, it is no wonder that some families decide to buy now and pay later. There are over 300 million retail credit cards, 133 million gasoline credit cards, 93 million bank credit cards, and 6 million general purpose credit cards in circulation in the United States.[21] It is estimated that half of all retail purchases are made by using credit.

Credit cards are primarily used for convenience, because many persons do not like to carry sizable sums of cash with them and because credit card records provide a convenient way to keep track of expenditures. In addition, credit cards have an advantage over writing checks for purchases because they are more easily negotiable (many merchants will not take personal checks, particularly out-of-town checks). In some instances, using a credit card is like borrowing interest-free money for a period of twenty-five to thirty days. Of course, if the card utilized is from a company that does charge interest immediately, the loan can be an expensive one.

Sometimes, but not always, an item or service has an inflated price to make up for the cost to the vendor of providing credit card service. Some merchants have very competitive prices and do not give discounts to cash-paying customers, so that whether or not one uses credit does not affect the price. Most of the general or single-use credit card companies that do not charge interest if the bill is paid within a specified period (department stores, oil companies, hotels, and car rental firms) also do not charge a membership fee. American Express,

Carte Blanche, and Diner's Club charge a small annual fee but require accounts to be kept current and thus do not serve as lending institutions and do not charge interest. Bank credit cards such as VISA and Master Charge now charge for the card and charge a service fee each time the card is used. These cards are still convenient but no longer have the economic advantages they once had.

Expensive items such as cars, major household appliances, furniture, and vacations are often paid for in credit installments. Payments include the regular cost of the item or service plus interest charges and any insurance that is deemed necessary. Usually such credit buying involves high interest rates of at least $1\frac{1}{2}$ percent on the unpaid balance each month or 18 percent true annual interest, compounded monthly.

Retailers are required to state specifically what their finance charges are, but in most states there is no limit on what they can ultimately charge. There are countless cases in which the fees have run between 30 and 40 percent true annual interest. Some credit issuers have *balloon payments* at the end of the contract, meaning that the customer pays small monthly payments until a specified date, at which time the entire balance must be paid all at once. It is always wise to read any contract very carefully and to get a copy of it. Some contracts have an "add on" clause providing that all items purchased may be repossessed, if any one is not paid for promptly—no matter what the total amount is that has already been collected. If you do not understand a contract, get a qualified person to look it over, and cancel the contract within the three-day limit that is allowed if there are parts that you wish not to agree to.

It is generally recommended that one have some kind of credit established. Using credit wisely and paying all bills when they are due establishes a good credit rating, which may be necessary at some future date for major purchases. There are over two thousand credit bureaus in the United States that keep files on credit users. A good credit rating is based on past credit history, current capability of paying off what is purchased on credit, and overall capital worth. Buying everything with cash does not establish such a rating; although many couples prefer to remain on a cash basis, most will eventually need an item and want to defer at least part of the payment. Purchase of a home, for example, is rarely accomplished without borrowing part of the cost.

In the mid-1970s the Equal Credit Opportunity Act was passed. This law prohibits creditors from disqualifying credit applicants because of certain sources of personal income (alimony, child support, or part-time wages, for instance). Under this regulation, accounts cannot be closed down because of a divorce if both parties are able to pay the bills they incur. This legislation has been a great boon to families who wish to count a wife's part-time income as evidence that they can pay their bills. It has also allowed women, whose credit previously was closely tied to their husbands' incomes, to establish credit in their own names.

With credit easily established for most adults and with family needs frequently straining the family budget, it is no surprise to find that many couples overextend themselves. Some are impulse spenders to begin with and with credit cards can easily become "crediholics." Financial experts recommend that no more than 20 to 25 percent of one's annual take-home income should be charged to future payments. A rule of thumb is that credit card balances should be able to be reduced in no more than sixty days without hurting the family budget. The cash advances or "instant money" offered by some lenders may be so tempting that couples find themselves with runaway debts before they realize what is happening to them.

Some couples turn to a debt consolidation loan from a bank or finance company, which pays off all their outstanding credit bills and requires them to make a payment each month on this loan. Sadly, these loans may carry some of the highest interest rates charged, although these may be justified by the poor credit ratings of the applicants. Couples in this kind of financial difficulty are better advised to see a credit counselor—a nonprofit community service in many areas—to arrange regular payments to creditors while curtailing any further credit purchases—tearing up credit cards, if necessary.

If couples have a good credit rating, they may be able to borrow money at a reasonable rate to pay off high-interest debts. Borrowing against savings, if they have any, or against investments or life insurance, they may be able to negotiate a loan at lower interest rates than the finance charges that creditors charge. Credit unions are excellent sources of low-interest loans for those who qualify, as some 24 million Americans do. Depending on the credit union's financial solvency, members usually can qualify for up to $2,500 at an interest rate well below the rate most banks charge. The problem with borrowing to pay off creditors is that bills are likely to pile up again unless a moratorium is called on using credit.

Some couples get into such financial straits that they are forced to file *bankruptcy*. This is the formal recognition of their inability to pay their debts or other obligations that they owe. The Federal Bankruptcy Reform Act of 1979 liberalized laws and established uniform rules that permit individuals declaring bankruptcy to exempt certain possessions from being claimed by creditors. Formerly many bankruptcy courts ordered debtors to repay as much as possible by selling any personal possessions they had.

The Federal Bankruptcy Reform Act of 1979 allows a person to declare bankruptcy while not being completely insolvent and while retaining considerable equity in a home or other property. The intent of the law, of course, was to permit families to hang on to some assets while getting a fresh start after disastrous financial expenditures or losses. Many families have been helped by these new laws, but it also appears that they have made bankruptcy a more common occurrence. In the first full year following passage of the legislation, personal bankruptcies rose 82 percent. The number of VISA credit card holders who filed bankruptcy was multiplied by five during that period.[22]

Conclusion

No single budget or financial plan will solve every family's financial problems. Much depends on the ages and sexes of the members, the point in the career cycle of each, the region in which they live, and even the part of town or rural area in which they live. Perhaps most of all, the life-style of the family and the habits with which they are comfortable affect their proportionate expenditures.

Every family has extravagances and economies that other families have trouble understanding. One family with two color television sets "can't afford" an encyclopedia; another family can spend several thousand dollars on a wedding or a funeral but "can't afford" to help a child with college expenses. Even advice to keep one's expenditures below one's earnings may not hold at some points in one's family life cycle or one's own career cycle.

The number, sexes, and ages of children affect food, clothing, and housing costs. In cold climates, winter coats, hats, boots, and snowsuits often can be handed down from year to year between children of the same sex who are not too far apart in age, but styles and sizes may limit passing clothing on to children who are much younger or of the opposite sex. A family with two boys or two girls may be adequately housed in a two-bedroom, two-bathroom house, but a comparable family with one boy and one girl may feel inadequately housed unless they have a three-bedroom, three-bathroom house; in cold climates this means two more rooms to heat.

Needs for medical care are high, but fairly predictable, during pregnancy and the early years of child rearing. As the family life cycle progresses, average costs may be lower but also less predictable. Some budgetary strains may be relieved by health insurance programs. which are likely to require more predictable budgeted amounts.

A periodic accounting for expenditures is a necessity in most families. If a record is kept, the items can be categorized (food, clothing, housing, insurance, and so forth) so that the family can at least be aware of how their money has been spent and decide whether the proportional amounts reflect the life-style they want. If not, it may be a necessary step to modify the figures in the accounting to make a budget for the coming year and to try to adjust expenditures to match the desired life-style as nearly as possible. In most regions of the United States an annual budget is preferable to a monthly one because many expenses vary with the seasons. In the northern and eastern states there are drastic differences in the necessary expenditures for heating, clothing, dry cleaning, and so forth from season to season. Vacations are usually once-a-year expenses. Holiday expenses are often exceptional. Property taxes are usually payable once or twice a year.

Generally speaking, budgeting is better than not budgeting for most families. Budgets fail when they are not comprehensive enough, are unrealistic, or subject the family to an uncomfortable change in life-style. A great deal of flexibility is usually necessary to keep family finances stabilized.

Notes

Chapter 1

1. U.S. Bureau of the Census, *Current Population Reports,* series P-23, no. 107 (October 1980), p. 40.
2. T. Hoult, *Dictionary of Modern Sociology* (Totowa, N.J.: Little-field, Adams, 1969).
3. G. Murdock, "World Ethnographic Sample," *American Anthropologist* 59 (1957), p. 686.
4. H. Christensen, ed., *Handbook of Marriage and the Family* (Chicago: Rand McNally, 1964), pp. 3–32.
5. E. Burgess, H. Locke, and M. Thomes, *The Family: From Institution to Companionship* (New York, Van Nostrand Reinhold, 1963).
6. U.S. Bureau of the Census, *Current Population Reports,* series P-20, no. 352 (July 1980), p. 7.
7. P. Jacobsen, *American Marriage and Divorce* (New York: Rinehart and Company, 1959).
8. U.S. Bureau of the Census, *Current Population Reports, Projections of the Population of the United States, 1977 to 2050,* series P-25, no. 704 (1977).
9. Jacobsen, *American Marriage.*
10. G. Streib and R. Beck, "Older Families: A Decade Review," *Journal of Marriage and the Family* 42 (November 1980), pp. 937–956.
11. Department of Health and Human Services Publication no. (PHS) 80-1120, vol. 29, no. 4, Supplement (July 31, 1980).
12. U.S. Bureau of the Census, *Current Population Reports,* series P-20, no. 336 (April 1979).
13. U.S. Bureau of the Census, *Current Population Reports,* series P-20, no. 338 (May 1979), p. 1.
14. Ibid.
15. S. Rawlings, *Perspectives on American Husbands and Wives* (Washington, D.C.: U.S. Department of Commerce, Bureau of the Census, Special Studies, series P-23, no. 77, December 1978).
16. Ibid.
17. U.S. Bureau of the Census, *Current Population Reports,* series P-20, no. 336 (April 1979).
18. Ibid.
19. Jacobsen, *American Marriage.*
20. U.S. Bureau of the Census, *Current Population Reports,* series P-20, no. 336 (April 1979), p. 1.
21. G. Elder, Jr., "Family History and the Life Course," *Journal of Family History* 2 (1977), pp. 279, 304.
22. G. Elder, Jr., "Approaches to Social Change and the Family: A Sociological Perspective," in J. Demos and S. Boocock, eds., *Turning Points: Historical and Sociological Essays on the Family* (Chicago: University of Chicago Press, 1978). Supplement to *American Journal of Sociology.*
23. W. Goode, *World Revolution and Family Patterns* (New York: Free Press, 1963).
24. L. Duberman, *Marriage and Other Alternatives,* 2nd ed. (New York: Praeger, 1977), p. 22.
25. U. Bronfenbrenner, "Nobody Home: The Erosion of the American Family," *Psychology Today* 10 (May 1977), pp. 41–47.
26. M. Bane, "Marital Disruption and the Lives of Children," *Journal of Social Issues* 32 (1976), pp. 103–117.
27. M. Levy, *Modernization and the Structure of Societies* (Princeton, N.J.: Princeton University Press, 1966).
28. Research and Forecasts, Inc., Survey for Connecticut Mutual Life Insurance Company (New York: Connecticut Mutual Life Insurance Company, 1980).
29. R. Moroney, "The Issue of Family Policy: Do We Know Enough to Take Action?" *Journal of Marriage and the Family* 41 (August 1979), pp. 461–463.
30. H. Pardes, "Foreword," in *Families Today,* vol. 1, Science Monographs (Washington, D.C.: National Institute of Mental Health, 1979), p. 1.
31. Burgess, Locke, and Thomes, *The Family from Institution to Companionship.*
32. L. Pratt, *Family Structure and Effective Health Behavior: The Energized Family* (Boston: Houghton Mifflin, 1976).
33. N. Stinnett, "Strengthening Families" (Paper presented at the National Symposium on Building Family Strengths, University of Nebraska, Lincoln, May 1978).
34. C. Backman and P. Secord, "The Effect of Perceived Liking on Interpersonal Attraction," *Human Relations* 12 (1959), pp. 379–384.
35. M. Shaw, *Group Dynamics: The Psychology of Small Group Behavior* (New York: McGraw-Hill, 1976).
36. F. M. Esfandiary, *Up-Wingers* (New York: Popular Library, 1977), pp. 46, 47.
37. R. Whitehurst, "Alternate Life-Styles," *The Humanist* (May–June 1975), pp. 23–26.
38. V. Packard, *A Nation of Strangers* (New York: David McKay, 1972).
39. National Opinion Research Center poll, 1973–1975.
40. U.S. Bureau of the Census, *Current Population Reports,* series P-23, no. 77 (December 1978), p. 1.
41. M. Bane, *Here to Stay: America —Families in the Twentieth Century* (New York: Basic Books, 1976).
42. E. Corfman, "Introduction and Overview," *Families Today,* vol. I, Science Monographs (Washington, D.C.: National Institute of Mental Health, 1979), p. 1.
43. W. Burr, *Theory Construction and the Sociology of the Family* (New York: Wiley, 1973).

44. T. Holman and W. Burr, "Beyond the Beyond: The Growth of Family Theories in the 1970's," *Journal of Marriage and the Family* 42 (November 1980), pp. 729–741.

45. R. Hill, "Contemporary Developments in Family Theory," *Journal of Marriage and the Family* 28 (February 1966), pp. 10–25.

46. D. Klein, "A Social History of a Grass-Roots Institution: The Case of the NCFR Workshop on Theory Construction and Research Methodology" (Paper presented to the NCFR Workshop on Theory Construction and Research Methodology, Boston, August 1979).

47. Holman and Burr, "Beyond the Beyond."

48. D. Klein, J. Schaneveldt, and B. Miller, "The Attitudes and Activities of Contemporary Family Theorists," *Journal of Comparative Family Studies* 8 (Spring 1977), pp. 5–27.

49. I. Nye, "Is Choice and Exchange Theory the Key?" *Journal of Marriage and the Family* 40 (May 1978), pp. 219–233.

50. P. Blau, *Exchange and Power in Social Life* (New York: Wiley, 1964), p. 91.

51. M. Osmond, "Reciprocity: A Dynamic Model and a Method to Study Family Power," *Journal of Marriage and the Family* 40 (February 1978), pp. 49–61.

52. R. Stuart, "An Operant Interpersonal Program for Couples," in D. Olson, ed., *Treating Relationships* (Lake Mills, Iowa: Graphic Publishing Company, 1976), pp. 119–132.

53. B. Murstein, M. Cerreto, and M. McDonald, "A Theory and Investigation of the Effects of Exchange-Orientation on Marriage and Friendships," *Journal of Marriage and the Family* 39 (August 1977), pp. 543–548.

54. D. Hobbs and S. Cole, "Transition to Parenthood: A Decade Replication," *Journal of Marriage and the Family* 38 (November 1976), pp. 723–731.

55. C. Broderick and J. Smith, "The General Systems Approach to the Family," in W. Burr, R. Hill, I. Nye, and I. Reiss, eds., *Contemporary Theories about the Family*, vol. 2 (New York: Free Press, 1979), pp. 112–129.

56. Holman and Burr, "Beyond the Beyond."

57. Broderick and Smith, *The General Systems Approach.*

58. J. Heiss, "Family Theory—20 Years Later," *Contemporary Sociology* 8 (1980), pp. 201–204.

59. B. Rollins and K. Cannon, "Marital Satisfaction over the Family Life Cycle: A Reevaluation," *Journal of Marriage and the Family* 36 (May 1974), pp. 271–283.

60. J. Sprey, "Conflict Theory and the Study of Marriage and the Family" in W. Burr et al., eds., *Contemporary Theories about the Family*, vol. 2 (New York: Free Press, 1979), pp. 130–159.

61. R. Collins, "A Conflict Theory of Sexual Stratification," *Social Problems* 19 (1971), pp. 3–12.

62. M. Mahoney, *Cognition and Behavior Modification* (Cambridge, Mass.: Ballinger, 1974).

63. Ibid.

64. R. Jewson, "The National Council on Family Relations: Decade of the Seventies," *Journal of Marriage and the Family* 42 (November 1980), pp. 1017–1028.

65. From *Marriage and Divorce Today: The Professionals' Newsletter* September 1, 1980, p. 4.

66. E. Macklin, "Nontraditional Family Forms: A Decade of Research," *Journal of Marriage and the Family* 42 (November 1980), pp. 905–922.

67. S. Keller, "Does the Family Have a Future?" *Journal of Comparative Family Studies* (Spring 1971), pp. 1–14.

68. R. Whitehurst, "Alternate Life-Styles."

69. R. Ryder, "The Future of American Fertility," *Social Problems* 26 (February 1979), pp. 359–370.

70. M. Bane, *Here to Stay.*

71. H. Carter and P. Glick, *Marriage and Divorce: A Social and Economic Study*, rev. ed. (Cambridge, Mass.: Harvard University Press, 1976).

Chapter 2

1. K. Mason and J. Czajka, "Change and U.S. Women's Sex-Role Attitudes 1964–1974," *American Sociological Review* 41 (August 1976), pp. 573–596.

2. Yankelovich, Skelly and White, Inc., *The General Mills American Family Report 1976–1977* (Minneapolis, Minn.: General Mills, 1977), pp. 68–69.

3. J. Money, *Love and Love Sickness: The Science of Sex, Gender Difference, and Pair-Bonding* (Baltimore, Md.: Johns Hopkins University Press, 1980), p. 133.

4. R. Stoller, *Sex and Gender: On the Development of Masculinity and Femininity* (New York: Science House, 1968), p. 9.

5. S. Wachtel, "Genes and Gender," *The Sciences* (May–June 1978), pp. 16–17, 32–33.

6. Money, *Love and Love Sickness*, p. 134.

7. M. Martin and B. Voorhies, *Female of the Species* (New York: Columbia University Press, 1975), pp. 84–107.

8. Stoller, *Sex and Gender*, p. 9.

9. Ibid., p. 10.

10. J. Bardwick, *Psychology of Women: A Study of Biocultural Conflict* (New York: Harper & Row, 1971); cf. also P. Weintraub, "The Brain: His and Hers," *Discover* 2 (April 1981), pp. 14–20.

11. E. Maccoby and C. Jacklin, *The Psychology of Sex Differences* (Stanford, Calif.: Stanford University Press, 1974).

12. Money, *Love and Love Sickness*, p. 159.

13. W. Hale, *Ancient Greece* (New York: American Heritage Press, 1970).

14. J. Gagnon and W. Simon, "Sexual Deviance in Contemporary America," *Annals of the American Academy of Political and Social Science* (March 1968).

15. A. Bell and M. Weinberg, *Homo-*

sexualities (New York: Simon and Schuster, 1978).

16. M. Saghir and E. Robbins, *Male and Female Homosexuality* (Baltimore, Md.: Williams and Wilkins, 1973).

17. G. Dorner et al., "A Neuroendocrine Predisposition for Homosexuality in Men," *Archives of Sexual Behavior* 4 (1975), pp. 1–8.

18. J. Spence and R. Helmreich, *The Psychological Dimensions of Masculinity and Femininity: Their Correlates and Antecedents* (Austin: University of Texas Press, 1978).

19. S. Bem, "Beyond Androgyny: Some Presumptuous Prescriptions for a Liberated Sexual Identity," in A. Skolnick and J. Skolnick, eds., *Family in Transition,* 2nd ed. (Boston: Little, Brown, 1977).

20. C. Tavis, *The Longest War: Understanding Sex Differences* (New York: Harcourt Brace Jovanovich, 1978).

21. A. Korner, "Methodological Considerations in Studying Sex Differences in the Behavioral Functioning of Newborns," in R. C. Friedman, R. M. Richart, and R. L. Van de Wiele, eds., *Sex Differences in Behavior* (New York: Wiley, 1974).

22. A. Bandura, *Social Learning Theory* (Morristown, N.J.: General Learning Press, 1971).

23. A. Bandura, "Influence of Model's Reinforcement Contingencies on the Acquisition of Imitative Responses," *Journal of Personality and Social Psychology* 1 (1965), pp. 589–595.

24. J. Kagan, "Acquisition and Significance of Sex Typing and Sex Role Identity," in M. Hoffman and L. Hoffman, eds., *Review of Child Development Research,* vol. 2 (New York: Russell Sage, 1964).

25. E. Hetherington and G. Frankie, "Effects of Parental Dominance, Warmth, and Conflict on Imitation in Children," *Journal of Personality and Social Psychology* 6 (1967), pp. 119–125.

26. D. Lynn, *Parental and Sex-Role Identification: A Theoretical Formu-*

lation (Berkeley, Calif.: McCutchan, 1969).

27. L. Kohlberg, "Stage and Sequence: The Cognitive Developmental Approach to Socialization," in D. A. Goslin, ed., *Handbook of Socialization Theory and Research* (Chicago: Rand McNally, 1969).

28. R. Sears, L. Rau, and R. Alpert, *Identification and Child Rearing* (Stanford, Calif.: Stanford University Press, 1965).

29. E. Hetherington, "Effects of Father Absence on Personality Development in Adolescent Daughters," *Developmental Psychology* 7 (1972), pp. 313–326.

30. H. Biller, "Father-Absence and Personality Development of the Male Child," *Developmental Psychology* 2 (1970), pp. 181–201.

31. E. Hetherington, "Effects of Father Absence."

32. R. D. Hess, "Social Class and Ethnic Influence upon Socialization," in P. H. Mussen, ed., *Carmichael's Manual of Child Psychology,* vol. 2 (New York: Wiley, 1970).

33. A. Bandura, "Social-Learning Theory of Identificatory Processes," in D. Goslin, ed., *Handbook of Socialization:Theory and Research* (Chicago: Rand McNally, 1969).

34. S. Freud, *An Outline of Psychoanalysis* (New York: Norton, 1949).

35. B. Fagot, "Sex Differences in Toddlers' Behavior and Parental Reaction," *Developmental Psychology* 10 (1974), pp. 554–558.

36. A. Bandura and R. Walters, *Adolescent Aggression* (New York: Ronald Press, 1959).

37. M. Mead, *Sex and Temperament in Three Primitive Societies* (New York: William Morrow, 1935, 1961), p. 935.

38. J. Money and P. Rucker, *Sexual Signatures: On Being a Man or a Woman* (Boston: Little, Brown, 1975), p. 83.

39. Maccoby and Jacklin, *Psychology of Sex Differences.*

40. P. McGuiness and K. Pribram, "The Origins of Sensory Bias

in the Development of Gender: Differences in Perception and Cognition," in M. Bortner, ed., *Cognitive Growth and Development: Essays in Memory of Herbert G. Birch* (New York: Brunner/Mazel, 1979).

41. S. Weitz, *Sex Roles: Biological, Psychological, and Social Foundations* (New York: Oxford University Press), 1977.

42. M. Horner, "Toward an Understanding of the Achievement Related Conflicts in Women," *Journal of Social Issues* 28 (1972), pp. 157–175.

43. Spence and Helmreich, *Psychological Dimensions.*

44. B. Rosen and C. Aneshensel, "The Chameleon Syndrome: A Social Psychological Dimension of the Female Sex Role," *Journal of Marriage and the Family* 38 (1976), pp. 605–617.

45. L. Pogrebin, *Growing Up Free: Raising Your Child in the Eighties* (New York: McGraw-Hill, 1980).

46. T. Parsons and R. Bales, *Family Socialization and Interaction Process* (Glencoe, Ill.: Free Press, 1955).

47. Survey by *Marriage and Divorce Today,* reported in vol. 6, no. 3 (August 25, 1980).

48. J. Pleck and R. Brannon, "Male Roles and the Male Experience," *Journal of Social Issues* 34 (1978), p. 1.

49. T. Skovholt, J. Gormally, P. Schauble, and R. Davis, eds., "Counseling Men," *The Counseling Psychologist* 7 (1978), p. 4.

50. R. Lewis and J. Pleck, eds., "Men's Roles in the Family," *The Family Coordinator* 28 (October 1979), p. 4.

51. S. Julty, *Men's Bodies, Men's Selves* (New York: Dell, 1979), p. 21.

52. B. Friedan, "Their Turn: How Men Are Changing," *Redbook* (May 1980), p. 23.

53. Personal communication with Laura Schlessinger, Ph.D.

Chapter 3

1. A. Bernstein, "How Children Learn about Sex and Birth,"

Psychology Today 9 (January 1976), pp. 31–36, 66.

2. A. Bernstein and P. Cowan, "Children's Concepts of How People Get Babies," *Child Development* 46 (1975), pp. 77–92.

3. W. Masters, "Sex Therapy in a Clinical Setting" (Paper presented to the International Congress of Sexology, Philadelphia, 1976).

4. W. Gadpaille, *The Cycles of Sex* (New York: Scribner's, 1975).

5. M. Diamond and A. Karlen, *Sexual Decisions* (Boston: Little, Brown, 1980).

6. H. Thornburg, "Age and First Sources of Sex Information as Reported by 88 College Women," *Journal of School Health* 40 1970), pp. 156–158.

7. S. McCary, and J. McCary, "A Measure of Level of Sex Information," *Journal of Sex Education and Therapy* 3 (1977), pp. 26–28.

8. S. McCary, "Ages and Sources of Information for Learning about and Experiencing Sexual Concepts as Reported by 43 University Students." *Journal of Sex Education and Therapy* 4 (1978), pp. 50–53.

9. R. Sorenson, *Adolescent Sexuality in Contemporary America* (New York: World Publishing Company, 1973).

10. W. Reevy, "Adolescent Sexuality," in A. Ellis and A. Abarbanel, eds., *Encyclopedia of Sexual Behavior* (New York: Jason Aronson, 1973), pp. 52–68.

11. A. Kinsey, W. Pomeroy, C. Martin, and P. Gebhard, *Sexual Behavior in the Human Female* (Philadelphia: W. B. Saunders, 1953).

12. D. West, *Homosexuality* (Chicago: Aldine, 1968).

13. C. Broderick, "Socio-sexual Development in a Suburban Community," *Journal of Sex Research* 2 (1966), pp. 1–24.

14. Diamond and Karlen, *Sexual Decisions*, pp. 171–187.

15. R. Bell and K. Coughey, "Premarital Sexual Experience among College Females, 1958,

1968, and 1978," *Family Relations* 29 (July 1980), pp. 353–357.

16. Ibid.

17. J. Udry, *The Social Context of Marriage* (Philadelphia: Lippincott, 1971).

18. Reevy, "Adolescent Sexuality." Reprinted by permission of Hawthorn Properties (Elsevier-Dutton Publishing Co., Inc.) from *Encyclopedia of Sexual Behavior*, edited by Dr. Albert Ellis and Dr. Albert Abarbanel. Copyright © 1961 by Hawthorn Books, Inc.

19. Gadpaille, *Cycles of Sex*, pp. 268–269.

20. G. Wilson and D. Nias, *The Mystery of Love* (New York: Quadrangle/New York Times, 1976).

21. A. Comfort, ed., *The Joy of Sex: A Cordon Bleu Guide to Lovemaking* (New York: Crown, 1972); and *More Joy: A Lovemaking Companion to The Joy of Sex* (New York: Crown, 1974).

22. A. Ellis, *Sex without Guilt* (Alhambra, Calif.: Borden, 1958).

23. M. Hunt, *Sexual Behavior of the 1970s* (Chicago: Playboy Press, 1974).

24. C. Tavris and S. Ladd, *The Redbook Report on Female Sexuality* (New York: Delacorte, 1977).

25. J. Gagnon, *Human Sexualities* (Glenview, Ill.: Scott, Foresman, 1977), p. 130.

26. Kinsey, Pomeroy, Martin, and Gebhard, *Sexual Behavior in the Human Female.*

27. R. Greenblatt and V. McNamara, "Endocrinology of Human Sexuality," in B. Sadock, H. Kaplan, and A. Freedman, eds., *The Sexual Experience* (Baltimore: Williams and Wilkins, 1976).

28. W. Masters and V. Johnson, *Human Sexual Response* (Boston: Little, Brown, 1966).

29. Ibid.

30. Sorenson, *Adolescent Sexuality.*

31. A. Kinsey, W. Pomeroy, and C. Martin, *Sexual Behavior in the Human Male* (Philadelphia: W. B. Saunders, 1948).

32. Kinsey, Pomeroy, Martin, and

Gebhard, *Sexual Behavior in the Human Female.*

33. Diamond and Karlen, *Sexual Decisions*, pp. 175–182.

34. Sorenson, *Adolescent Sexuality.*

35. I. Arafat and W. Cotton, "Masturbation Practices of Males and Females," *Journal of Sex Research* 10 (1974), pp. 293–307.

36. M. De Martino, *Sex and the Intelligent Woman* (New York: Springer, 1974).

37. P. Abramson, "The Relationship of the Frequency of Masturbation to Several Personality Dimensions and Behavior," *Journal of Sex Research* 9 (1973), p. 139.

38. Masters, "Sex Therapy."

39. N. Friday, *My Secret Garden: Women's Sexual Fantasies* (New York: Trident Press, 1973).

40. M. Stein, *Lovers, Friends, Slaves . . . The Nine Male Sexual Types: Their Psycho-Sexual Transactions with Call Girls* (New York: G. P. Putnam's Sons, 1974).

41. Friday, *My Secret Garden.*

42. Gagnon, *Human Sexualities.*

43. Hunt, *Sexual Behavior.*

44. L. Humphreys, *Out of the Closet: The Sociology of Homosexual Liberation* (Englewood Cliffs, N.J.: Prentice-Hall, 1972).

45. A. Kopkind, "Gay Rock: The Boys in the Band." *Ramparts* 11 (1973), pp. 49–50.

46. *Newsweek*, May 27, 1974, p. 90.

47. C. Warren and B. Ponse, "The Existential Self and the Gay World," in J. Douglas, ed., *Existential Sociology* (Cambridge, Mass.: Harvard University Press, 1979).

48. J. Ramey, *Intimate Friendships* (Englewood Cliffs, N.J.: Prentice-Hall, 1976).

49. L. Yablonsky, *The Extra-Sex Factor: Why Over Half of America's Married Men Play Around* (New York: New York Times Book Company, 1979).

50. Kinsey, *Sexual Behavior in the Human Male* and *Sexual Behavior in the Human Female.*

51. Hunt, *Sexual Behavior.*

52. L. Wolfe, "The Sexual Profile of That Cosmopolitan Girl,"

Cosmopolitan (September 1980), pp. 254–265.

53. J. De Lamater and P. MacCorquodale, *Premarital Sexuality: Attitudes, Relationships, Behavior* (Madison: University of Wisconsin Press, 1979).

54. I. Reiss, *Family Systems in America*, 3rd ed. (New York: Holt, Rinehart and Winston, 1980), pp. 272–279.

55. Hunt, *Sexual Behavior.*

56. Yablonsky, *The Extra-Sex Factor.*

57. M. Maykovich, "Attitudes versus Behavior in Extramarital Sexual Relations," *Journal of Marriage and the Family* 38 (November 1976), pp. 693–699.

58. Hunt, *Sexual Behavior.*

59. Ibid., p. 270.

60. H. Strean, *The Extramarital Affair* (New York: Free Press, 1980).

61. Gadpaille, *Cycles of Sex*, pp. 371–372.

62. J. Sprey, "Extramarital Relationships," *Sexual Behavior* 2 (1972), pp. 34–36.

63. A. Pietropinto and J. Simenauer, *Beyond the Male Myth* (New York: Quadrangle/New York Times, 1977).

64. R. Bell, R. Turner, and L. Rosen, "A Multi-Variate Analysis of Female Extra-Marital Coitus," *Journal of Marriage and the Family* 37 (May 1975), pp. 375–384.

65. Maykovich, "Attitudes versus Behavior."

66. J. Knapp and R. Whitehurst, "Sexually Open Marriage and Relationships: Issues and Prospects," in R. Libby and R. Whitehurst, eds., *Marriage and Alternatives: Exploring Intimate Relationships* (Glenview, Ill.: Scott, Foresman, 1977), pp. 147–160.

Chapter 4

1. I. Reiss, *Family Systems in America*, 3rd ed. (New York: Holt, Rinehart and Winston, 1980), p. 121.

2. D. Hinkle and M. Sporakowski,

"Attitudes toward Love: A Reexamination," *Journal of Marriage and the Family* 37 (1975), pp. 764–767.

3. M. Lasswell and N. Lobsenz, *Styles of Loving* (Garden City, N.Y.: Doubleday, 1980), p. 2.

4. W. Kephart, "Some Correlates of Romantic Love," *Journal of Marriage and the Family* 29 (1967), pp. 470–474.

5. M. Mahler, F. Pine, and A. Bergman, *The Psychological Birth of the Human Infant: Symbiosis and Individuation* (New York: Basic Books, 1975).

6. R. Lax, S. Bach, and J. Burland, eds., *Rapprochement: The Critical Subphase of Separation-Individuation* (New York: Jason Aronson, 1980).

7. E. Erikson, *Childhood and Society* (New York: Norton, 1963).

8. H. Sullivan, *The Interpersonal Theory of Psychiatry* (New York: Norton, 1953).

9. C. Broderick, "Sexual Behavior among Pre-Adolescents," *Journal of Social Issues* 22 (April 1966), pp. 6–21.

10. Ibid.

11. C. Broderick and G. Rowe, "A Scale of Pre-Adolescent Heterosexual Development," *Journal of Marriage and the Family* 30 (February 1968), pp. 97–101.

12. W. Simon and J. Gagnon, "Selected Aspects of Adult Socialization" (Unpublished paper, 1967).

13. E. Erikson, *Identity, Youth and Crisis* (New York: Norton, 1968).

14. R. Driscoll, K. Davis, and M. Lipetz, "Parental Interference and Romantic Love: The Romeo and Juliet Effect," *Journal of Personality and Social Psychology* 24 (1972), pp. 1–10.

15. E. Walster and W. Walster, *A New Look at Love* (Reading, Mass.: Addison-Wesley, 1978), p. viii.

16. F. Galton, "Measurement of Character," *Fortnightly Review* 36 (1884), pp. 179–185.

17. D. Byrne, C. Ervin, and J. Lambeth, "Continuity Between the

Experimental Study of the Attraction and 'Real Life' Computer Dating," *Journal of Personality and Social Psychology* 16 (1970), pp. 157–165.

18. Z. Rubin, "Measurement of Romantic Love," *Journal of Personality and Social Psychology* 16 (1970), pp. 265–273.

19. T. Hatkoff and T. Lasswell, "Love and Age, Sex, and Life Course Experiences" (Paper presented at the Meeting of the National Council on Family Relations, October 1977).

20. J. Lynch, *The Broken Heart: The Medical Consequences of Loneliness in America* (New York: Basic Books, 1977), p. 197.

21. G. B. Shaw, personal communication to Mrs. Patrick Campbell.

22. Walster and Walster, *New Look at Love*, p. 135.

23. B. Murstein, *Theories of Attraction and Love* (New York: Springer, 1971).

24. G. Wilson and D. Nias, *The Mystery of Love* (New York: Quadrangle/New York Times, 1976).

25. E. Sutherland and D. Cressey, *Principles of Criminology* (Philadelphia: Lippincott, 1960), pp. 171–187.

26. E. Bogardus, *Social Distance* (Los Angeles: E. S. Bogardus, 1959), pp. 7–13.

27. E. Berne, *Sex in Human Loving* (New York: Simon and Schuster, 1970).

28. K. Davis, "Final Note on a Case of Extreme Isolation," *American Journal of Sociology* 52 (March 1947), pp. 432–437.

29. H. Harlow, "The Heterosexual Affectional System in Monkeys," *American Psychologist* 17 (1962), pp. 1–9.

30. R. Byrd, *Alone* (New York: Putnam, 1938).

31. M. Zuckerman, R. Albright, C. Marks, and G. Miller, "Stress and Hallucinatory Effects of Perceptual Isolation and Confinement," *Psychology Monographs* 76 (1962).

32. Berne, *Sex in Human Loving.*
33. W. Sze, "Social Variables and Their Effect on Psychiatric Emergency Situations among Children," in W. Sze, ed., *Human Life Cycle* (New York: Jason Aronson, 1975), pp. 207–215.
34. Berne, *Sex in Human Loving.*
35. Wilson and Nias, *Mystery of Love,* p. 1.
36. A. Iliffe, "A Study of Preferences in Feminine Beauty," *British Journal of Psychology* 51 (1960), pp. 267–273.
37. J. Udry, *The Social Context of Marriage* (Philadelphia: Lippincott, 1971).
38. Wilson and Nias, *Mystery of Love.*
39. Z. Rubin, *Liking and Loving: An Invitation to Social Psychology* (New York: Holt, Rinehart and Winston, 1973), p. 33.
40. Ibid.
41. T. Pear, *English Social Differences* (London: George Allen and Unwin, 1955).
42. T. Van de Velde, *Ideal Marriage: Its Physiology and Technique* (New York: Random House, 1957).
43. E. Brecher, *The Sex Researchers* (New York: New American Library, 1971), p. 45.
44. Van de Velde, *Ideal Marriage,* pp. 27–28.
45. Ibid., p. 27.
46. D. Morris, *Intimate Behavior* (New York: Random House, 1971), p. 35.
47. H. Kelley and J. Thibaut, *Interpersonal Relations: A Theory of Independence* (New York: Wiley, 1978).
48. E. Berscheid and E. Walster, *Interpersonal Attraction,* 2nd ed. (Reading, Mass.: Addison-Wesley, 1978).
49. E. Hess, "Attitude and Pupil Size," *Scientific American* 212 (1965), pp. 46–54.
50. Rubin, *Liking and Loving,* p. 37.
51. E. Aronson, *The Social Animal,* 3rd ed. (San Francisco: W. H. Freeman, 1980).
52. B. Murstein, "Self-Ideal-Self Discrepancy and the Choice of Marital Partner," *Journal of Consulting and Clinical Psychology* 37 (1971), pp. 47–52.
53. M. Snyder, E. Tanke, and E. Berscheid, "Social Perception and Interpersonal Behavior: On the Self-Fulfilling Nature of Social Stereotypes," in E. Aronson, ed., *Readings about the Social Animal* (San Francisco: W. H. Freeman, 1981), pp. 391–406.
54. H. Harlow, "The Nature of Love," *American Psychologist* 13 (1958), pp. 673–685.
55. Kephart, "Correlates of Romantic Love."
56. Rubin, *Liking and Loving.*
57. Ibid.
58. I. Reiss, *Family Systems in America,* 3rd ed. (New York: Holt, Rinehart and Winston, 1980), p. 129.
59. D. Tennov, *Love and Limerence: The Experience of Being in Love* (New York: Stein and Day, 1979).
60. Wilson and Nias, *Mystery of Love.*
61. J. Lee, *Colours of Love* (Toronto: New Press, 1973).
62. S. Schachter, "The Interaction of Cognitive and Physiological Determinants of Emotional State," in L. Berkowitz, ed., *Advances in Experimental Social Psychology,* vol. I (New York: Academic Press, 1964), pp. 49–80.
63. T. Lasswell, M. Lasswell, and L. Goodman, "What Biofeedback Can Tell Us about Love" (Paper presented at meeting of American Association of Marriage and Family Counselors, Las Vegas, Nevada, 1976).

Chapter 5

1. P. Glick, "Future American Families," *Washington COFO Memo* 2 (Summer–Fall 1979), pp. 2–5.
2. U.S. Bureau of the Census, "Marital Status and Living Arrangements, March 1976," *Current Population Reports,* series P-20, no. 306 (1977).
3. P. Stein, "The Lifestyles and Life Chances of the Never-Married," *Marriage and Family Review* 1 (July–August 1978), pp. 1–11.
4. R. Spreitzer and L. Riley, "Factors Associated with Singlehood," *Journal of Marriage and the Family* 36 (August 1974), pp. 533–542.
5. J. Barkas, *Single in America* (New York: Atheneum, 1980).
6. P. Stein, *Single* (Englewood Cliffs, N.J.: Prentice-Hall, 1976).
7. C. Bird, "Women Should Stay Single," in H. Hart, ed., *Marriage: For and Against* (New York: Hart, 1972).
8. S. Roberts, "The 'Living Alone' Phenomenon," *New York Times,* January 31, 1971, p. 56.
9. P. Stein, *Single.*
10. G. Knupfer, W. Clark, and R. Room, "The Mental Health of the Unmarried," *American Journal of Psychiatry* 122 (1966), pp. 841–851.
11. D. Heer and A. Grossbard-Schectman, "The Impact of the Female Marriage Squeeze and the Contraceptive Revolution on Sex Roles and the Women's Liberation Movement in the United States, 1960 to 1975." *Journal of Marriage and the Family* 43 (February 1981), pp. 49–65.
12. "Rise of the Singles—40 Million Free Spenders," *U.S. News and World Report,* October 7, 1974, pp. 54ff.
13. P. Stein, *Single,* p. 68.
14. M. Lasswell, "Is There a Best Age to Marry? An Interpretation," *The Family Coordinator* 23 (1974), pp. 237–242.
15. S. Jacoby, "Forty-Nine Million Singles Can't Be All Right," in S. Feldman and G. Thieller, eds., *Life Styles: Diversity in American Society,* 2nd ed. (Boston: Little, Brown, 1975), pp. 115–123.
16. Stein, "Lifestyles of the Never-Married," pp. 10–14.
17. A. Campbell, "The American Way of Mating: Marriage, Si; Children, Maybe," *Psychology Today,* May 8, 1975, pp. 37–43.
18. W. Gove and J. Tudor, "Adult Sex Roles and Mental Illness,"

American Journal of Sociology 78 (January 1973), pp. 50–73.

19. Campbell, "American Way of Mating," p. 38.

20. U.S. Bureau of the Census, *Current Population Reports,* series P-20, no. 363 (June 1981).

21. J. Pleck, "Man to Man: Is Brotherhood Possible?" in N. Glazer-Malbin, ed., *Old Family/New Family* (New York: Van Nostrand, 1975), pp. 229–244.

22. U.S. Bureau of the Census, "Social and Economic Characteristics of Americans during Midlife," *Current Population Reports,* series P-23, no. 111 (June 1981), pp. 3–4.

23. W. Gove, "The Relationship between Sex Roles, Marital Status and Mental Illness," *Social Forces* 51 (1972), pp. 34–44.

24. J. Bernard, *The Future of Marriage* (New York: Bantam, 1973).

25. Ibid.

26. Ibid.

27. Campbell, "American Way of Mating," p. 38.

28. I. Bengis, "Being Alone," *New York* magazine (1973).

29. M. Schwartz, "Career Strategies of the Never Married" (Paper presented at the 71st Annual Meeting of the American Sociological Association, New York, September 1976).

30. R. Francoeur, *Eve's New Rib* (New York: Delta Press, 1972).

31. M. Hunt, *Sexual Behavior in the 1970s* (New York: Dell, 1974).

32. Ibid., p. 154.

33. P. Gebhard, "Postmarital Coitus among Widows and Divorcees," in P. Bohannon, ed., *Divorce and After* (Garden City, N.Y.: Doubleday, 1970), pp. 81–96.

34. R. Weiss, *Marital Separation: Managing after a Marriage Ends* (New York: Basic Books, 1975).

35. Hunt, *Sexual Behavior,* p. 154.

36. M. Zelnik and J. Kantner, "Sexual and Contraceptive Experience of Young Unmarried Women in the United States, 1976 and 1971," *Family Planning Perspectives* 9 (1977), pp. 55–71.

37. I. Reiss, *Family Systems in Amer-*

ica, 3rd ed. (New York: Holt, Rinehart and Winston, 1980).

38. C. Williams, "The New Morality," *Time,* November 21, 1977, pp. 111–116.

39. J. Sandler, M. Myerson, and B. Kinder, *Human Sexuality: Current Perspectives* (Tampa, Fla.: Mariner, 1980).

40. I. Reiss, *The Social Context of Premarital Permissiveness* (New York: Holt, Rinehart and Winston, 1967).

41. Zelnik and Kantner, "Sexual and Contraceptive Experience."

42. R. Udry, K. Bauman, and N. Morris, "Changes in Premarital Experience of Recent Decades of Birth Cohorts of Urban American Women," *Journal of Marriage and the Family* 37 (1975), pp. 783–787.

43. S. Queen and R. Habenstein, *The Family in Various Cultures,* 4th ed. (Philadelphia: Lippincott, 1974).

44. D. Marshall, *Human Sexual Behavior: Variations in the Ethnographic Spectrum* (New York: Basic Books, 1971).

45. M. Edwards and E. Hoover, *The Challenge of Being Single* (New York: New American Library, 1974).

46. Ibid., p. 164.

47. Ibid., p. 175.

48. C. Safilios-Rothschild, *Love, Sex, and Sex Roles* (Englewood Cliffs, N.J.: Prentice-Hall, 1977).

49. Zelnik and Kantner, "Sexual and Contraceptive Experience."

50. Safilios-Rothschild, *Love, Sex, and Sex Roles,* p. 117.

51. U.S. Bureau of the Census, *Current Population Reports,* series P-20, no. 352 (July 1980).

52. C. Cole, "Cohabitation in Social Context," in R. Libby and R. Whitehurst, eds., *Marriage and Alternatives: Exploring Intimate Relationships* (Glenview, Ill.: Scott, Foresman, 1977), pp. 62–79.

53. R. Clayton and H. Voss, "Shacking Up: Cohabitation in the 1970s," *Journal of Marriage and the Family* 39 (1977), pp. 273–284.

54. E. Macklin, "Review of Research on Nonmarital Cohabitation in the United States," in B. Murstein, ed., *Exploring Intimate Lifestyles* (New York: Springer, 1978).

55. E. Macklin, "Nontraditional Family Forms: A Decade of Research," *Journal of Marriage and the Family* 42 (November 1980), pp. 907–908.

56. P. Glick and G. Spanier, "Married and Unmarried Cohabitation in the United States," *Journal of Marriage and the Family* 42 (February 1980), pp. 19–30.

57. L. Henze and J. Hudson, "Personal and Family Characteristics of Cohabiting and Noncohabiting College Students," *Journal of Marriage and the Family* 36 (1974), pp. 722–726.

58. D. Peterman, C. Ridley, and S. Anderson, "A Comparison of Cohabiting and Noncohabiting College Students." *Journal of Marriage and the Family* 36 (1974), pp. 344–354.

59. Clayton and Voss, "Shacking Up."

60. D. Bower and V. Christopherson, "University Student Cohabitation: A Regional Comparison of Selected Attitudes and Behavior," *Journal of Marriage and the Family* 39 (1977), pp. 447–454.

61. Ibid.

62. Macklin, "Nontraditional Family Forms," p. 907.

63. U.S. Bureau of the Census, "Marital Status and Living Arrangements: March, 1979," *Current Population Reports,* series P-20, no. 349 (1980), pp. 3–5.

64. Ibid.

65. Macklin, "Nonmarital Cohabitation," p. 16.

66. J. Makepeace, "The Birth Control Revolution: Consequences for College Student Life Styles" (Ph.D. diss., Washington State University, 1975).

67. N. Glenn and C. Weaver, "Attitudes toward Premarital, Extramarital, and Homosexual Relations in the U.S. in the 1970s," *Journal of Sex Research* 15

(May 1979), pp. 108–118.

68. J. De Lamater and P. MacCorquodale, *Premarital Sexuality: Attitudes, Relationships, Behavior* (Madison: University of Wisconsin Press, 1979).

69. Bower and Christopherson, "University Student Cohabitation."

70. Macklin, "Nonmarital Cohabitation."

71. Peterman et al., "A Comparison."

72. Macklin, "Nonmarital Cohabitation."

73. Macklin, "Nontraditional Family Forms," p. 907.

74. J. Trost, *Unmarried Cohabitation* (Vasteras, Sweden: International Library, 1979).

75. J. Jacques and K. Chason, "Cohabitation: Its Impact on Marital Success," *Family Coordinator* (January 1979), pp. 35–39.

76. Macklin, "Nonmarital Cohabitation."

77. Clayton and Voss, "Shacking Up."

78. Macklin, "Nonmarital Cohabitation."

79. Reiss, *Family Systems in America*, pp. 106–107.

80. Peterman et al., "A Comparison."

81. E. Walster, W. Walster, and J. Traupmann, "Equity and Premarital Sex." *Journal of Personality and Social Psychology* 36 (1978), pp. 82–92.

82. Henze and Hudson, "Personal and Family Characteristics."

83. E. Markowski, J. Croake, and J. Keller, "Sexual History and Present Sexual Behavior of Cohabiting and Married Couples," *Journal of Sex Research* 14 (1978), pp. 27–39.

84. Macklin, "Nonmarital Cohabitation."

85. Peterman et al., "A Comparison."

86. B. Risman, C. Hill, Z. Rubin, and L. Peplau, "Living Together in College: Implications for Courtship," *Journal of Marriage and Family* 43 (February 1981), pp. 77–83.

87. Macklin, "Nonmarital Cohabitation."

88. D. Knox, *Exploring Marriage and the Family* (Glenview, Ill.: Scott, Foresman, 1979), p. 210.

89. R. Stafford, E. Backman, and P. DiBona, "The Division of Labor among Cohabiting and Married Couples," *Journal of Marriage and the Family* 39 (1977), pp. 43–57.

90. Jacques and Chason, "Cohabitation."

91. C. Hill, Z. Rubin, and L. Peplau, "Breakups Before Marriage: The End of 103 Affairs," *Journal of Social Issues* 32 (1976), pp. 147–168.

92. Ibid. p. 165.

93. L. Budd, "Problems, Disclosure, and Commitment of Cohabiting and Married Couples" (Ph.D. diss., University of Minnesota, 1976).

94. J. Trost, "Married and Unmarried Cohabitation: The Case of Sweden with Some Comparisons," *Journal of Marriage and the Family* 37 (August 1975), pp. 677–682.

95. N. Lavori, *Living Together, Married or Single: Your Legal Rights* (New York: Harper & Row, 1976).

96. Macklin, "Review of Research," p. 300.

97. N. Myricks, "Palimony: The Impact of Marvin v. Marvin," *Family Coordinator* (April 1980), pp. 210–215.

98. "Marvin v. Marvin." *Family Law Reporter* 5 (1979), p. 3109.

99. Myricks, "Palimony."

100. S. Macovsky, "Coping with Cohabitation," *Money* (May 1979).

101. Ibid.

102. P. Ashley, *Oh Promise Me, but Put It in Writing: Living-Together Agreements without, before, during, and after Marriage* (New York: McGraw-Hill, 1978).

103. R. Jones and J. Bates, "Satisfaction in Male Homosexual Couples," *Journal of Homosexuality* 3 (Spring 1978), pp. 217–224.

104. D. Tanner, *The Lesbian Couple* (Lexington, Mass.: Lexington Books, D. C. Heath, 1978).

105. A. Bell and M. Weinberg, *Homosexualities* (Bloomington, Ind.: Institute for Sex Research, 1979).

106. J. Lee, "Forbidden Colors of Love: Patterns of Gay Love and Gay Liberation," *Journal of Homosexuality* 4 (1976), pp. 401–418.

107. C. Silverstein, *A Family Matter: A Parent's Guide to Homosexuality* (New York: McGraw-Hill, 1977).

108. D. Hitchens, "Social Attitudes, Legal Standards, and Personal Trauma in Child Custody Cases," *Journal of Homosexuality* 5 (Fall–Winter 1979–80), pp. 89–95.

109. B. Voeller and J. Walters, "Gay Fathers," *Family Coordinator* 27 (April 1978), pp. 149–157.

Chapter 6

1. G. Fox, "Love Match and Arranged Marriage in a Modernizing Nation: Mate Selection in Ankara, Turkey," *Journal of Marriage and the Family* 37 (February 1975), pp. 180–193.

2. G. Adams, "Mate Selection in the United States: A Theoretical Summarization," in W. Burr, R. Hill, I. Nye, and I. Reiss, eds., *Contemporary Theories about the Family*, vol. 1 (New York: Free Press, 1979), pp. 259–267.

3. B. Murstein, "Mate Selection in the 1970s," *Journal of Marriage and the Family* 42 (November 1980), p. 779.

4. W. Goode, "The Theoretical Importance of Love," *American Sociological Review* 24 (February 1959), pp. 38–47.

5. R. Winch, *Mate Selection: A Study of Complementary Needs* (New York: Harper and Brothers, 1958).

6. S. Saegert, W. Swap, and R. Zajonc, "Exposure, Context and Interpersonal Attraction,"

Journal of Personality and Social Psychology 25 (1973), pp. 234–242.

7. G. Cretser and J. Leon, "Intermarriage in the U.S.: The Last Fifty Years" (Paper presented to the Pacific Sociological Association, Anaheim, California, April 1979).

8. F. Heider, *The Psychology of Interpersonal Relations* (New York: Wiley, 1958).

9. Murstein, "Mate Selection," p. 786.

10. J. Trost, "Some Data on Mate Selection: Homogamy and Perceived Homogamy," *Journal of Marriage and the Family* 29 (November 1967), pp. 739–755.

11. N. Glenn, A. Ross, and J. Tully, "Patterns of Intergenerational Mobility of Females through Marriage," *American Sociological Review* 39 (October 1974), pp. 683–699.

12. R. Centers, *Sexual Attraction and Love: An Instrumental Theory* (Springfield, Ill.: Charles C Thomas, 1975).

13. Murstein, "Mate Selection," p. 789.

14. I. Nye, "Choice, Exchange, and the Family," in W. Burr, R. Hill, I. Nye, and I. Reiss, eds., *Contemporary Theories about the Family*, vol. 2 (New York: Free Press, 1979), pp. 1–41.

15. Murstein, "Mate Selection," p. 785.

16. J. Scanzoni, "Social Exchange and Behavioral Interdependence," in R. Burgess and T. Houston, eds., *Social Exchange in Developing Relationships* (New York: Academic Press, 1979).

17. J. Thibaut and H. Kelley, *The Social Psychology of Groups* (New York: Wiley, 1959).

18. E. Walster, G. Walster, and J. Traupmann, "Equity and Premarital Sex," *Journal of Personality and Social Psychology* 36 (1978), pp. 82–92.

19. P. Blau, *Exchange and Power in Social Life* (New York: Wiley, 1964).

20. Walster, Walster, and Traupmann, "Equity and Premarital Sex."

21. F. Hall and D. Hall, *The Two-Career Couple* (Reading, Mass.: Addison-Wesley, 1979).

22. Winch, *Mate Selection*.

23. S. Freud, "Some Psychological Consequences of Anatomical Distinction between the Sexes," *International Journal of Psychological Analysis* 8 (1927), pp. 133–142.

24. A. Aron et al., "Relationships with Opposite-Sex Parents and Mate Choice," *Human Relations* 27 (1974), pp. 17–24.

25. W. Toman, *Family Constellation: Its Effect on Personality and Social Behavior* (New York: Springer, 1969).

26. J. Birtchnell and J. Mayhew, "Toman's Theory: Tested for Mate Selection and Friendship Formation," *Journal of Individual Psychology* 33 (May 1977), pp. 18–36.

27. M. Hayes, "Family Ordinal Position of Status Offenders," unpublished monograph, Department of Sociology, University of Southern California (1981).

28. L. Forer, with Henry Still, *The Birth Order Factor: How Your Personality Is Influenced by Your Place in the Family* (New York: David McKay, 1976).

29. Toman, *Family Constellation*.

30. Forer, *Birth Order Factor*.

31. Ibid., p. 286.

32. R. Lewis, "A Developmental Framework for the Analysis of Premarital Dyadic Formation," *Family Process* 11 (1972), pp. 17–48.

33. Centers, *Sexual Attraction and Love*.

34. B. Wilson, "First Marriages: United States," U.S. National Center for Health Sciences, series 21, no. 35 (September 1979).

35. *World Almanac Book of Facts 1981* (New York: Newspaper Enterprise Association, Inc., 1980), p. 149.

36. P. Glick, "Remarriage: Some Recent Changes and Variations," *Journal of Family Issues* 1 (December 1980), pp. 455–478.

37. M. Lasswell, "Is There a Best Age to Marry? An Interpretation," *Family Coordinator* 23 (1974), pp. 237–242.

38. E. Burgess, H. Locke, and M. Thomes, *The Family* (New York: Van Nostrand Reinhold, 1971).

39. A. Kinsey, W. Pomeroy, C. Martin, and P. Gebhard, *Sexual Behavior in the Human Female* (New York: Pocket Books, 1969), p. 265.

40. B. Lindsey, *The Companionate Marriage* (Garden City, N.Y.: Garden City Publishers, 1927).

41. M. Mead, "Marriage in Two Steps," *Redbook* (July 1966), pp. 48–49.

42. U.S. Bureau of the Census, *Current Population Reports*, series P-20, no. 338 (May 1979), pp. 4, 5.

43. E. Macklin, "Nontraditional Family Forms: A Decade of Research," *Journal of Marriage and the Family* 42 (November 1980), pp. 905–922.

44. D. Bower and V. Christopherson, "University Student Cohabitation: A Regional Comparison of Selected Attitudes and Behaviors," *Journal of Marriage and the Family* 39 (August 1977), pp. 447–453.

45. R. Lewis and G. Spanier, "Theorizing about the Quality and Stability of Marriage," in W. Burr et al., eds., *Contemporary Theories about the Family*, vol. 2 (New York: Free Press, 1979), pp. 268–294.

46. U.S. Bureau of the Census, *Current Population Reports*, series P-20, no. 297 (October 1976), p. 2.

47. National Center for Health Statistics, "Final Marriage Statistics, 1977" *Monthly Vital Statistics Report* 28, no. 4, (1979).

48. Glick, "Remarriage."

49. M. Schulman, "Communication between Engaged Couples" (Ph.D. diss., University of Southern California, 1970).

50. Ibid.
51. T. Lasswell and M. Lasswell, "I Love You, but I'm Not in Love with You," *Journal of Marriage and Family Counseling* 2 (July 1976), pp. 211–224.
52. C. Cooley, *Human Nature and the Social Order* (New York: Charles Scribner's Sons, 1902).
53. Schulman, "Communication."
54. National Center for Health Statistics, "Divorce and Divorce Rates," *Vital and Health Statistics,* series 21, no. 29 (March 1978).
55. C. Hill, Z. Rubin, and L. Peplau, "Breakups Before Marriage: The End of 103 Affairs," *Journal of Social Issues* 32 (1976), pp. 147–168.
56. S. Schrader, "Commitment: A Conceptualization and an Empirical Demonstration in the Courtship Process" (Ph.D. diss., University of Southern California, 1980).
57. Ibid., pp. 90–92.
58. C. Broderick, *Marriage and Family* (Englewood Cliffs, N.J.: Prentice-Hall, 1979), p. 140.
59. Schrader, "Commitment," pp. 8, 94.
60. B. Risman, C. Hill, Z. Rubin, and L. Peplau, "Living Together in College: Implications for Courtship," *Journal of Marriage and the Family* 43 (February 1981), pp. 77–83.
61. Ibid., p. 79.
62. J. Money, *Love and Love Sickness: The Science of Sex, Gender Difference and Pair-Bonding* (Baltimore: Johns Hopkins University Press, 1980).
63. A. Calhoun, *A Social History of the American Family* (New York: Barnes and Noble, 1960).
64. Money, *Love and Love Sickness,* pp. 62–63.
65. L. Benson, *The Family Bond: Marriage, Love and Sex in America* (New York: Random House, 1971).
66. M. Seligson, *The Eternal Bliss Machine: America's Way of Wedding* (New York: William Morrow, 1973).
67. B. Blumberg and P. Paul, "Continuities and Discontinuities in Upper-Class Marriages," *Journal of Marriage and the Family* 37 (February 1975), pp. 63–77.
68. J. Gagnon and C. Greenblat, *Life Designs: Individuals, Marriages and Families* (Glenview, Ill.: Scott-Foresman, 1978), pp. 224–225.

Chapter 7

1. E. Erickson, *Identity: Youth and Crisis* (New York: Norton, 1968), pp. 217–220.
2. R. Turner, "The Real Self: From Institution to Impulse," *American Journal of Sociology* 81 (March 1976), pp. 989–1016.
3. H. Zerof, *Finding Intimacy: The Art of Happiness in Living Together* (New York: Random House, 1978).
4. M. Lasswell and N. Lobsenz, *No-Fault Marriage* (Garden City, N.Y.: Doubleday, 1976).
5. L. Singer and B. Stern, *Stages: The Crises That Shape Your Marriage* (New York: Grosset and Dunlap, 1980), p. 36.
6. M. McGoldrick, "The Joining of Families through Marriage: The New Couple," in E. A. Carter and M. McGoldrick, eds., *The Family Life Cycle: A Framework for Family Therapy* (New York: Gardner Press, 1980), pp. 95–96.
7. M. Gernstein and M. Papen-Daniel, *Understanding Adulthood* (Fullerton, Calif.: California Personnel and Guidance Association Monograph, no. 15, 1981), p. 2.
8. W. Meisner, "The Conceptualization of Marriage and Family Dynamics from a Psychoanalytic Perspective," in T. Paolino and B. McCrady, eds., *Marriage and Family Therapy* (New York: Brunner/Mazel, 1978), p. 47.
9. C. Broderick, *Couples: How to Confront Problems and Maintain Loving Relationships* (New York: Simon and Schuster, 1979), p. 23.
10. A. Maslow, *The Farther Reaches of Human Nature* (New York: Viking Press, 1971), pp. 379–390.
11. E. Berne, *Transactional Analysis in Psychotherapy* (New York: Grove Press, 1961).
12. D. Warren, "How to Use Transactional Analysis in Counseling," in P. Popenoe, ed., *Techniques of Marriage and Family Counseling* (Los Angeles: American Institute of Family Relations, 1972), pp. 101–103.
13. Broderick, *Couples,* p. 71.
14. J. Pearce and L. Friedman, *Family Therapy* (New York: Grune and Stratton, 1980), p. 43.
15. R. Stuart, "An Operant Interpersonal Program for Couples," in D. Olson, ed., *Treating Relationships* (Lake Mills, Iowa: Graphic Publishing Company, 1976).
16. U.S. Bureau of the Census, *Current Population Reports,* series P-20, no. 297 (1976), p. 15.
17. Singer and Stern, *Stages.*
18. B. Montgomery, "The Form and Function of Quality Communication in Marriage," *Family Relations* 30 (January 1981), pp. 21–30.
19. S. Miller, R. Corrales, and D. Wackman, "Recent Progress in Understanding and Facilitating Marital Communication," *Family Coordinator* 24 (1975), pp. 143–152.
20. V. Satir, *Conjoint Family Therapy* (Palo Alto, Calif.: Science and Behavior Books, 1964).
21. I. Altman and D. Taylor, *Social Penetration: The Development of Interpersonal Relationships* (New York: Holt, Rinehart and Winston, 1973).
22. S. Witkin and S. Rose, "Group Training in Communication Skills for Couples: A Preliminary Report," *International Journal of Family Counseling* 6 (1978), pp. 45–56.
23. C. Wilder, "From the Interactional View—A Conversation with Paul Watzlawick," *Journal of Communication* 28 (1978), p. 41.
24. G. Levinger and D. Senn, "Disclosure of Feelings in Marriage," *Merrill-Palmer Quarterly* 13 (1967), pp. 237–249.

25. R. Stuart, "An Operant Interpersonal Program."

26. P. Watzlawick, J. Beavin, and D. Jackson, *Pragmatics of Human Communication: A Study of Interactional Patterns, Pathologies, and Paradoxes* (New York: Norton, 1967).

27. M. Lasswell and N. Lobsenz, "When and How to Be Honest," *McCall's* (July 1979), p. 70.

28. F. Clarke, "Interpersonal Communication Variables as Predictors of Marital Satisfaction-Attraction" (Ph.D. diss., University of Denver, 1973).

29. Watzlawick, Beavin, and Jackson, *Pragmatics of Human Communication.*

30. D. Sprenkle and D. Olson, "Circumplex Model of Marital Systems: An Empirical Study of Clinic and Nonclinic Couples," *Journal of Marriage and Family Counseling* 4 (1978), pp. 59–74.

31. B. Fisher and D. Sprenkle, "Therapists' Perceptions of Healing Family Functioning," *International Journal of Family Counseling* 6 (1978), pp. 9–17.

32. Levinger and Senn, "Disclosure of Feelings."

33. Montgomery, "Form and Function," p. 28.

34. Ibid., p. 24.

35. Fisher and Sprenkle, "Therapists' Perceptions."

36. P. Schauble and C. Hill, "A Laboratory Approach to Treatment in Marriage Counseling: Training in Communication Skills," *The Family Coordinator* 25 (July 1976), pp. 227–284.

37. C. Kelly, "Empathic Listening," in J. Steward, ed., *Bridges, Not Walls* (Reading, Mass.: Addison-Wesley, 1977).

38. T. Scheff, "Toward a Sociological Model of Consensus," *American Sociological Review* 32 (1967), pp. 32–46.

39. M. Schulman, "Idealization in Engaged Couples," *Journal of Marriage and the Family* 36 (1974), pp. 139–147.

40. Watzlawick, Beavin, and Jackson, *Pragmatics of Human Communication.*

41. L. Navron, "Communication and Adjustment in Marriage," *Family Process* 6 (1967), pp. 173–184.

42. D. Orthner, "Patterns of Leisure and Marital Interaction," *Journal of Leisure Research* 9 (1976), pp. 98–111.

43. M. Argyle, *Social Interaction* (Chicago: Aldine Atherton, 1969).

44. D. Jackson, "Family Rules: Marital Quid pro Quo," in P. Watzlawick and J. Weakland, eds., *The Interactional View* (New York: Norton, 1977).

45. A. L. Scoresby, *The Marriage Dialogue* (Reading, Mass.: Addison-Wesley, 1977).

46. S. Gilbert, "Self-Disclosure, Intimacy and Communication in Families," *Family Coordinator* 25 (1976), pp. 221–230.

47. E. Zerin and M. Zerin, "Four Styles of Communication" (Unpublished paper, 1980).

48. J. Hawkins, G. Weisberg, and D. Ray, "Marital Communication Style and Social Class," *Journal of Marriage and the Family* 39 (August 1977), pp. 479–490.

49. M. Komarovsky, *Blue-Collar Marriage* (New York: Random House, 1964).

50. B. Montgomery, "Form and Function," p. 27.

51. R. Bell and N. Lobsenz, "Marital Sex," in J. Gagnon, ed., *Human Sexuality in Today's World* (Boston: Little, Brown, 1977).

52. Scoresby, *Marriage Dialogue.*

53. D. Kantor, "Critical Identity Image: A Concept Linking Individual, Couple, and Family Development," in J. Pearce and L. Friedman, eds., *Family Therapy* (New York: Grune and Stratton, 1980), pp. 137–167.

54. B. Chadwick, S. Albrecht, and P. Kunz, "Marital and Family Role Satisfaction," *Journal of Marriage and the Family* 38 (August 1976), pp. 431–440.

55. Broderick, *Couples*, p. 13.

56. B. Marshall and C. Marshall, *The Marriage Secret* (Maplewood, N.J.: Hammond, 1980).

57. Ibid.

58. R. Gould, *Transformations: Growth and Change in Adult Life* (New York: Simon and Schuster, 1978).

59. D. Levinson with C. Darrow, E. Klein, M. Levinson, and B. McKeen, *The Seasons of a Man's Life* (New York: Knopf, 1978).

60. B. Rollins and H. Feldman, "Marital Satisfaction over the Family Life Cycle," *Journal of Marriage and the Family* 32 (1970), pp. 20–28.

61. A. Campbell, "The American Way of Mating: Marriage Si, Children, Only Maybe," *Psychology Today*, (May 1975), pp. 39–42.

62. R. Rappoport and R. Rappoport, *Dual-Career Families* (Baltimore: Penguin, 1971).

63. Rollins and Feldman, "Marital Satisfaction."

64. M. Lasswell and N. Lobsenz, *No-Fault Marriage* (Garden City, N.Y.: Doubleday, 1976).

65. J. Cuber and P. Harroff, *The Significant Americans: A Study of Sexual Behavior among the Affluent* (New York: Appleton-Century-Crofts, 1965).

66. Ibid., p. 142.

67. J. Scanzoni, *Sex Roles, Life Styles, and Childbearing* (New York: Free Press, 1975).

68. B. Forisha, *Sex Roles and Personal Awareness* (Morristown, N.J.: General Learning Press, 1978).

69. R. Stuckert, "Role Perception and Marital Satisfaction—A Configurational Approach," *Marriage and Family Living* 25 (November 1963), pp. 415–419.

70. Forisha, *Sex Roles.*

71. L. Pratt, Conjugal Organization and Health," *Journal of Marriage and the Family* 34 (February 1972), pp. 85–95.

72. J. Bernard, *The Future of Marriage* (New York: Bantam Books, 1972).

73. R. Lewis and G. Spanier, "Theorizing about the Quality and Stability of Marriages," in W. Burr, R. Hill, I. Nye, and I. Reiss, eds., *Contemporary Theories about the Family*, vol. 1 (New York: Free Press, 1979).

74. E. Burgess and L. Cottrell, *Pre-

dicting Success or Failure in Marriage (Englewood Cliffs, N.J.: Prentice-Hall, 1939).

75. H. Locke, *Predicting Adjustment in Marriage: A Comparison of a Divorced and a Happily Married Group* (New York: Henry Holt, 1951).

76. R. Blood and D. Wolfe, *Husbands and Wives* (New York: Macmillan, 1960).

77. I. Nye and S. McLaughlin, "Role Competence and Marital Satisfaction," in I. Nye et al., eds., *Role Structure and Analysis of the Family* (Beverly Hills, Calif.: Sage Publications, 1976).

78. D. Haun, and N. Stinnett, "Does Psychological Comfortableness between Engaged Couples Affect Their Probability of Successful Marriage Adjustment?" *Family Perspective* 9 (1974), pp. 11–18.

79. G. Spanier, "Measuring Dyadic Adjustment: New Scales for Assessing the Quality of Marriage and Similar Dyads." *Journal of Marriage and the Family* 38 (February 1976), pp. 15–28.

Chapter 8

1. D. Olson, D. Sprenkle, and C. Russell, "Circumplex Model of Marital and Family Systems: I. Cohesion and Adaptability Dimensions, Family Types, and Clinical Applications," *Family Process* 18 (1979), pp. 3–28.

2. R. Blood and D. Wolfe, *Husbands and Wives: The Dynamics of Married Living* (New York: Free Press, 1960).

3. G. McDonald, "Family Power: Reflections and Direction," *Pacific Sociological Review* 20 (October 1977), pp. 607–621.

4. C. Willie and S. Greenblatt, "Four 'Classic' Studies of Power Relationships in Black Families: A Review and Look to the Future," *Journal of Marriage and the Family* 40 (November 1978), pp. 691–694.

5. C. Safilios-Rothschild, "A Macro- and Micro-Examination of Family Power and Love: An Exchange Model," *Journal of Marriage and the Family* 37 (May 1976), pp. 355–362.

6. J. Scanzoni and K. Polonko, "A Conceptual Approach to Explicit Marital Negotiation," *Journal of Marriage and the Family* 42 (February 1980), pp. 31–44.

7. H. Blalock and P. Wilken, *Intergroup Processes: A Micro-Macro Perspective.* (New York: Free Press, 1979).

8. J. Sprey, "Family Power Structure: A Critical Comment," *Journal of Marriage and the Family* 33 (May 1972), pp. 722–733.

9. Safilios-Rothschild, "Family Power and Love."

10. G. McDonald, "Family Power: The Assessment of a Decade of Theory and Research, 1970–1979," *Journal of Marriage and the Family* 42 (November 1980), pp. 841–854.

11. McDonald, "Family Power: Reflections and Direction."

12. W. Pearson, Jr., and L. Hendrix, "Divorce and the Status of Women," *Journal of Marriage and the Family* 41 (May 1979), pp. 375–385.

13. T. Kolb and M. Straus, "Marital Power and Marital Happiness in Relation to Problem-Solving Ability," *Journal of Marriage and the Family* 36 (November 1974), pp. 757–766.

14. R. Corrales, "Power and Satisfaction in Early Marriage," in R. Cromwell and D. Olson, eds., *Power in Families* (New York: Wiley, 1975), pp. 197–216.

15. S. Wilson, *Informal Groups* (Englewood Cliffs, N.J.: Prentice-Hall, 1978).

16. M. Richmond, "Beyond Resource Theory: Another Look at Factors Enabling Women to Affect Family Interaction," *Journal of Marriage and the Family* 38 (May 1976), pp. 257–266.

17. J. Scanzoni, "Social Processes and Power in Families," in W. Burr, R. Hill, I. Nye, and I. Reiss, eds., *Contemporary Theories about the Family,* vol. I: *Research Based Theories* (New York: Free Press, 1979), pp. 295–316.

18. R. Cromwell and D. Olson, *Power in Families* (New York: Wiley, 1975).

19. D. Gillespie, "Who Has the Power? The Marital Struggle," *Journal of Marriage and the Family* 33 (August 1971), pp. 445–458.

20. M. Lasswell and N. Lobsenz, "The Right (and Wrong) Way to Make Decisions," *McCall's* (August 1979), pp. 70–74.

21. R. Bales, and F. Strodtbeck, "Phases in Group Problem Solving," *Journal of Abnormal and Social Psychology* 46 (1951), pp. 485–495.

22. J. Aldous, "A Framework for the Analysis of Family Problem Solving," in J. Aldous, T. Condon, R. Hill, M. Straus, and I. Tallman, eds., *Family Problem Solving: A Symposium on Theoretical, Methodological, and Substantive Concerns* (Hinsdale, Ill.: Dryden Press, 1971), p. 266.

23. I. Tallman, "The Family as a Small Problem Solving Group," *Journal of Marriage and the Family* 32 (February 1970), pp. 94–104.

24. F. Hall and D. Hall, *The Two-Career Couple* (Reading, Mass.: Addison-Wesley, 1979).

25. Lasswell and Lobsenz, "The Right (and Wrong) Way."

26. J. Sprey, "Conflict Theory and the Study of Marriage and the Family," in W. Burr, R. Hill, I. Nye, and I. Reiss, eds., *Contemporary Theories about the Family,* vol. 2 (New York: Free Press, 1979), pp. 130–159.

27. I. Charney, "Marital Love and Hate," in S. Steinmetz and M. Straus, eds., *Violence in the Family* (New York: Dodd, Mead, 1974), p. 55.

28. J. Cuber and P. Harroff, "The More Total View: Relationships among Men and Women of the Upper Middle Class," *Marriage and Family Living* 25 (May 1963), pp. 140–145.

29. P. Watzlawick, J. Weakland,

and R. Fisch, *Change: Principles of Problem Formation and Problem Resolution* (New York: Norton, 1974).

30. M. Lasswell and N. Lobsenz, "When Someone You Love Suddenly Changes," *McCall's* (May 1978), pp. 120–124.

31. D. Terkelson, "Toward a Theory of the Family Life Cycle," in E. Carter and M. McGoldrick, eds., *The Family Life Cycle: A Framework for Family Therapy* (New York: Gardner Press, 1980), pp. 21–52.

32. C. Broderick and J. Smith, "The General Systems Approach to the Family," in W. Burr, R. Hill, I. Nye, and I. Reiss, eds., *Contemporary Theories about the Family*, vol. 2 (New York: Free Press, 1979), pp. 112–129.

33. L. Hoffman, "The Family Life Cycle and Discontinuous Change," in E. Carter, and M. McGoldrick, eds., *The Family Life Cycle: A Framework for Family Therapy* (New York: Gardner Press, 1980), p. 55.

34. N. Jacobsen and G. Margolin, *Marital Therapy: Strategies Based on Social Learning and Behavior Exchange Principles* (New York: Brunner/Mazel, 1979).

35. M. Lasswell and N. Lobsenz, "Can You Really Change the One You Love?" *McCall's* (June 1979), pp. 78–81.

36. D. Kantor, "Critical Identity Image: A Concept Linking Individual, Couple, and Family Development," in J. Pearce and L. Friedman, eds., *Family Therapy: Combining Psychodynamic and Family Systems Approaches* (New York: Grune and Stratton, 1980).

37. Ibid.

38. J. Coleman, *Contemporary Psychology and Effective Behavior*, 4th ed. (Glenview, Ill.: Scott, Foresman, 1979).

39. E. Berne, *Games People Play* (New York: Grove Press, 1967).

40. M. Lasswell and N. Lobsenz, *No-Fault Marriage* (Garden City, N.Y.: Doubleday, 1976), p. 122.

41. M. Lasswell and N. Lobsenz, "The 'Little Things' That Can Destroy a Marriage," *McCall's* (February 1978), pp. 66–70.

42. J. Gottman, H. Markman, and C. Notarius, "The Topography of Marital Conflict: A Sequential Analysis of Verbal and Nonverbal Behavior," *Journal of Marriage and the Family* 39 (August 1977), pp. 461–477.

43. D. Klein and R. Hill, "Determinants of Family Problem Solving Effectiveness," in W. Burr, R. Hill, I. Nye, and I. Reiss, eds., *Contemporary Theories about the Family*, vol. I (New York: Free Press, 1979), pp. 493–548.

44. G. Bach and P. Wyden, *The Intimate Enemy: How to Fight Fair in Love and Marriage* (New York: Avon, 1970).

45. V. Mathews and C. Mihanovich, "New Orientations on Marital Adjustment" *Marriage and Family Living* 25 (August 1963), pp. 300–305.

46. M. Lasswell and N. Lobsenz, *No-Fault Marriage* (Garden City, N.Y.: Doubleday, 1976), p. 122.

47. I. Charney, "Marital Love and Hate," pp. 211–212.

48. D. Cartwright, "The Nature of Group Cohesiveness," in D. Cartwright and A. Zander, eds., *Group Dynamics: Research and Theory*, 3rd ed. (New York: Harper & Row, 1968).

49. M. Deutsch, "An Experimental Study of the Effects of Cooperation and Competition upon Group Process," *Human Relations* 2 (1949), pp. 199–231.

50. M. Shaw, *Group Dynamics*, 2nd ed. (New York: McGraw-Hill, 1976).

51. A. Lott and B. Lott, "Group Cohesiveness as Interpersonal Attraction: A Review of Relationships with Antecedent and Consequent Variables," *Psychological Bulletin* 64 (1965) pp. 259–309.

52. Shaw, *Group Dynamics*.

53. R. Stuart, *Helping Couples Change* (New York: Guilford Press, 1980).

54. Deutsch, "Effects of Cooperation and Competition."

55. B. Raven and J. Rubin, *Social Psychology: People in Groups* (New York: Wiley, 1976).

56. M. Deutsch, *The Resolution of Conflict: Constructive and Destructive Processes* (New Haven: Yale University Press, 1973).

57. Ibid.

58. Ibid.

59. N. Voissem and F. Sistrunk, "Communication Schedule and Cooperative Game Behavior," *Journal of Personality and Social Psychology* 19 (1971), pp. 160–167.

60. D. Schoeninger, and W. Wood, "Comparison of Married and Ad Hoc Mixed-Sex Dyads Negotiating the Division of a Reward," *Journal of Experimental Social Psychology* 5 (1969), pp. 483–499.

61. L. Wrightsman, Jr., "Personality and Attitudinal Correlates of Trusting and Trustworthy Behaviors in a Two-Person Game," *Journal of Personality and Social Psychology* 4 (1966) pp. 328–332.

62. M. Lasswell and N. Lobsenz, *No-Fault Marriage.*

63. Ibid.

64. F. Pepitone-Rockwell, ed., *Dual Career Couples* (Beverly Hills, Calif.: Sage Publications, 1980).

65. R. Weiss, *Marital Separation* (New York: Basic Books, 1975).

66. A. Skolnick, *The Intimate Environment: Exploring Marriage and the Family* (Boston: Little, Brown, 1973), p. 213.

Chapter 9

1. V. Bullough and B. Bullough, *Sin, Sickness, and Sanity* (New York: New American Library, 1977).

2. T. Malthus, *An Essay on Population*, 2 vols. (New York: Dutton, 1914).

3. T. Hoult, L. Henze, and J. Hudson, *Courtship and Marriage in America* (Boston: Little, Brown, 1978), p. 396.

4. U.S. Bureau of the Census, *Current Population Reports,* series P-20, no. 363 (June 1981), p. 19.

5. E. Whelan, *A Baby . . . Maybe?* (New York: Bobbs-Merrill, 1975), pp. 171–173.

6. B. Linner, *Sex and Society in Sweden* (New York: Pantheon, 1976).

7. J. M. Eekelaar, "Reforming the English Law Concerning Illegitimate Persons," *Family Law Quarterly* 14 (Spring 1980), pp. 41–58.

8. R. Rindfuss and L. Bumpass, "Fertility during Marital Disruptions," *Journal of Marriage and the Family* 39 (August 1977), pp. 517–528.

9. National Center for Health Statistics, *Monthly Vital Statistics Report* 21, no. 15 (February 1968), p. 4; also *Monthly Vital Statistics Report* 27, no. 11 (February 1979), p. 19.

10. U.S. Bureau of the Census, *Current Population Reports,* series P-20, no. 340 (July 1979), p. 1.

11. U.S. Bureau of the Census, *Current Population Reports,* series P-20, no. 350 (May 1980), p. 9.

12. A. Campbell, "The Role of Family Planning in the Reduction of Poverty," *Journal of Marriage and the Family* 30 (May 1968), pp. 236–245.

13. M. Zelnik and J. Kantner, "Sexual and Contraceptive Experience of Young Unmarried Women in the U.S., 1976 and 1971," *Family Planning Perspectives* 9 (March–April 1977), pp. 55–71.

14. U.S. Bureau of the Census, *Current Population Reports,* series P-20, no. 338 (May 1979), p. 2.

15. M. Zelnik, "Sex Education and Knowledge of Pregnancy Risk among U.S. Teenage Women," *Family Planning Perspectives* 11 (November 1979), pp. 355–357.

16. Personal communication.

17. M. Zelnik and J. F. Kantner, "Reasons for Non-Use of Contraception by Sexually Active Women Aged 15–19," *Family Planning Perspectives* 11 (September–October 1979), pp. 289–298.

18. G. Cvetkovich, B. Grote, J. Lie-berman, and W. Miller, "Sex Role Development and Teenage Fertility-Related Behavior," *Adolescence* 13 (1978), pp. 231–236.

19. F. Shah and M. Zelnik, "Parent and Peer Influence on Sexual Behavior, Contraceptive Use, and Pregnancy Experience of Young Women," *Journal of Marriage and the Family* 43 (May 1981), p. 345.

20. L. Fosburgh, "The Make-Believe World of Teenage Maternity," *The New York Times Magazine,* August 7, 1977, pp. 29–34.

21. M. Zelnik and J. Kantner, "First Pregnancies to Women aged 15–19 in 1976," *Family Planning Perspectives* 10 (May–June 1978), pp. 135–142.

22. F. Furstenberg, *Unplanned Parenthood* (New York: Free Press, 1976), p. 174.

23. D. Knox, *Exploring Marriage and the Family* (Glenview, Ill.: Scott, Foresman, 1979), p. 412.

24. Commission on Population Growth in America, *Population and the American Future* (New York: New American Library, 1972), p. 163.

25. L. Hoffman and M. Hoffman, "The Value of Children to Parents," in J. Fawcett, ed., *Psychological Perspectives on Population* (New York: Basic Books, 1973).

26. R. Rapoport, R. Rapoport, and Z. Strelitz, with S. Kew, *Fathers, Mothers and Society: Perspectives on Parenting* (New York: Vintage Books, 1980), pp. 139–140.

27. U.S. Bureau of the Census, *Current Population Reports,* series P-20, no. 308 (1977), Tables 2, 12, and 13.

28. J. Blake, "Is Zero Preferred? American Attitudes toward Childlessness in the 1970s," *Journal of Marriage and the Family* 41 (May 1979), pp. 245–257.

29. U.S. Bureau of the Census, *Current Population Reports,* series P-20, no. 341 (1979), p. 27.

30. U.S. Bureau of the Census, *Current Population Reports,* series P-20, no. 341 (1979), p. 27.

31. L. Silka and S. Kiesler, "Couples Who Choose to Remain Childless," *Family Planning Perspectives* 9 (January–February 1977), pp. 16–25.

32. U.S. Bureau of the Census, *Current Population Reports,* series P-20, no. 341 (1979), p. 27.

33. U.S. Bureau of the Census, *Current Population Reports,* series P-20, no. 350 (May 1980), p. 6.

34. G. Sabagh, "Fertility Planning Status of Chicano Couples in Los Angeles," *American Journal of Public Health* 70 (January 1980), pp. 56–61.

35. J. Veevers, "Voluntary Childlessness: A Review of Issues and Evidence," *Marriage and Family Review* 2 (1979), pp. 1, 3–24.

36. R. Nason and M. Poloma, *Voluntary Childless Couples: The Emergence of Variant Lifestyles* (Beverly Hills, Calif.: Sage Publications, 1976).

37. Ibid.

38. Silka and Kiesler, "Couples Who Choose."

39. S. Houseknecht, "Timing of the Decision to Remain Voluntarily Childless: Evidence for Continuous Socialization," *Psychology of Women Quarterly* 4 (Fall 1979), pp. 81–96.

40. S. Houseknecht, "Reference Group Support for Voluntary Childlessness: Evidence for Conformity," *Journal of Marriage and the Family* 39 (May 1977), pp. 285–292.

41. S. Houseknecht, "Childlessness and Marital Adjustment," *Journal of Marriage and the Family* 41 (May 1979), pp. 259–265.

42. R. Ryder, "Longitudinal Data Relating to Marriage Satisfaction and Having a Child," *Journal of Marriage and the Family* 35 (November 1973), pp. 604–606.

43. Houseknecht, "Childlessness."

44. U.S. Bureau of the Census, *Current Population Reports,* series P-20, no. 352 (July 1980), p. 81.

45. U.S. Bureau of the Census, *Current Population Reports,* series P-20, no. 324 (1978), p. 5.

46. *Family Planning Perspectives* (July–August 1975), pp. 147–148.

47. M. McGoldrick, "The Joining of Families through Marriage:

The New Couple," in E. Carter and M. McGoldrick, eds., *The Family Life Cycle: A Framework for Family Therapy* (New York: Gardner Press, 1980), p. 95.

48. U. Stannard, "The Male Maternal Instinct," *Transaction* 8 (November–December: 1970), pp. 24–35.

49. N. Himes, *Medical History of Contraception* (New York: Gamut Press, 1963).

50. V. Bullough and B. Bullough, *Sin, Sickness and Sanity* (New York: New American Library, 1977).

51. Reported in *The Los Angeles Times*, September 29, 1980, part I, p. 1.

52. I. Reiss, *Family Systems in America*, 3rd ed. (New York: Holt, Rinehart and Winston, 1980), p. 364.

53. B. Vaughn, J. Trusell, J. Menken, and E. Jones, "Contraceptive Failure among Married Women in the United States, 1970–1973," *Family Planning Perspectives* 9 (November–December 1977), pp. 251–258.

54. M. Diamond and A. Karlen, *Sexual Decisions* (Boston: Little, Brown, 1980), p. 400.

55. C. Dreifus, "Sterilizing the Poor," *The Progressive* 39 (1975), pp. 13–19.

56. C. Westhoff and E. Jones, "Contraception and Sterilization in the United States, 1965–1975," *Family Planning Perspectives* 9 (September–October 1977), pp. 52–157.

57. Ibid.

58. "Forum International" (editorial), *Forum: International Journal of Human Relations* 10 (February 1981), p. 10.

59. Ibid.

60. R. Hatcher, G. Stewart, F. Stewart, F. Guest, P. Stratton, and A. Wright, *Contraceptive Technology: 1978–79*, 9th ed. (New York: Irvington Publishers, 1978).

61. Diamond and Karlen, *Sexual Decisions*, p. 419.

62. W. Masters and V. Johnson, *Human Sexual Response* (Boston: Little, Brown, 1966).

63. "Forum International," *loc. cit.*

64. "Oral Contraceptives: OC's Update on Usage, Safety, and Side Effects," *Population Reports*, series A, no. 5 (Washington: George Washington University, January 1979).

65. K. Ford, "Contraceptive Use in the U.S. 1973–1976," *Family Planning Perspectives* 10 (September–October 1978), pp. 264–269.

66. Boston Women's Health Book Collective, *Our Bodies, Our Selves* (New York: Simon and Schuster, 1976).

67. F. Stewart, F. Guest, G. Stewart, and R. Hatcher, *My Body, My Health: The Concerned Woman's Guide to Gynecology* (New York: Wiley, 1979).

68. A. Rosenfeld, "Controls on Male Fertility Now Seem to Be within Our Reach," *Smithsonian* (July 1977), pp. 36–43.

69. S. Julty, *Men's Bodies, Men's Selves* (New York: Dell, 1979), p. 385.

70. Hatcher et al., *Contraceptive Technology*.

71. Julty, *Men's Bodies, Men's Selves*, p. 371.

72. Himes, *Medical History of Contraception*.

73. "Forum International," *op. cit.*, November 1980, pp. 6–7.

74. M. Levin, "Let George Do It: Male Contraceptives," *Ms.* (January 1976), pp. 91–94.

75. P. Piotrow, W. Rinehart, and J. Schmidt, "IUD's—Update on Safety, Effectiveness, and Research," *Population Reports*, series B, no. 3 (May 1979), p. 48.

76. F. Brayer, L. Chiazze, and B. Duffy, "Calendar Rhythm and Menstrual Cycle Range," *Fertility/Sterility* (1969).

77. J. McCary, *Human Sexuality*, 3rd ed. (New York: Van Nostrand, 1978).

78. B. Seaman and G. Seaman, *Women and the Crisis in Sex Hormones* (New York: Rawson and Associates, 1977).

79. J. Sandler, J. Myerson, and L. Kinder, *Human Sexuality: Current Perspectives* (Tampa, Fla.: Mariner, 1980), p. 110.

80. Personal communication from J. A. Zimmerman.

81. R. Crooks and K. Baur, *Our Sexuality* (Menlo Park, Calif.: Benjamin/Cummings, 1980), p. 519.

82. J. Forrest, C. Tietze, and E. Sullivan, "Abortion in the United States, 1976–1977," *Family Planning Perspectives* 10 (1978), pp. 271–279.

83. D. W. Stewart and J. B. Nicholson, "Abortion Policy in 1978: A Follow-up Analysis," *Publius* 9 (Winter 1979), pp. 161–167.

84. M. J. Field, "Determinants of Abortion Policy in Developed Nations," *Policy Studies Journal* 7 (Summer 1979), pp. 771–781.

85. Sandler, Myerson, and Kinder, *Human Sexuality*, p. 119.

86. J. Christensen, *The Church of Jesus Christ of Latter-Day Saints: In Support of the Family* (Salt Lake City, Utah: Church Educational System, 1979), p. 4.

87. Hatcher et al., *Contraceptive Technology*.

88. Forrest, Tietze, and Sullivan, "Abortion."

89. M. Diamond, P. Steinhoff, J. Palmore, and R. Smith, "Sexuality, Birth Control and Abortion: A Decision-Making Sequence," *Biosocial Science* 5 (1973), pp. 347–361.

90. P. Steinhoff et al., "Women Who Obtain Repeat Abortions: A Study Based on Record Linkage," *Family Planning Perspectives* (1979), pp. 30–38.

91. C. Tietze, "Induced Abortion: 1977 Supplement," *Reports on Population and Family Planning* 14 (1977).

92. Diamond et al., "Sexuality."

93. J. Osofsky, H. Osofsky, and R. Rajan, "Psychological Effects of Abortion," in H. Osofsky and J. Osofsky, eds., *The Abortion Experience: Psychological and Medical Impact* (New York: Harper & Row, 1973), pp. 188–205.

94. Stewart et al., *My Body, My Health*.

95. E. Sandberg, "Psychological Aspects of Contraception," in

B. Sadock, H. Kaplan, and A. Freedman, eds., *The Sexual Experience* (Baltimore: Williams and Wilkins, 1976), pp. 335–347.

96. J. Kasindorf, "The Case against IUDs," *New West*, May 5, 1980, pp. 21–33.

97. L. Crawley, A. Malfetti, E. Stewart, and N. Vas Dass, *Reproduction, Sex, and Preparation for Marriage*, 2nd ed. (Englewood Cliffs, N.J.: Prentice-Hall, 1973), p. 218.

98. R. Dougherty, quoted in *Sexual Medicine Today* (November 1979), p. 14.

99. J. Rodgers, "Special Report on the Third International Congress on Twin Studies," *Los Angeles Herald Examiner*, June 22, 1980, p. A-7.

100. *Sexual Medicine Today* (May 1979), p. 17.

101. *Sexual Medicine Today* (January 1980), p. 29.

102. D. Havron and P. Smith, "In Vitro Fertilization in the U.S.," *Sexual Medicine Today* (April 1980), p. 12.

103. J. Cipriano, "Childless—Not by Choice: The Poignant Plight of the Infertile Couple," *Sexual Medicine Today* 4 (May 1980), pp. 14–17.

104. A. L. Podolski, "Abolishing Baby Buying: Limiting Independent Adoption Placement," *Family Law Quarterly* 9 (Fall 1975), pp. 547–554.

105. S. Katz and U. Gallagher, "Subsidized Adoption in America," *Family Law Quarterly* 10 (Spring 1976), p. 3.

106. C. Jones and J. Else, "Racial and Cultural Issues in Adoption," *Child Welfare* 58 (June 1979), pp. 373–382.

Chapter 10

1. A. Bernstein, "How Children Learn about Sex and Birth," *Psychology Today* (January 1976), pp. 31–36, 66.

2. A. Bernstein and P. Cowan, "Children's Concepts of How People Get Babies," *Child Development* 46 (1975), pp. 77–92.

3. M. Diamond and A. Karlen, *Sexual Decisions* (Boston: Little, Brown, 1980), p. 368.

4. *Los Angeles Times*, July 10, 1980.

5. M. Blehar, "Preparation for Childbirth and Parenting," *Families Today*, vol. I, National Institute of Mental Health Science Monographs, (Washington, D.C.: U.S. Government Printing Office, 1980), p. 144.

6. U.S. Bureau of the Census, *Current Population Reports*, series P-20, no. 324 (June 1978).

7. M. Gerson, "Motivation for Motherhood" (Ph.D. diss. no. 7818420, New York University, 1978), p. 153.

8. S. Lichtendorf, and P. Gillis, *The New Pregnancy* (New York: Random House, 1979).

9. W. Davenport, "Sex in Cross-Cultural Perspective," in F. Beach, ed., *Human Sexuality in Four Perspectives* (Baltimore: Johns Hopkins University Press, 1977), pp. 115–163.

10. A. Meigs, "Male Pregnancy and the Reduction of Sexual Opposition in a New Guinea Highlands Society," *Ethnology* 15 (1976), pp. 393–407.

11. M. Trause, J. Kennel, and M. Klaus, "Parental Attachment Behavior," in J. Money and H. Mustaph, eds., *Handbook of Sexology, Procreation and Parenthood*, vol. 3 (New York: Elsevier, 1978).

12. S. Doering and D. Entwisle, *The First Birth*, Final Report, U.S. Public Health Service, National Institute of Mental Health, Rockville, Md. (July 1977).

13. Reported in *Marriage and Divorce Today*, July 28, 1980, p. 2.

14. J. Butler, D. Reisner, and N. Wagner, "Sexuality: During Pregnancy and Parturition," in R. Green, ed., *Human Sexuality: A Health Practitioner's Text*, 2nd ed. (Baltimore: Williams and Wilkins, 1979), pp. 176–190.

15. Doering and Entwisle, *First Birth*.

16. D. Larned, "Caesarean Births: Why They Are Up 100 Percent," *Ms.* (October 1978), pp. 24–30.

17. Doering and Entwisle, *First Birth*.

18. E. Hurlock, *Child Development* (New York: McGraw-Hill, 1972), p. 87.

19. B. E. Menning, *Infertility: A Guide for the Childless Couple* (Englewood Cliffs, N.J.: Prentice-Hall, 1977).

20. S. Arms, *Immaculate Deception* (San Francisco: San Francisco Book Company, 1975).

21. J. Scanlon, "Obstetric Anesthesia as a Neonatal Risk Factor in Normal Labor and Delivery," *Clinics in Perinatology* 1 (1974), pp. 465–482.

22. G. Corea, *The Hidden Malpractice* (New York: Harcourt, Brace, Jovanovich, 1977).

23. Arms, *Immaculate Deception*.

24. C. Norwood, "A Humanizing Way to Have a Baby," *Ms.* (May 1978), pp. 89–91.

25. G. Dick-Read, *Childbirth without Fear*, 2nd rev. ed. (New York: Harper & Row, 1944).

26. M. Klaus and J. Kennell, *Maternal Infant Bonding* (St. Louis: C. V. Mosby, 1976).

27. C. Spezzano and J. Waterman, "The First Day of Life," *Psychology Today*, December 11, 1977, p. 110.

28. F. Lamaze, *Painless Childbirth*, L. Celestin, trans. (Chicago: Regnery, 1970).

29. V. Apgar, "Proposal for a New Method of Evaluation of Newborn Infants," *Anaesthesia and Analgesia* 32 (1953), pp. 260–267.

30. Klaus and Kennell, *Maternal Infant Bonding*.

31. F. Le Boyer, *Birth without Violence* (New York: Knopf, 1975).

32. W. Nelson, V. Vaughn, and R. McKay, *Textbook of Pediatrics*, 9th ed. (Philadelphia: W. B. Saunders, 1969).

33. W. Masters and V. Johnson, *Human Sexual Response* (Boston: Little, Brown, 1968).

34. Doering and Entwisle, *First Birth*.

35. Ibid.
36. R. LaRossa, *Conflict and Power in Marriage* (Beverly Hills, Calif.: Sage Publications, 1977).
37. E. LeMasters, "Parenthood as Crisis," *Marriage and Family Living* 19 (November 1957), pp. 352–355.
38. D. Hobbs and S. Cole, "Transition to Parenthood: A Decade Replication," *Journal of Marriage and the Family* 38 (November 1976), pp. 723–731.
39. C. Russell, "Transition to Parenthood: Problems and Gratifications," *Journal of Marriage and the Family* 36 (May 1974), pp. 294–302.
40. M. McGoldrick, "The Joining of Families through Marriage: The New Couple," in E. Carter and M. McGoldrick, eds., *The Family Life Cycle: A Framework for Family Therapy* (New York: Gardner Press, 1980), p. 114.
41. A. Rossi, "Transition to Parenthood," *Journal of Marriage and the Family* 30 (February 1968), pp. 26–39.
42. Personal communication.
43. Blehar, "Preparation for Childbirth."
44. LaRossa, *Conflict and Power.*
45. Personal communication.
46. M. Bowen, *Family Therapy in Clinical Practices* (New York: Jason Aronson, 1978), p. 199.
47. M. Blehar, "Working Couples as Parents," *Families Today*, vol. 1, Institute of Mental Health Science Monographs (Washington, D.C.: United States Government Printing Office, 1980), pp. 299–321.
48. I. Reiss, *Family Systems in America*, 3rd ed. (New York: Holt, Rinehart and Winston, 1980), p. 375.
49. T. Brazelton, "The Importance of Mothering the Mother," *Redbook* (October 1980), pp. 112–115.
50. J. Bradt, "The Family with Young Children," in E. Carter and M. McGoldrick, eds., *The Family Life Cycle: A Framework for Family Therapy* (New York: Gardner Press, 1980), pp. 121–146.
51. Personal communication.

Chapter 11

1. S. Feldman and M. Ingham, "Attachment Behavior: A Validation Study in Two Age Groups," *Child Development* 46 (1975), pp. 319–330.
2. J. Framo, "The Integration of Marital Therapy and Sessions with Family of Origin," in A. Gurman and D. Kniskern, eds., *Handbook of Family Therapy* (New York: Brunner/Mazel, 1981), pp. 133–158.
3. C. Broderick and J. Smith, "The General Systems Approach to the Family," in W. Burr, R. Hill, I. Nye, and I. Reiss, eds., *Contemporary Theories about the Family*, vol. 2 (New York: Free Press, 1979), pp. 112–129.
4. D. Gottlieb and J. Chafetz, "Dynamics of Familial, Generational Conflict and Reconciliation: A Research Note," *Youth and Society* 9 (1977), pp. 213–224.
5. E. Erickson, *Identity: Youth and Crisis* (New York: Norton, 1968).
6. H. McCubbin, C. Joy, A. Cauble, J. Comeau, J. Patterson, and R. Needle, "Family Stress and Coping: A Decade Review," *Journal of Marriage and the Family* 42 (November 1980), p. 865.
7. D. Sollie and B. Miller, "The Transition to Parenthood as a Critical Time for Building Family Strengths," in N. Stinnett, B. Chesser, J. Defrain, and P. Knaub, eds., *Family Strengths: Positive Models for Family Life* (Lincoln: University of Nebraska Press, 1980), pp. 149–169.
8. P. Kunz and E. Peterson, "Parental Control over Adolescents According to Family Size," *Adolescence* 10 (Fall 1975), pp. 419–427.
9. J. Zussman, "Relationship of Demographic Factors to Parental Discipline Techniques," *Developmental Psychology* 14 (1978), pp. 685–686.
10. E. Erikson, *Identity.*
11. Ibid.
12. R. Spitz, "Hospitalism: The Genesis of Psychiatric Conditions in Early Childhood," in W. Sze, ed., *Human Life Cycle* (New York: Jason Aronson, 1975), pp. 29–43.
13. D. Thomas, V. Gecas, A. Weigert, and E. Rooney, *Family Socialization and the Adolescent* (Lexington, Mass.: D. C. Heath, 1974).
14. E. Erikson, *Childhood and Society* (New York: Norton, 1963), pp. 248–249.
15. W. Sze, ed., *Human Life Cycle* (New York: Jason Aronson, 1975).
16. B. Spock, *Baby and Child Care* (New York: Pocket Books, 1976).
17. Roper Organization *The Virginia Slims' American Women's Opinion Poll* (New York: Roper Organization, 1974), p. 77.
18. J. Willis, J. Crowder, and J. Willis, *Guiding the Psychological and Educational Growth of Children* (Springfield, Ill.: Charles C Thomas, 1975).
19. B. White, J. Watts, I. Barnett, et al., *Experiences and Environment: Major Influences on the Development of the Young Child*, vol. I (Englewood Cliffs, N.J.: Prentice-Hall, 1973).
20. M. Pinsker and K. Geoffroy, "A Comparison of Parent Effectiveness Training and Behavior Modification Parent Training," *Family Relations* 30 (January 1981), pp. 61–68.
21. H. Yahraes and D. Baumrind, "Parents as Leaders: The Role of Control and Discipline," *National Institute of Mental Health Science Monographs* 1 (1980), pp. 289–297.
22. D. Baumrind, "The Contributions of the Family to the Development of Competence in Children," *Schizophrenia Bulletin* 14 (1975), pp. 12–37.
23. M. Kohn, "Social Class and Parental Values," *American Jour-*

nal of Sociology 64 (1959), pp. 337–351.

24. K. Bartz and E. Levine, "Child-rearing by Black Parents: A Description and Comparison to Anglo and Chicano Parents," *Journal of Marriage and the Family* 40 (1978), pp. 709–719.

25. M. Rosenberg, *Society and the Adolescent Self-Image* (Princeton: Princeton University Press, 1965).

26. S. Glueck and E. Glueck, *Delinquents and Nondelinquents in Perspective* (Cambridge, Mass.: Harvard University Press, 1968).

27. E. LeMasters, *Parents in Modern America* (Homewood, Ill.: Dorsey Press, 1974).

28. L. Sims and B. Paolucci, "An Empirical Reexamination of the Parent Attitude Research Instrument, part I, *Journal of Marriage and the Family* 37 (1975), pp. 724–732.

29. S. Wood, R. Bishop, and D. Cohen, *Parenting* (New York: Hart, 1978).

30. D. Baumrind, "Socialization Determinants of Personal Agency" (Paper presented to the Society for Research in Child Development, New Orleans, March 1977).

31. B. Rollins and D. Thomas, "Parental Support, Power and Control Techniques in the Socialization of Children," in W. Burr, R. Hill, I. Nye, and I. Reiss, eds., *Contemporary Theories about the Family*, vol. 1 (New York: Free Press, 1979).

32. D. Jackson, "The Eternal Triangle," in J. Haley and L. Hoffman, eds., *Techniques of Family Therapy* (New York: Basic Books, 1967), pp. 174–264.

33. V. Satir, "A Family of Angels," in J. Haley and L. Hoffman, eds., *Techniques of Family Therapy* (New York: Basic Books, 1967), pp. 97–173.

34. D. Sawin and R. Parke, "Fathers' Affectionate Stimulation and Caregiving Behaviors with Newborn Infants," *Family Coordinator* (October 1979), pp. 509–513.

35. R. Parke and D. Sawin, "The Father's Role in Infancy: A Reevaluation," *Family Coordinator* (October 1976), p. 368.

36. H. Biller and D. Meredith, *Father Power* (New York: David McKay, 1974).

37. J. Pleck, "Men's Roles in the Family: A New Look" (Paper for Sex Roles in Sociology Conference, Merrill-Palmer Institute, Detroit, Mich., November 1975).

38. M. Lamb, "The Role of the Father: An Overview," in M. Lamb, ed., *The Role of the Father in Child Development* (New York: Wiley, 1977), pp. 1–63.

39. K. Clarke-Stewart, "And Daddy Makes Three: The Father's Impact on Mother and Young Child," *Child Development* 49 (1978), p. 475.

40. Lamb, "Role of the Father."

41. W. Mackey and R. Day, "Some Indicators of Fathering Behaviors in the United States: A Cross-Cultural Examination of Adult Male-Child Interaction," *Journal of Marriage and the Family* 41 (May 1979), pp. 287–298.

42. R. Parke and S. O'Leary, "Father-Mother-Infant Interaction in the Newborn Period: Some Findings, Some Observations, and Some Unresolved Issues," in K. Riegel and J. Meacham, eds., *Developing Individual in a Changing World*, vol. II, Social and Environmental Issues (Chicago: Aldine, 1975), pp. 653–663.

43. Ibid.

44. L. Pogrebin, *Growing Up Free: Raising Your Child in the 80's* (New York: McGraw-Hill, 1980).

45. M. Kohn, *Class and Conformity: A Study in Values*, 2nd ed. (Chicago: University of Chicago Press, 1977).

46. D. Lynn, *The Father: His Role in Child Development* (Belmont, Calif.: Brooks/Cole, 1974).

47. Lamb, "Role of the Father."

48. Clarke-Stewart, "And Daddy Makes Three."

49. Parke and O'Leary, "Father-Mother-Infant Interaction."

50. J. Walters and L. Walters, "Parent-Child Relationships: A Review, 1970–1979," *Journal of Marriage and the Family* 42 (November 1980), pp. 807–822.

51. Ibid.

52. M. Hicks and M. Platt, "Marital Happiness and Stability: A Review of the Research in the Sixties," *Journal of Marriage and the Family* 32 (August 1970), pp. 553–574.

53. E. Luckey and J. Bain, "Children: A Factor in Marital Satisfaction," *Journal of Marriage and the Family* 32 (January 1970), pp. 43–44.

54. B. Rollins and R. Galligan, "The Developing Child and Marital Satisfaction of Parents," in R. Lerner and G. Spanier, eds., *Child Influences on Marital and Family Interaction* (New York: Academic Press, 1978), pp. 71–105.

55. R. Rapoport, R. Rapoport, and Z. Strelitz, *Fathers, Mothers, and Society: Perspectives on Parenting* (New York: Random House, 1980), pp. 27–28.

56. Group for the Advancement of Psychiatry, *Joys and Sorrows of Parenthood* (New York: Charles Scribner's Sons, 1973), pp. 131–132.

57. Rapoport, Rapoport, and Strelitz, *Fathers, Mothers, and Society*, p. 21.

58. Group for the Advancement of Psychiatry, *Joys and Sorrows*.

59. R. Arnold, R. Bulato, C. Buripakdi, B. Chung, J. Fawcett, T. Iritani, S. Lee, and T. Wu, *The Value of Children: A Cross-National Study*, vol. I: *Introduction and Comparative Analysis* (Honolulu: East-West Population Institute, East-West Center, 1975).

60. J. Ferbolt and A. Solnit, "Counseling Parents of Mentally Retarded and Learning Disordered Children," in L. Arnold, ed., *Helping Parents Help Their Children* (New York: Brunner/Mazel, 1978), pp. 157–173.

61. R. Bell, "The Effect on the Family of a Limitation in Coping Ability in the Child: A Re-

search Approach and Finding,"
Merrill-Palmer Quarterly 10
(1964), pp. 129–142.

62. T. Jordan, "Research on the
Handicapped Child and the
Family," *Merrill-Palmer Quarterly*
8 (1962), pp. 354–260.

63. B. Farber, "Effects of a Severely
Mentally Retarded Child on
Family Integration," *Monographs
of the Society for Research in Child
Development* 24 (1959).

64. U.S. Bureau of the Census,
"Families Maintained by Female
Householders, 1970–79," *Current
Population Reports*, series P-23,
no. 106 (October 1980), p. 1.

65. Ibid, p. 7.

66. Ibid.

67. Ibid.

68. M. Rutter, *Helping Troubled Children* (New York: Plenum Press,
1975).

69. R. Chester, "The One-Parent
Family: Deviant or Variant," in
R. Chester and J. Peel, eds.,
*Equalities and Inequalities in Fam-
ily Life* (New York: Academic
Press, 1977).

70. B. Braen and J. Forbush,
"School-Age Parenthood, A
National Review," *Journal of
School Health* 45 (May 1975).

71. I. Nye, "School-Age Parent-
hood: Consequences for Babies,
Mothers, Fathers, Grandparents,
and Others," *Washington State
University Extension Bulletin* 667
(April 1976).

72. Ibid.

73. F. Furstenberg, "Family Support: Helping Teenagers Cope,"
Family Planning Perspectives 10
(November–December 1978),
pp. 323–333.

74. L. Bacon, "Early Motherhood,
Accelerated Role Transition,
and Social Pathologies, *Social
Forces* 52 (March 1974).

75. Ibid.

76. Nye, "School-Age Parenthood."

77. Ibid.

Chapter 12

1. H. McCubbin and D. Olson,
"Beyond Family Crisis: Family

Adaptation" (Paper presented at
the Families in Disaster Conference, Uppsala, Sweden, June
1980).

2. Ibid.

3. P. Moen, "Family Impacts of
the 1975 Recession: Duration of
Unemployment," *Journal of Marriage and the Family* 41 (August
1979), pp. 561–573.

4. R. Hill, *Families under Stress*
(New York: Harper & Row,
1949).

5. W. Burr, *Theory Construction and
the Sociology of the Family* (New
York: Wiley, 1973).

6. J. Lewis, *How's Your Family?*
(New York: Brunner/Mazel,
1979), pp. 142–143.

7. L. Pratt, *Family Structure and Effective Health Behavior: The Energized Family* (Boston: Houghton
Mifflin, 1976).

8. Personal communication with
Leon Webber, Family Institute
of Alaska, Anchorage.

9. G. Grace and M. Steiner,
"Wives' Attitudes and the Retention of Navy Enlisted Personnel," in E. Hunter and
E. Nice, eds., *Military Families*
(New York: Praeger, 1978), pp.
42–54.

10. D. Lund, "Junior Officer Reten-
tion in the Modern Volunteer
Army: Who Leaves and Who
Stays?" in E. Hunter and E.
Nice, eds., *Military Families*
(New York: Praeger, 1978), pp.
32–41.

11. A. Bebbington, "The Function
of Stress in the Establishment
of the Dual-Career Family,"
Journal of *Marriage and the Family*
(August 1973), pp. 530–537.

12. D. Dudley and E. Welke, *How
to Survive Being Alive* (New York:
Doubleday, 1977).

13. U.S. Bureau of the Census, *Current Population Reports*, series
P-23, no. 77 (1978), p. 24.

14. D. Kimmel, "Adult Development: Challenges for Counseling," *Personnel and Guidance Journal* 55 (1976), pp. 103–105.

15. U.S. Bureau of the Census, *Current Population Reports*, series
P-20, no. 363 (June 1981), p. 29.

16. L. Haverstein, "Married Wom-
en: Work and Family," *Family
Today* 1 (May 1980), pp. 365–
386.

17. D. Mason and L. Bumpass,
"U.S. Women's Sex Role Ideology, 1970," *American Journal of
Sociology* 80 (March 1975), pp.
1212–1220.

18. R. Rapoport and R. Rapoport,
"Dual-Career Families: Progress
and Prospects," *Marriage and
Family Review* 1 (September–
October 1978), pp. 3–12.

19. L. Wallum, *The Dynamics of Sex
and Gender: A Sociological Perspective* (Chicago: Rand McNally,
1977).

20. M. Van Sell, A. Brief, and R.
Addag, "Job Satisfaction among
Married Working Women,"
Journal of Employment Counseling
16 (March 1979), pp. 38–42.

21. U.S. Bureau of the Census, *Current Population Reports*, series
P-23, no. 77 (1978), p. 33.

22. U.S. Bureau of the Census, *Current Population Reports*, series
P-20, no. 363 (June 1981), p. 39.

23. Ibid.

24. W. Gove and M. Greerken,
"The Effects of Children and
Employment on the Mental
Health of Married Men and
Women," *Social Forces* 56 (1977),
pp. 66–76.

25. W. Arkin and L. Dobrofsky,
"Shared Labor and Love: Job
Sharing Couples in Academia,"
Alternative Lifestyles 1 (November
1978), pp. 492–512.

26. C. Cole, "Split-Shift Marriages"
(Paper presented at the Groves
Conference, Gatlinburg, Ten-
nessee, May 1980).

27. T. Rodes, *National Child Care
Consumer Study: 1975*, vols. I–II:
*Basic Tabulation, Current Pattern
of Child Use in the United States,
American Consumer Attitudes and
Opinion on Child Care* (Prepared
by U.S. Department of Health,
Education, and Welfare, Wash-
ington, D.C., 1976).

28. M. Rowe, "Choosing Child
Care: Many Options," in R.
Rapoport and R. Rapoport, eds.,
Working Couples (New York:

Harper & Row, 1978), pp. 89–99.

29. L. Hoffman, "Effects on Children: Summary and Discussion," in L. Hoffman and I. Nye, eds., *Working Mothers* (San Francisco: Jossey-Bass, 1974), pp. 190–212.

30. Ibid.

31. R. Rapoport and R. Rapoport, *Dual-Career Families Re-examined* (New York: Harper & Row, 1976).

32. J. Hopkins and P. White, "The Dual-Career Couple: Constraints and Supports," *The Family Coordinator* 27 (July 1978), pp. 253–259.

33. Rapoport and Rapoport, *Dual-Career Families Re-examined*.

34. L. Pogrebin, "There's More Than One Way to Slice the Pie . . . and Clean Up Afterward," *Ms* (October 1978), p. 52.

35. A. Booth, "Does Wives' Employment Cause Stress for Husbands?" *Family Coordinator* 28 (October 1979), pp. 445–450.

36. S. Orden and N. Bradburn, "Working Wives and Marital Happiness," *American Journal of Sociology* 74 (January 1969), pp. 392–407.

37. T. Nadelson and L. Eisenberg, "The Successful Professional Woman: On Being Married to One," *American Journal of Psychiatry* 134 (1977), pp. 1071–1076.

38. J. Wright, "Are Working Women Really More Satisfied? Evidence from Several National Surveys," *Journal of Marriage and the Family* 40 (May 1978), pp. 301–313.

39. I. Reiss, *Family Systems in America*, 3rd ed. (New York: Holt, Rinehart and Winston, 1980), pp. 403–404.

40. A. Booth, "Wife's Employment and Husband's Stress: A Replication and Refutation," *Journal of Marriage and the Family* 39 (November 1977), pp. 645–650.

41. R. Burke and T. Weis, "Relationship of Wives' Employment Status to Husbands', Wife Pair Satisfaction and Performance," *Journal of Marriage and the Family* 38 (May 1976), pp. 279–287.

42. J. Richardson, "Wife Occupational Superiority and Marital Troubles: An Examination of the Hypothesis," *Journal of Marriage and the Family* 41 (February 1979), pp. 63–72.

43. A. Macke, W. Bohrnstedt, and I. Bernstein, "Housewives' Self-Esteem and Their Husbands' Success: The Myth of Vicarious Involvement," *Journal of Marriage and the Family* 41 (February 1979), pp. 51–57.

44. K. Moore and I. Sawhill, "Implications of Women's Employment for Home and Family Life," in J. Knaps, ed., *Women and the American Economy: A Look to the 1980's"* (Englewood Cliffs, N.J.: Prentice-Hall, 1976), pp. 102–122.

45. G. McDonald, "Family Power: Reflection and Direction." *Pacific Sociological Review* 20 (October 1977), pp. 607–621.

46. D. Rice, *Dual-Career Marriage: Conflict and Treatment* (New York: Free Press, 1979).

47. C. Ridley, "Exploring the Impact of Work Satisfaction and Involvement on Marital Interaction When Both Partners Are Employed," *Journal of Marriage and the Family* 35 (1973), pp. 229–237.

48. L. Holmstrom, *The Two-Career Family* (Cambridge, Mass.: Schenkman, 1972).

49. C. Safilios-Rothschild, "The Influence of the Wife's Degree of Work Commitment upon Some Aspects of Family Organization and Dynamics," *Journal of Marriage and the Family* 32 (1970), pp. 681–691.

50. M. Poloma and T. Garland, "The Married Professional Woman: A Study of the Tolerance of Domestication," *Journal of Marriage and the Family* 33 (1971), pp. 531–540.

51. T. Martin, K. Berry, and R. Jacobsen, "The Impact of Dual-Career Marriages on Female Professional Careers: An Empirical Test of a Parsonian Hy-

pothesis, *Journal of Marriage and the Family* 37 (1975), pp. 734–742.

52. "Commuting: A Solution for Two Career Couples," *Business Week,* April 3, 1978, p. 68.

53. R. Duncan and C. Perrucci, "Dual Occupational Families and Migration," *American Sociological Review* 41 (1976), pp. 252–261.

54. R. Hall and D. Hall, *The Two Career Couple* (Reading, Mass.: Addison-Wesley, 1979), pp. 51–53.

55. Ibid.

56. N. Heckman, R. Bryson, and J. Bryson, "Problems of Professional Couples: A Content Analysis," *Journal of Marriage and the Family* 39 (1977), pp. 323–330.

57. J. Pleck, "The Work-Family Role System," *Social Problems* 24 (April 1977) pp. 417–427.

58. M. Lasswell and N. Lobsenz, *No-Fault-Marriage* (New York: Doubleday, 1976), p. 231.

59. G. Clanton and L. Smith, eds., *Jealousy* (Englewood Cliffs, N.J.: Prentice-Hall, 1977).

60. R. Bringle and S. Evenback, "The Study of Jealousy as a Dispositional Characteristic," in M. Cook and G. Wilson, eds., *Love and Attraction* (Oxford: Pergamon Press, 1979).

61. J. Bernard, "Jealousy in Marriage," *Medical Aspects of Human Sexuality* 5 (1971), pp. 200–215.

62. Personal communication from Alexander Taylor, past president of the Southern California Association for Marital and Family Therapy.

63. T. Parsons, *The Social System* (New York: Macmillan, 1951).

64. M. Sussman, "Relations of Adult Children with Their Parents," in E. Shanas and G. Streib, eds., *Social Structure and the Family: Generational Relations* Englewood Cliffs, N.J.: Prentice-Hall, 1965), pp. 62–92.

65. E. Shanas, "Family-Kin Networks and Aging in Cross-Cultural Perspective," *Journal of Marriage and the Family* 35 (August 1973), pp. 505–511.

66. Ibid.
67. "The Redbook Poll on In-Laws," *Redbook* (June 1980), p. 62.
68. B. Adams, *Kinship in an Urban Setting* (Chicago: Markham, 1968).
69. B. Adams, "Isolation, Function and Beyond," *American Family* 32 (November 1970), pp. 575–597.
70. "Redbook Poll on In-Laws."
71. R. Ward, "Limitations of the Family as a Supportive Institution in the Lives of the Aged," *Family Coordinator* 47 (October 1978), pp. 365–373.
72. M. Liberman and G. Liberman.
73. Personal communication.
74. E. Martin and J. Martin, *The Black Extended Family* (Chicago: University of Chicago Press, 1978).
75. B. Adams, *Kinship in an Urban Setting*.
76. W. Mitchell, *Mishpokhe: A Study of New York City Jewish Family Clubs* (New York: Mouton, 1978).
77. "Redbook Poll on In-Laws," p. 62.
78. Ibid.

Chapter 13

1. M. Lasswell and N. Lobsenz, *No-Fault Marriage* (New York: Doubleday, 1976), p. ix.
2. Ibid., pp. 235–239.
3. L. Meyers, "Battered Wives, Dead Husbands," *Student Lawyer* 6 (March 1978), pp. 46–51.
4. *Vital Statistics Reports* (annual summary for the United States) vol. 24, no. 13 (1976).
5. S. Steinmetz, *The Cycle of Violence: Assertive, Aggressive, and Abusive Family Interaction* (New York: Praeger, 1977).
6. *San Fernando* (California) *Valley News*, November 1, 1979, p. 12.
7. R. Gelles and J. Straus, "Violence in the American Family," *Journal of Social Issues* 35 (1979), p. 12.
8. E. Kinard, "The Psychological Consequences of Abuse for the Child," *Journal of Social Issues* 35 (1979), pp. 82–100.
9. J. Weston, "A Summary of Neglect and Traumatic Cases," in C. Kempe and R. Helfer, eds., *The Battered Child*, 2nd ed. (Chicago: University of Chicago Press, 1974).
10. S. Steinmetz, "Violence between Siblings" (Paper presented at the Second World Conference of the International Society of Family Law, Montreal, June 1977).
11. S. Steinmetz, "Battered Parents," *Society* 15 (July–August 1978), pp. 54–55.
12. M. Freeman, *Violence in the Home* (Westmead, England: Saxon House, 1979).
13. L. Beckman, "Women Alcoholics: A Review of Social and Psychological Studies," *Journal of Studies on Alcohol* 36 (1975), pp. 797–824.
14. B. Greene, *A Clinical Approach to Marital Problems* (Springfield, Ill.: Charles C Thomas, 1970).
15. S. Zimberg, J. Wallace, and S. Blume, eds., *Practical Approaches to Alcoholism Psychotherapy* (New York: Plenum Press, 1978).
16. National Center for Health Statistics, "Births, Marriages, Divorces, and Deaths for 1979," *Monthly Vital Statistics Report* 28, no. 12 (Washington, D.C.: U.S. Department of Health, Education, and Welfare, 1980).
17. A. Cherlin, "Remarriage as an Incomplete Institution," *American Journal of Sociology* 84 (November 1978), pp. 634–650.
18. I. Reiss, *Family Systems in America*, 3rd ed. (New York: Holt, Rinehart and Winston, 1980).
19. L. Bumpass and J. Sweet, "Differentials in Marital Instability: 1970," *American Sociological Review* 37 (December 1972), pp. 754–767.
20. F. Furstenberg, "Premarital Pregnancy and Marital Instability," *Journal of Social Issues* 32 (Winter 1976), pp. 67–86.
21. U.S. Bureau of the Census, *Current Population Reports*, series P-20, no. 312 (1977), Table H.
22. L. Burchinal and L. Chancellor, "Survival Rates among Religiously Homogamous and Interreligious Marriage," *Iowa Agricultural and Home Economics Station Research Bulletin* 512 (1962), pp. 743–770.
23. J. Landis, "The Pattern of Divorce in Three Generations," *Social Forces* 34 (March 1956), pp. 213–216.
24. C. Mueller and H. Pope, "Marital Instability: The Study of Its Transmission between Generations," *Journal of Marriage and The Family* 39 (February 1977), pp. 83–92.
25. R. Gould, *Transformations, Growth, and Change in Adult Life* (New York: Simon and Schuster, 1978).
26. M. Hetherington, M. Cox, and R. Cox, "Divorced Fathers," *Family Coordinator* 25 (1976), pp. 417–428.
27. Personal communication.
28. Hetherington, Cox, and Cox, "Divorced Fathers."
29. B. Bloom, S. Asher, and S. White, "Marital Disruption as a Stressor: A Review and Analysis," *Psychological Bulletin* 85 (1978), pp. 867–894.
30. K. Kressel, "Patterns of Coping in Divorce and Some Implications for Clinical Practice," *Family Relations* 29 (April 1980), pp. 234–240.
31. S. Price-Bonham and J. Balswick, "The Noninstitutions: Divorce, Desertion, and Remarriage," *Journal of Marriage and the Family* 42 (November 1980), p. 963.
32. A. Falek and S. Britton, "Coping: The Hypothesis and Its Implications," *Social Biology* 2 (1974), pp. 1–7.
33. L. Pearlin and J. Johnson, "Marital Status, Life Strains and Depression," *American Sociological Review* 42 (October 1977), pp. 704–715.
34. P. Bohannan, *Divorce and After* (New York: Doubleday, 1970).
35. S. Kessler, *The American Way of Divorce: Prescriptions for Change*. (Chicago: Nelson-Hall, 1975).

36. K. Kressel and M. Deutsch, "Divorce Therapy: An In-Depth Survey of Therapists' Views," *Family Process* 16 (1977), pp. 413–443.

37. Personal communication.

38. H. Raschke, "The Role of Social Participation in Postseparation and Postdivorce Adjustment," *Journal of Divorce* 1 (Winter 1977), pp. 129–139.

39. Ibid.

40. A. Grossman, "Divorced and Separated Women in the Labor Force—An Update," *Monthly Labor Review* 101 (October 1978), pp. 43–45.

41. M. Hetherington, M. Cox, and R. Cox, "The Aftermath of Divorce," in J. Stevens and M. Matthews, eds., *Mother-Child, Father-Child Relations* (Washington, D.C.: National Association for the Education of Young Children, 1978).

42. K. Rosenthal and H. Keshet, "The Impact of Child Care Responsibilities on Part-time or Single Fathers," *Alternate Lifestyles* 1 (November 1978), pp. 465–491.

43. J. Santrock and R. Warshak, "Father Custody and Social Development in Boys and Girls," *Journal of Social Issues* 35 (1979), pp. 112–125.

44. S. Abarbanel, "Shared Parenting after Separation and Divorce: A Study of Joint Custody," *American Journal of Orthopsychiatry* 49 (April 1979), pp. 320–329.

45. M. Cox and L. Cease, "Joint Custody," *Family Advocate* (Summer 1978), pp. 10–13.

46. Personal communication.

47. C. R. Ahrons, "The Binuclear Family: Two Households, One Family," *Alternate Lifestyles* 2 (November 1979), pp. 499–515.

48. R. Hess and K. Camara, "Postdivorce Family Relationships as Mediating Factors in the Consequences of Divorce for Children," *Journal of Social Issues* 35 (1979), pp. 79–96.

49. D. Chambers, *Making Fathers Pay: The Enforcement of Child Support* (Chicago: University of Chicago Press, 1979).

50. Personal communication.

51. R. Weiss, *Marital Separation* (New York: Basic Books, 1975).

52. Personal communication.

53. R. Robertiello, *A Man in the Making: Grandfathers, Fathers, Sons* (New York: R. Marek Publishers, 1979).

54. M. Hunt, *The World of the Formerly Married* (New York: McGraw-Hill, 1966).

55. M. Hunt and B. Hunt, *The Divorce Experience* (New York: McGraw-Hill, 1977).

56. G. Gurin, J. Veroff, and S. Feld, *Americans View Their Mental Health* (New York: Basic Books, 1960).

57. G. Spanier and R. Casto, "Adjustment to Separation and Divorce: An Analysis of 50 Case Studies," *Journal of Divorce* 2 (Spring 1979), pp. 241–253.

58. E. Fisher, *Divorce: The New Freedom* (New York: Harper & Row, 1974), p. 119.

59. U.S. Bureau of the Census, *Current Population Reports*, series P-20, no. 352 (July 1980), p. 3.

60. P. Glick, "Children of Divorced Parents in Demographic Perspective," *Journal of Social Issues* 35 (1979), pp. 170–182.

61. R. Gardner, *The Parents' Book about Divorce* (Garden City, N.Y.: Doubleday, 1977).

62. A. Parks, "Children and Youth of Divorce in Parents without Partners, Inc.," *Journal of Clinical Child Psychology* 6 (1977), pp. 44–48.

63. J. McDermott, W. Tseng, W. Char, and C. Fukunaga, "Child Custody Decision Making: The Search for Improvement," *Journal of the American Academy of Child Psychiatry* 17 (1978), pp. 104–116.

64. M. Hetherington, M. Cox, and R. Cox, "The Aftermath of Divorce," in J. Stevens and M. Matthews, eds., *Mother-Child, Father-Child Relations* (Washington, D.C.: National Association for the Education of Young Children, 1978).

65. J. Wallerstein and J. Kelly, "The Effects of Parental Divorce: Experiences of the Preschool Child," *Journal of the American Academy of Child Psychiatry* 14 (1975), pp. 600–616.

66. J. Wallerstein and J. Kelly, "The Effects of Parental Divorce: Experiences of the Child in Later Latency," *American Journal of Orthopsychiatry* 46 (1976), pp. 256–269.

67. J. Wallerstein and J. Kelly, "The Effects of Parental Divorce: The Adolescent Experience, " in E. Anthony and C. Koupernik, eds., *The Child in His Family: Children at Psychiatric Risk* (New York: Wiley, 1974).

68. R. Kulka and H. Weingarter, "The Long-Term Effects of Parental Divorce in Childhood on Adult Adjustment," *Journal of Social Issues* 35 (1979), pp. 50–78.

69. N. Kalter, "Children of Divorce in an Outpatient Psychiatric Population," *American Journal of Orthopsychiatry* 47 (1977), pp. 40–51.

70. T. Parish and T. Copeland, "The Relationship between Self-Concepts and Evaluations of Parents and Stepfathers," *Journal of Psychology* 101 (January 1979), pp. 135–138.

71. H. Raschke and V. Raschke, "Family Conflict and Children's Self-Concept: A Comparison of Intact and Single-Parent Families," *Journal of Marriage and the Family* 41 (May 1979), pp. 367–374.

72. L. Bumpass and R. Rindfuss, "Children's Experiences of Marital Disruption," *Institute for Research on Poverty Discussion Papers*, no. 512-78 (Madison: University of Wisconsin, 1978).

73. P. Glick, cited in *Marriage and Divorce Today*, April 21, 1980, p. 1.

Chapter 14

1. S. Price-Bonham and J. Balswick, "The Noninstitutions: Divorce,

Desertion, and Remarriage," *Journal of Marriage and the Family* 42 (November 1980), pp. 959–972.

2. A. Norton and P. Glick, "Marital Instability: Past, Present, and Future," *Journal of Social Issues* 32 (June 1976), pp. 5–20.

3. National Center for Health Statistics, "Births, Marriages, Divorces and Deaths for 1979," *Monthly Vital Statistics Report* 28, no. 12, U.S. Department of Health, Education, and Welfare (1980).

4. Ibid.

5. W. Goode, *After Divorce* (New York: Free Press, 1956).

6. U.S. Bureau of the Census, *Current Population Reports*, series P-20, no. 297 (1976), p. 15.

7. P. Landis, "Sequential Marriage," *Journal of Home Economics* (October 1950), p. 626.

8. M. Hunt and B. Hunt, *The Divorce Experience* (New York: McGraw-Hill, 1977), p. 223.

9. L. Westoff, *The Second Time Around: Remarriage in America* (New York: Viking Press, 1977).

10. J. Peters, "A Comparison of Mate Selection and Marriage in the First and Second Marriages in a Selected Sample of the Remarried Divorced," *Journal of Comparative Family Studies* 7 (Autumn 1976), pp. 483–491.

11. Personal communication.

12. R. Weiss, *Marital Separation* (New York: Basic Books, 1975), pp. 305–309.

13. Ibid.

14. S. Albrecht, "Correlates of Marital Happiness among the Remarried," *Journal of Marriage and the Family* (November 1979), pp. 857–867.

15. N. Glenn and C. Weaver, "The Marital Happiness of Remarried Divorced Persons," *Journal of Marriage and the Family* 39 (May 1977), pp. 331–337.

16. P. Glick and A. Norton, "Frequency, Duration, and Probability of Marriage and Divorce," *Journal of Marriage and the Family* 33 (May 1971), pp. 307–317.

17. P. Glick and A. Norton, "Marrying, Divorcing and Living Together in the U.S. Today," *Population Bulletin* 32 (October 1977), pp. 1–41.

18. Norton and Glick, "Marital Instability."

19. Hunt and Hunt, *Divorce Experience.*

20. R. Weiss, *Marital Separation*, pp. 305–309.

21. U.S. Bureau of the Census, *Current Population Reports*, series P-20, no. 297 (1976).

22. Albrecht, "Correlates of Marital Happiness."

23. J. Bernard, *Remarriage: A Study of Marriage* (New York: Russell and Russell, 1971).

24. L. Duberman, *The Reconstituted Family: A Study of Remarried Couples and Their Children* (Chicago: Nelson Hall, 1975).

25. U.S. Bureau of the Census, *Current Population Reports*, series P-23, no. 106 (September 1980), p. 1.

26. Clinical files.

27. L. White, "Sex Differentials in the Effect of Remarriage on Global Happiness," *Journal of Marriage and the Family* 41 (November 1979), pp. 869–876.

28. L. Messinger, "Remarriage between Divorced People with Children from Previous Marriages," *Journal of Marriage and Family Counseling* 2 (April 1976), pp. 193–200.

29. Bernard, *Remarriage.*

30. J. Spicer and G. Hampe, "Kinship Interaction after Divorce," *Journal of Marriage and the Family* 37 (February 1975), pp. 113–119.

31. Spicer and Hampe, "Kinship Interaction," p. 115.

32. L. Westoff, *Second Time Around* pp. 43, 46.

33. M. Elkin, "Post-divorce Counseling in a Conciliation Court" (Paper presented at the Third Invitational Conference on Marriage Counselors' Education, San Francisco, October 9, 1976).

34. *Los Angeles Times*, August 8, 1980, p. 7.

35. C. Ahrons, "The Coparental Divorce: Preliminary Research Findings and Policy Implica-

tions" (Paper presented at the Annual Meeting of the National Council on Family Relations, Philadelphia, October 1978).

36. P. Bohannan, "Divorce Chains, Households of Remarriage and Multiple Divorces," in P. Bohannan, ed., *Divorce and After* (New York: Doubleday, 1970), pp. 127–139.

37. A. Goetting, "Former Spouse–Current Spouse Relationships," *Journal of Family Issues* 1 (March 1980), pp. 58–80.

38. J. Dovidio and W. Morris, "Effects of Stress and Commonality of Fate on Helping Behavior," *Journal of Personality and Social Psychology* 31 (1975), pp. 145–149.

39. Goetting, "Former Spouse–Current Spouse Relationships."

40. H. Raschke, "Sex Differences in Voluntary Post Marital Dissolution Adjustment" (Paper presented at the American Sociological Association Annual Meeting, New York, August 1976).

41. Clinical files.

42. B. Maddox, *The Half Parent* (New York: Evans, 1975).

43. P. Stern, "Stepfather Families: Integration around Child Discipline," *Issues in Mental Health Nursing* 1 (1978), pp. 50–56.

44. E. Visher and J. Visher, *Stepfamilies: A Guide to Working with Stepparents and Stepchildren* (New York: Brunner/Mazel, 1979), p. 91.

45. P. Bohannan and R. Erickson, "Steppin In," *Psychology Today* (January 1978), pp. 53–59.

46. Stern, "Stepfather Families."

47. H. Goldstein, "Reconstituted Families: The Second Marriage and Its Children," *Psychiatric Quarterly* 48 (Fall 1974), pp. 433–440.

48. Bohannan and Erickson, "Steppin In."

49. O. Spann and N. Spann, *Your Child? I Thought It Was My Child!* (Pasadena, Calif.: Ward Ritchie Press, 1977), p. 152.

50. Duberman, *The Reconstituted Family.*

51. Goldstein, "Reconstituted Families."
52. A. Simon, *Stepchild in the Family: A View of Children in Remarriage* (New York: Odyssey Press, 1964).
53. Maddox, *The Half Parent*, p. 16.
54. I. Sardanis-Zimmerman, "The Stepmother: Mythology and Self-Perception" (Ph.D. diss., May 1977), reported in Visher and Visher, *Step-families*, p. 81.
55. G. Schulman, "Myths That Intrude on the Adaptation of the Stepfamily," *Social Casework* 49 (1972), pp. 131–139.
56. R. Roosevelt and J. Lofas, *Living in Step* (New York: Stein and Day, 1976), p. 69.
57. Simon, *Stepchild in the Family*, p. 201.
58. M. Draughon, "Stepmother's Model of Identification in Relation to Mourning in the Child," *Psychological Reports* 36 (1975), pp. 183–189.
59. J. Lewis, R. Beavers, J. Gossett, and V. Phillips, *No Single Thread: Psychological Health in Family Systems* (New York: Brunner/Mazel, 1976).
60. Personal communication.
61. Duberman, *The Reconstituted Family*.
62. Ibid.
63. Ibid.
64. Clinical observations.
65. P. Glick, "Remarriage: Some Recent Changes and Variations," *Journal of Family Issues* 1 (December 1980), pp. 455–478.
66. W. Cleveland and D. Gianturco, "Remarriage Probability after Widowhood: A Retrospective Method," *Journal of Gerontology* 31 (January 1976), pp. 99–103.
67. J. Treas and A. Van Hilst, "Marriage and Remarriage Rates among Older Americans," *The Gerontologist* 16 (April 1976), pp. 136–143.
68. H. Lopata, *Widowhood in an American City* (Cambridge, Mass.: Schenkman, 1973).
69. I. Glick, R. Weiss, and C. Parkes, *The First Year of Bereavement* (New York: Wiley, 1974).

70. Ibid.
71. U.S. Bureau of the Census, *Current Population Reports*, series P-20, no. 312 (August 1977), pp. 13–14.
72. L. Tessman, *Children of Parting Parents* (New York: Jason Aronson, 1978), p. 417.
73. U.S. Bureau of the Census, *Current Population Reports*, series P-20, no. 312 (August 1977), p. 15, Table P.
74. W. McKain, "A New Look at Older Marriages," *Family Coordinator* 21 (January 1972), pp. 61–69.
75. Ibid.

Chapter 15

1. L. Beard, "Are the Aged Ex-Family?" *Social Forces* 27 (1949), pp. 274–279.
2. U.S. Bureau of the Census, *Current Population Reports*, series P-23, no. 43 (February 1973), p. 15, Table 13.
3. P. Dressel and W. Avant, "Aging and College Family Textbooks," *Family Coordinator* 27 (October 1978), pp. 427–435.
4. G. Neubeck, "Getting Older in My Family: A Personal Reflection," *Family Coordinator* 27 (October 1978), pp. 445–447. © 1978 by the National Council on Family Relations. Reprinted by permission.
5. E. Shanas, "Older People and Their Families," *Journal of Marriage and The Family* 42 (February 1980), pp. 9–15.
6. U.S. Bureau of the Census, *Current Population Reports*, series P-20, no. 363 (June 1981), p. 9.
7. Shanas, "Older People."
8. H. Maas, and J. Kuypers, *From Thirty to Seventy* (San Francisco: Jossey-Bass, 1974).
9. D. Baldwin, "Poverty and the Older Woman: Reflections of a Social Worker," *Family Coordinator* 27 (October 1978), pp. 448–450.
10. Shanas, "Older People," p. 10.
11. S. McKinlay and M. Jeffreys,

"The Menopausal Syndrome," *British Journal of Preventive and Social Medicine* 28 (1974), p. 108.
12. J. Hyde and B. Rosenberg, *Half the Human Experience: The Psychology of Women* (Lexington, Mass.: D. C. Heath, 1980), p. 198.
13. H. Feldman and M. Feldman, "Marriage in Later Years: Cohort and Parental Effect" (Unpublished paper, Department of Human Development and Family Studies, Cornell University, 1976).
14. N. Glenn, "Psychological Well-Being in the Post-Parental Stage: Some Evidence from National Surveys," *Journal of Marriage and the Family* 37 (1975), pp. 105–110.
15. S. Albrecht, H. Bahr, and B. Chadwick, "Changing Family and Sex Roles: An Assessment of Age Difference," *Journal of Marriage and the Family* 41 (February 1979), pp. 41–50.
16. M. Huyck, *Growing Older* (Englewood Cliffs, N.J.: Prentice-Hall, 1974).
17. B. Neugarten, "The Awareness of Middle Age," in B. Neugarten, ed., *Middle Age and Aging: A Reader in Social Psychology* (Chicago: University of Chicago Press, 1968).
18. D. Levinson, C. Darrow, E. Klein, M. Levinson, and B. McKee, "The Psychosocial Development of Men in Early Adulthood and Mid-Life Transition," in D. Ricks, A. Thomas, and M. Roff, eds., *Life History Research in Psychotherapy*, vol. 3 (Minneapolis: University of Minnesota Press, 1974).
19. M. Mead, *Blackberry Winter* (New York: William Morrow, 1972), p. 275.
20. E. Burgess, *Aging in Western Societies* (New York: Thomas Crowell, 1958).
21. B. Neugarten and K. Weinstein, "The Changing American Grandparent," in Neugarten, ed., *Middle Age and Aging*.
22. S. Clavan, "The Impact of Social Class and Social Trends on the Role of Grandparent," *Fam-*

ily Coordinator 27 (October 1979), pp. 351–357.

23. J. Robertson, "Grandmother-hood: A Study of Role Conceptions," *Journal of Marriage and the Family* 39 (February 1977), pp. 165–174.

24. Neugarten and Weinstein, "Changing American Grandparent."

25. Ibid.

26. G. Streib and C. Schneider, *Retirement in American Society: Impact and Process* (Ithaca, N.Y.: Cornell University Press, 1971).

27. A. Entine, "Mid-Life Counseling: Prognosis and Potential," *Personnel and Guidance Journal* 55 (November 1976), pp. 112–114.

28. G. Leslie and E. Leslie, *Marriage in a Changing World*, 2nd ed. (New York: Wiley, 1980).

29. Study prepared by Research and Forecasts, Inc., for American Healthcare Corporation, New York City, reported by Associated Press, Pomona, California, *Progress Bulletin*, June 11, 1980, p. 1.

30. Huyck, *Growing Older.*

31. R. Atchley, "Selected Social and Psychological Differences between Men and Women in Later Life," *Journal of Gerontology* 31 (1976), pp. 204–211.

32. D. Heyman, "Does a Wife Retire?" *The Gerontologist* 10 (Spring 1970), pp. 54–56.

33. B. Adamcik, "An Examination of the Comparability of Morale Measures among Working and Retired Blacks, Mexican-Americans and Whites" (Unpublished research paper, University of Southern California, 1980).

34. G. Streib, "Older Families and Their Troubles: Familial and Social Responses," *Family Coordinator* 21 (January 1972), pp. 5–19.

35. E. Cumming and W. Henry, *Growing Old* (New York: Basic Books, 1961).

36. A. Rose, "A Current Theoretical Issue in Social Gerontology," in B. Neugarten, ed., *Middle Age and Aging.*

37. R. Havighurst, "Personality and Patterns of Aging," *The Gerontologist* 8 (Spring 1968), pp. 20–23.

38. E. Shanas, "Family-Kin Networks and Aging in Cross-Cultural Perspective," *Journal of Marriage and the Family* 35 (August 1973), pp. 505–511.

39. L. Troll and J. Smith, "Attachment through the Life Span: Some Questions about Dyadic Relationships in Later Life," *Human Development* 19 (1976), pp. 156–171.

40. E. Johnson and B. Bursk, "Relationships between the Elderly and Their Adult Children," *The Gerontologist* 17 (February 1977), pp. 90–96.

41. R. Hill, *Family Development in Three Generations* (Cambridge, Mass.: Schenkman, 1970).

42. C. Swensen, R. Eskew, and K. Kohlhepp, *Factors in the Marriages of Older Couples* (Unpublished report on NIMH Research Grant no. R01-MH-26933, Purdue University, 1977).

43. U.S. Office of Human Development, Administration on Aging, Publication no. OHD 77-2006 (1976).

44. *Guinness Book of World Records* (New York: Sterling, 1980).

45. D. Elevenstar, "Happy Couple a Tribute to Old-Fashioned Virtues," *The Los Angeles Times*, January 8, 1980, p. 2.

46. A. Roberts and W. Roberts, "Factors in Life-Styles of Couples Married over Fifty Years" (Paper presented at Annual Meeting of National Council on Family Relations, Salt Lake City, August 1975).

47. M. Sporakowski and G. Jughston, "Prescriptions for Happy Marriage: Adjustments and Satisfaction of Couples Married for 50 or More Years," *Family Coordinator* 27 (1978), pp. 321–327.

48. G. Spanier, R. Lewis, and C. Cole, "Marital Adjustment over the Family Life Cycle: The Issue of Curvilinearity," *Journal of Marriage and the Family* 37 (May 1975), pp. 263–375.

49. Ibid.

50. A. Friedman and J. Todd, "Power, Intimacy, and Happiness in Long Term Marriages" (Unpublished paper, 1979).

51. R. Schram, "Marital Satisfaction over the Family Life Cycle," *Journal of Marriage and the Family* 41 (February 1979), pp. 7–12.

52. N. Stinnett, L. Carter, and J. Montgomery, "Older Persons' Perceptions of Their Marriages," *Journal of Marriage and the Family* 32 (November 1972), pp. 665–670.

53. I. Hutchison, "The Significance of Marital Status for Morale and Life Satisfaction among Lower Income Elderly," *Journal of Marriage and the Family* 37 (May 1975), pp. 287–293.

54. R. Hill, "Methodological Problems with the Developmental Approach to Family Study, *Family Process* 3 (March 1964), pp. 186–206.

55. R. Rodgers, "Toward a Theory of Family Development," *Journal of Marriage and the Family* 26 (August 1964), pp. 262–270.

56. C. Swensen, "Marriage Relationship and Problems of Retired Married Couples" (Unpublished manuscript, Purdue University, 1978), reported in *Families Today*, National Institute of Mental Health Monographs, vol. 1 (1979), pp. 249–286.

57. J. Loevinger, *Ego Development: Conceptions and Theories* (San Francisco: Jossey-Bass, 1976).

58. Swensen, "Marriage Relationship."

59. Personal communication.

60. R. Kalish and D. Reynolds, *Death and Ethnicity: A Psychocultural Study* (Los Angeles: University of Southern California Press, 1976).

61. W. McKain, *Retirement Marriages*. Storrs, Conn.: Storrs Agricultural Experiment Station, monograph 3 (January 1969).

62. A. Comfort, "Sexuality in Old Age," *Journal of American Geriatrics Society* 22 (1974), pp. 440–442.

63. C. Tavris, "The Sexual Lives of Women over Sixty," *Ms* 6 (July 1977), pp. 62–65.

64. S. Schumacher (Reported from a symposium on Sex for the Mature Adult, Miami, Florida, 1973).

65. H. Lopata, *Widowhood in an American City.* (Cambridge, Mass.: Schenkman, 1973).

66. G. Arling, "The Elderly Widow and Her Family, Neighbors, and Friends," *Journal of Marriage and the Family* 38 (August 1976), pp. 757–768.

67. V. Kivett, "Loneliness and the Rural Widow," *Family Coordinator* 27 (October 1978), pp. 389–394.

68. R. Weiss, ed., *Loneliness: The Experience of Emotional and Social Isolation* (Cambridge, Mass.: MIT Press, 1973).

69. S. Cutler, "Transportation and Changes in Life Satisfaction," *The Gerontologist* 15 (1975), pp. 155–159.

70. G. Hansen, "Meeting Housing Challenges: Involvement—The Elderly," in *Housing Issues*, Proceedings of the Fifth Annual Meeting, American Association of Housing Educators (Lincoln: University of Nebraska Press, 1975).

71. J. Hendricks and E. Hendricks, *Aging in Mass Society: Myths and Realities* (Cambridge, Mass.: Winthrop Publishers, 1977).

72. G. Streib and M. Hilker, "The Cooperative 'Family': An Alternative Lifestyle for the Elderly," *Alternate Lifestyle* 3 (May 1980), pp. 167–184.

73. J. Peterson and B. Payne, *Love in the Later Years* (New York: Association Press, 1975).

74. T. Eaton, "Social Functioning and Personal Autonomy in Black and White OAS Recipients" (Ph.D. diss., University of Southern California, 1974).

75. K. Smith and V. Bengtson, "Positive Consequences of Institutionalization: Solidarity between Elderly Patients and Their Middle-Aged Children," *The Gerontologist* 19 (October 1979), pp. 438–447.

76. G. Streib, "An Alternative Family Form for Older Persons: Need and Social Context," *Family Coordinator* 27 (October 1978), pp. 413–420.

77. C. Bourg, "Elderly in a Southern Metropolitan Area," *The Gerontologist* 15 (February 1975), pp. 15–22.

78. E. Erikson, *Childhood and Society* (New York: Norton, 1963).

79. R. Butler, *Why Survive? Being Old in America* (New York: Harper & Row, 1975).

80. Personal communication.

Appendix A

1. J. DeLora and C. Warren, *Understanding Sexual Interaction* (Boston: Houghton Mifflin, 1977), p. 23.

2. R. Rimmer, *Thursday, My Love* (New York: New American Library, 1972).

3. B. Dodson, *Liberating Masturbation: A Meditation on Self Love* (New York: Betty Dodson, 1976).

4. W. Masters and V. Johnson, *Human Sexual Response* (Boston: Little, Brown, 1966), p. 41.

5. F. Netter, "Reproductive System," *Ciba Collection of Medical Illustrations*, vol. 2 (Summit, N.J.: Ciba, 1965), p. 90.

6. T. Van de Velde, *Ideal Marriage: Its Physiology and Technique* (New York: Random House, 1957), p. 169.

7. Student Health and Counseling Center, *Herpes II*, Bulletin Number HEC 055, University of Southern California, Los Angeles (January 1979).

8. Masters and Johnson, *Human Sexual Response*, pp. 28–30.

9. H. Katchadourian and D. Lunde, *Fundamentals of Human Sexuality* (New York: Holt, Rinehart and Winston, 1972), p. 28.

10. Masters and Johnson, *Human Sexual Response*, p. 190.

11. C. Urion, "Circumcision and Sexual Conduct: A Cross-Cultural Comparison" (Paper presented to the International Conference on Love and Attraction, Swansea, Wales, September 7, 1977).

12. Katchadourian and Lunde, *Fundamentals*, pp. 27, 66–67.

13. DeLora and Warren, *Understanding Sexual Interaction*, p. 32.

14. Katchadourian and Lunde, *Fundamentals*, pp. 66–67, 78.

15. Masters and Johnson, *Human Sexual Response*, pp. 286–293.

16. Ibid.

17. Katchadourian and Lunde, *Fundamentals*, pp. 37, 38.

18. Ibid., pp. 101–102.

19. Ibid., p. 38.

20. Ibid., p. 40.

21. Ibid., p. 88.

22. Ibid., p. 106.

23. B. Kogan, *Human Sexual Expression* (New York: Harcourt, Brace Jovanovich, 1973), p. 38.

24. Ibid.

25. Katchadourian and Lunde, *Fundamentals*, p. 64.

26. H. Singer Kaplan, *Disorders of Sexual Desire: And Other New Concepts and Techniques in Sex Therapy, The New Sex Therapy*, vol. II (New York: Brunner/Mazel, 1979), pp. 24–25.

27. A. Kinsey, W. Pomeroy, C. Martin, and P. Gebhard, *Sexual Behavior in the Human Female* (New York: Pocket Books, 1965), pp. 372–373.

28. Masters and Johnson, *Human Sexual Response*, p. 211.

29. Ibid., pp. 212–213.

Appendix B

1. J. Lee, *The Colours of Love* (Toronto: New Press, 1975).

2. T. Lasswell and M. Lasswell, "I Love You but I'm Not in Love with You," *Journal of Marriage and Family Counseling* 2 (July 1976), pp. 211–224.

3. T. Hatkoff, "Cultural and Demographic Differences in Persons' Cognitive Referents of Love" (Ph.D. diss., University of Southern California, 1978).

4. M. Lasswell and N. Lobsenz, *Styles of Loving: Why You Love the Way You Do* (Garden City, N.Y.: Doubleday, 1980).

5. D. Bem, *Beliefs, Attitudes and Human Affairs* (Belmont, Calif.: Brooks-Cole, 1970).

6. I. Reiss, *Family Systems in America* (New York: Holt, Rinehart and Winston, 1980), pp. 126–132.

7. Hatkoff, "Cultural and Demographic Differences."

8. D. Underwood, "The Use of the Lasswell Profile in Marital Therapy: A Study of Re-defining Dissimilarities in Relationship Treatment (Ph.D. diss., Fielding Institute, Santa Barbara, Calif., 1979).

9. Lasswell and Lobsenz, *Styles of Loving*, pp. 195–196.

Appendix C

1. J. Kilgore and D. Highlander, *Getting More Family Out of Your Dollar* (Irvine, Calif.: Harvest House, 1976).

2. F. Feldman, *The Family in Today's Money World* (New York: Family Service Association of America, 1976).

3. Feldman, *The Family.*

4. E. Bergler, *Money and Emotional Conflicts* (New York: International Universities Press, 1970).

5. Ibid., pp. 18–19.

6. S. Porter, *Sylvia Porter's Money Book* (New York: Doubleday, 1975).

7. Gallup poll, "1981 Cost of Living Audit."

8. S. Rawlings, *Perspectives on American Husbands and Wives*, Bureau of the Census, series P-23, no. 77 (December 1978), p. 23.

9. Gallup poll, "1981 Cost of Living Audit."

10. J. Quinn, *Everyone's Money Book* (New York: Delacorte, 1979).

11. U.S. Bureau of the Census, *Current Population Reports*, series P-23, no. 78 (1979), p. 11.

12. Shana Alexander, *State-By-State Guide to Women's Legal Rights* (Los Angeles: Wollstonecraft, 1975).

13. Ibid.

14. Ibid.

15. U.S. Bureau of the Census, "Characteristics of Households and Persons Receiving Noncash Benefits: 1979 (Preliminary Data from the March 1980 Current Population Survey)," *Current Population Reports*, series P-23, no. 110 (March 1981), p. 23.

16. Ibid., pp. 9, 12, 15.

17. D. Helms, and J. Turner, *Exploring Child Behavior*, 2nd ed. (New York: Holt, Rinehart and Winston, 1981), p. 234.

18. J. Williams and M. Stith, *Middle Childhood*, 2nd ed. (New York: Macmillan, 1980).

19. Ibid.

20. U.S. Department of Commerce, *Price Index of New One-Family Houses Sold, Fourth Quarter, 1977*; and U.S. Department of Labor, *CPI Detailed Report* (February 1978).

21. Kilgore and Highlander, *Getting More Family*, p. 95.

22. A. Clausen, president of the Bank of America (Paper presented to the American Bankers Association Installment Credit Conference, quoted in *The Los Angeles Times* financial section, March 1981).

Index

Boldface page number indicates text page on which indexed term is defined.